Effective Justice

Ius, Lex et Res Publica
Studies in Law, Philosophy and Political Cultures

Edited by Barbara Janusz-Pohl

Volume 39

Barbara Janusz-Pohl (ed.)

Effective Justice. International and Comparative Approaches

Volume 2

PETER LANG

Berlin · Bruxelles · Chennai · Lausanne · New York · Oxford

Library of Congress Cataloging-in-Publication Data

Names: Janusz-Pohl, Barbara, editor.
Title: Effective justice, international and comparative approaches. Volume 2 / Barbara Janusz-Pohl (ed.).
Description: Oxford ; New York : Peter Lang, 2025. | Series: Ius, lex et res publica, 2191-3250 ; volume 39 | Includes bibliographical references.
Identifiers: LCCN 2025000637 | ISBN 9783631901427 (hardback) | ISBN 9783631935095 (ebook)
Subjects: LCSH: Effectiveness and validity of law--European Union countries. | Remedies (Law)--European Union countries. | International and municipal law--European Union countries. | Conflict of laws--European Union countries. | Justice, Administration of--European Union countries. | Comparative law--European Union countries.
Classification: LCC KJE5087 .E345 2025 | DDC 340/.114094--dc23/eng/20250113
LC record available at https://lccn.loc.gov/2025000637

Bibliographic Information published by the Deutsche Nationalbibliothek
The Deutsche Nationalbibliothek lists this publication in the Deutsche Nationalbibliografie; detailed bibliographic data is available in the internet at http://dnb.d-nb.de.

Cover illustration: Courtesy of Benjamin Ben Chaim.

This publication was financially supported by the Faculty of Law and Administration, University of Warsaw, Poland.

ISSN 2191-3250
ISBN 978-3-631-90142-7 (Print)
E-ISBN 978-3-631-93509-5 (E-PDF)
E-ISBN 978-3-631-93510-1 (E-PUB)
DOI 10.3726/b22742

Published by Peter Lang GmbH, Berlin (Germany)

info@peterlang.com

This publication has been peer reviewed.

www.peterlang.com

Table of Contents

Introduction

The following monograph is the culmination of the collaborative efforts of dedicated researchers within the Effective Justice International and Comparative Approaches Platform, which officially launched its activities in December 2021. This platform led Prof. UAM Dr. hab. Barbara Janusz-Pohl from the Faculty of Law and Administration at Adam Mickiewicz University and Prof. Unibo Dr. Daniele Vicoli, representing the Department of Legal Sciences at the University of Bologna.

The platform's endeavours were made possible through the generous support of various sources, including grant funds from Adam Mickiewicz University and the University of Bologna and the prestigious Excellent Science Grant provided by the Polish Ministry of Science and Higher Education. The platform was dedicated to advancing scientific knowledge through a wide range of activities, including hosting international seminars and spearheading initiatives aimed at consolidating research efforts in the field of effectiveness, particularly in criminal proceedings at large. Emphasising the comparative and international aspects analysis, the platform attracted a diverse and global community of researchers. This resulted in a robust network of over 40 individuals representing more than 20 scientific centres, fostering both permanent and periodic cooperation. The platform's activities can be followed at www.effective-justice.com.

The book captures works on the effectiveness of evidentiary issues, summary and abbreviated proceedings, as well as those related to the issue of access to an effective remedy. The common theme throughout the collection is the concept of effectiveness. Within the framework of the EJ Platform, effectiveness was the primary focus, and its meaning was outlined against the background of other closely related terms such as efficacy, effectivity, or efficiency. The effectiveness presented in this collection's chapters is seen in a multi-layered dimension related to the achievement of the goals inherent to a given procedure, institution, or process activity.

The publication of this work was made possible due to the tremendous professional discipline of all authors, as well as the persons responsible for leading the "Evidence, Special and Abbreviated Procedure" section and the "Effective Remedies" section.

Mr. Michał Wawrzyńczak, a PhD student at the School of Social Sciences of the UAM and the Doctoral School of the Department of Legal Sciences of the University of Bologna, carried out critical activities related to preparing all papers for publication and technical layout.

This monograph is financed by the Adam Mickiewicz University Faculty of Law and Administration.

Prof. UAM Dr. hab. Barbara Janusz-Pohl[1]

Editorial

This book is divided into two parts. The first part focuses on special, abbreviated procedures and evidence, while the second covers the effective remedies system. The topics discussed in both parts are related to the effectiveness of criminal proceedings, procedural actions, and selected legal institutions. The chapters address a range of issues, including national and international themes, particularly those relevant to modern European standards. The section on special and abbreviated procedures highlights alternative methods of resolving disputes in criminal cases and also touches on specific proceedings related to the liability and protection of juveniles. The section on evidence focuses on the admissibility and legality of evidence while also examining issues related to effective remedies. The analysis of evidentiary issues is viewed through the lens of guarantees established by the ECHR and the standards developed by European tribunals. Additionally, the section on effective remedies contains interdisciplinary chapters that expand beyond the effectiveness of criminal proceedings. In most chapters, the authors analyse the issue of efficiency using the example of national systems. The presented overview can be used for comparative study.

The considerations of part one begin with the work entitled ***Between Efficiency Urges and Expectations of Justice in the Italian System. Deflation profiles of case dismissal for particular tenuity of the criminal act and for oblation by Italian Scholars*** by Prof. Chiara Gabrielli and Dr. Andrea Zampini.

In this work, effectiveness is characterised by the examples of a few institutions. The authors explore the regulations for case dropping requested by the public prosecutor (richiesta di archiviazione) at the end of preliminary investigations in Italian criminal procedure. They discuss the conformity of this regulation with the constitutional standards. Article 112 of the Italian Constitution mandates criminal prosecution, limiting the public prosecutor's discretion in dismissing a case through legally prescribed formulas. A common trait of traditional dismissal cases is a prognosis of trial superfluity due to grounds that may lead to subsequent acquittal. The Authors state that - recently, the Italian legislature expanded the operational boundaries of this legal feature to relieve a procedural system in severe

1 ORCID no. 0000-0002-7135-4960. Associate professor of Criminal Procedure at Adam Mickiewicz University.

and chronic distress. The institution of the request for dropping a case might be observed as an example of opportunism in criminal proceedings, as such a request is also now allowed in cases where the outcome of a trial would likely result in a conviction for minor offences punishable by a penalty that doesn't exceed a certain threshold of gravity, has modest consequences, and is not habitual (archiviazione per particolare tenuità del fatto). Additionally, this institution shall be seen as an tool for restorative justice, as in specific criminal fields, such as minor criminal offences against the environment and safety and health in workplaces, the request to drop a case is allowed after specific compensation (oblazione "condizionata"). The Authors expound upon these peculiar hypotheses of dismissal through the lens of constitutional and legitimacy jurisprudence. They elucidate these hypotheses' underlying objectives, prerequisites, and operational mechanics while highlighting their problematic aspects regarding systemic interpretation. Discussing the effectiveness of criminal proceedings in Italy, the thesis is formulated that this system "has become stuck in a chronic impasse", causing proceedings to drag on well beyond a reasonable timeframe guaranteed by the Italian Constitution. As a result, criminal liability is often impossible to determine in court due to the expiration of the statute of limitations. Minor offences significantly burden the justice system: fines or short prison sentences make up 90% of the total. Particularly, the Authors focus on the so-called "Cartabia reform" (Legislative Decree No. 150 of October 10th, 2022), which has narrowed the path to the preliminary hearing or direct trial by reshaping the concept of "unfoundedness of *the notitia criminis*". The authors, especially, refer to Article 408 c.p.p. This provision currently requires the public prosecutor to request dismissal "when the elements acquired during the preliminary investigation do not allow a reasonable prediction of conviction or application of a security measure other than confiscation". They point out that before the reform, the prosecution had to determine whether to pursue charges based on the investigative discoveries and their prospective integration into the trial. In contrast, the new regulation bounds prosecution with the existence of solid and converging evidence at the conclusion of the investigation. It is said that the Cartabia reform (No. 150 of 2022) extended the possibility of obtaining the dismissal thanks to the offender's restorative activities for contravention issued by Law No. 283/1962 and by other regulations on hygiene, production, traceability and sale of food and beverages. As mentioned, this law seeks to remove insignificant infractions from the criminal justice system, which would be "costly for the community and demanding for the offender".

In this study, the Italian scholars explore how dismissal can be used as a tool for special and abbreviated procedures and how fundamental principles entailed by this choice can be balanced to ensure, at the same time, procedural efficiency and adequate protection of individual rights connected with the justice system. Consequently, this study is a description of the regulations that supposed to speed up Italian criminal proceedings. The Authors highlight the constitutional dilemmas associated with these new regulations. Thus, the chapter contains considerations that can serve for further comparative studies.

The next chapter analyses the Croatian system and the general model for the formation of restorative justice in criminal cases. In its interesting inquiries on **Restorative Justice in Croatia: A Potential for an Effective Criminal Justice System** Prof. Aleksandar Maršavelski provides an overview of Croatian restorative justice literature, which is quite optimistic concerning the effectiveness of restorative justice. Ultimately, the effectiveness of restorative justice models depends on a lot of factors, such as the type of model used, legal framework, state support, implementation etc. The author states that there is no one-size-fits-all solution, and this contribution reveals the possibility of restorative justice in the Croatian legal system. The main argument is that the greatest potential of improving the effectiveness of the Croatian criminal justice system is to expand the application of restorative justice not just in juvenile cases, but also to find ways of its application to adult offenders. Despite the fact that restorative justice has a very limited use in the pre-trial stage because the real mediation between the offender and the victim, which avoids trial, is limited to a small portion of criminal cases – mainly juvenile cases or cases in which the victim has a decisive role in the initiation of the prosecution. In cases where the initiation of proceedings depends on the victim's initiative, restorative justice is mostly used informally, and there is a lack of data about it. Access to restorative justice is also very limited, as specialised out-of-court settlement services are available only in three Croatian cities. It is said that in Croatian law, elements of restorative justice are also present at the court proceedings level, especially in the context of special obligations that can be imposed along with a suspended sentence. The Author rightly observes that the use of restorative justice tools as obligations under suspended sentences has the greatest potential to expand the restorative. Based on the current Croatian legal framework, restorative justice also has the potential to be used in the stage of sanctions enforcement, including while serving prison sentences.

What seems to be crucial is that the Author states that the lenient sentencing policy in Croatia indicates that the judicial system treats most crimes as less serious in nature. The suspended sentences is by far the most frequently used sanction in Croatia, amounting to approximately 80%. Unfortunately, this is in line with the defense tactics. Based on the presented research, one shall argue that restorative justice tools are rarely used as obligations under suspended sentences. As Prof. Marsavelski stated, the Croatian judges are reluctant to impose them because they would need to control their execution in the post-conviction stage. Waiting for the suspended sentence to expire is a much simpler task for judges to close the case.

Analysing the layers of restorative justice mechanisms through the prism of stages of Croatian criminal procedure, it is pointed to the enforcement phase, including serving prison sentences. The Author diagnoses that victim-offender mediation is rarely initiated in reality post-conviction due to the fact that good behaviour without re-offending is sufficiently credited, so no effort to seek reconciliation with the victim is needed. Looking at the reasons for this state of affairs, it is said that the insufficient use of restorative justice mechanisms in criminal practice, despite the legal framework's vast options, primarily indicates inadequate training and a lack of motivation. Consequently, the remedy might be connected with promoting restorative justice mechanisms and proper training of professional actors. Prof. Marsavelski goes further by suggesting that regulations governing the monitoring and evaluation of the work of judges will certainly facilitate the work of judges as mediators. It is also necessary to ensure monitoring of restorative justice practices to evaluate their success and problems.

The other work that fits into the characteristics of national restorative justice regulations is a chapter under the title of **Mediation in Criminal Proceedings as a Potentially Effective Tool for Restorative Justice** by Prof. US Dr. hab. Magdalena Kowalewska-Łukuć. The Author characterises the institution of mediation as a specific tool in criminal proceedings, which can be an effective alternative to the "classic" - non-consensual - course of criminal proceedings. The work presents the legal framework and functioning of mediation in Polish criminal proceedings and Scandinavian countries, particularly Finland and Denmark. This Author has selected two radically different systems in terms of the popularity of mediation. Her considerations have been subjected to verification of the hypothesis that significant differences in the legal regulation and practice of mediation in these countries translate into its effectiveness and scope of impact. Adequately, therefore, the two systems were first described and then tried to find out what might be the reasons for the low use of the VOM in Poland.

Describing the mediation in Poland, Prof. Kowalewska-Łukuć refers to the Polish Code of Criminal Procedure (CCP) and the relevant regulation of the Minister of Justice, and based on these provisions, stated that the mediation seems to be regulated in such a general and at the same time flexible manner that one can assume that the legislative framework should even encourage its frequent application. She mentioned that statistics concerning mediation in Polish criminal proceedings show a rather surprising picture. Only a negligible number of criminal cases go to mediation. To be precise, it is less than 1%. At the same time, however, the effectiveness of mediation proceedings that have already begun is at a relatively good level - about 60–70% of them end with a settlement agreement. Thus, the statistical data show that mediation in criminal cases occurs very rarely. On the other hand, if it is launched, it has quite a high success rate. This leads her to the thesis that mediation can be a valuable tool of restorative justice, however, there are some severe problems or limitations in its application in the Polish criminal procedure. She rightly pointed out that the institutional constraints to mediation in Poland include the lack of tangible benefits for the offender when mediation was employed in criminal cases.

She diagnoses that even more far-reaching or simply obligatory, rather than merely optional, effects of mediation on the reduction of the offender's sentence could contribute to greater interest in it on the part of offenders and, consequently, to its more frequent use. It is, of course, uncertain how the greater influence of the mediation procedure on the outcome of criminal proceedings would work in the Polish criminal process. Discussing and describing the Polish system of mediation, a special focus was on so-called victim-sensitive mediation. Based on her professional experiences, she exposed the psychological features of this procedure, and she proposes some changes that represent a certain shift of emphasis in the current formula of mediation, which does not properly focus on the needs of the victim. When describing the Scandinavian model of mediation and its role in restorative justice panorama, this Author concluded that approaching the Polish system to Scandinavian might positively influence the effectiveness of mediation in Polish criminal courts. She suggests that without greater interest on the part of the potential parties to mediation and the criminal procedure authorities, the significance of mediation in Poland will not increase. One of the neglected fields – as the Author says, might be linked with building greater trust towards mediators (through their professional preparation), increasing the impact of mediation on the outcome of criminal proceedings (by offering suspects/accused persons a real reduction of criminal liability) and adapting the mediation procedure to the expectations, needs and specific situation of persons victimised by crime.

The next two chapters of the monograph address the issue of procedures related to the legal protection and responsibility of juveniles.

Work on **Life Path Lessons of Children in Closed Childcare Institution Service in Estonia: Experiences and Practices Related to Interprofessional Collaboration Based Support** by Dr. Koidu Saia that is part of a more extensive, five-objective study 'Study to Improve the System of Timely Identification and Effective Assistance to Children at Risk: Life Course Lessons for Children in a Closed Childcare Institution', which was conducted in Estonia with the participation of the CIRIC research group of the School of Governance, Law and Society of Tallinn University. This main study describes the empirical results of children's "journeys" to a closed childcare institution service (CCIS).

This chapter aims to analyse the cooperation between the child protection, education, social and law enforcement systems for the benefit of children in the CCIS, including identifying bottlenecks in the system and possible solutions. The focus is on the CCIS, which replaced special schools as a result of the 2018 reforms in Estonia. CCIS means temporarily restricting a minor's freedom of movement away from home in a safe and supportive environment. It is intended as a measure of last resort for children whose behaviour poses a serious threat to their own life, health or development or to the life or health of others. Consequently, CCIS might be the response for criminally oriented behaviours and demoralisation of juveniles. The CCIS means that the child's fundamental rights, including freedom of movement, are significantly restricted. It is reported that the assessment and decision-making process that underpins a referral to services, whether under the Social Welfare Act or criminal procedure, is complex and ultimately reserved for the court. One can apply for the CCIS for a maximum of one year at a time, and the court decides on the referral. It must be noted that for a child, an arrest is replaced by the CCIS.

Dr. Koidu observes that the number of applications for the CCIS has increased every year, from 93 applications in 2018 to 137 applications in 2020, even though this solution shall be ultima ratio. Behind the scenes, the abuse use of this measure might be discussed.

In this work, it is said that children referred to the service are characterised by complex problems and risky behaviour, including repeatedly committed offenses; therefore and, referring to the outputs of the systematic literature review – the CCIS families and children need positive parenting and family strengths focuse, early identification and prevention, participation and child-centred, interdisciplinary collaboration, services, methods. The discussion is kept around the characteristics of significant changes that have taken place in the Estonian child protection, education, social welfare, and justice systems in recent years, which have affected the well-being of children and families in vulnerable, fragile situations (including those involved in CCIS) and posed new challenges for professionals working in the system, sector developers, and policymakers.

The last piece of work devoted to the abbreviated procedure contains a discussion on: Proceed with caution? Human rights concerns arising from the use of out-of-court disposals to improve efficiency in the criminal justice system by Dr. Stephen Terrett offers an overview of out-of-court disposals that offer an alternative to traditional criminal prosecutions and court proceedings. As the Author argues, these formulas are quick, cheap and capable of producing better rehabilitation results than formal trials and punitive sentences. Nonetheless, such efficiency is produced by sacrificing many of the procedural safeguards that apply during traditional prosecutions and trials. This chapter explores the non-trial alternatives that are available in the English legal system and discusses some of the human rights concerns that they spawn.

Out-of-Court Disposals (OOCDs) are mechanisms for dealing with ('disposing of') criminal cases without a formal prosecution. As the Author explains the 'non-court' location at which OOCDs are administered is generally the police station where the suspected offender is taken following arrest. In most cases, the police are empowered to issue OOCD mechanisms directly. The OOCD's is based on the voluntary decision of the offender who must admit to having committed the offence and freely accept the OOCD proposed by the police. Still, there is a marge of manoeuvre for the Police to proceed in more formalised way. One may say that the OOCD's are consensual modes. The Author rightly observes the dangers that are at the same times consequences of renouncing the formal prosecution.

In Dr. Terrett's deliberations, effectiveness is clearly split between time and cost factors, which are the benefits of using OOCD's, and factors related to protecting procedural values and principles. This is because the reduction of formalism combines with a drastic decrease in the guarantees of criminal procedure. The author describes in detail the evolution of the operation of out-of-court solutions on the one hand and their current form on the other. Stressing that from a formal point of view any OOCD can be applied to any offense, though the law may modify this general rule, and though additional procedures apply if the police wish to apply OOCDs to serious offenses. Nevertheless, the Author indicates that the police are unlikely to apply OOCDs to the most severe (indictable) crimes, or to mid-ranking offenses (triable either way) committed in circumstances which would probably see the courts impose a lengthy imprisonment period for anyone who might be prosecuted. This makes the OOCD's a very flexible mechanism of action that could support the fight against lengthy cases or reduce costs. The quantitative analysis presented in this chapter reveals clearly that consensual dispute resolutions create the dominant model in GB and Wales.

The remaining five chapters of Part One are dedicated to evidentiary issues. They address the issue of the relationship between the principle of elimination of illegal evidence and the principle of material truth. The problem of special types of evidence, proof obtained through deep fake technology, or so-called chain of custody, was considered.

In a work entitled **Procedural treatment of prohibited evidence: its evolution in Spain** by a group of scholars Prof. Dr. Dr.h.c. Juan-Luis Gómez Colomer; Prof. Dr. Andrea Planchadell Gargallo; Dr. Christa M. Madrid Boquín, the Authors discuss the fundamental question of the legality and admissibility of evidence in Spain. They present the actual standard and its evolution by focusing on the approaches given by the Spanish Constitutional Court. They state that the Spanish Constitution does not include such a rule or evidentiary prohibition in any of its provisions. The Authors observe that since 1998 onwards, the Spanish Constitutional Court has confirmed the reductionist tendency in this area. The Constitutional Court opens up new lines of jurisprudence, which either imply changes to the already established doctrine of prohibited evidence or formulate new exceptions in addition to those linked with the doctrine of the fruits of the poisonous tree. Among these exceptions, the most important is the theory of the connection of unlawfulness and the exception of the voluntary confession of the defendant and the so-called "good faith exception". Authors argue that current reality is based on the idea of the prevalence of the principle of substantive truth and the non-punity argument. With the criticism, the Authors reflect that the Spanish courts consider that society would never understand that a criminal, especially if he is a savage terrorist, a brutal murderer, a ruthless drug trafficker, an important corrupt politician, an inhuman facilitator of human trafficking, or a despicable corrupter of minors, that is, if we are dealing with socially very relevant cases, would be set free on a "mere legal technicality". These exceptions to exclusionary rules, in addition to avoiding impunity, are also intended to protect the public investigating authority against possible failures that would, if the initial theories of prohibited evidence were maintained, inevitably lead to the acquittal of the accused.

The main observation in this study says that Spanish jurisprudence and doctrine have gone from assuming the prohibition of evidence for its effect of deterring the police from acting against the law and constitutionally protecting the rights of the defendant against the interventionist power of the State in the individual sphere, to purely utilitarian considerations of punishing anyone who is "evidently" guilty of a horrendous crime in any way possible.

The Authors share their criticism of this development. However, it must be mentioned that in recent times, one can find few rulings in the Spanish Constitutional Court or the Spanish Supreme Court, in which an appeal is granted or where the initial ruling is overturned because the process is null and void. After all, evidence has been declared to have been obtained unlawfully. Subsequently, the Authors ask: Quo Vadis, then, unlawful evidence?

The Authors suggest that: The truth is that there is no precise answer to this question, although one might intuitively suggest something. In any case, it is necessary to take up the reins once again and urgently in such a delicate matter and return to positions of guarantee, this time taking into account the practical experiences that caused us to stray from the path we had taken, without ignoring the social demands that motivated them, reinforcing the legality of criminal investigation so that all those who intervene in it are sufficiently trained and qualified to avoid those technical failures that cause procedural nullities and subsequently motivate undesired acquittals.

In an effectiveness framework, values come into play with objective and measurable efficiency parameters, such as time and cost. In the study by the Spanish authors, the focus is clearly centred. At the same time, the conclusion of the text calls for the most serious violation of the law of evidence, i.e. all the cases of possible evidential illegality which violate the Constitution were to be regulated, that is to say, expressly regulated in ordinary law. Their infringement would be considered either a cause for the nullity of the whole process (and, therefore, the release of the accused without charge or acquittal) or the nullity only of the act (allowing conviction in the case of the existence of other evidence obtained lawfully). The Authors rightly observe that this would also help to simplify the process, particularly in the area of evidence, in view of the clarity of the rules achieved.

In the chapter: **The use of spy software as a means of obtaining evidence in criminal investigations and the need for effective remedies to safeguard fundamental rights: the case of Portugal, Eduardo Bolsoni Riboli** examines the nature of spy software and the risks that its use for investigative purposes poses to the fundamental rights of those under investigation. Subsequently, examples of the implementation of this measure in the European Union are to be inquired, drawing from the legal frameworks established in Germany and Italy; and elucidate the requirements that the ECtHR deems necessary for the use of covert means for evidence collection, particularly the interception of communications. Finally, the Author concludes how this method of evidence gathering has been implemented in Portugal, subsequently assessing its constitutionality and verifying whether Portugal guarantees the right to remedies against measures that violate fundamental rights, such as the use of spy software for collecting evidence, in compliance with the right to an effective remedy established in Article 13 of the ECHR.

In this work, specific terminological assumptions are adopted, and consequently, "Spyware" encompasses a class of computer programs engineered to extract information from digital devices or computer systems without the user's consent or awareness regarding their installation and operation. While different types of spyware exist, each tailored to fulfill one or more specific function(s), they all share the common trait of masking their installation and operation. They are often referred to as "Trojan horses" or "malware" (a contraction of the term "malicious software"). The Author rightly observes that in the context of secret surveillance and covert investigations, one shall opt for the terminology "spy software" as (1) not all malware is designed for the extraction of digital information (some serve commercial purposes like generating pop-up ads)12; (2) Trojan horses are just one of the multiple forms of spyware available, and (3) to avoid the presumption that all spy software is necessarily illegal, inappropriate, or harmful, as when adequately regulated and employed, they can be a valuable tool for investigative purposes.

The main part of the discussion is based on the acknowledgement that the use of spy software as a means of obtaining evidence raises conflicts between different legal interests and fundamental rights: due process of law, freedom of expression and information, the right to image, the right to privacy; the right to self-determination and communication; the right to professional secrecy; the integrity of technical-informational systems; and informational self-determination. Conflicts also arise at the procedural level, impacting, among others, the right to refuse testimony or interrogations and the principle of *nemo tenetur*. Such rights and principles are a cornerstone of the European legal order, especially the right to privacy, as established in Article 8 of the European Convention on Human Rights.

The Author reports that within the European Union, several countries, ie. Germany and Italy have incorporated the use of spy software for evidence collection into their legal frameworks.

A large part of this study discusses the jurisprudence of the ECHR based on the Art. 8 of the Convention—which establishes the need for legal provisions in order to restrict fundamental rights inherent to private and family life and determines the cases in which these rights can be limited by the state. Among the cases under discussion, one shall point to the cases Amann v. Switzerland Weber and Saravia v. Germany, when the ECtHR established six minimum requirements to assess the "quality of law" in secret surveillance legislation. In the case of Roman Zakharov v. Russia, the Court updated the concept of necessary predictability for fulfilling the "quality of law" and in the case Big Brother Watch And Others v. The United Kingdom, the ECtHR would return to the subject. A large part of this study discusses the recent case (2022) Ekimdzhiev and Others v. Bulgaria, when the Court ruled that the laws governing secret surveillance in Bulgaria did not meet the minimum safeguards against arbitrariness and abuse as established in Article 8 of the ECHR. In short, the ECtHR recognises the possibility of limitations of fundamental rights but only if they are justified (e.g. prevention of serious crimes) and if the domestic law meets the required criteria of "quality of law" to ensure the necessary safeguards to protect the rights affected. Spy software, with its ability to access a wide range of information, has proven to be a valuable tool in criminal investigations. However, its use raises concerns related to the restriction of fundamental rights. As a result, the use of spy software must be established by adequate legal provisions to avoid violating the rights of those under investigation.

The last part of the analysis is devoted to Portuguese regulations or, rather, the lack of proper regulations in Portugal on the use of spy software in criminal investigations. This creates legal gaps and lacks the "quality of law" required by the ECtHR. The author clearly states that special investigative techniques should adopt clear and effective laws regulating them, including procedural guarantees, controls, oversight, and judicial review mechanisms. As such, the use of spy software as a means of obtaining evidence in Portugal, under the current version of the Cybercrime Law, is incompatible with the principles set out by the Portuguese Constitution, rendering Article 19(2) of the Cybercrime Law unconstitutional.

The following chapter by Federico C. La Vattiata discusses **Crimes of Harmful Consequences and Artificial Intelligence: Causation at the Bar**.

Firstly, the Author refers to the terminological controversies, as there is no unique definition of AI by European law as states: "means software that (…) can, for a given set of human-defined objectives, generate outputs such as content, predictions, recommendations, or decisions influencing the environments they interact with".

The Author reminds that the Commission has launched the aforementioned Draft AIA, aiming at harmonising the rules on AI, and in particular at reaching four goals: ensure that AI systems placed on the Union market and used are safe and respect existing law on fundamental rights and Union values; ensure legal certainty to facilitate investment and innovation in AI; enhance governance and effective enforcement of existing law on fundamental rights and safety requirements applicable to AIs; and facilitate the development of a single market for lawful, safe and trustworthy AIs and prevent market fragmentation.

La Vattiata is following Fabio Basile by distinguishing four research pathways concerning AI in criminal law theory: i) AI and law enforcement activities; ii) AI-based judicial decisions in criminal matters (robot-judge); iii) AI-based crime-risk assessment; and iv) AI and criminal liability. The Author searches for responses to the question of whether the 'good old criminal law', grounded upon a notion of causation related to classical 'Newtonian' physics, is still a useful tool for managing AI-risks. He says: "To answer such a question, human capacity to etiologically govern AI is crucial. In other words, its theoretical categories turn out to be no more useful only as long as the 'black box dilemma' is radically unsolvable". The Author discusses details aspect of challenges for substantive criminal law based on AI developments. In conclusion, it seems to be neither necessary nor appropriate to renounce classical criminal law as one of the state's risk management tools and protection of fundamental legal values. In fact, as clarified above, except for some residual cases of 'opaque' AI algorithms, a problem relating to causation either is not posed, or is solvable. Criminal law shall not be used to merely 'sedate' (control) social fears of technological innovation.

Some AI features can jeopardise the 'functioning' of criminal law. In this respect the Author calls for criminal law tools should be integrated with civil law and administrative law instruments, thus providing for an AI-product liability framework that is 'balanced' and inspired by subsidiarity and proportionality principles. In conclusion, it is said that as for substantive law, "minimum rules concerning the definition of criminal offences and sanctions" might be established through directives under Article 83 TFEU. As the Author rightly observed - they cannot be established under paragraph 1, as the regulation of AI is not among the "areas of particularly serious crime with a cross-border dimension" explicitly enlisted therein – unless we consider it as a species included within the genus 'computer crime'. Finally, under the procedural law perspective, the legal framework in question could be effectively completed by including the AI-crime within the matters for which the European Public Prosecutor's Office (EPPO) is competent.

Next chapter is prepared by Dr. Marcin Galiński, and concerns **Detection of usage deepfake technology in evidentiary proceedings on the ground of the Polish Code of Criminal Procedure**.

At the outset, the Author says that technical development gives plenty of profits and previously unknown opportunities for the improvement of everyday life, nevertheless it has negative aspects as well, among them, the newest technology is partially a source of new forms of criminal activity. It has consequences not only in the area of substantive criminal law but also in the field of procedural law. One of the newest technologies that can be used for unlawful purposes is deepfake technology, which allows for the realistic modification of video materials. Based on this Author's opinion – deepfake technology might be used for the production of false pieces of evidence in court proceedings. One might disagree with this Author, by seeing that the use of deep fake technology is more of a threat to the effectiveness of the procedure, as it shall increase the costs and cause a delay when it comes to the need for expert witnesses' opinions in those cases when the use of deep fake technology by the privet parties to the trail is suspected.

On the contrary, the Author maintains that the continual improvement of deepfake technology, which will provide more possibilities for content modification, impacts the need for regulations that would allow judicial organs to detect modification of evidence and react to cases of usage of deepfake materials.

In this chapter, firstly, the Author will briefly present Polish regulations creating a legal framework for the detection and usage of deepfake technology in criminal proceedings, and secondly, propose some amendments (rather general). The author says that the binding provisions of CCP provide several significant possibilities for detecting the usage of deepfake technology in an evidentiary proceeding. CCP creates legal frameworks for trustworthy video verification. The major instruments which can be used in the mentioned goal are the opinion of expert witnesses and the examination of carriers containing video material.

The Author concludes that due to the current modest scale of the use of deefake technology, the existing tools are sufficient, while there are not many cases that can be used to create a pattern. However, it seems that the development of deepfake technology will force some changes in the methodology of dealing with electronic evidence produced illegally.

The last chapter in part one is entitled **Message Applications Mirroring, Jurisprudential Interpretation, and the Challenging Chain of Custody in a Criminal Case** by Dr. Rodrigo da Silva Brandalise; Décio Alonso Gomes.

The Authors focus their debate on the jurisprudential analysis, emphasising that in Brazil, the jurisprudential debate on the chain of custody (initial and generally linked to telephone and telematic interception techniques) precedes regulations of the Brazilian Code of Criminal Procedure. To explain the terminological aspect, one must notice that the essence of the chain of custody concept is to provide the integrity of the source of evidence and the evidence itself, enabling the exercise of adversarial and probative evaluation of evidence. In other words, the primary purpose of the chain of custody is to ensure that the evidence left in the material world by a criminal offence corresponds exactly to those collected by the police, examined and presented in Court. It must be added that this characteristic depends on the type of evidence generated by the conduct. In this regard, the Brazilian Superior Court of Justice (also called the Citizenship Court) decided that the quantitative real evidence divergence does not automatically break the chain of custody. Thus, situations like these should be analysed case by case. In summary, it is not any alteration of the chronological history documentation of the collected evidence that causes nullity. If the alteration – merely quantitative - does not affect the essence of the source or the evidence itself, the Court will not declare the violation of the procedural guarantee. However, if there is a qualitative alteration, it breaks the guarantee matrix, it does not assure the parties (and the judge) the integral knowledge of the evidence, and it affects its evaluation. Considering these perceptions about quantitative and qualitative aspects as premises, the Authors focus on a critical analysis of the Brazilian judicial decisions about the chain of digital evidence.

Initially, the Authors mention the encryption (as a result, telephone and telematic interceptions lose effectiveness and are unable to access the content of the messages in an understandable and helpful way to the criminal procedure), which forces the investigation and intelligence agencies to seek alternatives to overcome this technological barrier as the use of mirroring or data replication (that is the synchronous reflection of physical objects on a distinct monitor that allows access to a faithful copy of the data in another location - physical or logical). It must be observed that for prosecutorial purposes, mirroring permits data availability at the source without alerting the investigated person during the observation of exchange messages. The Authors say that, the first question must be responded directly: the mirroring service does not necessarily use a different smartphone because it must be limited to the visualisation feature without interaction. Thus, data replication does not necessarily lead to editing or manipulating the source data. There is conceptual corruption due to the wide use of a particular message application in Brazil instead of other apps: the widespread use of WhatsApp narrows the technology knowledge to the possibilities and limitations of this app.

At first, the Authors ask the question: "without ignoring the relevance of freedom of expression and the guarantee of privacy, would it be correct to permit operating technologies that are completely immune to prosecution?"

The whole discussion is focused on the recent court decision by the Brazilian Superior Court of Justice that revisited its precedents and overruled the illegitimacy of the mirroring decision. In the introduction, it is said what exactly mirroring is. The Authors refer to definition based on it is an investigation technique to collect evidence that must occur with the trust of the agents, especially the agent provocateur, who must obtain information from the rest of the people involved in the crime; For this reason, the agent provocateur needs to perform direct action in crime commitment. It must be clarified that the Brazilian Law also allows access to and interference in the so-called communications flow through the internet since it is duly authorised. This recent decision presents that covert actions or agent provocateurs during criminal investigations, especially in virtual media, must be combined with proportionality (utility, necessity) and subsidiarity when they cannot be produced by other available means, which it expressly recognises. After all, the defendant's right not to self-incriminate and the right to remain silent are conferred by the State to avoid any obligation for the defendant to produce the evidence that incriminates him, except if the defendant himself, voluntarily, carries it out. What is crucial in this discussion is the court decision at hand stated that the expert examination is unnecessary to verify the recording's reliability because they must presume authenticity, considering the public faith of state agents. For this reason, the chain of custody, per se, cannot decide about the inadequacy of the evidence. Nevertheless, the WhatsApp Web's evidence analysis must be combined with the rest of the evidentiary context, like any other type of evidence. The Authors criticise a part of court interpretation that says - it is up to those who allege the violation of the chain of custody to demonstrate it and, even more so, the adulteration of its contents, notably, because there is a sequence that the conversation itself demonstrates, even when arising from screen capture. The features of WhatsApp tell a path of messages and exchange of information and the smartphones and the application background register what is, in fact, the chain of custody, and there must be the obligation of those who make the allegation of violation (who sustains it must exercise the burden of proving it). The point of view presented by the Brazilian court admittedly has the potential to be controversial as creating a basis for weakening the right to defense, at the same time, the ruling can be seen as advantageous from the point of view of the efficiency of investigative activities.

The deliberations contained in Part Two: Systems of effective remedies consist of 5 studies of a quite diverse format. The main focus of reflection remains the European context, related to the exploration of the right to effective remedies.

In the chapter on The right to an effective remedy in the light of the length of the proceedings in the Polish criminal process according to the jurisprudence of the ECtHR, Prof. UW Dr. hab. Szymon Pawelec, states that the practical realisation of the right specified in Article 13 of the ECHR raises a number of issues stemming not only from the problematic general wording of that particular provision but also from its systemic position and relation to other regulations of the Convention. Crucial issue concerns the violation of the "reasonable time" requirement in criminal proceedings, which has been frequently analysed by the Strasburg Court. The ponderings of this chapter focus on the landmark judgment in the case Kudła v. Poland on October 26th, 2005. In this case, the Court adopted the interpretation that the right to an effective remedy under Art. 13 ECHR is distinct from the reasonable time requirement under Art. 6 § 1 ECHR. Moreover, the national legal orders of the Member States must include remedies within the meaning of Art. 13 ECHR, enabling a challenge to the excessive length of the proceedings. In his discussion, Prof. Pawelec examines the realisation of the Strasbourg standard of the right to an effective remedy in the Polish criminal process stemming from the judgement in Kudła v. Poland case. In that judgment, the ECtHR changed its assessment of the relationship between Art. 6 § 1 and Art. 13 ECHR. The ECtHR found that in this case there had been a violation of Article 13 of the Convention, in that the applicant did not have a domestic remedy by which he could have enforced his right to a "hearing within a reasonable time" guaranteed by Article 6 § 1 of the Convention. As a result, there can be no doubt that there must be an effective remedy to bring before the national authorities a breach of the guarantees arising from Article 6 § 1 ECHR, including the right to have the case heard "within a reasonable time", and additionally that the ECtHR has the power to assess whether such a legal remedy in a given legal system is effective within the meaning of Art. 13 ECHR. The judgment of ECtHR in the Kudła v. Poland case obliged Poland to introduce into its national legal systems a measure enabling a challenge to the excessive length of proceedings. In implementation of this judgment Poland enacted the Law of June 17th, 2004 on complaint about breach of the right to have a case examined in judicial proceedings without undue delay. The Author rightly observes that despite many years that passed since the entry into force of the Act, there is still a problem in Poland with the lengthiness of court proceedings and the possible ineffectiveness of the created measure. This is noticeable, among others, in the number of complaints about unfinished proceedings taken into consideration by the ECtHR, and submitted after using national measures to counteract excessive length of proceedings. As Prof. Pawelec rightly indicates, one of the key decisions in this regard is the judgment issued by the ECtHR in the case Rutkowski v. Poland. In this case the ECtHR noticed a general systemic problem in Poland regarding the length of court proceedings. In terms of violations of Art. 6 § 1 ECHR, the Court noted that they are most often related to too slow submission of opinions by court experts and defective process management – in particular, too frequent postponements of hearings and long breaks between subsequent hearings. In turn, under Art. 13 of the Convention, the Court noticed a structural problem in the functioning of the remedy created in the form of a complaint about excessive length. In this judgment, the Strasburg Court criticised the Polish law adopted on June 17th, 2004, specifically problematic the aspect of compensation mentioned. In the Author's opinion, as regards the above position of the Tribunal on the amount that can be awarded by Polish courts to the applicant if a complaint about the length of proceedings is upheld, there seems to be a clear necessity for changes in the Polish regulations.

More general view of **Fair trial rights violations and effective remedies in criminal proceedings—The ECHR perspective** is presented by Ph. D. Lorenzo Bernardini. The Author offers a thorough exploration of the concept of 'effective remedy' as outlined in Article 13 ECHR. It then focuses on its application in the context of criminal proceedings, analyzing how the ECtHR approaches cases where fair trial rights are allegedly breached. Specifically, it offers an updated analysis of the ECtHR's legal reasoning regarding the necessity of guaranteeing effective remedies in cases involving violations of Article 6(1) ECHR (right to a trial within a reasonable time) and Article 6(2) ECHR (presumption of innocence). The chapter concludes by addressing any lingering unresolved questions in this regard. At the outset, the Author rightly diagnosed problems related to the interpretation of the concept "effective remedy." As he says: "(…) which specific measures must domestic systems establish in order to qualify as a 'remedy'? What types of authorities (including judicial, administrative, political, and disciplinary bodies) are capable of providing an effective remedy? What attributes define an 'effective remedy' in the context of criminal proceedings and how is its efficacy may be quantified? Can the mere acknowledgment of a violation suffice as an 'effective remedy', or must such a remedy offer redress or relief for the contested circumstance? And, in this latter case, what may constitute the suitable form of redress for a violation of fundamental rights?"

Defining the notion of "effective remedy" Dr. Bernardini noticed that the Strasbourg Court has provided an interpretation of the notion of 'effective remedy' in concrete terms. Noteworthy topics scrutinized by the Court include the definition of 'remedy', 'effectiveness' of the latter, 'national authority' and 'violation' as stipulated in Article 13 ECHR. The Author also highlighted the importance of judgement in case Kudła v. Poland, which was discussed in an earlier chapter by Prof. Pawelec in the context of Polish regulations. As it was mentioned, in case Kudła the Court overturned its prior case law and for the first time, the autonomous importance of the right to an effective remedy for a breach of the reasonable time requirement stemming from Article 6(1) ECHR was expressly acknowledged. The well-established ECtHR's case-law has consistently upheld the admissibility of combining this aforementioned provision with Article 13 ECHR. Regarding the breach of the reasonable time requirement, it recognized that Article 6(1) ECHR and Article 13 thereof could be regarded as distinct and separate. Dr. Bernarding calls this perspective "defensible," but he admits that it is rooted in pragmatic considerations. By criticising the Court's interpretation, the Author reminds us that judicial decisions should be grounded in a thorough examination of the relevant provisions, considering their literal meaning, their context and their purpose.

On the other hand, as the Author underlines, the right to an effective remedy has consistently preserved its substantive autonomy where breaches of the presumption of innocence are alleged. Unfortunately, the ECtHR's case-law has not followed a uniform pattern in this aspect. However, it is observed that the Court tried to delineate the fundamental grounds that a remedy must satisfy to be deemed 'effective' when analysing the effective remedy for the presumption of innocence. Dr. Bernardini speaks about three elements, and one of them refers to the claim for civil damages arising from a breach of the presumption of innocence that could only serve as a partial remedy, as it could not 'fully' redress the alleged infringement. Thus, for a civil law remedy to be considered 'effective', it must be complemented by additional procedures aimed at recognising or rectifying the violation of the presumption of innocence.

In this chapter, another argument is leaping out, Dr. Bernardini states that if the Court continues to embrace this functionalistic approach, it appears that there is still room within the realm of fair trial rights to fully recognise the significance of Article 13 ECHR. He argues that this is particularly evident when considering the rights of the defence outlined in Article 6(3) ECHR. In conclusion, the observation is made that the matter of providing effective remedies for violations of fair trial rights is an evolving concern before the ECtHR, but the principle of subsidiarity creates a self-limit for the ECtHR to adopt a stronger approach, which means it opens more possibility to demand redress directly before this court.

The subsequent chapter on **Non-appealable nature of evidentiary decisions in appeal proceedings in Polish criminal trial from the perspective of the right to an effective remedy under Art. 13 ECHR** is delivered by Dr. Aleksandra Komar-Nalepa.

Dr. Komar Nalepa indicates that the Polish legal system lacks appealability of evidentiary decisions at the stage of appeal proceedings, although evidence unknown in the first-instance proceedings may be carried out in these proceedings. This, in her opinion, raises doubts about the realization of the right to effective remedy resulting from Art. 13 ECHR.

First, the Author presented the necessary scope of the Polish regulation contained in the 1997 Criminal Procedure Code, noting that, on the one hand, in appeal proceedings, the court may carry out extensive evidentiary proceedings, and, on the other hand, that recently Polish legislator has also introduced new evidentiary restrictions, including the inadmissibility to present evidence that the applicant could have called before the first-instance court, or if the circumstance to be proven by a given evidence concerns a new fact that is not the subject of the proceedings before the first-instance court, and the applicant could then indicate it (Article 452 § 2 point 2 CCP in connection with Article 427 § 3 CCP). Notwithstanding these provisions, it should be mentioned that their interpretation is not straightforward. The legislator continues to give primacy to the principle of material truth; certainly, full evidentiary preclusion has not been adopted. However, it is strictly stipulated that the request for evidence cannot be dismissed on the basis of the above premises in a situation where the circumstance to be proven, within the limits of the consideration of the case by the appellate court, is of significant importance for determining whether a prohibited act was committed at all, and if so, under what conditions it was committed, in order to impose an appropriate penalty. The Author of this chapter argues that the legislator should have introduced a remedy, interlocutory appeal for this decision, namely a decision on evidence admissibility. As a side note, one must add that in Polish CCP there is no interlocutory measure against the decision on evidence admissibility, also based on the basic provision of this Code. The Author notes that in Polish criminal procedure, the court in the appellate proceedings can conduct new evidence, and these, in turn, can be the basis for a new merit decision, which is no longer appealable in the course of the instances. For this reason, in the Author's opinion, due to the inadmissibility to appeal in Polish criminal proceedings against the decision to dismiss an application for evidence by the appellate court at the stage of the proceedings pending before it, should be assessed as inconsistent with Art. 13 ECHR. Due to the fact that the appellate court may also take evidence unknown to the first-instance court and, on its basis, issue a substantive decision in the case, the party should be able to have the court's specific position in the above respect verified by another independent body. It is important that an appropriate appeal can be brought during this particular proceedings so as to remedy the effects of the defective decision as quickly as possible.

In the next subsection, the issue of **Evidentiary misbehaviours and their consequences by Dr. Emanuele Toma** is presented.

The Author starts his consideration by reminding us that in Italian criminal procedure, the domain of inadmissibility of evidence is partially regulated. The evidence is only required to be suitable for the ascertainment of facts (i) and not to affect moral freedom (ii). The first requirement says nothing about the lawfulness of the evidence itself, and – if no other exclusionary rules were provided – it would only exclude the unreliable ones. The concept of moral freedom is very limited by Article 188, which defines it as "methods or techniques able to influence the freedom of self-determination or to alter the ability to remember and evaluate facts". Moreover, the Author explains that the theory of constitutional exclusionary rules has not been strictly adopted in Italian procedure. The main reasons that bring judges to oppose a wider application of exclusionary rules usually lie in the struggle to find a good balance between the collective interests and the fundamental rights of the citizens, further complicated by the moral dilemmas implied by the choice between admitting unlawfully obtained evidence and letting a guilty person free. The Toma says, that the Corte di Cassazione (1.11.2023, n. 15836) seemed to open to a new approach and expressly stated that violations of fundamental rights do have an effective and immediate remedy inside of Italian trials. Violations of Constitutional rights would cause un-usability of the evidence as provided by Article 191, c.p.p., as such irremediable. Following this thought, Dr. Toma tried to discover an effective remedy to this kind of evidentiary misbehaviour in criminal procedure. To do so, we will examine the implication of fair trial and due process principles and of Constitutional exclusionary rules. Although more closely focused on an effective remedy, Dr. Tom's analysis shares a common denominator with the Spanish authors' analysis in Part One of this monograph. How to resolve the collision of reaching the material truth while ensuring procedural fairness of the process. An effective process is a process based on values, but what to do when these values compete with each other, whether in such cases parameters such as efficiency features, purely related to the economics of action, shall be decisive.

The Author rightly observes that if the law provides for the procedure for taking evidence, it should also provide for the consequences of its violations. Unfortunately, codes of criminal procedures in this sphere operate on formula leges non-perfecta, which means no sanctions for the infringements.

Dr. Toma proposes the following solutions: "i) If the misbehaviour causes a violation that harms a fundamental right guaranteed by the country's constitution and there is the possibility of appealing to the Constitutional Court, it will be possible to proceed by bringing ordinary law to its attention, arguing that it is illegitimate because it poses a threat to the rights protected by the Fundamental Chart (indirect remedy). ii) If the violation concerns other rights but still renders the trial unfair as a whole, an effective remedy should be found challenging the decision before a domestic or a supranational court (as would be the case in the ECHR) and, consequently, the trial reopened. iii) If the violation ultimately concerns any other right, the collective interest in criminal prosecution should prevail and there would be no need to grant any remedy."

However, it must be underlined that the Author puts some additional restrictions when it comes to the application of this pattern on the one hand when it comes to countries based on adversarial and mixed criminal justice systems, and on the other hand, when the system is inquisitorially oriented. In countries based on the inquisitorial model, the judicial discretion should be greater; a judge may still admit the evidence later (if it's not radically excluded as such) even if it was previously acquired in violation of fundamental rights. The only other circumstance in which such evidence could be excluded due to such violations would be when they rendered the trial unfair as a whole, and only as long as a domestic or supernational remedy is provided. In countries shaped on an adversarial system, however, the provision of a fundamental constitutional right should constitute, by itself, a valid source of exclusionary rules, regardless of whether it has made the trial unfair, and the parties should, therefore, be guaranteed access to an effective remedy, whether it is direct or indirect. At the end of his discussion, Dr. Toma pointed out that the diversity of national systems is not supportive for establishing general principles, due to the fact that the rules of inadmissibility of evidence are likely to vary substantially. Let us note that this would be most dangerous in a situation where the jurisdictions of such countries compete.

Michał Wawrzyńczak presents the work on **Securing Effective Collection of Evidence: An Overview of Various Approaches to Interrogation Techniques**.

Although a suspect's confession is no longer the 'queen of evidence' one cannot overestimate the value of testimony provided by personal sources of evidence in criminal proceedings. After all, defendants and witnesses, including expert witnesses, are the primary source of factual findings in the vast majority of pending cases. Only the correct reconstruction of events makes it possible to establish the real culprit and the basis of their responsibility. For that purpose, it is essential to obtain statements that are truthful.

This study focuses on analysing the interrogation techniques used to obtain evidence in the form of testimony at the pre-trial proceedings. Typically, interrogation activities are carried out by police officers or their equivalent; less frequently, the prosecutor or other supervising or prosecuting authority will be responsible for the interrogation. There are many interrogation techniques and their variants. In the chapter at hand, the focus is on the most important proposals of the doctrine, practice and legislature. Both so-called coercive techniques and those based on the rapport&trust building mechanism will be analysed. The main idea of the paper is to evaluate the commonly used interrogation techniques and to identify those that should provide a universal basis for shaping the ways of interrogation in the future. In this perception, an effective interrogation technique is the guarantee-oriented modus.

The last chapter in this par focuses on more selected issues. Dr. Katarzyna Zombory highlights **Effective Remedies for the Violation of Cultural Human Rights under International Law**. The Author discusses the concept of effective remedies and the international framework for the protection of cultural rights, especially by identifying different approaches to remedies for the violation of cultural rights in the jurisprudence of the international treaty bodies at the universal and regional levels, specifically within the Inter-American, African, and European systems for human rights protection.

The Author points out that cultural rights aim at the preservation, maintenance, and development of culture, which are the specific elements of the social or cultural life of a group that contributes to its separate identity. The effective legal protection of cultural rights is important for national minorities and indigenous people. Dr. Zombory discusses the right to participate in cultural life, which has been recognised in all fundamental human rights instruments at the universal and regional levels (ICESCR, ICCPR, ACHR, ACHPR). The critical point is linked with the argument that the ECHR does not explicitly protect cultural rights. However, it allows for the protection of cultural rights by the evolutionary interpretation of some of its other provisions. Cultural human rights, either recognised explicitly or implicitly, need to be given effect in the first place at the domestic level, which is the idea embodied in the concept of the right to an effective remedy and manifested by the subsidiary role of human rights treaty bodies.

Dr. Zombory presents an overview of the international mechanisms to secure the effective enjoyment of cultural human rights comprising inter-state and individual complaint procedures before the human rights treaty bodies (CCPR, CESCR, IACtHR, ACmHPR and ECtHR). As a main argument, the diversity of regional bodies jurisprudence is highlighted, as regional organs vary significantly in terms of the scope and types of redress awarded, ranging from declaratory judgments and compensation to specific actions and non-monetary remedies. As it was emphasised at the outset in Europe, the ECtHR is more restrained towards awarding redress for cultural rights violations and leaves it to the requested state to decide on how to remedy the wrongful situation. Remedies ordered by the ECtHR in cases involving cultural rights commonly amount to moderate compensation. While ordering compensation, the ECtHR is specific about the payment modalities, such as the default interest rate. As Dr. Zombory states, at other times, the ECtHR does not hesitate to refuse the applicants' claim for compensation, in which case, the declaratory judgment must suffice for a just satisfaction for non-pecuniary damage.

One must agree with the main thesis of this article that the proper implementation of cultural human rights is of utmost importance for the peaceful coexistence of different cultures, which cannot be achieved without the existence of effective remedies at the domestic and supra-national levels.

The presented overview of this book's contents indicates that the issue of effectiveness is (intuitively) seen by the Authors as a clash in the realisation of the various goals of the criminal proceedings. Whether a given Author analysed an evidentiary or restorative justice issue or sought an effective remedy, his point of reference was, on the one hand, the particular goals associated with a given legal institution and, on the other hand, the goals that a given legislator under the analyzed legal system has established for a given model of procedure. Thus, the effectiveness of criminal proceedings is a measure of the realisation of these goals. The dilemma, however, is that the individual values that materialise within the framework of the goals of criminal proceedings: the drive to detect the perpetrator of the crime and bring him to criminal justice, the adequate application of procedural institutions, guarantee-oriented application of the procedure law, endeavour to take into account legally protected interests of victims, economic efficiency of the trial, speed of the proceedings, all these values very, fortunately, compete with each other. The crucial issue of effectiveness, therefore, is to determine the clear need for prioritization of the various goals, and this seems to be an unresolvable dilemma as it always depends on the assumptions adopted as the ground for such an evaluation.

Part I
Special, Abbreviated Procedure and Evidence

Prof. Chiara Gabrielli,[1] Dr. Andrea Zampini[2]

I. Between efficiency urges and expectations of justice in the Italian system. Deflation profiles of case dismissal for particular tenuity of the criminal act and for oblation

Abstract: In the Italian legal system, case dismissal is requested by the public prosecutor (*richiesta di archiviazione*) at the end of preliminary investigations. Its acceptance means the end of criminal proceedings before indictment and trial. However, Article 112 of the Constitution mandates criminal prosecution, limiting the public prosecutor's discretion in dismissing a case through legally prescribed formulas. A common trait of traditional dismissal cases is a prognosis of trial superfluity due to grounds that may lead to subsequent acquittal.

Recently, the Italian legislature expanded the operational boundaries of this legal feature to relieve a procedural system in severe and chronic distress. The request to drop a case is also now allowed in cases where the outcome of a trial would likely result in a conviction for minor offences punishable by a penalty that doesn't exceed a certain threshold of gravity, has modest consequences, and is not habitual (*archiviazione per particolare tenuità del fatto*). Additionally, in specific criminal fields, such as minor criminal offences against the environment and against safety and health in workplaces, the request to drop a case is allowed after payment of a reduced fine and restoration of legality (*oblazione "condizionata"*).

The Authors expound upon these peculiar hypotheses of dismissal through the lens of constitutional and legitimacy jurisprudence. They elucidate these hypotheses' underlying objectives, prerequisites, and operational mechanics while highlighting their problematic aspects in terms of interpretation and system.

Keywords: dismissal, oblation, procedural effectiveness, italian criminal procedure

---

1 ORCID no. 0000-0003-4605-2319. Associate professor of criminal procedure, University of Urbino 'Carlo Bo'. Wrote paragraphs 1–5.

2 ORCID no. 0000-0002-8117-1842. Fellow researcher of criminal procedure, University of Urbino. Juridical assistant at the Supreme Council for Judiciary. Wrote paragraphs 6–12.

1. Dismissal as a tool for procedural deflation

Dismissal results in the premature halt of criminal proceedings started after lodging a *notitia criminis* in the register outlined in Article 335 of the Code of Criminal Procedure (hereafter also referred to as c.p.p.). This entails the abandonment of bringing the accused person to trial. In other terms, this measure "validates the lack of transition to *res iudicata*", which is the "definitive judicial determination about the existence of a criminal offence and liability".

The Constitution provides some indirect guidance on the topic of dismissal. Article 112 of the Constitution, which is the procedural projection of the principle of equality set out in Article 3 of the Constitution, mandates criminal prosecution. This does not mean the public prosecutor must prosecute any accused person automatically. Instead, they must bring the accused to trial where the conditions outlined in the Criminal Procedure Code do not permit them to abstain from action. Essentially, "the dismissal is used to determine whether the necessary prerequisites for the obligation to prosecute are absent, and the dismissal may be used to release the public prosecutor from this obligation in exceptional circumstances".[3]

A further implication lies in the fact that the decision not to prosecute must be approved by someone other than the public prosecutor. An impartial control over the decision is crucial not to disregard the duty to proceed. In this perspective, avoiding unintentional mistakes or favouring the accused person based on personal connections, political beliefs, social and economic status, or institutional role is mandatory. The judge for preliminary investigations has been entrusted with the authority to control and react to any prosecutor's evasive behaviour. In these cases – at the end of a chamber hearing eventually attended by the prosecutor himself, the accused, his defence counsel, and the victim – the judge may impose on the public prosecutor two decisions. When the judge finds out that the decision not to prosecute is due to some investigation deficiency, they order to investigate further. The other option is to impose the prosecutor to formally charge the accused if the investigations have already uncovered evidence that excludes the possibility of the crime being baseless.

Systematically speaking, the Constitutional Court has clarified that the "implicit limit" to the mandatory nature of criminal prosecution, "rationally understood, is that the trial should not be started when it appears objectively superfluous". The Court also reminded us that "trial deflation" and "procedural economy" goals

---

3 G. Giostra, *L'archiviazione. Lineamenti sistematici e questioni interpretative*, Giappichelli 1994, p. 4.

should not be pursued through dismissal. Instead, special procedures should be prioritised to achieve such goals.[4]

Unfortunately, things went differently. The Italian justice system has become stuck in a chronic impasse, causing proceedings to drag on well beyond a reasonable timeframe, guaranteed by Article 111 comma 2 of the Constitution. As a result, criminal liability is often impossible to determine in court due to the expiration of the statute of limitations. This outcome can be attributed to the detrimental effects of short-sighted legislative policies. Moreover, the justice sector has traditionally received limited resources, personnel, facilities, and technological equipment. In these conditions, defendants often wait for their trial, as the reasonable prospect of benefiting from the statute of limitations makes it more advantageous than seeking abbreviated procedures.

Moreover, there has been an overabundance of criminalisation policies, ignoring that the principle of subsidiarity advocates for criminal sanctions to be used as a last resort and that non-criminal sanctions – such as administrative or civil penalties – better suit minor offences (such penalties should be designed to provide sufficient retribution and overall preventative impact). As a result, minor offences significantly burden the justice system: fines or short prison sentences make up 90% of the total.[5]

Given all these unforeseen circumstances, it's not surprising that deflationary goals started affecting the dismissal rationale. Dismissal presents an opportunity for terminating criminal proceedings, and broadening its reach would effectively lessen the judicial burden.

In the past, at the end of an investigation, the public prosecutor was authorised to discontinue prosecution based on a list of hypotheses. They included insufficient evidence to support the accusation in court (Articles 408 and 125 of the implementation rules of the criminal procedure – from now on: c.p.p.i.r.), the lack of a requirement for prosecuting, the extinction of the offence, the circumstance that the fact is not foreseen by law as an offence (Article 411 c.p.p.), and the inability to identify the author of the crime even with continued investigation (Article 415 c.p.p.).

---

4 Constitutional Court, February 15th, 1991, No. 88.

5 Final report of the Lattanzi Commission (*Relazione finale e proposte di emendamenti al d.d.l. a.c. 2435*, p. 22), quoting several researches by independent institutes); available at https://www.giustizia.it/cmsresources/cms/documents/commissione_LATTANZI_relazione_finale_24mag21.pdf [accessed on September 19th, 2023].

The recent Cartabia reform (Legislative Decree No. 150 of October 10th, 2022) has narrowed the path to the preliminary hearing or direct trial by reshaping the concept of unfoundedness of the *notitia criminis*.

Article 408 c.p.p. currently requires the public prosecutor to ask for dismissal "when the elements acquired during the preliminary investigation do not allow a reasonable prediction of conviction or application of a security measure other than confiscation". Before the reform, the prosecution had to determine whether to pursue charges based on the investigative discoveries and their prospective integration into the trial. In contrast, the new regulation bounds prosecution with the existence of solid and converging evidence at the conclusion of the investigation.

The list of conditions that allow the public prosecutor to dismiss a case was expanded by Legislative Decree No. 28/2015. This update included the new requirement of the offence being particularly tenuous, as specified in Article 131-*bis* of the Criminal Code (hereafter referred to as c.p.). It provides non-punishment for offences not exceeding a specific severity level if the behaviour is not habitual.

Ultimately, the lawmaker has recognised the value of dismissal in redirecting resources and energy towards more serious criminal offences rather than tying them up in minor cases. However, it would be simplistic to see this strategy solely as a means to reduce the burden on the justice system. When an individual commits a minor offence that only marginally violates the interests protected by criminal law, subjecting them to criminal sanctions may not be appropriate. This is especially true in a legal system where punishment serves a rehabilitative purpose, as Article 27, comma 3 of the Constitution outlines. Penalties should be proportional to the committed offence, considering the severity and quantity of the sanction.[6] Not taking the accused to court may be justifiable, recognising the harsh consequences of a trial, both in terms of human impact and financial burden. This approach seeks to remove insignificant infractions from the criminal justice system, which would be "costly for the community and demanding for the offender".[7] That's why, ultimately, even the Supreme Court's Jointed Chambers

---

6 M. Daniele, 'L'archiviazione per tenuità del fatto fra velleità deflattive ed equilibrismi procedimentali', [in:] S. Quattrocolo (ed.), *I nuovi epiloghi del procedimento penale per particolare tenuità del fatto*, Giappichelli 2015, p. 49.

7 T. Padovani, 'Un intento deflattivo dal possibile effetto boomerang', *Guida al diritto*, 2015 (15), p. 19.

observed that non-punishment for a particular tenuity creates an intimate link between proportionality and deflation goals.[8]

By utilising the broad range of legal categories outlined in Article 411 c.p.p., the dismissal application was expanded to include a variety of circumstances that could lead to the extinction of the offence. These include the offender's death, the statute of limitations, amnesty, and scenarios where the suspect resolves a low-level criminal case and requests an early conclusion of the proceedings during the preliminary investigation stage. One of these cases is oblation (*oblazione*, from the Latin *offerre-oblatum*). Thanks to this legal institution, a contravention can be extinguished by paying a sum of money. The amount of the sum and the assessment powers attributed to the judge to whom the request is made vary depending on whether the oblation is "automatic" (Article 162 c.p.) or "optional" (Article 162-*bis* c.p.).

For some specific offences, a particular hypothesis of "oblation" extinguishes the contravention upon fulfilling a non-exclusively financial obligation. In such scenarios, an individual must undertake corrective measures concerning the discovered breach alongside the administrative payment of money. Supervisory bodies responsible for ascertaining the violation are involved in the proceeding because of their technical expertise, which enables them to exercise the judicial police functions outlined in Article 55 c.p.p. and indicate the action that must be realised. By granting the undoubted advantage of an early conclusion of the proceedings, the intention is to favour the re-establishment of the legal situation compromised by the unlawful conduct. The mechanism is known as "conditional" oblation, a wording that expresses the idea of prioritising restorative behaviour over economic fulfilment; it entered our legal system in the field of hygiene, health, and safety at work thanks to Legislative Decree No. 758/1994. A similar procedural scheme waives the offender's prosecution in exchange for a counter-conduct of re-establishing the previous state of things in the environmental field (Legislative Decree No. 152/2006). More recently, the Cartabia reform (Legislative Decree No. 150 of 2022) extended the possibility of obtaining the dismissal thanks to the offender's restorative activities for contravention issued by Law No. 283/1962 and by other regulations on hygiene, production, traceability and sale of food and beverages.

8 Court of Cassation, Jointed Chambers, February 25th, 2016, Tushaj, and Court of Cassation, Jointed Chambers, February 25th, 2016, Coccimiglio, *Diritto penale contemporaneo*, April 29th, 2016, with a comment by E. Andolfatto.

The Lattanzi Commission[9] – which drafted the Cartabia reform –proposed to incorporate the institution of "conditional" or "deserved" dismissal into the Code of Criminal Procedure. The intention was to apply it to minor offences. The basic idea was that if a suspect takes corrective measures that adequately compensate for the harm done to public and private interests, proceeding with a trial may no longer be necessary.

In the scheme drawn up by the Lattanzi Commission, the public prosecutor and the person under investigation could ask the judge for preliminary investigations to dismiss the case under the condition of performing one or more services in favour of the victim or the community. The proper performance would lead to the extinction of the offence.[10] The waiver of prosecution would have been based on the "possibility for the suspect, given the seriousness of the offence and the capacity to commit offences, to compensate the public interest arising from the offence by carrying out a series of positive conduct in favour of the community (e.g. payment of a sum of money to the State, performance of work in the public interest, or job training or education courses) and/or of the victim (compensation for damages, mediation activities)".[11] Reasons for short-sighted compromise with political parties' supporters of a strict criminal policy led to the renunciation of a mechanism that would have combined the deflating and restorative functions from the final version of the reform.[12]

It should now be understood that these instruments are highly flexible and typically activated by the public prosecutor with the accused's consent. These instruments are designed to achieve multiple goals, including re-socialization and restoration, both of which have been recognised by the Committee of Ministers of the Council of Europe since the late 1980s.[13] In this article, we will explore how dismissal can be used as a tool for special and abbreviated procedures and how

---

9 Study Commission to draw up reform proposals on the criminal trial and penalty system, as well as on the statute of limitations of criminal offences, through the formulation of amendments to Bill A.C. 2435, on the delegation to the Government for the efficiency of the criminal trial and provisions for the speedy definition of judicial proceedings pending at the courts of appeal (March 16th, 2021).

10 When proceeding for offences punishable by a fine alone or by a maximum term of imprisonment of no more than four years, alone, in conjunction with or as an alternative to a fine.

11 M. Gialuz, 'L'archiviazione meritata come terza via tra archiviazione ed esercizio dell'azione penale', *Processo penale e giustizia*, 2021, p. 309.

12 Delegation Law No. 134/2021

13 Rec. (87)18.

fundamental principles entailed by this choice can be balanced to ensure, at the same time, procedural efficiency and adequate protection of individual rights connected with the justice system.

2. Particular tenuity of the criminal act and oblation: when the trial is unnecessary

Dismissal is ordinarily justified by failing to find enough evidence to expect a conviction (Article 408 c.p.p.). On the contrary, dismissal based on the particular tenuity of the criminal act or a successful oblation procedure has a distinguishing feature in the panorama of the hypotheses grounding dismissal. They imply the criminal liability of the accused person, drawn from the investigative findings, and, at the same time, the waiver to bring them to trial. It follows that it is possible to frame these dismissal figures within the horizon of diversion. While it is true that they are related to rewarding logic for the suspect and to reasons of economy for the system, the qualifying feature lies in recognising the inadequacy of the criminal trial as an answer to the case. An inadequacy with different nuances in the two cases: in the first, it is an excessively afflictive reaction against an occasional perpetrator of a mild crime; in the second, the response doesn't help to restore the lawful *status quo*. This is not the only difference.

Regarding tenuity, dismissal follows a mainly static judgement formulated on the offence's characteristics and the person considered to be its author. At the same time, the legislator recently included the conduct that follows the crime as one of the factors to consider when evaluating the nature of the action and the harm or danger it has caused. Regarding oblation, to ensure that the prosecutor drops the case against a person under investigation, they must comply with the legal requirements and instructions given by a supervisory body. Being proactive in this regard is crucial.

However, it's important to note that opting for a particular tenuity dismissal may result in less favourable legal treatment on both the premises and the consequences. About the premises, it implies a "crypto-conviction", based on the evidence unilaterally gathered during the investigation, that a criminal offence was committed by the accused person;[14] an offence which, unlike in the event of

14 The measure "undoubtedly" implies an articulated assessment, which has its logical premise in the "acknowledgement of the commission of the offence", clearly states Court of Cassation, IIIrd Chamber, January 26th, 2017, Vanzo, *Cassazione penale*, 2018, p. 1656, with a comment by V. Vasta.

a "pure" extinction clause, remains intact "in its historical and legal existence".[15] As regards the consequences, although it does not have the force of *res iudicata* in civil or administrative proceedings, particular tenuity is the only dismissal decision that must be entered in the criminal record based on Article 3 comma 1 letter *f* of Presidential Decree No. 313/2002.[16] Characteristics that place the case in question, in the ideal hierarchy of grounds for dismissal, at the "lowest level" of attractiveness for the person under investigation.[17]

3. The particular tenuity offence

Article 131-*bis* c.p. outlines the specific conditions that constitute tenuousness in a criminal offence. This involves two factors: the harm caused to the protected legal asset and the non-recurring nature of the offence. While both factors are crucial, they only pertain to cases prosecuted under a special legal framework, which has recently changed under the "Cartabia reform" (Legislative Decree No. 150 of 2022).

Article 131-*bis* c.p. is responsible for identifying a range of offences that can be judged as irrelevant due to the penalties imposed by law, also following what's socially felt. This excludes more serious crimes.[18] The original version authorised the exclusion of punishability for offences providing "a term of imprisonment not exceeding a maximum of five years or a fine, either alone or in conjunction with imprisonment". The general application perimeter has been considerably expanded:[19] the threshold is now set for offences punished with a minimum imprisonment of two years. The minimum edictal range generally defines, at best, the

15 Court of Cassation, IIIrd Chamber, May 26th, 2015, p.c. in proc. Sorbara, *C.e.d. Cass.*, No. 263885; Court of Cassation, VIth Chamber, 27 gennaio 2016, Carnevale, *Guida al diritto*, 2016 (17), p. 63.

16 The Jointed Chambers, overcoming the uncertainties that emerged due to an ambiguous regulatory formulation, have solved the issue: Court of Cassation, Jointed Chambers, May 30th, 2016, p.m. in proc. De Martino, *Guida al diritto*, 2019 (47), p. 64 ss., with a comment by C. Minnella.

17 S. Quattrocolo, 'L'altra faccia della medaglia: l'impatto della particolare tenuità del fatto sul processo penale', *Criminalia*, 2016, p. 229.

18 For all, C. Cesari, 'Le clausole di irrilevanza del fatto nel sistema processuale penale', [in:] R.E. Kostoris (ed.), *La ragionevole durata del processo. Garanzia ed efficienza della giustizia penale*, Giappichelli 2005, p. 101.

19 The amendment makes the ground for non-punishment applicable to, for example, aggravated theft (Article 625 c.p.), receiving stolen goods (Article 648 c.p.), and material falsity of a public official in public deeds (Article 476 c.p.).

gravity of the crime and sets the lowest punishment that the judge can determine as a penalty. This is a solution urged by the Constitutional Court:[20] it appears more rational because it expresses "the threshold of indefectibility to which the protection is anchored, and therefore the disvalue necessarily recognised in the offence".[21]

To determine the penalty limit in question, lawmakers specify that certain circumstances should be considered, namely those for which the law establishes a penalty of a different type from the ordinary one and those with a special effect. These categories are deemed worthy of special regulation since they "reveal a particular significance" that makes them "autonomous sub-species of criminal offence".[22] The final comma of Article 131-*bis* c.p. clarifies that the exclusion of punishment still applies even if the law explicitly punishes minimal damage or danger. This helps prevent confusion for interpreters.

Within the aforementioned edictal *range*, non-punishability may operate if the offence is particularly tenuous and the offender's non-habitual conduct. This legal clarification is necessary to prevent the judicial body from exercising unchecked discretion, which would conflict with the mandatory prosecution outlined in Article 112 of the Constitution. To avoid confusion and ensure compliance with this principle, assessment criteria have not been defined with vague references to preventive reasons that could be influenced by the judge's personal biases or the needs of the administration. Also, the coordinates drawn by the legislator try to prevent eccentric factors from entering the judicial horizon, such as the prejudices against the offender, the victim's resentment, and the convenience of prosecuting the crime. Although the law attempts to restrict judges' discretion, it is not always effective.

---

20 Constitutional Court, July 21st, 2020, No. 156, declared the non-conformity to the Constitution of Article 131-*bis* c.p. because it doesn't allow the application of the cause of non-punishability to offences punished with a sanction that has no minimum edictal standard (i.e., imprisonment up to six months).

21 T. Padovani, 'Un intento deflativo', *op.cit.*, p. 20. See also D. Brunelli, 'La tenuità del fatto nella "riforma Cartabia": scenari per l'abolzione dei minimi edittali', *Sistema penale*, January 13th, 2022.

22 Schema di decreto legislativo recante: "Disposizioni in materia di non punibilità per particolare tenuità del fatto, a norma dell'articolo 1, comma 1, lettera m), della legge aprile 28th, 2014, n. 67, § 5. Available at: https://www.giustizia.it/giustizia/it/mg_1_2_1.page?facetNode_1=0_39&facetNode_2=1_8%282015%29&contentId=SAN1108598&previsiousPage=mg_1_2_0# [accessed on September 19th, 2023].

The concept of the offence of particular tenuity focuses on ensuring that the assessment is based on objective profiles. This requires considering both the conduct involved and the degree of harm or danger caused. If the event or the criminal action is serious, it cannot be considered a minor offence. Article 133 comma 1 c.p. represents the judge's guidance, which generally provides factual criteria to determine the appropriate penalty.

The regulation emphasises that when assessing the severity of harm caused by an offence, the focus should be on the impact on personal legal assets rather than financial ones. Additionally, factors such as the nature, method, object, time, and place of the offence, as well as any other relevant aspects of the conduct, should be considered to determine the level of harm. It's important to note that using specific methods of offence, violence or deception, and exploitation of circumstances related to the crime's location, time, or victim might hinder the legal institute's application.

When evaluating a particular tenuity, it's crucial to consider the perpetrator's level of intentionality or negligence. Although Article 131-bis c.p. doesn't explicitly cover this topic, examining how the crime was committed can offer insight into the perpetrator's mindset. Negligence can be determined by analysing how the typical illegal behaviour was carried out, while intentionality can be inferred from the specific actions taken by the offender. Only a significant degree of psychological adherence to the offence can hinder access to non-punishability; while this does not happen, the preclusion cannot be derived from comma 2 of Article 133 c.p., which lists indicators of the capacity to commit offences since Article 131-*bis* c.p. doesn't explicitly refer to it.

Due to the lack of reference to comma 2 of Article 133 c.p.,[23] the judge cannot consider the offender's behaviour after the crime. Some legal experts tried to legitimise it as an evaluation criterion by stating that Article 133 comma 1 c.p. is a mandatory, but not exclusive, assessment standard.[24] This minority interpreta-

---

23 "The judge must also take into account the offender's capacity to commit offences, deduced: 1) from the offender's motives for committing offences and his character; 2) from the offender's criminal and judicial record and, in general, from his conduct and life before the offence; 3) from the offender's conduct during or after the offence; 4) from the offender's individual, family and social conditions of life".

24 V. Bove, *Particolare tenuità del fatto*, Giuffrè 2019, p. 191, does not consider the textual obstacle insuperable, taking into account, in particular, the "scope that the Constitutional Court attributes to conduct subsequent to the crime, which takes the form of restorative behaviour"; so also R. Dies, 'Questioni varie in tema di irrilevanza penale del fatto per particolare tenuità', *Diritto penale contemporaneo*, September 13th, 2015, p. 23, footnote 51).

tion did not breach the jurisprudence, and the Supreme Court's ruling remained unaffected. As a result, the legislature clarified that the assessment of the severity of the crime should also include consideration of the offender's behaviour after the crime.[25] These behaviours may include restitution, compensation for damages, reparative actions, and access to restorative justice programs. However, it's essential to remember that these actions alone cannot imply the tenuity of the offence. They should be viewed in conjunction with an overall evaluation of the offence, according to the guidelines set out in Article 133 comma 1 c.p.[26]

An offence cannot be deemed particularly tenuous in the hypotheses listed in comma 2 of Article 131-*bis* c.p., which number increased over time. Anyone who has acted with abject or futile motives, or with cruelty, even towards animals, or exploited the victim's vulnerability, including age or diminished defence, cannot benefit from the regulation. Also, it cannot operate when the action has caused or resulted in a person's death or serious injury as an unintended consequence. It is essential to acknowledge that these exemptions are typically linked to one's internal beliefs, which do not diminish the severity of the offence but rather heighten personal accountability.[27] Some consider this choice poorly considered, possibly influenced by a desire to avoid being seen as too lenient in enforcing the law. This perception is supported by subsequent regulatory actions that have expanded the inapplicability of the tenuity clause. In the first place, Law Decree No. 53/2019 excluded from the scope of application crimes committed on the occasion of or because of sports events when punished with an imprisonment penalty exceeding a maximum of two years and six months. Then, Law No. 77/2019 added to the list the violence, threat, resistance, and outrage against a public official (Articles 336, 337 and 341-*bis* c.p.). Right after, these offences were joined by the outrage against a magistrate during a hearing (Article 343 c.p.). Most of these hypotheses are not necessarily highly offensive and do not generate such a social alarm to justify the inclusion in the list of Article 133 comma 2 c.p. Unfortunately, the rule attracted offences perceived as alarming during each "social emergency" season. The substantial additions made by the "Cartabia reform" confirm that this tendency has not ended. According to delegation law No. 134 of 2021, domestic

---

25 The insertion is due to Legislative Decree No. 159/2022. For example, if a driver hits a person and causes injury, it is restorative conduct to immediately accompany them to the emergency room.

26 Court of Cassation, IIIrd Chamber, April 4th, 2023, Hu Qinglian, *C.e.d. Cass.*, No. 284497.

27 T. Padovani, 'Un intento deflativo', *op.cit.*, p. 21.

violence offences attributable to the Istanbul Convention of May 2011 are now also excluded from the potential application of particular tenuity.

Moreover, the generic possibility, questionably conferred by the delegation law, of extending the hypotheses in which the offence cannot be considered particularly minor "if considered appropriate based on empirical-criminological evidence or for reasons of systematic consistency" has resulted in the exclusion of the offences relating to non-petty narcotics selling (Article 73 of Presidential Decree No. 309/1990); and to insider trading and market manipulation (Articles 184 and 185 Legislative Decree No. 58/1998).

4. The non-habitual nature of the behaviour

The second criterion given by Article 131-*bis* c.p. is the absence of habitual behaviour, which serves a special prevention purpose. If we only consider the nature of the action, individuals who commit minor offences will not be afraid of the consequences of future offences and could be encouraged to offend again.

Article 131-bis c.p. provides judges with three strict presumptions that opposing evidence cannot challenge in determining whether conduct is habitual. This list is exhaustive, as constitutional reasons require a strictly defined scope for non-punishability.

Those who have been declared habitual, professional, or trendy delinquents, as defined respectively in Articles 102, 103, 105, and 108 c.p., are considered socially dangerous and, therefore, cannot benefit from particular tenuity. Likewise, habituality exists when the accused "has committed several offences of the same nature, even if each fact, considered separately, is of particular tenuousness". The "same nature" is defined in Article 101 c.p. as either violating the same rule more than once or different rules that share fundamental features about the "nature of the facts constituting them or the motives that determined them". The same nature must be "assessed by the judge in relation to the examined case".[28]

The reference to "several offences" appeared somewhat ambiguous, so the Jointed Chambers of the Court of Cassation were called to intervene.[29] To establish a habitual pattern of behaviour, at least two offences of the same nature, in addition to the one *sub iudice*, must be present. The time between the previous

---

28 Court of Cassation, Vth Chamber, May 30th, 2018, M., *C.e.d. Cass.*, No. 274186; Court of Cassation, IVth Chamber, April 4th, 2017, Garbocci, *C.e.d. Cass.*, No. 270107.

29 Court of Cassation, Jointed Chambers, February 25th, 2016, Thusaj, *Sistema penale*, Novembrer 19th, 2021.

and current offences is irrelevant, as there is no normative indication stating otherwise.

Lastly, individuals who have committed "offences involving multiple, habitual and repeated conducts" - a redundant formula that has generated various interpretative doubts – cannot benefit from non-punishability because of the particular tenuity. The prevailing interpretation considers the three adjectives to express a unified logic, referring primarily to offences committed through multiple acts (i.e., habitual offences[30]). The Jointed Chambers of the Court of Cassation made a noteworthy attempt to elucidate the meaning of "multiple conducts". This term pertains to situations where several instances of distinct behaviour contribute to the progression of events. For example, in cases of culpable injuries that violate workplace safety regulations, the offence may be due to a failure to take separate preventative measures and a consistent disregard for security. Such negligent conduct, which persists over time, may give the offence a habitual or repeated character.[31]

The relationship between the "habitual nature" of the conduct referred to in Article 131-*bis* c.p. and the "continued criminal offence" under Article 81 c.p. has proved rather complex: it presupposes more than one criminal conduct aimed at realising a unitary criminal plan.[32] Such a phenomenon could have breached multiple regulatory barriers provided for in Article 131-*bis* c.p. However, a part of the jurisprudence has emphasised the specific features of the episodes linked by continuation to avoid the excessive rigidity of always considering the continued offence as an index of criminal habituality. This solution was shared by the Jointed Chambers of the Supreme Court, according to which "the plurality of offences unified by the continuation link is not an obstacle to the activation of the cause of exclusion of punishability due to the particular tenuity of the fact". The judge

30 Habitual offences are those that require a person to repeatedly commit the same type of conduct over a period of time. This means that at least two unlawful actions must occur within a short time frame, such as in cases of stalking or family abuse.

31 Again, Court of Cassation, Jointed Chambers, February 25th, 2016, Thusaj, quoted above.

32 When a person has a single intention to commit multiple law violations, it is considered one criminal act. This is because the legislative body deems this type of behaviour less severe and allows for a legal cumulation of penalties, meaning the penalty for the most severe offence is increased by up to three times but never more than the penalty that would result if the penalties for each violation were added together. Therefore, the continuing offence is an exception to the usual regime of material concurrence of crimes.

must conduct an overall assessment of the concrete case, considering a series of indicators, such as the nature and seriousness of the offences in continuation, the type of protected legal assets, the extent of the provisions of the law infringed, and the purposes and methods of execution of the conduct. The judge must also consider the motivations and consequences of the behaviour, the moment and context in which the various actions take place, the intensity of the intent, and the relevance attributable to conduct after the facts.[33]

5. An unprecedented dismissal itinerary

To optimise the potential deflation of particular tenuity in the dismissal procedure, Legislative Decree No. 28/2015 implemented a specialised procedural pathway in cases where evidence has emerged indicating both the culpability of the accused and the relative insignificance of the charges. When the new provisions show some lack of regulation, the standard rules for dismissal proceedings must be applied in a manner consistent with the unique characteristics of this innovative legal feature.

According to Article 411 comma 1-*bis* c.p.p., it is mandatory for the public prosecutor to notify both the accused person and the victim about the submitted dismissal request. This notification serves as a warning, allowing them to access the investigation file and submit an opposition within ten days. If the complaint is deemed admissible, the judge is required to hold a hearing in chambers.

For a complaint to be admissible, the party must present reasons for disagreeing with the prosecutor's decision to dismiss. Supporting documents must also be attached to validate these assumptions. This means that parties involved can challenge the dismissal request by presenting a different interpretation of evidence or proposing a fresh interpretation based on innovative evidence.

The accused and the victim typically have opposite reasons for presenting their cases. The accused will aim to obtain a more favourable outcome by submitting evidence that the alleged crime did not take place, that they are not responsible, that the act is not considered a crime under the law, that the statute of limitations has expired, or that the necessary procedural conditions have not been met. Conversely, the victim will attempt to refute the particular tenuousness, perhaps by arguing that a legal prohibition exists, to advocate for compensation as a civil party during the trial. However, the term of only ten days granted to build these strategies is wholly insufficient for obtaining a defence counsel, reviewing the

---

33 Court of Cassation, Jointed Chambers, January 27th, 2022, Ubaldi, *Sistema penale*, December 6th, 2022.

file at the prosecutor's office, obtaining a copy of the documents, and eventually conducting investigations.

After admitting an opposition, the judge must notify the public prosecutor, victim, person under investigation, and counsel of the scheduled hearing in the chamber. Attendance is not mandatory for any of the parties.

After the hearing, the judge may choose to dismiss the case in response to the prosecutor's request or return the case to the prosecutor for further investigation if the initial inquiries were inadequate or there is sufficient evidence to suggest that the suspect committed the offence, but not all of the requirements outlined in Article 131-*bis* c.p. have been met. In the latter scenario, an order to lay charges will be issued along with the returned case file.

The decision made by lawmakers regarding the dismissal of cases based on particular tenuity without considering the victim's wishes has sparked a debate. Some argue that it undermines the victim's role in the proceedings.[34] In contrast, others believe preventing them from making excessive claims is necessary to achieve an early end of the proceedings.[35] Allowing the victim to have high procedural rights standards hurts the system's efficiency. Moreover, victims can always seek compensation through civil proceedings for damages due to the offence. This ensures that the right to take legal action to safeguard one's claims, as guaranteed by Article 24 comma 1 of the Constitution, is upheld.

While it may be argued that fulfilling the constitutional obligation to allow the victim and suspect the ability to request a hearing in the chamber is sufficient, concerns arise regarding Article 111 comma 4 of the Constitution. This article specifies that to determine the accused's responsibility evidence must be formed through an adversarial process. The most reliable way to gather evidence is through a hearing where both parties can question witnesses before the judge. Exceptions to this rule are only permitted in cases of the accused's consent, unlawful conduct, or objective impossibility, as outlined in Article 111 comma 5 of the Constitution.

Although dismissal because of particular tenuity is not equal to a guilty verdict, it requires careful consideration of the evidence, somehow implying the defendant's responsibility and the existence of the offence, followed by a verification of the indicators of the tenuousness – and it is meant to enter in the criminal record. Is this possible, considering that the prosecution unilaterally forms the evidence,

34 R. Muzzica, 'Il ruolo della vittima negli istituti riparativi', [in:] *Legislazione penale*, November 22nd, 2019, p. 22.

35 C. Santoriello, *La clausola di particolare tenuità del fatto*, Dike giuridica 2015, p. 80.

while the defence may only discuss it in the chamber? In this case, evidence is not formed with the contribution of all parties before the judge, who decides on the merits. The Constitutional Court has ruled that the accused has the right to a fair trial and cannot be held liable based on unilateral evidence gathered by the prosecutor. This right is more important than the need for a speedy trial. Ultimately, decisions based solely on the investigation collide with several constitutional principles: the adversarial nature of evidence (Article 111 comma 4 of the Constitution), the inviolability of the right of defence (Article 24 comma 2 of the Constitution), and the presumption of innocence (Article 27 comma 2 of the Constitution).

Two potential solutions can be found in Article 111, comma 5 of the Constitution to address the inconsistencies, specifically regarding the defendant's consent. A reformulation of the rules is necessary to ensure that dismissal on the grounds of a particular tenuity can only occur with the person under investigation's informed consent. Under this new system, the prosecutor should notify the person under investigation of their intention and offer them the choice between consenting to dismissal for a particular tenuity or having a hearing in chambers. During this hearing, the person under investigation could persuade the prosecutor to order dismissal for a more favourable reason. If the person under investigation gives their consent, the victim should also be notified so that they can attend the hearing or submit any pleadings. Alternatively, the person under investigation could be given the right to oppose the dismissal order, which would prevent the early closure of the proceedings and ensure a fair trial. Failure to activate this remedy could be seen as implicit consent, bringing the dismissal procedure in line with the constitutional dictate.

6. A traditional deflating answer to milder crime: oblation

Since 1930, the Criminal Code has included legal mechanisms for dealing with less severe offences without resorting to full-fledged criminal proceedings. One such mechanism is oblation (in Italian, *oblazione*). Etymologically, the term draws from Catholic religious jargon and initially referred to monetary or material offerings made for charitable purposes.[36] Juridically, however, the term oblation names a means of extinguishing less serious offences by paying a fraction of the maximum amount provided by law (along with any associated legal fees). This approach

36 On historical aspects, see C. Carini, 'Oblazione', [in:] A. Gaito-G. Spangher-F. Giunchedi-C. Santoriello (eds.), *La giustizia penale differenziata. I procedimenti speciali*, vol. I, Giappichelli, 2011, p. 485.

offers a flexible and equitable alternative to conventional criminal proceedings, allowing for a more tailored response to less serious transgressions.

The institution operates in a formulation close to the original.[37] Article 162 c.p. regulates the ordinary (or automatic) oblation, which is an option to settle quickly those proceedings opened for contraventions that are only punishable by a fine. By meeting this requirement, the defendant can pay a sum equal to one-third of the maximum penalty prescribed by law at the start of the trial or before the criminal decree's enforceability. It is crucial to ensure that the payment term is included in the judge's ordinance:[38] as the statute of limitations is notably lenient in contravention cases, and it is imperative not to allow the accused to exploit this loophole.[39] If the payment is made within the specified timeframe, the criminal offence is extinguished, and the judge must declare it without any discretion.[40] Following this path, the accused person forgoes the ordinary criminal proceedings and their corresponding safeguards.[41] That's why oblation represents a "double-faced instrument, with simultaneously substantive and procedural effects".[42]

---

37 According to the original text contraventions punished with a maximum fine exceeding 10 000 lire couldn't be defined through oblation. The sum is approximately the actual equivalent of 9 000 euros. The provision was abolished by Article 7 of the Lieutenancy Legislative Decree No. 679/1945.

38 G. Piziali, 'Il procedimento di oblazione', [in:] M. Pisani (ed.), *I procedimenti speciali in materia penale*, Giuffrè 2003, p. 577.

39 According to Article 157 comma 1 c.p. the statute of limitations cancels out a crime after an amount of time equal to the maximum penalty foreseen by law that can't be in any case shorter than six years for a *delitto* and four years for a *contravvenzione*, regardless of whether the punishment only consists in a fine.

40 In general, the extinguishing effect takes place as soon as the agreed-upon amount is paid. This effect is not determined by a jurisdictional pronouncement that declares it but instead by the payment of the sum of money. The judge's primary role is to verify the existence of the conditions laid down by law and to confirm the absence of the duty to punish rather than determining the existence of the offence and its commission by the defendant (in these terms, see M. Bontempelli, 'Il procedimento di oblazione' [in:] Spangher et al. (eds.), *Procedura penale. Teoria e pratica del processo*, vol. III, 2015, p. 473). On the general features of oblation, see also E. Selvaggi, Comment to article 141 of the implementation rules of the code of criminal procedure in: M. Chiavario, *Commentario Chiavario, La normativa complementare*, vol. I, Norme di attuazione, UTET 1992, p. 537.

41 In these terms, under the old inquisitorial code, F. Bricola, 'In tema di rapporti tra oblazione e conciliazione amministrativa', *Rivista italiana di diritto e procedura penale*, 1961, p. 1103.

42 F. Cordero, *Contributo allo studio dell'amnistia nel processo*, Giuffrè 1957, p. 43.

While at the beginning addressed defining milder crimes punished only with a fine, the oblation perimeter was widened by the introduction of Article 162-*bis* c.p., which allows it for crimes punished alternatively with a fine or detention.[43] In this "extended version", the payment regulation is different and more detailed. Firstly, the amount is raised to half the maximum foreseen by the law; moreover, the defendant must deposit the sum with the oblation request. If the request is rejected, the amount will be refunded.[44]

Article 162-*bis* c.p. outlines several restrictions on the use of the oblation. Recidivists, professional criminals, and those with a tendency towards criminal behaviour (as defined in Articles 99, 104, and 105 c.p.) are not eligible to opt for the oblation. Additionally, the oblation cannot be granted when the harmful or dangerous consequences of the offence persist, although they could have been eliminated. Moreover, the judge has discretion to deny the oblation in front of the "seriousness of the offence". Unlike automatic oblation, Article 162-bis c.p. allows the magistrate to consider the social stigma of the offence and the offender's characteristics.[45] The final procedural terms for the application remain the trial's opening and the criminal decree's enforceability.

The legal regulation of this "judicial decriminalisation"[46] feature was only addressed by the Criminal Code until 1988 when the still-in-force Code of Criminal Procedure was approved. The legislature recognised the need to establish a procedural framework, which was absent in the previous code. Article 141 c.p.p.i.r. now offers important coordinates to rule a legal institution representing a "middle ground" between investigations and trial.[47] Essentially, the procedure involves making a request, obtaining the public prosecutor's opinion, receiving approval from the judge, making payment, and finally, the extinction of the offence with a judicial declaration.[48]

---

43 This Article was introduced by Law No. 689/1981, which deeply reformed the criminal system.

44 E. Selvaggi, 'Comment to article 141 of the implementation rules of the code of criminal procedure', *op.cit.*, p. 537.

45 A. Cadoppi, 'Oblazione "vecchia" e "nuova" e principi costituzionali', *Rivista italiana di diritto e procedura penale*, 1983, p. 185.

46 A. Bernardi, 'La depenalizzazione e le sue diverse forme', [in:] A. Bernardi-I. Zoda (eds.), *Depenalizzazione. Profili teorici e pratici*, Cedam 2008, p. 10.

47 G. Conti-A. Macchia, 'Introduzione alle norme di attuazione del 1989' [in:] G. Conso-V. Grevi-G. Neppi Modona (eds.), *Il nuovo codice di procedura penale. Dalle leggi delega ai decreti delegati*, vol. VI, Cedam 1990, p. 91.

48 In similar terms, see F.M. Molinari, *I procedimenti alternativi per reati minori*, Giuffrè 2018, p. 186.

Before this legislative action, Articles 162 and 162-*bis* c.p. stated that the request must be made before the formal opening of the trial. A wording which did not exclude the pre-trial phase. Now, Article 141 c.p.p.i.r. clarifies that the oblation proceedings can also be activated during the investigations and defines the role of the public prosecutor at this juncture. If the person under investigation requests oblation, the prosecutor forwards it to the judge (comma 1); it's not specified but seems systematically coherent that the request shall be filed at the Public Prosecutor's office.[49] The present tense might lead to thinking that the request made during investigations must always be addressed to the judge.[50] However, systematic interpretation leads to the opposite solution: the investigation ending is an exclusive prerogative of the public prosecutor in the first instance. Only this magistrate can decide whether to promote prosecution or ask the judge to dismiss a case.[51] If the person under investigation could promote an action that leads to the dismissal himself, and if the judge agrees on the oblation, the prosecutor would be forced to ask for the dismissal because of the offence extinction. This case would represent a kind of "compulsory dismissal",[52] not foreseen in the system.[53]

Furthermore, it is within the prosecutor's competence to apprise the subjects of an investigation about their eligibility for oblation (Article 141 comma 2 c.p.p.i.r.). In the event that the prosecutor requests a criminal decree, the presiding judge must also include details about the possibility of settling the case through oblation.

49 F. Galluzzo, *Il consenso dell'imputato nei procedimenti speciali*, Wolters Kluwer 2020, p. 198; F.M. Molinari, *I procedimenti alternativi per reati minori*, *op.cit.*, p. 198.

50 A. Sabatino, 'Il procedimento di oblazione', [in:] G. Dalia (ed.), *Procedimenti alternativi per reati minori*, Giuffrè 2018, p. 187. The prosecutor's opinion is not binding only once the trial phase has already started (in these terms, see Constitutional Court, ordinance February 18th, 1992, No. 58).

51 If the accused submits the application without prior notice from the public prosecutor, it can represent "a sort of self-imputation" (A. Martini, "Il procedimento per oblazione" [in:] S. Nosengo (ed.), *Giurisprudenza sistematica di diritto processuale penale. Riti camerali e speciali*, Utet 2006, p. 707).

52 E. Selvaggi, *Comment to article 141*, *op.cit.*, p. 537.

53 On the contrary, in the dismissal proceeding, the judge can force the promotion of the prosecution when – disagreeing with the prosecutor – he finds that the request was based on elements that could lead to the high possibility of a conviction at the end of the trial (in these terms the new formulation of Article 125 c.p.p.i.r., modified by the Legislative Decree No. 150/2022).

Failure to do so would nullify the decree, as it would violate the general rule in Article 178 comma 1 letter *c* c.p.p. regarding the right to defensive assistance.[54]

Looking at it from another angle, Article 141 comma 4 c.p.p.i.r. states that judges must obtain the public prosecutor's opinion. This is because the lawmakers wanted to create a single regulation for oblations requested before and after the decision to prosecute, which includes during the investigations or the trial.[55] The rule is straightforward when applied in the trial phase, where the public prosecutor is present at the hearing or in written form, when the judge can ask for the prosecutor's opinion after the criminal decree has been opposed. However, when the prosecutor sends the request to the judge during investigations, it implies that the prosecutor's opinion has already been expressed and is positive. Otherwise, the prosecutor would not have forwarded the request in the first place.

At this stage, the judge for preliminary investigation verifies if the requirements stated in Articles 162 and 162-*bis* c.p. are met. For ordinary oblation, the judge's role is "marginal" and limited to ascertaining formal elements, the nature of the offence, and its legal framework correctness.[56] However, "conditional" oblation requires the judge to conduct a more thorough review, analysing additional factors, some objective, such as the existence of one of the legal preclusions, and some subjective, such as the assessment of the crime's seriousness.

Suppose the judge decides to endorse the assessment made by the public prosecutor. In that case, the applicant will be admitted to the oblation with an order that will specify the amount to be paid, which will be communicated to the applicant. Once the judge is notified of the payment, the file will be sent back to the prosecutor for further "determinations". Since the payment extinguishes the offence, the determination in question is somewhat "bound", and the only way out is to submit a dismissal request to the preliminary investigation judge. Ultimately, when the oblation is accorded during the investigation phase, the proceeding is meant to end with a dismissal decision.[57]

On the contrary, if the judge's decision is adverse, the file will be returned to the public prosecutor to proceed in ordinary ways.

Unfortunately, the introduction of Article 141 c.p.p.i.r. has also caused some difficulties in interpretation. According to the rule, the judge must "set" (*fissare*)

54 A. Scalfati, 'Decreto di citazione pretorile e mancato avviso circa le scelte alternative al dibattimento', *Giurisprudenza costituzionale*, 1995, p. 4241.

55 S. Sottani, 'L'oblazione nel nuovo processo penale: caratteristiche, struttura e ipotesi', *La giustizia penale*, 1990, III, c. 673.

56 A. Sabatino, 'Il procedimento di oblazione', *op.cit.*, p. 187.

57 E. Selvaggi, Comment to article 141, *op.cit.*, p. 536–537.

the amount of the sum to be paid with an order (comma 4). Based on this provision, the jurisprudence has drawn two conclusions about the overall regulation in force, both based on the general principle of the silent abrogation of old laws by new ones (*lex posterior derogat priori*). On the one hand, the reference to the need to set the sum amount implies the abrogation of the fixed calculation based on the maximum fine, allowing the judge to operate freely within the range of the possible monetary sanction. On the other hand, the necessity of the sum to be settled implies the silent abrogation of the mandatory payment in advance of the sum, foreseen by Article 162-*bis* c.p., as a necessary requirement for the admissibility of the request.[58]

However, this legal reasoning may not be based on solid foundations.[59] In the first place, a silent abrogation of a clear disposition of the Criminal Code made through a subsequent disposition inserted in the implementing regulation of the Code of Criminal Procedure is an interpretative slippery slope. This is especially true considering that Article 141 c.p.p.i.r. is not logically incompatible with Articles 162 and 162-*bis* c.p.p. The judge is required to indicate the sum in the admission order, which may be redundant but not inconsistent with the existence of a binding arithmetic formula for calculation. Additionally, the "setting" of the sum can also be explained by the need to add procedural expenses to the oblation, which the judge must determine.

Two more systematic arguments lean towards different interpretative positions. In the first place, there's the excess of delegation. The Code of Criminal Procedure results from a legislative delegation procedure: the Parliament delegated the Government to rewrite the code following specific and binding guidelines. The outcome of government activity not foreseen or beyond these guidelines is not compliant with the Fundamental Law because of the violation of the special legislative procedure provided by Article 76 of the Constitution. In other words, the government cannot act in contrast or beyond parliament's will. In our case,

58 In these terms, see Court of Cassation, March 11th, 2015, No. 18991, *C.e.d. Cass.*, No. 263515: "Article 141 of c.p.p.i.r. has implemented a standardised set of regulations for the oblation. These regulations pertain to the cases mentioned in Articles 162 and 162-*bis* c.p. This Article has established a different procedure, as opposed to the one established by Article 162-*bis* comma 2 paragraph, c.p. As a result, depositing the sum while applying in the cases outlined by the latter provision is no longer mandatory". F.M. Molinari, *I procedimenti alternativi per reati minori*, *op.cit.*, p. 190, shares this interpretative position.

59 An opinion shared by E. Selvaggi, *Comment to article 141*, *op.cit.*, p. 538.

delegation Law No. 81 of 1987[60] allowed the government to give a procedural frame to oblation in the general context of a whole new procedural regulation. But it didn't mention the power to step in the criminal substantial matter, to which oblation belongs as a means to extinguish the offence, which still remains a matter linked to the sanctioning power. Since interpreters must always consider the constitutional conformity parameter when reading a legal text, it may be wiser not to view Article 141 comma 4 c.p.p.i.r. as a silent abolishment clause.[61]

In addition, the lawmaker has consistently used a fixed-amount formula to regulate oblation-like legal institutes. A systemic approach should consider this fact, as all proceedings of oblation approved since 1994 have adopted the same arithmetic fixed criterion to determine the amount needed to extinguish the offence and the subsequent dismissal of the proceeding, with no exceptions.

7. The need for an update in the oblation regulation

If we aim to make the justice system more efficient through the oblation procedure, it may seem counterintuitive to split it into two parts: one for extinguishing the offence and another for dismissing the case. However, in practice, separating these phases is necessary since payment in the oblation procedure leads to the extinction of the offence, which funds the dismissal decision.

One way to simplify the system is to combine the offence extinguishing and dismissal procedures. To do so, it's important to legally clarify that the fixed amount provided by Articles 162 and 162-*bis* c.p. must be paid in advance as a condition for the request's admissibility. The regulation outlined in Article 162-*bis* c.p. should also apply to Article 162 c.p.

At this stage, the prosecutor may request the judge's dismissal. For ordinary oblation, the judge only has to control timely payment and legitimate requests to extinguish the offence and dismiss it, which is an applicant's right. Hence, recurring the legal objective requirements, the prosecutor has no choice but to request dismissal. However, Article 162-*bis* c.p. has a different approach. Here, it's the prosecutor who can disagree with the applicant's assessment about removing harmful or dangerous consequences of the offence or about its seriousness.

---

60 The law is entitled "Legislative delegation to the Government of the Republic for the enactment of the new Code of Criminal Procedure".

61 "The sum of money to be paid is strictly prescribed by law, therefore the economic conditions of the offender pursuant to Article 133-bis of the criminal code cannot be taken into account and the sum cannot be made payable in instalments" (A. Sabatino, 'Il procedimento di oblazione', *op.cit.*, p. 176).

In this case, the prosecutor may refuse to forward the request to the judge, and the applicant must wait for the formal prosecution act to directly ask the judge for access to oblation before the trial opening. On the contrary, if the public prosecutor is persuaded about the requirements for the oblation, they will address the request to the judge along with the dismissal request, which is equivalent to his (positive) opinion on the oblation's admissibility.

Therefore, the procedures for Articles 162 and 162-*bis* c.p. should differ since the former only necessitates verifying formal requirements, while the latter also involves deciding the offence's severity.

If an oblation under Article 162 c.p. can utilise traditional dismissal proceedings, then Article 162-bis c.p. oblation should use the special and particular tenuity dismissal proceedings.

Both procedures allow victims to participate and oppose dismissal requests. However, in the traditional procedure, victims can only suggest new investigations or assessments to overturn the prosecutor's prognosis; in the special procedure, the victim can provide a dissenting reason. Similarly, in oblations *ex* art. 162-*bis* c.p.p., the victim could explain to the judge why the harmful or dangerous consequences of the offence still persist or why the case must be considered serious and, therefore, not eligible for oblation.

Double judicial passages can be avoided by unifying the proceedings without compromising the victims' right to defence or prosecution determinations.

8. Special "conditioned" oblation: new features for an old institution

Oblation can be a dismissal tool with high potential. However, while traditional methods, such as those outlined in articles 162 and 162-*bis* c.p., may suffice for settling minor infractions, they may not be suitable for more complex cases.

To address this, lawmakers have created a "conditioned" or "bargained"[62] oblation mechanism, which balances the need to alleviate the burden on the criminal justice system, provide beneficial treatment to the offender, and generate public revenue with the goal of restoring legality. In this scheme, diversion adequately

62 M. Donini, *Alla ricerca di un disegno. Scritti sulle riforme penali in Italia*, Cedam 2003, p. 359, is credited with coining this latter and less used definition.

meets restoration strategies because "it is more important to achieve a useful result than the obtuse imposition of a penalty as an end in itself".[63]

These new solutions were first introduced with Legislative Decree No. 758/1994. The decree aimed to rewrite criminal sanctions in the occupational safety field. Since then, similar rules have been extended to cover environmental and food safety crimes. All these regulations reach contraventions meant to punish violations of precautionary rules, which are called to prevent damage before it occurs.

As the fundamental principles behind these mechanisms are essentially the same, we will examine them together.

Specialised bodies designated by law to oversee each mentioned field are responsible for initiating such proceedings. In the Italian system, these bodies possess specific expertise in their area of focus. Their primary function is to uncover any illegal activities that ordinary bodies may not have the expertise to identify. If such a discovery is made, they alert the public prosecutor to initiate a criminal case.

In this situation, the supervising body takes the lead in the initial step of the proceeding. Either the surveillance body,[64] when exercising police competencies, or the police itself issues a prescription to the offender, establishing a deadline for its accomplishment. The deadline may be extended in certain circumstances. Prescriptions are recommendations aimed at eliminating any detected violation. Along with the prescription, the supervising body may also impose specific measures to end dangerous situations or continue potentially harmful activities.

The supervising body has two reporting obligations. It must forward the prescription to the legal representative of the offender's workplace and notify the head of the corporation (on the assumption that they are different persons). This is because prescriptions often require financial and managerial resources to be fulfilled.

---

63 A. Culotta, 'Il nuovo sistema sanzionatorio in materia di sicurezza ed igiene del lavoro e le responsabilità penali in caso di attività date in appalto', *Rivista italiana di diritto e procedura penale*, 1996, p. 967. According to G. Fidelbo-M. Pacini, 'Commento al nuovo apparato sanzionatorio in materia di lavoro', *Diritto penale e processo*, 1995, p. 529, the priority was to establish an effective and efficient system for workplace safety and hygiene, rather than focusing on reducing criminal proceedings.

64 Called *organo di vigilanza* by Legislative Decree No. 758/94 and in art. 318-*ter* Legislative Decree No. 152/06; *organo accertatore* by art. 12-*ter* Law No. 238/62.

Furthermore, the supervising body is required to report the *notitia criminis* to the public prosecutor as per Article 347 c.p.p. *Notitia criminis* inscription in the dedicated register set up by Article 335 c.p.p. sets – as usual – the formal beginning of the criminal proceeding. However, its course is meant to be immediately suspended until the public prosecutor "receives one of the notifications" regarding successful or unsuccessful prescription compliance.[65] The lawmaker made an unfortunate decision by referring to the moment the public prosecutor received the notification. This term depends on the supervising body's will and is not easily verifiable. It is better to interpret the rule as if it refers to the maximum time within which the vigilance organs must notify the public prosecutor of the procedure's outcome. The actual notification date can be counted only if the notification is made within this term. This timing has significant consequences, especially on the statute of limitations, which does not run while the proceedings are suspended.

In general, the proceeding suspension allows the public prosecutor to ask for the ordinary dismissal of the case if one of the legal hypotheses recurs.[66]

The prescription must also be submitted to the magistrate. In this regard, the latest regulation on food safety specifies that the prosecutor – who has control powers "linked to his general prerogatives of directing and coordinating the judicial police" – may order by decree that the supervising body amends the prescriptions (art. 12-*ter* comma 6 Law No. 238/62).[67] Although the law is silent, this power also exists in other legal regulations, as the public prosecutor fully governs criminal investigations.[68]

65 Articles 23 Legislative Decree No. 758 del 1994, 318-*sexies* Legislative Decree No. 152/06, and 12-*septies* Law No. 283/1962.

66 Articles 23 Legislative Decree No. 758 del 1994, 318-*sexies* comma 3 Legislative Decree No. 152/06, and 12-*septies* comma 3 Law No. 283/1962.

67 Court of Cassation, Ufficio del Massimario, "Relazione su novità normativa la 'riforma Cartabia'", Report No. 2/2023, p. 264.

68 In matters of safety and hygiene at work, the prescription issued by the supervisory body is not an administrative measure but a typical act of the judicial police, characterised by no discretion, not even technical, and issued under the functional direction of the judicial authority pursuant to Article 55 c.p.p. This implies that the prescriptions cannot be challenged before the administrative court and any issue remains under the jurisdiction of the ordinary criminal court (Court of Cassation, Third Chamber, November 13th, 2019, No. 14214, in C.e.d. Cass., No. 279294). G. Fidelbo-M. Pacini, 'Commento al nuovo apparato sanzionatorio in materia di lavoro', cit., p. 529, highlight the existence of a "constant control of the judicial authority over the regularisation subprocedure, from the moment of the ascertainment of the contravention until the compliance verify".

The structure of these proceedings allows the supervising body and police to take the initiative, but two opposing incidents could result in the public prosecutor taking the lead. In one scenario, the subjects called to give the prescriptions could not have fulfilled their duty and only notified the prosecutor about the *notitia criminis*.[69] If all legal requirements are met, the magistrate may direct the supervising body or police to issue the prescriptions, eventually upon indication of the same perpetrator who aspires to access the deflating mechanism. Conversely, prescriptions may be issued in cases where oblation is not permitted under the law. This can occur when agents incorrectly assess the nature of the crime, a decision that ultimately falls under the jurisdiction of the public prosecutor. If the magistrate reclassifies the offence as more severe and outside the scope of oblation, the extinction mechanism must be halted.

Also, suppose the public prosecutor takes notice of an offence on his initiative or receives it from individuals, public officials, or persons in charge of a public service other than the supervisory body and the police. In this case, the magistrate is explicitly required to notify the supervising body or the police so that the prescriptions can be processed and ordered.[70]

This leads us to the second important step of the procedure, which lies in verifying the elimination of the violation in accordance with the given prescriptions. This happens within a specific timeframe after the given time has elapsed. This step represents a "due act of the proceeding", which the supervising body "must unquestionably carry out whenever it has issued a prescription to the offender".[71] Also, the inspecting organism cannot burden the offender with communication tasks about the accomplishment: Article 23 of the Constitution forbids not lawfully grounded personal obligations.[72]

Once the prescriptions have been fulfilled, the supervising body admits the offender to pay, within thirty days, a sum that is determined with a fixed formula

69 S. Dovere, 'Il progetto di riassetto e riforma delle norme in materia di salute e sicurezza sul lavoro: l'estinzione delle contravvenzioni', *Diritto penale e processo*, 2007, p. 670, affirms that the legislator failed to regulate some aspects in the 1994 regulation, beginning with the response to the supervisory body's misbehavior.

70 Articles 22 Legislative Decree No. 758/94, 318-*quater* Legislative Decree No. 152/06, and 12-*sexies* Law No. 283/1962.

71 C. Gabrielli, 'L'estinzione delle contravvenzioni mediante "oblazione condizionata": questioni interpretative risalenti e soluzioni giurisprudenziali innovative', *Cultura giuridica e diritto vivente*, 2018 (5), p. 7.

72 Court of Cassation, Third Chamber, January 8th, 2009, No. 12483, *C.e.d. Cass.*, No. 243091.

with regard to the maximum fine inflicted by law. After the payment and within another term given by law, the supervising body informs the prosecutor of fulfilling the prescriptions and completing the payment. According to the specific regulation, the magistrate will request the judge to dismiss the case because of the extinction of the offence.

On the contrary, when the prescriptions are not precisely met or the sum is not paid, the supervising body must inform the prosecutor and the offender within a specific timeframe. In this case, another diversion strategy is possible, and it's common to all the analysed schemes before the criminal proceeding continues its ordinary course. The lawmaker created a specific way out under Article 162-*bis* c.p. To do so, the prosecutor and the judge shall consider two factors when assessing the elimination of harmful or dangerous consequences of the offence. Firstly, they must evaluate positively whether the defendant has complied with the specified requirements within a reasonable timeframe, even after the prescribed term has expired. Secondly, they must consider positively whether the harmful consequences of the offence have been eliminated, even if in a manner other than the prescribed ones.

In summary, conditioned oblation represents a multifaceted approach to dismissal, providing a flexible framework to address a wide range of cases while upholding the principles of justice and restoration.

9. In workplaces, safety, and hygiene crime

The first application area of the special conditioned oblation mechanism was represented by the contraventions provided within the Legislative Decree No. 758/1994, in the labour field.[73] Since the experience was positive, in 2004 the lawmaker extended it to all the contraventions provided by labour and social security laws.[74] This all-inclusive clause allows the interpreter to apply

73 S. Dovere, 'I procedimenti definitori nella tutela penale della salute', [in:] G. Garuti (ed.) *Modelli differenziati di accertamento* in: G. Spangher (ed.), *Trattato di procedura penale*, book VII, vol. II, UTET 2011, p. 767.

74 Article 15 Legislative Decree No. 124/2004: "with reference to the laws on labour and social legislation, the application of which is entrusted to the supervision of the provincial labour directorate, if the inspection staff detects criminal offences punishable by the alternative penalty of imprisonment or a fine or by a fine only, they shall issue the offender with a specific mandatory prescription pursuant to Articles 20 and 21 Legislative Decree No. 758/1994, for the purposes of Articles 23 and 24 and Article 25 of the same decree".

the regulation to the Legislative Decree No. 81/2008, also known as the unique-text-law on labour safety, which provides most of the still-in-force criminal offences in the field.

In this regulatory framework, only a limited number of analyses will be conducted as the key features have already been outlined in the preceding paragraph.

Regarding the subject responsible for issuing prescriptions, Article 19 of Legislative Decree No. 758/1994 refers to the overseeing body with police functions (Article 55 c.p.p.), but not the police itself.

About the first step, the term for fulfilling prescriptions should be, at most, the technically necessary time. It may be extended due to the complexity or difficulty of the task. This term is capped at six months. If circumstances beyond the offender's control delay regularisation, the offender can request an extension of up to six months, which the supervising body will decide upon and communicate to the public prosecutor (Article 20 Legislative Decree No. 758/1994).

The second step must be completed within sixty days before the given deadline expires. The supervising body is responsible for verifying that the contravention has been eliminated in accordance with the prescribed guidelines (Art. 21 comma 1 Legislative Decree No. 758/1994).

If the task is accomplished, the vigilance organ admits the offender to the payment of a sum equal to one-quarter of the maximum fine foreseen by the contravention within thirty days. If payment is made within 120 days, it is reported to the public prosecutor (Art. 21 comma 2 Legislative Decree No. 758/1994). As the payment extinguishes the contravention, the prosecutor may request that the case be dismissed (Article 24 commas 1 and 2 Legislative Decree No. 758/1994).

However, the supervising body must report failure to comply with regulations to the prosecutor within ninety days of the original deadline. The criminal proceedings will then continue as normal. Nonetheless, Article 24 comma 3 Legislative Decree No. 758/1994 provides one last opportunity to make amends. It allows for positive evaluation of the non-prescribed methods or late elimination of the contravention in applying Article 162-*bis* c.p.: in this case, the oblation sum is reduced to one-quarter of the maximum fine (rather than one-half).

10. In environmental crime

Law No. 68/2015 extended the conditioned oblation mechanism to contraventions punished by Legislative Decree No. 152/2006, a unique-text-law on the environment. Within this legal source, Article 318-*bis* Legislative Decree No. 152/2006 represents a distinctive trait of this procedure.[75] It specifies that its scope of application does not include contraventions that "have caused damage or a *concrete* and *actual* risk of damage to protected environmental, town-planning or landscape resources".[76] This may seem at odds with Articles 318-*ter* and 318-*septies* Legislative Decree No. 152/2006, which permit authorities to take action to halt dangerous or potentially harmful activities. To reconcile this inconsistency, it may be appropriate to limit the application of these articles to violations that pose a non-concrete and non-actual threat. This is likely because most of the contraventions in this field punish misconducts that are far from actually damaging the environment in order to prevent *potential* damages.[77]

---

75 This rule – and the others in the part VI-*bis* of Legislative Decree No. 152/2006 – has been introduced by Law No. 68/2015. C. Ruga Riva, *I nuovi ecoreati*, Giuffrè 2015, p. 74: it appears that the direction of the reform contradicts the tightening of discipline for environmental crimes and allows for non-punishment of various environmental offences. However, upon closer examination, it is actually a complementary strategy, as non-punishment is tied to the restoration of legality and the elimination of hazardous situations. See also on this point: L. Siracusa, 'La legge 22 maggio 2015, n. 68, sugli "ecodelitti": una svolta "quasi" epocale', *Diritto penale contemporaneo*, July 9th, 2015; M. Telesca, 'Osservazioni sulla legge n. 68/2015 recante "disposizioni in materia di delitti contro l'ambiente", ovvero i chiaroscuri di una agognata riforma', in *Diritto penale contemporaneo*, July 17th, 2015; A. Merlin-R. Losengo, "Ambiente. Il nuovo modello per la tutela penale", *Ambiente&Sicurezza*, 2015 (12).

76 This is on the shared assumption that the term "protected" is intended in the dogmatic sense of "protected as legal interest" and not in the sense of "protected as places subject to legal constraints". This opinion is shared by most of the authors (see, among others, V. Paone, 'La prescrizione dei reati ambientali secondo la l. 68/2015: non mancano dubbi interpretativi', *Ambiente & Sviluppo*, 2016, p. 501; M. Caterini, 'Le implicazioni sistematiche della nuova causa di estinzione delle contravvenzioni del Testo Unico dell'ambiente', in *Rivista trimestrale di diritto penale dell'economia*, 2016, p. 591). *Contra*, V.B. Muscatiello, 'L'entropia ambientale. Dal boia (improbabile) all'esattore (incerto)', *Diritto penale contemporaneo*, 21 ottobre 2016, p. 6.

77 On the expansive tendency of criminal law, see J.M. Silva Sanchez, *L'espansione del diritto penale. Aspetti della politica criminale nelle società postindustriali*, Giuffrè 2004, *passim*. M. Caterini, 'L'ambiente "penalizzato". Storia e prospettive dell'antagonismo tra esigenze preventive e reale offensività' [in:] K. Aquilina-P. Iaquinta (eds), *Il sistema ambiente, tra etica, diritto ed economia*, Cedam 2013, p. 110, is critical of the extensive use of incrimination by offences of abstract danger.

Another peculiarity lies in the new provisions that the applicant is responsible for covering the costs associated with prescriptions (Article 318-*ter* comma 4-*bis* Legislative Decree No. 152/2006).[78] Additionally, any payments made for "oblations" are allocated to the State budget, whereas the supervising body collects any payment made for the realisation of prescriptions. These funds are then utilised to enhance environmental control and verification activities performed by the relevant bodies and entities (Article 318-*quater* comma 2 Legislative Decree No. 152/2006).

Besides these ground boundaries, the fundamental features of the procedure leading to the extinction of the offences are very similar to the labour one. Between the differences: in this context, the police are given the competence to release prescriptions even without the involvement of the environmental supervisory body.

Moreover, the terms and requirements of the prescription procedure have some peculiarities.

The first step, defined in Article 318-*ter* Legislative Decree No. 152 of 2006, mandates that offenders eliminate the ascertained contravention within a reasonable timeframe for technical reasons. This timeframe does not have a formal maximum length, and offenders may request an extension if specific, documented circumstances beyond their control delay the regularisation process. Extensions are limited to a maximum of six months.

In the second step, the supervising body is called to verify that the contravention has been eliminated within sixty days of the expiration of the given deadline.

If the offender succeeds, he gains admission to the payment of a sum equal to one-quarter of the maximum fine foreseen by the contravention within thirty days. The payment must then be communicated to the public prosecutor, who is entitled to ask for the dismissal (Article 318-*septies* comma 2 Legislative Decree No. 152/2006).

In front of non-compliance, the prosecutor must be informed within ninety days so that the criminal proceeding can continue (Article 318-*sexies* comma 1 Legislative Decree No. 152/2006). Also, at this juncture, it's possible to achieve the oblation ordinarily foreseen by Article 162-*bis* c.p.: Article 318-*septies* comma 3 Legislative Decree No. 152/2006 allows the positive assessment of contravention elimination through non-prescribed methods or with a delay. In the environmental field, the oblation sum is not reduced as in labour one: Article 318-*septies*

78 The rule was introduced by Article 26-*bis* Law Decree No. 36/2022 (Further urgent measures to implement the National Recovery and Resilience Plan). On the new regulation, see G. Amarelli, 'Il decreto "PNRR 2" e le modifiche (minime) della procedura estintiva delle contravvenzioni ambientali', *Sistema penale*, July 12th, 2022.

comma 3 Legislative Decree No. 152/2006 uses the same criterion adopted by Article 162-*bis* c.p., so the sum to pay is equal to one-half of the maximum fine. The difference between regulations has been brought to the Constitutional Court's attention, which affirmed that the difference is not grossly unreasonable since the lawmakers can fix different thresholds in different fields.[79] In this case, the regulatory gap could also be explained by the fact that the lawmaker wants to encourage environmental offenders to comply precisely with the prescription given the nature of the protected interest. Environmental health is a shared interest, and even minor infractions can have potentially exponential effects.[80]

11. In the food production and trade crime

The lawmaker proposed a comprehensive overhaul of criminal trials to enhance efficiency and meet the targets set by P.N.R.R., which aims to reduce the average trial duration by 25% by 2026. To implement this reform, Law Decree No. 150/2022 (known as the "*Cartabia reform*" after the Minister of Justice appointed by the Draghi government) was passed, affecting all aspects of the criminal justice system, including the criminal code, criminal procedure code, and several related laws.

In this field, the government worked based on a delegation law, which allowed substantial changes in the overall regulation of conditioned oblation. Article 1 comma 23 letter *a* of Delegation Law No. 134/2021 aimed to establish a general procedure for the extinction of contraventions. This procedure would operate during the preliminary investigation stage, provided that the offender fulfilled the prescribed conditions and paid a sum of money calculated as a fraction of the maximum fine for the contravention. However, this detail was unnecessary since the prescription implies that intervention can remove the consequences of the violation. Irreparable harm or danger is incompatible with this type of procedure.

Despite the potential benefits offered by the delegation law, the lawmaker decided to limit the mechanism of conditioned oblation to a specific field, lacking the courage to explore its potential fully. The legislative action was limited to an

79 Constitutional Court, April 9th, 2019, No. 76. On the decision, see G. Amarelli, 'Proporzionalità e *tertium comparationis*: la maggiore onerosità dell'oblazione tardiva ambientale rispetto a quella antinfortunistica non è irragionevole', *Giurisprudenza costituzionale*, 2019, p. 928.

80 On this aspect, A. Zampini, 'L'oblazione in materia ambientale supera lo scrutinio di legittimità costituzionale ma sulla disciplina restano alcune perplessità', Giurisprudenza costituzionale, 2019, p. 1005.

insertion in Law No. 283/1962. New Article 12-*ter* Law No. 283/1962 states that the new procedure can be applied to contraventions "concerning hygiene, production, traceability and sale of food and beverages, which have caused damage or danger susceptible that can be eliminated through restorative or compensatory conduct and for which the punishment is a fine only, or a fine as an alternative or joint punishment with imprisonment".

However, the alternative set between restoration and compensation has raised some doubts. Monetary compensation is difficult to assess, and usually there is no individual victim for this type of crime, only public health, and the market.

Moreover, some contraventions sanctioned by Law No. 283/1962 instantly result in damages that cannot be amended. For example, Article 5 Law No. 283/1962 prohibits selling food prepared with the addition of non-authorised chemical additives. According to the new regulation, though, the only violations susceptible to regularisation are those with a material possibility of eliminating unlawful hygienic and sanitary conditions.[81] This situation can occur if someone violates Article 8 of Law No. 283/1962, regarding the proper labelling of food products. In such a case, it is possible to correctly re-label existing and future goods.

The procedural *iter* is similar to those previously analysed. Here, the procedure experiences shorter and accelerating deadlines and lower amounts to be paid as an incentive.[82] The first step involves fulfilling the prescription within the technically necessary timeframe, which can be up to six months. If objective circumstances beyond the offender's control cause a delay in regularisation, an extension of up to six months may be requested. The supervising body must make this decision and communicate it to the public prosecutor.

The second step must be completed within thirty days after the initial deadline. The supervising body is responsible for verifying that the contravention has been eliminated according to the prescribed rules (Article 12-*quater* comma 1 Law No. 283/1962). If the verification is positive, the supervising body allows the offender to pay one-sixth of the maximum foreseen fine within thirty days. If the payment is made, the supervising body must communicate, within sixty days of the payment deadline, to the prosecutor that all conditioned oblation requirements have been fulfilled (Article 12-*quater* commas 2 and 3 Law No. 283/1962).

---

81 Court of Cassation, Ufficio del Massimario, "Relazione su novità normativa la 'riforma Cartabia'", Report No. 2/2023, p. 264.

82 *Ibidem.*

The prosecutor will then ask the judge to dismiss the case since the contravention has been extinguished (Article 12-*octies* Law No. 283/1962).

On the contrary, non-compliance to prescriptions shall be communicated by the supervising body to the prosecutor within sixty days from the final term, and the criminal proceeding resumes its course (Article 12-*septies* comma 1 Law No. 283/1962). As it happens in the labour field, it's possible to achieve an oblation according to Article 12-*nonies* Law No. 283/1962. This allows for a positive evaluation of the non-prescribed methods or late elimination of the contravention in applying Article 162-*bis* c.p. In this case, the oblation sum is reduced to one-quarter of the maximum fine (instead of one-half).

At this juncture lies the most interesting innovation of the new rules. Indeed, following the indication of delegation law,[83] the reform provided a variant in the procedure when the offender cannot pay the sum for oblation because of "economic or patrimonial conditions" (Article 12-*quinquies* Law No. 283/1962). Within the term to pay the oblation sum, the offender can ask the public prosecutor to do "public utility work for the State, Regions, Metropolitan Cities, Provinces, Municipalities or with social assistance and voluntary bodies or organisations".

It is worth noting that failure to pay can be proven through a declaration according to Article 46 comma 1 letter *o* of Presidential Decree No. 445/2000. False statements made in such declarations lead themselves to criminal liability. Also, a statement of willingness of the public or social organ that will host the offender must be attached to the request. This means that the offenders must find this institution on their own.

According to the law, the prosecutor cannot reject the public utility request. When the prosecutor doubts the offender's ability to pay, investigations may be initiated to determine if the offender's statement is false. The prosecutor may then proceed to charge the offender if necessary.

Additionally, the law requires the public prosecutor to issue a decree specifying the duration and deadlines for the public utility work, which must be communicated to both the offender and the supervising body. Also, the law gives the public prosecutor an arithmetic formula to set the duration of the work: 250 euro of the sum set according to Article 12-*quinquies* comma 3 Law No. 283/1962 is equal

83 Article 1 comma 23 Law No. 134/2021.

to one day of public utility work; and one day of public utility work is equivalent to 2 hours of actual work.[84]

To ensure fairness, public utility work must be completed within six months, preferably in the offender's region. Unless otherwise agreed upon, the weekly service should be at least six hours and must not interfere with work, study, family, or health needs. Additionally, the daily duration of the service can be at most eight hours.

The request for public utility work must also be communicated to the supervising body. The provision aims to relieve the organ of his duties, such as the check of the effective payment. Moreover, the supervising body is not burdened with reviews over the actual accomplishment of the public work programme. This duty weighs on the general security organisms: police (12-*quinquies* comma 6 Law No. 283/1962). This provision is coherent with the territorial relevance of public work: supervising bodies need help controlling small contexts, while public security offices are present even in small communities.[85] Also, the public security organisms must communicate with the supervising body and the public prosecutor the programme's outcome (12-quinquies comma 7 Law No. 283/1962); at this moment, the proceeding suspension stops.

As well as in other conditioned oblation regulations, the proceeding suspension allows the public prosecutor to ask for the dismissal of the case because of ordinary hypotheses. If this happens while the public utility work is ongoing, its performance must be suspended until the judge decides over the ordinary dismissal request (12-*septies* comma 4 Law No. 283/1962).

Since this type of activity cannot be coerced, Article 12-*quinquies* comma 6 Law No. 283/1962 specifies that the offender can stop the public utility work at any time by paying the originally agreed sum minus the amount corresponding to the completed work duration. This situation could arise if the economic conditions change. Once the supervisory body has verified payment, a notification is sent to the prosecutor, and the case can be dismissed.

---

84 Yet known pattern to avoid inequalities. The standard used to compare the offering of a fine to the number of days of community service is the same one applied in the criminal code for converting fines to imprisonment (as stated in Article 135 c.p.) and in instances when a convicted person is unable to pay (Article 103 comma 2 Law No. 689/1981).

85 For instance, Carabinieri are present also in small towns with tenancies and stations, while inspecting bodies are only present in major cities.

12. Conclusive remarks on "deserved" oblation

It is crucial that lawmakers implement the oblation operative perimeter.[86] Over time, some authors highlighted the need for "a cautious application widening" of such an instrument.[87] One way to do so is represented by the establishment of a list of minor offences that could be "settled" using Article 162-*bis* c.p. mechanism[88] (for instance, the damaging of properties *ex* Article 635 c.p.; or defamation *ex* Article 595 c.p.). Another way to pursue the goal is represented by a legislative action to transform some of those offences (*delitti*) into contraventions (*contravvenzioni*), enabling the oblation procedure to resolve them.

Alongside this path, which affects traditional forms of oblation, there is also the one initially taken and then abandoned by the Cartabia reform. The combination of the traditional oblation profiles (payment and contravention extinguishment) and the restorative model (take action to remove negative consequences and access a reduced pecuniary sanction) has been successfully tested in a few narrow legal fields. Although Article 1 comma 23 letter *a* of the delegation Law No. 134/2021 pointed towards this direction, the lawmaker only extended the mechanism to the food production and trade field, creating new disparities between special regulations. For instance, choosing public utility work instead of paying a sum to extinguish the offence is unreasonably possible only for food production and trade contraventions.[89]

Generalising the "conditioned" oblation mechanism may be beneficial in addressing the issue. Article 162-*bis* c.p.p. could be utilised to specify that oblation can be achieved during the preliminary investigation phase per the public authorities' prescription. The payment amount should be lower than the standard amount for Article 162-*bis* oblation to encourage proper compliance. Moreover, the procedural regulations should be added to the criminal procedure code, providing an opportunity to resolve any remaining interpretation issues from Art. 141 c.p.p.i.r.

---

86 The Constitutional court affirmed the constitutionality of Article 162-bis c.p. even if it does not extend oblation to *delitti* punishable only by a fine; as well of Article 162 c.p. even if it excludes contraventions punishable by imprisonment, either alone or in conjunction with a fine (decision of the December 3rd, 1987, No. 462).

87 R. Orlandi, 'L'insostenibile lunghezza del processo penale e le sorti progressive dei riti speciali', *Rivista di diritto processuale*, 2012, p. 35.

88 *Ibidem*. The Author, in footnote No. 30, highlights that "some special laws already allow for the oblation of *delitti* only punishable by a fine: this is the case, for example, of Article 171 comma 1-*bis* Law No. 633/1941 on copyright infringement".

89 I. Giugni, 'Procedura estintiva delle contravvenzioni antinfortunistiche: verso una questione di costituzionalità all'indomani della c.d. riforma Cartabia?', *Sistema penale*, June 6th, 2023.

Bibliography

Amarelli G., 'Il decreto "PNRR 2" e le modifiche (minime) della procedura estintiva delle contravvenzioni ambientali', *Sistema penale*, July 12th, 2022, available at https://www.sistemapenale.it/it/scheda/il-decreto-pnrr2-e-le-modifiche-minime-della-procedura-estintiva-delle-contravvenzioni-ambientali.

Amarelli G., 'Proporzionalità e *tertium comparationis*: la maggiore onerosità dell'oblazione tardiva ambientale rispetto a quella antinfortunistica non è irragionevole', *Giurisprudenza costituzionale*, 2019.

Bernardi A., 'La depenalizzazione e le sue diverse forme', [in:] Bernardi A.-Zoda I. (eds.), *Depenalizzazione. Profili teorici e pratici*, Cedam 2008.

Bontempelli M., 'Il procedimento di oblazione', [in:] Spangher et al. (eds.), *Procedura penale. Teoria e pratica del processo*, vol. III, 2015.

Bove V., *Particolare tenuità del fatto*, Giuffrè 2019.

Brunelli D., 'La tenuità del fatto nella "riforma Cartabia": scenari per l'abolizione dei minimi edittali', *Sistema penale*, January 13th, 2022, available at https://www.sistemapenale.it/it/opinioni/brunelli-tenuita-del-fatto-riforma-cartabia.

Cadoppi A., 'Oblazione "vecchia" e "nuova" e principi costituzionali', *Rivista italiana di diritto e procedura penale*, 1983.

Carini C., 'Oblazione', [in:] Gaito A.-Spangher G.-Giunchedi F.-Santoriello G., *La giustizia penale differenziata. I procedimenti speciali*, vol. I, Giappichelli, 2011.

Caterini M., 'L'ambiente "penalizzato". Storia e prospettive dell'antagonismo tra esigenze preventive e reale offensività', [in:] K. Aquilina K.-Iaquinta P. (eds.), *Il sistema ambiente, tra etica, diritto ed economia*, Cedam 2013.

Caterini M., 'Le implicazioni sistematiche della nuova causa di estinzione delle contravvenzioni del Testo Unico dell'ambiente', *Rivista trimestrale di diritto penale dell'economia*, 2016.

Cesari C., 'Le clausole di irrilevanza del fatto nel sistema processuale penale', [in:] R. E. Kostoris (ed.), *La ragionevole durata del processo. Garanzia ed efficienza della giustizia penale*, Giappichelli 2005.

Conti G.-Macchia A., 'Introduzione alle norme di attuazione del 1989', [in:] Conso G.-Grevi V.-Neppi Modona G. (eds.), *Il nuovo codice di procedura penale. Dalle leggi delega ai decreti delegati*, vol. VI, Cedam 1990.

Culotta A., 'Il nuovo sistema sanzionatorio in materia di sicurezza ed igiene del lavoro e le responsabilità penali in caso di attività date in appalto', *Rivista italiana di diritto e procedura penale*, 1996.

Daniele M., 'L'archiviazione per tenuità del fatto fra velleità deflattive ed equilibrismi procedimentali', [in:] S. Quattrocolo (ed.), *I nuovi epiloghi del procedimento penale per particolare tenuità del fatto*, Giappichelli 2015.

Dies R., 'Questioni varie in tema di irrilevanza penale del fatto per particolare tenuità', *Diritto penale contemporaneo*, September 13th, 2015, available at https://archiviodpc.dirittopenaleuomo.org/d/4128-questioni-varie-in-tema-di-irrilevanza-penale-del-fatto-per-particolare-tenuita.

Donini M., *Alla ricerca di un disegno. Scritti sulle riforme penali in Italia*, Cedam 2003.

Dovere S., 'I procedimenti definitori nella tutela penale della salute', [in:] G. Garuti (ed.) *Modelli differenziati di accertamento* in: G. Spangher (ed.), *Trattato di procedura penale*, book VII, vol. II, UTET 2011.

Dovere S., 'Il progetto di riassetto e riforma delle norme in materia di salute e sicurezza sul lavoro: l'estinzione delle contravvenzioni', *Diritto penale e processo*, 2007.

Fidelbo G.-Pacini M., 'Commento al nuovo apparato sanzionatorio in materia di lavoro', *Diritto penale e processo*, 1995.

Gabrielli C., 'L'estinzione delle contravvenzioni mediante "oblazione condizionata": questioni interpretative risalenti e soluzioni giurisprudenziali innovative', *Cultura giuridica e diritto vivente*, 2018 (5).

Galluzzo F., *Il consenso dell'imputato nei procedimenti speciali*, Wolters Kluwer 2020.

Gialuz M., 'L'archiviazione meritata come terza via tra archiviazione ed esercizio dell'azione penale', *Processo penale e giustizia*, 2021.

Giostra G., *L'archiviazione. Lineamenti sistematici e questioni interpretative*, Giappichelli 1994.

Giugni I., 'Procedura estintiva delle contravvenzioni antinfortunistiche: verso una questione di costituzionalità all'indomani della c.d. riforma Cartabia?', *Sistema penale*, June 6th, 2023, available at https://www.sistemapenale.it/it/scheda/giugni-procedura-estintiva-delle-contravvenzioni-antinfortunistiche-verso-una-questione-di-costituzionalita-allindomani-della-cd-riforma-cartabia.

Martini A., 'Il procedimento per oblazione' [in:] S. Nosengo (ed.), *Giurisprudenza sistematica di diritto processuale penale. Riti camerali e speciali*, Utet 2006.

Merlin A.-Losengo R., 'Ambiente. Il nuovo modello per la tutela penale', *Ambiente&Sicurezza*, 2015 (12).

Molinari F. M., *I procedimenti alternativi per reati minori*, Giuffrè 2018.

Muscatiello V. B., 'L'entropia ambientale. Dal boia (improbabile) all'esattore (incerto)', *Diritto penale contemporaneo*, 21 ottobre 2016, available at https://archiviodpc.dirittopenaleuomo.org/d/4991-lentropia-ambientale-dal-boia-improbabile-allesattore-incerto.

Muzzica R., 'Il ruolo della vittima negli istituti riparativi', *Legislazione penale*, November 22nd, 2019, available at https://www.lalegislazionepenale.eu/wp-content/uploads/2019/11/2019-MUZZICA-Il-ruolo-della-vittima-negli-istituti-riparativi-_def.pdf.

Orlandi R., 'L'insostenibile lunghezza del processo penale e le sorti progressive dei riti speciali', *Rivista di diritto processuale*, 2012.

Padovani T., 'Un intento deflattivo dal possibile effetto boomerang', *Guida al diritto*, 2015/15.

Paone V., 'La prescrizione dei reati ambientali secondo la l. 68/2015: non mancano dubbi interpretativi', *Ambiente & Sviluppo*, 2016.

Piziali G., 'Il procedimento di oblazione', [in:] M. Pisani (ed.), *I procedimenti speciali in materia penale*, Giuffrè 2003.

Quattrocolo S., 'L'altra faccia della medaglia: l'impatto della particolare tenuità del fatto sul processo penale', *Criminalia*, 2016.

Ruga Riva C., *I nuovi ecoreati*, Giuffrè 2015.

Sabatino A., 'Il procedimento di oblazione', [in:] G. Dalia (ed.), *Procedimenti alternativi per reati minori*, Giuffrè 2018.

Santoriello C., *La clausola di particolare tenuità del fatto*, Dike giuridica 2015.

Scalfati A., 'Decreto di citazione pretorile e mancato avviso circa le scelte alternative al dibattimento', *Giurisprudenza costituzionale*, 1995.

Selvaggi E., 'Comment to article 141 of the implementation rules of the code of criminal procedure', [in:] M. Chiavario, *Commentario Chiavario, La normativa complementare*, vol. I, Norme di attuazione, UTET 1992.

Silva Sanchez J. M., *L'espansione del diritto penale. Aspetti della politica criminale nelle società postindustriali*, Giuffrè 2004.

Siracusa L., 'La legge 22 maggio 2015, n. 68, sugli "ecodelitti": una svolta "quasi" epocale', *Diritto penale contemporaneo*, July 9th, 2015, available at https://archiviodpc.dirittopenaleuomo.org/d/4050-la-legge-22-maggio-2015-n-68-sugli-ecodelitti-una-svolta-quasi-epocale-per-il-diritto-penale-dell-a.

Sottani S., 'L'oblazione nel nuovo processo penale: caratteristiche, struttura e ipotesi', *La giustizia penale*, 1990, III.

Telesca M., 'Osservazioni sulla legge n. 68/2015 recante "disposizioni in materia di delitti contro l'ambiente", ovvero i chiaroscuri di una agognata riforma', in *Diritto penale contemporaneo*, July 17th, 2015, available at https://archiviodpc.dirittopenaleuomo.org/d/4071-osservazioni-sulla-l-n-682015-recante--disposizioni-in-materia-di-delitti-contro-l-ambiente--ovvero.

Zampini A., 'L'oblazione in materia ambientale supera lo scrutinio di legittimità costituzionale ma sulla disciplina restano alcune perplessità', *Giurisprudenza costituzionale*, 2019.

Prof. Aleksandar Maršavelski[1]

II. Restorative Justice in Croatia: A Potential for an Effective Criminal Justice System

Abstract: This study provides an overview of Croatian restorative justice literature, which is quite optimistic concerning the effectiveness of restorative justice. Ultimately, the effectiveness of restorative justice models depends on many factors, such as the type of model used, legal framework, state support, implementation etc. The main argument is that the greatest potential of improving the effectiveness of the Croatian criminal justice system is to expand the application of restorative justice not just in juvenile cases, but also to find ways of its application to adult offenders. Restorative justice has very limited use in the pre-trial stage because the real mediation between the offender and the victim, which avoids trial, is limited to a small portion of criminal cases. In cases where the initiation of proceedings depends on the victim's initiative, restorative justice is mostly used informally, and there is a lack of data about it. Access to restorative justice is also very limited, as specialized out-of-court settlement services are available only in three Croatian cities.

The Author states that proper education is especially important to ensure the wider application of restorative justice in criminal matters. This will eliminate doubts among practitioners about the application of available mechanisms. With increased investment and support, restorative justice can play a significant role in making the Croatian criminal justice system more effective and just.

Keywords: restorative justice, effective criminal procedure, Croatian criminal procedure

1. Introduction

Restorative justice scholars are not always concerned with its overall effectiveness. Note that Howard Zehr wrote that "*reduced recidivism is not the reason for operating restorative justice programs. Reduced recidivism is a byproduct, but restorative justice is done first of all because it is the right thing to do*".[2] Such absolute statements are in fact typical for retributivists who would object and say that justice is done only when the offender is punished for the wrongdoing. On the other hand, utilitarians would be concerned about the effectiveness of restorative justice. The understanding of restorative justice, however, should not be limited to its typical

---

1 ORCID no. 0000-0002-6196-4212. Associate Professor of Criminal Law at the University of Zagreb.

2 H. Zehr, *The Little Book of Restorative Justice*, Good Books 2014.

form such as out-of-court victim-offender mediation, because restorative justice elements exist in many forms and even within punishment. This enables us to think broadly about how to reform criminal justice into victim-friendly justice beyond strong procedural rights acknowledged to victims of crime across Europe. Restorative justice elements existed even in periods of history characterised by severe punishments and even for the most severe crimes, such as homicide.[3]

The origins of restorative justice in Croatia can be traced back to Medieval times when it was practised most often in the form of extrajudicial mediation, which preceded court proceedings. For example, in 1451, in Zagreb, "*a certain Antun, after an unsuccessful attempt at reconciliation, was sentenced to pay medical expenses and 25 pence to the blacksmith Pavlo, whom he beat so badly with a wooden club that Pavalo barely survived his injuries*".[4] At that time, no clear distinction was made between criminal and civil proceedings, so proceedings to determine tort liability often combined civil and criminal elements. Although in the mentioned example the mediation was not successful, the outcome of the procedure had a multiple restorative character because not only did the perpetrator pay the victim's treatment costs, but he also paid her an additional sum of money as a sanction of a punitive nature, which was paid to the victim.[5]

However, the historical origins had little or no impact on the modern Croatian development of restorative justice. The theoretical foundations for the application of restorative justice in criminal matters in Croatia first came in the context of the global victimological movement, as the funder of Yugoslav and Croatian victimology was Zvonimir Šeparović, who also touched upon restorative justice in his work.[6] The person who pioneered restorative justice in Croatia, both in

---

3 The most recent example of large-scale restorative justice practices addressing homicides in Europe are reconciliation processes addressing blood feuds rooted in Albanian customary law. See A. Marsavelski, F. Sheremeti, J. Braithwaite, 'Did nonviolent resistance fail in Kosovo?', *The British Journal of Criminology*, 2018/58 (1), pp. 218–236.

4 K. Judaš, *Nasilni zločini protiv osoba u sudskim spisima zagrebačkog Gradeca u kasnom srednjem vijeku* (Violent crimes against persons in the court files of Zagreb's Gradec in the late Middle Ages), Sveučilište u Zagrebu, Filozofski fakultet, Zagreb 2013, p. 59.

5 A. *Maršavelski, K. Ivanušić*, 'Restorativna Pravda u kaznenopravnoj teoriji i praksi' (Restorative justice in Croatian criminal law theory and practice), *Hrvatski ljetopis za kaznene znanosti i praksu*, 28(2), p. 481.

6 For an overview of Zvonimir Šeparović's work, see K. Turković, A. Maršavelski, S. Roksandić Vidlička, *Liber Amicorum Zvonimir Šeparović: Od kaznenog prava do viktimologije* (Liber Amicorum Zvonimir Šeparović: From Criminal Law to Victimology), *Zbornik radova u čast 80. rođendana profesora emeritusa Zvonimira Šeparovica*, Pravni fakultet Sveučilišta u Zagrebu, Zagreb 2009.

academic and practical terms, was Nivex Koller Trbović, who started the first restorative justice project in Croatia in 2000 and was one of the founders of the Association for Extrajudicial Settlement, which was the first to promote victim-offender mediation.[7]

Mass atrocities, such as the ones that occurred during the war in Croatia in 1991–1995 are always challenging in terms of transitional justice effectiveness. The whole post-war justice process in Croatia was focused on bringing all war criminals to justice while neglecting the needs of victims and their families. Almost three decades later, most war criminals did not face justice, victims were mostly unsatisfied, 1,410 persons were missing, and an additional 395 persons were killed in the war, but their bodies were never found.[8] Although there were initiatives to establish a regional truth reconciliation commission across former Yugoslavia, it never received political support.[9]

The post-war development of restorative justice in Croatia must be understood in the context of the ongoing modernisation of its criminal justice system and the challenges it faces.[10] Restorative justice serves as a promising model in several aspects, including as an alternative or complementary to retributive and re-socializing justice.[11] This approach prioritises the victim's role in the criminal procedure and responds adequately to the contemporary criminal justice system's difficulties, such as large case-loads, lengthy procedures, reduced efficiency, and negative public perception.[12]

Various comparative studies across the world have shown the effectiveness of restorative justice in reducing recidivism, improving victim satisfaction, and building community relationships.[13] This paper also provides an overview of

---

7 See: M. Meštrović, *Dobitnica medijacijske nagrade "Medijator restorativne pravde" – dr. sc. Nivex Koller Trbović* (Interview), available at: https://medijacija.hr/dobitnica-medijacijske-nagrade-medijator-restorativne-pravde-dr-sc-nivex-koller-trbovic/ [accessed on January 31st, 2024].

8 Source: Republic of Croatia, Ministry of War Veterans, available at: https://branitelji.gov.hr/mjere-14/nestale-osobe/nestale-osobe-u-domovinskom-ratu-834/834 [accessed on October 10th, 2023].

9 A. Maršavelski, J. Braithwaite, 'Transitional Justice Cascades', *Cornell International Law Journal*, 2020/53 (2), p. 243.

10 I. Bojanić, 'Croatia' [in:] F. Dünkel, J. Grzywa-Holten, P. Horsfield (eds.) *Restorative Justice and Mediation in Penal Matters*, Vol. 1, Mönchengladbach 2015, p. 145

11 Ibidem.

12 Ibidem.

13 For a detailed overview of these studies see J. Braithwaite, 'Restorative justice and responsive regulation: the question of evidence', *RegNEt Research Papers*, 2016/51.

Croatian restorative justice literature, which is quite optimistic concerning the effectiveness of restorative justice. Ultimately, the effectiveness of restorative justice models depends on a lot of factors, such as the type of model used, legal framework, state support, implementation etc. There is no one-size-fits-all solution and this paper reveals the restorative justice possibilities in the Croatian legal system.

In Croatia, restorative justice has been primarily utilised in the pre-trial procedure, where the state attorney decides whether to prosecute based on conditional prosecutorial discretion. Juvenile delinquency is an area where the effectiveness of responses is most needed to avoid reoffending. Conditional prosecutorial discretion, which involves non-prosecution if certain conditions are met, is used to resolve 35–45% of juvenile offender cases, but out-of-court settlements make up less than 10% of the special obligations ordered by prosecutors. Between 2004 and 2012, 1,237 juvenile cases were referred for out-of-court settlements, which was, on average, 137 cases per year. However, due to the entry of the new Criminal Code in force in 2013 – which increased the prescribed sentences for some of the most common offences, such as theft – there was a reduction in the applicability of restorative justice in juvenile cases. Thus, there was a significant decline from 2013 onwards – almost by half in comparison with the period 2004–2012.[14]

The main argument of this paper is that the greatest potential of improving the effectiveness of the Croatian criminal justice system is to expand the application of restorative justice not just in juvenile cases, but also to find ways of its application to adult offenders. Despite the fact that restorative justice has a very limited use in the pre-trial stage because the real mediation between the offender and the victim, which avoids trial, is limited to a small portion of criminal cases – mainly juvenile cases or cases in which the victim has a decisive role in the initiation of the prosecution. In cases where the initiation of proceedings depends on the victim's initiative, restorative justice is mostly used informally, and there is a lack of data about it. Access to restorative justice is also very limited, as specialised out-of-court settlement services are available only in three Croatian cities.

---

14 A. Mirosavljević, *Izvansudska nagodba-perspektiva oštećenika i mladih u sukobu sa zakonom* (Out-of-court settlement - the perspective of victims and juveniles in conflict with the law), Pravni fakultet Sveučilišta u Zagrebu, Zagreb 2015.

This does not mean, however, that restorative justice is not possible in other criminal cases. This paper provides an analysis of a broad restorative justice potential within the existing legal framework. According to Croatian law, elements of restorative justice are also present at the court proceedings level, especially in the context of special obligations that can be imposed along with a suspended sentence. Suspended sentences are by far the most frequently used sanction in Croatia, amounting to approximately 80% of all imposed sanctions. The use of restorative justice tools as obligations under suspended sentences, thus, has probably the greatest potential of expanding the restorative justice elements. Based on the current Croatian legal framework, restorative justice also has the potential for use in the stage of sanctions enforcement, including while serving prison sentences.

The aim of this paper is to identify restorative justice tools under the Croatian legal framework at all levels of administration of criminal cases and what could be done to expand their use.

2. The overview of Croatian restorative justice literature

Some Croatian scholars tend to interpret restorative justice as a tool to restore the victim's sense of dignity and safety, the offender takes responsibility for his behaviour, and the reconciliation of the parties leads to faster and easier resolution of social conflicts.[15] Other scholars see restorative justice as a replacement for retributive justice in cases of less serious crimes, particularly for interpersonal conflicts.[16] In any case, the research on restorative justice in Croatia is interdisciplinary, so the authors on this topic include lawyers, criminologists, victimologists, sociologists, social pedagogues, social workers, etc. Most of the studies are published in the Croatian language and, as such, are incomprehensible to the international audience, so the forthcoming paragraphs provide an overview of the Croatian restorative justice research.

15 A. Carić, 'Počinitelji i žrtve – odgovornost i pravednost u kaznenom postupku' (Offenders and victims – responsibility and justice in criminal proceedings), *Zbornik radova Pravnog fakulteta u Splitu*, 2000/37, p. 280.

16 B. Pavišić, *Komentar Zakona o kaznenom postupku* (Commentary on the Criminal Procedure Act). Rijeka: Dušević & Kršovni d.o.o. 2011, p. 20.

Koller-Trbović, Gmaz-Luški, Mirosavljević and Lalić Lukač specifically dealt with restorative justice in the context of out-of-court settlements;[17] Mirosavljević provided an overview of models of restorative justice and undertook a qualitative research;[18] Turković, Roksandić Vidlička and Maršavelski initiated a recommendation on alternative dispute resolution in medical liability cases,[19] Maršavelski and Berneš developed a theoretical model for the application of restorative justice in borderline cases between conviction and acquittal, as determined in cases of necessity;[20] Grozdanić and Škorić gave a theoretical concept for the application of restorative justice as an alternative to punishment;[21] Gospodnetić analyzed the use of mediation in the Croatian judiciary in general by analysing opinions

---

17 See N. Koller-Trbović, V. Gmaz-Luški, V., 'Primjena izvansudske nagodbe (medijacija) u pretkaznenom postupku prema maloljetnicima i mlađim punoljetnim osobama' (Application of out-of-court settlement in preliminary criminal procedure to minors and younger adult offenders), *Hrvatski ljetopis za kazneno pravo i praksu*, 2006/13, pp. 933–956; A. Mirosavljević, A., N. Koller-Trbović, D. Lalić-Lukač, 'Evaluacija uspješnosti izvansudske nagodbe u stručnoj službi za izvansudsku nagodbu Zagreb' (Evaluation of the efficiency of victim-offender mediation in Zagreb professional service for victim-offender mediation in cases of juvenile offenders), *Kriminologija i socijalna integracija*, 2010/18, pp. 77–95.

18 A. Mirosavljević, 'Modeli restorativne pravde u svijetu za mlade u sukobu sa zakonom i pregled istraživanja njihove učinkovitosti' (Restorative justice models in the world for youth in conflict with the law and overview of its efficiency studies), *Kriminologija i socijalna integracija* 2010/18, pp. 53–64; A. Mirosavljević, *Izvansudska nagodba-perspektiva oštećenika i mladih u sukobu sa zakonom* (Out-of-court settlement - the perspective of victims and juveniles in conflict with the law), Zagreb 2015, Pravni fakultet Sveučilišta u Zagrebu.

19 K. Turković, S. Roksandić Vidlička, A. Maršavelski, 'Recommendation on alternative dispute resolution in medical liability in Council of Europe member states' [in:] K. Turković, S. Roksandić Vidlička, A. Maršavelski (eds.), *Book of proceedings of the 18th World Congress on medical law*, Faculty of Law, University of Zagreb, Zagreb 2010, CD, paper No. 15, pp. 1–15.

20 A. Maršavelski, A. Berneš, 'Temeljni aktualni problemi krajnje nužde u kontekstu primjenjivosti restorativne pravde' (Fundamental Contemporary Problems of Necessity in the Context of Application of Restorative Justice), in: K. Turković, M. Munivrana Vajda, M. Dragičević Prtenjača (eds.), *Kazneno pravo: sinergija teorije i prakse (Zbornik radova u čast profesora Petra Novoselca)*, Zagreb 2019, Pravni fakultet u Zagrebu, pp. 299–333.

21 V. Grozdanić, M. Škorić, 'O kaznenom pravu i kazni zatvora' (On criminal law and prison sentence), in: K. Turković, M. Munivrana Vajda, M. Dragičević Prtenjača (eds.), *Kazneno pravo: sinergija teorije i prakse (Zbornik radova u čast profesora Petra Novoselca)*, Zagreb 2019, Pravni fakultet u Zagrebu, pp. 205–227.

of lawyers, judges and court users on mediation as an alternative dispute resolution;[22] Maršavelski and Braithwaite did a major interview-based research on the applicability of restorative justice in the context of transitional justice and peacebuilding after the war in Croatia;[23] Maršavelski and Ivanušic identified the restorative justice models in the Croatian legal framework and practice and made recommendations how to advance the application of restorative justice.[24] The following research contains the most relevant research data about the use of restorative justice in Croatia.

The first two evaluations on the implementation of victim-offender mediation through the out-of-court settlement procedure focused on the work of the Service for Out-of-Court Settlement in Zagreb.[25] The first evaluation covered the period 2001–2006 and analysed a sample of 175 cases involving suspects.[26] The study evaluated the basic criteria for referring to the out-of-court settlement procedure, the success of the process, and the satisfaction of the parties involved. The study found that the criteria for voluntary participation were respected, with a high degree of willingness to participate, as only 4% of suspects and 6% of victims did not agree to participate. The majority of cases referred were property offences (60%) and offences against life and limb (25%), with none being insignificant. The victims were physical persons in 95% of the cases. Most of the perpetrators were first-time offenders (94%) and male (95%). The State Attorney decided not to institute criminal proceedings in 86% of the cases. The out-of-court settlement procedure was completed within one month in 49% of the cases. Agreements were reached in 88% of cases where there was consent, and the agreement was successfully fulfilled in 92% of those cases. The most common means of repairing or compensating the damage were an apology followed by material compensation (58%), only an apology (26%), and only material compensation (6%). The second evaluation

---

22 F. Gospodnetić, *Medijacija u pravosuđu: Analiza mišljenja odvjetnika, sudaca i korisnika sudova o medijaciji kao alternativnom rješavanju sporova* (Mediation in the judiciary: Analysis of opinions of lawyers, judges and court users on mediation as an alternative dispute resolution), Datafit, Zagreb 2021.

23 A. Maršavelski, J. Braithwaite, *Transitional Justice*, *op.cit.*, pp. 207–260.

24 A. Maršavelski, K. Ivanušić, 'Restorativna Pravda u kaznenopravnoj teoriji i praksi' (Restorative justice in Croatian criminal law theory and practice), *Hrvatski ljetopis za kaznene znanosti i praksu*, 2021/28(2), pp. 473–505.

25 See N. Koller-Trbović, V. Gmaz-Luški, *Primjena izvansudske*, *op.cit.*, pp. 933–956; A. Mirosavljević, A., N. Koller-Trbović, D. Lalić-Lukač, *Evaluacija uspješnosti izvansudske*, *op.cit.*, pp. 77–95.

26 N. Koller-Trbović, V. Gmaz-Luški, *Primjena izvansudske*, *op.cit.*, pp. 933-956

covered the period 2006–2009 and analysed a sample of 209 suspects.[27] It found no substantial differences from the first evaluation. However, more comprehensive evaluations with more adequate methodology are needed to encompass out-of-court settlements throughout all of Croatia.

Another evaluation study of juvenile out-of-court settlements in eleven Croatian cities for 2015 included 110 persons, consisting of 60 minors and 50 underage offenders.[28] Property (58%) and violent crimes (32%) were the most common offences. 70% of cases resulted in an agreement between suspects and victims, of which 97% were successfully executed. The most common way of repairing damage was through an apology and financial compensation. The process typically took 1–3 months and was successfully implemented in 66% of cases.

A qualitative research involving 14 injured parties and 17 juvenile offenders exploring their perspectives on out-of-court settlements.[29] Initially, both parties felt tension, fear, and embarrassment, but at the end of the joint meeting and reaching an agreement, they expressed positive emotions of happiness, relief, and satisfaction. Injured parties found an apology, an answer to the question of why the crime was committed, and a guarantee that the suspect would not repeat criminal acts against them as key gains. Suspects valued formal and legal benefits of out-of-court settlements, such as avoiding court and not being entered into the criminal record. However, some injured parties considered out-of-court settlements as "easy" and insufficient, and there was an impression that the process was favorable and focused on the suspect. It is essential to respect the principles and standards of the process to ensure a positive experience for both parties.

Another qualitative study of 5 mediators in out-of-court settlements in Zagreb and Osijek who describe their experience and role in the process.[30] The mediators are intrinsically motivated and see the usefulness of an out-of-court settlement. Their role is crucial in preparing participants, encouraging suspects to take responsibility, and focusing on the emotional resolution of the conflict.

---

27 Mirosavljević, A., N. Koller-Trbović, D. Lalić-Lukač, *Evaluacija uspješnosti izvansudske, op.cit.*, p. 89.

28 A. Modrić, *Provjera uspješnosti izvansudske nagodbe za mlade u sukobu sa zakonom u Hrvatskoj* (Evaluation of the success of out-of-court settlements with juveniles in conflict with the law in Croatia), Zagreb 2016, Edukacijsko-rehabilitacijski fakultet Sveučilišta u Zagrebu.

29 A. Mirosavljević, *Izvansudska nagodba-perspektiva, loc.cit.*

30 A. Markulj, *Izvansudska nagodba iz perspektive posrednika* (Out-of-court settlement from mediator's perspective), Zagreb 2016, Edukacijsko-rehabilitacijski fakultet Sveučilišta u Zagrebu.

Success criteria include competence, compliance with legal criteria, acceptance by participants, and working conditions. Helpful factors include consultation with colleagues, supervision, and good preparation, while difficult factors include maintaining neutrality, demanding participants, and poor working conditions.

In the context of war crimes and post-war transitional justice in Croatia, there was an initiative called RECOM with an aim to establish a regional commission tasked with establishing the facts about all victims of war crimes and other serious human rights violations committed during the 1990s. Despite receiving considerable popular support, with more than half a million citizens signing the petition for RECOM, bringing together more than 2 thousand NGOs, it lacked international pressure on governments to join, so the commission was never established.[31]

An analysis of the opinion of lawyers, judges and court users on mediation in Croatia based on a sample of 438 respondents shows that "conciliation/mediation is still an unknown way of resolving disputes in the judicial system of the Republic of Croatia. Despite the ambition of lawyers and judges to familiarise themselves with the conciliation/mediation process, it seems that the judicial system's openness to conciliation/mediation is the main obstacle to its implementation."[32] Still, respondents positively evaluated mediation in terms of increasing the efficiency of the courts, more pleasant interaction with the parties, faster and cheaper dispute resolution and increased satisfaction of the parties. Finally, the analysis points to the need to invest additional effort in the education of all actors of the justice system.

In the most recent evaluation of the success of out-of-court settlements in Zagreb from 2016 to 2021, more than 90% of suspects and victims voluntarily agreed to participate in the mediation process.[33] The agreement was reached in 86% of cases, of which 93% were executed by the offender. More than 90% of agreements included an apology to the victim.

The latest research on restorative justice in Croatia, using interviews and case studies, identified various areas allowing restorative justice in the existing legal framework.[34] However, despite these possibilities, the implementation of restorative justice remains infrequent in Croatia.

---

31 A. Maršavelski, J. Braithwaite, *Transitional Justice*, *op.cit.*, p. 243.

32 F. Gospodnetić, *Medijacija u pravosuđu*, *op.cit.*, p. 23.

33 K. Đukes, *Provjera uspješnosti izvansudske nagodbe u Zagrebu* (Evaluation of the success of out-of-court settlements in Zagreb), Zagreb 2022, Edukacijsko-rehabilitacijski fakultet, Sveučilište u Zagrebu.

34 A. Maršavelski, K. Ivanušić, *Restorativna Pravda*, *op.cit.*, pp. 473–505.

3. Legal framework of restorative justice in Croatia

Implementing out-of-court settlements in the pre-trial procedure against juveniles and young adults is of significant importance in the historical development of restorative justice in Croatia. While victim-offender mediation was not explicitly prescribed by law, its practical application was supported by the provisions of the 1997 JCA, which regulated special obligations in the context of conditional dischargement under prosecutorial discretion.

In Croatia, restorative justice elements can be found in the following four legislative sources: the 2008 Criminal Procedure Act (CPA), the 2011 Criminal Code (CC), the 2011 Juveniles Courts Act (JCA), and the 2021 Prison Sentence Execution Act (PSEA).

Restorative justice mechanisms typically require flexibility with regard to the initiation of criminal proceedings. However, one of the basic principles of the Croatian criminal procedure is the principle of mandatory prosecutions (Art. 2(3) CPA). As an exception to this principle, however, the CPA also regulates the conditions for the application of the principle of prosecutorial discretion, known in Croatian literature as the "principle of purposefulness" (*načelo svrhovitosti*) or the principle of opportunity (*načelo oportuniteta*), regulated in Art. 206d CPA. This exceptional principle enables the state attorney to conditionally postpone prosecution or discharge the defendant for less severe offences punishable by imprisonment of up to five years. The main condition is to fulfil one or more of the six listed obligations, among which are those of a restorative nature: repairing or compensating for damage caused by a criminal offence, payment of overdue obligations and payment in favour of a public institution, humanitarian or charitable purpose. Another important restorative justice condition is that both the defendant and the victim must consent to this arrangement. If any of them does not consent or the defendant fails to fulfill the obligation imposed, the state attorney shall initiate prosecution.

Furthermore, Articles 71 and 72 JCA regulate a broader application of the principle of prosecutorial discretion in juvenile justice cases. If a minor (a person below 18) commits a crime for which a prison sentence of up to five years is prescribed, and if it would not be purposeful to conduct proceedings against the minor, the state attorney may condition the decision to suspend the proceedings based on the willingness of the minor to perform certain obligations from the list. Many of the listed obligations are restorative in character: an apology to the victim, repair of the damage caused by the criminal offence, involvement in the mediation process through an out-of-court settlement, involvement in the work of humanitarian organisations, as well as other obligations that are appropriate in view of the committed criminal offence and the personal and family circumstances of the minor (Art. 72(1) JCA). After the minor fulfills the obligations, the state attorney makes a final decision to drop the charges against him (Art. 72(2) JCA). This prosecutorial discretion in juvenile justice cases is the most common restorative justice practice in Croatia.

Restorative justice also has a potential in the context of plea bargaining. According to the CPA, the state attorney has the power and duty to negotiate and agree with the defendant on a plea of guilty and a sanction. If there is a signing of a statement for the rendering of judgment based on the agreement between the state attorney and the defendant, as a rule, the state attorney is obliged to inform the victim about it (Art. 360(5) CPA). However, the state attorney must obtain the consent of the victim for the plea bargain in cases of crimes against life and body (e.g. murder and battery) and crimes against sexual freedom (e.g. rape) for which a prison sentence of more than five years is prescribed. As the consent of the victim is required in such cases, there is space for the application of restorative justice.

Restorative justice is applicable through mediation in the context of private criminal lawsuits (*privatna tužba*), which are exceptional for crimes where there is no ex officio duty of the state attorney to prosecute, such as petty theft, insult and defamation. When the criminal court receives a private lawsuit, it can refer the parties to mediation, where it will set a deadline in which the mediation will be attempted and will pause the procedure, and upon expiry of that term or if the mediation fails, the procedure will continue (Art. 527(1) CPA).

Furthermore, mediation-based restorative justice schemes are possible in cases of criminal offences that require the victim to file a motion for the state attorney to prosecute (*kazneni progon po prijedlogu*). According to Art. 47 CPA, for such offences, the motion for prosecution must be submitted within three months from the day the victim learned about the crime and the perpetrator. At this pre-prosecution stage, the victim can reconcile with the perpetrator and not submit the motion to the state attorney. Furthermore, they can reconcile even later during the proceedings as the victim can withdraw the motion. Then, the state attorney must drop the criminal prosecution. In practice, judges sometimes informally advise the parties to undergo a mediation process.

Extrajudicial restorative justice models are also applicable in cases when the victim takes over the prosecution as a subsidiary plaintiff (*supsidijarni tužitelj*) under Art. 55 CPA. When the state attorney dismisses or withdraws the charges, he is obliged to inform the victim, who can decide to take over the criminal prosecution. By taking over the criminal prosecution, the subsidiary plaintiff actually takes the place of the state attorney, which means that the continuation of criminal proceedings and its outcome depend to a significant extent on the subsidiary plaintiff himself.

The sentencing rules in Croatia also potentially promote restorative justice practices. The restorative justice sentencing factors include the relationship between the defendant and the victim as well as compensation for damages, which mitigate the sentence under Art. 47 CC. Furthermore, under Art. 50 CC, the court can mitigate or even exonerate the offender from punishment in the following two situations: if he tried to eliminate or reduce the consequences of a negligent offence and compensated for the damage; and if he, in case of a petty offence, i.e. punishable by fine or imprisonment up to one year, reconciled with the victim and compensated the damage.

According to Art. 62 CC, in addition to a suspended or partially suspended sentence, the court may impose special obligations on the offender, some of which are of a restorative nature: repairing the damage caused by the criminal offence, paying a certain amount of money into the fund for compensation of damages to victims of crime, fulfilling alimony obligation, or any other obligation that is appropriate in view of the crime committed. If the offender is a minor, special obligations can be imposed as independent educational measures – including *inter alia* repairing the damage caused by the criminal offence, an apology to the victim, and any other obligation appropriate to the crime committed (Art. 10(2) JCA).

Initiation of restorative justice arrangements is possible even when the convicted person is in prison. According to Art. 14(2) PSEA prisons shall encourage and assist prisoners in repairing the damage caused by criminal acts and reconciling with the victims. Successful restorative outcomes can affect the decision to grant parole, i.e. the conditional release of the prisoner. While granting the parole, the aforementioned special obligations from Art. 62 CC can be imposed on the prisoner to fullfill during the parole period. In addition, when deciding on individual prisoner's benefits, the attitude of the victim or the victim's family shall be taken into account (Art. 138(4) PSEA). This provision has the potential to motivate the prisoner to enter a restorative justice process.

If we look beyond the legal framework, restorative justice can occur informally – for example, before the filing of criminal charges. Such attempts to reconcile are common in Croatia, although they remain unrecorded. Typically, they take place with the help of lawyers who try to reach a settlement so that no criminal charges are filed. Mediators are not normally involved in these processes. Another example of informal restorative justice occurs after the sentence has been served. In this phase, the chances of application of restorative justice are lower because, in this phase, the offender is no longer motivated to avoid criminal prosecution or to receive a lighter punishment. Still, he may be motivated to enter a restorative justice process to avoid civil litigation and subsequent enforcement.

4. European restorative justice standards

At the European and international levels, there is a clear trend for the wider application of restorative justice in criminal matters. The European and international restorative justice standards were first promoted in the following three documents, acknowledged in the Croatian literature. The first was the Council of Europe's Recommendation No. R (99) 19 of the Committee of Ministers concerning mediation in penal matters, but it had a non-binding character. The second is the EU Council Framework Decision 2001/220/JHA of March 15th, 2001 on the standing of victims in criminal proceedings.[35] The latter stipulated in Art. 10 that each member state encourages mediation between victims and perpetrators of criminal offences. However, it had little influence as Croatia was not an EU member state at the time. The third document referenced in the Croatian literature is the ECOSOC Resolution 2002/12. Basic principles on the use of restorative justice programmes in criminal matters also had little influence and were non-binding.

At the European Union level in 2012, the Framework Decision was replaced by the Directive 2012/29/EU, establishing minimum standards on the rights, support and protection of victims of crime, which provided for the so-called restorative justice services. Restorative justice services are regulated explicitly in Art. 12 of the Directive, which foresees for victims of criminal offences access to safe and professional services for restorative justice, that these services are used only if they are in the interests of the victim and that member states facilitate the referral of cases to these services (by establishing procedures or guidelines on the conditions for such referral). Also, according to Art. 25 (4) of the Directive, member states are obliged to encourage the training of restorative justice service workers.

In 2018, the Committee of Ministers of the Council of Europe adopted a new Recommendation CM/Rec(2018)8 concerning restorative justice in criminal matters. That Recommendation and its commentary explain the ways in which states can use restorative justice to increase the effectiveness of reconciliation between victims and perpetrators and is the most advanced and sophisticated international legal instrument in this area. It is recommended that all victims and perpetrators have access to restorative justice processes and advocate a cultural change towards

35 See e.g. A. Maršavelski, K. Ivanušić, *Restorativna Pravda, op.cit.*, p. 483.

a more restorative approach to the processing of criminal offences at all levels of policy and practice.

Although these international documents are cited in Croatian literature, their influence on Croatian restorative justice practices is far from satisfactory. There is also one international convention that limits the use of restorative justice in certain cases. The 2011 Council of Europe Convention on Preventing and Combating Violence against Women and Domestic Violence, ratified by Croatia in 2018, prohibits mandatory alternative dispute resolution processes for such crimes. However, Croatia never introduced mandatory alternative dispute resolution processes in cases of violence against women and domestic violence, so there was no need to change the law in this regard to conform with the Convention.

5. Restorative justice at different stages of Croatian criminal procedure

To ensure the use of restorative justice measures throughout all phases of criminal proceedings, the Croatian legal system incorporates specific provisions to facilitate its implementation. The principle of prosecutorial discretion, which is applicable to both juveniles and adults at the pre-trial level, is considered essential to the implementation of restorative justice in Croatian law. However, differences between the treatment of adults and juveniles persist at the court level regarding the criminal sanctions with restorative elements that can be applied. Despite the potential benefits of restorative justice, it is still underrepresented in all areas except juvenile justice cases.

The Croatian model, part of out-of-court settlement, is based on the provisions of the JCA, which provide for conditional prosecutorial discretion and the special obligation of mending or compensating damage caused by the criminal offence. The goal of the out-of-court settlement is to achieve a successful agreement that is acceptable to both parties, forming a basis for peaceful coexistence and preventing recidivism.[36]

The out-of-court settlement in Croatia involves the State Attorney, who decides which cases should be referred and whether a case should be dismissed after the out-of-court settlement procedure has been completed.[37] The project to introduce the out-of-court settlement resulted in the establishment of the Services for the Out-of-Court Settlement in Zagreb, Osijek, and Split, which operate within the Center of Social Care. Mediators are paid by the Ministry of

---

36 N. Koller-Trbović, V. Gmaz-Luški, *Primjena izvansudske, op.cit.*, p. 936.

37 I. Bojanić, *Croatia, op.cit.*, p. 153.

Health and Social Care and receive training based on international practices and positive experiences, particularly from Germany and Austria. The mediators are employees of the Ministry from fields such as social work, law, psychology, and social pedagogy.[38]

When a criminal report is filed in the municipal State Attorney's office, and the basic conditions for a potential application of the prosecutorial discretion are fulfilled, the State Attorney passes the case to an associate, such as social pedagogues, social workers, or psychologists. The associate then examines the records of the Social Care Services and forwards the motion for mediation to the Services for Out-of-Court Settlement. The Service invites the offender to a conversation and, if they accept responsibility and express a readiness to continue with the process of mediation, consults the victim. If the victim agrees to mediation, a joint conversation is set up, and specially trained professionals support them. These professionals help them come to an agreement regarding the demands of the victim for the harm done, follow up on the fulfillment of the agreement, check if the victim is satisfied, and send a report to the State Attorney, who decides whether to initiate criminal proceedings or not.[39]

5.1. Pre-court level

In the pre-trial phase, the most significant aspect of restorative justice is the state attorney's conditional prosecutorial discretion. The conditions for its application for adult offenders are set out in the CPA, while for juveniles and young adults they are specified in the JCA. Apart from that, restorative justice can also take place informally at the pre-court level without involving the legal framework before the filing of criminal charges. In Croatia, reconciliation attempts are common, often facilitated by lawyers who aim to reach a settlement to avoid criminal charges.

5.1.1. Adult criminal justice

The State Attorney has the authority under Art. 206d CPA to drop charges or abstain from prosecuting a suspect for a criminal offence punishable by a maximum sentence of five years imprisonment or a fine if the suspect agrees to fulfill

38 Ibidem.

39 A. Žižak, 'Mediation in Cases of Juvenile Offenders in Croatia' [in:] Afford Ltd., M. Gyokos, K., Lanyi (eds.), *European Best Practices of Restorative Justice in Criminal Procedure. Ministry of Justice and Law Enforcement of the Republic of Hungary*, Budapest 2010, p. 175.

certain obligations such as compensating the damage caused by the offence, paying a sum of money to a charitable institution or compensation fund, paying the alimony, doing community service work, undergoing treatment for drug addiction or psycho-social therapy aimed at addressing violent behaviour. The State Attorney specifies a period, not exceeding one year, within which the offender must complete the obligations (Art. 206d(2) CPA). The decision of the State Attorney is communicated to the suspect, the victim, and the person who reported the crime. The victim is informed that she may pursue civil action for compensation. The state attorney's decision is final and cannot be appealed (Art. 206d(3) CPA).

Restorative justice has the potential to be utilised in plea bargaining situations. The state attorney, in accordance with the Criminal Procedure Act (CPA), has the power and responsibility to negotiate and agree with the defendant on a guilty plea and corresponding sentence. If a judgment based on the agreement between the state attorney and defendant is reached, the state attorney is required to inform the victim under Art. 360(5) of the CPA. However, in cases of crime against life and body or sexual freedom punishable by a prison sentence of more than five years, the state attorney must obtain the victim's consent for the plea bargain. This is an opportunity for restorative justice to be employed, given the need for the victim's agreement.

Mediation-based restorative justice can be utilised also in private criminal lawsuits, which are only applicable to crimes where the state attorney has no obligation to prosecute, such as defamation, petty theft, and insult. It can also be applied in cases where the victim must file a motion for the state attorney to prosecute. Under Art. 47 of the CPA, the victim must submit the motion within three months of learning about the crime and perpetrator. However, at this pre-prosecution stage, the victim can reconcile with the perpetrator and not submit the motion to the state attorney.

Out-of-court restorative justice models are applicable when the victim becomes a subsidiary plaintiff, taking over the prosecution if the state attorney dismisses or withdraws the charges. In such cases, it is up to the subsidiary plaintiff to decide on the continuation of the criminal proceedings.

Finally, the court can exonerate or reduce punishment for the offender who tried to eliminate or reduce the consequences of a negligent offence, compensated for damages, or reconciled with the victim in cases of a petty offence (Art. 50 CC). Additionally, in the context of probation, the court can impose special obligations on the offender, such as repairing the damage caused by the crime or paying a specific amount of money into a fund for compensation for victims of criminal offences (Art. 62 CC).

5.1.2. *Juvenile justice*

The principle of prosecutorial discretion is an essential aspect of Croatian juvenile criminal law that aims to provide rational and humane policies for social reactions towards juvenile offenders. This principle allows for providing assistance, care, and protection through out-of-court measures within the framework of social care. In Croatian juvenile criminal law, the state attorney plays a crucial role in the application of the principle of prosecutorial discretion by deciding whether or not to charge offenders.[40]

If the offence is punishable by imprisonment for up to five years or a fine, the State Attorney can choose not to initiate criminal proceedings, even if there is reasonable suspicion that the juvenile committed the crime. This decision is based on various factors, such as the nature of the offence, the circumstances surrounding the offence, the juvenile's earlier life, and personal traits. The state attorney can request information from the juvenile's guardian, parents, other persons, and institutions or ask an associate in the state attorney's office to provide relevant data (Art. 71(1) JCA).

In cases where a juvenile is reported for multiple criminal offences, but it is purposeful to impose a juvenile sanction for only one offence, the state attorney can decide not to conduct criminal proceedings for the other offences. This decision is only applicable to criminal offences punishable by a fine or imprisonment of up to five years (Art. 71(2) JCA). The state attorney will notify the injured person, the center for social care, and the police authorities (if they filed the charge) about the decision not to initiate criminal proceedings and the underlying reasons (Art. 71(3) JCA).

When applying prosecutorial discretion, the state attorney can condition his decision not to institute criminal proceedings on the readiness of the juvenile to fulfill specific obligations, which could result in informal sanctions. The obligations may include apologising to the injured person, correcting or compensating the harm caused by the offence, being involved in the mediation process of an out-of-court settlement, or participating in rehabilitation programs or social services (Art. 72 JCA). If the juvenile fulfills his obligations under the supervision of the center for social care, the state attorney will make a final decision not to initiate criminal proceedings (Art. 72(2) JCA). The state attorney will notify the center for social care, the injured person, and the police authorities (if they filed

40 A. Carić, I. Kustura, 'Kamo ide hrvatsko maloljetničko kazneno pravo? – 1. dio' (Which direction is juvenile criminal legislation taking? – Part 1), *Zbornik radova Pravnog fakulteta u Splitu*, 2010/47, pp. 614–615.

the charge) of the decision not to institute criminal proceedings and the reasons for the decision (Art. 72(3) JCA). The Principal State Attorney of Croatia provides detailed instructions on the application of the provisions of conditional prosecutorial discretion (Art. 72(4) JCA).

Unlike the legal provisions for adult offenders, the state attorney's decision to apply the principle of conditional prosecutorial discretion in the proceedings against juvenile offenders is not dependent on the victim's prior consent. Furthermore, offenders cannot appeal such diversionary decisions, and they are not entitled to a full criminal trial in which their guilt must be tested.

5.2. Court level

5.2.1. Adult criminal justice

The Croatian law offers community service and probation as an alternative to short-term imprisonment. This option can be supplemented with special obligations, such as paying restitution or repairing the damage caused by the offence, as long as they are appropriate to the case or offender (Art. 62 CC).

The criminal court also needs to evaluate the perpetrator's relationship with the victim and their efforts to compensate for any damages caused by the crime when determining the type and range of punishment (Art. 56(2) CC). The court can view a perpetrator's behaviour towards the injured person after the crime as a mitigating factor and reduce their punishment accordingly (Art. 48 CC). If an offender commits a negligent crime, he may be exempted from punishment if he tried to reduce the consequences of his actions and compensate for the damage or if he reconciled with the victim in cases of petty crimes i.e. punishable by fine or imprisonment of up to one year (Art. 50(1) CC).

As noted earlier, restorative justice through mediation can be employed in private criminal lawsuits. In cases where private lawsuits are filed, the criminal court can direct the parties to engage in mediation within a specific timeframe. If the mediation attempt fails, the proceedings will proceed as usual, in line with Art. 527(1) of the CPA.

In cases where the victim must file a motion for the state attorney to prosecute, under Art. 47 CPA, the victim can also withdraw the motion at any point during the court proceedings, potentially leading to a settlement. Judges may informally encourage mediation in these situations.

When the state attorney withdraws the charges, and the state attorney is required to inform the victim about it, the victim can take over the prosecution as a subsidiary plaintiff (Art. 55 CPA). The victim, as the subsidiary plaintiff, then assumes the prosecutorial role, so the continuation and outcome of the proceedings depend significantly on the victim's actions. For instance, in a case involving threats via text messages, after the state attorney dismissed the charges, the victim took over the prosecution as the subsidiary plaintiff. Ultimately, the victim and defendant reached an agreement, with the defendant paying the victim €2,000 and the victim withdrawing the accusation.[41]

Restorative justice practices can also be promoted by the sentencing rules. Mitigation of sentences can be achieved by considering restorative justice factors such as compensation for damages and the relationship between the defendant and the victim under Art. 47 CC. Additionally, Art. 50 CC allows the court to reduce or waive the punishment entirely if the offender attempted to mitigate the consequences of a negligent offence, compensated for the damage, or reconciled with the victim in the case of a petty offence punishable by a fine or imprisonment of up to one year.

5.2.2. Juvenile justice

According to Art. 88(2) JCA, the Juvenile Council of the court has the power to terminate criminal proceedings, regardless of the gravity of the offence, if it finds that neither an educational measure nor juvenile imprisonment would be purposeful. The law does not specify the circumstances that are relevant for this evaluation. However, the behaviour of the juvenile towards the victim, including actions such as apologising, working in the victim's interest, or reconciling with the victim, may be considered in this regard.

When choosing an educational measure, the court must consider the behaviour of the juvenile after the offence, especially whether the juvenile has attempted to repair any damage caused and their behaviour towards the victim (Art. 8 JCA). Special obligations, such as those outlined in Art. 10 of the JCA, can include restorative justice measures such as requiring the juvenile to apologize or compensate the damage to the victim.

The court will select obligations that are suitable for the offender. If an obligation to repair damage is selected, the court will determine the scope, form, and nature of the restitution, and the juvenile cannot be required to work more than 60 hours within a three month period (Art. 10(7) JCA). The obligations must be organized in a manner that do not disrupt the juvenile's schooling or employment.

41 A. Maršavelski, K. Ivanušić, *Restorativna Pravda*, *op.cit.*, p. 490–491.

5.3. Restorative elements while serving sentences

As noted earlier, in the context of suspended and partially suspended sentences, the court can impose special obligations on offenders. These special obligations may include restorative measures, such as repairing the damage caused by the criminal offence, paying compensation to victims of crime, fulfilling alimony obligations, or other appropriate obligations. For minors, independent educational measures may be imposed, including repairing the damage caused by the criminal offense, apologizing to the victim, and other appropriate obligations. While serving the suspended sentence the offender needs to fulfill these restorative obligations to avoid prison.

Restorative justice processes can be initiated even if the offender is sentenced to prison. As per Art. 14(2) of the PSEA, prisons are required to support and encourage prisoners to make amends for the harm caused by their criminal acts and reconcile with the victims. Successful restorative outcomes may influence the decision to grant parole, which is a conditional release from prison. Moreover, when granting parole, the offender may be imposed with special obligations outlined in Art. 62 of the CC to fulfill during the parole period. Furthermore, the attitude of the victim or the victim's family can be considered when deciding on individual prisoner benefits, according to Art. 138(4) of the PSEA. This provision has the potential to incentivise offenders to engage in restorative justice practices. Regenerate response. Consequently, the realisation of restorative justice in this area has been largely neglected.[42]

6. Restorative justice projects aimed at making restorative justice more effective

The first restorative justice project on "Special obligation - extrajudicial settlement" promoted a mediation model based on Austrian and German mediation concepts. The first out-of-court settlements were initiated in mid-2001 in the offices for out-of-court settlements in the Croatian cities of Osijek, Zagreb, and Split.[43]

42 Z. Šeparović, Kazneno izvršno pravo i uvod u penologiju (Criminal enforcement law and penology). Zagreb 2003: Pravni fakultet u Zagrebu, Poslijediplomski studij iz kaznenopravnih znanosti, p. 200; A. Carić, *Počinitelji i žrtve*, *op.cit.*, p. 287.

43 B. Cvjetko, 'Hrvatski projekt posebne obveze – izvansudske nagodbe u prethodnom postupku prema maloljetnim i mlađim punoljetnim počiniteljima kaznenih djela' (The Croatian specific obligations project - out-of-court settlement in preliminary proceedings related to juvenile criminal offenders and young adult criminal offenders), *Hrvatski ljetopis za kazneno pravo i praksu*, 2003/10, p. 59.

In 2001, the State Attorney's Office of the Republic of Croatia published the Guidelines on the implementation of the experimental project of out-of-court settlement.[44] These directives outline criteria and assumptions for the application of the principle of prosecutorial discretion and special obligations of the out-of-court settlement. For instance, the out-of-court settlement should apply if the victim is a physical person, there is a high degree of certainty that the juvenile or young adult committed the criminal offence, and the criminal offence is one for which the law foresees a prison sentence of up to five years or a fine. The gravity of the offence must not be of minor significance, and being a recidivist is not a ground to exclude a juvenile or young adult from out-of-court settlement. However, the out-of-court settlement should not be applied in cases where the offender had harmed more than one person when the offence was planned in advance or demonstrated brutality and coldness, when criminal proceedings for other criminal offences are ongoing, or when offenders have shown severe behavioural problems.[45] The successful results of the project influenced the new 2011 JCA within the framework of conditional prosecutorial discretion.[46]

The expansion of the out-of-court settlement in Croatia followed training of new mediators, but also employees of social care centers, state attorneys and associates at state attorney's offices, conducted in 2013–2014. In 2014, the pilot project "Mediation between a victim and a minor perpetrator of a misdemeanour" was launched, which provided a mediation tutorial in 20 misdemeanour cases involving minors as perpetrators.

Finally, there is an ongoing project of the Ministry of Justice and Administration titled "Reinforcing the system of court-annexed mediation". The project involves international collaboration with the aim of improving the Croatian mediation system. An analysis of the current mediation system was already conducted in comparison to other European countries to identify opportunities for enhancement, including study visits to some of these countries. Additionally, a sociological-legal analysis will be conducted to determine the reasons behind the underutilisation of mediation and a manual on court-annexed mediation. Furthermore, 500 professionals, including judges, lawyers, civil servants, court advisors, and state

---

44 I. Bojanić, *Croatia*, *op.cit.*, p. 153.

45 Ibidem.

46 M. Božičević-Grbić, S. Roksandić-Vidlička, 'Reforma maloljetničkog prava i sudovanja' (Reform of juvenile criminal law and adjudication), *Hrvatski ljetopis za kazneno pravo i praksu*, 2011/18, p. 710.

attorneys, will receive training on mediation, and the awareness-raising campaign will target both judicial staff and the general public.[47]

7. Discussion and conclusion

Half a century ago, Nils Christie concluded that crime victims lost the property of their conflicts to the state.[48] The solution, however, is not necessarily to return the property of the conflict to the victim, but to seek ways to empower victims, including those within existing criminal justice systems. Restorative justice is a proven and effective way to reduce crime, heal victims, and build stronger communities – but most importantly – it is a humane and compassionate approach to justice that transforms the lives of everyone involved. If restorative justice operates within the criminal justice system, its effectiveness partially depends on the effectiveness of the overall system. In Croatia, restorative justice has been primarily utilised in the pre-trial procedure, where the state attorney decides whether to prosecute based on prosecutorial discretion. However, this approach has been consistently applied only in the mediation procedure for juveniles. Juvenile delinquency is indeed an area where the effectiveness of responses is most needed in order to avoid reoffending, but restorative justice has a much greater potential, especially to enable broader application to adult offenders. Financial resources are required to achieve these goals, including funds for establishing mediation services and educating new mediators and state attorneys who ultimately decide on criminal prosecutions.

The reality is that restorative justice in Croatia can mostly serve as an alternative for less serious criminal offences. The lenient sentencing policy in Croatia indicates that the judicial system treats most crimes as less serious in nature. The suspended sentences is by far the most frequently used sanction in Croatia, amounting to approximately 80%. Unfortunately, this is the ultimate goal of defence attorneys as they want to save their clients from being sent to prison. Although the use of restorative justice tools as obligations under suspended sentences has the greatest potential, such obligations are currently used rarely in practice. Croatian judges are reluctant to impose them because they would need to control their execution in the post-conviction stage. Waiting for the suspended sentence to expire is a much simpler task for judges to close the case. Restorative justice can also be used in the stage of sanctions enforcement, including during

47 *See: https://mpu.gov.hr/highlights/projects/norwegian-financial-mechanism/reinforcing-the-system-of-court-annexed-mediation/25430* [accessed on January 10th, 2024]

48 N. Christie, 'Conflicts as Property', *British Journal of Criminology*, 1977/17(1), pp. 1–15.

serving prison sentences, but mediation between the offender and the victim is rarely initiated in reality post-conviction. Good behaviour without re-offending is sufficiently credited, so no effort to seek reconciliation with the victim is needed.

Insufficient use of restorative justice mechanisms in criminal practice, despite the wide options that the legal framework provides, primarily indicates insufficient training and insufficient motivation. In order to ensure the wider application of restorative justice in criminal matters, education is especially important, as it will eliminate doubts about the application of available mechanisms among practitioners. Part of the infrastructure in the courts already exists because some judges, that is, court counsellors, are already trained mediators. With so many specific provisions in the legislation, changing the law to boost restorative justice would probably not be of much help. However, the legislator could encourage legal practitioners to use restorative justice options within the criminal justice system by adding *victim satisfaction* as a general purpose of punishment to the Criminal Code.

Support is also needed at other levels. First of all, it is necessary to ensure the appropriate valorisation of the use of restorative justice mechanisms through the framework benchmarks for the operation of the judges and the methodology of assessing the refereeing duties. In this way, simple intervention in regulations governing the monitoring and evaluation of the work of judges will certainly facilitate the work of judges as mediators. It is also necessary to ensure monitoring of restorative justice practices to evaluate their success and problems that occur in order to eliminate them. With increased investment and support, restorative justice can play a significant role in making the Croatian criminal justice system more effective and more just. This is also applicable to other jurisdictions whose criminal justice practitioners have not explored the restorative justice possibilities within their national systems.

Bibliography

Bojanić I., 'Croatia', [in:] Frieder Dünkel, Joanna Grzywa-Holten, Philip Horsfield (Eds.), *Restorative Justice and Mediation in Penal Matters*, 2015, Vol. 1.

Božičević-Grbić, M., Roksandić-Vidlička, 'Reforma maloljetničkog prava i sudovanja' (Reform of juvenile criminal law and adjudication), *Hrvatski ljetopis za kazneno pravo i praksu*, 2011/18.

Braithwaite J., 'Restorative justice and responsive regulation: the question of evidence', *RegNEt Research Papers* No 51, 2016.

Carić, A.; 'Počinitelji i žrtve – odgovornost i pravednost u kaznenom postupku (Offenders and victims – responsibility and justice in criminal proceedings)', *Zbornik radova Pravnog fakulteta u Splitu*, 2000/37.

Carić, A., Kustura, I., 'Kamo ide hrvatsko maloljetničko kazneno pravo? – 1. Dio' (Which direction is juvenile criminal legislation taking? – Part 1), *Zbornik radova Pravnog fakulteta u Splitu*, 2010/47.

Carić, M., 'Uvjetni odustanak od kaznenog progona' (Conditional waive of criminal prosecution), *Zbornik radova Pravnog fakulteta u Splitu*, 2009/46.

Christie N., 'Conflicts as Property', *British Journal of Criminology*, 1977, Vol. 17, No. 1.

Cvjetko, B., 'Hrvatski projekt posebne obveze – izvansudske nagodbe u prethodnom postupku prema maloljetnim i mlađim punoljetnim počiniteljima kaznenih djela' (The Croatian specific obligations project - out-of-court settlement in preliminary proceedings related to juvenile criminal offenders and young adult criminal offenders), *Hrvatski ljetopis za kazneno pravo i praksu*, 2003/10.

Cvjetko, B., Singer, M., *Kaznenopravna odgovornost mladeži u praksi i teoriji* (Criminal responsibility of youth in the practice and theory). Zagreb: Organizator 2011.

Đukes, K., 'Provjera uspješnosti izvansudske nagodbe u Zagrebu' (Evaluation of the success of out-of-court settlements in Zagreb), *Zagreb, Edukacijsko-rehabilitacijski fakultet, Sveučilište u Zagrebu*, 2022.

Gospodnetić, F., *Medijacija u pravosuđu: Analiza mišljenja odvjetnika, sudaca i korisnika sudova o medijaciji kao alternativnom rješavanju sporova* (Mediation in the judiciary: Analysis of opinions of lawyers, judges and court users on mediation as an alternative dispute resolution), Datafit, Zagreb, 2021.

Grozdanić, V., Škorić, M.; 'O kaznenom pravu i kazni zatvora' (On criminal law and prison sentence), [in:]Turković, K., Munivrana Vajda, M., Dragičević Prtenjača, M. (eds.), *Kazneno pravo: sinergija teorije i prakse*, Liber Amicorum Petar Novoselec, 2019.

Judaš, K.; *Nasilni zločini protiv osoba u sudskim spisima zagrebačkog Gradeca u kasnom srednjem vijeku* (Violent crimes against persons in the court files of Zagreb's Gradec in the late Middle Ages), Sveučilište u Zagrebu, Filozofski fakultet, Zagreb 2013.

Koller-Trbović, N., Cvjetko, B., Koren-Mrazović, M., Žižak, A.; *Model izvansudske nagodbe u kaznenom postupku prema maloljetnicima i mlađim punoljetnicima* (Out-of-court settlement model in criminal procedure against juvenile and younger adult criminal offenders). Ministarstvo zdravstva i socijalne skrbi, Državno odvjetništvo Republike Hrvatske, Edukacijsko-rehabilitacijski fakulet. Zagreb 2003.

Koller-Trbović, N., Gmaz-Luški, V, 'Primjena izvansudske nagodbe (medijacija) u pretkaznenom postupku prema maloljetnicima i mlađim punoljetnim osobama' (Application of out-of-court settlement in preliminary criminal procedure to minors and younger adult offenders), *Hrvatski ljetopis za kazneno pravo i praksu*, 2006/13.

Markulj, A., *Izvansudska nagodba iz perspektive posrednika* (Out-of-court settlement from mediator's perspective), Zagreb, Edukacijsko-rehabilitacijski fakultet Sveučilišta u Zagrebu 2016.

Maršavelski, A., Berneš, A., 'Temeljni aktualni problemi krajnje nužde u kontekstu primjenjivosti restorativne pravde' (Fundamental Contemporary Problems of Necessity in the Context of Application of Restorative Justice), [in:] K. Turković, M. Munivrana Vajda, M. Dragičević Prtenjača (eds.), *Kazneno pravo: sinergija teorije i prakse (Zbornik radova u čast profesora Petra Novoselca)*, Zagreb: Pravni fakultet u Zagrebu 2019.

Maršavelski, A., Braithwaite, J., 'Transitional Justice Cascades', *Cornell International Law Journal*, 2020 vol. 53, No. 2.

Maršavelski A., Ivanušić K., 'Restorativna Pravda u kaznenopravnoj teoriji i praksi' (Restorative justice in Croatian criminal law theory and practice), *Hrvatski ljetopis za kaznene znanosti i praksu*, 2021 vol. 28, No. 2.

Marsavelski, A., Sheremeti, F., Braithwaite, J., 'Did nonviolent resistance fail in Kosovo?', *The British Journal of Criminology*, 2018 58(1).

Mirosavljević, A., Koller-Trbović, N., Lalić-Lukač, D., 'Evaluacija uspješnosti izvansudske nagodbe u stručnoj službi za izvansudsku nagodbu Zagreb' (Evaluation of the efficiency of victim-offender mediation in Zagreb professional service for victim-offender mediation in cases of juvenile offenders), *Kriminologija i socijalna integracija*, 2010/18.

Mirosavljević, A., 'Modeli restorativne pravde u svijetu za mlade u sukobu sa zakonom i pregled istraživanja njihove učinkovitosti' (Restorative justice models in the world for youth in conflict with the law and overview of its efficiency studies), *Kriminologija i socijalna integracija*, 2010/18.

Mirosavljević, A., *Izvansudska nagodba-perspektiva oštećenika i mladih u sukobu sa zakonom* (Out-of-court settlement - the perspective of victims and juveniles in conflict with the law), Zagreb, Pravni fakultet Sveučilišta u Zagrebu 2015.

Modrić, A., *Provjera uspješnosti izvansudske nagodbe za mlade u sukobu sa zakonom u Hrvatskoj* (Evaluation of the success of out-of-court settlements with juveniles in conflict with the law in Croatia), Zagreb, Edukacijsko-rehabilitacijski fakultet Sveučilišta u Zagrebu 2016.

Novoselec, P.; *Opći dio kaznenog prava* (General part of criminal law). Zagreb: Pravni fakultet Sveučilišta u Zagrebu 2009.

Pavišić, B., *Komentar Zakona o kaznenom postupku* (Commentary on the Criminal Procedure Act). Rijeka: Dušević & Kršovni d.o.o. 2011.

Šeparović, Z.; *Kazneno izvršno pravo i uvod u penologiju* (Criminal enforcement law and penology). Zagreb: Pravni fakultet u Zagrebu, Poslijediplomski studij iz kaznenopravnih znanosti 2003.

Turković, K.; Maršavelski, A.; Roksandić Vidlička, S., Liber Amicorum Zvonimir Šeparović: Od kaznenog prava do viktimologije (Liber Amicorum Zvonimir Šeparović: From Criminal Law to Victimology), Zbornik radova u čast 80. rođendana profesora emeritusa Zvonimira Šeparovica, Pravni fakultet Sveučilišta u Zagrebu, Zagreb 2009.

Turković, K.; Roksandić Vidlička, S. and Maršavelski, A., 'Recommendation on alternative dispute resolution in medical liability in Council of Europe member states', [in:] Turković, K.; Roksandić Vidlička, S. and Maršavelski, A. (eds.), *Book of proceedings of the 18th World Congress on medical law*, Faculty of Law, University of Zagreb, Zagreb, CD, 2010, paper No. 15.

Zehr, H., *The Little Book of Restorative Justice*, Good Books, 2014.

Žižak, A., 'Nove mogućnosti u izvršavanju maloljetničkih sankcija (New perspectives in the enforcement of juvenile sanctions)', *Hrvatski ljetopis za kazneno pravo i praksu*, 2006/13.

Žižak, A., 'Mediation in Cases of Juvenile Offenders in Croatia' [in:] Afford Ltd., Gyokos, M., Lanyi, K. (eds.) *European Best Practices of Restorative Justice in Criminal Procedure. Ministry of Justice and Law Enforcement of the Republic of Hungary*. Budapest 2010.

Croatian Legislation

Kazneni zakon (2011) Narodne novine (Official Gazette), no. 125/11, 144/12, 56/15, 61/15, 101/17, 118/18, 126/19, 84/21

Zakon o izvršavanju kazne zatvora (2021). Narodne novine (Official Gazette), no. 14/21

Zakon o kaznenom postupku (2008). Narodne novine (Official Gazette), no. 152/08, 76/09, 80/11, 121/11, 91/12, 143/12, 56/13, 145/13, 152/14, 70/17, 126/19, 126/19, 130/20, 80/22

Zakon o probaciji (2018). Narodne novine (Official Gazette), no. 99/18

Zakon o sudovima za mladež (2011). Narodne novine (Official Gazette), no. 84/11, 143/12, 148/13, 56/15, 126

Prof. US Dr. hab. Magdalena Kowalewska-Łukuć[1]

III. Mediation in Criminal Proceedings as a Potentially Effective Tool for Restorative Justice

Abstract: This chapter is an attempt to analyse the institution of mediation as a specific tool in criminal proceedings, which can be an attractive and at the same time effective alternative to the "classic" - non-mediation - course of criminal proceedings. The article will present the legal framework and functioning of mediation in Polish criminal proceedings and in Scandinavian countries - in particular Finland and Denmark. These countries were chosen for the analysis because in Poland mediation is a tool that is marginally used by the authorities or the parties to the proceedings, while in Scandinavia it enjoys greater popularity. This paper will verify the hypothesis that there are significant differences in the legal regulation and practice of mediation in these countries that translate into its effectiveness and scope of impact. Then, after identifying these significant differences, an attempt will be made to formulate proposals for certain standards that mediation should meet so that it can be a truly, and not just potentially, effective tool in criminal proceedings, reflecting the ideas of restorative justice. The research methods that have been used in the work on this study are primarily the dogmatic-legal method, the comparative-legal method, the sociological-legal method and the psychological-legal method.

Keywords: mediation, restorative justice, criminal proceedings, mediation in criminal proceedings

1. Mediation in criminal proceedings as a tool of restorative justice

The link between mediation and the idea of restorative justice is quite obvious. The definition of restorative justice formulated by T. Marshall, states that restorative justice is a process in which all parties related to a specific crime come together to work out how to remedy the consequences of the crime and its effects on the future,[2] could de facto also be part of the definition of mediation in criminal

---

1 ORCID no. 0000000266633674. Associate Professor at Faculty of Law and Administration, University of Szczecin.

2 T. Marshall, 'The evolution of restorative justice in Britain', *European Journal on Criminal Policy and Research*, 1996/4, p. 36.

proceedings. If we add to this the fact that one of the main objectives of restorative justice is the reparation by the offender of the damage or harm caused by the crime[3] the link between mediation and restorative justice becomes even more clear and inseparable.

The definitional elements of restorative justice given above also fully correspond with the definition formulated by the Council of Europe, according to which restorative justice refers to any process which enables those harmed by crime, and those responsible for that harm, if they freely consent, to participate actively in the resolution of matters arising from the offence, through the help of a trained and impartial third party. In turn, the process is intended to encourage offenders to take responsibility for their actions, to enable them to change for the better, to reintegrate, and to compensate and understand towards the victim. Mediation is identified, along with conferences and circles, as one of the main tools of restorative justice.[4]

It is pointed out that mediation is the simplest[5] and, at the same time, probably the closest tool of restorative justice to the main parties involved, i.e. the victim and the offender. Mediation is intended to enable the victim and the offender to attempt a voluntary resolution of the conflict caused by the offence, to reconcile and to agree on a binding method of reparation for the harm caused by the offence and of compensation for the harm suffered as a result. This is to be achieved with the help of an impartial mediator.

The utility of mediation in criminal proceedings is supported by the fact that it can carry a number of far-reaching benefits for its participants. The results of some studies indicate that, following mediation, offenders' levels of compassion and empathy towards victims increase and the risk of recidivism decreases.[6]

---

3 Cf. P. Kozłowska, 'Wykorzystanie sprawiedliwości naprawczej w sprawach o przestępstwa z nienawiści – szanse i ograniczenia', *Probacja* 2023/2, p. 137.

4 Recommendation CM/Rec (2018) 8 of the Committee of Ministers to member States concerning restorative justice in criminal matters.

5 Cf. P. Kozłowska, *Wykorzystanie sprawiedliwości naprawczej*, *op.cit.*, p. 139.

6 J. Jonas-van Dijk, S. Zebel, J. Claessen, H. Nelen, 'Victim–Offender Mediation and Reduced Reoffending: Gauging the Self-Selection Bias', *Crime & Delinquency*, 2020/6–7, *passim*. It should be noted, however, that the lower recidivism rate among offenders who have used mediation in the criminal process may be due to their specific criminological profile, the sign of which is already indicated by the simple fact that they have agreed to take part in the mediation procedure – cf. Ibidem, 965.

The results of the research also remain very promising in terms of the benefits of mediation for victims. Indeed, these studies show that victims of crime who use mediation, compared to victims who go through 'normal' criminal proceedings and who have suffered the same type of crime, show a significant decrease in post-traumatic stress symptoms. These individuals also have lower scores on stress and anxiety scales. Furthermore, the results show a significant reduction in the negative emotions expressed by victims after their participation in mediation, such as fear, anger, guilt and anxiety. In addition, mediation promotes a reduction in feelings of helplessness in the face of what happened and correlates positively with increased feelings of safety and self-esteem. It is also very important that the interviewed victims indicate that mediation gave them a sense of emotional overcoming of the trauma, a certain closure based on relief after working through the emotions, which enabled them to return to normal functioning.[7] Summarising the benefits of mediation for victims of crime, therefore, it can be said that mediation helps them to cope with victimisation in the broadest sense.

2. Mediation in criminal cases in Poland and in Scandinavia

Taking into account the above-described research results, there is, therefore, no doubt that launching a mediation procedure in criminal proceedings may bring a number of benefits, not only for the offender but also for the victim of a criminal act. It can accordingly be concluded that mediation is a very attractive tool of restorative justice and should be used relatively often as an alternative to the 'standard' course of criminal proceedings. In reality, however, this is not always the case. An example is the institution of mediation in Polish criminal proceedings. In the Polish Code of Criminal Procedure (CCP) and in the relevant regulation of the Minister of Justice, mediation seems to be regulated in such a general and,

---

7 A. Nascimento, J. Andrade, A. de Castro Rodrigues, 'The Psychological Impact of Restorative Justice Practices on Victims of Crimes – a Systematic Review', *Trauma, Violence, & Abuse*, 2022/1–19, DOI: 10.1177/15248380221082085, p. 2 and 12, available at: https://repositorio.ispa.pt/bitstream/10400.12/8674/1/The%20psychological%20impact%20of%20restorative%20justice....pdf, [accessed on September 22nd, 2023].

at the same time, flexible manner[8] that one can assume that the legislative framework should even encourage its frequent application. Meanwhile, statistics concerning mediation in Polish criminal proceedings show a rather surprising picture. Only a negligible number of criminal cases go to mediation. To be precise, it is less than 1%.[9] At the same time, however, the effectiveness of mediation proceedings that have already begun is at a relatively good level - about 60–70% of them end with a settlement agreement. Thus, the statistical data show that mediation in criminal cases occurs very rarely. On the other hand, if it is launched, it has quite

8 The current regulation of Article 23a of the Code of Criminal Procedure defines the authorities that can refer a case to mediation, the premises that allow it, the maximum period of mediation and the entities that cannot act as mediators. Other regulations concerning mediation in criminal proceedings are contained in the aforementioned regulation of the Minister of Justice, which additionally defines in more detail the procedure for conducting mediation proceedings, the conditions to which institutions and persons authorised to conduct mediation should conform; the manner of appointing and dismissing mediators; the scope and conditions for making case files available to the mediator; and the form and scope of the report on the results of mediation proceedings. The basic prerequisite for referring a case to mediation is that the victim and the accused give their consent in this respect. A given case may be referred to mediation by a court or a court referendary (clerk), while at the stage of pre-trial proceedings, it may also be referred by a public prosecutor or another authority conducting such proceedings, e.g. the police. Referral to mediation is made by means of a decision. There is no right of appeal against it. Mediation proceedings should generally not last longer than one month, although this is an instructional deadline. Upon appointment to mediate, the mediator should immediately establish contact with the accused and the victim and set a date and place for a meeting with each of them. The mediator should then conduct individual or joint preliminary meetings with the accused and the victim at a time and place convenient to them, during which he or she explains to them the objectives and principles of the mediation proceedings and instructs them on the possibility of withdrawing their consent to participate in the mediation proceedings. Following these preliminary activities, the mediator conducts a mediation meeting with the accused and the victim at a place and time convenient for the participants. In an ideal arrangement, the mediation proceedings end with the conclusion of a settlement agreement between the victim and the accused. When defining who can be a mediator, it should be noted first of all that mediation proceedings can only be conducted by an institution or an authorised person entered in a special list. Such a list is kept by the chairmen of the particular district courts. The mediator, all in all, must be impartial and inspire confidence in both the victim and the accused. The requirements for mediators in criminal cases are not particularly extensive.

9 Cf. 'Mediacje karne w latach 1998–2021', available at: https://isws.ms.gov.pl/pl/baza-statystyczna/opracowania-wieloletnie/, [accessed on September 22nd, 2023].

a high success rate.[10] Thus, it is possible to put forward the thesis that mediation can be a very valuable tool of restorative justice. However, there are some serious problems or limitations in its application in the Polish criminal procedure.

Supplementing the statistics cited above, it should also be pointed out that, according to a report prepared in 2015 at the request of the Minister of Justice, both judges and prosecutors are not interested in referring cases to mediation.[11] The doctrine indicates that the reason for this may be the schematic, established way of conducting proceedings, which does not assume the use of mediation, and the lack of trust in the quality of mediation itself,[12] the qualifications of mediators and the value of a mediated settlement.[13]

Furthermore, as research carried out for the purposes of the aforementioned report indicates, neither are the potential parties to mediation - the perpetrators of crimes and the victims - interested in it. A pessimistic conclusion irresistibly arises that in Polish criminal proceedings, no one is interested in launching a mediation procedure - neither the parties to these proceedings nor their bodies.[14]

It may, therefore, be interesting to take a look at what the legal regulation of mediation and the practice of its use in criminal cases looks like in other countries. A good example, contrasting with the picture outlined above from Polish criminal proceedings, seems to be the Nordic countries, where the use of the mediation procedure is at a completely different level. First of all, mediation in Scandinavia has a much longer tradition than in Polish criminal proceedings, as it already dates

---

10 E. Zielińska, J. Klimczak, *Zakres stosowania mediacji w sprawach karnych w praktyce wymiaru sprawiedliwości*, 2020, p. 39, available at: https://iws.gov.pl/wp-content/uploads/2020/04/IWS_Zieli%C5%84ska-E.-Klimczak-J-Zakres-stosowania-mediacji-w-sprawach-karnych-w-praktyce-wymiaru-sprawiedliwo%C5%9Bci.pdf. [accessed on September 23rd, 2023].

11 A. Rudolf, M. Cichowicz-Major, M. Matysiak, S. Pałka, W. Pieniążek, C. Przybył, *Diagnoza stanu stosowania mediacji oraz przyczyn zbyt niskiej w stosunku do oczekiwanej popularności mediacji – Raport końcowy*, available at: https://www.gov.pl/attachment/cb132c4a-8e40-401d-9bdb-57c73427578d, [accessed on September 23rd, 2023].

12 Cf. M. Hacia-Groticka, P. Czarnecki, 'Opinie ekspertów na temat barier instytucjonalnych oraz promocji mediacji w środowiskach prawniczych', [in:] M. Araszkiewicz, J. Czapska, M. Pękala, K. Płeszka (eds.), *Mediacja. Teoria, normy, praktyka*, Warszawa 2017, pp. 449–453.

13 The problem of mediators' qualifications is highlighted by mediators themselves, pointing to a lack of financial resources and motivation to improve their qualifications – cf. A. Rudolf, M. Cichowicz-Major, M. Matysiak, S. Pałka, W. Pieniążek, C. Przybył, *Diagnoza stanu stosowania*, *op.cit.*, pp. 6–7 and 20–31.

14 Cf. M. Hacia-Groticka, P. Czernecki, *Opinie ekspertów*, *op.cit.*, p. 474.

back to the 19th or even 18th century. At the same time, mediation in criminal cases between offender and victim, so-called victim-offender mediation (VOM), is only one of many types of mediation practised in the Nordic countries.[15]

VOM was introduced in Scandinavia already in the 1980s. What is noteworthy is that the mediators who conduct it undergo thorough training and receive both theoretical and practical preparation for mediation. As in Poland, mediation in criminal cases is always voluntary and cases for mediation are most often referred by law enforcement agencies. Compared to the reality of Polish mediation, the very high number of cases referred to mediation is noteworthy. In Finland and Norway, it is around 20%. Slightly smaller results are recorded in Denmark. It should be noted, however, that in Denmark, mediation in criminal cases, as in Poland, can be a supplementary element in criminal proceedings. However, a settlement agreement concluded between the offender and the victim cannot replace a court ruling. On the other hand, in Finland, for example, a mediation procedure may replace the 'ordinary' justice system - the prosecutor, taking into account the results of the mediation procedure, may drop the charges or the indictment, and the court may refrain from issuing a conviction, imposing a sentence or mitigating the punishment.[16]

3. Discussion

The immeasurably longer tradition of mediation in Scandinavian countries translates not only into its greater prevalence than, for example, in Poland but also into the fact that mediation in criminal cases in Finland, Norway or Denmark seems to be at a completely different stage of development - both at the practical level, i.e. its application, and at the theoretical level, i.e. reflection and research. In Scandinavia, the lack of full coherence between the theoretical basis of a mediation system and the behaviour of mediators, as well as the evaluative style of mediation or

15 Cf. K. Ervasti, 'Past, Present and Future of Mediation in Nordic Countries', [in:] A. Nylund, K. Ervasti, L. Adrian (eds.), *Nordic Mediation Research*, Berlin 2018, pp. 226–233.

16 K. Ervasti, *Past, Present*, *op.cit.*, p. 234. Interestingly, in other aspects, mediation in criminal cases is in Finland, regulated in a way similar to Polish legislation – it can be used if both the victim and the suspect consent to it. It is required that the suspect confirms the course of events and that mediation is in the best interests of the victim. Mediation is free of charge and always voluntary, and it can, if desired, be discontinued at any stage. The main legal source regulating mediation in criminal cases in Finland is Act on Mediation in Criminal Matters (Laki rikosasioiden sovittelusta). Some provisions are also included in the Finnish Code of Criminal Procedure.

the excessive focus on the offender identified in some studies, are seen as some of the problems with mediation.[17] Consideration is also being given to how to adapt mediation appropriately to an increasingly multicultural society.[18] Meanwhile, in Poland, we are wondering what to do to go beyond the 'magic' border of 1% of cases referred to mediation, and one of the main problems identified is the lack of confidence of the authorities of the proceedings in the competence of mediators in general, rather than the full consistency of their attitude with the accepted theoretical model of mediation.

Thus, what definitely differentiates mediation in criminal matters in Poland and in the Nordic countries, apart from history and tradition, is certainly the different emphasis placed on the appropriate preparation of mediators. In Poland, in accordance with § 4 of the aforementioned regulation of the Minister of Justice, a mediator can be a person who enjoys full public rights and has full capacity to perform legal acts, is at least 26 years old, has verbal and written knowledge of the Polish language and has not been sentenced by final conviction for an intentional crime or an intentional fiscal crime. Moreover, such a person must have skills and knowledge in conducting mediation proceedings, conflict resolution and establishing interpersonal relations, and must be able to guarantee the proper performance of his or her duties. The penultimate of these conditions, i.e. that the candidate mediator has the skills and knowledge to conduct mediation proceedings, resolve conflicts and establish interpersonal contacts, seems to be crucial. The fulfillment of this condition by a future mediator is unfortunately not adequately verified in Poland.

Meanwhile, in VOM, the mediator's competence and role are crucial to the success of the entire mediation process, from the first - initial - meetings with the accused and the victim to the final settlement. The mediator must be adequately prepared to conduct these meetings. Therefore, it is necessary that he or she has the appropriate level of experience and knowledge so that he or she is able to conduct the mediation procedure and guide the participants through it. This experience and knowledge should be verified before a person is included in the list of mediators. The most sensible form of this verification seems to be simply an exam. It also seems quite obvious that mediators should be required to improve their qualifications, for example, by attending training courses, in order

17 K. Ervasti, *Past, Present*, *op.cit.*, p. 240.

18 B. Albrecht, 'Multicultural Challenges for Restorative Justice: Mediators' Experiences from Norway and Finland, Journal of Scandinavian Studies in Criminology and Crime Prevention', *Journal of Scandinavian Studies in Criminology and Crime Prevention*, 2010/1, pp. 3–24, DOI: 10.1080/14043851003616204, *passim*.

to keep their knowledge up to date and develop their competencies.[19] In short, if mediation in Polish criminal proceedings is to be a useful tool of restorative justice, bringing real benefits to the victim, not only economic ones, it must be conducted by a person adequately prepared for this. Currently, on the basis of the current 2015 Regulation of the Minister of Justice, this preparation remains only a certain postulate and is not adequately verified. It is, therefore, difficult to perceive them as a condition for admission to the list of mediators. The need for changes in this area has also been signalled by the mediators' community in Poland itself, pointing out that "the criteria are too liberal, the verification rules are too vague, there is no possibility of verifying persons included in the lists of mediators, and there is no possibility of deleting a mediator who has already been included and is not providing services at the appropriate level".[20]

The second aspect worth noting is the strength of the impact of mediation on the outcome of criminal proceedings and the possible benefits that the suspect/accused may gain from it. As mentioned above, in Finland, for example, the outcome of mediation proceedings can have very far-reaching consequences for the scope of the criminal legal response to the crime, or even its implementation at all. In Poland, meanwhile, pursuant to Article 53 § 3 of the Criminal Code (CC), the court takes the positive results of mediation into account when determining the punishment. Pursuant to Article 60 § 2 of the Criminal Code, a positive result of mediation may affect extraordinary mitigation of punishment. The most far-reaching effects a positive result of mediation can achieve in private prosecution proceedings. Indeed, in private prosecution proceedings, the effect of a positive result of mediation is to discontinue the proceedings (Article 492 of the Code of Criminal Procedure). In cases of offences prosecuted on request, on the other hand, a positive result of mediation may translate into withdrawal of the request. It seems that even more far-reaching or simply obligatory, rather than merely optional, effects of mediation on the reduction of the offender's sentence could contribute to greater interest in it on the part of offenders and, consequently,

---

19 Cf. M. Pękala, 'Dobry mediator – czyli kto? Kwalifikacje zawodowe mediatorów w świetle opinii ekspertów', [in:] M. Araszkiewicz, J. Czapska, M. Pękala, K. Płeszka (eds.), *Mediacja. Teoria, normy, praktyka*, Warszawa 2017, pp. 497–500.

20 Ibidem, p. 488.

to its more frequent use.[21] It is, of course, uncertain how the greater influence of the mediation procedure on the final outcome of criminal proceedings would work in the Polish criminal process. In-depth research is needed in this regard. However, based on the example of Finland, a hypothesis can be proposed that such a de lege ferenda postulate would be worth considering.

Taking into account the above considerations, it can be concluded that legislative changes in the scope of a more significant influence of mediation on the shaping of decisions made in criminal proceedings in Poland and in the scope of better preparation of mediators should go hand in hand and would perhaps contribute to an increase in the number of cases referred to mediation. A greater influence of mediation on the outcome of criminal proceedings could encourage perpetrators of crimes to use it, while better preparation of mediators, as the results of the research show, above all the organs of criminal proceedings. However, the question of how to make the prospect of mediation more attractive in the perception of the victims of crime is irresistible.

It seems that an appropriate design of the VOM procedure itself may be one answer. If by VOM we mean a specific process whereby the victim of a crime meets the perpetrator in a structured and safe environment, and the purpose of the process is to provide the victim and the perpetrator with an opportunity to engage in a dialogue about their emotional needs, talk about the crime, and discuss its impact on both parties, then it is clear that the process needs special conditions in order to take place. The emphasis on these conditions is placed within a special formula of VOM - the so-called victim-sensitive mediation. This is a mediation carried out in criminal cases, which, however, is not limited to the conclusion of a settlement, but is primarily geared towards dialogue and working through the psychological effects of the crime by both parties, the victim and the accused. Central to this formula is ensuring that the victim feels safe throughout the mediation process. Manuals and guidelines on victim-sensitive mediation point out that an appropriate organisation of the mediation meeting - in a place where the victim will feel comfortable and safe and with the participation of some person accompanying the victim, such as a relative - is important for this

21 Greater interest in mediation on the part of offenders is desirable, for instance because of the above-mentioned mediation effect, i.e. the possibility of reducing the risk of recidivism – cf. J. Jonas-van Dijk, S. Zebel, J. Claessen, H. Nelen, *Victim-Offender Mediation*, loc.cit. As an aside, it can also be added that the other consensual modes, which are very popular in Polish criminal proceedings, i.e. conviction without trial and voluntary submission to punishment, do not seem to show positive effects on the level of risk of recidivism.

feeling. The meeting between the victim and the accused should be preceded by individual, preparatory meetings between the mediator and each party. Such preliminary meetings are already explicitly provided for in the provisions of the 2015 Polish Regulation of the Minister of Justice on mediation proceedings in criminal cases (§ 14 of the Regulation). It seems that also the other indications from victim sensitive mediation, i.e. the participation in the mediation meeting of a person accompanying the victim and flexibility in the choice of the place of this meeting, could be implemented in this regulation.

The postulated changes that may adapt the current form of the Polish regulation of the Minister of Justice to the victim-sensitive mediation formula are certainly not revolutionary and may even be perceived as certain nuances. They do, however, represent a certain shift of emphasis in the current mediation formula, which does not properly focus on the needs of the victim.

4. Conclusion

There is no guarantee that changes in the legal regulation of mediation and the practice of its application in Poland in the 'Scandinavian' direction would be fully effective. Further research is, of course, needed for cautious guarantees in this regard. However, there is also probably no other way to implement mediation more widely in Polish criminal proceedings than its reform. Without greater interest from the potential parties to mediation and the criminal procedure authorities, we will continue to refer about 1% of cases to mediation. It seems that this interest, on the other hand, can be strengthened by building greater trust towards mediators (through their professional preparation), increasing the impact of mediation on the outcome of criminal proceedings (by offering suspects/accused persons a real reduction of criminal liability) and adapting the mediation procedure to the expectations, needs and specific situation of persons victimised by crime. These changes will obviously not be effective overnight. It seems more realistic to forecast their effects over several years. However, the Scandinavian tradition of mediation, including VOM, has also not been created in a year.

Bibliography

Albrecht B., 'Multicultural Challenges for Restorative Justice: Mediators' Experiences from Norway and Finland, Journal of Scandinavian Studies in Criminology and Crime Prevention', *Journal of Scandinavian Studies in Criminology and Crime Prevention*, 2010/ 1, DOI: 10.1080/140438510036 16204.

Ervasti E., 'Past, Present and Future of Mediation in Nordic Countries', [in:] A. Nylund, K. Ervasti, L. Adrian (eds.), *Nordic Mediation Research*, Berlin 2018.

Hacia-Groticka M., Czarnecki P., 'Opinie ekspertów na temat barier instytucjonalnych oraz promocji mediacji w środowiskach prawniczych', [in:] M. Araszkiewicz, J. Czapska, M. Pękala, K. Płeszka (eds.), *Mediacja. Teoria, normy, praktyka*, Warszawa 2017.

Jonas-van Dijk J., Zebel S., Claessen J., Nelen H., 'Victim–Offender Mediation and Reduced Reoffending: Gauging the Self-Selection Bias', *Crime & Delinquency*, 2020/6–7.

Kozłowska P., 'Wykorzystanie sprawiedliwości naprawczej w sprawach o przestępstwa z nienawiści – szanse i ograniczenia', *Probacja*, 2023/2.

Marshall T., 'The evolution of restorative justice in Britain, *European Journal on Criminal Policy and Research* 1996, no 4.

Mediacje karne w latach 1998–2021', https://isws.ms.gov.pl/pl/baza-statystyczna/opracowania-wieloletnie.

Nascimento H., Andrade J., de Castro Rodrigues A., 'The Psychological Impact of Restorative Justice Practices on Victims of Crimes – a Systematic Review', *Trauma, Violence, & Abuse*, 2022/1–19, DOI: 10.1177/15248380221082085.

Pękala M., 'Dobry mediator – czyli kto? Kwalifikacje zawodowe mediatorów w świetle opinii ekspertów', [in:] M. Araszkiewicz, J. Czapska, M. Pękala, K. Płeszka (eds.), *Mediacja. Teoria, normy, praktyka*, Warszawa 2017.

Recommendation CM/Rec (2018) 8 of the Committee of Ministers to member States concerning restorative justice in criminal matters.

Rudolf A., Cichowicz-Major M., Matysiak M., Pałka S., Pieniążek W., Przybył C., 'Diagnoza stanu stosowania mediacji oraz przyczyn zbyt niskiej w stosunku do oczekiwanej popularności mediacji – Raport końcowy', https://www.gov.pl/attachment/cb132c4a-8e40-401d-9bdb-57c73427578d

Zielińska E., Klimczak J., 'Zakres stosowania mediacji w sprawach karnych w praktyce wymiaru sprawiedliwości', 2020, p. 39, https://iws.gov.pl/wp-content/uploads/2020/04/IWS_Zieli%C5%84ska-E.-Klimczak-J-Zakres-stosowania-mediacji-w-sprawach-karnych-w-praktyce-wymiaru-sprawiedliwo%C5%9Bci.pdf

Dr. Koidu Saia[1]

IV. Life Path Lessons of Children in Closed Childcare Institution Service in Estonia: Experiences and Practices Related to Interprofessional Collaboration-Based Support

Abstract: This analysis is part of a larger, five-objective study 'Study to Improve the System of Timely Identification and Effective Assistance to Children at Risk: Life Course Lessons for Children in a Closed Childcare Institution', which was conducted in Estonia with the participation of the CIRIC research group of the SOGOLAS of Tallinn University.

The focus of the current study is on the CCIS, which replaced special schools as a result of the 2018 reforms. The CCIS created in 2018 to replace special schools, is the last measure for children in need. The service means that the child's fundamental rights, including freedom of movement, are significantly restricted. The assessment and decision-making process that underpins a referral to services, whether under the Social Welfare Act or criminal procedure, is complex and affects the lives of both the child in need and the family. The need for public support services is statistically on the rise, including the need for CCIS. The aim of the service in a CCIS is to support the child's psychological, emotional, social, educational, and cognitive development, in order to achieve lasting changes that will enable the child to cope successfully in the normal environment after the end of the restriction of their freedom, without behaviour that is detrimental to their own life, health, and development and to the life and health of others. on the referral.

Keywords: Child Protection Services, Closed Childcare Institution Service, SOGOLAS, Childcare in Estonia

1. Introduction

This analysis is part of a larger, five-objective study, 'Study to Improve the System of Timely Identification and Effective Assistance to Children at Risk: Life Course Lessons for Children in a Closed Childcare Institution', which was conducted in Estonia with the participation of the CIRIC research group of the School of

1 ORCID no. 0000-0002-4248-9022. Assistant professor at Tallinn University of Technology.

Governance, Law and Society of Tallinn University. The main study describes the empirical results of children's "journeys" to a closed childcare institution service (CCIS) and the assistance/support provided for the children from the perspectives of children, parents, and practitioners. The sub-study carried out under the responsibility of the CIRIC research group, aimed to analyse the cooperation between the child protection, education, social and law enforcement systems for the benefit of children in the CCIS, including identifying bottlenecks in the system and possible solutions, and the following text is based on the data and materials from the study carried out and the final report.

The focus of the current sub-study is on the CCIS, which replaced special schools as a result of the 2018 reforms. CCIS means temporarily restricting a minor's freedom of movement away from home in a safe and supportive environment. It is intended as a measure of last resort for children whose behaviour poses a serious threat to their own life, health or development or to the life or health of others. However, the number of applications for the CCIS has increased every year: from 93 applications in 2018 to 137 applications in 2020. As CCIS is a measure restricting the child's liberty, referral to CCIS should not be made prematurely or when the child's need for assistance is too low. Therefore, prevention, i.e. early identification of the child's and family's need for help, responding to it, and providing appropriate assistance, is crucial.

2. International Practices Concerning CCIS

A systematic review[2] of evidence-based intervention programmes in the UK, Norway, the Netherlands, Denmark, and Ireland in support of the CCIS target group was one section of the study. It revealed the following good practices: (i) positive parenting: strengthening parenting skills to promote children's stability, development, and well-being and effective family functioning (e.g. the parenting programme 'Aiming for Adorable V: A Review of 17 Years' in all five countries; 'Preparing for Life' in Ireland; 'A Sure Start' in Ireland and the UK, 'Parent Training: Oregon Model' in Denmark, Norway, and the Netherlands), but also interventions specifically designed to improve positive parenting skills of foster carers and kinship carers (e.g. KEEP in the UK). Some parental support programmes are web-based (e.g. Parenting Wisely and EasyPeasy in Ireland and the UK); (ii) prevention and early identification of families and children at risk

---

2 K. Toros, A. Schults, R. Lehtme, *Kirjandusanalüüs riskis laste varajase tuvastamise ja toetamise võimalustest ning parimatest praktikatest välisriikides*, Tallinna Ülikool: CIRIC 2022.

was a key principle of the child protection system in all five countries, as can be seen from the nature of the evidence-based programmes implemented. In prevention and early identification, in addition to the child protection system, the education system also has an important role to play (e.g. 'School-Wide Positive Behaviour Support' in Denmark and the UK; School Care and Advice Groups in the Netherlands); (iii) participatory approaches with children and families – different models and programmes aim to support family participation, e.g. different types of conference models (Family Solution Ring in Norway and the UK; Child Protection Conference and Strengthening Family Child Protection Conference model in the UK; Family Wellbeing Conference in Ireland); (iv) a child-centred perspective that encourages children to express their needs and wishes and to participate (e.g. solution-focused case work in Norway; 'Signs of Safety' in Ireland, UK, Denmark, the Netherlands); (v) child safety – models and programmes that build on safety and permanence (e.g. solution-focused casework in Norway; 'Safety Signs' in Ireland, the UK, Denmark, the Netherlands; Strengthening Family Child Protection conference model in the UK; Mandatory Child Abuse and Domestic Violence Protocol to identify potential child abuse in the Netherlands); (vi) specific support for children with behavioural difficulties – various interventions are implemented for children with behavioural and emotional problems (e.g. 'Parent Training: Oregon Model' in the Netherlands; special focus on children with ADHD in Denmark; multi-systemic therapy in Ireland and the UK, Norway, the Netherlands; functional family therapy in the Netherlands, Ireland and the UK; multi-dimensional family therapy in Norway; trauma-informed approach in Norway); (vii) family strengths and skills – different programmes and intervention models based on family strengths ('Parent Training: Oregon Model' in Denmark, Norway, and the Netherlands; Solution Focused Case Work in Norway; 'Signs of Safety' in Ireland, the UK, Denmark, the Netherlands; Strengthening Family Child Protection Conference Model in the UK; Trauma Informed Approach in Norway; Family Wellbeing Conference in Ireland); (viii) interdisciplinary collaboration – an integrated method for agencies and professionals to work together to identify risks early and provide effective support (e.g. at-risk youth index and school care and advice groups in the Netherlands; family solution circles in Norway and the UK; child protection conference and the Strengthening Family Child Protection conference model in the UK).

Children referred to the service are characterised by complex problems and risky behaviour, including repeatedly committed offences; therefore, referring to the outputs of the systematic literature review – the CCIS families and children need positive parenting and family strengths-focused, early identification and prevention, participation and child-centred, interdisciplinary collaboration centred approaches, services, methods.

3. CCIS in Estonian Context

Significant changes have taken place in the Estonian child protection, education, social welfare, and justice systems in recent years, which have affected the well-being of children and families in vulnerable, fragile situations (including those involved in CCIS) and posed new challenges for professionals working in the system, sector developers, and policymakers. The CCIS created in 2018 to replace special schools is the last measure for children in need whose behaviour is assessed as posing a serious risk to the child's life, health, and development. The service means that the child's fundamental rights, including freedom of movement, are significantly restricted. The assessment and decision-making process that underpins a referral to services, whether under the Social Welfare Act or criminal procedure, is complex and affects the lives of both the child in need and the family. The need for public support services is statistically on the rise, including the need for CCIS.[3]

The service in a CCIS aims to support the child's psychological, emotional, social, educational, and cognitive development in order to achieve lasting changes that will enable the child to cope successfully in the normal environment after the end of the restriction of their freedom, without behaviour that is detrimental to their own life, health, and development and to the life and health of others. CCIS provides temporary 24-hour support and security for a child whose behaviour poses a serious threat to their own life, health, and development or to the life and/or health of others. Also for a child for whom an arrest is replaced by the CCIS. The service restricts the child's freedom of movement, which is one of the most important fundamental rights, so the need for the service must be carefully considered beforehand. A child can only be subjected to the CCIS through court. One can apply for the CCIS for a maximum of one year at a time, and the court decides on the referral. In Estonia, four service providers have 100 service vacancies to offer as of 2023.

The main reasons for referral are the following, occurring in combination with each other, are systematic, long-term, and continuous: the child is violent and aggressive towards other people or property, the child abuses addictive substances,

---

3 K. Gornischeff, E. Linnas, *Innovatsioon seisneb koostöös – kinnise lasteasutuse jätkutoe pilootprojekti kogemus*, Sotsiaaltöö 2020.

the child has a history of risky sexual behaviour, e.g. over-sexualisation, the child has a long history of truancy, the child has a history of non-consensual overnight absences, the child is violent towards themselves, e.g. cutting themselves and attempting suicide. The CCIS is not suitable if the child needs constant medical supervision and intervention because of a physical or mental health condition (e.g. acute psychosis).

In a CCIS, children and young people are provided with a structured environment that is supportive, caring, and organised meaningfully. Sleep and wake time, as well as time spent in a group or on one's own, studying or working, and time spent using the screen, are regulated. Individual and group activities, physical activity, balanced nutrition, leisure activities, and other similar activities are offered, and trauma recovery is supported. The child is given the opportunity to experience a sense of achievement through appropriate activities. A team of professionals works around the child to support the child's development. The staff in the group's educational area ensure the child's safety and developmental activities around the clock. In addition to educational staff, support professionals (therapists, psychologists, social pedagogues, etc.) are involved in supporting children and families. The child is also offered educational support. The service builds on the child's strengths and is based on their individual needs. Activities are aimed at providing stability and support, encouraging development and change of difficult-to-understand behaviours, including new attitudes and skills. The aim of all activities is for the child to be able to cope in the community and in the regular environment without harming others or themselves when they leave the CCIS.

The children live in groups of up to six, with shared social areas and usually each in their own room. The specific number of people in a group will depend on the level of coping and compatibility. The aim is to support the child's relationships in the community and a smooth return from the childcare institution to their home environment, thus gradually giving the child more freedom while at the same time trusting them with more responsibility. The children go on outings and, where appropriate and possible, also attend training outside the centre. The child will start to have a regular stay at home as soon as they have settled in a CCIS and it has been assessed during the service that the child's risky behaviour towards themselves and/or others has decreased to such an extent that temporarily removing the child from the service does not endanger themselves and/or the people around them. The service must be as short as possible and as long as necessary to achieve the basic therapeutic objectives.

Assessing the needs of a child and family in a situation of such serious and complex need requires multidisciplinary, highly professional, and well-functioning collaboration.[4] The assessment of the cooperation between child protection, education, social, and law enforcement systems, possible bottlenecks and proposed solutions, which is derived from the purpose of this study, is of particular importance for the development of CCIS and the child-friendly and effective support of children and families referred to the service.

4. Theoretical Framework

Timely, appropriate, and effective assistance to support the well-being and coping of children / young people in need and their families is important to prevent or at least mitigate potential subsequent problems that place additional burdens on welfare, justice, labour market, health and economic sectors.[5] Methods of working with children and young people with complex needs (including offenders with behavioural difficulties and other special needs) have evolved significantly over time, from positivist and treatment-oriented medical-psychological approaches to community-based, risk assessment, and intervention programmes and evidence-based methods and from there to reintegration, restorative justice and psychosocial, therapeutic, and integrated approaches. We have moved on to the importance of the child's perspective and experiences,[6] child well-being, mental health and supportive environment, proportionate interventions, and early

4 K. Toros, *Assessment of Child Well-Being: Child Protection Practice in Estonia*, Tallinn: Tallinn University 2011; K. Gornischeff, E. Linnas, *Innovatsioon seisneb koostöös…*; K. Gornischeff, K. Saia, K. Toros, E. Ülviste, 'Lapsesõbraliku õigusemõistmise põhimõtete rakendamine Eesti õigussüsteemis ja alaealiste õigusrikkujate juhtumite kohtulahendite näitel', *Acta Politica Estica* 2018/9, pp. 24–62; K. Saia, K. Toros, D. DiNitto, M. Leino, I. Sindi, E. Teresteegen, 'Juvenile offender rehabilitation in Estonia: interprofessional collaboration in written assessments and specialists' perceptions', *European Journal of Social Work*, 2019/22(01), pp. 121–133. DOI: 10.1080/13691457.2017.1357022; K. Saia, K. Toros, D. DiNitto, 'Interprofessional collaboration in social rehabilitation services for dually-involved Estonian youth: Perceptions of youth, parents, and professionals', *Children and Youth Services Review*, 2020/113, pp. 1–12. DOI: 10.1016/j.childyouth.2020.104945.

5 A. Graham, *Early Intervention: The Next Steps. An Independent Report to Her Majesty's Government*, Cabinet Office, 2011, available at: https://dera.ioe.ac.uk//14161/ [accessed on October 10th, 2023].

6 K. Farrow, K. Gill, B. Wilkinson, Bristol: Policy Press 2007.

prevention.[7] However, we understand that, according to the neoliberal discourse, we cannot put all the responsibility for the child's coping on the child,[8] all the more so in the case of traumatised children who need complex support for their well-being, the protection of their rights, and their growth as citizens.

A child in need in a vulnerable situation must receive the help they need, which must be needs-based, of high quality, and trauma-informed.[9] Children are influenced by risk and protective factors related to the individual, family, friends, school, and community protective factors, and children's resilience needs to be strengthened.[10] All children have the right to have their well-being, development, dignity, and other rights protected and supported.

In order to conceptualise interdisciplinary and interprofessional collaboration, we adapted the frameworks of the Reeves, Lewin, Espin, and Zwarenstein model[11] and the PINCOM model[12] as theoretical starting points. The first of these helped to understand and make sense of cross-disciplinary and cross-functional teamwork by synthesising key factors under four domains/areas: relational, process, organisational, and contextual. The PINCOM model is an instrument to support

---

7 R. Loeber, D.P. Farrington, D. Petechuk, 'Child Delinquency: Early Intervention and Prevention', *Child Delinquency Bulletin Series*, OJJDP: May 2003, available at: https://eric.ed.gov/?id=ED477922 [accessed on October 10th, 2023]; D.P. Farrington, H. Gaffney, F. Lösel, M.M. Ttofi, 'Systematic reviews of the effectiveness of developmental prevention programs in reducing delinquency, aggression, and bullying', *Aggression & Violent Behavior*, 2017/33, pp. 91–106, https://doi-org.ezproxy.tlu.ee/10.1016/j.avb.2016.11.003. [accessed on October 10th, 2023].

8 D. Huges 'Time and space on the hospital ward: shaping the scope of nursing practice' [in:] D. Allen, D. Huges (eds), *Nursing and the Division of Labour in Healthcare*, Palgrave: Basingstoke 2002.

9 B. Goldson, J. Muncie, 'Towards a global 'child-friendly' juvenile justice?', *International Journal of Law, Crime and Justice*, 2012/40(1), pp. 47–64. https://doi.org/10.1016/j.ijlcj.2011.09.004; M. Ekendahl, J. Månsson, P. Karlsson, 'Risk and responsibilization: resistance and compliance in Swedish treatment for youth cannabis use', *Drugs: Education, Prevention & Policy*, 2020/27(1), pp. 60–68.

10 M. Turliuc, C. Mairean, O. Danila, 'Risk and resilience in children, family and community. A Research Review' in: I. Rogobete, A. Neagoe (eds.), *Contemporary issues facing families: An interdisciplinary dialogue*, Bonn: Verlag fur Kultur und Wissenshaft 2013, pp. 33–53.

11 S. Reeves, S. Lewin, S. Espin, M. Zwarenstein, *Interprofessional Teamwork for Health and Social Care*, Wiley-Balckwell 2010.

12 A. Ødegard, J. Strype, 'Perceptions of interprofessional collaboration within child mental health care in Norway', *Journal of Interprofessional Care*, 2009/23(3), pp. 286–296. https://doi.org/10.1080/13561820902739981. [accessed on October 10th, 2023].

research on perceptions of inter-professional collaboration, which allows for the analysis of different aspects of interdisciplinary collaboration and is well suited for research on children.

The following theoretical frameworks, evidence-based approaches, emerged from objective V of the study, a survey of knowledge and practice in other countries,[13] which helped to shape the research design for objective IV: (a) positive parenting and strengthening parenting skills; (b) early identification, prevention, and early recognition of the need for help, including in collaboration between social and educational systems; (c) supporting child and family participation; (d) a child-centred (including solution-centred) perspective; (e) ensuring child safety (e.g. conference model); (f) support for children with behavioural and emotional problems (e.g. MDFT); (g) models and interventions focusing on family strengths (including a trauma-informed approach); (h) multidisciplinary collaboration to identify risks and provide effective support (including the Strengthening Families conference model).

In addition, we consider the concept of a child-friendly approach, according to which every child has the right to protection and developmental support for their well-being, development, self-determination and other rights, to be a critical theoretical starting point. The concept is linked to the changing legal status of children and includes child-friendly components in the administration of justice and in the preceding and subsequent stages.[14] The child-friendly approach is linked to child-centredness, the principle of safeguarding the best interests of the child, which is based on the involvement of the child in need and their participation in decisions affecting their life.

5. Design of the Study and Methodology

For the analysis, individual (n = 16) and focus group interviews (6) were conducted with children and young people who had been in CCIS, parents, the CCIS service managers, counsellors from the Social Insurance Board (SKA), judges, child protective workers, and network members (including child protective worker, district police officer, youth worker, district social worker, youth guarantee case manager, foster home worker, CCIS social worker, hospital social worker,

13 K. Toros, A. Schults, R. Lehtme, *Kirjandusanalüüs riskis op.cit.*

14 Guidelines of the Committee of Ministers of the Council of Europe on child friendly justice (Adopted by the Committee of Ministers on November 17th, 2010 at the 1098th meeting of the Ministers' Deputies), available at: https://www.justice.gov.sk/dokumenty/2021/05/Guidelines-child-friendly-justice.pdf [accessed on December 10th, 2023].

CCIS career counsellor). The PINCOM model of child-friendly justice and multidisciplinary cooperation was used as a theoretical framework. Thematic analysis was applied to the data analysis by coding the interviews, forming key codes/categories, and placing them under key themes. The central research questions were the following: 1) Based on the survey results, what can be said about the system cooperation for the benefit of children? 2) Based on the survey results, what are the main bottlenecks in cooperation? 3) What are the possible solutions to the bottlenecks in the system?

The empirical basis of the study consists of datasets, sources of information, and methods of analysis involving the following target groups as a sample. The use of the data is subject to and based on the decision of the Research Ethics Committee of the National Institute for Health Development No 1047.

We used a qualitative approach, which allowed us to delve into the lives of specific children and young people who received CCIS, their families, the cases, events, descriptions, and reasons given by professionals to understand people's behaviour and/or to make sense of what happened. The aim was to understand the experiences, interpretations, and opinions of children, young people, and parents / legal guardians with experience of CCIS in-depth from different perspectives, thus creating a more holistic picture of bottlenecks and possible solutions. Data analysis was carried out by four authors (Koidu Saia, Kadi Liik, Astra Schults, and Jaana Malmberg) using the principles of thematic analysis described by Braun and Clarke,[15] which consisted of generating initial codes and searching, reviewing, and naming themes.

Prior to the data analysis, three main themes and sub-themes were defined according to the study's research questions. Data analysis started with coding the interviews (L – child, LV – parent, FG – focus group), multiple readings of interview transcripts and listening to audio recordings to gain a general understanding of the interviewees' experiences. This was followed by the identification of initial codes from the data (including the coding of key meta-citations) and the categorisation of the codes into possible themes, bearing in mind the predefined main theme and their sub-themes based on the study's baseline. The codes were reviewed again, including with research group II. The details of each theme were refined, and the codes were combined into themes based on the three main themes.

15 V. Braun, V. Clarke, 'Using thematic analysis in psychology', *Qualitative Research in Psychology*, 2006/3(2), pp. 77–101. ISSN1478-0887, available at: http://eprints.uwe.ac.uk/11735 [accessed on October 10th, 2023].

The main limitations of the present study, and important to consider when reviewing the results, are the following: low number of interviews with children / young people with the CCIS experience (12) and parents/guardians (4); low representation of children in substitute care with the CCIS experience in the sample; interview data collection instruments could have had a similar structure when interviewing different subgroups of the sample, analogy of topics in order to draw out the opinions of different subgroups of the sample on the same issues (e.g. who is the child / young person referred to CCIS, etc.); the qualitative empirical data (interviews) did not form comprehensive case-based (child / young person with the CCIS experience, their legal representative and the CCIS service provider, their child protective workers as a case manager, and other professionals) datasets, but were unrelated interviews; time constraints in conducting the study, time pressure.

The main strengths of the survey include interdisciplinarity of the research team (developmental, organisational, environmental psychology; social work; social pedagogy; juvenile delinquency and rehabilitation; youth police competences); involvement of a practitioner (formerly a youth police officer, now a school social pedagogue) in the research team and feedback from a practising child protective worker (including a practitioner with experience of children / young people cases referred to CCIS) to validate the final report; long and diverse experience of the research group (CIRIC) in designing, conducting, and publishing research on children and families; triangulation applied (close collaboration with the objective II and V research groups, and mutual consultation and learning from the working process, adapting research activities as necessary).

In the following sections, we will analyse the current practices of CCIS in Estonia. More precisely the experiences of the children and parents in CCIS and the specialists concerning the perceived interprofessional collaboration based support, child-friendly justice principles and the good practices for supporting the life paths of children based on best available knowledge.

6. Implementing Child-Friendly Justice Principles in KLAT

6.1. Relevance

According to L2, her mother was offered many support services and options, which she quickly accepted (due to child protective worker), but the child did not comply with the agreements. L2 was referred to the CCIS on two occasions, at around 10 years old and at around 15 years old, and they feel that the service has changed a lot. L2 was able to devote more time and focus on their studies through CCIS (they had a problem with school attendance, mainly due to computer game addiction).

Young interviewee: L4 (18 years old at the time of the interview, was supposed to be in CCIS for 1 month and 4 days, but decided to finish 9th grade of their own free will) highlighted from their experience the fact that they did not know where they would be referred and under what conditions they would be released from the service.

> L4: *'Well, they do not have to explain. It is always 'now we decided, we say, and so it happens, so it goes'. […] You can ask […], but they do not want to answer, because most of the time they do not have a reason. Most of the time, it is that they are just taking an idea and 'now it is going to happen'.*

> L4: *'Well, in that respect it is kind of weird that… I also had a kind of… one time I got an email saying to come to the police to talk. And then… it was the beginning of the year, the end of the year – that now it was the time to go to the court. What happened in the meantime – no idea; just off to the court. And then there was also a kind of, oh well, we think they should be put there [CCIS] for that period. And then this judge at the beginning was like 'No!' […] that, basically, 'that is like too much, we are not going to do it'. But in the end, somehow, they still decided to put me there [CCIS]. I do not know what changed exactly. I do not know who to ask what happened. But they have made that decision – it remains. Somehow it actually got to be like that… if you dig into it all the time… because otherwise I would have had to be there for a month longer, but because it took them a week to get a new answer, well, […] so many times to shorten the time actually. So, if you compare it to what would have been maybe two months and a bit, then it is like only one month, then it is actually… Or well, it does not really matter in the end, because […] I was finally… well, I got home at the beginning of March, and then I was gone for a week, and I finally came back to do schoolwork […].'*

The focus group interviews with FG4 judges revealed that in most cases, going to court is the last option to be referred to CCIS, and that other measures have already been taken but have not been successful. According to the judges, there have been some referrals after placement, but this is not the predominant practice and the experience of judges may vary from region to region. The practice of the judges shows that the documents have been drawn up in sufficient detail and that the necessary relevant material has been compiled, including the opinion of the Social Insurance Board (SKA). The judges consider that the actions or inactions of the child protective worker will influence what happens to the child.

In the focus group interviews, the FG5 child protective workers highlighted the need for and importance of taking into account children's interests and well-being when intervening and applying for and referring to CCIS. Referral to a service is a last resort if various prevention and intervention measures have been implemented beforehand (counselling, therapies, specialist involvement, referral to social programmes, etc.). The prerequisites for access to the service are usually lack of parental competence in raising and supporting the child, mental health problems of both the child/young person and the parents, self-harming and/or dangerous behaviour.

In the network focus groups, it was pointed out that it is important to consider that the child should be in contact with a specialist with whom they have a better contact and relationship, for example, when introducing CCIS. It is important to keep an ethical and professional distance, but also to be open and understanding. Both the child / young person and the parent(s) need to be involved, including so that important information from network meetings can be summarised and communicated unambiguously. Children / young people and families need to feel that they are trusted, that they are welcome to ask for advice, whatever happens.

> Focus group_2: *'If we could give these young people, who have endured a lot, the information that they are still welcome and believed in – just that blue-eyed, but also, so to speak, well, good life experience, right – I think that is maybe the key. Because by turning the back on them, they go even further in a direction we do not want them to go. So yes… and that if they feel they belong somewhere.'*

The network must be made up of members, taking into account the needs of the child / young person, and the composition may change over time. Each network member brings their own perspective on the child's / young person's story, up-to-date information, competences, and additional opportunities in the field.

> Focus group_1: *'There is no point in involving a whole army who are not really contributing at this point because it devalues the credibility of the network. And what has been really nice about the networks is that each participant has their own view of the young person's story, and then the puzzle is put together.'*

In addition, it was pointed out that it is important for the child and the family, as well as for the network as a whole, to know the next steps after CCIS, such as which school the child will continue in and under which curriculum.

> Focus group_1: *'Since I had the best rapport with one of the young people in the network before I went to CCIS and it was very difficult with them, we decided that I would talk to them about why they should go to CCIS and what could be there.'*

6.2. Being informed

According to the young person (L1), they were not aware of the procedures (including what would happen next and where they could have a say). They saw the assessment of the child protective worker, for example, but they had no say in it, even though they noticed the mistakes. The problems with CCIS were the long duration (while in the service, they were in contact with only the advocate, e.g. not the child protective worker, in addition to the educators, the psychiatrist about once a month, and the psychologist outside), no work on their reintegration into society was observed. They considered the meeting(s) with the MDFT therapist to be important – it allowed them to get clarity about the reasons why they had got into this situation and the support of CCIS, their mother, and the psychologist (who was not from inside the CCIS system, but from outside).

A similar experience is shared by L4, whose interview revealed that they were not informed in advance and during the procedure about what they were facing and why the procedure was necessary.

> L4: *'And then the funny thing is that... then it is like I am sitting on one side of the table. There is this defender sitting next to me who does not understand what is going on at all; who does not understand why they are there and what they are supposed to do. They were no help at all. They did not understand at all what was happening. And on the other side of the table, there are two 'dudes' [officials] who for some reason just hate me and want to make my life as miserable as possible. And then the judge – I did not understand them at all in the end. They seemed normal at first. In the end... in the end it is like... in the end it is like... like completely out of the blue, like [I] was not even there... the decision comes a week later, and then it is like... And they do not have to justify it... they just said out of the blue that we are going to do it this way and that's how it was.'*

6.3. Best interests, non-discrimination

Focus group members have seen cases where the municipality does not want to take back children who have been removed from CCIS, because the community is not ready, there is no person in charge of the case, and the young people feel this. It is important for a child / young person to have someone waiting for them at home, someone they can talk to if they have a problem, someone who believes in them. One good practice is the 'Out of the Circle Model' and the support person as a confidant.

> Focus group_1: *so that this young person actually feels that, despite what they may have done previously, they are welcome back and will not be labelled. We who are in the network and sort of standing up for their good with them, we have the power to actually also protect that child in that sense and say... well, give them another chance and not think of them as 'oh, you see'.*

6.4. Environment and Relations

Serious areas of concern were the difficult relationships with other children (who were very different, with very different problems and needs, and who were seriously difficult to manage) and the feeling (including from the children's own tested and evidenced experience) that the CCIS educators and staff could not be trusted. One young person mentioned attempted suicides and repeated attempts to run away with no one to confide in, followed by the use of sanctions (punishments).

The image communicated in case of CCIS (that it was not a prison) did not correspond to reality, according to the young person, as CCIS was more lenient than a detention centre, but with a longer duration and unclear rules and sanctions. The young person's suggestion was that a single offence and one interview with a child protective worker should not lead to a referral to CCIS (including that the next steps are based on the child protective worker's assessment, which may be flawed) and that in some cases a shock detention of about 2 months or CCIS of about 2 months could be more effective than a 1-year duration in CCIS. According to L2, for example, children who are small (about 10 years old) and older and behave aggressively should not be grouped together (they were once among the old ones when they were small). L2 sees it as a very big problem that the CCIS children often do not have a reliable, supportive, and helpful adult (parent). L2 had a supportive first therapist (therapist-psychologist-psychiatrist) with whom they had good contact, but after their parental leave, the therapist assigned to them did not fit – there could have been an opportunity to change if the cooperation was not suitable.

When children leave the service, they should be in a safe and supportive environment; often, they are back in an old and unchanged environment where old roles and behaviours are triggered. According to the FG2 CCIS leaders, the CCIS young people are frustrated and do not know how to behave or cope with their emotions and end up back on the streets and in trouble. The FG4 judges pointed out that the existing CCIS may not be suitable for all young people with special needs, including those with intellectual disabilities. It is important to support parents to understand and step by step fulfil their role as parents.

> Focus group_1: '*We actually have some positive cases where really, let's say, in the course of the year, the parent was still transformed into, well, a parent – no longer a girlfriend or a friend, but they were like a parent and they took on their role as a parent.*'

6.5. Interdisciplinary cooperation

According to L2, professionals working with the CCIS children should be adequately prepared, professional, and genuine. According to the CCIS managers, many necessary services are available, but they are not accessible to the child / young person / family as a necessary, logical, and flexible service.

> CCIS_leaders_North: '*If these services are offered in different ways, well, it is quite difficult to get a complete service. Anyway, some bits and pieces…*'

The FG5 child protective workers think that cooperation with the SKA could be faster so that they do not have to wait 30 days for an opinion from the SKA (decisions concerning children should be faster). The needs of the CCIS children are multifaceted, and both children / young people and parents often need interdisciplinary help, networking support, and support measures from different fields.

6.6. Supporting participation

According to the network specialists and the CCIS leaders, the weak link – the willingness of the family to be involved and participate – is rather low because parents are tired, do not understand children's diagnoses, and do not know or dare to ask for help. It can also be difficult to involve parents who need help to cope with their lives (alcohol and drug addicts, etc.) and parents with mental health problems – who cannot find solutions to their problems and do not accept help for themselves or their child. On the professional side and in networking, it is important to be attentive and in-depth in order to understand what comes from what, and this will also help find solutions. For example, either the parent does not want to work together as part of CCIS, or the parent has serious problems (e.g. health or economic problems, etc.) that would first need support in finding solutions. Then, the parents could focus on the next issue that is most important to them – CCIS cooperation.

> Focus group_judges: *'And with the parents, on the contrary, there's less cooperation, because the parents have given up a little bit – or well, not a little bit; really given up. They are overwhelmed by this child because I have not had any experience where a parent has objected, at least to the initial referral. In one extension, yes, the guardian still fought to get the child out, so to speak, and then we stopped the service anyway. But in general, the parents have always been in favour of these children being assigned there.'*

> L7: *'My mum has been in touch, yes, but at the moment it is just alimony. But that's all.'*

6.7. Involvement

The young person's (L2) involvement and opinion was to ask if they were sure they wanted to go to CCIS, and if they had said no, they would still have been referred. According to L3, there were a number of false accusations in the court order (on the basis of which CCIS was involved), which they could not do anything about. At the same time, professionals claim that they are involved in, listen to, and take into account the views of children / young people and families. In the focus group interviews with the FG5 child protective workers, it was confirmed that the child and the family are involved in the discussion and that the content and necessity of CCIS is explained to the child's family according to the child's / young person's and parent's understanding, age, and special needs. The FG4 judges confirm that the child, their family and, where appropriate, other relevant persons are always heard according to the (different) needs of the child and parents. The child is interviewed in a setting/room that suits them whenever possible.

From the focus group interviews, it emerged that the key issue is to ensure the child's / young person's real and meaningful involvement and participation – that they can be an informed participant in processes that affect their lives, either through their guardian or through their own participation. Although not everyone may be ready, participation must be given a chance, as only plans made together with the child / young person are more likely to work, as they will then take responsibility.

> Focus group_1: *'This is so important – to take into account the readiness of the young person. And well, we can still do our best to make sure that their voice is heard, whatever it is... whether it is through a trusted person or through the young person's own participation. But there's no point in us making plans that the young... the young person does not believe in.'*

Much depends on the child's development and readiness, but also on the values and communication skills of the convener. The starting point is to establish good contact, which may not be easy for children / young people. The child / young person and parent(s) can be involved, and unjustified fears and resistance can be reduced if the whole process is explained to them before the service starts and decisions are made. They need to feel that their voice has been heard and taken into account, that their willingness is taken into account, that fears are respected, and that additional partners are brought in where necessary. Young people who are ready for networking should and must be fully involved.

> Focus group_1: *'Well, it is the same with going to CCIS – if they know what to expect, they won't be afraid; then maybe there won't be that reluctance, that reluctance to go. When they come back, the same way, he won't do any tricks again. After all, this solid plan provides security for all.'*

7. Experiences and Perceptions Concerning Interprofessional Collaboration

In the following, we will focus on the perceived aspects and components of inter-professional cooperation based on the theoretical framework of the PINCOM model.

7.1. Motivation

Through the eyes of L1 (young person), the CCIS educators were not motivated; they were bitter and took their anger out on the children. Neither the young person interviewed nor, according to them, the other children who had been in CCIS trusted the teachers or other CCIS staff because when tested for trust, the staff passed on the information they had been entrusted with, and sanctions followed. In addition, the young person's confidence was undermined by the fact that the CCIS educators accused the young person of pretending in order to get diagnoses. According to the CCIS leaders, CCIS is understaffed, has few training opportunities and low wages, and has difficult work.

7.2. Power relations

L1 felt that officials have a lot of power. In their opinion, the children / young people are not informed about procedures, time dimension, decision logic, and timeframe; they rather cannot have a say in assessments. As for the psychiatrist's assessments, the court system doubted their validity, but still, according to the young person, they were taken into account, and they received the necessary treatment and psychiatric counselling during CCIS. However, it seems that young people do not see that they can have a say, a voice, or a role in the assessments and decisions of the officials. They seriously questioned how a child protective worker could assess on the basis of one meeting, on which the officials and decision-makers (prosecutor, judge, etc.) at the next stage would base their judgement. According to L3, there were several false accusations in the court order (referred to CCIS) (incitement to suicide of classmates, exploitation of a special needs peer), but the child felt powerless before the system. Also, they expressed their hope that they will not, however, be left with a scar from these false accusations that would prevent them from working with young people with complexities in the future.

7.3. Communication

Communication between officials and the child and the parent about what is happening with the child and the family is, when listening to the young person's story, worryingly poor and inadequate. Network members know little about whether, with whom, and what work is done during CCIS. The young person and the parent are just like part of the process; they are valued and judged but have insufficient voice and opportunity. According to L3, thanks to the young people who had been in CCIS, they knew a lot about CCIS and how life was organised there. Both the child and the parent, as well as the network members, need to know what will happen after CCIS and what is expected of them.

Focus group_1: *'Perhaps the most important thing is that the parent is actually ready by the time the child comes back. This kind of maybe work plan could just be put in place with the network, where we are then... where we are with certain things; how far away our school things are; maybe in the meantime to communicate with the Pathfinder, whether there are any learning differences needed... The important thing is that everyone is ready and the child is also aware of what things are going to be... how things are going to be when they come back.'*

Interviews with the FG5 child protective workers confirmed that cooperation and networking between them is generally good and operational where necessary. On average, networking meetings take place online or in real life once a month. A shortcoming was the slow processing of documents by the SKA, the review of the application. In one region where a family commission is working, the experience was positive, as the commission's decision to refer a child to the service is reviewed by the SKA and you do not have to wait long for the decision. If necessary, the SKA will advise, for example, if a decision is received not to refer to CCIS.

7.4. Purpose and culture of the organisation

According to young people, the official description of CCIS (as if it were not a prison) does not correspond to its actual content in practice. Young people's views differ – some do not see CCIS as a supportive measure. Rather, the sanctions and punishments run through the story, which are milder than detention. Still, the young person doubts the effectiveness of CCIS (he would prefer prison as a shock imprisonment for 2 months to 1 year of CCIS), while several children find that thanks to CCIS they are able to stay within the necessary limits, that it is a safe and structured environment that helps to get out of previous behavioural patterns and start again.

L7: *'Two years [in CCIS]. Then it finally dawns on you what a normal life is... If you leave here and you feel that you do nor have that support around you anymore – that you are not in a safe environment – then you are going to end up back in that hole.'*

A few years ago, CCIS was a children's prison for L2; the new system (like a sanatorium) has brought a change (including a reference to the change of director – the importance of leadership). Among the FG5 child protective workers, one specialist pointed out that the conditions in CCIS are good and that there are children who, living at home, do not have the opportunity to benefit from some of the conditions services that CCIS provides to the child (living and learning environment, support and services provided on the spot). As an example of good practice, the professionals mentioned the Kaagvere unit, where the necessary services and supportive housing are available on-site.

CCIS for young people with special needs requires to be reviewed and improved – there is a lack of pre-services and post-services. Lille Home has a problem with school placement, as it is a private school, which has to be paid for separately. The local government has the additional task of organising the school, despite the fact that the referral to CCIS has taken place. The child has a place in the service (this does not mean a school place is automatically guaranteed).

7.5. Wider context

Young people tended not to complain about school or the health system during CCIS. At the same time, the descriptions made it clear that the assessment was rather inadequate and the information and involvement of the child and the family were low before CCIS; during CCIS, the young person had contact only with the school, the CCIS educators and staff and the advocate, and after CCIS mainly with the probation officer (plus a psychologist and a psychiatrist, for which it was unclear whether this was a systematic follow-up to CCIS or a support service at the initiative of the parent). Before, during, and after the referral to CCIS, work with child and family support should be systematic, there should be effective information exchange between key areas, and follow-up support should be ensured to avoid backsliding. According to L2, they received the treatment they needed through CCIS and the school was supportive, while the role of the child protective worker was seen as rigid and formal.

8. For Future Perspectives: Life Path Lessons of Children in CCIS

Based on the analysis of the interviews conducted, we can learn from the life path lessons of Children in CCIS the following keypoints.

In many CCIS cases, case management is poorly coordinated and inconsistent, and there is a fragmented understanding and coordination of the whole process. It is a prerequisite that the child protective worker in the local government fulfils and assumes the role of case manager and that there is systematic coordination of multidisciplinary networking.

Parents and families are the weak link, needing help themselves to be able to help their child and to participate in networking. Their coping skills tend to be poor, and their willingness to cooperate is low, but this may be due to the parent's own coping difficulties and the need for additional support. If the parents and the home environment, the communication patterns in the family do not change during the provision of CCIS (and this should be addressed by the local government, child protection in particular, including in cooperation with the CCIS team) – the child / young person leaving CCIS will not be adequately supported. The results achieved will not be sustainable.

The CCIS children / young people do not have a stable, safe, supportive support person / trusted person/contact person, an adult – to trust. The family often fails to fulfil this role in many homes. This person could be a child protective worker, but their workload is heavy, they themselves feel a conflict of roles (CCIS tough assessor v supporter), and their professionalism is different. Children / young people referred to CCIS and parents / legal representatives must be involved in the cooperation at an early stage, ensuring their participation and information and the opportunity to have their say.

Children and young people referred to CCIS do not perceive support from different actors (even when support is offered) and feel negative labelling. There should be a fast-track procedure for referral to CCIS, and a sufficient number of CCIS vacancies (currently queues) should be guaranteed.

Children have different needs, diagnoses, and backgrounds at home and would, therefore, require different types of support services and facilities (including different forms of CCIS, especially residential care), which are unavailable today. CCIS should not be a service to which a child / young person is referred because there are no alternative services on offer. Children / young people in a vulnerable position and their well-being and development should not be at risk when they are referred to CCIS (e.g. when different mismatched target groups are in CCIS together).

Access to professionals and services to support children and families varies across regions and is often intermittent, with long waiting times. There should be a wider choice of professionals, and the child and family should be able to get the support they need quickly when needed. Providers and stakeholders (including teachers, educators, etc.) need training to enhance their qualifications and competences – this requires regular mapping of needs and cooperation with trainers (including universities).

The CCIS exit support needs to be strongly developed. If no work is done with the family during CCIS, and the child returns to the old, unchanged environment after CCIS, this will actualise the old patterns of behaviour, and the positive effects of the interim service provision are likely to be lost. A phase/services would provide help to support the transition to normal life.

The search for solutions should be solution-oriented. On the one hand, it is understandable that resources and possibilities are limited and that not all problems can be solved simultaneously, but making excuses (heavy workload, lack of suitable services, etc.) is not a step towards a solution. It is worthwhile to learn from good practices (there are regions and local governments where case management and networking work, service needs are mapped and possibilities for covering the necessary services are sought in cooperation with partners) and to look for and implement development opportunities in a systemic, holistic way, ensuring that the necessary and adequate resources (financial, human resources, supporting regulations, etc.) are available.

The role of child protective workers as case managers for children and young people in CCIS and as evaluator(s) is important. At the same time, child protective workers are overburdened and perceive a conflict of roles (defending children's interests and applying to criminal or civil judges for CCIS). The judges will assess, hear, and decide on a pass/dismiss decision on the application.

According to professionals, 'all available services and support options have been tried before CCIS'. At the same time, the range and availability of services vary widely from region to region. Effective networking is a critical factor in getting noticed and providing effective assistance, but to keep networks informed about CCIS, there needs to be consistent outreach and cooperation with networks.

In several cases, the weak link was cooperation with parents. Parents (including children) also have a duty and responsibility to accept the help offered. Cases were identified where the support provided by the local government to parents during the period of the CCIS provision remains insufficient (including by trusted educators in substitute homes). A child / young person who has undergone a change in CCIS will, therefore, return to the old, unchanged environment, and this is a high risk of relapse.

The CCIS reputation is rather poor, and children and young people feel threatened by it. They also feel that the real practice does not match the official image. The CCIS image needs to be modernised, both among professionals and among parents and children, so that it is seen as a modern welfare service and not as a special school and punishment in the old sense. Consideration should be given to transferring CCIS from the Ministry of Education and Research to the Ministry of Social Affairs.

Officials are in a position of power, and children / young people and parents do not feel meaningfully involved in the CCIS process. There are 'holes' in the system, with a lack of a residential care home and crisis family and other support services. Children / young people who have nowhere else to go are referred to CCIS. Therefore, CCIS brings together children and young people who do not fit together, and this jeopardises the development and well-being of both the CCIS target group and the other service users.

The advisory role of the Social Insurance Board (SKA) is sometimes unclear to professionals, and the SKA as an additional link in the CCIS referral process takes a lot of time. According to several professionals interviewed, in order to mitigate the role conflict of child protective workers (in case of CCIS, the roles of family separator and support worker in one professional), it would be worth considering assigning the task of referring a CCIS application to another institution (e.g. the SKA). On the other hand, a child protective worker's role includes defending the interests of children and families, for better or for worse, always taking the child's side, including in such complex situations of role conflict.

The CCIS follow-up services, follow-up support as a whole, needs to be systematically developed. Needs-based follow-up support could be provided by professionals with whom the child / young person has developed a relationship of trust in CCIS.

Good practices include early identification of need (e.g. social pedagogues in kindergartens), systematic and strong networking and case management in specific areas/communities of practice, finding solutions to support children and families despite resource constraints, regional differences, etc., interdisciplinary collaboration (including the involvement of child psychiatrists, MDFT therapists, etc.).

Training needs for professionals working with the CCIS children / young people: case management, networking, involving and informing the child and parents, working with coercive clients, trauma-informed approach. Children / young people referred to CCIS, their families, and network members need helpful information materials about CCIS.

When referring cases to CCIS, consideration could be given to creating a fast-track option for complex and critical cases. From the point of view of supporting child development, it is crucial to ensure that the CCIS children and young people have a flexible educational pathway while waiting for a CCIS decision, during the CCIS period, and after leaving CCIS.

The pre-CCIS and post-CCIS processes are not sufficiently child-friendly, lacking child and family involvement, access to necessary support services, effective case management, and networking. Interdisciplinary cooperation, and more specifically networking, is a critical factor in supporting CCIS children and families (from the identification of the need for support to the follow-up support of CCIS). Still, case management needs to be developed (so that the local government's child protective worker has the time and, on the other hand, the skills to play the role of the case manager systematically and robustly, in addition to the heavy workload), in a strong and multidisciplinary way) and training needs for network members (on case management, networking, working with coercive clients, child/young person and family involvement and building trust, mental health issues).

9. Conclusions and Practical Implications

For the children in CCIS, a pervasive problem is relapse: CCIS deals effectively with children's problems, but when they return to the family and community, the same concerns are repeated – the child has changed, but the environment has not. Providing consistent and effective support to the child requires networking with the family during CCIS and with the child and family after CCIS. Children reaching adulthood and for whom services are coming to an end are vulnerable. A remarkable number of network members do not have a common understanding of the content of modern CCIS; also, assessing a child's need and effective assistance requires that representatives of different disciplines have an adequate understanding of the trauma experience. Providing effective support for the child also requires continuous involvement of the child and family in the work of the network, which is currently rather lacking – officials are in a position of power, and neither children nor parents feel meaningfully involved in the CCIS process.

Based on international (UK, Norway, Denmark, the Netherlands, Ireland) practice, CCIS is a key factor in (potentially) targeting children, young people, and their families for support: (1) strengthening parenting skills to promote the stability, development, and well-being of children and the effective functioning of families, including support for kinship carers, prevention and early identification of families and children at risk, including the role of the education system; (2) participatory approaches with children and families – different models and programmes aim to support family participation, e.g. different types of conferencing models; (3) child-centred perspective encouraging children to express their needs and wishes, child safety – models and programmes; (4) specific support for children with behavioural difficulties – a range of interventions are implemented to address children's behavioural and emotional problems, e.g. special attention to children with ADHD; MST and MDFT; (5) family's strengths and skills – different programmes and intervention models that build on family strengths; (6) intersectoral collaboration – an integrated method for agencies and professionals to work together to identify risks early and provide effective support, e.g. school advisory groups and family solution circle. Therefore, consistent interdisciplinary cooperation allows for identifying and assessing needs, identifying appropriate support measures from different sectors before and after the CCIS, and supporting the child/family through different resources. However, in Estonia, the case management of many CCIS cases is poorly coordinated and lacks consistency, partly due to the excessive workload of the child protective workers.

Several practical implications can be outlined based on the findings. Firstly, to notice cases where assistance is needed as early as possible, it is necessary to make early identification in CCIS families-related institutions a part of everyday work. It is necessary to increase the availability of mental health services and client-friendly and non-judgemental treatment. More attention should be paid to the existence of proper values in recruitment processes and the development of curriculums in educational institutions. The uniform method of work with CCIS children and families must be child-friendly, trauma-informed, and collaborative with the child and family. The decisions must be understood and acceptable to all parties involved, including the child and family, at all stages, and the solutions must be sought in full collaboration. There is a need for a wider selection of open care services for children with specific needs (e.g. for children with intellectual disabilities and mental disorders), timely home-type assistance for families and treatment in home-type institutions.

Bibliography

Braun, V. and Clarke, V., 'Using thematic analysis in psychology', *Qualitative Research in Psychology*, 2006/3 (2) ISSN1478-0887 Available from: http://eprints.uwe.ac.uk/11735.

Ekendahl, M., Månsson, J., & Karlsson, P., 'Risk and responsibilization: resistance and compliance in Swedish treatment for youth cannabis use', *Drugs: Education, Prevention & Policy*, 2020/27(1), https://doi-org.ezproxy.tlu.ee/10.1080/09687637.2018.1544224

Farrington, D. P., Gaffney, H., Lösel, F., & Ttofi, M. M.; 'Systematic reviews of the effectiveness of developmental prevention programs in reducing delinquency, aggression, and bullying' *Aggression & Violent Behavior*, 2017/33, https://doi-org.ezproxy.tlu.ee/10.1016/j.avb.2016.11.003.

Farrow, K., Gill, K., & Wilkinson, B., *Offenders in Focus*. Bristol: Policy Press 2007.

Goldson, B., & Muncie, J., 'Towards a global 'child friendly' juvenile justice?' *International Journal of Law, Crime and Justice*, 2012/40(1), https://doi.org/10.1016/j.ijlcj.2011.09.004.

Gornischeff, K., Linnas, E.; *Innovatsioon seisneb koostöös – kinnise lasteasutuse jätkutoe pilootprojekti kogemus*; Sotsiaaltöö 2020.

Gornischeff, K., Saia, K., Toros, K., & Ülviste, E.; 'Lapsesõbraliku õigusemõistmise põhimõtete rakendamine Eesti õigussüsteemis ja alaealiste õigusrikkujate juhtumite kohtulahendite näitel', *Acta Politica Estica*, 2018/9.

Graham, A.; Early Intervention: The Next Steps. An Independent Report to Her Majesty's Government. Cabinet Office 2011, https://dera.ioe.ac.uk//14161/

Huges, D., 'Time and space on the hospital ward: shaping the scope of nursing practice', [in:] Allen, D., Huges, D., (eds)., *Nursing and the Division of Labour in Healthcare*, Palgrave: Basingstoke 2002.

Lee, S-Y., 'Psychometric tests of the risk and resiliency check-up', *Youth Violence and Juvenile Delinquency*, 2013/11(2), 165–177. https://doi.org/10.1177/1541204012460875.

Loeber, R., Farrington, D. P., & Petechuk, D., 'Child Delinquency: Early Intervention and Prevention'. *OJJDP, Child Delinquency Bulletin Series* 2003, https://eric.ed.gov/?id=ED477922

Nash, J. K., & Kim, J. S., 'Patterns of change over time in beliefs legitimizing aggression in adolescents and young adults: Risk trajectories and their relationship with serious aggression', *Social Work Research*, 2007/31(4), https://doi.org/10.1093/swr/31.4.231.

Ødegard, A., & Strype, 'Perceptions of interprofessional collaboration within child mental health care in Norway', *Journal of Interprofessional Care*, 2009/23(3), https://doi.org/10.1080/13561820902739981.

Raudkivi, M., & Linnas, E.; *Teadlik kogukond aitab muuta kinnise lasteasutuse teenusele jõudnud lapse eluted*, Sotsiaaltöö. 24.03.2023. https://tai.ee/en/node/13043.

Reeves, S., Lewin, S., Espin, S., & Zwarenstein, M., *Interprofessional Teamwork for Health and Social Care*, Wiley-Balckwell 2010.

Saia, K., Toros, K., DiNitto, D., Leino, M., Sindi, I., & Teresteegen, E., 'Juvenile offender rehabilitation in Estonia: interprofessional collaboration in written assessments and specialists' perceptions', *European Journal of Social Work*, 2019/22 (1), DOI: 10.1080/13691457.2017.1357022.

Saia, K., Toros, K., DiNitto, D., 'Interprofessional collaboration in social rehabilitation services for dually-involved Estonian youth: Perceptions of youth, parents, and professionals', *Children and Youth Services Review*, 2020/113, DOI: 10.1016/j.childyouth.2020.104945

Saia, K., Liik, K., Schults, A., Malmberg, J., *Lastekaitse-, haridus, sotsiaal- ja õiguskaitsesüsteemi koostöö kinnise lasteasutuse teenuse laste hüvanguks: kitsaskohad ja lahendused*, Uuringuraport. Tallinn: Tallinna Ülikool, CIRIC 2022.

Toros, K., *Assessment of Child Well-Being: Child Protection Practice in Estonia*, Tallinn: Tallinn University 2011.

Toros, K., Schults, A., Lehtme, R., *Kirjandusanalüüs riskis laste varajase tuvastamise ja toetamise võimalustest ning parimatest praktikatest välisriikides*, Tallinna Ülikool: CIRIC 2022.

Turliuc, M., Mairean, C., & Danila, O., 'Risk and resilience in children, family and community. A Research Review', [in:] *Contemporary issues facing families: An interdisciplinary dialogue*, Bonn: Verlag fur Kultur und Wissenschaft 2013.

van der Put, C. E., ‚The development of a risk and needs assessment instrument for truancy', *Children & Youth Services Review*, 2020/109 https://doi.org/10.1016/j.childyouth.2019.104721.

Dr. Stephen Terrett[1]

V. Proceed with caution? Human rights concerns arising from the use of out-of-court disposals to improve efficiency in the criminal justice system

Abstract: Out-of-court disposals offer an alternative to traditional criminal prosecutions and court proceedings. They are quick, cheap and capable of producing better rehabilitation results than formal trials and punitive sentences. Nonetheless, such efficiency is produced by sacrificing many of the procedural safeguards that apply during traditional prosecutions and trials. This chapter explores the non-trial alternatives that are available in the English legal system and discusses some of the human rights concerns which they spawn.

Keywords: Criminal justice, out-of-court disposals, police, cautions, human rights

1. Introduction

Every country aims to create an efficient criminal justice system. This invariably creates tension between, on the one hand, dealing with cases as quickly as possible whilst, on the other hand, ensuring that criminal procedures are not unfair to the accused. Most debate focuses on the balance between efficiency and fairness during the criminal trial process, but this chapter discusses the system for out-of-court disposals (OOCDs), which operates in in England and Wales[2] and how it seeks to strike that balance outside the courtroom.

It begins by explaining the philosophy and historical evolution of the OOCD system before outlining the various types of OOCDs and the procedures for

---

1 ORCID no. 0000-0002-1149-1939. Adjunct Professor at University of Warsaw, Faculty of Law & Administration, British Law Centre.

2 Although the United Kingdom is a unitary state, it has extensive devolution arrangements, so its constituent parts (i.e. England, Wales, Scotland and Northern Ireland) enjoy considerable governmental freedom to implement their own legislative regimes. Although many legal issues are regulated differently between the regions, England and Wales have been regarded as a single legal jurisdiction, since the *Act of Union (Wales) 1536*, whereas Scotland and Northern Ireland more often have different laws. For further detail, see D. Birrell, P. Carmichael, and D. Heenan, *Devolution in the UK: Politics, Powers and Policies*, Bloomsbury 2023.

administering them. It then discusses the latest data to highlight the prevalence of OOCDs as a method for disposing of criminal cases. Finally, it highlights some of the concerns resulting from the system, using case law to illustrate them. It suggests that, despite the system's many advantages, concerns remain about whether sufficient safeguards exist to protect the rights and legitimate expectations of those receiving OOCDs as an alternative to prosecution.

2. What are OOCDs?

Out-of-Court Disposals (OOCDs) are mechanisms for dealing with ('disposing of') criminal cases without a formal prosecution. No trial is commenced, no evidence is heard by a judge or jury, and no court hands down judgment or punishment. Instead, the case is handled entirely out-of-court.[3] The 'non-court' location at which OOCDs are administered is generally the police station where the suspected offender is taken following arrest. In most cases, the police are empowered to issue OOCD mechanisms directly, without involving other state bodies, but sometimes the law requires the involvement or approval of other bodies. For example, the Crown Prosecution Service must *ex ante* approve 'conditional cautions' issued by the police. A Youth Offence Team (YOT) may need to send an 'appropriate adult'[4] to accompany a minor or 'vulnerable adult'[5] and safeguard their rights after arrest, including by explaining the consequences of

---

3 See M. Rowe, A. Amankwaa, P. Biddle, & L. Bengtsson, 'Streamlining out-of-court disposals: Assessing the impact on reoffending and police practice', *Criminology & Criminal Justice* 2024/24(1), pp. 204–225; A. Crawford, 'The pattern of policing in the UK: Policing beyond the police', [in:] T. Newburn (ed.) *Handbook of Policing*, 2003, pp. 136–168; J. Brown, G. Sturge, and R. McInnes, *House of Commons Briefing Paper on the Police, Crime, Sentencing and Courts Bill*, HMSO 2021; House of Commons Home Affairs Committee, *Out-Of-Court Disposals. Fourteenth Report of Session 2014–15*, HMSO 2015; R. Allen, *Less Is More: The Case for Dealing with Offences*, 2017; P. Neyroud, M.P. Slothower, 'Wielding the Sword of Damocles: The Challenges and Opportunities in Reforming Police Out-of-Court Disposals in England and Wales', [in:] M. Wasik, S. Santatzoglou, (eds.) *The Management of Change in Criminal Justice: Who Knows Best?*, Basingstoke: Palgrave MacMillan 2015, pp. 275–292; HMIC and HMCPSI, *Exercising Discretion: The Gateway to Justice A Study on Cautions, Penalty Notices for Disorder and Restorative Justice*, 2011.

4 See the *Police and Criminal Evidence Act 1984*, for the definition of an 'appropriate adult'.

5 Essentially this means an adult who, due to a mental disorder or other reason, may have difficulty understanding the information given to them by the police. See *PACE 1984*, s. 45ZA.

any proposed OOCDs.[6] Nevertheless, even if other bodies are involved, OOCDs are ultimately issued by the police.

The police's central role in OOCDs is matched by the importance of the offender's consent. Subject to a few exceptions, discussed below, OOCDs cannot be *imposed*. The offender must admit to having committed the offence and freely accept the OOCD proposed by the police. If the police believe that an OOCD would be inappropriate, or if the offender refuses to accept it, the arrested person will either be released or formally prosecuted.[7]

The OOCD system can yield many advantages. It can improve the criminal justice system's efficiency by providing cost-effective ways to end a criminal investigation as swiftly as possible, freeing up the police, prosecutors and courts to deal with more serious cases. This helps reduce delays in criminal courts and the need for pre-trial detention (remand). OOCDs also help offenders to acknowledge their guilt, take responsibility for their actions and desist their criminal behaviour before it becomes a lifestyle. They produce better rehabilitation rates compared to formal prosecutions, particularly with youth-orientated OOCDs which divert minors away from crime, avoid stigmatisation, and decrease re-offending rates.[8]

---

6 For further details, see *PACE 1984 Code C*, 2023, available at https://www.gov.uk/government/publications/pace-code-c-2023/pace-code-c-2023-accessible [accessed on June 10th, 2024].

7 See Chapter D2 *'The Decision to Prosecute and Diversion'* [in:] D. Ormerod, D. Perry, *Blackstone's Criminal Practice, 34th ed.*, OUP 2024; and *Code for Crown Prosecutors*, paras 7.1–7.2, available at https://www.cps.gov.uk/publication/code-crown-prosecutors [accessed on June 10th, 2024].

8 Almost 50% of adults released from prison re-offend within a year of their release. Thoe who receive short sentences have even higher re-offending rates. The re-offending rate for those receiving non-custodial sentences is about 29%. See Ministry of Justice *Guide to proven reoffending statistics: April 2024*; L.N. Pappas, A.L. Dent, 'The 40-year debate: a Meta-Review on What Works for Juvenile Offenders', *Journal of Experimental Criminology*, 2023/19, pp. 1–30; S.C. Noah Uhrig, K. Atherton, *Reoffending Following Custodial Sentences or Community Orders, by Offence Seriousness and Offender Characteristics, 2000–2018*, Ministry of Justice 2020; P. Neyroud, *Out of Court Disposals Managed by the Police: A Review of the Evidence*, NPCC 2018; J. Gormley, M. Hamilton, I. Belton, *The Effectiveness of Sentencing Options on Reoffending*, Sentencing Council, London 2022; Ministry of Justice, *Consultation on Out of Court Disposals*, 2014; D. Wilson, I. Brennan, A. Olaghere, 'Police Initiated Diversion for Youth to Prevent Future Delinquent Behaviour', *Campbell Systematic Reviews*, 2018/14(1), pp. 1–88; S. Case, A. Browning, *Child First Justice: the Research Evidence-Base*, Loughborough 2021.

From the offender's perspective, OOCDs obviate the need for a formal prosecution and public trial. It can be extremely stressful awaiting trial, even for those not on remand. Those who are awaiting a trial may consider it futile to make changes to their lives, such as seeking new employment or moving home, until the results of their trial are known, whereas someone who accepted an OOCD can rebuild their life immediately, knowing that no trial or potential imprisonment awaits them.

Financially speaking, OOCDs are much less costly than court trials.[9] The costs of the police, courts, prisons and rehabilitation caused by re-offending place significant demands on the state budget and can cause systemic logistical problems. In June 2024, HM Prison and Probation Service announced that it expected jails in England and Wales to be so overcrowded by July 2024 that it would be impossible to accommodate more inmates, whether on remand (pre-trial) or post-conviction.[10] Traditional trials can also be costly for convicted offenders

9 It is notoriously difficult to accurately calculate the total public costs of an average trial, because such costs combine numerous elements, such as those of the police and the CPS, defence lawyers (who may be funded via the legal aid system), magistrates' costs (most are unpaid but are entitled to expenses), professional judges and juries, witness, experts, the maintenance of court buildings, staff and many other factors. In November 2023, the Ministry of Justice stated that, although the full average cost of a trial "cannot be reliably quantified", the average cost of a Crown Court sitting day in 2022–23 was £3,036 per day (see: https://questions-statements.parliament.uk/written-questions/detail/2023-11-30/4726) [accessed on June 10th, 2024]. This excluded all other costs related to the trial process. The CPS estimates that its staff preparation costs for magistrates' court trials are £650 and £4,380 for Crown Court trials (see https://www.cps.gov.uk/legal-guidance/costs-annex-1) and a defence lawyer's fees may cost somewhere in the region of £15,000-£30,000 + VAT for a typical Crown Court trial (see https://brittontime.com/2021/10/05/what-is-the-crown-court-and-what-type-of-cases-go-there) [accessed on June 10th, 2024]. Put simply, it is indisputable that the costs of criminal litigation are significantly higher than the costs of the OOCD system.

10 Ministry of Justice data from 14/6/2024 showed a total prison capacity of 88,815 and a prison population of 87,347. Such "operational capacity breaking point" can trigger a crisis mechanism called Operation Early Dawn, whereby offenders are detained in police cells until prison spaces are available. Those currently in prison may be released early to free up space. Prosecutors may delay trials and the courts are encouraged to delay imposing custodial sentences. See R. Syal, 'Prisons in England and Wales will be at 'breaking point' in July, governors told', Guardian, June 20th, 2024, available at: https://www.gov.uk/government/publications/prison-population-figures-2024 [accessed on June 10th, 2024].

who are ordered to pay a fine, compensation and/or the Victim Surcharge.[11] The court can also require convicted offenders to contribute towards the prosecution and trial costs.[12]

In essence, OOCDs can provide a quick, cost-efficient and effective alternative to traditional trial-orientated methods for disposing of criminal cases. They are broadly supported by the police, legal practitioners, victims' organisations, judges and all political parties. However, despite their undeniable advantages, OOCDs can cause concern as to whether the pursuit of efficiency sometimes comes at the cost of fairness. The remainder of this chapter explores such concerns, firstly by explaining how the informal development of the OOCD system placed informality and police discretion at its epicentre. These characteristics are central to the OOCD system's functionality but they are also the root cause of concerns regarding its fairness.

3. Development of the OOCD system

The OOCD system did not spring into existence on one rainy English morning, following the adoption or amendment of a Code of Criminal Law, not least because the United Kingdom has never had a Criminal Code, nor any other meta-level code.[13] Rather, like much of the English common law, it developed incrementally and organically, as a "constructive and pragmatic response"[14] to perceived societal problems and needs.

The seeds of a fledgling OOCD system can be traced back to police warnings. If a police officer detained or arrested someone whom they felt had committed a crime (or, perhaps, simply acted inappropriately), an officer might 'have a word'

11 This was created by the *Criminal Justice Act 2003*. Convicted offenders may be required to pay money to the Victim and Witness General Fund, which is used to fund victim/witness support and restorative justice programmes. See details, see Ministry of Justice, *Victims and Witnesses Funding Awards*, MoJ 2012.

12 Section 18 of the *Prosecution of Offences Act 1985* entitles the CPS to ask the court to order a convicted defendant, or unsuccessful appellant to contribute to the trial costs, which the CPS routinely does. For details of the standard requested amounts, see: *CPS Prosecution Guidance, Annex 1: Costs*, at https://www.cps.gov.uk/legal-guidance/costs-annex-1#.[accessed on June 10th, 2024].

13 For a discussion of England's unique legal history, see *inter alia* R.C. Van Caenegem, *The Birth of the English Common Law*, CUP 1988; J. Baker, *An Introduction to English Legal History, 5th ed*, OUP 2019; Holdsworth, W.S., *A History of English Law* (1923), Methuen & Co.

14 Per Lord Bingham in *R (R) v Durham Constabulary* [2005] UKHL 2, at para 3.

with the wrongdoer rather than arrest them. It is sensible for such an informal option to exist, otherwise police officers might be forced to choose between two possibly inappropriate extremes, namely ignoring the wrongdoing altogether or arresting and prosecuting the wrongdoer. Naturally, the 'system' of warnings was non-statutory. It relies on officers' common-sense assessments of situations, including their seriousness, the harm involved and the wrongdoer's response. A comparable 'system' probably exists in every country, albeit in the extra-legal world outside the statute books. It is impossible to know precisely when it began or how many such warnings have been issued over time.

Warnings of this kind had no formal consequences, but officers might record them in their note-books and check these if they encountered the wrongdoer again. Over time, regional police forces made collective records of their individual officers' notes. If the same wrongdoer was arrested, even by different officers, these collective records could help the police to decide whether to prosecute. A person with multiple previous warnings would be more likely to be prosecuted.

Police 'warnings' were later joined by police 'cautions', issued to people who were arrested but not formally prosecuted.[15] They would be released and 'cautioned' that if they re-offended, they would be prosecuted in the future. Such 'cautions' were recorded on the local police station's records. Originally, police records were paper notes, stored and available only locally or regionally. As time and technology progressed, however, they became electronic records. At first, these were stored on local police computers and accessible solely by the relevant police station but, by 1995, all warnings and cautions were recorded on the Police National Computer ("PNC")[16] and accessible by police forces nationwide.

Cautions were more 'formal' than warnings. They were only issued at police stations to people who had been arrested and admitted to having committed the relevant offence. Cautions needed to be expressly accepted by the offender after having been informed that accepting a caution could increase the likelihood of

15 For further details, see D. Steer, *Police Cautions – A Study in the Exercise of Police Discretion*, Blackwells Penal Research Unit, Oxford 1970; J.A. Ditchfield, *Police Cautioning in England and Wales*, HMSO 1976; E. Campbell,'Two Futures for Police Cautioning', [in:] P. Francis, P. Davies, V. Jupp (eds), *Policing Futures*, Palgrave Macmillan, London 1997, pp. 51–79.

16 The PNC is a national police database that was created in the 1970s. It became central to the Criminal Records Certificate ('disclosure') system created by *Part V* of the *Police Act 1997*, discussed later in this chapter. Alongside the PNC, the UK police also use other national databases: the Police National Database (PND), IDENT1 (a fingerprint database) and the National DNA Database (NDNAD).

prosecution if he/she offended again. The offender was usually made to sign a declaration to this effect. In contrast, 'street warnings' could be issued anywhere, without requiring an arrest, and to someone who denied any wrongdoing. In other words, warnings could be *imposed*, whereas cautions required mutual *consent*.

Although it is unclear when the police first started to issue cautions, they have a significant lineage. In *R (ex parte L) v Chief Constable of Kent*,[17] Tasker Watkins LJ suggested that the practice may have begun in 1928, around the time that the Home Office first started to publish statistics on cautions, whereas in *R (Stratton) v Chief Constable of Thames Valley Police*, Sir John Thomas LJ thought that it dated back to the early nineteenth century.[18] The *Habitual Criminal Act 1859* required local police forces to monitor recidivists by keeping a register of convicts in their area,[19] so the practice of registering cautions probably developed alongside this. A parallel, informal 'system' of issuing youth warnings and cautions also developed over time, with the earliest records coming from Glasgow in 1905.[20]

This nascent OOCD system continued for numerous decades, with only minor alterations. Any policies or practices on warnings and cautions were developed locally by the Chief Constable of each regional police force. Inevitably, this created inconsistencies in how OOCDs were used, including fundamental issues such as which rank of officer could issue cautions, how the consequences of cautions should be explained, and how long warnings, cautions and other information gained during investigations should be retained on police records. In 1962 a Royal Commission on the Police noted that the considerable discretion available to local police had produced significant inconsistencies in the use of cautions. In 1981, the Royal Commission on Criminal Procedure made similar remarks.[21]

In 1978, the Home Office issued its first guidelines ('circulars') aimed at reducing such inconsistencies and in 1985, it issued *Guidance on Cautioning*

---

17 [1991] 93 Cr App R 416, at 418.

18 [2013] EWHC 1561 (Admin), para 21.

19 See M.W. Melling, 'Cleaning House in a Suddenly Closed Society: The Genesis, Brief Life and Untimely Death of the Habitual Criminals Act, 1869', 21 Osgoode Hall Law Journal 1983, pp. 273–308; T. Thomas, 'A Short History of Criminal Records', *Criminal Records*, Palgrave Macmillan, London 2007.

20 2013] EWHC 1561 (Admin), para 22.

21 C. Phillips, The Royal Commission on Criminal Procedure Report, House of Commons 1981, paras 4.54–4.57. See also R. Evans, C. Wilkinson, 'Variations in police cautioning policy and practise in England and Wales', *Howard Journal of Criminal Justice* 1990/29, pp. 155–176; H. Giller, N. Tutt, 'Police cautioning of juveniles: The continuing practice of diversity', *Criminal Law Review*, 1987 pp. 367–374.

for Adults. However, the British police are constitutionally independent from the government, so ministerial guidelines do not bind them.[22] Instead, regional Chiefs of Police were responsible for creating guidelines for their own regions. These perhaps took account of ministerial guidelines but were not obliged to. For example, although the 1985 guidelines recommended that cautions be kept on record for 3 years, regional practice varied considerably. Likewise, neither the Association of Chief Police Officers ("ACPO")[23] nor the National Police Chiefs' Council ("NPCC") which replaced it,[24] can adopt rules which bind regional police forces. These organisations were intended to provide a forum for regional police forces to discuss policies or best practices but not to generate rules which bind regional forces or remove their discretion.

The next evolutionary step in the OOCD system was statutory intervention. The *Street Offences Act 1959* contained the first explicit statutory reference to cautions,[25] but did not seek to regulate how cautions were issued. It merely acknowledged that cautions existed in police practice. As inconsistent practice became more apparent, however, Parliament adopted more interventionist techniques. One Parliamentary tactic in this regard is illustrated by *s. 37A* of the *Police and Criminal Evidence Act ("PACE") 1984*. This permits the chief officer of the Crown Prosecution System ("CPS"), the Director of Public Prosecutions ("DPP"), to issue guidance on various matters which bind prosecutors and which the police must "have regard to" when deciding whether to caution someone. Although

---

22 Lord Denning MR famously said in *Blackburn v Commissioner of the Police for the Metropolis [1968] 2 QB 118*, paras 135–6, that a Chief of Police is "*...independent of the executive. He is not subject to the orders of the Secretary of State... No minister of the Crown can tell him that he must, or must not... prosecute this man or that one. [....]. The responsibility for law enforcement lies on him. He is answerable to the law and to the law alone.*"

23 The ACPO was created in 1948. Technically, it was a private company which organised meetings between representatives of regional police forces. It was not entitled to instruct regional police forces how to act, but it operated as forum for o discuss and agree standard policies on police-related matters, which could then be adopted or adapted by regional forces.

24 The NPCC replaced the ACPO in 2015, following criticism of the ACPO's lack of transparency, in a review conducted by General Sir Nick Parker in 2013. As a private company, the ACPO was not subject to the *Freedom of Information Act 2000*, and it had suggested policies which were found to be unlawful by the European Court of Human Rights. See *S. and Marper v. the United Kingdom (Applications nos. 30562/04 and 30566/04) [2008]*.

25 s.2(1) of that Act (now repealed) applied to a women who was "cautioned for loitering or soliciting" on the basis that the police suspected her to be a prostitute.

this normative obligation perhaps strengthened the *de facto* impact of the DPP's guidelines, it does not make it unlawful for the police's cautioning decisions to depart from them. Moreover, the CPS's role in the OOCD system is limited,[26] so the DPP's guidelines had limited impact.

Parliament has also broadened the scope of the OOCD system by creating new types of warnings, cautions and other OOCD mechanisms. It has also broadened the ways in which information stored on the PNC is used. Originally, police records were used solely to decide whether to prosecute re-offenders. With time, such information was also supplied to the courts to help them pass appropriate sentences on offenders who were convicted after prosecution.[27] It was also provided to employers or organisations for whom a person with a criminal record, including OOCDs, wished to perform paid or unpaid work.

The final evolutive step to date is that Parliament has adopted certain OOCD-related rules, which allow the police no discretion in how to apply them. Examples include the disclosure rules in the *Police Act 1997* (as amended). These dictate when the police and the Disclosure and Barring Service ("DBS"),[28] must inform employers about a person's criminal record, including any OOCDs. They include numerous *"bright line rules…[which leave]… no room for case by case consideration…"*,[29] such as those requiring the disclosure of serious offences, regardless of when they were committed or any mitigating circumstances surrounding them.[30] Nonetheless, on other issues, discussed further below, the Act permits significant police discretion, such as whether lesser offences, or even acquittals and other information about a person possessed by the police, should be disclosed during enhanced criminal record checks.

In summary, the OOCD system evolved from informal police practice, devoid of any legislative basis. It reflected a sensible compromise between prosecuting and taking no action whatsoever. Its *raison d'être* was to facilitate police discretion. However, discretion can result in inconsistency and the creation of some

---

26 As discussed further below, the CPS must be consulted before a conditional caution can be issued, but otherwise the police need not consult or seek the approval of the CPS when issuing OOCDs.

27 2013] EWHC 1561 (Admin), para 47.

28 The DBS was created by *s. 87* and *Schedule 8* of the *Protection of Freedoms Act 2012*. Its website is: https://www.gov.uk/government/organisations/disclosure-and-barring-service

29 Lady Hale in *Gallagher and others (P, W, G) v Secretary of State for the Home Department and another [2019] UKSC 3*, at para 77.

30 See, for example, *s. 113A* on Criminal Record Certificates.

harmonising rules by Parliament should not distract from the huge scope of police discretion that remains, just as the existence of the Galápagos Islands should not distract from the breadth of the surrounding ocean. Various governments have struggled to decide the proper balance between, on the one hand, harmonising police practice (which is only truly achievable via prescriptive legislative rules) and, on the other hand, retaining the police discretion and informality at the heart of the OOCD system. The present system is a complex and confusing patchwork of primary and secondary legislation,[31] court judgments, important but non-binding guidelines and a remaining ocean, or at least a sea, of police discretion. This short chapter merely scratches the surface of the issues involved.

4. OOCD mechanisms

A variety of OOCD mechanisms exist. Generally, any OOCD can be applied to any offence, although legislation may modify this general rule.[32] There is no crime which is, according to statute, so serious that it cannot be disposed of by way of an OOCD, although additional procedures apply if the police wish to apply OOCDs to serious offences.[33] In reality, the police are unlikely to apply OOCDs to the most serious (indictable) offences, or to mid-ranking offences (triable either way)

---

31 The complex web of statutory instruments includes at least the following: the *Misuse of Drugs Act 1971*; the *Rehabilitation of Offenders Act 1974* and *Rehabilitation of Offenders Act 1974 (Exceptions) Order 1975*, both of which are amended on an almost annual basis; the *Road Traffic Offenders Act 1988*; the *Crime and Disorder Act 1998*; the *Police Act 1997* (and related secondary legislation including the *Police Act 1997 (Criminal Records) (Amendment) Regulations 2013* and subsequent amendments); the *Criminal Justice and Police Act 2001*; the *Police Reform Act 2002*; the *Criminal Justice Act 2003*; the *Road Traffic Safety Act 2006*; the *Criminal Justice and Immigration Act 2008*; the *Legal Aid, Sentencing and Punishment of Offenders Act ("LASPO") 2012*; the *Fixed Penalty Offences Order 2013*; the *Antisocial Behaviour Crime and Policing Act 2014*; the *Criminal Justice and Courts Act 2015*; the *Policing and Crime Act 2017; the Domestic Abuse Act 2021*; and the *Police, Crime, Sentencing and Courts Act 2022.*

32 E.g. PNDs, discussed below, can only be applied to "penalty offences", as defined by the *Criminal Justice and Police Act 2001*. This includes things such as "failing to remove immediately any faeces deposited by an animal of which that person is in charge", contrary to *Regulation 3(6)* of the *Royal Parks and Other Open Spaces Regulations 1997.*

33 For example, *p. 17* of the *Criminal Justice and Courts Act 2015* stipulates that a caution shall not be given for indictable-only or certain either-way offences (e.g. those involving carrying an offensive weapon; child cruelty; certain sexual and drug-related offences) unless there are "exceptional circumstances relating to the person or the offence" and, as regards indictable offences, where the Director of Public Prosecutions has consented.

committed in circumstances which would probably see the courts impose a lengthy period of imprisonment to anyone who might be prosecuted.[34] Nonetheless, this is due to the police's commonsensical practice rather than formal legal limitations.

The National Police Chiefs Council (NPCC) has published a "gravity matrix"[35] to help police forces decide whether to prosecute or to propose an OOCD. It is a points-based system for calculating the seriousness of an offence and any mitigating or aggravating factors.[36] A comparable "Child Gravity Matrix" exists in relation to youth OOCDs.[37] These matrices are used in conjunction with the National Decision-Making Model and various guidelines issued by the College of Policing and the Home Office.[38] As noted above, however, such guidelines are non-binding. Some police forces have developed local versions of these "gravity matrices" and policies on using particular OOCD mechanisms (e.g. cannabis warnings), which may differ from the guidelines.

4.1. Warnings and notices

Originally, 'street warnings' merely involved officers noting that they had reprimanded a wrongdoer for their behaviour. This need not entail an arrest nor any admission of guilt. Indeed, warnings of this kind may be issued in relation to behaviour that is not even unlawful. Other, more 'formal' types of warning have since developed, either as a result of police practice or statutory intervention.

Police Information Notices (PINs), known colloquially as 'Harassment Warning Notices', are non-statutory. Various police forces started issuing them following the adoption of the *Protection from Harassment Act 1997*, if an officer deemed someone's behaviour to be harassment. No admission of guilt is required. PINs have no formal consequence, so they cannot be appealed against. Data on the number of PINs issued is only available on local police records rather than via the PNC, but a House of Commons Home Affairs Committee has noted that

34 Account will be taken of the *Sentencing Act 2020* and the Sentencing Code it created. However, more, concrete answers can be seen in the Magistrates' Court and Crown Court sentencing guidelines, available at https://www.sentencingcouncil.org.uk/offences/ and https://www.sentencingcouncil.org.uk/court-type/crown-court/ [accessed on June 10th, 2024].

35 National Police Chief's Council, *Gravity Matrix (Adult): Two-Tier Framework* (2019), NPCC.

36 J. Brown, G. Sturge, R. McInnes, *House of Commons*, *op.cit.*, p. 8.

37 National Police Chief's Council, *Child Gravity Matrix* (2023), NPCC.

38 Available at: https://www.college.police.uk/app/national-decision-model/national-decision-model [accessed on June 10th, 2024].

thousands of PINs are issued annually.[39] They may be disclosed in the 'enhanced' disclosure procedure, discussed below.

Community Protection Notices (CPNs) were created by the *Anti-Social Behaviour, Crime and Policing Act 2014*. They can be imposed on anyone aged over 16 or on any legal body whose "unreasonable" conduct has "*...a detrimental effect, of a persistent or continuing nature, on the quality of life of those in the locality...*".[40] CPNs can demand that particular conduct be ceased, or specify conduct that must be done. Failure to comply is a criminal offence.[41] Comparable rules apply to *Criminal Behaviour Orders* (CBOs), *Public Spaces Protection Orders* (PSPOs) and *Closure of Nuisance Premises Orders*, all of which are regulated by the 2014 Act. Other Acts entitling the police (and certain other state bodies) to issue notices and warnings include the *Environmental Protection Act 1990*, which regulates *Noise Abatement Orders*.[42] The police must issue the wrongdoer a written warning before issuing any of the special warnings discussed in this paragraph.

Penalty Notices for Disorder[43] ("PNDs") are fixed penalties (typically ranging from £60 to £90) that the police can impose for a specified range of low-level offences.[44] Some wrongdoers are invited to undertake educational training instead of paying a fine (these are known as PND-Es). The offender has 21 days to pay the PND or to request a court hearing to challenge it. Paying the penalty is not an admission of guilt, but failure to pay may result in prosecution. PNDs cannot be issued to anyone who is under 18 or unable to understand why the PND was issued.[45]

---

39 See House of Commons Home Affairs Committee, *Police Information Notices*, HMSO 2015, para 4.

40 See s. 43. See also Home Office, *Anti-social Behaviour, Crime and Policing Act 2014: Anti-social behaviour powers - Statutory guidance for frontline professionals* (2023), HMSO.

41 Ibidem, p. 48.

42 See *Environmental Protection Act 1990, s. 80A*, as inserted by the *Noise and Statutory Nuisance Act 1993*.

43 PNDs were introduced by the *Criminal Justice and Police Act 2001* (pp. 1–11) and later amended by p. 132 and *Schedule 23* of the *Legal Aid, Sentencing and Punishment of Offenders Act 2012*.

44 This includes shoplifting (property not exceeding £100), criminal damage (not exceeding £300), throwing fireworks, misuse of the 999 service or making threatening calls, possession of cannabis or khat For a full list of relevant offences, see the table at p. 25 of Ministry of Justice, *Penalty Notices for Disorder*, HMSO 2014.

45 *Legal Aid, Sentencing and Punishment of Offenders Act 2012, s. 132* and *Schedule 23*.

Fixed Penalty Notices (FPNs) are similar to PNDs, but they can also be issued to youths and by a variety of non-police bodies (e.g. traffic wardens, local council enforcement officers, train conductors).[46] FPNs are commonly used in relation to minor traffic offences or regulatory breaches.

Two more 'formal' warnings were created after the *Misuse of Drugs Act 1971* was amended to downgrade cannabis and khat to Class C drugs in 2004 and 2014, respectively.[47] *Cannabis warnings* and *khat warnings* are the most 'formal' types of warnings, because they can only be imposed on adults who admits to having committed the relevant 'drug possession' offence. Also, they are recorded on the PNC. Unlike other warnings, only one cannabis/khat warning can be given, so anyone who reoffends will probably receive a PND and then be prosecuted for any third offence.[48] In most other respects, the rules applicable to warnings are comparable. The common denominator is that they do not form part of a person's formal 'criminal record', so employees need not disclose them to employers. However, the police may disclose them during enhanced criminal records checks, as discussed below.

4.2. Community Resolutions

Community Resolutions (CRs) are non-statutory, informal OOCDs developed by police practice. They do not result in a criminal record and are not recorded on the PNC, but are recorded on local police computers and may be disclosed during enhanced criminal records checks.

CRs are essentially contracts between the police and offenders who admit to having committed the relevant crime and agree to undertake specified activities to rehabilitate or punish them or to provide reparation to the victim or to the community (e.g. apologising to a victim or repairing damaged or vandalised property).[49] CRs are typically administered to non-serious, first-time offenders, but no

46 FPNs may apply to things such as breaches of noise restrictions, littering, dog fouling, cycling on pavements, smoking in prohibited areas etc. For Cambridge City Council's FPN policy, see https://democracy.cambridge.gov.uk/documents/s63640/FPN%20Review%202023%20Report.pdf [accessed on June 10th, 2024].

47 The *Misuse of Drugs Act 1971 (Modification) (No. 2) Order 2003* took effect from 29/1/2004. See Explanatory Memorandum to the *Misuse of Drugs Act 1971 (Amendment) Order 2014.*

48 CoP Description of OOCD outcomes, J. Brown, G. Sturge, R. McInnes, *House of Commons… loc.cit.*

49 See National Police Chiefs' Council *Community Resolutions Guidelines*, 2022; and J. Brown, G. Sturge, R. McInnes, *House of Commons, loc.cit.*

formal limits prevent them from being used in relation to more serious crimes, and reports exist of police inconsistencies in this respect.[50] Victims are usually consulted about whether to issue a CR, but their views do not bind the police.

4.3. Cautions

As noted above, cautions have a long history. Currently, two types of cautions exist. *Simple cautions* (sometimes called 'formal' cautions[51]) do not require the offender to undertake (or refrain from) any action other than admitting guilt and accepting the caution.[52] They can be applied to any offence but are unlikely to be used in sexual, violent or serious offences. The offender must voluntarily and clearly admit to the offence, and there must be reliable, credible and admissible evidence[53] which gives a realistic prospect that the offender would be convicted if prosecuted. There must be no inducement or coercion to accept the caution, and the offender must be given time to consider and take independent legal advice if necessary.

The police must consider it in the public interest to issue a caution rather than prosecuting,[54] taking into account a range of factors, such as the seriousness of the offence, the offender's culpability, age, maturity level and previous criminal record, the harm suffered by any victim or the community, the victim's views etc. If so, the custody officer, not the arresting officer, explains the implications of a caution and asks for the offender's consent to issue the caution. No harmonised version exists of the words that custody officers use when issuing a caution, but it should be clear that, although a caution is not a conviction, it will be stored on the PNC and may have consequences in the future. For many years, regional police practices differed as to whether offenders were required to sign a formal Caution

---

50 See N. Westmarland, K. Johnson, C. McGlynn, 'Under the radar: The widespread use of 'out of court resolutions' in policing domestic violence and abuse in the United Kingdom', *The British Journal of Criminology*, 2017/58(1), pp. 1–16.

51 This term ceased to be used after the *Criminal Justice Act 2003* created conditional cautions.

52 See MoJ, *Simple Cautions: Guidance for Police and Prosecutors*, HMSO 2013; and MoJ, *Simple Cautions for Adult Offenders*, 2015, which should be read together with the *Director's Guidance on Charging issued by the Director of Public Prosecutions under section 37A of the PACE 1984*, available at https://www.cps.gov.uk/legal-guidance/directors-guidance-charging-sixth-edition-december-2020-incorporating-national-file [accessed on June 10th, 2024].

53 Para 4.7 of the Crown Prosecution Service, *Code for Crown Prosecutors*, 2018.

54 *Ibid*, paras. 4.9–4.13

Acknowledgement Declaration, but this is now universal practice, although the precise wording of such a declaration differs between regions.[55]

Conditional cautions were created by the *Criminal Justice Act 2003*. The Ministry of Justice has issued a Code of Practice regarding adult conditional cautions[56] and the CPS has published guidance which binds prosecutors but is non-binding for the police.[57] For present purposes, it suffices to say that conditional cautions resemble simple cautions in all but two important aspects. Firstly, they impose conditions on the offender which the police deem, and the offender agrees, are suitable to the particular offender, offence and circumstances (e.g. attending rehabilitation programs, avoiding certain places or people, complying with a curfew, apologising and/or paying compensation to the victim etc.) Non-compliance can result in prosecution. Secondly, the caution and conditions must be approved by the CPS, to ensure that they are appropriate, proportionate, and enforceable. Neither the police nor the prosecution can issue a caution without the other's approval. Ultimately, the police issue the caution but if the CPS consider that a caution is appropriate yet the police wish to prosecute, the CPS can refuse to accept the case for prosecution, leaving the police to either issue a caution or release the offender.

4.4. Youth OOCDs

Many adult OOCD mechanisms have equivalent versions that can be applied to youth offenders. The minimum age of criminal responsibility in England and Wales and Northern Ireland is 10 years old,[58] so youth OOCDs can be applied to anyone aged between 10–17. These include *Community Resolutions, Youth Cautions* and *Youth Conditional Cautions* each of which mirrors the requirements of their adult counterparts. They must be issued in the presence of an "appropriate adult",[59] and only after consulting the Youth Offending Team.[60] Until the *Legal Aid,*

55 *Supra* n. 52, para 80.

56 MoJ, *Code of Practice for Adult Conditional Cautions*, HMSO 2013.

57 Available at https://www.cps.gov.uk/legal-guidance/conditional-cautioning-adults-dpp-guidance [accessed on June 10th, 2024].

58 In Scotland, the minimum age of criminal responsibility is 12. Lord Bingham, in para. 2 of *R (ex parte F) v. Durham Constabulary and others [2005] UKHL 21*, noted that this is a younger age than in most European countries.

59 See *Legal Aid, Sentencing and Punishment of Offenders Act 2012*, pp. 135 and 135(7).

60 See N. Pamment, 'Youth Offending Teams: a multi-agency success or system failure?' [in:] A. Pycroft, D. Gough, *Multi-agency working in criminal Justice*, Bristol University Press 2010, pp. 217–230.

Sentencing and Punishment of Offenders Act 2012 entered into force, youth OOCDs also included reprimands and warnings, including *Cannabis Warnings*, but these have now been replaced so all that remains are cautions and youth CRs.

5. The statistical significance of OOCDs

The most recent crime statistics indicate that, in the reporting year ending March 2023, 7.7 million crimes were reported.[61] Of these, 135,439 'informal' OOCDs were issued, comprising Cannabis/Khat Warnings (3,761) and Community Resolutions (131,678). This represented 2.47% of all offences. A further 52,433 'formal' OOCDs were issued, comprising all Adult Cautions (40,937), Youth Cautions (5,148) and Penalty Notices for Disorder (6,348). This represented 0.96% of all offences. Another 32,383 offenders agreed to undertake diversionary activities instead of being prosecuted or receiving a caution.[62] Combined, the various OOCD mechanisms were used in 3.43% of the total reported cases, with cautions issued in 1% of them.[63] These numbers may seem insignificant until one realises that, for varying reasons, in over 80% of reported cases, no further action is taken and the case is dropped after being reported.[64]

---

61 Ministry of Justice, *Crime Outcomes in England and Wales 2022–2023*, HMSO 2023.

62 This includes restorative justice actions (e.g. meeting with victims to discuss the impact that the offender's actions had on the victim or their family, and how the offender can atone for this); https://www.gov.uk/government/collections/restorative-justice-action-plan [accessed on June 10th, 2024] community payback activities (e.g. performing unpaid work which benefits the community, such as cleaning public areas) – see https://www.gov.uk/community-sentences/community-payback; educational or vocational training or rehabilitation programmes (e.g. drug or alcohol awareness courses) or other intervention programmes (e.g. anger management courses, mental health workshops etc.). For further details on restorative justice and its efficacy, see: L.W. Sherman, H. Strang, *Restorative Justice: the Evidence*, Smith Institute 2007.

63 Ministry of Justice, *Crime Outcomes…*, Table 2.

64 Ibidem. This is most frequently due to evidential difficulties because the police were unable to identify a suspect (2,155,288 cases – almost 40% of all reported crimes). Also, a victim may indicate that they do not wish further action with a view to identifying a suspect (320,038 cases – 5.9%). Even in cases where the police have identified a suspect, a victim may not support further action (1,145,617 cases – 21%). Even when the victim supports further action, other evidential difficulties may result in a case being dropped (698,855 cases – 12.8%). Other reasons for discontinuing a action include the offender having been too young (i.e. under 10 years old), or being too ill or having died (collectively these represented 54,024 cases – 1% of all reported cases); or the time limit for prosecution having expired (15,901 - 0.3% of all reported cases).

Once the distorting effect of this 'no action' category is removed, a different picture arises. OCD mechanisms were applied in 220,255 cases (4.02% of reported crimes),[65] while prosecutions were initiated in 312,167 cases (5.7% of reported crimes).[66] Viewed this way, OOCDs represent an extremely common way for disposing of reported crimes.

6. Concerns regarding OOCDs

Having demonstrated their statistical significance and outlined the justifications commonly cited for their central role in the criminal justice system, it remains to discuss some concerns produced by OOCDs.

Firstly, the police have considerable discretion in deciding whether to propose OOCDs which results in inconsistent practice that is only partially remedied by NPCC and Home Office guidelines. Since the 1990s, police forces are obliged to reveal how many reported crimes in their region ended with an 'action' outcome (i.e. rather than 'inaction' which ends an investigation). OOCDs represent an 'action' outcome and their growing use may reflect a desire for the police to achieve targets more easily, without needing to conduct prosecutions.[67]

The OOCD system is complex and frequently amended by legislation, national guidelines and regional police policies. The resulting system can be remarkably confusing. The content of oral and written explanations given by police to offenders when discussing OOCDs is not harmonised, so it varies between regions. This includes the declaration signed by offenders to show that they have understood a caution's consequences. The Home Office itself has noted the existence of "*...confusion regarding the impact of a caution on a criminal record*."[68] Put simply, people who accept OOCDs may not appreciate the full wide scope of their repercussions. An understandable desire to be released from the police

65 i.e. the total of 'informal' (135,439) and 'formal' OOCDs (52,433), plus diversionary, educational or intervention activities (32,383).

66 Ibidem, Table 2.2. This low percentage is typical. The equivalent percentage in the previous year was 5.5%. Within this number, there are significant difference between various categories, such as between crimes involving the possession of weapons (27.74% of cases ended in charges being brought) or drugs (19.76%) and those involving sexual offences (3.61%) or rape (2.09%)

67 For a study on how imposing Offences Brought to Justice (OBTJ) targets impacted on police performance, see S. Grace, 'The perverse impact of performance measures on policing: Lessons from the rise and fall of out of court disposals', *Policing and Society* 2022/32, pp. 200–220.

68 College of Policing, *Review of Simple Cautions*, HMSO 2013, para 5.

station, combined with a mistaken impression that OOCDs are merely formal warnings which avert the need for a trial, in exchange for some momentary embarrassment at the police station, may result in people underestimating their potential consequences.

Such consequences may relate to the offence in respect of which the caution was issued. For example, any victim of the crime may initiate civil litigation against the offender. Furthermore, if new evidence comes to light (e.g. indicating that the circumstances of the offence are more serious), the police can withdraw the caution and prosecute. If that happens, offenders would find it very difficult to deny a crime which they had already confessed to when accepting the caution.

Other consequences may include travel restrictions. OOCDs do not *per se* limit travel unless travel restrictions form part of a *conditional* caution, but some countries may refuse to grant entry visas or residence permits to anyone whose criminal record includes an OOCD.[69] The UK immigration authorities can refuse permission for someone to enter/leave the UK on the same basis.

Depending upon the nature of the underlying offence, an OOCD may result in the person being added to the Children's Barred List or the Vulnerable Adult's Barred List, pursuant to the *Safeguarding Vulnerable Groups Act 2006*.[70] This precludes offenders from working or volunteering with such vulnerable groups, or from studying on courses which may bring them into contact with such groups.

OOCDs can also be disclosed during future court proceedings, whether to help the court pass sentence on an offender with a previous criminal record or as evidence of the offender's 'bad character' when assessing the credibility of their offender's evidence, given either as the defendant or as a witness in someone else's trial. For example, in *R. v. Olu, Wilson and Brooks*[71] the prosecution challenged the veracity of the defendant's evidence, given in a murder trial, by referring to a caution he had for possessing a weapon 5 years earlier.

Most frequently, however, OOPCs impact on an offender's future employment prospects, via a process called 'disclosure'. Employers or volunteer-based institutions (e.g. sports clubs, churches, etc.) may ask workers to disclose if they have a criminal record and may use this information to decide on their suitability for

69 The USA, Canada, Australia, New Zealand and Japan all have very strict immigration rules which may result in a visa being refused to someone who has a police caution. China, the United Arab Emirates and many other countries also require cautions to be disclosed on visa applications.

70 See p. 2 and also the *Education (Prohibition from Teaching or Working with Children) Regulations 2003*.

71 [2011] 1 Cr. App. R. 33. See also Criminal Procedure Rules 2010, r.35.4.

work. To prevent offenders from being permanently disadvantaged by their past, most convictions become 'spent' after a defined period (depending on the crime), so workers can lawfully withhold information about such convictions. Cautions are not technically convictions and originally were never deemed to be 'spent', regardless of when they occurred. The *Criminal Justice and Immigration Act 2008* (CJIA 2008) changed this, so that simple cautions are 'spent' immediately and conditional cautions become 'spent' three months later,[72] or earlier if the relevant conditions cease to apply sooner.[73] However, cautions never become 'spent' and still need to be disclosed by persons working in a long list of certain professions (lawyers, medics, accountants, etc.), positions (teachers, police constables, traffic wardens, etc.) or regulated occupations (firearms dealers, insurance company managers, securities dealers etc.)[74]

Moreover, employers can also obtain information about an employee's criminal record from the police, pursuant to the *Police Act 1997*. The police's disclosure duty was narrowed over time to exclude many 'spent' convictions and cautions,[75] but these are still disclosed to certain types of employers and in relation to certain professions, as noted above.[76] Moreover, if an offender wishes to undertake work involving contact with children or vulnerable adults, an 'enhanced' criminal records certificate ("ECRC") is required and the police may disclose not only convictions and cautions, but also any other OOCD history, including 'informal' OOCDs such as warnings, PINs, CPNs, PNDs, FPNs, cannabis/khat warnings and CRs, many of which did not even require an admission of guilt. Furthermore, the police may disclose any other information they possess,[77] including "soft intelligence"[78] going far beyond what many might imagine could be lawfully retained or disclosed. The test for disclosing such information is that the Chief of Police must reasonably believe that it might be relevant to the employment position and so ought to be included.[79] This test is a 'beefed-up' version from the one originally

---

72 *Criminal Justice and Immigration Act 2008, s. 49* and *para 6* of *Schedule 10.*

73 See *Rehabilitation of Offenders Act 1972, Schedule 2* and *Legal Aid, Sentencing and Punishment of Offenders Act 2012, s. 139(7)(a).*

74 See *Schedule 1* of the *Rehabilitation of Offenders Act 1974 (Exceptions) Order 1975.*

75 *Criminal Justice and Immigration Act 2008, p. 50(2)(b).*

76 See *Regulation 5A* of the *Police Act 1997 (Criminal Records) Regulations 2002 (SI 2002/233)* and *Rehabilitation of Offenders Act 1974 (Exceptions) Order 1975*, as amended.

77 *Police Act 1997, 113B(4).*

78 Per Lord Wilson in *R (ex parte T and another) v SSHD [2014] UKSC 35* at paras 10–12.

79 *Protection of Freedoms Act 2012 p. 82(1)(b).*

enacted, which did not require the Chief's opinion to be a reasonable one, but it still remains remarkably discretionary. Such discretion, combined with the breadth of information that ECRCs can reveal, can produce shocking results. At the very least, it focuses attention on the balance stuck between, on the one hand, protecting children and vulnerable groups from potentially dangerous people and, on the other hand, allowing offenders to leave their criminal pasts behind them and start afresh.

Many cases show how difficult it can be to create a test that is flexible enough to retain some necessary police discretion whilst being clear enough to produce predictable, proportionate results based on something more than mere police discretion.[80] In *R v Local Authority and Police Authority in the Midlands, Ex p LM*[81] an ECRC included allegations of child sexual abuse made against an employee. Following an investigation by the employer, no action was taken and the police felt that the allegations were unsubstantiated by evidence, so did not prosecute. Nonetheless, the allegations were disclosed and the employer terminated an offer of work. In *R (X) v Chief Constable of the West Midlands Police*,[82] an ECRC noted that the police had discontinued an investigation into an alleged indecent exposure after the victim failed to identify X as the perpetrator. No charges were brought and no caution was issued, but the fact that the allegation was made against X was disclosed on the ECRC, which resulted in him being rejected for a teaching job. In *YZ v Chief Constable of South Wales Police*,[83] an ECRC disclosed that YZ had been charged with rape 10 years earlier, but unanimously acquitted. An acquittal is not a sufficient reason for removing data from police files. As Andrews LJ put it: "*...the fact of an acquittal establishes no more than that, on the evidence adduced at trial, the jury were not sure that the individual committed the offence. The fact that there was sufficient evidence to charge the person with that offence, particularly if it is a serious offence of violence, may be highly relevant to an assessment of the risks that they might pose in the future.*"[84] ECRCs can disclose information that "...could not be described as criminal behaviour at all",[85] such as a person being related to a third party who has committed a criminal offence. The disclosed information can, in reality, be little more than "*...rumour, conjecture*

80 See C. Ventham, B. Collier, R. Cohen, R. Talalay, J. Wright, 'Judicial Reviews Claims Involving the Police', *Judicial Review* 2018/27(3), pp. 209–242.

81 *[2000] 1 FLR 612.*

82 *[2005] 1 WLR 65.*

83 *[2022] EWCA Civ 683.*

84 YZ, *supra* n. 83, at para 68.

85 *Supra* n. 86, at para 27.

and uncorroborated allegations"[86] but it can have the same effect as if it were a conviction and represent "*...something close to a killer blow...*"[87] to a person's chances of being allowed to work, study or volunteer.

7. Conclusion

The OOCD system has developed from historical and informal police practice into something which is an integral part of the British criminal justice system. It is probably indispensable, as it not only offers potential benefits to offenders and victims but also eases the pressure that would otherwise exist on the police, courts and government to prosecute the quarter-of-a-million crimes that are currently disposed of by OOCDs.

In some respects, the OOCD is system is unremarkable. Most, if not all, countries have informal systems for issuing police warnings and fines. The ubiquity of a non-judicial system for imposing penalties does not automatically make it untroublesome, however, and further consideration should be given to the safeguards built-in to such systems. The British OOCD model, originally designed by the police with the aim of increasing their discretion, remains influenced more by local practices and non-binding guidelines than clear statutory rules, which perhaps falls short of the safeguards that ought to exist. Traditional trials are regulated by numerous, binding rules to ensure that the accused enjoys due process, an equality of arms and the right to a reasoned decision. Each of these is significantly weakened by OOCDs, which enables the police to impose a variety of warnings and fines on people who may deny any wrongdoing and to issue cautions which can have such wide-ranging repercussions, even decades after they were issued. Some have gone so far as to suggest that, by delegating so many aspects of the dispensation of justice to the police, traditional trials have "*...become an accident in the smooth administration of criminal justice.*"[88]

Furthermore, inconsistencies in police practice between regions are regularly noted, both as regards the extent and ways in which OOCDs are used and the

86 Lord Hope in *R (ex parte L) v Commissioner of Police of the Metropolis [2009] UKSC 3*, at para 33.

87 Ibidem, at para 75.

88 T. Weigend, 'Why have a Trial when you can have a Bargain?', [in:] A. Duff, L. Farmer, S. Marshall, V. Tadros, (eds.) *The Trial on Trial Vol. 2: Judgment and Calling to Account*, Hart Publishing 2006, p. 369. See also M. Langer, 'Plea Bargaining, Conviction Without Trial, and the Global Administratizarion of Criminal Convictions', *Annual Review of Criminology* 2021/4, pp. 377–411.

procedures followed when administering them. Moreover, the OOCD system has become increasingly complex as consecutive governments have tinkered with the system by creating new OOCD mechanisms or modifying guidance on how existing OOCD options should be applied. This can undermine public confidence in the system itself. The *Police, Crime, Sentencing and Courts Act 2022* includes provisions to replace the "*unwieldy… patchwork of statutory and non-statutory cautions, warnings and penalties that has been added to piecemeal over the years*."[89] with a two-tier framework, consisting of (i) Diversionary Cautions (more serious disposals involving conditions which, if infringed, can lead to prosecution for the original offence); and (ii) Community Cautions (less serious disposal with conditions which, if infringed, can result in a fine being imposed). This would end the use of simple cautions, PNDs and cannabis/khat warnings and limit OOCD options to conditional cautions and CRs. In other words, all OOCDss would involve a conditional element. However, although this 'streamlined' OOCD system was successfully piloted in 3 regional areas,[90] its nationwide entry into force was is conditional upon the adoption of secondary legislation. This did not occur before the UK elections on July 4th, 2024 and it remains unclear whether the new government will continue with these streamlining reforms, abandon them or develop new ones. Whatever happens, it seems inevitable that the OOCD system will remain an important part of British criminal justice.

Some aspects of the British OOCD model are more far-reaching than in other countries. It permits an extremely wide scope of information to be stored on police records and authorises the disclosure of such information to potential employers, including information that a person was acquitted of a crime, or not prosecuted because the police and/or prosecutors deemed the evidence insufficient. Numerous cases indicate that, as common sense would suggest, employers frequently refuse employment to someone when such information is disclosed by the police. They may feel that, as the saying goes, 'there is no smoke without fire' and prefer to play it safe by employing someone about whom the police have no derogatory information on file. Admittedly, the enhanced disclosure system

---

89 Ministry of Justice, *Diversionary and Community Cautions: Draft Code of Practice - Part 6 of the Police, Crime, Sentencing and Courts Act 2022*, HMSO 2023, at p. 3. See also J. Brown, G. Sturge, and R. McInnes, *House of Commons op.cit.*

90 See A. Ames et al., *Adult Out of Court Disposal Pilot Evaluation – Final Report*, Ministry of Justice Analytical Series 2018; R. Sturrock, A. Mews, *Analytical Summary 2018, Out of Court Disposals Pilot: Cautions Re-offending Analysis*, 2018; Ministry of Justice, *Reforms to the adult out of court disposals framework in the Police, Crime, Sentencing and Courts Bill*, HMSO 2023.

represents the exception rather than the rule, but it is a significant and frequent exception which can impact on thousands of people's lives, including those who accepted an OOCD, considering it to be a 'slap on the wrist'[91] without understanding the "*...serious adverse consequences that would follow...*".[92] The fact that such a wide scope of information, which has "*...not been tested at trial or led to a conviction...*"[93] can be retained on police records and disclosed to potential employers is certainly unusual when compared to other European countries.[94]

In a number of cases, the UK's senior courts have already declared aspects of the OOCD system to be incompatible with the ECHR, given the absence of procedural safeguards.[95] The Strasbourg court has also declared that aspects of the system reveal "*...the absence of a clear legislative framework... and the lack of clarity as to the scope, extent and restrictions of the... powers of the police to retain and disclose caution data.*"[96] The UK Parliament has adopted legislation to remedy the problems highlighted by the courts but, even after such legislative ping-pong, elements of the OOCD system remain open to criticism. Such reforms demand ongoing analysis of whether the system strikes the right balance between efficiency and procedural fairness and between the protection of vulnerable groups and the right to privacy, not only of convicted offenders but also those who accepted cautions without realising their consequences or even people who were acquitted at trial or never even prosecuted. The OOCD is here to stay, but its potential impact on the human rights of those who accept OOCDs or have an OOCD imposed on them against their will demands constant vigilance.

91 See https://unlock.org.uk/personal_story/is-a-caution-really-a-slap-on-the-wrist-not-if-you-need-a-police-certificate/

92 Per Thomas LJ in R. v. Olu, Wilson and Brooks [2011] 1 Cr. App. R. 33, at p. 404.

93 *Supra* n. 86, at paras 1 and 27. See also Lord Scott at para 51.

94 See E.L. Pijoan, 'Criminal Record Disclosure and the Right to Privacy', *Crim. L.R.* 2014/10, pp. 726–728; and A. Pivaty, 'Out-of-Court Disposals in the Dutch Criminal Process' in: E. Johnston, S. Marsh, (eds.) *Contemporary Issues in Global Criminal Justice*, 2022, p. 196.

95 See, for example, Lord Reed's reference to the absence of "...safeguards which have the effect of enabling the proportionality of the interference to be adequately examined..." in *R (ex parte T and another) v SSHD [2014] UKSC 35*, paras 108–114.

96 *M.M. v. the United Kingdom*, Case 24029/07 [2012], at para 206.

Bibliography

Allen, R., *Less Is More: The Case for Dealing with Offences* (2017), Transform Justice, available at: https://www.transformjustice.org.uk/wp-content/uploads/2017/12/November2017_Less-is-more.pdf.

Ames, A., Di Antonio, E., Hitchcock, J., Webster, S., Wong, K., Ellingworth, D., Meadows, L., McAlonan, D., Uhrig, N and Logue, C., *Adult Out of Court Disposal Pilot Evaluation – Final Report* (2018), Ministry of Justice Analytical Series, available at: https://assets.publishing.service.gov.uk/government/uploads/system/uploads/attachment_data/file/718947/adult-outof-court-disposal-pilot-evaluation.pdf

Baker, J., *An Introduction to English Legal History, 5th ed* (2019), Oxford University Press.

Blakeborough, L. and Pierpont, H., *Conditional Cautions: An Examination of the Early Implementation of the Scheme* (2007). London: Ministry of Justice.

Brown, J., Sturge, G. and McInnes, R., *House of Commons Briefing Paper on the Police, Crime, Sentencing and Courts Bill* (2021), available at: https://research-briefings.files.parliament.uk/documents/CBP-9165/CBP-9165.pdf.

Campbell, E.' 'Two Futures for Police Cautioning' in Francis, P., Davies, P., Jupp, V. (eds) *Policing Futures* (1997), Palgrave Macmillan, London.

Case, S. and Browning, A., *Child First Justice: the Research Evidence-Base* (2021), Loughborough University Report, available at https://hdl.handle.net/2134/14152040.v1.

College of Policing, *Review of Simple Cautions* (2013), HMSO, available at: https://assets.publishing.service.gov.uk/media/5a748b8840f0b616bcb17593/report-of-the-simple-cautions-review.pdf.

Crawford, A., 'The pattern of policing in the UK: Policing beyond the police' in Newburn, T., (ed.) *Handbook of Policing*, (2003).

Crown Prosecution Service, *Code for Crown Prosecutors* (2018) CPS, available at: https://www.cps.gov.uk/publication/code-crown-prosecutors -

Ditchfield, J. A., *Police Cautioning in England and Wales* (1976), HMSO.

Evans, R. and Wilkinson, C. 'Variations in police cautioning policy and practise in England and Wales (1990)' *Howard Journal of Criminal Justice*, 29.

Giller, H. and Tutt, N. 'Police cautioning of juveniles: The continuing practice of diversity', *Criminal Law Review* (1987),

Gormley, J., Hamilton, M. and Belton, I., *The Effectiveness of Sentencing Options on Reoffending* (2022), Sentencing Council, London, available at https://www.sentencingcouncil.org.uk/wp-content/uploads/Effectiveness-of-Sentencing-Options-Review-FINAL.pdf.

Grace, S., 'The perverse impact of performance measures on policing: Lessons from the rise and fall of out of court disposals', *Policing and Society* (2022), Vol 32.

HM Inspectorate of Constabulary (HMIC) and HM Crown Prosecution Service Inspectorate (HMCPSI), *Exercising Discretion: The Gateway to Justice A Study on Cautions, Penalty Notices for Disorder and Restorative Justice* (2011), available at: https://www.justiceinspectorates.gov.uk/cjji/inspections/exercising-discretion-the-gatewayto-justice-a-study-by-her-majestys-inspectorate-of-constabulary-and-her-majestys-crownprosecution-service-inspectorate-on-cautions-penalty-notices-for-disorder/

Holdsworth, W. S., *A History of English Law* (1923), Methuen & Co.

Home Office, *Anti-social Behaviour, Crime and Policing Act 2014: Anti-social behaviour powers - Statutory guidance for frontline professionals* (2023), HMSO, available at: https://assets.publishing.service.gov.uk/media/6422a19b60a35e00120cae63/2023_Update_ASB_Statutory_Guidance_-_FINAL__1_.pdf.

House of Commons Home Affairs Committee, *Out-Of-Court Disposals. Fourteenth Report of Session 2014–15* (2015), HMSO, London.

House of Commons Home Affairs Committee, *Police Information Notices* (2015), HMSO, London.

Langer, M. 'Plea Bargaining, Conviction Without Trial, and the Global Administratizarion of Criminal Convictions', *Annual Review of Criminology*, 2021/4.

Melling, M. W., 'Cleaning House in a Suddenly Closed Society: The Genesis, Brief Life and Untimely Death of the Habitual Criminals Act, 1869', *Osgoode Hall Law Journal*, 1983/21'

Ministry of Justice, *Victims and Witnesses Funding Awards* (2012), HMSO, available at: https://www.gov.uk/government/publications/victims-and-witnesses-funding-awards

Ministry of Justice, *Simple Cautions: Guidance for Police and Prosecutors* (2013), HMSO, available at: https://www.gov.uk/government/publications/simple-cautions-guidance-for-police-and-prosecutors

Ministry of Justice, *Code of Practice for Adult Conditional Cautions* (2013), HMSO, available at: https://consult.justice.gov.uk/digital-communications/code-adult-conditional-cautions/results/code-practice-adult-conditional-cautions.pdf.

Ministry of Justice *Consultation on Out of Court Disposals* (2014), HMSO, available at: https://consult.justice.gov.uk/digital-communications/out-of-court-disposals/results/out-of-court-disposals-response.pdf

Ministry of Justice, *Penalty Notices for Disorder* (2014), HMSO, available at: https://assets.publishing.service.gov.uk/media/5a7f48d6ed915d74e33f57b9/penalty-notice-disorder-police-guidance.pdf

Ministry of Justice, *Simple Cautions for Adult Offenders* (2015), HMSO, available at: https://www.gov.uk/government/publications/simple-cautions-guidance-for-police-and-prosecutors

Ministry of Justice, *Crime Outcomes in England and Wales 2022–2023* (2023), HMSO, available at https://www.gov.uk/government/statistics/crime-outcomes-in-england-and-wales-2022-to-2023/crime-outcomes-in-england-and-wales-2022-to-2023

Ministry of Justice, *Reforms to the adult out of court disposals framework in the Police, Crime, Sentencing and Courts Bill* (2023), HMSO, available at: https://www.gov.uk/government/publications/police-crime-sentencing-and-courts-bill-2021-equality-statements/reforms-to-the-adult-out-of-court-disposals-framework-in-the-police-crime-sentencing-courts-bill-equalities-impact-assessment

Ministry of Justice, *Diversionary and Community Cautions: Draft Code of Practice - Part 6 of the Police, Crime, Sentencing and Courts Act 2022* (2023), HMSO, available at: https://consult.justice.gov.uk/probation-policy/out-of-court-disposals-consultation/supporting_documents/diversionaryandcommunitycautionscodeofpractice.pdf

Ministry of Justice *Guide to proven reoffending statistics: April 2024* (2024), HMSO, available at: https://www.gov.uk/government/collections/proven-reoffending-statistics

National Police Chiefs' Council, *Gravity Matrix (Adult): Two-Tier Framework* (2019), available at: https://npcc.police.uk/2019%20FOI/Counter%20Terrorism/061%2019%20Gravity%20Matrix.pdf

National Police Chiefs' Council *Community Resolutions Guidelines* (2022), available at: https://www.npcc.police.uk/SysSiteAssets/media/downloads/publications/publications-log/criminal-justice/2023/npcc-community-resolution-guidance-2022-v.1.1.pdf

Noah Uhrig, S. C. and Atherton, K., *Reoffending Following Custodial Sentences or Community Orders, by Offence Seriousness and Offender Characteristics, 2000–2018*, (2020), Ministry of Justice, available at: https://assets.publishing.service.gov.uk/media/5f688b18e90e072b9bd0a79c/reoffending-custodial-sentences-community-orders-research-report.pdf

Neyroud, P. *Out of Court Disposals Managed by the Police: Review of the Evidence* (2018), NPCC, available at: https://www.npcc.police.uk/Publication/NPCC%20Out%20of%20Court%20Disposals%20Evidence%20assessment%20FINAL%20June%202018.pdf

Neyroud, P., Slothower, M. P., 'Wielding the Sword of Damocles: The Challenges and Opportunities in Reforming Police Out-of-Court Disposals in England and Wales', [in:] Wasik, M. and Santatzoglou, S. (eds.) *The Management of Change in Criminal Justice: Who Knows Best?* (2015), Basingstoke: Palgrave MacMillan.

Ormerod, D. and Perry, D., *Blackstone's Criminal Practice, 34th ed.* (2024).

Pamment, N., 'Youth Offending Teams: a multi-agency success or system failure?' in Pycroft, A. and Gough, D., *Multi-agency working in criminal Justice* (2010), Bristol University Press.

Pappas, L. N. and Dent, A. L., 'The 40-year debate: a Meta-Review on What Works for Juvenile Offenders', *Journal of Experimental Criminology*, 2023/19.

Phillips, C., The Royal Commission on Criminal Procedure Report (1981), House of Commons.

Pivaty, A. 'Out-of-Court Disposals in the Dutch Criminal Process', [in:] Johnston, E. and Marsh, S. (eds.) *Contemporary Issues in Global Criminal Justice* (2022).

Rowe, M., Amankwaa, A., Biddle, P., & Bengtsson, L. 'Streamlining out-of-court disposals: Assessing the impact on reoffending and police practice' in *Criminology & Criminal Justice*, 2024/24(1); https://doi.org/10.1177/17488958221087492

Sherman, L. W. and Strang, H., *Restorative Justice: the Evidence* (2007), Smith Institute, available at https://research.tees.ac.uk/ws/portalfiles/portal/6854074/600940.pdf

Steer, D., *Police Cautions – A Study in the Exercise of Police Discretion* (1970), Blackwells Penal Research Unit, Oxford University.

Sturrock, R. and Mews, A., *Analytical Summary 2018, Out of Court Disposals Pilot: Cautions Re-offending Analysis* (2018), available at: https://assets.publishing.service.gov.uk/media/5b34c671e5274a0c4ffc37de/out-of-court-disposals-pilot-cautions-reoffending-analysis.pdf

Thomas, T. 'A Short History of Criminal Records' in *Criminal Records* (2007), Palgrave Macmillan, London.

Van Caenegem, R. C. *The Birth of the English Common Law* (1988), Cambridge University Press.

Ventham, C., Collier, B., Cohen, R., Talalay, R. and Wright, J., 'Judicial Reviews Claims Involving the Police' i*Judicial Review*, 2018/27(3).

Weigend, T., 'Why have a Trial when you can have a Bargain?', in Duff, A., Farmer, L., Marshall, S and Tadros, V., (eds.) *The Trial on Trial Vol. 2: Judgment and Calling to Account*, Hart Publishing, Oxford 2006.

Westmarland, N., Johnson, K. and McGlynn, C., 'Under the radar: The widespread use of 'out of court resolutions' in policing domestic violence and abuse in the United Kingdom', *The British Journal of Criminology*, 2017/58(1).

Wilson, D., Brennan, I. and Olaghere, A., *Police Initiated Diversion for Youth to Prevent Future Delinquent Behaviour, Campbell Systematic Reviews*, 2018/14(1), available at: https://onlinelibrary.wiley.com/doi/full/10.4073/csr.2018.5.

Prof. Dr. Dr.h.c. Juan-Luis Gómez Colomer,[1]
Prof. Dr. Andrea Planchadell Gargallo,[2]
Dr. Christa M. Madrid Boquín[3]

VI. Procedural treatment of prohibited evidence: its evolution in Spain

Abstract: This comprehensive study thoroughly examines the complex issue of the legality and admissibility of evidence in the context of Spanish law. It meticulously analyzes the evolution of the standards and focuses on the interpretations provided by the Spanish Constitutional Court. The authors critically observe and highlight the reductionist trend affirmed by the Court in this field. Moreover, they emphasize the Court's groundbreaking contributions to jurisprudence, which either entail modifications to established doctrines regarding prohibited evidence or the formulation of new exceptions, particularly in connection with the doctrine of the fruits of the poisonous tree. The authors contend that the current landscape is underpinned by the overarching principle of substantive truth and the non-punitive argument.

Keywords: evidence, Spanish constitution, exclusionary rules, impunity argument

1. By way of introduction: the evolution of the issue of admissibility of evidence up to the democratic Spanish Constitution of 1978

Before there was a proposed dogmatic organisation of the institution of prohibited evidence, derived directly from the democratic principles and fundamental rights of citizens established in the 1978 Spanish Constitution (SC), developed by the organic and ordinary legislation regulating criminal proceedings, on the problem of whether any evidence, no matter where it came from or how it was found, could be obtained during the phase of criminal investigation and, if necessary, could be later produced and used in the oral trial against an accused person, the laws of prosecution already allowed a systematic conclusion to be reached in the sense that not every piece of evidence could be used to find a person guilty.

1 ORCID no. 0000-0003-4661-7324. Professor of Procedural Law, Jaume I University of Castellón (Spain).
2 ORCID no. 0000-0002-0448-0326. Professor of Procedural Law, Jaume I University of Castellón (Spain).
3 ORCID no. 0000-0003-1875-5690. Lecturer in Procedural Law, Jaume I University of Castellón (Spain).

Until 1989, in fact, the Spanish Criminal Procedure Act (CPA), which dates from 1882, established certain cases in which the gathering, introduction and practice of means of investigation that were later to become evidence was in no case possible, causing either the absolute nullity of the diligence and in all probability that of the criminal proceedings themselves considered as a whole, or relative nullity, which could lead to its annulment and removal from the proceedings.

A typical example of the first case, and practically the only one for almost a hundred years, was the obtaining of a confession from the accused by means of torture, since Article 389, III CPA, based on the maximum protection required by respect for the right to life and the right to physical integrity, above all in criminal proceedings, excludes this inhumane method of obtaining confessions from the accused by torture (art. 15 SC), in line with the most recent international standards.[4] This law proscribes coercion or threats against the accused when giving evidence, and it also excludes the results of the statement of the accused or defendant under these conditions as evidence, apart from the criminal liability of the authority that had taken the statement, therefore making the subsequent criminal proceedings useless in most cases, as the nullity affected it completely. This was because the rights to life and physical integrity were considered sacred and intangible, and no procedural act could be valid if it was produced as a direct or indirect consequence of a violation of those rights.[5]

A typical example of the second case was the failure to warn the wife of the accused that she could legally refuse to testify against her husband, according to Art. 416-1° CPA.[6] She, who was obliged to appear before the examining magistrate,

---

4 Such as the 1948 UN Universal Declaration of Human Rights (arts. 3 and 5); the 1950 European Convention for the Protection of Human Rights and Fundamental Freedoms (arts. 2 and 3); the 1966 International Covenant of Civil and Political Rights (arts. 6 and 7); the 1969 American Convention on Human Rights (Pact of San José) (arts. 4 and 5); the 1984 UN Convention against Torture and Other Cruel, Inhuman or Degrading Treatment or Punishment; and the 1987 European Convention for the Prevention of Torture and Inhuman or Degrading Treatment or Punishment; among others.

5 This was the understanding of the doctrine of the time. See E. Reus, *Ley de Enjuiciamiento Criminal de 14 de septiembre de 1882, concordada y anotada extensamente*, IRL, Madrid, 1883, vol I, p. 266; and E. Aguilera de Paz, *Comentarios a la Ley de Enjuiciamiento Criminal*, 2nd ed., Reus, Madrid, 1924, vol. III, p. 604.

6 In Spain, the spouse of an offender who is not legally separated (or divorced) is also exempt from the obligation to report his or her husband or wife to the authorities (art. 261-1° CPA). According to the same precept, the exemption also protects the unmarried partner or the person who lives with him/her in an analogous relationship of affectivity.

could nevertheless excuse herself from testifying, but she was not banned from testifying (art. 416-1°, I CPA). Therefore, if, after the warning had been given, the wife testified as a witness, the evidence was legal and valid. But if the warning was not given by the public prosecution authority and the wife testified, there was no express legal provision. The most relevant doctrine prior to the SC was in favour, at most, of excluding the witness's statement as a means of investigation for being prejudicial (art. 311, I CPA), or, subsequently, as a means of evidence for being impertinent (art. 659, I CPA), which if accepted by the judge or court should have meant that the statement should have been excluded from the process, as it was annullable but not null and void, with the other means of evidence being valid.

However, such rules were not enough, as they were always isolated and did not allow for clear conclusions to be reached in all cases. The interpretative chaos regarding their effectiveness in criminal proceedings, in particular, was and is also notable. What is more, in fact, in practice, it was more frequent in these cases to observe how the criterion of finding the material truth was imposed on the illegally obtained evidence, which meant its admission and evaluation.[7] The Spanish situation was comparable to that of other countries, especially those with French influence. For this reason, Beling, the first continental European author to deal directly with the subject of prohibited evidence, proposed an ordered classification of it in accordance with the legislation in force at the time in Germany, basically the StPO (Criminal Procedure Act of 1877), with six possibilities, many of which are still in force today.[8] Nowadays, this need for systematisation is even more pressing because the modern world has been evolving for some decades now due to today's very serious, highly technical and devastating criminality towards unimaginable approaches, which require that this field of tension between democracy, freedom and security, i.e. between the effectiveness of criminal prosecution by the State and respect for the constitutional rights of the accused, which is criminal procedure, be better defined and dogmatically constructed in such a way that the appropriate practical solution can be found at any given time. It was, therefore, necessary to establish an adequate legal framework for this problem, which has generally been called "prohibited evidence" or "unlawful evidence" in

---

7 See T. Armenta Deu, 'Prueba ilícita y reforma del proceso penal', *Revista del Poder Judicial* 2006, special issue XIX "Propuestas para una nueva Ley de Enjuiciamiento Criminal", F. Gutiérrez-Alviz y Conradi (ed.), pp. 186 and 187.

8 E. Beling, *Die Beweisverbote als Grenzen der Wahrheitserforschung im Strafprozess*, Schletter'sche Buchhandlung, Breslau, 1903 (reprinted in Scientia Verlag, Aalen 1968), pp. 5 et seq.

continental Europe and "exclusionary rule" in common law, as a direct reference to the limits of investigation in criminal proceedings.[9]

The basis for the existence of prohibited evidence is thus very clear in a democracy that relishes a criminal process proper to the rule of law, since it is the democratic State itself which, by enshrining a catalogue of fundamental rights in its Constitution, to which it grants the value of inviolability and priority over all others (art. 10.1 SC), is demanding that any act that violates one or some of these fundamental rights has no evidential value in the court proceedings. Therefore, judicially assessing prohibited evidence simply means that the constitutional guarantees on which the process itself is based, particularly the criminal process, are being ignored; in other words, the right to a process with all the guarantees of art. 24.2 SC, or the principle of due, equitable or fair process, is being directly attacked.

Legal and jurisprudential recognition has two transcendental effects. On the one hand, the effect of protection, since a correct theory of prohibited evidence contributes effectively to better protection of the fundamental rights of the accused or defendant guaranteed by the Constitution that mandates such democracy; and on the other hand, the deterrent effect, which ensures that the conduct of the criminal prosecution authorities, especially during the investigation of the crime and particularly those carried out by the police, will be in accordance with the Constitution itself.[10]

However, the development of this issue in Spain has been neither original nor first in time. We are trailing behind Anglo-Saxon law, undoubtedly,[11] with our sights set on what Germany and Italy are suggesting[12] and, more recently, adapting our jurisprudence to that of the European Court of Human Rights (ECtHR).[13] In any case, we all agree on something transcendental: from the initial dazzlement, whereby any constitutional violation that occurred in obtaining or using a means

9 In this regard, comparative law citations are constant in our case law, see, for example, the Judgement of the Supreme Court (JSC) of June 2nd, 2014 (TOL4.394.463).

10 This double effect, particularly the deterrent one, which brings us closer to the basis of this rule in the United States, can be found, for example, in the JSC of February 17th, 2014 (TOL4.125.685).

11 See, among many others, C. Fidalgo Gallardo, *Las "pruebas ilegales": De la exclusionary rule estadounidense al art. 11.1 LOPJ*, Centro de Estudios Políticos y Constitucionales, Madrid, 2003, pp. 87 et seq.

12 Also in Latin America, for example in Colombia, see O.J. Guerrero Peralta, *Institutos probatorios del nuevo proceso penal*, Nueva Jurídica, Bogotá, 2009.

13 This occurs, as we will explain below, with Judgement of the Constitutional Court (JCC) 97/2019, of 16 July (TOL7446118).

of evidence in criminal proceedings meant the exclusion of the evidence affected from the process practically automatically, in other words, from a clearly *pro* "freedom and fundamental rights" situation, we are moving on to a regrettable and worrying theoretical-practical reductionism in which anything is valid if there is a loophole in legality. The pendulum is now clearly swinging in favour of "effectiveness and security". Let us see what has happened and demonstrate the conclusion that has just been advanced.

2. The beginning of the shift towards guarantism: the recognition of the institution of prohibited evidence by the Spanish Constitutional Court

The primary source, the 1978 Constitution, neither directly nor indirectly regulates evidentiary prohibitions, nor is an exclusionary rule indubitably evident from any of its precepts.

It is one thing for the Constitution to contain fundamental rights of the parties of the proceedings, especially the accused, which refer directly or indirectly to evidentiary issues, such as the right to procedural equality (art. 14), the right to be informed of the reasons for their detention (art. 17.3), the right to be informed of the charges brought against them (art. 24.2), the right to legal assistance during police and judicial detention (art. 17.3), the right to a technical defence during the proceedings (art. 24.2), the right not to testify during detention (art. 17.3), the right to effective judicial protection (art. 24.1), the right not to be defenceless (art. 24.1 and 2), the right to a trial with all guarantees (art. 24.2), the right to use the means of evidence relevant to his defence (art. 24.2), the right not to testify against himself (art. 24.2), the right not to confess guilt (art. 24.2), and the right to the presumption of innocence (art. 24.2). All these fundamental rights, institutional guarantees and public freedoms enshrined in the Constitution have come into play in some way when our Constitutional Court (CC) has tried to establish a rule of exclusion in a process, generally criminal, above all in relation to the protection of the secrecy of the communications of the accused persons, but not only in relation to this, and to the explicit protection of their presumption of innocence.

Another thing is that among its fundamental rights, institutional guarantees and public freedoms, it recognises the rights to life (art. 15), physical integrity (art. 15), freedom of movement (art. 17.1), honour (art. 18.1), personal and family privacy (art. 18.1), inviolability of the home (art. 18.2), secrecy of communications (art. 18.3) and the protection of personal data (art. 18.4), which, if violated in the process, will undoubtedly give rise to an exclusionary rule.

The Spanish Constitution does not include such a rule or evidentiary prohibition in any of its provisions. However, we will see immediately that this does not mean at all that the prohibitions of evidence cannot be solidly based on constitutional rules, precisely those we have just mentioned, with the laudable aim that the citizen whose fundamental rights have been violated through prohibited evidence may have access, if necessary, to the maximum procedural protection that our legal system provides for, the appeal for protection before the Constitutional Court.

Thus, in 1984, the Constitutional Court had the opportunity to hear a case that led to the first Spanish ruling on the subject of prohibited evidence, a case, curiously enough, not of criminal origin but of labour origin (JCC 114/1984, of 29 November, TOL79.403).[14]

An editor of a newspaper in Alicante was dismissed for disloyalty and lack of good faith towards the newspaper's publishing company because, in a private conversation with a technical advisor of the Ministry of Transport and Communications, he made certain statements without knowing that the conversation was being recorded. This was subsequently used as evidence in the labour proceedings that led to his dismissal, a labour sanction confirmed by the Supreme Court (SC). Before the CC, the dismissed appellant alleged a violation of the right to secrecy of communications under art. 18.3 SC and violation of the right to due process under art. 24.2 SC. The CC denied the constitutional appeal.

Well, the legal grounds of this judgement establish as a starting doctrine several considerations that should be considered. In the first place, it recognizes knowledge of the American doctrine of the *exclusionary rule*, although it does not cite the truly important case law, as well as the situation in France and Italy. Curiously, it says nothing about Germany.

Secondly, the CC understands that there is no rule in the SC that enshrines an autonomous constitutional right to the rejection of unlawful evidence and that, therefore, the reception of unlawfully obtained evidence does not necessarily imply the infringement of a fundamental right:[15]

14 See J.M. Asencio Mellado, 'La prueba prohibida en Jurisprudencia Constitucional (S.T.C. 114/84, de 29 de noviembre)', *Revista Valenciana de Estudios Autonómicos* 1985/1, pp. 289 et seq.; and A. Planchadell-Gargallo, *La prueba prohibida: Evolución jurisprudencial (Comentario a las sentencias que marcan el camino)*, Thomson-Reuters Aranzadi, Cizur Menor (Navarra), 2014, pp. 15 et seq.

15 A. Planchadell Gargallo, *La prueba prohibida: Evolución jurisprudencial*, *op.cit.*, pp. 32 et seq.

> *The impossibility of procedural estimation may exist in some cases, but not by virtue of a fundamental right that may be considered to be originally affected, but as an expression of an objective and implicit guarantee in the system of fundamental rights, whose validity and preferential position in the legal system may require the rejection of any evidence obtained in violation of them. It should, therefore, be made clear that the hypothetical reception of unlawfully obtained evidence does not necessarily imply an infringement of a fundamental right. This is not to say that the admission of unlawfully obtained evidence -and the decision based on it- must always be indifferent to the scope of the fundamental rights guaranteed by the constitutional remedy of appeal. Such an effect - and the consequent possible harm- cannot be ruled out in the abstract, but will only occur by reference to the rights that come into existence in the scope of the process (art. 24.2 of the Constitution).*

In fact, it states that we are at a crossroads of interests, on the one hand, finding the material truth in the process and, on the other hand, guaranteeing the rights of citizens:

> *The latter* [referring to the rights or subjective legal situations of citizens] *may perhaps yield to the first requirement when their basis is strictly infra-constitutional, but not when they are fundamental rights that derive their direct and immediate cause from the first rule of the legal system. In such a case, the priority requirement of attending to their full effectiveness can be affirmed, relegating to second place the public interests linked to the evidentiary phase of the process.*

Thirdly, if evidentiary illegality were to exist and if there were a rule imposing its procedural ineffectiveness, it would have to be concluded that the jurisdictional decision based on such evidentiary material could affect the following fundamental rights:

1. The right to a due process with all guarantees (art. 24.2 SC). The reason is that, once the inadmissibility of evidence obtained in violation of fundamental rights has been established, its procedural reception implies ignorance of the guarantees inherent to the process;[16] and
2. To the principle of equality between the parties (Art. 14 SC), since this violation entails an unacceptable institutional confirmation of the inequality between the parties in the trial, an inequality that has been unlawfully procured to their advantage by those who have sought evidentiary instruments in disregard of the fundamental rights of another.

16 The ECtHR also bases the prohibited evidence on art. 6.2 ECHR, linking it to the right to a fair trial. See, among others, ECtHR Judgements 4/1988, December 16th, 1988 (*Case Schenk v. Switzerland*, TOL216.238); May 12th, 2000 (*Case Kahn v. United Kingdom*); 552/2001, September 25th, 2001 (*Case P.G and J.H. v. United Kingdom*); 64/2002, November 5th, 2002 (*Case Allan v. United Kingdom*).

Consequently, for our CC and in accordance with the aforementioned 1984 ruling, the interdiction of the admission of evidence obtained in violation of fundamental rights derives directly from the Constitution due to the collision that this would entail with the right to a trial with all guarantees and the equality of the parties, and is directly linked to the preferential nature of fundamental rights in the legal system and their inviolable condition, in accordance with what is stated in art. 10.1 SC.

Therefore, based on this ruling, it is impossible for evidence obtained by violating a fundamental right, an institutional guarantee or public freedom of the accused or defendant to be admitted in the process -in any process, be it criminal, civil, labour or administrative- and it is established as precedent that "the concept of relevant means of evidence that appears in art. 24.2 of the Constitution itself, thus incorporates, over its essentially technical-procedural content, a scope that is also substantive, in merit of which an evidential instrument obtained in this way can never be considered relevant".

Finally, it should be noted that in this case the CC did not base the possible rule of exclusion on the defendant's right to the presumption of innocence (art. 24.2 SC), probably because the facts that motivated it belonged to the labour jurisdiction; a presumption of innocence whose violation has subsequently been upheld in most of the rulings on prohibited evidence by our CC that arose from criminal proceedings, due to the fact that the prohibited evidence does not rebut the presumption of innocence of the defendant and, therefore, is not sufficient evidence for the court to be able to convict him.

Nor does the Spanish Constitutional Court make any reference to the deterrent effect on which the US Federal Supreme Court bases the exclusionary rule, probably because it has a very difficult constitutional fit in the Spanish system, although as an *obiter dicta* argument it is impeccable.[17]

The constitutional basis originally given to the exclusionary rule in our system differs from the initial construction of the same rule in the United States, whose application is conditioned by the need to prevent police actions that may violate fundamental rights, with such application being ruled out when this purpose cannot be achieved, such as when the police act in good faith.[18] Although in the

---

17 See A. Planchadell-Gargallo, *La prueba prohibida: Evolución jurisprudencial*, *op.cit.*, pp. 39 and 40. We find such references, combining both grounds, for example in the JSC of November 26th, 2003 (TOL352.273), or in the more recent JSC of January 22nd, 2013 (TOL3.010.880).

18 A. Planchadell Gargallo, *La prueba prohibida: Evolución jurisprudencial*, loc. cit.

United States, the exclusionary rule is directly linked to Amendments IV[19] (right to be free from unreasonable searches and seizures) and V (right not to testify against oneself) of the Constitution, it soon begins to refer to the deterrent effect.[20] Indeed, the United States Supreme Court in *US v. Leon* [468 U.S. 897 (1984)] recognised this:[21]

> *The Fourth Amendment contains no express exclusionary provision against the use of evidence obtained in violation of its terms, and an evaluation of its origin and purpose makes clear that the use of the 'fruits' of a prior illegal search or seizure is not contrary to the Fourth Amendment. Because of the Amendment, the wrongful conviction is 'fully realised' by the illegal search or seizure itself, and the principle of prohibited evidence neither attempts, nor is capable, 'to remedy the violation of the defendant's rights which he has already suffered'. The principle thus functions as 'a judicial remedy created and designed to safeguard Fourth Amendment rights through its deterrent effect, rather than as a personal constitutional right of the aggrieved individual' (...).*
>
> *If the exclusion of evidence obtained pursuant to a subsequently invalidated warrant is intended to have a deterrent effect, it must therefore alter the particular behaviour of police officers in the application of the law or the policies of their departments.*

---

19 However, the Fourth Amendment does not contain an express prohibition on the use of illegally obtained evidence either, but it must be understood as an instrument to protect the guarantees provided for therein, focusing on the substantive right and its needs for protection. This is recognised in the cases of *Mapp v. Ohio*, 367 U.S. 643 of 1961 and *United States v. Leon*, 468 U.S. of 1984. See J.L. Gomez Colomer (ed.), *Introducción al proceso penal federal de los Estados Unidos de Norteamérica*, Tirant lo Blanch, Valencia, 2013, pp. 361 et seq.

20 See J.L. Gómez Colomer (ed.), *Introducción al proceso penal federal de los Estados Unidos de Norteamérica, op.cit.*, pp. 358 et seq.; J.L. Gómez Colomer (ed.), *Proceso Penal y Constitución de los Estados Unidos de Norteamérica (Casos destacados del Tribunal Supremo y Texto introductorio)*, Tirant lo Blanch, Valencia, 2012, pp. 123 et seq., where the judgements of the US Supreme Court can be found translated; and J.M. Alcaide González, *La prueba ilícita penal. Decadencia y extinción (Jurisprudencia práctica comparada con EEUU)*, La Ley, Málaga, 2013, pp. 13 et seq., T. Armenta Deu, *La prueba ilícita (Un estudio comparado)*, Marcial Pons, Madrid, 2011, p. 30, that the rationale for the exclusionary rule also refers to the necessary preservation of judicial integrity (*Elkins v. United States*, 364 U.S. 206, 1960), to the reliability of the evidence or to constitute a remedy for an error against a person (*Linkletter v. Walzer* 381 U.S. 618, 1965).

21 J.L. Gómez Colomer (ed.), *Introducción al Proceso Penal Federal de los Estados Unidos de Norteamérica*, cit., pp. 758 et seq.; the full judgement is available in Spanish in J.L. Gómez Colomer (ed.), *Proceso penal y Constitución de los Estados Unidos de Norteamérica (Casos destacados del Tribunal Supremo y Texto introductorio)*, loc.cit.

A clear manifestation of this conception can be found in the 1974 *US v. Calandra* decision, which stated that the exclusionary rule is a judicially created remedy designed to safeguard Fourth Amendment rights generally through its deterrent effect, rather than a personal constitutional right of the aggrieved party. Two years later in *US v. Manis*, this non-constitutional nature of the exclusionary rule is confirmed, stating that "the primary purpose of the exclusion of unlawful evidence, if not the sole purpose, is to prevent unlawful police conduct" and adding that "the rule excluding evidence obtained in violation of the Fourth Amendment through a deterrent effect (of the violation itself) rather than as an expression of a subjective constitutional right of the aggrieved party…". The exclusionary rule is thus a constitutional requirement not in and of itself, but insofar as it serves to prevent police conduct contrary to constitutional amendment rights.[22]

In contrast to this rationale, and although in the end these rules will follow parallel paths in the United States and Spain, in the latter country, let us remember, the exclusion of evidence obtained by violating fundamental rights is based on the preponderant value that these rights have in our legal system, relating it both to the right to a trial with all guarantees and the principle of equality, and to the principle of the presumption of innocence. However, as we shall see in the following pages, the introduction of the different exceptions to the exclusion rule, clearly influenced by North American jurisprudence, above all, but also by European jurisprudence, has led our courts to move towards the deterrent effect,[23] focusing on the specific violation of substantive law, not on the fundamental procedural rights.[24]

---

22 Salas L. Calero, 'Aspectos materiales y procesales del principio acusatorio: Problemas probatorios, prueba ilícita y procesos penales socialmente relevantes. La exclusión de las pruebas ilícitamente obtenidas en el Derecho Procesal de los Estados Unidos', *Revista Poder Judicial* 2006/66, pp. 367–401; E. Velasco Nuñez, 'Prueba obtenida ilícitamente. Doctrina del "fruto del árbol envenenado": Correcciones actuales y tendencias de futuro', [in:] *Medidas restrictivas de derechos fundamentales*, Cuadernos de Derecho Judicial, Consejo General del Poder Judicial, Madrid, 1996/12, pp. 425–463; and E. Martinez Garcia, *Eficaciacia de la prueba ilícita en el proceso penal (a la luz de la S TS 81/1998, de 2 de abril)*, Tirant lo Blanch, Valencia, 2003, pp. 84 et seq.

23 This is clearly reflected in the JSC of November 26th, 2003 (TOL352.273).

24 Thus JSC of November 26th, 2003 (TOL352.273).

3. The dogmatic consolidation of the theory of prohibited evidence: trajectory and difficulties

This doctrine had a sudden enormous impact, because it was immediately included in art. 11.1 of the Organic Law on the Judiciary (OLJ), which was passed in July 1985, that is, less than a year after the first ruling of our Constitutional Court mentioned above. The legal text is, however, too caustic, given that, according to this precept "evidence obtained, directly or indirectly, by violating fundamental rights or freedoms shall not be effective".[25]

From this point onwards, important doctrinal studies began to be published which tried to explain the scope of this rule,[26] focusing above all on the understanding of the adverb "indirectly",[27] not introduced by the CC in Judgement 114/1984, of 29 November (TOL79.403), but which in the end was confirmed by the CC itself that its meaning was none other than to concentrate in a brief summary the evolution of the "reflect effect" of prohibited evidence, or the North American "fruits of the poisonous tree" doctrine.

---

25 On its parliamentary *iter*, practically without interesting data due to the lack of discussion, see A. Oliva Santos, 'Sobre la ineficacia e las pruebas ilícitamente obtenidas', *Revista Tribunales de Justicia* 2003/8–9, pp. 1–3.

26 From e.g. B. Pastor Borgoñón, 'Eficacia en el proceso de las pruebas ilícitamente obtenidas. A propósito de la sentencia núm. 114/1984, de 29 de noviembre (BOE del 21 de diciembre de 1984), dictada por el Tribunal Constitucional en el recurso de amparo 167/1984', *Revista Justicia* 1986/2, pp. 337 et seq.; M. Miranda Estrampes, 'La regla de exclusión de la prueba ilícita: historia de su nacimiento y de su progresiva limitación', *Revista Jueces para la Democracia*, 2003/47, pp. 55 and 56.

27 See J.M. Asencio Mellado, *Prueba prohibida y prueba preconstituída*, Trivium, Madrid, 1989, p. 89; J. L. González Montes, 'La prueba obtenida ilícitamente con violación de los derechos fundamentales (El Derecho constitucional a la prueba y sus límites)', *Revista de Derecho Procesal*, 1990/1, pp. 39 and 40; J.L. González Montes, 'Nuevas reflexiones en torno a la prueba ilícita', *Revista Derechos y Libertades del Instituto Bartolomé de las Casas*, 1993/2, pp. 67 et seq.; J. Vegas Torres, *Presunción de inocencia y prueba en el proceso penal*, La Ley, Madrid, 1993, pp. 120 et seq.; J. Picó i Junoy, 'Nuevas perspectivas sobre el alcance anulatorio de las pruebas ilícitas', *Revista Justicia*, 1997/3 pp. 890 et seq.; and M. Fernández López, *Prueba y presunción de inocencia*, Iustel, Madrid, 2005, pp. 150 et seq. This issue has also attracted criminal lawyers such as F. Muñoz Conde, 'Prueba prohibida y valoración de las grabaciones audiovisuales en el proceso penal', *Revista Penal*, 2004/14, pp. 101 and 102 (also published [in:] "Estudios sobre Justicia Penal" in homage to Professor Julio B.J. Maier (ed.). del Puerto, Buenos Aires 2005, pp. 381 and 382).

The Spanish OLJ thus enshrines in this norm the expansive or more protective criterion of the theory of prohibited evidence, as interpreted by the Spanish Constitutional Court from the first moments after its promulgation, a doctrine that we could summarise as follows:[28]

a) Evidence directly obtained violating fundamental rights (which are those enshrined in the SC) has no effect on the proceedings;
b) Evidence indirectly obtained by violating fundamental rights also has no effect on the proceedings (reflect effectiveness or fruit of the poisonous tree doctrine);
c) It does not matter who obtained the illicit evidence;
d) It does not matter in which stage of the proceedings the prohibited evidence was obtained, whether at the investigation stage or at any other stage;
e) Regardless of the type of proceeding in which it is sought to be asserted (criminal, or non-criminal); and
f) If it is prohibited evidence, it is excluded from the proceedings, i.e. its admission, use and assessment is prohibited.

However, it was in 1994 when an even more protectionist step was taken,[29] confirming the unstoppable expansion of the theory of prohibited evidence since its constitutional recognition in 1984 and legal recognition in 1985. It was in that year when in a case in which a telephone tapping of two people was carried out (judicially ordered through a non-motivated resolution) on suspicion of committing crimes against public health (drug trafficking). This tapping was extended twice by the police without the required judicial authorisation and a crime was discovered during its course. The CC established in its judgement 85/1994, of 14 March (TOL82.493), the doctrine of the reflect effectiveness of prohibited evidence, recognising it in Spanish procedural law,[30] in a similar way to other American and European courts.

---

28 JCC 107/1985, of 7 October (TOL79.522), reiterated the doctrine established by JCC 114/1984, of 29 November (TOL79.403), which was also upheld in JCC 64/1986, of 21 May (TOL79.610).

29 This is surprising, since the ECtHR had already delivered its famous judgement in the *Schenk* case (ECtHR judgement of July 12th, 1988, TOL216.238), where it had stated that admitting unlawful evidence does not in principle imply a violation of article 6 of the ECHR (right to a fair trial).

30 M. Miranda Estrampes, *El concepto de prueba ilícita y su tratamiento en el proceso penal*, 2nd ed., J.M. Bosch, Barcelona, 2004, pp. 107 et seq.; and by the same author, 'La regla de exclusión de la prueba ilícita: historia de su nacimiento y de su progresiva limitación, loc.cit.

According to this judgement, where the key question was whether or not there had been a violation of the right to secrecy of the convicted persons' communications, and therefore, whether the evidence of their crime had been obtained unlawfully, the CC, after stating that the evidence had been obtained in violation of art. 18.3 SC, because the first judicial authorisation of the telephone tapping had been made without proper judicial motivation, which made it impossible to know whether the measure was proportionate, without considering that the extension of the telephone tapping had not been judicially authorised, undoubtedly due to the legal precept in force at that time (art. 579 CPA), now reformed in this sense, and bearing in mind that it is as a result of the telephone conversation that the police came to know that a girl was going to pick up a package from the appellants' home to take it home, which the police themselves deduced to be drugs (as it was, heroin of high purity), they established the following doctrine:

> *Once it has been established that the tapping of the appellants' telephone during the period between 5 August and November 17th, 1987 violated their right to secrecy of communications, recognised in art. 18.3 SC, we must conclude that any evidentiary element that sought to be deduced from the content of the tapped conversations should not have been subject to evidentiary assessment, since the impossibility of admitting evidence obtained by violating a fundamental right into the proceedings not only derives directly from the nullity of any act violating the rights recognised in Chapter Two of Title I of the Constitution, and the need not to confirm, by recognising them as effective, the contraventions thereof [JCC 114/1984], but now also in terms of legality by virtue of the provisions of art. 11.1 of the Organic Law of the Judiciary.*
>
> *... Thus, the occupation of the drug by the minor M.J.P. is not assessed by the Second Chamber of the Supreme Court as direct evidence of the appellants' guilt, but as evidence which, together with the transcript of the tapes recorded by the police and the interpretation of the terms used in them, forms the logical reasoning used to base the conviction on the existence of sufficient circumstantial evidence to rebut the presumption of innocence. However, as it is not possible to assess, given their constitutionally unlawful origin, the evidence considered as such by the court, it is clear that that logical reasoning is thereby undermined, since the possession of the drugs in the possession of the minor alone cannot be considered sufficient evidence to prove the trafficking of which the appellants are accused. All the more so when, as in the present case, that evidence could not have been obtained without prior knowledge that the minor was going to make the route indicated, transporting 'something' from the appellants' home to her own, a fact which came to light through the infringement of the fundamental right to secrecy of communications.*
>
> *This immediate derivation of the unconstitutionally obtained evidence prevents this evidence from being considered as independent, legally obtained evidence. Consequently, it must be concluded that there has been no evidential activity that can be considered sufficient to undermine the right to the presumption of innocence initially in favour of the appellants (...).*

This is the first judgement in which the effects of the appeal claim being upheld in a case of prohibited evidence are clearly determined, as not only is the evidence excluded from the process (in this case the illegal telephone conversation), but also that which is its consequence (in this case the circumstantial evidence). The consequence of this is that the CC annulled the two judgements being challenged, that of the Provincial Court and that of the Supreme Court, or in other words, in material terms, this meant the acquittal of the two convicted persons.

Therefore, what is truly being done is to recognise in our criminal procedural system the American doctrine of the fruit of the poisonous tree,[31] which is certainly not named directly in the judgement but which undoubtedly implies the same thing. Although it was the CC resolution *(Auto)* 155/1999, of 14 June (TOL48.488), which referred expressly for the first time to such a plastic American terminology, a few years earlier our highest ordinary court in JSC 814/1992, of 7 April (TOL400.474), had already brought this foreign terminology to our judicial practice, which has been followed by this court, sometimes referring to it as the doctrine of the "domino effect".[32] As indicated in the JSC of November 26th, 2003 (TOL352.273) and those cited therein:

The justification for this so-called 'domino effect' (JSC of December 15th, 1994, June 19th, 1999; 457/1999, January 31st, 2000; 65/1999, December 29th, 2000; 1850/2000, July 18th, 2002; 1203/2002, among others), which overturns and drags down all the evidence derived from the constitutional violation, is to be found in the fact that this is the only way to ensure that the initial unlawful evidence has no effect on the proceedings. When the initial prosecution evidence has been obtained through an action that violates fundamental rights, its evidential effectiveness must be annulled and, as a consequence of this 'domino effect', this determines the decay of all subsequent evidence derived from it (JSC October 6th, 1999, 1380/1999).

As has already been pointed out, among others, in the judgements of this Court (numbers) 448/97 of 4 March, 472/97 of 14 April, 974/1997 of 4 July, 290/1999 of 17 February, 369/1999 of 13 March and 1203/2002 of 18 July, prohibiting the direct use of these means of evidence and tolerating their indirect use would constitute a proclamation void of effective content, and even an incitement to the use of unconstitutional procedures which, indirectly, would end up having an effect in the process, from which one can already sense the disincentive or deterrent effect which is going to be the most important element to consider in order to exclude unlawful evidence.

31 E. Velasco Núñez, 'Prueba obtenida ilícitamente. Doctrina del "fruto del árbol envenenado": Correcciones actuales y tendencias de futuro', [in:] E. Velasco Núñez, Medidas restrictivas de derechos fundamentales, *Cuadernos de Derecho Judicial* 1996/12, CGPJ, Madrid, pp. 427–446.

32 See e.g. JSC 1284/1994 of June 17th, 1994 (TOL403.949) and JSC of November 26th, 2003 (TOL352.273).

The extensive interpretation (the prohibited evidence also includes the fruits of the poisonous tree), remained unchanged for a very short time, until 1995, the year immediately after the theory of reflexive effectiveness was adopted, which indicates that Spanish jurisprudence did not take long to realise that, in practice, the adoption of the reflect doctrine left major criminals, who had committed horrendous crimes, free and began to look for a way to ensure that this did not happen, without discussing the essence of the CC's 1984 doctrine on prohibited evidence, only focusing on denying the consequences of reflect effectiveness, thus seeking a way to ensure that not all evidence derived or existing in the process, apart from the truly unlawful, would be fruit of the poisonous tree. And it did so by establishing restrictive criteria, some determined by the CC itself, such as the so-called exception of legally independent evidence, and others by the SC, such as the exception of inevitable discovery and the theory of chance discovery. Neither did the two Spanish high courts contributed anything new in this respect, as the US Federal Supreme Court had already applied these theories.[33]

Thus, during this period, and through the jurisprudence of the SC and the CC, the following exceptions were adopted in relation to the rule of exclusion of prohibited evidence that had been established a few years earlier in Article 11.1 OLJ:

1. *The independent evidence exception*: already formulated in cases such as *Segura v. United States* [468 U.S. 796 (1984)] and *Murray v. United States* [487 U.S. 533 (1988)], it was incorporated into Spanish jurisprudence in JCC 86/1995, of 6 June (TOL8285) and reaffirmed a year later in JCC 54/1996, of 26 March (TOL82988). This theory suggests that evidence that has a different and autonomous origin to the diligence that violated the fundamental right should be assessed as independent evidence, unaffected by the contaminating effect of the

33 Regarding the American origin of these theories and their incorporation into Spanish jurisprudence, see C.M. Madrid Boquín, *La prueba ilícita en el proceso civil*, Tirant lo Blanch, Valencia, 2020, pp. 199 et seq. In relation to their application and development in Spain, J.L. Gómez Colomer, 'La evolución de las teorías sobre la prueba prohibida aplicadas en el proceso penal español: del expansionismo sin límites al más puro reduccionismo. Una meditación sobre su desarrollo futuro inmediato', [in:] J.L. Gómez Colomer (ed.), *Prueba y proceso penal: análisis especial de la prueba prohibida en el sistema español y en el derecho comparado*, Tirant lo Blanch, Valencia, 2008, pp. 121–126; A. Planchadell Gargallo, *La prueba prohibida: Evolución jurisprudencial, loc.cit*; J.L. Gómez Colomer and A. Planchadell Gargallo, 'Prueba Prohibida', [in:] M.I. González Cano, M.I. Romero Pradas (eds.), *La prueba. Tomo II. La prueba en el proceso penal*, Tirant lo Blanch, Valencia, 2017, pp. 377–393.

prohibited evidence. The problem lies in the practical difficulty of delimiting which evidence is causally linked and which is not.

2. *The inevitable discovery exception*: Similarly, the theory of inevitable discovery, originally applied in *Nix v. Williams* [467 U.S. 431 (1984)], was accepted by the SC in its judgement 974/1997 of 4 July (TOL408447). According to this theory, it will be possible to assess evidence derived from the prohibited evidence when it is shown that it would have been equally obtained if the infringement of the fundamental right had not occurred (for example, because a parallel line of investigation already existed, which would have allowed the same results to be obtained in a lawful manner).
3. *The chance discovery exception*: this doctrine is inspired by the *plain view doctrine* formulated in *Coolidge v. New Hampshire* [403 U.S. 443 (1971)] and was taken up by the SC in judgement 462/1999, 22 March. It is important to mention that chance discovery is the only exception to the doctrine of reflect effect that has been expressly regulated by the Spanish legislator.[34] This doctrine refers to evidence that has been found "accidentally" or "by chance" while carrying out an authorised investigation in order to find different evidence.

---

34 In this sense, it was incorporated into articles 579 bis and 588 bis (i) of the CPA through Organic Law 13/2015, of 5 October, amending the Criminal Procedure Act to strengthen procedural guarantees and regulate technological investigative measures. In accordance with this reform, the theory of chance discovery will be applied in relation to different investigative measures that have an impact on article 18 SC. Article 579 bis CPA establishes that information and chance discoveries produced in another procedure may be used in a process. Thus: *1. The result of the arrest and opening of written and telegraphic correspondence may be used as a means of investigation or evidence in another criminal proceeding. 2. To this end, testimony shall be taken from the individuals necessary to prove the legitimacy of the interference. This shall include, in any event, the initial application for the adoption, the judicial decision granting it and all the petitions and judicial decisions for the extension of the original proceedings. 3. The continuation of this measure for the investigation of the offence discovered by chance requires the authorisation of the competent judge, for which the latter shall verify the diligence of the action, assessing the framework in which the chance discovery took place and the impossibility of having requested the measure that included it at the time. Likewise, it will be informed if the proceedings continue to be declared secret, so that this declaration is respected in the other criminal proceedings, communicating the moment in which this secrecy is lifted.* In relation to this subject, see C.M. Madrid Boquín, 'Los hallazgos casuales en la investigación criminal: actualidad legislativa y jurisprudencial en España', [in:] J.L. Gómez Colomer, C.M. Madrid Boquín (eds.), *La instrucción del crimen: algunos problemas procesales*, Sepín, Madrid, 2020, pp. 119–158.

4. The current restrictive anti-guaranteeing trend

The current state of the issue is even more restrictive, in theory, and practice, because it is from 1998 onwards that the Spanish Constitutional Court has confirmed the clearly reductionist tendency in this area, denying not only any possibility of expanding the doctrine of prohibited evidence, but also, and more seriously, of at least preserving what had been achieved until now. The reductionism of this procedural guarantee is produced when the CC opens up new lines of jurisprudence, which either imply changes to the already established doctrine of prohibited evidence or formulate new exceptions, in addition to those already mentioned, to the doctrine of the fruits of the poisonous tree which completely annul the reflect effectiveness. Among these exceptions, the most important is the theory of the connection of unlawfulness, which we will explain shortly, but we should also mention the exception of the voluntary confession of the defendant and the good faith exception.[35]

a) *The exception of the voluntary confession of the defendant*: This theory is partly derived from the *attenuated taint doctrine*, applied by the American courts in the cases of *Wong Sun v. United States* [371 U.S. 471 (1963)] and *Brown v. Illinois* [422 U.S. 590 (1975)] and which was later accepted by Spanish jurisprudence in JCC 86/1995, of 6 June (TOL82825). More specifically, the voluntary confession of the investigated person is referred to in JCC 161/1999, of 27 September (TOL81208). According to this doctrine, a confession may be granted evidential value, even when it has been made in violation of a fundamental right, as long as the statement has been voluntary, spontaneous and complies with certain requirements established by case law.
b) *The good faith exception*: This theory was applied in *United States v. Leon* [468 U.S. 897 (1984)] and subsequently adopted in Spain in JCC 22/2002, of 10 February (TOL239218), which allows not only derivative or reflect evidence to be assessed, but also prohibited evidence directly obtained due to the violation of the fundamental right. This will be possible when such violation has occurred "in good faith", that is, in those cases in which the police act in

---

35 These are discussed in depth in J.L. Gómez Colomer, 'La evolución de las teorías sobre la prueba prohibida aplicadas en el proceso penal español… opc.cit., pp. 127–144, ff.; A. Planchadell Gargallo, *La prueba prohibida: Evolución jurisprudencial*, op, cit., pp. 137 et seq. ff;. J.L. Gómez Colomer, A. Planchadell Gargallo, 'Prueba Prohibida', *op.cit.*, pp. 409 et seq., ff.; C.M. Madrid Boquín, *La prueba ilícita en el proceso civil*, *op.cit.*, pp. 213–236, ff.

the objective belief that they are acting in accordance with the Constitution (for example, when carrying out a judicially authorised search and entry procedure, but which is subsequently annulled due to a lack of sufficient motivation in the judicial order).

Additionally, we must refer to the most recent of the exceptions, the *theory of evidence obtained by private parties*, which we will analyse below, also of American origin as can be seen in the case of *Burdeau v. McDowell* [256 U.S. 465 (1921)], but which in Spain was raised by the SC in its Judgement 116/2017, of 23 February (TOL5969881) and which was subsequently reconsidered in JCC 97/2019, of 16 July (TOL7446118), as we will analyse below.

Utilitarian and procedural economy considerations are not unrelated to all of these exceptions, as the new doctrines also aim to preserve the process.[36] As the decision as to whether or not evidence was prohibited (and therefore should be excluded) could not be taken by the court until the end of the proceedings, that is, once the evidence had been taken in the oral trial at the time of sentencing, the declaration of nullity was the worst procedural situation imaginable, as everything that had been done beforehand would have been of no use. Perhaps for this reason, the Spanish Civil Procedure Act of 2000, which is supplementary for all proceedings (art. 4), therefore also for criminal proceedings,[37] included in its article 287 a rule of great importance,[38] because it established the way of immediately asserting in the process the violation of fundamental rights, both in the obtention and the origin of any evidence admitted.[39] This rule is complemented with the

36 On these issues, see the JSC of October 31st, 2012 (TOL2.703.526).

37 The rules governing the exclusion of unlawful evidence in criminal proceedings are few and brief. For example, the CPA, at the beginning of the trial in abbreviated proceedings, allows for the parties to make a statement regarding the violation of fundamental rights and the nullity of the evidence (art. 786.2 CPA). The issue is also shortly regulated in Article 36.1.b of the Organic Law of the Jury Court and in Article 37.1 of the Organic Law regulating the criminal responsibility of minors.

38 Precept that has its immediate reference in Spain in art. 549, I (Inadmissible means of evidence) of the *Propuesta de Profesores Españoles de Derecho Procesal*, which can be consulted in "Corrección y Actualización de la Ley de Enjuiciamiento Civil", Ed. Tecnos, Madrid 1974, t. II, pp. 272 and 273.

39 For the situation immediately prior to the Civil Procedure Act of 2000, see J. Pico I Junoy, *El derecho a la prueba en el proceso civil*, Bosch, Barcelona, 1996, pp. 283 et seq.

provisions of article 230 on nullity, which recognises the maxim of preservation of procedural acts.[40]

4.1. The exception of the connection of unlawfulness

Among the different jurisprudential exceptions to the exclusionary rule of article 11.1 OLJ, we will proceed to analyse two of them in more detail. Firstly, the connection of unlawfulness doctrine, due to its indisputable practical significance. This theory has basically managed to leave the exclusion of unlawful evidence to the discretion of the sentencing court. As we will see below, the judge must justify, from a double internal and external perspective, whether or not the way in which the violation occurred, its intensity and the need to protect the fundamental right merit the procedural expulsion of the evidence. This analysis and its justification, in each case, will be carried out at the discretion of the corresponding judge and this may, in the end, undermine the legal security of the parties who will not know, until the judgement is handed down, whether the flawed evidence can be assessed or not. Moreover, if the decision can be appealed, the *ad quem* court can reconsider the analysis and rule on the admissibility or invalidity of the prohibited evidence, so that the uncertainty about the effectiveness of the evidence can continue beyond one instance.

Secondly, in the next section, we will study the most recent paradigmatic case of unlawful evidence in Spain, which refers to the unlawfulness of evidence obtained by private individuals, which was analysed in JSC 116/2017, of 23 February (TOL5969881) and subsequently in JCC 97/2019, of 16 July (TOL7446118).[41] This analysis is necessary, on the one hand, because it is the most recent jurisprudential line of the CC in relation to prohibited evidence and, on the other hand, because in the aforementioned JCC of 2019, an important systematisation and reinterpretation of the most relevant constitutional jurisprudence on the subject of prohibited evidence is carried out. This judgement highlights the theory of the connection of unlawfulness and also incorporates a two-tier analysis technique similar to that applied in these cases by the European Court of Human Rights.

---

40 We deal extensively with this procedural incident for unlawful evidence, regulated in art. 287 of the Civil Procedure Act in C.M. Madrid Boquín, *La prueba ilícita en el proceso civil, loc.cit.*

41 This jurisprudential position has been endorsed in subsequent judgements, for example, JNA 23/2019, of 20 November (TOL7.602.138); JSC, Third Chamber, 1174/2021, of 27 September (TOL8.610.928); JSC, Second Chamber, 807/2022, of 7 October (TOL9.259.913); and JSC, Third Chamber, 722/2023, of 29 May (TOL9 594.642).

Thus, the theory of the connection of unlawfulness was first included in JCC 81/1998, of 2 April (TOL80.937). In this case, the CC refused to grant protection to a person convicted of a crime against public health (drug trafficking), having carried out an illegal wiretap in the process, but with the existence of four witnesses (civil guards) and having seized the drugs during the surveillance operation that ended in his arrest, an operation that was articulated by what was heard during the wiretap. The question was, therefore, to decide whether the causal connection existing in the latter evidence contaminated it by the illegal wiretapping or whether, on the contrary, it could support the conviction because it was legally independent.[42] The CC reasoned, in essence, as follows:

> *Consequently, if from the natural perspective, the evidence in question had no connection whatsoever with the event constituting the infringement of the substantive fundamental right, that is, if it had a different and totally unrelated real cause, its validity and the consequent possibility of assessment for the purpose of overriding the presumption of innocence would, from this perspective, be indisputable.*
>
> *The problem arises, therefore, when taking into consideration the event as it actually occurred, the evidence in question is linked to the infringement of the right, because it has been obtained from the knowledge derived from it.*
>
> *Well, in such cases, the general rule, as we have expressed on several occasions and expressly reaffirm now, is that any evidential element that is intended to be deduced from a fact that violates the fundamental right to the secrecy of telephone communications is subject to the prohibition of assessment ex-art. 24.2 of the Spanish Constitution.*
>
> *However, while establishing the general doctrine we have just outlined and bearing in mind that, as we have repeatedly stated, fundamental rights are neither unlimited nor absolute, in exceptional cases we have admitted that, although the evidence against the prosecution was naturally linked to the event constituting the violation of the fundamental right because it derived from the knowledge acquired from it, it was legally independent of it and, consequently, we recognised it as valid and, therefore, apt to undermine the presumption of innocence(…).*
>
> *As has been said, such reflect evidence is, from an intrinsic point of view, constitutionally legitimate. Therefore, in order to conclude that the prohibition of assessment also extends to them, it must be specified that they are linked to those that directly violated the substantive fundamental right, that is, a link must be established between the former and the latter that allows it to be affirmed that the constitutional illegitimacy of the former also extends to the latter (connection of unlawfulness). In the presence or absence of this connection lies,*

---

42 This judgement is explained in detail by its own rapporteur, see T. Vives Antón, 'Consideraciones constitucionales sobe la exclusión de los "frutos del árbol emponzoñado"', *Revista Jurídica de la Comunidad Valenciana*, 2002/4, pp. 12 et seq. See also A. Planchadell Gargallo, *La prueba prohibida: Evolución jurisprudencial*, loc.cit.

therefore, the ratio of the prohibition to assess evidence obtained from knowledge derived from other evidence that violates the right to secrecy of communications.

(...), the Supreme Court understands that given the circumstances of the case and, in particular, the observation and monitoring of the appellant, the suspicions against him and the irrelevance of the data obtained through the telephone tapping, the knowledge derived from the interference with the fundamental right contrary to the Constitution was neither indispensable nor in itself decisive of the occupation of the drug or, what is the same, that this occupation would also have been reasonably obtained without the infringement of the right.

That statement which, from the legal perspective we are now considering, breaks, according to the appreciation of the Supreme Court, the link between the original and the derivative evidence, is not, in itself, a fact, but a judgement of experience about the degree of connection that determines the relevance or irrelevance of the questioned evidence. Therefore, it is not exempt from our control; but, given that, in principle, it is the responsibility of the ordinary Judges and Courts, the examination of this Court must be limited to verifying the reasonableness of the same and that, in the present case, it cannot be considered to be unreasonable or arbitrary, we must conclude that, from the point of view set out above, the assessment of the evidence in this case does not infringe the right to a fair trial (...).

The connection of unlawfulness is undoubtedly, in addition to a refined technical evolution of the theory of legally independent evidence that we already mentioned, the most important exception to the rule of the reflect effectiveness of unlawful evidence (theory of the fruit of the poisonous tree),[43] and the doctrine states not without reason that in fact this exception practically means the disappearance of the reflect effectiveness of unlawful evidence in criminal proceedings.[44]

---

43 An extensive jurisprudential summary see C. Climent Durán, *La prueba penal* (2nd ed.), Tirant lo Blanch, Valencia, 2005, t. I, pp. 423 et seq.; and E. Urbano Castrillo, M.A. Torres Morato, *La prueba ilícita penal. Estudio jurisprudencial* (3rd ed.), Thomson-Aranzadi, Pamplona 2003, pp. 75 et seq.

44 J.J. López Ortega, 'Prueba y proceso penal. El alcance derivado de la prueba ilícita en la jurisprudencia constitucional (A propósito de la STC 81/1998)', *Revista de Derecho y Proceso Penal*, 1999/1, pp. 133 et seq.; A. Juanes Peces, 'La prueba prohibida (análisis de la Sentencia de 7 de 7 de abril de 1999 del Tribunal Constitucional)', *Repertorio Aranzadi del Tribunal Constitucional*, 1999/2, pp. 1682–1686; M. Cedeño Hernán, M., 'Algunas cuestiones suscitadas en torno al derecho a la presunción de inocencia a la luz de la jurisprudencia constitucional', *Cuadernos de Derecho Público*, 2000/10, p. 206; M. Miranda Estrampes, 'La regla de exclusión de la prueba ilícita: historia de su nacimiento y de su progresiva limitación', *op.cit.*, p. 59, ff.; and I. López-Barajas Perea, 'La prueba ilícitamente obtenida y su eficacia refleja', *Revista Actualizad Jurídica Aranzadi*, 2006/708, p. 1. Also, very critical is N. Martí Sánchez, 'La llamada "prueba ilícita" y sus consecuencias procesales', *Actualidad Penal*, 1998/7, pp. 154 et seq.

This doctrine has subsequently been maintained in numerous judgements of the CC,[45] and followed practically without nuance by the Spanish SC.[46] The latter has made a precise summary of the theory of unlawfulness connection in JSC 9/2004, of 19 January (TOL352.433), in a case of a crime against public health in which telephone tapping was ordered without declaring the procedural proceedings secret, in the following terms:

> *The greatest difficulties are to be found when determining the scope of this evidential ineffectiveness in relation to the evidence produced subsequently and which derives from this unconstitutional telephone observation, an ineffectiveness which must reach all other evidence which has the so-called connection of unlawfulness with that evidence. This is what we said in ground 3.2 of our judgement 666/2003, of 17 June:*
>
> *The Constitutional Court's thesis on this issue of the connection of unlawfulness is well known, initially set out in its judgement 81 of April 2nd, 1998, which examines the problem of the possible contamination of later evidence by the constitutional unlawfulness of earlier evidence in which a fundamental substantive right was violated.*
>
> *As a general rule, the unconstitutionality of the second piece of evidence (reflect evidence) must be extended to the unconstitutionality of the first piece of evidence with the consequence that it cannot be considered as evidence, provided that there is a natural connection or causal link between the two.*
>
> *By way of exception, such reflect evidence can be considered as evidence for the prosecution when, despite the existence of this natural connection, what the Constitutional Court calls the connection of unlawfulness is lacking, that is, when, due to the assessment of the different elements in play, this subsequent evidence can be considered legally independent and, in itself considered, must be considered as having been lawfully obtained and brought to the proceedings.*
>
> *The following elements can be considered in this judgement 81/1998 in order to determine this connection of unlawfulness:*
>
> 1. *The nature or importance of the constitutional violation that appears as the basis for the unlawfulness of the first test.*
> 2. *The result achieved with this unconstitutional evidence, that is to say, the relevance of the data or information known through this unlawful evidence in the practice of the subsequent lawful test.*

---

45 For example, judgements of the CC 49/1999, of 5 April (TOL528.614); 94/1999, of 31 May (TOL81.159); 239/1999, of 20 December (TOL81.266); 136/2000, of 29 May (TOL26.502); 299/2000 of December 11th, 2000 (TOL81.725); 14/2001 of January 29th, 2001 (TOL81.394); 167/2002 of September 18th, 2002 (TOL205.001); and 26/2006 of January 30th, 2006 (TOL817.646).

46 For example, judgements of the SC 2011/2002, of 3 December (TOL4.922.052); 2210/2001, of 20 November (TOL129.225); 229/2008, of 15 May (TOL 1.320.837); of October 31st, 2012 (TOL129.225); of January 22nd, 2013 (TOL3.010.880) and June 11th, 2013 (TOL3.888.381).

3. *Whether there were other elements, apart from this unlawful evidence, by means of which it could reasonably be thought that the very thing that could have been known through the practice of this unconstitutional evidence would have been known.*
4. *If the fundamental right infringed needed special protection, particularly because of the greater ease of such an infringement, so that it could remain clandestine.*
5. *Finally, the mental attitude of the person or persons who caused the violation, specifically whether there was the intention or just a mere error on the part of the perpetrators, bearing in mind that the deterrent effect, one of the bases of the prohibition on the assessment of unconstitutional evidence, is of less significance in these cases of error(…).*

The connection of unlawfulness is therefore based on the fact that a piece of lawful derivative evidence is the fruit of the poisoned tree if there is a causal connection between the independent evidence and the unlawful evidence (a natural relationship between them so that the first is obtained from the second), and if there is also a connection of unlawfulness (the two pieces of evidence are constitutionally unlawful).[47] It should be noted, therefore, that it is no longer sufficient, as the CC had maintained until that moment, for the causal connection or natural relationship between the second piece of evidence and the first prohibited piece of evidence for the second piece of evidence to be considered as prohibited evidence by application of the reflect effect, but that another kind of connection is also necessary, this one not of a natural but of a legal nature, the connection of unlawfulness.[48]

The assessment of the connection of unlawfulness will depend on the nature and characteristics of the original infringement of the fundamental right produced in the first place since if it is not serious and the evidence can be obtained by other means there will be no such connection; as well as on its result and the essential needs of protection of the fundamental right affected by the unlawfulness in the second place, so that this fundamental right is not deprived of any of its essential guarantees by the obtaining of the derived evidence, in which case there will also be no such connection of unlawfulness.[49]

47 See the differences between evidence that is different but derived from that obtained unlawfully, and independent evidence for the purposes of the connection of unlawfulness in the aforementioned JSC 1203/2002, of 18 July (TOL203.139).

48 Thus, T. Vives Antón, *Consideraciones constitucionales sobre la exclusión de los "frutos del árbol emponzoñado"*, loc.cit.

49 See M. Cedeño Hernán, *Algunas cuestiones suscitadas en torno al derecho a la presunción de inocencia a la luz de la jurisprudencia constitucional*, pp. 206–207 et seq.

The existence or not of intentionality or serious negligence in the original violation, as well as the objective nature of the violation committed, must, therefore, be analysed in the specific case. Thus, the aforementioned JCC 66/2009, of 9 March (TOL1.468.758) states that:

> *(...) we also established a dual perspective of analysis to determine whether or not there is a connection of unlawfulness: an internal perspective, which takes into account the nature and characteristics of the infringement of the right to secrecy of communications in the original test (which guarantees of the interference with the right have been undermined and in what way), as well as the immediate result of the infringement (the knowledge acquired through the unconstitutionally practised interference), and another external perspective, which takes into account the essential needs of protecting the reality and effectiveness of the right to secrecy of communications. Specifically, we have said that: These two perspectives are complementary, since only if the reflect evidence is legally unrelated to the infringement of the right and the prohibition to assess it is not required by the essential needs for its protection will it be understood that its effective assessment is constitutionally legitimate, as it does not have a negative impact on either of the two aspects that make up the content of the substantive fundamental right (JCC 81/1998, of 2 April, FJ 4; in the same sense, among others, judgements of the CC 121/1998, of 15 June, FJ 6; 49/1999, of 5 April, FJ 14; 94/1999, of 31 May, FJ 6; 166/1999, of 27 September, FJ 4; 171/1999, of 27 September, FJ 4; 136/2000, of 29 May, FJ 6).*

Doctrinally, this judgement has been criticized for the fact that the CC has made use of a contrived construction[50] to avoid impunity: A technical flaw in the process, it is said, cannot let a murderer go free. It could also mean a disproportionate extension of the exceptions because, given the terms in which it has been formulated, the possibilities of finding cases in which the required connections of unlawfulness do not exist are theoretically many.

4.2. Incorporating the doctrine of the ECtHR: integrity of the fair trial and the instrumentality of unlawful evidence

Having reviewed the evolution of the different theories on the exclusion of prohibited evidence in Spain and the jurisprudential exceptions that subsequently qualified it, we will conclude this analysis by studying the most recent jurisprudential development on the application of the rule of exclusion of article 11.1 OLJ,

50 J.A. Díaz Cabiale, R. Martín Morales, *La garantía constitucional de la inadmisión de la prueba ilícitamente obtenida*, Civitas, Madrid, 2001, p. 104; and M. Miranda Estrampes, 'La regla de exclusión de la prueba ilícita: historia de su nacimiento y de su progresiva limitación', *op.cit.*, p. 61, et seq. Also, T. Armenta Deu, *Prueba ilícita y reforma del proceso penal*, *op.cit.*, p. 196, et seq.

contained in JCC 97/2019, of 16 July (TOL7.446.118). By means of this decision, the CC rejected the constitutional appeal brought against JSC, Second Chamber, 116/2017 of 23 February (TOL5.969.881) which, by way of background, we must comment on previously.

JSC, Second Chamber, 116/2017 of 23 February (TOL5.969.881), analyses the admissibility of the evidence used to convict the accused as the perpetrator of two crimes against the Public Treasury. The origin of the contested evidence goes back to the internationally known "Falciani list", drawn up by a computer expert, an employee of a bank in Switzerland, who collected personal and financial information on thousands of the bank's clients. It is unclear whether his purpose was to profit from the subsequent sale of that information or whether, on the contrary, he had collected the data for the purpose of exposing corruption in the banking system, since many of the institution's customers were apparently involved in illicit activities.

According to the judgement, Falciani had obtained the clients' information "in breach of his duty of confidentiality" and had taken advantage of his access to it "to draw up, by means of the appropriate cross-referencing of data, a profile of taxpayers - including the defendant - who had concealed their earnings from the tax authorities". However, the SC concluded that it will not be necessary to exclude unlawful evidence obtained by a private individual as long as this person, in violating the fundamental right, was not acting for the purpose of obtaining evidence or collaborating with the authorities in the criminal investigation. The exclusion of unlawful evidence, the SC held, should not be done automatically, but rather by analysing the context and the protection needs of the specific case.

> *In its historical origin and in its jurisprudential systematisation, the exclusionary rule only makes sense as an element of prevention against the excesses of the State in the investigation of crime. This idea has been expressed in all the doctrines that have been formulated in recent decades with the aim of restricting the automatism of the exclusionary rule. Whether by resorting to the exceptions of good faith, independent source or attenuated connection, the aim is to avoid an understanding which, due to its rigidity, separates the exclusionary rule from its true basis. The prohibition on assessing evidence obtained in violation of fundamental rights takes on its genuine meaning as a mechanism to restrain police excesses in the search for the hidden truth in the commission of any crime.*

Thus, in order to be able to assess evidence unlawfully obtained by a private individual, it will be necessary to analyse two main aspects: first, the scope and intensity of the infringement of the fundamental right; second, the significance of the activity of the private individual, i.e. that he has not acted with the purpose of obtaining evidence and that he has not collaborated with the State in the criminal investigation. The SC explains it as follows:

> *Decisive, therefore, are the extent and intensity of the infringement of the fundamental right undermined. But it is also important to consider the significance of the activity of the private individual who, as a result of his actions, discovers documents or a computer file of singular evidential value. Only in this way will the decision on the exclusionary rule not run the risk of deviating from its genuine basis. Whoever seeks to obtain documents for financial gain or whoever seeks to denounce injustice in the financial system is certainly not becoming a State agent who spontaneously joins in the exercise of ius puniendi. The rules of exclusion of evidence are distanced from their true meaning when they have no connection with the purpose that is at the origin of their formulation. It is a question of limiting the State's zeal in the prosecution of criminal offences, of keeping the agents of authority away from the temptation to make use of means of evidence which, due to their high degree of interference in the circle of fundamental rights, are subject to constitutional guarantees designed to safeguard them. It has been rightly said that the proscription of unlawful evidence is explained by the deterrent effect for the official State apparatus of being fully aware that it will never be able to make use of evidence obtained in violation of the constitutional rules at stake.*

In synthesis, we can observe that this new line of reasoning stems from the deterrent effect as the basis of the exclusionary rule, to establish that the evidence can be assessed if the person who violated the fundamental right was a private individual who did not act with the purpose of obtaining evidence and who did not collaborate with public authorities in obtaining it.

Nonetheless, the JSC, Second Chamber, 116/2017 of 23 February (TOL5.969.881) was appealed before the CC. Departing from the analysis that the SC had carried out, which focused, as we have stated, on the possibility of using evidence that had been obtained unlawfully by private individuals in the context of criminal proceedings, the CC used this opportunity to carry out an important systematisation and reinterpretation of its thirty-five years of case law on the exclusion of unlawful evidence. With this, the jurisprudential doctrine on prohibited evidence underwent a major change in Spain, as the CC decided to move away from the guidelines established by American jurisprudence and to adopt the position that the ECtHR had been upholding for some decades.

In this sense, the central axis will be the link between the unlawful evidence and the breach of due process as a necessary requirement to determine its exclusion, also highlighting the instrumental nature of the violation of the substantive fundamental right. In addition, the CC clarifies that the public or private origin of the violation of the fundamental right will be irrelevant, which rules out the exception of unlawful evidence obtained by private individuals that had been formulated in JSC, Second Chamber, 116/2017 of 23 February (TOL5.969.881).

Thus, in Judgement 97/2019, of 16 July (TOL7.446.118), the CC brought its position closer to that of the ECtHR in relation to the exclusion of unlawful evidence, accepting the doctrine of the ECtHR which holds that the analysis of the unlawfulness of evidence must be carried out at two levels.[51] In the first level of analysis, it will be necessary to determine whether there has been a violation of a fundamental right at the time of obtaining the source of evidence. If the answer is positive, the court must determine, in the second level of analysis, whether the procedural use of this illegally obtained evidence has led to a violation of the right to a fair trial. Only if the second level of analysis shows that the right to a fair or equitable process has also been violated will the evidence be excluded or the proceedings annulled.[52]

In the analysed judgement, the CC begins by explaining the basic idea, already formulated in that first judgement of 1984, that "the constitutional prohibition of the judicial assessment of unlawfully obtained evidence constitutes an objective guarantee of our system of fundamental rights, linked to the idea of a fair trial (art. 24.2 CE)". It then continues to review the historical background to this figure in his own case law, referring to a judgement and two orders from 1984, in which it was initially considered that the exclusion of unlawful evidence was a question of mere ordinary legality and, therefore, lacked constitutional relevance.[53] However, it recognises that it was with JCC 114/1984, of 29 November (TOL79.403), that the analysis of the unlawfulness of evidence and its procedural consequences was really addressed from a constitutional point of view. The Constitutional Court

51 See, inter alia, ECtHR judgements of March 26th, 1982 (*Case Adolf v. Austria*, TOL164.152); of July 12th, 1988 (*Case De Cubber v. Belgium*, TOL168.780); 4/1988, of December 16th, 1988 (*Case Schenk v. Switzerland*, TOL216.238); of May 12th, 2000 (*Case Kahn v. United Kingdom*); 552/2001, of September 25th, 2001 (*Case P.G and J.H. v. United Kingdom*); 64/2002 of November 5th, 2002 (*Allan v. United Kingdom*); July 11th, 2006 (*Jalloh v. Germany*, TOL965.144); April 3rd, 2003 (*Copland v. United Kingdom*) and 45/2008 of July 1st, 2008 (*Liberty v. United Kingdom*, TOL1.331.869). The position and jurisprudence of the ECtHR in relation to prohibited evidence is further explained in C.M. Madrid Boquín, 'La prueba prohibida ante el Tribunal Europeo de Derechos Humanos: luces y sombras del caso Zherdev c. Ucrania', *Revista de Estudios Europeos*, 2017/1, pp. 78–93.

52 On this point we can also refer to J.M. Asencio Mellado, 'La STC 97/2019, de 16 de julio. Descanse en paz la prueba ilícita', *Diario La Ley*, 2019/9499; and J.I. Zaragoza Tejada, D.A. Gutiérrez Azanza, 'La exclusión de la prueba ilícita tras la sentencia del Tribunal Constitucional de 16 de julio de 2019 sobre la "Lista Falciani"', *Revista Aranzadi de Derecho y Proceso Penal*, 2019/56.

53 JCC 9/1984 of January 30th, 1984 (TOL79.299); also resolutions (autos) CC 173/1984 of March 21st, 1984 and 289/1984 of May 16th, 1984 (TOL242.199).

then reinterpreted its 1984 ruling and emphasised that it formulated three guiding principles, which can be summarised as follows:

a) The procedural inadmissibility of evidence obtained in violation of a substantive fundamental right does not constitute a requirement deriving from the content of the fundamental right affected. In other words, the fundamental right violated at the time of obtaining a source of evidence does not incorporate within its content the obligation to deprive of all legal effectiveness the consequences of any act that violates it.
b) The claim to exclude unlawful evidence derives from the preferential position of fundamental rights in the legal system, is strictly procedural in nature and must be approached from the point of view of the guarantees of a fair trial (art. 24.2 SC). There is, therefore, no autonomous right to the exclusion of unlawful evidence, but rather this guarantee forms part of the right to a trial with all guarantees. Along these lines, and building on its 1984 ruling, the CC takes advantage of the 2019 ruling to qualify the importance of the exclusion of unlawful evidence, in the following sense:

   The hypothetical reception of unlawfully obtained evidence does not necessarily imply a violation of a fundamental right. Rather, we are faced with 'an objective and implicit guarantee in the system of fundamental rights', whose validity and preferential position in the legal system may require the rejection of evidence obtained in violation of these rights; therefore, if there is a violation of the Constitution, it occurs within the process and in accordance with the rights and procedural guarantees provided in art. 24.2 CE.

c) The violation of the procedural guarantees of Art. 24.2 SC must be determined, in relation to the unlawfully obtained evidence, by means of a balancing judgement aimed at ensuring the balance and equality of the parties, that is, the integrity of the process in question as a fair and equitable process.

While it is true that the requirement of a balancing test to determine the unlawful nature of evidence is not alien to the Spanish courts, the novelty of this line of jurisprudence lies in the emphasis placed on "the integrity of the fair trial", that is, in the adoption of the doctrine of the ECtHR, according to which the nullity of unlawfully obtained evidence is made dependent on the breach of the guarantee of a fair or equitable trial, considering the process as a whole. Thus, the CC indicates that it must be analysed whether "the integrity of the criminal proceedings as a fair trial, in which fundamental rights cannot be violated as an instrumental method of obtaining evidential advantages" is compromised. Therefore, the ineffectiveness of the unlawful evidence will only be necessary if this integrity of the process is compromised; otherwise, "the exclusion of the evidence is revealed as an impertinent and excessive remedy which, therefore, must be rejected".

It is interesting to note how JCC 97/2019 systematises the exceptions previously formulated by the CC, bringing together the different approaches developed over 35 years in relation to unlawful evidence. The judgement especially includes and broadens the field of application of the theory of the connection of unlawfulness, highlighting as elements to be weighed up the integrity of due process and the instrumentality of the unlawful evidence. In this sense, the requirement of instrumentality of unlawful evidence means that, in order to merit procedural exclusion, it will be necessary for the violation of the fundamental right to have been committed "instrumentally", that is, as a means of obtaining a source of evidence. Contrariwise, if the infringement is not motivated by a desire to obtain evidence, then it will not be constitutionally relevant from a procedural point of view and, therefore, will not merit exclusion of the unlawfully obtained evidence.[54] The judgement explains it as follows:

> *Once the previous violation of the substantive fundamental right has been established, the second step is to determine its link or connection with the procedural rights of the parties from the perspective of a fair and equitable process, or, in the words of JCC 114/1984 itself, the 'link' of the disputed evidence with 'a right of freedom of those that can be protected constitutionally'. Such a nexus or link exists if the decision to incorporate it into the body of evidence evidences a rupture in the procedural balance between the parties, that is, an 'inequality between the parties in the trial (art. 14 of the Constitution), an inequality that has been unlawfully sought for its own benefit by those who have obtained evidential instruments in disregard of the fundamental rights of another' (JCC 114/1984, 29 November, FJ 4, and 49/1999, 5 April, FJ 12). The constitutional prohibition on the admission of unlawful evidence is thus revealed as an instrumental prohibition, that is, as a constitutional mandate to identify those violations of fundamental rights committed precisely to undermine the integrity of the process, that is, aimed at obtaining procedural advantages to the detriment of the integrity and balance required in a fair and equitable process insofar as it generates 'an unacceptable institutional confirmation of inequality between the parties' (JCC 114/1984, 29 November, FJ 5, and 49/1996, 26 March, FJ 2).*

---

54 Thus, for example, in the case analysed, it is considered that Mr. Falciani violated the right to privacy of bank clients, but not with the purpose of obtaining a source of evidence to be used in a certain trial against a certain defendant. According to the SC, it could be that he was trying to expose corruption in the banking system or that he intended to profit from the sale of the information. Therefore, in the case analysed, the violation of the fundamental right that made it possible to obtain the source of inculpatory evidence was not carried out instrumentally in order to prove something in that specific criminal proceeding. Consequently, despite the fact that a fundamental right was violated in obtaining the information (violation at the first level of analysis), the fair process as a whole would not be violated (lack of violation at the second level of analysis) and therefore it would not be necessary to exclude the unlawfully obtained evidence.

Then, returning to the two-tier analysis necessary to weigh the exclusion of spurious evidence, the CC states that:

> *As has been seen, in the doctrine of this Court two steps are necessary to determine the possible violation of art. 24.2 SC as a consequence of the evidentiary reception of unlawfully obtained evidence: A) it must be determined, firstly, whether the original unlawfulness has consisted of the violation of a substantive fundamental right or of freedom; B) it must be clarified, in the event that the fundamental right has indeed been compromised, whether between said original violation and the integrity of the guarantees of the fair trial that our Constitution guarantees (art. 24.2 SC) there is a nexus or link that shows a specific need for protection, substantiated in the radical exclusion of the evidence of the unlawfully obtained material (24.2 SC) there is a nexus or link that evidences a specific need for protection, substantiated in the radical exclusion of unlawfully obtained material from the body of evidence.*

In the case analysed by the judgement, it is assumed that there has been an infringement of the right to privacy, which occurred at the time the source of the evidence was obtained. This was determined by the *a quo* court and, not being part of the subject matter of the debate, the CC cannot rule on this point *ex officio* and even less so to the appellant's detriment. It is therefore assumed, at the first level of analysis, that there has been a violation of the fundamental right to privacy; it only remains to be determined whether or not, at the second level of analysis, there has been a violation of the right to a fair trial. According to the CC:

> *The finding of the original violation of the substantive fundamental right (in this case, the right to privacy) does not, however, in itself determine the automatic violation of the right to due process (art. 24.2 SC), generating the imperative need to inadmit the corresponding evidence. The appeal to art. 24.2 SC would be superfluous if every violation of a substantive fundamental right entailed, per se, the consequent impossibility of using the materials derived from it. If this were the case, the use of such materials in criminal proceedings would be, per se, a violation of the substantive right itself (in this case, privacy) without the appeal to art. 24.2 SC to justify the exclusion having any relevance or scope. Our doctrine, as has already been explained, does not impose such automatism, but rather leads to a weighing up of the interests involved.*

The statement that the violation of a fundamental right does not in itself entail the need to exclude unlawfully obtained evidence cannot be overlooked. In our opinion, this position directly contradicts the rule established in Article 11.1 OLJ, according to which "evidence obtained, directly or indirectly, in violation of fundamental rights or freedoms shall have no effect". However, the CC considers that if article 11.1 OLJ is interpreted in the literal sense that evidence obtained in violation of fundamental rights will be ineffective, this would constitute an undesirable "automatism" that would prevent the two-level balancing test from being carried out. Therefore, the CC proceeds to explain, from the point of view of the instrumentality of unlawful evidence and the protection of the integrity of the fair trial, how the exclusion rule of article 11.1 OLJ should be interpreted.

> *[Article 11.1 OLJ] does not refer to any violation of fundamental rights but, as corresponds to the strict procedural sphere in which its effectiveness is deployed, to the proscription of the instrumental use of means of investigation that harm these primordial rights (…).*
>
> *Art. 18.1 SC (which protects privacy) and art. 24.2 SC (which protects the procedural rights of the parties) are precepts that have different aims, the specific aim of the 'process with all the guarantees' provided for in art. 24.2 SC being to preserve the integrity of the process, prohibiting evidence from being obtained by instrumentally violating fundamental rights. The specific meaning of the guarantee of due process included in art. 24.2 SC is, therefore, to protect citizens from the instrumental violation of their fundamental rights that has been verified precisely in order to obtain evidence. This protects the integrity of the justice system, the equality of the parties and discourages public bodies, in particular the police, but also private individuals themselves, from carrying out acts contrary to fundamental rights in order to obtain an evidentiary advantage in the proceedings. Apart from such cases, i.e. when there is no connection or link between the act determining the interference with the substantive fundamental right and the obtaining of sources of evidence, the needs for protection of this right are outside the procedural sphere and can be substantiated in criminal or civil proceedings directly aimed at sanctioning, restoring or compensating the effects of the infringement verified in the former.*

Consequently, the CC rejects the "automatic" application of article 11.1 OLJ -or rather, its literal interpretation- and opts for the application of a balancing test with a two-tier analysis. Now, focusing on the examination of the specific case analysed, derived from the Falciani List, we can highlight two important points.

Firstly, the CC opposes the exception of unlawful evidence obtained by private individuals, raised by the SC in the contested decision. In this regard, the judgement states that:

> *In general terms, it should be borne in mind that the fact that the original infringement of the substantive right was committed, in the case in question, by a private individual does not alter in any way the canon of constitutionality applicable from the point of view of the right to due process (art. 24.2 SC), so that the exclusion of the evidential elements obtained must also be, in this type of case, the starting point or general rule, although, in each specific case, the judicial body can assess, in accordance with the parameters that have already been set out, the absence of the need for procedural protection in relation to the violation committed, incorporating, in these exceptional cases, the disputed elements into the body of evidence.*

Secondly, the Constitutional Court developed the balancing test, considering both the criteria set out in JCC 81/1998, of 2 April (TOL80.937) on the connection of unlawfulness, and the new parameters formulated in the judgement now analysed. In this sense, from the internal point of view and considering the nature and characteristics of the violation of the fundamental right, it was considered that:

> *The protection of the privacy of the bank's customers against the violation committed by an employee of the bank is fully satisfied by the criminal or civil proceedings that may be carried out in the country in which the intrusion inter privatos has been committed, without there being any instrumental connection with the Spanish criminal proceedings that would imply, in accordance with art. 24.2 SC, an additional need for legal protection of privacy within those proceedings that must inevitably lead to a pronouncement of inadmissibility of the evidence.*

Moreover, considering the results of the infringement of the fundamental right, the CC found that the data used by the Spanish Treasury related only to "peripheral and innocuous" aspects of so-called "economic privacy".

On the other hand, from an external point of view, it was concluded that in this case there was no certain risk that the admission of the evidence in question would lead to practices that would compromise the effectiveness of the fundamental right violated in the future.

> *In Spain, the obtaining by the authorities of bank data for the purposes of tax or criminal investigations is provided for by law and is fully accessible through ordinary procedural instruments. It does not appear, therefore, from an external point of view, that there is any legal need to extend to criminal proceedings the protection of the right to privacy in relation to an intromission inter privatos such as the one verified in the case in question. Spain does not have a legal system of banking opacity that requires criminal proceedings to be used to prevent this type of violation of fundamental rights between private individuals.*

For all these reasons, the CC concluded that, despite the violation of the right to privacy, there had been no violation of the right to a fair trial, nor of the right to the presumption of innocence. Therefore, evidentiary exclusion would not be required and the contested information can validly be assessed by the courts.

5. Conclusions

Finally, there is no choice but to conclude that reality prevails. The current restrictions on the application of the initial doctrines on prohibited evidence are so important that what we are talking about today is not evidence but impunity, i.e. it does not matter so much whether the evidence is lawful or not as whether the real culprit is punished. When our highest courts come up with theories, for example, of good faith or the connection of unlawfulness, it is because the court considers that society would never understand that a criminal, especially if he is a savage terrorist, a brutal murderer, a ruthless drug trafficker, an important corrupt politician, an inhuman facilitator of human trafficking, or a despicable corrupter of minors, that is, if we are dealing with socially very relevant cases, would be set free on a "mere legal technicality".

However, this does not prevent us from criticising these restrictions to the exclusionary rule of the OLJ for being based on rather artificial constructions, without any legal support whatsoever. These exceptions, in addition to avoiding impunity, are also intended to protect the public investigating authority against possible failures that would, if the initial theories of prohibited evidence were maintained, inevitably lead to the acquittal of the accused. In addition, we must consider that even if the construction were artificial, we do not have consistent and certain dogmatic jurisprudence, so new surprises can occur at any time. This is why it can be said without hesitation that we have gone from assuming the prohibition of evidence for its effect of deterring the police from acting against the law and constitutionally protecting the rights of the defendant or accused citizens against the interventionist power of the State in the individual sphere, to purely utilitarian considerations of punishing anyone who is "evidently" guilty of a horrendous crime in any way possible.

In fact, in recent times, we can find few rulings in the Spanish Constitutional Court or in the Spanish Supreme Court in which an appeal is granted or where the initial ruling is overturned on the grounds that the process is null and void because evidence has been declared to have been obtained unlawfully.

Quo vadis, then, unlawful evidence? The truth is that there is no precise answer to this question, although intuitively one might intuitively suggest something. In any case, it is necessary to take up the reins once again and urgently in such a delicate matter and return to positions of guarantee, this time taking into account the practical experiences that caused us to stray from the path we had taken, without ignoring the social demands that motivated them, reinforcing the legality of criminal investigation so that all those who intervene in it are sufficiently trained and qualified to avoid those technical failures that cause procedural nullities and subsequently motivate undesired acquittals. In this sense, proper police training in these legal matters is the first goal to be achieved in order to return to the rule of law. This would also make a significant contribution to preparing the necessary instrument of prosecution to serve better and more effectively in the fight against the most heinous crimes and their ruthless perpetrators.

Furthermore, it would also be very useful if all the cases of possible evidential illegality which violate the Constitution were to be regulated, that is to say, expressly regulated in ordinary law, in such a way that their infringement would be considered either a cause for the nullity of the whole process and, therefore, the release of the accused without charge or acquittal, or the nullity only of the act, allowing conviction in the case of the existence of other evidence obtained lawfully. This is based on the useful German distinction between a prohibition on the taking of evidence and a prohibition on the use of evidence, as the two cases do not cover the same phenomenon. This would also help to simplify the process, particularly in the area of evidence, in view of the clarity of the rules achieved.

Among the first cases, i.e. those that cause nullity, the first should include the evidentiary violations that occurred during the detention of the defendant, and in particular in relation to his right of defence, as well as those that affect his constitutional rights to life, to physical integrity, to personal privacy, to the inviolability of his home, to the secrecy of communications and to the protection of his personal data, i.e. the non-procedural or substantive fundamental rights. On the other hand, all the others would fall into the second category (annulability due to procedural irregularities).

The reflect-effect of the prohibited evidence should also be elevated to legal status, so that it should be expressly stated by law, and not only with a brief adverb, that evidence obtained from the poisonous tree is also contaminated, defining whether or not it can be used in connection with the above classification.

The most important initial step to be taken in order to avoid greater evils, therefore, in the matter of evidentiary prohibitions, would be firstly to achieve adequate legal training of the criminal prosecution bodies, especially the police; and secondly, to legally regulate in detail all cases of evidentiary prohibitions, also establishing their procedural effects in law. This proposal would adequately respect the right to due process, fair trial or due process, a point that has been decisive for the analysis of prohibited evidence, according to the doctrine of the ECtHR, as well as providing undoubted legal certainty.

This would make it possible to respect something that should not go without saying, which is that the Constitution is above any ordinary law and any interpretation of it by a court, and that in order to return to a well-founded and sensible guarantee of rights, given the current imbalance between opting for the protection of the rights of the accused or for the exclusion of evidence from the process, it should be enough to apply it taking into account this criterion of normative superiority. True convergence and harmonisation in terms of rules of exclusion of evidence or prohibited evidence would be much easier to achieve if these proposals and others that could improve them were considered by the legislator, especially in view of the growing importance from a transnational point of view.

Bibliography

Alcaide González, J. M., *La prueba ilícita penal. Decadencia y extinción (Jurisprudencia práctica comparada con EEUU)*, La Ley, Málaga, 2013.

Armenta Deu, T., *La prueba ilícita (Un estudio comparado)*, Marcial Pons, Madrid, 2011.

Armenta Deu, T., 'Prueba ilícita y reforma del proceso penal', *Revista del Poder Judicial*, 2006, special issue XIX 'Propuestas para una nueva Ley de Enjuiciamiento Criminal', F. Gutiérrez-Alviz y Conradi (ed.).

Aguilera De Paz, E., *Comentarios a la Ley de Enjuiciamiento Criminal* (2nd ed.), Reus, Madrid, 1924.

Asencio Mellado, J. M., 'La STC 97/2019, de 16 de julio. Descanse en paz la prueba ilícita', in *Diario La Ley* 9499, 2019.

Asencio Mellado, J. M., *Prueba prohibida y prueba preconstituida*, Trivium, Madrid, 1989.

Asencio Mellado, J. M., 'La prueba prohibida en Jurisprudencia Constitucional (S.T.C. 114/84, de 29 de noviembre)', *Revista Valenciana de Estudios Autonómicos*, 1985/1.

Beling, E., *Die Beweisverbote als Grenzen der Wahrheitserforschung im Strafprozess*, Schletter'sche Buchhandlung, Breslau, 1903 (reprinted in Scientia Verlag, Aalen 1968).

Cedeño Hernán, M., 'Algunas cuestiones suscitadas en torno al derecho a la presunción de inocencia a la luz de la jurisprudencia constitucional', *Cuadernos de Derecho Público*, 2000/10.

Climent Durán, C., *La prueba penal* (2nd ed.), Tirant lo Blanch, Valencia, 2005.

Díaz Cabiale, J. A. and Martín Morales, R., *La garantía constitucional de la inadmisión de la prueba ilícitamente obtenida*, Civitas, Madrid, 2001.

Fernández López, M., *Prueba y presunción de inocencia*, Iustel, Madrid, 2005.

Fidalgo Gallardo, C., *Las "pruebas ilegales": De la exclusionary rule estadounidense al art. 11.1 LOPJ*, Centro de Estudios Políticos y Constitucionales, Madrid, 2003.

Gómez Colomer, J. L. (ed.), *Introducción al proceso penal federal de los Estados Unidos de Norteamérica*, Tirant lo Blanch, Valencia, 2013.

Gómez Colomer, J. L. (ed.), *Proceso Penal y Constitución de los Estados Unidos de Norteamérica (Casos destacados del Tribunal Supremo y Texto introductorio)*, Tirant lo Blanch, Valencia, 2012.

Gómez Colomer, J. L., 'La evolución de las teorías sobre la prueba prohibida aplicadas en el proceso penal español: del expansionismo sin límites al más puro reduccionismo. Una meditación sobre su desarrollo futuro inmediato'[in:],

Gómez Colomer, J. L. (ed.), *Prueba y proceso penal: análisis especial de la prueba prohibida en el sistema español y en el derecho comparado*, Tirant lo Blanch, Valencia, 2008.

Gómez Colomer, J. L. and. Planchadell Gargallo A., 'Prueba Prohibida', [in:] GONZÁLEZ CANO, M. I.; M. I. Romero Pradas (ed.), La prueba. Tomo II. La prueba en el proceso penal, Tirant lo Blanch, Valencia, 2017.

González Montes, J. L., 'La prueba obtenida ilícitamente con violación de los derechos fundamentales (El Derecho constitucional a la prueba y sus límites)', *Revista de Derecho Procesal*, 1990/ 1.

González Montes, J. L., 'Nuevas reflexiones en torno a la prueba ilícita', *Revista Derechos y Libertades del Instituto Bartolomé de las Casas*, 1993/2.

Guerrero Peralta, O. J., *Institutos probatorios del nuevo proceso penal*, Nueva Jurídica, Bogotá, 2009.

Juanes Peces, A., 'La prueba prohibida (análisis de la Sentencia de 7 de abril de 1999 del Tribunal Constitucional)', *Repertorio Aranzadi del Tribunal Constitucional*, 1999/2.

López-Barajas Perea, I., 'La prueba ilícitamente obtenida y su eficacia refleja', *Revista Actualizad Jurídica Aranzadi*, 2006/78.

López Ortega, J. J., 'Prueba y proceso penal. El alcance derivado de la prueba ilícita en la jurisprudencia constitucional (A propósito de la STC 81/1998)', *Revista de Derecho y Proceso Penal*, 1999/1.

Madrid Boquín, C. M., *La prueba ilícita en el proceso civil*, Tirant lo Blanch, Valencia, 2020.

Madrid Boquín, C. M., 'Los hallazgos casuales en la investigación criminal: actualidad legislativa y jurisprudencial en España', [in:] Gómez Colomer, J. L. Madrid Boquín, C. M. (eds.), *La instrucción del crimen: algunos problemas procesales*, Sepín, Madrid, 2020.

Madrid Boquín, C. M., 'La prueba prohibida ante el Tribunal Europeo de Derechos Humanos: luces y sombras del caso Zherdev c. Ucrania', *Revista de Estudios Europeos*, 2017/1.

Martí Sánchez, N., 'La llamada "prueba ilícita" y sus consecuencias procesales', *Actualidad Penal*, 1998/7.

Martínez García, E., *Eficacia de la prueba ilícita en el proceso penal (a la luz de la JSC 81/1998, de 2 de abril)*, Tirant lo Blanch, Valencia, 2003.

Miranda Estrampes, M., *El concepto de prueba ilícita y su tratamiento en el proceso penal*, 2nd edition, J. M. Bosch, Barcelona, 2004.

Miranda Estrampes, M., 'La regla de exclusión de la prueba ilícita: historia de su nacimiento y de su progresiva limitación', *Revista Jueces para la Democracia*, 2003/47.

Montero Aroca, *La prueba en el proceso civil*, 7th ed., Thomson-Civitas, Madrid, 2012.

Muñoz Conde, F., 'Prueba prohibida y valoración de las grabaciones audiovisuales en el proceso penal', *Revista Penal*, 2004/14.

Oliva Santos, A. de la, 'Sobre la ineficacia e las pruebas ilícitamente obtenidas', *Revista Tribunales de Justicia*, 2003/8–9.

Pastor Borgoñón, B., 'Eficacia en el proceso de las pruebas ilícitamente obtenidas. A propósito de la sentencia núm. 114/1984, de 29 de noviembre (BOE del 21 de diciembre de 1984), dictada por el Tribunal Constitucional en el recurso de amparo 167/1984', *Revista Justicia*, 1986/2.

Picó i Junoy, J., 'Nuevas perspectivas sobre el alcance anulatorio de las pruebas ilícitas', *Revista Justicia*, 1997/3.

Picó I Junoy, J., *El derecho a la prueba en el proceso civil*, Bosch, Barcelona, 1996.

Planchadell Gargallo, A., *La prueba prohibida: Evolución jurisprudencial (Comentario a las sentencias que marcan el camino)*, Thomson-Reuters Aranzadi, Cizur Menor, Navarra, 2014.

Reus, E., *Ley de Enjuiciamiento Criminal de 14 de septiembre de 1882, concordada y anotada extensamente*, IRL, Madrid, 1883.

Salas Calero, L., 'Aspectos materiales y procesales del principio acusatorio: Problemas probatorios, prueba ilícita y procesos penales socialmente relevantes. La exclusión de las pruebas ilícitamente obtenidas en el Derecho Procesal de los Estados Unidos', *Revista Poder Judicial*, 2006/66.

Urbano Castrillo, E. / Torres Morato, M. A., *La prueba ilícita penal. Estudio jurisprudencial* (3rd ed.), Thomson-Aranzadi, Pamplona 2003.

Vegas Torres, J., *Presunción de inocencia y prueba en el proceso penal*, La Ley, Madrid, 1993.

Velasco Nuñez, E., 'Prueba obtenida ilícitamente. Doctrina del "fruto del árbol envenenado": Correcciones actuales y tendencias de futuro', [in:] "Medidas restrictivas de derechos fundamentales", *Cuadernos de Derecho Judicial* 12, Consejo General del Poder Judicial, Madrid, 1996.

Vives Antón, T., 'Consideraciones constitucionales sobe la exclusión de los "frutos del árbol emponzoñado"', *Revista Jurídica de la Comunidad Valenciana*, 2002/4.

Zaragoza Tejada, J. I., Gutiérrez Azanza, D. A., 'La exclusión de la prueba ilícita tras la sentencia del Tribunal Constitucional de 16 de julio de 2019 sobre la "Lista Falciani"', *Revista Aranzadi de Derecho y Proceso Penal*, 2019/56.

Eduardo Bolsoni Riboli[1]

VII. The use of spy software as a means of obtaining evidence in criminal investigations and the need of effective remedies to safeguard fundamental rights: the case of Portugal

Abstract: In this section, we will delve into the nature of spy software and the potential threats it presents to the fundamental rights of individuals under investigation for investigative purposes. We will explore specific examples of how this measure is implemented in the European Union, drawing insights from the legal frameworks established in Germany and Italy. Furthermore, we will elaborate on the specific requirements outlined by the ECtHR for the use of covert means for evidence collection, with a focus on the interception of communications. Subsequently, we will analyze how this method of evidence-gathering has been put into practice in Portugal, conducting an assessment of its constitutionality. We will also examine whether Portugal ensures the right to remedies against measures that infringe upon fundamental rights, such as the use of spy software for evidence collection, in accordance with the right to an effective remedy as stipulated in Article 13 of the ECHR.

Keywords: evidence, right to effective remedy, spy software, AI, criminal proceedings

1. Introduction

Since the late 20th century, technological and scientific progress, coupled with globalisation, has fundamentally reshaped our world. The constant transformation brought about by these two phenomena is of undeniable social value; technological and computer advances have expanded and expedited communication and transportation channels, thus revolutionising the economy and the movement of people, goods, and information. We currently live in what is defined as the "information society",[2] a dynamic in which the continuous flow of information

---

1 ORCID no. 0000-0002-8691-3390. PhD Candidate (Criminal Law – Faculdade de Direito, University of Lisbon, Portugal), Master of Laws (Criminal Law – Faculdade de Direito, University of Coimbra, Portugal).

2 J.A.E. Vervaele, 'Surveillance and Criminal Investigation: Blurring of Thresholds and Boundaries in the Criminal Justice System?', [in:] S. Gutwirth, R. Leenes, P.D. Hert (eds.), *Reloading Data Protection: Multidisciplinary Insights and Contemporary Challenges*, New York: Springer 2014, pp. 118–119.

and knowledge are fundamental resources and play central roles in guiding social and political behaviour, particularly through the use of computer systems, digital devices, and the Internet. Everything is in constant (and rapid) change.

While a societal advancement, the widespread use of computer systems and digital devices, coupled with the digital environment's speed and anonymity, has led to the emergence of cybercrimes and enabled traditional crimes to extend into the digital world. Technological innovations are increasingly integrated into the enhancement of illicit practices,[3] and as a result, criminality has also adapted and shaped itself to new informational and communicational flows, adopting more organised, internationalised, and computerised forms.

In the following chapters, we will examine the nature of spy software and the risks that its use for investigative purposes poses to the fundamental rights of those under investigation. Subsequently, we will analyse examples of the implementation of this measure in the European Union, drawing from the legal frameworks established in Germany and Italy; and elucidate the requirements that the European Court of Human Rights (hereafter "ECtHR") deems necessary for the use of covert means for evidence collection, particularly the interception of communications. Finally, we will analyse how this method of evidence gathering has been implemented in Portugal, subsequently assessing its constitutionality and verifying whether Portugal guarantees the right to remedies against measures that violates fundamental rights, such as the use of spy software for collecting evidence, in compliance with the right to an effective remedy established in Article 13 of the European Convention on Human Rights (hereafter "ECHR").

2. The problem between the use of spy software as a means of obtaining evidence and the need of effective remedies to safeguard fundamental rights

The transition to an information society closely linked to cyberspace poses fresh challenges for law enforcement, judicial authorities, and legal systems, particularly regarding the collection of criminal evidence in the digital world. The diverse ways data is acquired, stored, and processed in computer systems challenge conventional investigative approaches.[4] Traditional evidence-collection methods are

3 A.L. Martins, 'Novas tecnologias, investigação criminal e o cidadão em vias de transparência', [in:] J.F. Costa, et al. (eds.), *Estudos em Homenagem ao Prof. Doutor Manuel da Costa Andrade*, Vol. II, Coimbra: Instituto Jurídico 2017, pp. 495–496.

4 J.A.E. Vervaele, *Surveillance and Criminal*, *op.cit.*, pp. 118–119.

proving increasingly inadequate for accessing data that no longer resides in a physical location but rather in a digital environment.

Information held on digital devices, computer systems, and communication networks can provide valuable data for law enforcement conducting criminal investigations.[5] This may encompass details like a suspect's whereabouts during a crime, communications with co-conspirators, documentation of criminal acts, or records of transactions tied to illicit activities.

To counter State surveillance in the digital world, anti-forensic tools, including encryption,[6] have been developed.[7] These tools encompass techniques and computer programs designed to conceal the user's identity and the information transmitted or stored in a computer system.[8] Apart from anti-forensic methods, the very framework of contemporary communication technologies presents hurdles for digital criminal investigations,[9] such as the nature of optical communication systems, cloud computing, and wireless Internet. They obstruct attempts to locate monitored devices or may unintentionally result in a simultaneous intrusion into the privacy of individuals not related to a criminal investigation.

Hence, in numerous legal systems, new evidence-collection methods are arising to align with this emerging paradigm, including the use of spy software for collecting evidence in criminal investigations. However, its use hinges on adequate legal provision, given its potential to significantly violate the fundamental rights of those under investigation.

3. The use of spy software as a means of obtaining evidence

To ensure a proper legal analysis in the context of computer science, it's essential to establish general technical concepts to avoid their misapplication to other evidence-collection methods.

5 N.G. Serrano, 'Garantías constitucionales de la persecución penal en el entorno digital', [in:] J.L.G. Colomer (ed.), *Prueba y Processo Penal (Análisis especial de la prueba prohibida en el sistema español y en el derecho comparado)*, Valencia: Tirant lo Blanch 2008, p. 151.

6 Defined by Marco Gercke as a "[T]echnique of turning a plain text into an obscured format by using an algorithm" (M. Gercke, *Understanding Cybercrime- A Guide for Developing Countries*, Geneva: International Telecommunication Union 2011, p. 146).

7 K. Conlan, I. Baggili, F. Breitinger, 'Anti-forensics: Furthering digital forensic science through a new extended, granular taxonomy', *Digital Investigation* 2016/18, p. 566.

8 M. Gercke, *Understanding Cybercrime…*, p. 146.

9 R.L.D. Pool, B.H.M. Custers, 'The Police Hack Back: Legitimacy, Necessity and Privacy Implications of The Next Step in Fighting Cybercrime', *European Journal of Crime, Criminal Law and Criminal Justice* 2017/25(2), p. 130.

3.1. Spyware: definition, nature, and operation

"Spyware" encompasses a class of computer programs engineered to extract information from digital devices or computer systems without the user's consent or awareness regarding their installation and operation.[10] While different types of spyware exist, each tailored to fulfill one or more specific function(s), they all share the common trait of masking their installation and operation. They are often referred to as "Trojan horses" or "malware" (a contraction of the term "malicious software").[11]

In the context of secret surveillance and covert investigations, we opt for the terminology "spy software" as (1) not all malware is designed for the extraction of digital information (some serve commercial purposes like generating pop-up ads);[12] (2) Trojan horses are just one of the multiple forms of spyware available, and (3) to avoid the presumption that all spy software is necessarily illegal, inappropriate, or harmful, as when adequately regulated and employed, they can be a valuable tool for investigative purposes.

Spyware can collect extensive information, including passwords, various file types, user location, audio, video, and text communications, real-time monitoring of the user (microphone, camera, GPS), typed content, device activities, and biometric data. Access to this data can be remote, not requiring physical retrieval. In the context of criminal investigations, the use of spy software, due to its inherent characteristics, can be an invaluable tool, granting access to an extensive array of information, including real-time data, prior to any endeavour to conceal or erase the information stored on the monitored device.

3.2. Spy software and limitations of fundamental rights

From the moment the spy software initiates the capture of data within the target device, it can gain access to numerous dimensions of the life of the person under investigation, such as their: lifestyle, routine, adoption of cultural habits, frequented locations, political beliefs, sexual orientation, financial transactions, interactions with family members, romantic relationships, business practices, and professional secrets.[13]

---

10 Cf. A. Marshall, *Digital Forensics – Digital Evidence in Criminal Investigation*, Chichester: Wiley-Blackwell 2008, p. 66; E. Filiol, *Computer viruses: from theory to application*, Paris: Springer 2005, p. 83.

11 J. Clough, *Principles of Cybercrime*, Cambridge: Cambridge University Press 2010, p. 33.

12 Federal Bureau of Investigation, 'Cybercrime', FBI.gov, Washington, available at: https://www.fbi.gov/investigate/cyber [accessed on: February 6th, 2023].

13 L.G. Velani, 'Trojan horse, strumenti investigativi e diritti fondamentali: alla ricerca di un difficile equilibrio', *Parola alla Difesa* 2016/1, p. 175.

Due to the intrusiveness of the measure, it is unquestionable that the use of spy software as a means of obtaining evidence raises conflicts between different legal interests and fundamental rights: due process of law, freedom of expression and information, the right to image, the right to privacy; the right to self-determination and communication; the right to professional secrecy; the integrity of technical-informational systems; and informational self-determination. Conflicts also arise at the procedural level, impacting, among others, the right to refuse testimony or interrogations and the principle of *nemo tenetur se ipsum accusare* and its ramifications.[14] Such rights and principles are a cornerstone of the European legal order,[15] especially the right to privacy, as established in Article 8 of the European Convention on Human Rights.

As it constitutes progress in criminal investigation and in light of the conflicts arising from its use, several foreign jurisdictions have incorporated spy software into their legal frameworks to advance criminal investigations.

4. The use of spy software as a means of obtaining evidence in criminal investigations in the European Union

Several countries within the European Union,[16] notably Germany and Italy, have incorporated the use of spy software for evidence collection into their legal frameworks.

14 P.S. Cunha, L. Chastre, 'L'utilizzo del captatore informatico "Trojan Horse" nella procedura penale portoghese', *Parola alla Difesa* 2016/1, p. 183; M.C. Andrade, '"Bruscamente no Verão passado", a reforma do código de processo penal: observações críticas sobre uma lei que podia e devia ter sido diferente', Coimbra: Coimbra Editora 2009, pp. 106–107; B.S. Rodrigues, *Da Prova Penal – Tomo II: Bruscamente... A(s) face(s) oculta(s) dos métodos ocultos de investigação criminal*, Cascais: Rei dos Livros 2010, pp. 471–472.

15 Cf. Q. Liger, M. Gutheil, *The use of Pegasus and equivalent surveillance spyware: The existing legal framework in EU Member State for the acquisition and use of Pegasus and equivalent surveillance spyware*, Brussels: Policy Department for Citizens' Rights and Constitutional Affairs (European Parliament) 2023, pp. 13 and 68, available at: https://www.europarl.europa.eu/RegData/etudes/STUD/2022/740151/IPOL_STU(2022)740151_EN.pdf [accessed on: June 11th, 2023].

16 At the time of this writing, the following European Union members have introduced the use of spy software as a means of obtaining evidence in their legal framework: Greece, Spain, Hungary, Poland, Germany, France, Italy, and Netherlands (Q. Liger, M. Gutheil, *The use of Pegasus...*, pp. 24–46).

4.1. Germany

In 2008,[17] the German Federal Constitutional Court (*Bundesverfassungsgericht*) examined the constitutionality of digital surveillance and acknowledged a novel fundamental right: the confidentiality and integrity of computer systems. The Court established that this right stems from the rights to personality and human dignity but noted that it is not absolute and can be limited for valid reasons related to prevention or criminal investigations.

Germany introduced the possibility of using spy software as a method of investigation in its legal framework through the *Bundeskriminalamtgesetz* (BKAG).[18] The law established the parameters for the operation of the software, limited to exceptional cases: in broad terms, apart from requiring judicial authorisation, there should be a concrete danger to a legitimate interest, such as threats to the physical integrity, life, or freedom of one or more individuals, or severe threats to the German state.

The BKAG was revised in 2017. In its current version, the use of spy software is outlined in § 49. In short, according to the provisions of § 49, the use of spy software in Germany is allowed under very specific conditions[19] and restricted to serious offences.

---

17 BVerfG, Urteil des Ersten Senats vom Februar 27th, 2008 - 1 BvR 370/07 - Rn. (1–333), available at: http://www.bverfg.de/e/rs20080227_1bvr037007.html [accessed on: February 6th, 2023].

18 N. Forgó *et al.*, 'The Collection of Electronic Evidence in Germany: A Spotlight on Recent Legal Developments and Court Rulings' in: M. Corrales, M. Fenwick, N. Forgó (eds.), *New Technology, Big Data and the Law*, Singapore: Springer Nature 2017, p. 269.

19 Such as, according to § 49 of the BKAG: (1) well-founded suspicion of a current or future threat to the physical integrity, life, or freedom of an individual, or a threat to the foundations or existence of a country or humanity (§ 49 (1)); (2) it must be limited to the essential changes in the targeted system necessary for obtaining the information (any alterations to the device need to be reversed at the end of the measure) (§ 49 (2)); (3) restricted to cases of serious criminality and terrorism (§ 49 (3)); (4) it requires a request from the authorities responsible for the investigation and a judicial authorization, with both cases mandating a description of the person to whom the measure is directed, a precise description of the computer system and/or digital device on which the software will be installed, the nature, extent, and duration of the measure, and the facts and reasons justifying its application (§ 49 (5) and (6)); (5) maximum duration of three months, which can be extended for an equal period (§ 49 (6)); among other detailed requirements that aim to ensure the least intrusion in the core are of the private life of the person under investigation.

4.2. Italy

In 2015, the Italian Court of Cassation issued a ruling regarding the use of hacking tools for intercepting communications,[20] where it emphasised the inviolability of the freedom and secrecy of communications, constitutional principles that could only be limited by a properly justified judicial order and in alignment with the guarantees established in the Italian law.

In 2016, the Court[21] addressed the legitimacy of intercepting conversations and communications among individuals using a "captatore informatico" ("digital wiretap") in cases related to organised crime and mafia activities. The discussion stemmed from a case in which an individual's conversations were intercepted and monitored through the hidden installation of spy software during a criminal investigation related to organised crime. The Court recognised the severity of using the *captatore informatico* as a means of obtaining evidence but expanded its scope of application, allowing its use in the individual's residence or private locations, strictly in cases involving organised crime and terrorism-related investigations.

Currently, the *captatore informatico* is established in Article 266(2) of the Italian Code of Criminal Procedure,[22] and the regulations for its use are detailed in Articles 267 to 270, 271, and subsequent articles. In short, it is only allowed in

20 Suprema Corte di Cassazione, sez. VI penale, judgement of May 26th, 2015 (dep. 26 giugno 2015), n. 27100, available at: http://www.penale.it/page.asp?IDPag=1201 [accessed on: February 6th, 2023].

21 Suprema Corte di Cassazione, sez. unite penali, judgement of April 28th, 2016 (dep. 01 giugno 2016), n. 26889, available at: http://www.giurisprudenzapenale.com/wp-content/uploads/2016/07/cass-pen-sez-un-2016-26889.pdf [accessed on: February 6th, 2023].

22 "Article 266(2): In the same cases, the interception of communications between individuals is allowed, which can also be carried out by placing a computer data capture device on a portable electronic device. However, if these interceptions take place in the locations indicated by Article 614 of the criminal code, interception is only permitted if there is reasonable cause to believe that criminal activity is occurring there".

cases involving organised crime and terrorism-related investigations under very specific conditions.[23]

5. The case law of the European Court of Human Rights on interception of communications and secret surveillance measures

In its article 8(2),[24] the ECHR establishes the need of legal provisions in order to restrict fundamental rights inherent to private and family life and determines the cases in which these rights can be limited by the state.

According to the ECtHR, as initially articulated in *Amann v. Switzerland*,[25] domestic laws restricting fundamental rights must possess what the Court defines as "quality of law": restrictive laws must be precise, accessible, predictable, and

---

23 In short: (1) its use is limited to cases related to organized crime, terrorism, and crimes listed in Article 266(1) of the Code of Criminal Procedure (such as drug trafficking, crimes related to weapons and explosives, insider trading, market manipulation, among others); (2) its use requires a request from the Public Prosecutor's Office and a properly justified judicial authorization (the request must demonstrate significant evidence of a crime and sufficient reasons justifying the necessity of the instrument for the investigation; the type of software to be employed; and the duration of the measure; while the judicial authority must analyze and provide sufficient grounds to authorize the measure and indicate the cases in which the device's functions can be activated); (3) its use must be extensively documented regarding its application, obtained data, and requests and authorizations for applying the measure; (4) it can intercept the flow of telephone and telematic communications from the monitored device; (5) it must observe the inviolability of the investigated person's residence, unless there are well-founded reasons to believe that criminal activity is taking place at that location (in exceptional cases it can be activated at the target's residence even if a criminal activity is not occurring at the moment, as long as authorized by a judicial authority), as established in the Italian law; (6) it must be limited to important data for the investigation, with the consequent exclusion of irrelevant data, especially sensitive personal data as defined by the law.

24 "Article 8: Right to respect for private and family life – 1. Everyone has the right to respect for his private and family life, his home and his correspondence. 2. There shall be no interference by a public authority with the exercise of this right except such as is in accordance with the law and is necessary in a democratic society in the interests of national security, public safety or the economic well-being of the country, for the prevention of disorder or crime, for the protection of health or morals, or for the protection of the rights and freedoms of others".

25 European Court of Human Rights, Case of Amann v. Switzerland, Application no. 27798/95, available at: https://hudoc.echr.coe.int/fre?i=001-58497 [accessed on: February 6th, 2023].

proportional. Citizens must have access to the content of the legislation not only to be aware of the situations in which their rights can be restricted but also to identify the investigative powers available to the state and the safeguards in place to prevent arbitrary use of these powers. Therefore, it is essential not only to publish the law but also to draft it with utmost precision, using clear language and detailed rules, especially concerning the methods or technologies that can be employed to restrict individual rights and freedoms. Legislation must also respect the principles of proportionality, necessity, and subsidiarity.

In *Weber and Saravia v. Germany*,[26] the ECtHR established six minimum requirements[27] to assess the "quality of law" in secret surveillance legislation, aiming to prevent abuses by authorities responsible for implementing such measures. Since *Weber and Saravia v. Germany*, subsequent decisions from the Court on the subject adhered to this understanding.

On 2015, in *Roman Zakharov v. Russia*,[28] the Court updated the concept of necessary predictability for fulfilling the "quality of law". The ECtHR started to understand that in the context of interception of communications, the restrictive law must be sufficiently clear to give citizens adequate indications of the circumstances and conditions under which public authorities are authorized to apply such measures. The legal text must specify, with sufficient clarity, any discretion granted to authorities at the time of application, enabling individuals to protect themselves from arbitrariness.

---

26 European Court of Human Rights, Case of Weber and Saravia v. Germany, no 54934/00, available at: https://hudoc.echr.coe.int/fre?i=001-76586 [accessed on: February 6th, 2023].

27 The Court determined that quality of law is only present when six minimum requirements are met: (1) specification of admissible cases for the interception of communications; (2) definition of individuals subject to the measure; (3) duration of the measure and its limits; (4) procedures to be followed during the analysis, use, and preservation of the data that was obtained; (5) precautions to be taken when sharing obtained data with other parties; and (6) provisions regarding the possibility or obligation to delete the information and destroy the physical media where the data (and/or its copies) were preserved.

28 European Court of Human Rights, Case of Roman Zakharov v. Russia, Application no. 47143/06, available at: https://hudoc.echr.coe.int/app/conversion/docx/pdf?library=ECHR&id=001-159324&filename=CASE%20OF%20ROMAN%20ZAKHAROV%20v.%20RUSSIA.pdf [accessed on: February 6th, 2023].

Three years later, in *Big Brother Watch And Others v. The United Kingdom*,[29] the ECtHR would return to the subject. The Court emphasized the significance of the "quality of law" in measures that impose restrictions on rights, particularly when the investigative method is covert and capable of accessing and capturing various aspects of an individual's private life, such as different forms of interception of communications. To comply with the ECHR, the Court highlighted the need for high-quality domestic law, in accordance with domestic legal order principles and the minimum requirements established in *Weber and Saravia v. Germany*, the updated predictability as defined in *Roman Zakharov v. Russia*, and other jurisprudential understandings of the Court regarding the subject.

Recently, on 2022, in *Ekimdzhiev and Others v. Bulgaria*,[30] the Court ruled that the laws governing secret surveillance in Bulgaria did not meet the minimum safeguards against arbitrariness and abuse as established in article 8 of the ECHR. In the ruling, the Court once again reiterated the need for States to fulfill the "quality of law" requirements when establishing laws governing secret surveillance.

In short, the ECtHR recognizes the possibility of limitations of fundamental rights but only if they are justified (e.g. prevention of serious crimes) and if the domestic law meets the required criteria of "quality of law" to ensure the necessary safeguards to protect the rights affected.

It's important to highlight that, as of the current writing, there is no case law regarding the use of spy software in the ECtHR.[31]

6. The use of spy software as a means of obtaining criminal evidence in Portugal

6.1. Preliminary notes: covert investigative methods in the Portuguese legal framework

In Portuguese law, covert investigative methods refer to means of obtaining evidence without the knowledge of the individual under investigation, with the most commonly used methods being wiretapping, the use of undercover agents, GPS tracking, and email interception.

---

29 European Court of Human Rights, Case of Big Brother Watch and Others v. The United Kingdom, Application nos. 58170/13, 62322/14, 24960/15, available at: https://hudoc.echr.coe.int/fre?i=001-210077 [accessed on: February 6th, 2023].

30 European Court of Human Rights, Case of Ekimdzhiev and Others v. Bulgaria, Application no. 70078/12, available at: https://hudoc.echr.coe.int/fre?i=001-214673 [accessed on: February 6th, 2023].

31 Q. Liger, M. Gutheil, *The use of Pegasus*, *op.cit.*, p. 74.

The Portuguese Code of Criminal Procedure, in its Article 125, establishes that "evidence that is not prohibited by law is admissible". The prohibited methods of obtaining evidence are listed in Article 126 of the same Code[32] and are directed at the organs of criminal prosecution, judicial authorities, and law enforcement agencies.[33]

While paragraphs 1 and 2 of Article 126 of the Criminal Procedure Code establish cases of absolute prohibition of obtaining evidence by the indicated means, paragraph 3 establishes the "relatively prohibited methods"[34] of evidence collection: "Except for cases provided for by law, evidence obtained by intrusion into private life, domicile, correspondence, or telecommunications without the consent of the respective holder is equally null and cannot be used". However, such prohibitions may be waived with the agreement of the rights holder in conflict or in cases where the Constitution expressly allows restrictions on conflicting rights, with such restrictions limited "to those needed to safeguard other constitutionally protected rights and interests" (Article 18(2), *in fine*, of the Constitution), provided that they do not diminish "the extent or scope of the essential content of the constitutional precepts" (Article 18(3), *in fine*, of the Constitution), known as the "inviolable nuclear area".[35] On this matter, Article 32(8) of the Portuguese Constitution establishes that "all evidence obtained by torture, coercion, infringement of personal physical or moral integrity, or improper intromission into

---

32 "Article 126 Prohibited Methods of Evidence – 1 - Evidence obtained through torture, coercion, or, in general, the violation of physical or moral integrity of individuals is null and cannot be used. 2 - Offensive to the physical or moral integrity of individuals are evidence obtained, even with their consent, through: a) Disturbance of free will or decision through mistreatment, bodily harm, administration of substances of any nature, hypnosis, or the use of cruel or deceptive means; b) Disturbance, by any means, of the capacity for memory or evaluation; c) The use of force beyond the cases and limits allowed by the law; d) Threat with measures legally inadmissible, as well as with the denial or conditioning of obtaining legally provided benefits; e) Promise of legally inadmissible advantage. 3 - Except for cases provided for by law, evidence obtained through intrusion into private life, domicile, correspondence, or telecommunications without the consent of the respective holder is equally null and cannot be used. 4 - If the use of evidence-gathering methods provided for in this article constitutes a crime, they may be used exclusively for proceedings against the perpetrators thereof.".

33 P.S. Mendes, *Lições de Direito Processual Penal*, Coimbra: Almedina 2015, p. 180.

34 P.S. Mendes, *Lições de Direito*, *op.cit.*, pp. 180–181.

35 M.C. Andrade, 'Métodos Ocultos de Investigação (Plädoyer para uma teoria geral)', [in:] M.F. Monte (ed.), *Que futuro para o Direito Processual Penal?*, Coimbra: Coimbra Editora 2009, p. 536.

personal life, the home, correspondence or telecommunications is null and void". As a logical consequence, when the intrusion into private life is not abusive, the evidence can be obtained and evaluated.

Therefore, restrictions can only operate through an objective and systematic interpretation of the Constitution.[36] Constitutional conformity will only be achieved if the eventual restriction is suitable and justified in light of the necessity to protect or promote a constitutional interest to the extent of the need in question.[37] In matters of methods of obtaining evidence, strict adherence to the principle of legality[38] is imperative, especially when dealing with covert investigative methods. It is worth noting, however, that mere legal provision is insufficient; there must be sufficient *density* in the norm, with effective *clarity* and *precise*[39] determination of its content, "to the highest degree".[40] The absence of gaps to be filled by the state power is imperative[41] to ensure determinability, process transparency, predictability of state action, and the creation of conditions of trust and reliability in control authorities.[42]

The more harmful potential a restrictive law has, the more precise and detailed its legal framework must be.[43] Furthermore, in addition to the restriction being limited to what is strictly necessary to safeguard other constitutional interests, it must adhere to the principles of proportionality and the prohibition of excess, with its scope of application not extending beyond the field in which it was initially deemed necessary.[44]

---

36 J. Miranda, *Direitos Fundamentais*, Coimbra: Almedina 2017, p. 463.

37 J.C.V. Andrade, *Os Direitos Fundamentais na Constituição Portuguesa de 1976*, 5 ed., Coimbra: Almedina 2012, p. 287.

38 J.G. Caires, 'O registo de som e imagem e as escutas ambientais', [in:] M.F. Palma et al. (eds.), *Direito da Investigação Criminal e da Prova*, Coimbra: Almedina 2014, p. 275.

39 J. Miranda, *Direitos Fundamentais*, *op.cit.*, p. 468.

40 C. Queiroz, *Direitos Fundamentais – Teoria Geral*, 2 ed., Coimbra: Coimbra Editora 2010, p. 260.

41 J.C.V. Andrade, *Os Direitos Fundamentais*, *op.cit.*, pp. 290–291.

42 J.R. Novais, *Direitos Fundamentais e Justiça Constitucional em Estado de Direito Democrático*, Coimbra: Coimbra Editora 2012, p. 124; C. Queiroz, *Direitos Fundamentais*, *op.cit.*, p. 260; J.C.V. Andrade, *Os Direitos Fundamentais...*, pp. 289–290; M.C. Andrade, *Bruscamente no Verão*, *op.cit.*, p. 112.

43 C. Queiroz, *Direitos Fundamentais*, *op.cit.*, p. 261.

44 J. Miranda, *Direitos Fundamentais*, *op.cit.*, p. 470.

Even if it is deemed legitimate in its conception, in the Portuguese legal system a law that does not adhere to these criteria should be declared unconstitutional.[45]

6.2. The Portuguese Cybercrime Law

In order to overcome the challenges arising from the proliferation of illicit practices and the increased flow of information in the digital environment, Portugal enacted Law No. 109/2009 on September 15 (the "Cybercrime Law"). The Cybercrime Law aims to establish substantive and procedural criminal provisions in the digital world, relating to international cooperation, electronic evidence collection, and issues pertaining to the domain of cybercrime.

The Cybercrime Law was responsible for regulating a range of previously unprecedented means of obtaining evidence in Portuguese law, such as online searches, access to computer data, seizure of electronic mail, interception of communications originating from a computer system, the use of undercover actions in the digital environment, and, most notably, the possibility of employing "computer means and devices" within the scope of undercover operations in the digital environment when necessary for the investigation.

While it enables the use of computer means and devices for investigative purposes, the Cybercrime Law does not regulate the procedure for these methods but rather subjects them to the "rules provided for the interception of communications" (Article 19(2), *in fine*, of the Cybercrime Law). The broad interpretation allowed by the terminology chosen by the legislator ("computer means and devices") has sparked discussions regarding the possibility of using spy software as a means of obtaining evidence in Portugal.

6.3. The use of spy software as a method of obtaining criminal evidence in Portugal

The Cybercrime Law, in its Article 19, establishes the possibility of resorting to undercover operations in a digital environment, which are admissible in crimes specified within the Cybercrime Law itself[46] and in crimes "committed through a computer system, when they, in abstract, are punishable by a maximum prison

---

45 Cf. J.R. Novais, *Direitos Fundamentais*, *op.cit.*, p. 123; C.V. Andrade, *Os Direitos Fundamentais*, *op.cit.*, p. 296.

46 Computer forgery (Article 3), damage related to computer programs or other computer data (Article 4), computer sabotage (Article 5), unauthorized access (Article 6), unauthorized interception (Article 7), and unauthorized reproduction of protected software (Article 8).

term exceeding 5 years; or, even if the penalty is lower, and when intentional, crimes against freedom and sexual self-determination in cases where the victims are minors or incapacitated; qualified fraud; computer fraud; racial; religious or sexual discrimination; economic and financial offenses; as well as crimes established in Title IV of the Copyright and Related Rights Code".[47]

The use of spy software can only be inferred from paragraph 2 of Article 19 ("When it is necessary to resort to *computer means and devices*, the rules provided for in the interception of communications shall be observed to the extent applicable"), and it would only be applicable in cases where there are "reasons to believe that the measure is indispensable for the discovery of truth or that the evidence would otherwise be impossible or very difficult to obtain".[48] Despite sharing similarities with other means of obtaining evidence, it is crucial to emphasize three distinctive characteristics setting spy software apart from other means of evidence collection: (1) the possibility of remote installation (though it can also be physically introduced into the digital device); (2) access to information prior to its destruction or encryption; and (3) the ability to execute different functions, sometimes concurrently.

The "computer means and devices" referred to in the Cybercrime Law are characterized by an important particularity: they are considered highly atypical investigative measures since they are subject to the principles and general provisions of the Constitution; the Criminal Procedure Code; and the legislation related to undercover operations (already an atypical investigative method regulated by Law No. 101/2001 of August 25). As such, spy software could only be employed in undercover operations in a digital environment.

Notwithstanding, they must still be supplemented, "to the extent applicable", by the rules established for the interception of communications, as outlined in Articles 187 and following of the Criminal Procedure Code, which set the rules for other highly atypical investigative methods.

Employing any investigative method without a well-defined legal framework that governs its safeguards, prerequisites, extent, and boundaries is impermissible. It cannot be justified by the argument of being incapable of countering developments in digital crime. The harmful potential of a spy software – surpassing that of other types of interception of communications – makes it what we define as an "extremely atypical" covert method of obtaining evidence. For this reason, special

47 Article 19(1)(b) of the Cybercrime Law.

48 Article 18(2) of the Cybercrime Law, applicable *ex vi* its Article 19(2).

legislative attention is needed in its regulation, with a focus on the principles of proportionality, necessity, adequacy, and subsidiarity.

The Cybercrime Law does not provide details nor establish a procedure for the installation and the use of spy software in criminal investigations. There are no details such as its operation; the acquisition, storage, and deletion of collected data; the individuals whose communications may be intercepted; and the duration and limits of the measure. Neither the Cybercrime Law, the Criminal Procedure Code, nor the law regulating the legal framework for covert actions address the necessary peculiarities inherent in the use of spy software for investigative purposes. In the case of the Cybercrime Law, it merely lists the catalog of crimes in which the measure would be applicable.

The gaps in the law cannot be filled through analogy;[49] the use of a new investigative method, especially an extremely atypical one, should only be allowed after its prior, explicit, and autonomous regulation.[50] The rules set for the interception of communications contained in the Criminal Procedure Code do not address these gaps, as spy software operates in an entirely different way. As previously mentioned, interception of communications is just one of the almost limitless functions that spy software can perform. Similarly, the rules outlined in Articles 187 and 188 of the Criminal Procedure Code do not apply, as they also do not foresee the inherent nature concerning the operation of spy software, resulting in similar gaps as observed in the Cybercrime Law. The same is true for the law that establishes the legal framework for covert actions.

All "relatively" prohibited methods of evidence, especially covert ones, are characterized by their atypical nature and must necessarily be regulated by law(s) with the utmost precision. These laws should detail how and under what circumstances the fundamental rights of the accused can be limited in favour of the interests of justice.[51] They should also specify the purpose and limits of state interference.[52] Still, these characteristics are absent in the current version of the Cybercrime Law.

It is clear that the Portuguese legislator attempted to introduce the use of spy software for criminal investigation through a "legislative patchwork", sewing

49 M.C. Andrade, *Métodos Ocultos de*, *op.cit.*, p. 541.

50 M.C. Andrade, *Bruscamente no Verão*, *op.cit.*, p. 113.

51 P.S. Mendes, *Lições de Direito*, *op.cit.*, p. 190; J.F. Dias, 'Revisitação de algumas ideias-mestras da teoria das proibições de prova em processo penal (Também à luz da jurisprudência constitucional portuguesa)', 146(4000) *Revista de Legislação e de Jurisprudência* 2016, Coimbra, p. 9).

52 M.C. Andrade, *Bruscamente no Verão*, *op.cit.*, p. 113.

together excerpts from different legislations. It lacks, as set by the ECtHR, *quality of law*.

As such, in the current version of the Cybercrime Law, the use of spy software as a means of obtaining evidence is not compatible with the principles established in the Constitution. As a result, Article 19(2) of the Cybercrime Law is unconstitutional.

Nevertheless, the subject is particularly problematic since it is possible that spy software are currently being used by the Portuguese government, as evidenced in documents released by WikiLeaks that show the interest of Portuguese law enforcement agents in acquiring a spy software in 2015.[53]

7. The right to an effective remedy in Portugal

In light of the intrusiveness of spy software, its impact on fundamental rights and particularly its operation without the knowledge of the person(s) under investigation, it is evident that any democratic government that wishes to implement this measure for investigative purposes needs to provide effective remedies and mechanisms capable of safeguarding the rights and freedoms of those surveilled.

Given, in our opinion, the absence of regulation regarding the use of spy software in Portugal and its consequent unconstitutionality, questions arise regarding the possibility of appealing the decision authorizing the implementation of this measure or the decision that evaluates the evidence obtained through this method. In this regard, we will analyze the available remedies for such case and

53 These documents, released in 2015, evidence email exchanges between an agent of the National Unit for Combating Cybercrime and Technological Crime of the Judicial Police and representatives of the European division of HackingTeam, a company known worldwide for selling spy software, especially to governments and law enforcement agencies. The disclosed documents clearly demonstrate the interest of the Judicial Police in obtaining an "active interception tool with 'special' options" and a "remote control solution", either "Wireless" or "Wi-Fi". There was an expression of intent by a police agent to arrange a meeting with a HackingTeam representative in Lisbon for a presentation and real-time demonstration of such tool (Wikileaks, 'Hacking Team – RE: [PJ CCU - Portugal] Remote IP Interc solution | request info, details, schedule, visit, etc – Email-ID 39666, available at: https://wikileaks.org/hackingteam/emails/emailid/39666 [accessed on: August 27th, 2023]). To date, there has been no official statement from the Judicial Police regarding the mentioned meeting or the leaked emails.

assess whether Portuguese legislation is in accordance with the right to an effective remedy established in Article 13 of the ECHR.

The Portuguese Constitution compels the State to "guarantee the fundamental rights and freedoms and respect for the principles of a democratic state based on the rule of law" (Article 9(b)) which are conferred to all citizens (pursuant to Article 12[54]).

In order to ensure that fundamental rights and freedoms are effectively protected, the Constitution establishes in its Article 18 that "the law may only restrict rights, freedoms and guarantees in cases expressly provided for in the Constitution, and such restrictions must be limited to those needed to safeguard other constitutionally protected rights and interests". To safeguard fundamental rights and freedoms, the Constitution guarantees effective judicial protection. In Article 20(1), the Constitution ensures that everyone has "access to the law and the courts in order to defend those of his rights and interests that are protected by law, and justice may not be denied to anyone due to lack of sufficient financial means". This right to a remedy encompasses both judicial and administrative decisions, whether they concern matters of fact or law. In this regard, the right to remedy guarantees that decisions and legal matters can be reviewed by a higher judicial instance (local Courts) or by the higher courts (the Supreme Court of Justice and the Constitutional Court).

The Constitution also establishes safeguards specifically related to criminal proceedings. In Article 32, the Constitution states that "criminal proceedings shall ensure all the safeguards of the defence, including the right to appeal" (Article 32(1)), along with the presumption of innocence of the accused, the right to appoint one's own defence counsel, the right of the accused to participate in the proceedings (as provided by law), and, particularly relevant to the present study, that "all evidence obtained by torture, coercion, infringement of personal physical or moral integrity, or improper intromission into personal life, the home, correspondence or telecommunications is null and void" (Article 32(8)).

54 "Article 12 (Principle of universality) 1. Every citizen enjoys the rights and is subject to the duties enshrined in the Constitution. 2. Legal persons enjoy the rights and are subject to the duties that are compatible with their nature".

The Code of Criminal Procedure also establishes a series of provisions[55] aimed at preventing unjustified limitations on fundamental rights and freedoms, with the purpose of elucidating and detailing constitutional principles. These provisions constitute an elaboration of constitutional principles.

As a Member State of the European Union, Portugal is required to establish the right to an effective remedy in its domestic legal system. By constitutional mandate, principles of general or common international law are part of Portuguese law (Article 8 of the Constitution). Particularly, "treaties that govern the European Union and the norms issued by its institutions in the exercise of their respective competences are applicable in Portuguese internal law in accordance with Union law and with respect for the fundamental principles of a democratic state based on the rule of law" (Article 8(4) of the Constitution).

Therefore, in Portugal, the right to an effective remedy is established both through a constitutional mandate and the obligations it assumes under international law and European Union law.

Regarding the unconstitutionality of using spy software as means of obtaining evidence, the right to an effective remedy is ensured due to the necessity for courts to examine allegations of unconstitutionality (Article 204 of the Constitution[56]) and also the provision of the constitutional remedy available for challenging the

55 Especially Articles 399, 401, 405, and 425, which, in short, guarantees the right to judicial remedies from Court decisions, even to decisions that deny their admissibility. Furthermore, concerning the case under study, Article 125 of the Code of Criminal Procedure establishes that "evidence that are not prohibited by law are admissible". The effects of nullity "invalidate the act in which they occur, as well as those dependent on it and those they may affect" (Article 122(1) of the Code of Criminal Procedure). Article 126(4), of the Code of Criminal Procedure makes it clear that "except as provided by law, evidence obtained through intrusion into private life, the home, correspondence, or telecommunications without the consent of the respective holder is also null and cannot be used".

56 "Article 204 (Compliance with the Constitution) In matters that are submitted for judgement the courts may not apply norms that contravene the provisions of the Constitution or the principles enshrined therein".

unconstitutionality of a norm: the concrete review of constitutionality and legality (Article 280 of the Constitution[57]).

The concrete review of constitutionality and legality is a remedy that must be filed with the Constitutional Court. It serves as an instrumental remedy to the main decision in which the incident of unconstitutionality (or illegality) arose,[58] being limited to the part in which the court ruled on the issue of unconstitutionality (or legality).[59] In other words, it involves the examination of one or more norms relevant to the decision of the case under trial.[60] As per Article 282 of the Constitution, its effects can be either general and extensive to the date of enactment

57 "Article 280 (Concrete review of constitutionality and legality) 1. Appeal may be made to the Constitutional Court against court decisions: a) That refuse the application of any norm on the grounds of its unconstitutionality; b) That apply a norm whose unconstitutionality has been raised during the proceedings. 2. Appeal may also be made to the Constitutional Court against court decisions: a) That refuse the application of a norm contained in a legislative act, on the grounds that it is illegal because it is in breach of a law which possesses superior legal force; b) That refuse the application of a norm contained in a regional legislative act, on the grounds that it is illegal because it is in breach of the autonomous region's statute; c) That refuse the application of a norm contained in a legislative act issued by an entity that exercises sovereignty, on the grounds that it is illegal because it is in breach of an autonomous region's statute; d) That apply any norm whose illegality on any of the grounds referred to in subparagraphs (a), (b) and (c) has been raised during the proceedings. 3. When the norm whose application has been refused is contained in an international convention, a legislative act or a regulatory decree, the Public Prosecutors' Office shall obligatorily lodge the appeal provided for in paragraph (1)(a) or 2(a). 4. The appeals provided for in paragraphs (1)(b) and (2)(d) may only be lodged by the party that raised the question of unconstitutionality or illegality, and the law must regulate the regime governing the admission of such appeals. 5. Appeal may also be made to the Constitutional Court, and the Public Prosecutors' Office shall obligatorily lodge such appeals, against court decisions that apply norms which the Constitutional Court itself has previously held unconstitutional or illegal. 6. Appeals to the Constitutional Court are restricted to the question of unconstitutionality or illegality, as appropriate".

58 J.J.G. Canotilho, V. Moreira, *Constituição da República Portuguesa Anotada – Volume IV*, Coimbra: Coimbra Editora 2010, p. 959.

59 J.M.M.C. Costa, *A Jurisdição Constitucional em Portugal*, Coimbra: Almedina 2007, p. 79; J.J.G. Canotilho, *Direito Constitucional e Teoria da Constituição*, Coimbra: Almedina 2003, p. 989.

60 V. Moreira, 'A «fiscalização concreta» no quadro do sistema misto de justiça constitucional', Volume Comemorativo do 75.º Tomo, *Boletim da Faculdade de Direito* 2003, Coimbra, p. 836.

of the declared unconstitutional norm or restricted to specific cases decided by the Constitutional Court.

Thus, Portugal ensures the right to an effective remedy established by Article 13 of the ECHR, as it provides the necessary means to prevent a violation of fundamental rights or to appeal from a decision that restricts fundamental rights or evaluates evidence obtained through prohibited methods, as it is currently the case of the use of spy software in criminal investigations.

8. Final remarks

The transition to an information society connected to cyberspace poses challenges for law enforcement and legal systems, particularly concerning the collection of digital evidence. Traditional methods are inadequate for accessing data stored in a digital device, and thus a necessity to develop methods and tools capable of obtaining information from the digital world arises. Spy software, with its ability to access a wide range of information, has proven to be a valuable tool in criminal investigations. However, its use raises concerns related to the restriction of fundamental rights. As a result, the use of spy software must be established by adequate legal provisions to avoid violating the rights of those under investigation.

The Portuguese Cybercrime Law does not establish the procedure for the use of spy software in criminal investigations, creating legal gaps and lacking the "quality of law" required by the ECtHR. Special investigative techniques should adopt clear and effective laws regulating them, including procedural guarantees, controls, oversight, and judicial review mechanisms. As such, the use of spy software as a means of obtaining evidence in Portugal, under the current version of the Cybercrime Law, is incompatible with the principles set out by the Portuguese Constitution, rendering Article 19(2) of the Cybercrime Law unconstitutional.

In the context of spy software's intrusiveness, its impact on fundamental rights, and its covert operation, any democratic government seeking to implement this measure for investigative purposes must establish effective remedies and mechanisms to safeguard the rights and freedoms of those under surveillance. The Portuguese Constitution compels the State to safeguard its citizens' fundamental rights and freedoms, and in addition, as a European Union Member State, Portugal is obliged to provide legal mechanisms to prevent them from being unlawfully restricted. The Portuguese legal framework guarantees the right to an effective remedy as established in Article 13 of the ECHR by offering the essential mechanisms to prevent fundamental rights violations or to challenge decisions that curtail these rights or assess evidence acquired through unauthorized methods, as exemplified by the use of spy software in criminal investigations.

Bibliography

Andrade, J. C. V., *Os Direitos Fundamentais na Constituição Portuguesa de 1976*, 5 ed., Coimbra: Almedina, 2012.

Andrade, M. C., 'Métodos Ocultos de Investigação (Plädoyer para uma teoria geral)', [in:] Monte, M. F. (ed.), *Que futuro para o Direito Processual Penal?*, Coimbra: Coimbra Editora, 2009.

Andrade, M. C., *"Bruscamente no Verão passado", a reforma do código de processo penal: observações críticas sobre uma lei que podia e devia ter sido diferente*, Coimbra: Coimbra Editora, 2009.

Caires, J. G., 'O registo de som e imagem e as escutas ambientais', [in:] Palma, M. F. *et al.* (eds.), *Direito da Investigação Criminal e da Prova*, Coimbra: Almedina, 2014.

Canotilho, J. J. G., *Direito Constitucional e Teoria da Constituição*, Coimbra: Almedina, 2003.

Canotilho, J. J. G., Moreira, V., *Constituição da República Portuguesa Anotada – Volume IV*, Coimbra: Coimbra Editora, 2010.

Clough, J., *Principles of Cybercrime*, Cambridge: Cambridge University Press, 2010.

Conlan, K., Baggili, I., Breitinger, F., 'Anti-forensics: Furthering digital forensic science through a new extended, granular taxonomy', *Digital Investigation*, New York, 2016/18.

Costa, J. M. M. C., *A Jurisdição Constitucional em Portugal*, Coimbra: Almedina, 2007.

Cunha, P. S., Chastre, L., 'L'utilizzo del captatore informatico "Trojan Horse" nella procedura penale portoghese', *Parola alla Difesa*, Pisa, 2016/1.

Dias, J. F., 'Revisitação de algumas ideias-mestras da teoria das proibições de prova em processo penal (Também à luz da jurisprudência constitucional portuguesa)', *Revista de Legislação e de Jurisprudência*, Coimbra, 2016/146(4000).

Federal Bureau of Investigation, 'Cybercrime', FBI.gov, Washington, available at: https://www.fbi.gov/investigate/cyber [accessed on: February 6th 2023].

Filiol, E., *Computer viruses: from theory to application*, Paris: Springer, 2005.

Forgó, N. *et al.*, 'The Collection of Electronic Evidence in Germany: A Spotlight on Recent Legal Developments and Court Rulings', [in:] Corrales, M., Fenwick, M., Forgó, N. (eds.), *New Technology, Big Data and the Law*, Singapore: Springer Nature, 2017.

Gercke, M., *Understanding Cybercrime: A Guide for Developing Countries*, Geneva: International Telecommunication Union, 2011.

Liger, Q., Gutheil, M., *The use of Pegasus and equivalent surveillance spyware: The existing legal framework in EU Member State for the acquisition and use of Pegasus and equivalent surveillance spyware*, Brussels: Policy Department for Citizens' Rights and Constitutional Affairs (European Parliament), 2023, available at: https://www.europarl.europa.eu/RegData/etudes/STUD/2022/740151/IPOL_STU(2022)740151_EN.pdf [accessed on: June 11th, 2023].

Marshall, A., *Digital Forensics – Digital Evidence in Criminal Investigation*, Chichester: Wiley-Blackwell, 2008.

Martins, A. L., 'Novas tecnologias, investigação criminal e o cidadão em vias de transparência', [in:] Costa, J. F. *et al.* (eds.), *Estudos em Homenagem ao Prof. Doutor Manuel da Costa Andrade – Volume II*, Coimbra: Instituto Jurídico, 2017.

Mendes, P. S., *Lições de Direito Processual Penal*, Coimbra: Almedina, 2015.

Miranda, J., *Direitos Fundamentais*, Coimbra: Almedina, 2017.

Moreira, V., 'A «fiscalização concreta» no quadro do sistema misto de justiça constitucional', Volume Comemorativo do 75.º Tomo, *Boletim da Faculdade de Direito*, Coimbra, 2003.

Novais, J. R., *Direitos Fundamentais e Justiça Constitucional em Estado de Direito Democrático*, Coimbra: Coimbra Editora, 2012.

Pool, R. L. D., Custers, B. H. M., 'The Police Hack Back: Legitimacy, Necessity and Privacy Implications of The Next Step in Fighting Cybercrime', *European Journal of Crime, Criminal Law and Criminal Justice*, Deventer, 2017/25(2).

Queiroz, C., *Direitos Fundamentais – Teoria Geral*, 2 ed., Coimbra: Coimbra Editora, 2010.

Rodrigues, B. S., *Da Prova Penal – Tomo II – Bruscamente… A(s) face(s) oculta(s) dos métodos ocultos de investigação criminal*, Cascais: Rei dos Livros, 2010.

Serrano, N. G., 'Garantías constitucionales de la persecución penal en el entorno digital', [in:] Colomer, J. L. G. (ed.), *Prueba y Processo Penal (Análisis especial de la prueba prohibida en el sistema español y en el derecho comparado)*, Valencia: Tirant lo Blanch, 2008.

Velani, L. G., 'Trojan horse, strumenti investigativi e diritti fondamentali: alla ricerca di un difficile equilibrio', *Parola alla Difesa*, Pisa, 2016/1.

Vervaele, J. A. E., 'Surveillance and Criminal Investigation: Blurring of Thresholds and Boundaries in the Criminal Justice System?', [in:] Gutwirth, S., Leenes, R., Hert, P. D. (eds.), *Reloading Data Protection: Multidisciplinary Insights and Contemporary Challenges*, New York: Springer, 2014.

Wikileaks, 'Hacking Team – RE: [PJ CCU - Portugal] Remote IP Interc solution | request info, details, schedule, visit, etc – Email-ID 39666, available at: https://wikileaks.org/hackingteam/emails/emailid/39666 [accessed on: August 27th, 2023].

Dr. Federico C. La Vattiata[1]

VIII. Crimes of Harmful Consequences and Artificial Intelligence: Causation at the Bar

Abstract: The development and the application of AI involve risks for fundamental legal values, mainly (but not only) the protection of human life and health. The Author when examining the relation between AI and criminal law follows the footsteps of Fabio Basile, and examines four research pathways concerning AI: i) AI and law enforcement activities; ii) AI-based judicial decisions in criminal matters (robot-judge); iii) AI-based crime-risk assessment; and iv) AI and criminal liability.

The Author asks whether the 'good old criminal law', grounded upon a notion of causation related to classical 'Newtonian' physics, is still a useful tool for managing AI-risks. And He states that to answer such a question, human capacity to etiologically govern AI is crucial. In other words, its theoretical categories turn out to be no more useful only as long as the 'black box dilemma' is radically unsolvable. included within the genus 'computer crime'. The article presents the collection of thoughts mainly focuse on the causation in criminal law.

Keywords: Artificial Intelligence, AI-crime, causation

1 ORCID no. 0000-0002-6750-812X. Assistant Professor of Criminal Law at the University of Catania.

1. Introductory remarks

The applications of artificial intelligence techniques (AI) are numerous (driverless cars,[2] lethal autonomous weapons,[3] medical devices,[4] etc.). Various disciplines, including law, address the questions posed by such a scientific and technological breakthrough.

There is no unique definition of AI. In general terms, we can refer to the definition given by the European Commission in the Communication *Artificial Intelligence for Europe* of the April 25th, 2018: AI *"refers to systems that display intelligent behaviour by analysing their environment and taking actions – with some degree of autonomy – to achieve specific goals"*.[5]

Also, on the April 21st, 2021, the European Commission issued a Proposal for a Regulation *"laying down harmonised rules on artificial intelligence (Artificial Intelligence Act) and amending certain Union legislative acts"* (hereinafter also

---

2 N.A. Greenblatt, 'Self-Driving Cars and the Law', 53(2) *IEEE Spectrum* 2016, pp. 46–51; S. Beck, 'Google Cars, Software Agents, Autonomous Weapons Systems – New Challenges for Criminal Law?', [in:] E. Hilgendorf, U. Seidel (eds.), *Robotics, Autonomics, and the Law: Legal Issues Arising from the AUTONOMICS for Industry 4.0 Technology Programme of the German Federal Ministry for Economic Affairs and Energy*, Baden-Baden: Nomos 2017, pp. 227–252.

3 V. Chiappini Koscina, 'Prosecuting Killer Robots: Allocating Criminal Responsibilities for Grave Breaches of International Humanitarian Law Committed by Lethal Autonomous Weapon Systems', [in:] B. Custers, E. Fosch-Villaronga (eds.), *Law and Artificial Intelligence: Regulating AI and Applying AI in Legal Practice*, The Hague: T.M.C. Asser Press 2022, pp. 149–167; L.A. Letendre, 'Lethal Autonomous Weapon Systems: Translating Geek Speak for Lawyers', *International Law Studies* 2020/96, pp. 274–294.

4 A.L. Caplan, B. Parent, *The Ethical Challenges of Emerging Medical Technologies*, Milton Park/Abingdon/Oxon-New York: Routledge 2020; J. Ordish, A. Hall, H. Murfet, *Algorithms as Medical Devices*, Cambridge: PHG Foundation 2019. Recently, I addressed the matter of regulating AI-based medical devices in the EU: F.C. La Vattiata, 'AI-Based Medical Devices: The Applicable Law in the European Union', *BioLaw Journal - Rivista Di BioDiritto* 2022/4, pp. 412–437, https://doi.org/10.15168/2284-4503-2484. [accessed on January 10th, 2023].

5 COMMUNICATION FROM THE COMMISSION TO THE EUROPEAN PARLIAMENT, THE EUROPEAN COUNCIL, THE COUNCIL, THE EUROPEAN ECONOMIC AND SOCIAL COMMITTEE AND THE COMMITTEE OF THE REGIONS Artificial Intelligence for Europe, Brussels 25.4.2018, COM(2018) 237 final, available at: https://eur-lex.europa.eu/legal-content/EN/TXT/?uri=COM%3A2018%3A237%3AFIN, [accessed on January 10th, 2023].

Draft AIA).[6] According to Article 3(1) of the Draft AIA, AI system *"means software that (...) can, for a given set of human-defined objectives, generate outputs such as content, predictions, recommendations, or decisions influencing the environments they interact with"*.

The development and the application of AI involve risks for fundamental legal values, mainly (but not only) the protection of human life and health. As a matter of fact, harmful events, such as death or injuries, can depend on one of the various phases of AIs' lifecycle. Also, the ubiquitous use of such technology (*i.e.*, beyond national boundaries) implies that its regulation cannot be nothing but at an international or at least a supranational level.

For this reason, in the EU, the Commission has launched the aforementioned Draft AIA, aiming at harmonising the rules on AI, and in particular at reaching four goals: ensure that AI systems placed on the Union market and used are safe and respect existing law on fundamental rights and Union values; ensure legal certainty to facilitate investment and innovation in AI; enhance governance and effective enforcement of existing law on fundamental rights and safety requirements applicable to AIs; and facilitate the development of a single market for lawful, safe and trustworthy AIs and prevent market fragmentation.

According to Fabio Basile, four research pathways concerning AI can be identified in criminal law theory: *i)* AI and law enforcement activities; *ii)* AI-based judicial decisions in criminal matters (robot-judge); *iii)* AI-based crime-risk assessment; and *iv)* AI and criminal liability.[7]

This article will address the latter, that is, AI's involvement in the perpetration of crimes and, specifically, causation in offences of harmful consequences.[8]

---

6 Proposal for a REGULATION OF THE EUROPEAN PARLIAMENT AND OF THE COUNCIL LAYING DOWN HARMONISED RULES ON ARTIFICIAL INTELLIGENCE (ARTIFICIAL INTELLIGENCE ACT) AND AMENDING CERTAIN UNION LEGISLATIVE ACTS, Brussels 21.4.2021, COM(2021) 206 final, available at: https://eur-lex.europa.eu/legal-content/EN/TXT/?uri=celex%3A52021PC0206, [accessed on January 10th, 2023].

7 F. Basile, 'Intelligenza artificiale e diritto penale: quattro possibili percorsi di indagine', *Diritto Penale e Uomo* 2019/10, pp. 1–34.

8 G.P. Fletcher, *Rethinking Criminal Law*, Oxford-New York: Oxford University Press 2000, pp. 385 ff. According to Fletcher, crimes of 'harmful consequences' – e.g. homicide, battery, and the destruction of property – do have some elements in common which are sufficient to generate a general patter of liability. First, "*[t]here is a concrete harm to a personal interest (death, bodily injury, destruction of property).*" Second, "*this harmful consequence might be brought about either by natural processes or by human conduct.*" Third, "*it is possible and plausible to punish both negligent infliction of the harmful consequence and the failure to intervene and prevent the harm's occurring.*"

2. Methodology

Having identified the scope of this article, some methodological considerations are worth mentioning. The main questions at stake, many of which will be addressed in this article, are the following.

a) The AI systems' legal nature, *i.e.*, whether they can be legal subjects or shall be treated as mere tools under criminal law. I will not analyse it, as, recently, I already did it in another article, the access to which is open. Here, it is worth being briefly restated what I maintain in such work: *i.e.*, in light of various (both techno-scientific and normative) arguments, AIs can only be considered as mere instruments, through which crimes can be committed.[9]
b) The extent to which humans can etiologically dominate an 'intelligent' system – hence, the abstract limits of an AI's predictability and control – with reference to the so-called 'but-for' (*i.e.*, scientific) causation.
c) The questions pertaining the so-called 'proximate' (*i.e.*, normative) causation.
d) The problem of the proof beyond any reasonable doubt (BARD) of all the liability's grounds.

The investigation will be conducted under the 'integrated' perspective of both substantive and procedural criminal law.[10] Also, the comparative research method[11] will be applied, with regards to common law and civil law traditions.

- As for common law, I will refer to the Anglo-American (both substantive and procedural) criminal law.
- As for civil law, I will mainly refer to Italian law, for both substantive and procedural questions. Regarding the latter, in fact, Italian law shares with Anglo-American systems the adoption of an adversarial procedural model. Also, I will refer to German law, but with regards to substantive law solely.

---

9 F.C. La Vattiata, 'AI Systems Involved in Harmful Events: Liable Persons or Mere Instruments? An Interdisciplinary and Comparative Analysis', *BioLaw Journal - Rivista Di BioDiritto* 2023/1, pp. 485–499, https://doi.org/10.15168/2284-4503-2646. [accessed on January 10th, 2023].

10 S. Fiore, *La teoria generale del reato alla prova del processo: spunti per una ricostruzione integrata del sistema penale*, Napoli: Ed. Scientifiche Italiane 2007.

11 K. Zweigert, H. Kötz, *Introduction to Comparative Law*, Oxford-New York: Clarendon Press-Oxford University Press 1998); M.D. Dubber, T. Hörnle, *Criminal Law: A Comparative Approach*, Oxford-New York: Oxford University Press 2014; J.E. Ross, S.C. Thaman (eds.), *Comparative Criminal Procedure*, Cheltenham-Northampton: Edward Elgar Publishing 2016.

The various solutions adopted in the aforementioned legal systems will be addressed under the twofold perspective of 'law in the books' and 'law in action',[12] so as to assess how legal theory's categories are concretely applied by courts, and the extent to which they actually either coincide or differ regardless of the different classification given to them in the two 'juridical families' as above.

3. Causation in AI-product liability and its proof BARD

3.1. Preliminary observations

If we assume that AIs are mere tools and that through them humans can perpetrate offences within the pattern of 'harmful consequences', the so-called causal question is crucial: *i.e.*, whether and how it is possible to provide evidence BARD that given harm (event 'β') is causally depending on a given step (antecedent 'α') of an AI's lifecycle in which one or more humans' conducts (that we can denominate 'α.1', 'α.2', 'α.3', etc.) are involved.

AIs' development and application implicate the summation and more often the integration of different 'spheres of competence and responsibility' to which different humans' actions and/or omissions refer.

Criminal liability is, by definition, personal, individual, and culpable, never collective (even at an international level). It follows that such spheres of competence and responsibility shall be circumscribed. Hence, in so far as it is possible that measures of the etiological domain of AI are not available, the issue of predictability and control by humans of 'intelligent' systems turns out to be paramount.

An example will clarify this point: Tom is using a driverless car which does have a degree of autonomy that requires the human to be constantly careful and to take charge of the vehicle under 'request/alert' by the AI embedded into it;[13] Dick, who is crossing the road at a pedestrian crossing, is run over by the driverless car, which does not stop at the red traffic light; because of the impact, Dick dies.

In cases like this, one shall assess whether the event (Dick's death) has been caused by *a)* upstream, a flaw in the driverless car's programming,

12 R. Pound, 'Law in Books and Law in Action', *American Law Review* 1910/44(1), pp. 12–36; J.-L. Halperin, 'Law in Books and Law in Action: The Problem of Legal Change', *Maine Law Review* 2011/64(1), pp. 45–76.

13 It is the level 3 of driving automation, according to the classification developed by Society of Automotive Engineers (SAE): see *amplius* On-Road Automated Driving (ORAD) committee, *Taxonomy and Definitions for Terms Related to Driving Automation Systems for On-Road Motor Vehicles*, SAE International, https://doi.org/10.4271/J3016_201806 [accessed on: August 23rd, 2023].

e.g., an incomplete training set lacking examples about the duty to stop at a red traffic light; *b)* an insufficient or omitted control over the vehicle by Tom; *c)* both the aforementioned factors, '*pro quota*' interacting on the causal chain; *d)* neither of the two, *e.g.*, for a fatal coincidence, exceptional weather conditions – that were not foreseeable by the AI's architect – determined a reduced view of the road both for the AI and for the user Tom; in particular, even if the latter were warned by the former, he could have not recognised the risk and, consequently, he could have not acted to avert the impact causing Dick's death.

However, it should be noted that, in cases like the one *sub d)*, the liability of AI's architect should not be established: not because causation lacks, in light of an '*ex post*' verification; but because it was '*ex ante*' impossible for him to comply with the duty to recognise the risk (the so-called *Erkennensollen*), as the risk-situation was exceptional and, as such, unforeseeable. In other words, what the Germanic criminal law theory defines "recognisability of risk" (*Erkennbarkeit*) consists in the possibility to recognise the fact's occurrence, taking into account certain circumstances. It refers to the objective probability of the fact's occurrence.[14] Thus, if the risk is unrecognisable, there can be neither a duty to recognise it, nor to avert the harm.

Such case shows that, in the AI sector, causation and the objective features of negligence/recklessness (*culpa*) are strongly linked. After all, the knowledge upon which *Erkennbarkeit*'s verification is grounded consists in the same scientific laws used to establish causation.[15] Nevertheless, even if such links need to be underlined, the two elements in question shall be conceptually separated, and their scrutiny shall be autonomous (albeit the offence is, as a whole, a 'conceptual *unicum*').

Preliminarily, we need to specify that both in Anglo-Saxon and Continental juridical traditions, two concepts of causation can be distinguished. In other words, despite some differences (which exist indeed), a parallelism can be found in the twofold theorisation of causation – scientific on the one hand, normative on the other – of both common law and civil law. *I.e.*, a parallelism between

---

14 H.-H. Jescheck, T. Weigend, *Lehrbuch des Strafrechts: Allgemeiner Teil*, Berlin: Duncker & Humblot 1996, pp. 563 ff.; G. Forti, *Colpa ed evento nel diritto penale*, Milano: Giuffrè 1990, p. 201; G. Fornasari, *I principi del diritto penale tedesco*, Milano: CEDAM 1993, pp. 220 et seq.; C. Piergallini, *Danno da prodotto e responsabilità penale: profili dommatici e politico-criminali*, Milano: A. Giuffrè 2004, p. 371.

15 G. Forti, *Colpa ed evento*, p. 208.

a) the Continental (Italian and Germanic) notion of '*condicio sine qua non*' on the one hand,[16] and the Anglo-Saxon 'but-for causation' on the other – they both refer to causation under a naturalistic/scientific and hypothetical perspective, *i.e.*, one should ask *"what the world would have been like had the actor not performed his conduct. Specifically, would the result still have occurred (when it did)? If the answer is no, then the actor's conduct was necessary for, was a 'but for' cause of, the result"*;[17]
b) the Anglo-Saxon notion of 'proximate causation' on the one hand, and the various ways the civil law tradition refers to causation under a normative perspective (which basically depend on – and can be differentiated according to – the numerous theoretical models that each scholar maintains),[18] *i.e.*, 'proximate' or

---

16 W. Naucke, 'Über Das Regreßverbot Im Strafrecht', 76 *Zeitschrift Für Die Gesamte Strafrechtswissenschaft* 1964, pp. 409 ff.; M. Maiwald, *Kausalität Und Strafrecht: Studien Zum Verhältnis von Naturwiss. u. Jurisprudenz*, Göttingen: Schwartz 1980; F. Stella, *Leggi scientifiche e spiegazione causale nel diritto penale*, Milano: Giuffrè 1990; F. Stella, *Giustizia e modernità: la protezione dell'innocente e la tutela delle vittime*, Milano: Giuffrè 2003; F. Stella, *Il giudice corpuscolariano: la cultura delle prove*, Milano: Giuffrè 2005; F. Toepel, *Kausalität Und Pflichtwidrigkeitszusammenhang Beim Fahrlässigen Erfolgsdelikt*, Berlin: Duncker & Humblot 1992; K. Summerer, *Causalità ed evitabilità: formula della condicio sine qua non e rilevanza dei decorsi causali ipotetici nel diritto penale*, Pisa: Ed. ETS 2013; S. Preziosi, *La causalità penale: nell'orizzonte della 'scienza nuova'*, Napoli: Jovene 2021.

17 P.H. Robinson, *Structure and Function in Criminal Law*, Oxford-New York: Clarendon Press-Oxford University Press 1997, p. 24. See also MPC § 2.03(l)(a).

18 The following are some examples.
- '*Kausalität im Rechtssinne*' or '*relevante Kausalität*' (G. Jakobs, *Strafrecht, Allgemeiner Teil: Die Grundlagen Und Die Zurechnungslehre. Lehrbuch*, Berlin-Boston: De Gruyter 1991, p. 226; I. Puppe, *Die Erfolgszurechnung im Strafrecht: dargestellt an Beispielsfällen aus der höchstrichterlichen Rechtsprechung*, Baden-Baden: Nomos 2000, p. 8).
- '*Kausalität zwischen Pflichtverletzung und Erfolg*' or '*Kausalität der Pflichtwidrigkeit*' (K. Ulsenheimer, *Das Verhältnis Zwischen Pflichtwidrigkeit Und Erfolg Bei Den Fahrlässigkeitsdelikten*, Bonn: Ludwig Röhrshceid Verlag 1965, p. 146); F. Toepel, *Kausalität Und Pflichtwidrigkeitszusammenhang Beim Fahrlässigen Erfolgsdelikt*, p. 49).
- '*Causalità della colpa*' – '*Kausalität der Sorgfaltspflichtverletzung*' (I. Puppe, *Die Erfolgszurechnung im Strafrecht*, pp. 73 ff.; M. Donini, *Imputazione oggettiva dell'evento: 'nesso di rischio' e responsabilità per fatto proprio*, Torino: Giappichelli 2006, pp. 93 ff.).
- '*Nesso di antigiuridicità*' – '*Rechtswidrigkeitszusammenhang*' (K. Engisch, *Die Kausalität Als Merkmal Der Strafrechtlichen Tatbestände*, Tübingen: Mohr Siebeck, 1931, p. 61; H.-H. Jescheck, T. Weigend, *Lehrbuch des Strafrechts*, p. 583; M. Romano, *Commentario Sistematico Del Codice Penale*, vol. 1, Milano: Giuffrè 2004, pp. 406 ff.).
- '*Realizzazione della colpa nell'evento*' – '*Realisierung der Sorgfaltsverletzung*' (G. Forti, *Colpa ed evento*, pp. 418 ff.).

'legal' causation assures that the strength and nature of the causal connection between the conduct and the result is sufficient, requiring that the harm is not too remote, or accidental, or unforeseeable in its occurrence to have a just bearing on the actor's liability or on the gravity of his offence.

Also, both Continental judges and Anglo-Saxon juries face the same problems when they shall determine whether someone, who does have a given role in a 'black-box' AI's lifecycle (*e.g.*, the user), is criminally liable beyond any reasonable doubt (BARD) for causing harm, so that should such proof is not satisfied in the trial – for instance, through an expert witness' testimony –, the outcome shall be only the defendant's acquittal.

Two main approaches can be distinguished with regards to AI.

In the first place, the so-called model-based AI, where systems imitate the behaviours of a given domain's experts. In short, the architect defines the knowledge representation about a phenomenon (*e.g.*, the need to stop at a red traffic light) and integrates such a model into the system. Thus, the AI can 'treat' the phenomenon (*e.g.*, analysis of the risk-factor regarding the possibility that pedestrians cross the road at the zebra crossing).

Two types of model-based AI can be identified: *a)* systems based upon if-then rules, where, given the premise 'α,' the system formulates the conclusion 'β,' to solve the question 'γ' that has been posed by the architect; *b)* systems based on the so-called 'trees,' where the knowledge is organised by reference to a model that evokes the shape of an ideal tree, whose 'fronds' correspond to the different data classification's alternatives, in such a way that, after the 'ramification,' an output is produced: *i.e.*, the software recognises the question 'γ' by virtue of a series of variables, that is, given the starting situation 'α,' the various possible alternatives 'ramify' until the conclusion 'β' is reached.

In the second place, another approach relates to AI, namely machine learning (ML)-based AI, where a phenomenon's model is obtained from data that, for instance, are made available on the Internet, by the numerous sensors in our cities, as well as by the sensors with which our smart watches are equipped. It is a technique that allows to realise complex knowledge representations, by way of statistics and the probability theory. The ML is grounded on different learning methods – that is, 'supervised learning,' 'unsupervised learning,' and 'reinforcement learning' – and several computational models (for example, 'artificial neural networks' or 'ANN) for data analysis. I analysed them extensively in the article I mentioned above.[19] However, stemming from the technical analysis therein, to

19 F.C. La Vattiata, 'AI Systems Involved in Harmful Events,' *op.cit.*, pp. 492 et seq.

which I hereby refer, it is worth being specified that a problem of systems' *explainability*[20] – *i.e.*, the possibility to understand 'how' and 'why', given the input 'x' the system produced the output 'y' – exists only with reference to ML techniques. For that matter, the ML-based AIs can be classified according to their degree of explainability. In fact, thanks to various techniques, also systems with a hidden inner structure can be made interpretable. Among such techniques, two test are worth mentioning: on the one hand, through the so-called 'black-box test', one can comprehend the software's function, in terms of input-output mapping, with no need to access to the source-code (with no need to 'open the black-box'); on the other hand, through the so-called 'white-box test', by accessing to the system's source-code, each code's lines can be tested, and the analysis is not limited to the input-output mapping.[21]

3.2. AI-Harm: Causation at the Bar

In light of the aforementioned, we can affirm that not all AIs are unexplainable, unforeseeable and uncontrollable, so that the problem of verifying the etiological nexus between the AI and a harm can be solved.

Hence, except for cases of radical opacity of AI systems (for which the *in dubio pro reo* principle shall apply and the defendant shall be accordingly acquitted – as detailed below), abstractly, not only one can identify cases of systems' faulty development (*e.g.*, because of its erroneous training), but also, as a consequence, where a harm allegedly reconnectable to the AI occurs, this should allow to clearly reconstruct the 'spheres of responsibility' by differentiating the judicial verifications

20 In the strict sense, some technical concepts can be differentiated: *a)* 'intelligibility' means the AI model's clarity under the functional viewpoint (how it works), regardless of an explanation about its inner structure; *b)* where referred to ML, 'comprehensibility' means the algorithm's suitability to represent the knowledge it has learnt, while 'interpretability' means the system's suitability to explain such a knowledge to humans in understandable terms; *c)* 'explainability' relates to the notion of explanation, as an interface between humans and the system capable of taking decisions; such a (humanly understandable) explanation also represents an accurate proxy of the system; last but not least *d)* a system is considered 'transparent' when it turns out to be *ictu oculi* (at first glance) intelligible.

On this point, see among others G. Montavon, W. Samek, K.-R. Müller, 'Methods for Interpreting and Understanding Deep Neural Networks', *Digital Signal Processing* 2018/73, pp. 1–15; M. Gleicher, 'A Framework for Considering Comprehensibility in Modeling', *Big Data* 2016/4(2), pp. 75–88.

21 J. Ordish, A. Hall, H. Murfet, *Algorithms as Medical Devices, op.cit.*, pp. 23 ff.

with regards, depending on the situation, to the liability of the various subjects involved in the AI's lifecycle (the architect, the manufacturer, the importer, the seller, the user, etc.).

Substantive and procedural law questions are the 'two sides of the same coin' and, as clarified below, they are closely interconnected and influence each other. However, for the purpose of explanatory order, the following subsections will respectively focus on first the former, then the latter.

3.2.1. Substantive criminal law questions

Cases of (also AI-) product liability can be differentiated as follows.

a) Liability for the 'type' of production, pertaining to fields where the risk-coefficient of harm's causation is so high that it cannot be significantly reduced, not even providing for precautionary measures.
b) Liability for the 'modality' of production, pertaining to productive activities which are allowed by the law as long as they are characterised by a lower risk-coefficient of harm's causation, that is, the available nomological knowledge allows to control it.

Having clarified this, we can affirm that, where AI techniques are applied to products for which the law requires an authorisation before they are put into the market/service, it is unlikely that a case of liability for the 'type' of production arises: *i.e.*, once the authorisation has been released – and except for cases of deceptive conducts aiming at eluding the controls that shall be performed in order for the authorisation to be issued –, the productive activity, though risky, is 'allowed'.[22] Rather, where some device's flaw has been found, one should wonder whether, in one or more phases of its lifecycle, cases of liability for the 'modality' of production arise.[23] Such a scrutiny shall be carried out according to the following checklist.

a) Does the AI-based product have a flaw that has determined its malfunctioning? If so,
b) is the harmful event to be explained etiologically linked to such malfunctioning?

---

22 W. Preuss, *Untersuchungen Zum Erlaubten Risiko Im Strafrecht*, Berlin: Duncker und Humblot 1974; K.L.L. Binding, *Die Schuld im deutschen Strafrecht. Vorsatz, Irrtum, Fahrlässigkeit: kurzes Lehrbuch*, Leipzig: Meiner 1919; K.L.L. Binding, *Die Normen Und Ihre Übertretung*, vol. IV. Die Fahrlässigkeit, Leipzig: Meiner 1919.

23 F. Bricola, 'Responsabilità penale per il tipo e per il modo di produzione' in: S. Canestrari, A. Melchionda (eds.), *Scritti Di Diritto Penale*, Milano: Giuffrè 1997, pp. 1231–1253.

c) Then, is the flaw that has caused the product's malfunctioning – and, consequently, the harmful event – in turn etiologically linked to one or more (either commissive or omissive)[24] conducts identifiable in the device's lifecycle?
d) As a matter of fact, did third causal factors – namely concurrent and independent causes suddenly developed, for instance identifiable in the device's application phase – determine the harm and interrupt the etiological development that had been 'activated' by the product's flaw in question? In general, in case the answer to the question *sub a)* is negative, has the harmful event been caused by one or more conducts of users concretely applying the AI-based product?

Specifically, the first step of the but-for causation consists in the event's (re-)description according to the criterion of the 'event in its concrete shape' ('*der Erfolg in seiner konkreten Gestalt*' or 'evento *hic et nunc*'). In other words, one shall refer to the event that constitutes the crime's requirement, by taking into account its characteristics that might reoccur (*e.g.*, someone's death), but at the same time as they concretely occurred in the case under scrutiny (*e.g.*, the death of a human, who crosses the road at a zebra crossing and is run over by a vehicle that does not stop at a red traffic light).[25]

Sometimes, there can be the need for a reference to some implicit assumptions according to the so-called '*coeteris paribus*' (literally 'all other things being equal') clause, *i.e.*, by assuming that the laws and an event's necessary conditions explicitly mentioned in a causal explanation can be used to understand how a given event occurred, provided that all other conditions, which are often unknown or only supposed, are equal.[26] It is worth being specified that one of the main reasons of the '*coeteris paribus*' clause's frequent application in scientific explanations is that, often, causal relationships are hypothesised between happenings that are spatially far and/or separated by some chronological hiatus.[27] Such a scenario is

24 G.P. Fletcher, *Basic Concepts of Criminal Law*, New York: Oxford University Press 1998, p. 63.
25 F. Stella, *Leggi scientifiche*, *op.cit.*, pp. 252 ff.; F. Stella, *La «descrizione» dell'evento. I: L'offesa – Il nesso causale*, Milano: Giuffrè 1970, pp. 87 ff.; K. Engisch, *Die Kausalität Als Merkmal Der Strafrechtlichen Tatbestände.*
26 G. Schurz, 'Ceteris Paribus Laws: Classification and Deconstruction', *Erkenntnis* 2002/57(3), pp. 351–372.
27 F. Stella, *Leggi scientifiche*, *op.cit.*, p. 285; G. P. Fletcher, *Basic Concepts of Criminal Law*, *op.cit.*, p. 61.

likely indeed with regards to AI products' lifecycle, which is usually characterised (at least) by numerous phases and expansion of time.[28]

In short, one shall wonder whether the but-for causation of the harm is effectively a system's flaw which is scientifically ascribable to the conduct performed for instance by the AI's architect (or by another subject involved in the AI's lifecycle). Such a verification shall be performed according to the scientific laws available at the time of trial (*ex post* perspective).

However, one should note that, in the field of AI, a solid nomological base is lacking. After all, a deep crisis, both epistemological and nomological, affects natural sciences, and determines the decrease of reliability on the traditional model of scientific explanation, *i.e.*, the so-called 'deductive-nomological' or 'D-N' model,[29] according to which a given phenomenon 'a' is explained by deducing its description from a law 'α' plus a description of the particular circumstances ('b1', 'b2', 'b3', etc.) in which the phenomenon in question occurs.[30] In the field of product liability, because of such a lack of solid knowledge base, both the description and the explanation of events turn out to be uncertain and unclear: it is a crisis that, with regards to AI, is deepened by the possibility that the 'black-box' algorithms are applied.

It would be erroneous to deal with such problems by trying to replace the D-N model with 'normative' models of liability's ascription, which are based upon, on the one hand, the mere chronological connection between the use of a product and the event's occurrence, and on the other the absence of alternative causal explanations (so-called 'negative causation').

In fact, there is a conceptual difference between, on the one hand, the '*ex ante* causation' – which, as such, can at the most help to predict (*i.e.*, for the future) the incidence of a given factor 'a' on the causation of a given event 'b' –, and on the other the so-called 'particularistic evidence' of causation, which is suitable to

---

28 *Contra* see K. Summerer, *Causalità ed evitabilità*, *op.cit.*, pp. 88 et seq.; I. Puppe, *Die Erfolgszurechnung im Strafrecht*, *op.cit.*, pp. 26 ff.

29 F. Stella, *Il giudice corpuscolariano, loc.cit.*; M. Maiwald, *L'evoluzione del diritto penale tedesco in un confronto con il sistema Italiano* (V. Militello ed.), Torino: Giappichelli 1993, pp. 143 et seq.

30 M. Esfeld, 'Explanation (Deductive-Nomological, Mereological, Reductive)', [in:] M.D. Binder, N. Hirokawa, U. Windhorst (eds.), *Encyclopedia of Neuroscience*, Berlin-Heidelberg: Springer 2009, pp. 1495–1498.

prove *ex post* whether a particular (single) event 'b' has been caused by a particular (single) antecedent 'a'.[31]

Also, as we have seen *supra*, even if the 'normative' viewpoint does have relevance in causation's scrutiny, 'proximate causation' requires that 'but-for causation' exists (and is proved). The former limits, under a normative perspective, the results to which but-for causation's verification leads under a scientific perspective. The former does not (*rectius*, shall not) replace the latter. The former integrates the latter: there can be no proximate causation without but-for causation.[32]

Of course, all the crime's requirements, including causation, shall be proved beyond any reasonable doubt.[33] The BARD rule pertains both to the evidence (it is the 'main' rule of evidence) and to the verdict overall.[34] However, it can amount to nothing if it is not 'given substance' by referring to reliable scientific laws. In particular, because of the nature itself of AI, laws of statistics are at stake.[35]

The questionable point regards what probabilistic coefficient of the relationship between happenings ($0 \leq x \leq 1$) can be considered sufficient to meet the BARD burden of proof. The question is: where – as it is likely in the cases in question – some high probabilistic coefficient (≈ 1) is not available, shall the jury/judge always acquit the defendant[36]?

It seems (by the way) reasonable to provide the following solution: 'not always."

As maintained by Justice Giovanni Canzio (Emeritus President of the Italian Supreme Court of Cassation) in the well-known precedent *Franzese*,[37] criminal trials' scrutiny is essentially based upon the inductive-inferential model of explanation. In other words, if we maintained that only the nomological-deductive model of explanation can be applied (according an utopistic idea of absolute certainty), criminal law's preventive and repressive purposes would not be likely realised, especially with regard to fundamental legal values (*Rechtsgüter*) like the

---

31 R.W. Wright, 'Liability for Possible Wrongs: Causation, Statistical Probability and the Burden of Proof', *Loyola of Los Angeles Law Review*, 2008/41, pp. 1295–1244.

32 G.P. Fletcher, *Basic Concepts of Criminal Law*, p. 64. See also W.R. LaFave, A.W. Scott, *Substantive Criminal Law*, St. Paul: West Pub. Co 1986, pp. 390 et seq.

33 Justia, *Stages of Criminal Trial*, available at: https://www.justia.com/criminal/procedure/stages-criminal-trial/ [accessed on: August 23rd, 2023].

34 F. Stella, *Giustizia e modernità*; F. Stella, *Il giudice corpuscolariano*; A.M. Dershowitz, *Reasonable Doubts: The Criminal Justice System and the O.J. Simpson Case*, New York: Simon & Schuster 1997.

35 S. Preziosi, *La causalità penale*, *op.cit.*, p. 262.

36 F. Stella, *Il giudice corpuscolariano*, *op.cit.*, pp. 76 et seq.

37 Corte suprema di Cassazione, Sezioni Unite penali, September 11th, 2002, *Franzese*.

protection of human life. Rather, the question shall be solved by materialising scientific laws[38] and by meeting, for the purposes of 'processual' certainty, a 'high reasonable reliability' (or 'logic probability') of a given explanation.[39] In *Franzese*, the Italian Supreme Court of Cassation affirmed that causation's existence can also be grounded upon low-to-medium probabilistic coefficients of relationship between happenings, as long as they are corroborated by positive evidence demonstrating the absence of alternative and interacting causal factors and conversely, in light of the available evidence, high coefficients can turn out to be inapplicable with reference to a particular harmful event's explanation. In short, the available evidence is what matters: insufficient, contradictory and/or uncertain evidence shall determine nothing but the defendant's acquittal: *in dubio pro reo*.

In summary, substantive criminal law fundamental principles and rules can never be sacrificed at the altar of evidentiary necessities or problems.[40] Specifically, the latter can never legitimise a 'weak' scrutiny of causation, and, therefore, a 'weak' notion of causation, which would imply a 'hypertrophic' area of liability. Also, the use of spurious scientific knowledge or even 'junk science' – which surely cannot be used to explain causal relationships – would not only imply the crisis of the deductive-nomological (D-N) model but also of the inductive-statistical (I-S) model of scientific explanation which is based upon a concept of *explanandum* anyway characterised by a high inductive probability of the *explanans*.[41]

Also, as already mentioned, to properly circumscribe the numerous 'spheres of liability' one should consider that AIs' lifecycle results from the summation/integration of numerous 'spheres of competence'. It is likely that the business paradigm more frequently involved in the development and application of AI-products is of corporate nature, where more people provide their (quantitatively and quantitatively) different contributions.

---

38 M. Romano, 'Nesso causale e concretizzazione delle leggi scientifiche in diritto penale', [in:] M. Bertolino, G. Forti (eds.), *Scritti per Federico Stella*, Napoli: Jovene 2007, pp. 891–922.

39 Federico Stella himself, before maintaining – in *Giustizia e modernità* and *Il Giudice corpuscolariano* – the need for a $\simeq 1$ probabilistic coefficient, had differentiated: *a)* on the one hand, the 'scientific' concepts of statistical probability and of 'synthetic' sentences (non-depending on logic observations, but on empirical investigations); *b)* on the other, the 'meta-scientific' concept of logic probability and of 'analytic' sentences (regarding the logic relationship between available evidence and hypothesis). In this regard, see F. Stella, *Leggi scientifiche, op.cit.*, pp. 222 et seq.

40 Corte suprema di Cassazione, *Franzese*.

41 F. Stella, *Il giudice corpuscolariano, op.cit.*, p. 7; F. Stella, *Leggi scientifiche, op.cit.*, p. 225.

If so, liability cannot be established only considering the position held by someone within a company's organogram or within the AI's lifecycle. It would be as 'convenient' as erroneous to consider fungible commissive and omissive conducts.

For instance, it would be as 'convenient' as erroneous to give relevance to a managerial decision's 'commissive' form (*e.g.*, being the result of a collective deliberation adopted by the company's directors board) rather than to its 'omissive' content (*e.g.*, the board of directors' inertia, waiting for more information about etiological factors determining harm, with reference to what is only allegedly a risky situation).[42] Furthermore, it would be as 'convenient' as erroneous to 'attribute' to manufacturers the failure of harm's prevention only on the grounds of their previous risky conduct – so-called '*ex Ingerenz Garantenstellungen*'[43] –, even more so where such activity (the production of AIs) is legally authorised.

In all the examples above, as it is self-evident, it would be a methodological error to let conduct be considered lawful (or unlawful) only because of harm's non-occurrence (or occurrence), rather than according to scientific investigations about the risk(s) posed by a given product:[44] the error consists in replacing the *explanans* with the *explanandum*.

Such a scenario turns out to be further complicated if one considers that omissive causation – *i.e.*, causation in omissive crimes of harmful consequences ('*unechte Unterlassungsdelite*') – is characterised by a significantly 'normative' structure (with both regards to but-for and proximate causation).

In fact, "*[t]here is no way to roll back history and to run the sequence again with one factor changed*".[45] While active causation's investigation is grounded upon a hypothesis, that is, a counterfactual conditional question ('α' causes an event 'β' if, but for 'α', 'β' would not have occurred: what would have happened if 'α' were absent? Would 'β' have happened anyway?), omissive causation's scrutiny is based on multiple hypotheses,[46] as follows.

---

42 C. Piergallini, *Danno da prodotto e responsabilità penale*, *op.cit.*, pp. 237 et seq.

43 G. Grasso, *Il reato omissivo improprio: la struttura obiettiva della fattispecie*, Milano: Giuffrè 1983, pp. 189 et seq. and pp. 287 et seq.

44 C. Piergallini, *Danno da prodotto e responsabilità penale*, *op.cit.*, p. 242.

45 G. P. Fletcher, *Basic Concepts of Criminal Law*, *op.cit.*, p. 63.

46 C.E. Paliero, 'La causalità dell'omissione: formule concettuali e paradigm prasseologici', *Rivista Italiana Di Medicina Legale* 1992/2, pp. 839 et seq.

a) First, was the defendant bound to some legal duty to act aimed at the event's prevention (*Garantenstellung*)? If so
b) secondly, one shall reconstruct the omitted (hypothetical) model of conduct, which would have averted the harm.
c) Third, one shall *ex post* reconstruct the etiological development that actually occurred and led to harm.
d) Finally, according to reliable scientific laws, one shall formulate a counterfactual hypothesis on the suitability to avert the harm of the mandatory model of conduct, which has not been performed by the defendant.[47]

3.2.2. Procedural criminal law questions

Therefore, all the trial's actors – especially prosecutors and judges/juries – shall deal with the BARD burden of proof.

With regards to the illustrative case mentioned above (car accident), we shall wonder how the judges/juries can verify whether, ultimately, Dick's death has been caused by a driverless car's flaw and not, for instance, by Tom's failure to control the vehicle. To this end, they likely need to investigate the AI system embedded in the vehicle, to 'open the black box' if need be.

Hence, a question is at stake: *i.e.*, whether ('*an*') and how ('*quomodo*') the so-called 'machine evidence' – that is, the evidence derivable from the AI system and regarding the man-machine interactions – can be admitted in the trial.[48]

As specified above, I will only refer to the adversarial criminal proceedings model, adopted in the United States of America, in the United Kingdom, and in Italy.

Adversarial systems' cornerstones are the following: hypotheses, evidence, facts, truth, doubts, and reasonable explanations of verdicts. The procedural paradigm in question is based upon evidence, criticism, and rationalism, as well as abductive and inductive reasonings, which are chiefly probabilistic: in short, "trial by probabilities".[49] In light of this, it is therefore worth wondering whether

47 F. Stella, *Il giudice corpuscolariano*, *op.cit.*, p. 216.

48 S. Gless, 'AI in the Courtroom: A Comparative Analysis of Machine Evidence in Criminal Trials', *Georgetown Journal of International Law* 2020/51(2), pp. 195–253.

49 G. Canzio, 'Intelligenza Artificiale, Algoritmi e Giustizia Penale', *Sistemapenale.it*, February 28th, 2021, available at: https://www.sistemapenale.it/it/articolo/canzio-intelligenza-artificiale-algoritmi-giustizia-penale [accessed on: August 28th, 2023]; G. Canzio, 'Scienza, Diritto e Processo Penale Nell'era Del Rischio', [in:] A. Amato, G. Flora, C. Valbonesi (eds.), *Scienza, diritto e processo penale nell'era del rischio*, Torino: Giappichelli 2019, pp. 45–59.

AI-harm causation, which is sometimes deeply 'dark', can effectively be verified in adversarial systems.

First and foremost, as we have seen above, except for cases where causation's verification turns out to be absolutely impossible, the causal question can be solved, especially where, in light of the admitted evidence, it can be established that no alternative causal factors (*i.e.*, other than, for example, either a faulty AI's programming or an omitted control by the user) interacted in the etiological development that determined the harmful event.

In order for the BARD burden of proof to be met, all the trial's actors shall be made capable of accessing to all the relevant information, *i.e.*, not only, in particular, the 'machine evidence', but also, in general, all the scientific knowledge regarding the type of AI each time in question, its 'modality of action', as well as – where it is a 'black box' – the techniques that can explain it and verify its output. In summary, it is a matter of scientific evidence:[50] there is the need for specialised knowledge, which comes into the trial scene through expert witnesses (*e.g.*, computer scientists). As things stand, in fact, it is unlikely that AIs themselves can be heard as witnesses.

The introduction into the trial of 'junk science'[51] shall be avoided. In this regard, some principles can be reminded. They have been first established by the US Supreme Court in *Daubert*,[52] then integrated by the Italian Supreme Court of Cassation in *Cozzini*.[53]

In short, the judge shall verify the evidence's relevance and reliability, not only for the purposes of its admissibility but also for its assessment. To this end, some criteria apply.

---

50 On this issue see among others S. Jasanoff, *Science at the Bar: Law, Science, and Technology in America*, Cambridge, Mass: Harvard University Press 1995; P. Roberts (ed.), *Expert Evidence and Scientific Proof in Criminal Trials*, London: Routledge 2016; O. Dominioni, *La prova penale scientifica: gli strumenti scientifico-tecnici nuovi o controversi e di elevata specializzazione*, Milano: Giuffrè 2005.

51 J. Hilbert, 'The Disappointing History of Science in the Courtroom: Frye, Daubert, and the Ongoing Crisis of Junk Science in Criminal Trials', *Oklahoma Law Review* 2019/71, pp. 759–821; J. M. Price, G. Gates Kelly, 'Junk Science in the Courtroom: Causes, Effects and Controls', *Hamline Law Review* 1996/19, pp. 395–408.

52 Supreme Court of the United States of America, June 28th, 1993, *Daubert v. Merrell Dow Pharmaceuticals, Inc*, 509 U.S. 579 (1993).

53 Corte suprema di Cassazione, Sez. IV penale, September 17th, 2010, *Cozzini*.

- As for the former: *a)* the controllability and falsifiability of principles upon which the evidence is based; *b)* whether the relevant scientific community has verified them; *c)* whether they have been addressed in publications of high scientific significance; *d)* whether the relative (certain or potential) margin of error is known; and, only after the aforementioned, *d)* whether they have been generally accepted by the relevant scientific community.
- As for the latter: *a)* the independence and reliability of the expert witness; *b)* the scope, the accuracy, and the purposes of the relative research; *c)* the research outcomes' suitability to provide an explanation to the specific question at stake.

4. Conclusive remarks

To conclude, we should wonder whether the 'good old criminal law', grounded upon a notion of causation related to classical 'Newtonian' physics, is still a useful tool for managing AI-risks. To answer such a question, the human capacity to etiologically govern AI is crucial. In other words, its theoretical categories turn out to be no more useful only as long as the 'black box dilemma' is radically unsolvable.[54]

In light of all the aforementioned, it seems to be neither necessary nor appropriate to renounce classical criminal law as one of the state's tools of risk management and protection of fundamental legal values. In fact, as clarified above, except for some residual cases of 'opaque' AI algorithms, a problem relating to causation either is not posed or is solvable.

Where evidentiary problems arise, the need for rigour in applying the BARD rule shall be reaffirmed, as it expresses the presumption of innocence,[55] which is in turn linked to *nullum crimen sine lege* (legality) and *nullum crimen sine culpa* (guilt) principles.[56] An authentic view of justice – which is 'bidirectional', not only for victims but also for defendants – implies a critical, rigorous and illuminated application of criminal law.

Criminal law shall not be used to merely 'sedate' (control) social fears of technological innovation.

---

54 M.U. Scherer, 'Regulating Artificial Intelligence Systems: Risks, Challenges, Competencies, and Strategies', *SSRN Electronic Journal* 2015, available at: https://doi.org/10.2139/ssrn.2609777. [accessed on January 10th, 2023]

55 Supreme Court of the United States of America, March 31st, 1970, *In re Winship*, 397 U.S. 358 (1970).

56 F. Stella, *Giustizia e modernità*, *op.cit.*, pp. 211 ff.; G. Grasso, 'La protezione dei diritti fondamentali nella Costituzione per l'Europa e il diritto penale: spunti di riflessione critica' in: M. Bertolino, G. Forti (eds.) *Scritti per Federico Stella*, pp. 242 et seq.

Some AI features can jeopardise the 'functioning' of criminal law. However, I find that the solution to such a problem cannot be to radically renounce the latter. Rather, as I already called for in another work, criminal law tools should be integrated with civil law and administrative law instruments,[57] thus providing for an AI-product liability framework that is 'balanced' and inspired by subsidiarity and proportionality principles.

For instance, a multilevel framework can be constructed upon the criterion of increasing harmfulness of conduct and relevance of legal values:

a) administrative sanctions, imposed by regulatory Agencies, for 'minor offences', that is, relating to legal values other than the protection of life or human health (*e.g.*, faulty programming of a device that causes its decreased performance, which turn out to be inconsistent with its 'quality' and market price);
b) criminal sanctions, imposed by the judiciary, for serious offences, *i.e.*, relating to the protection of life, human health, or other fundamental values.

Anyway, normative solutions are not sufficient. Also, the so-called 'technological' solutions proposed by Roger Brownsword, should be put in play: *i.e.*, "a broad range of measures that might supplement or supplant the rules" and that can be: *a)* 'architectural', that is, settings can be re-designed or *ex novo* designed in a way that allows to manage the risks posed by AI; *b)* incorporated in the design of AIs or their lifecycle, so that humans are removed from potentially risky situations; or *c)* incorporated in wearables or even in humans themselves.[58]

More generally, we can restate (cf. § 1) that, since AIs' lifecycle does not have national boundaries, its regulation cannot be nothing but at an international or at least a supranational level. In the EU, from the criminal law viewpoint, this would imply that even if the AIA were adopted and entered into force, for the four aforementioned goals pursued by the Commission to be reached, only non-criminal harmonised rules turn out to be insufficient. Also, supranational criminal law provisions are needed.

As for substantive law, "*minimum rules concerning the definition of criminal offences and sanctions*" might be established through directives under Article 83 of the Treaty on functioning of the EU (TFEU). They cannot be established under paragraph 1, as the regulation of AI is not among the "areas of particularly serious

57 F.C. La Vattiata, 'Artificial Intelligence in Healthcare: Risk Assessment and Criminal Law', [in:] I. Beridze, S. van de Meulengraaf, O. McCarthy, A. Rodriguez Tamayo (eds.), *Special Collection on Artificial Intelligence*, Torino: UNICRI 2020, pp. 48–58.

58 R. Brownsword, *Law 3.0: Rules, Regulation and Technology*, Abingdon/Oxon-New York: Routledge 2020, p. 2.

crime with a cross-border dimension" explicitly enlisted therein – unless we consider it as a *species* included within the *genus* 'computer crime'. However, to solve the question once and for all, the Council, acting unanimously after obtaining the consent of the European Parliament, might adopt a decision identifying AI crime as an area meeting the criteria of paragraph 1, *i.e.*, to be particularly serious and to have a cross-border dimension. Alternatively, minimum rules in question could be established under paragraph 2, as long as AIA is definitely adopted (thus becoming an area already "*subject to harmonisation measures*"): in fact, in the AI sector, "the approximation of criminal laws and regulations of the Member States proves essential to ensure the effective implementation" of the relative EU policy.

Finally, from a procedural law perspective, the legal framework in question could be effectively completed by including AI-crime in the matters for which the European Public Prosecutor's Office (EPPO)[59] is competent.[60]

Bibliography

Basile F., 'Intelligenza artificiale e diritto penale: quattro possibili percorsi di indagine', *Diritto Penale e Uomo* 2019/10.

Beck S., 'Google Cars, Software Agents, Autonomous Weapons Systems – New Challenges for Criminal Law?' [in:] E. Hilgendorf, U. Seidel (eds.), *Robotics, Autonomics, and the Law: Legal Issues Arising from the AUTONOMICS for Industry 4.0 Technology Programme of the German Federal Ministry for Economic Affairs and Energy*, Baden-Baden: Nomos 2017.

Binding K. L. L., *Die Normen Und Ihre Übertretung*, vol. IV. Die Fahrlässigkeit, Leipzig: Meiner 1919.

Binding K. L. L., *Die Schuld im deutschen Strafrecht. Vorsatz, Irrtum, Fahrlässigkeit: kurzes Lehrbuch*, Leipzig: Meiner 1919.

59 Regulation 2017/1939/EU of the Council of October 12th, 2017 implementing enhanced cooperation on the establishment of the European Public Prosecutor's Office ('the EPPO'), available at: https://eur-lex.europa.eu/legal-content/EN/TXT/?uri=celex%3A32017R1939 [accessed on: August 28th, 2023].

60 As things stand, EPPO's competence is limited to the protection of EU financial interests. About the EPPO, see among others V- Mitsilegas, F. Giuffrida, 'The European Public Prosecutor's Office and Human Rights', [in:] W. Geelhoed, L.H. Erkelens, A.W.H. Meij (eds.), *Shifting Perspectives on the European Public Prosecutor's Office*, The Hague: T.M.C. Asser Press 2018, pp. 59–98; K. Ligeti (ed.), *The European Public Prosecutor's Office at Launch: Adapting National Systems, Transforming EU Criminal Law*, Padova: CEDAM 2020.

Bricola F., 'Responsabilità penale per il tipo e per il modo di produzione' in: S. Canestrari, A. Melchionda (eds.), *Scritti Di Diritto Penale*, Milano: Giuffrè 1997.

Brownsword R., *Law 3.0: Rules, Regulation and Technology*, Abingdon/Oxon-New York: Routledge 2020.

Canzio G., 'Intelligenza Artificiale, Algoritmi e Giustizia Penale', *Sistemapenale.it*, February 28th, 2021, https://www.sistemapenale.it/it/articolo/canzio-intelligenza-artificiale-algoritmi-giustizia-penale.

Canzio G., 'Scienza, Diritto e Processo Penale Nell'era Del Rischio', [in:] A. Amato, G. Flora, C. Valbonesi (eds.), *Scienza, diritto e processo penale nell'era del rischio*, Torino: Giappichelli 2019.

Caplan A. L., Parent B., *The Ethical Challenges of Emerging Medical Technologies*, Milton Park/Abingdon/Oxon-New York: Routledge 2020.

Chiappini Koscina V., 'Prosecuting Killer Robots: Allocating Criminal Responsibilities for Grave Breaches of International Humanitarian Law Committed by Lethal Autonomous Weapon Systems', [in:] B. Custers, E. Fosch-Villaronga (eds.), *Law and Artificial Intelligence: Regulating AI and Applying AI in Legal Practice*, The Hague: T. M. C. Asser Press 2022.

Dershowitz A. M., *Reasonable Doubts: The Criminal Justice System and the O.J. Simpson Case*, New York: Simon & Schuster 1997.

Dominioni O., *La prova penale scientifica: gli strumenti scientifico-tecnici nuovi o controversi e di elevata specializzazione*, Milano: Giuffrè 2005.

Donini M., *Imputazione oggettiva dell'evento: 'nesso di rischio' e responsabilità per fatto proprio*, Torino: Giappichelli 2006.

Dubber M. D., Hörnle T., *Criminal Law: A Comparative Approach*, Oxford-New York: Oxford University Press 2014.

Engisch K., *Die Kausalität Als Merkmal Der Strafrechtlichen Tatbestände*, Tübingen: Mohr Siebeck, 1931.

Esfeld M., 'Explanation (Deductive-Nomological, Mereological, Reductive)', [in:] M. D. Binder, N. Hirokawa, U. Windhorst (eds.), *Encyclopedia of Neuroscience*, Berlin-Heidelberg: Springer 2009.

Fiore S., *La teoria generale del reato alla prova del processo: spunti per una ricostruzione integrata del sistema penale*, Napoli: Ed. Scientifiche Italiane 2007.

Fletcher G. P., *Basic Concepts of Criminal Law*, New York: Oxford University Press 1998.

Fletcher G. P., *Rethinking Criminal Law*, Oxford-New York: Oxford University Press 2000.

Fornasari G., *I principi del diritto penale tedesco*, Milano: CEDAM 1993.

Forti G., *Colpa ed evento nel diritto penale*, Milano: Giuffrè 1990.

Gleicher M., 'A Framework for Considering Comprehensibility in Modeling', *Big Data* 2016/4(2).

Gless S., 'AI in the Courtroom: A Comparative Analysis of Machine Evidence in Criminal Trials', *Georgetown Journal of International Law* 2020/51(2).

Grasso G., 'La protezione dei diritti fondamentali nella Costituzione per l'Europa e il diritto penale: spunti di riflessione critica' [in:] M. Bertolino, G. Forti (eds.) *Scritti per Federico Stella*.

Grasso G., *Il reato omissivo improprio: la struttura obiettiva della fattispecie*, Milano: Giuffrè 1983.

Halperin J.-L., 'Law in Books and Law in Action: The Problem of Legal Change', *Maine Law Review* 2011/64(1).

Hilbert J., 'The Disappointing History of Science in the Courtroom: Frye, Daubert, and the Ongoing Crisis of Junk Science in Criminal Trials', *Oklahoma Law Review* 2019/71. https://www.justia.com/criminal/procedure/stages-criminal-trial/

Jakobs G., *Strafrecht, Allgemeiner Teil: Die Grundlagen Und Die Zurechnungslehre. Lehrbuch*, Berlin-Boston: De Gruyter 1991.

Jasanoff S., *Science at the Bar: Law, Science, and Technology in America*, Cambridge, Mass: Harvard University Press 1995.

Jescheck H.-H., Weigend T., *Lehrbuch des Strafrechts: Allgemeiner Teil*, Berlin: Duncker & Humblot 1996.

Summerer K., *Causalità ed evitabilità: formula della condicio sine qua non e rilevanza dei decorsi causali ipotetici nel diritto penale*, Pisa: Ed. ETS 2013.

La Vattiata F. C., 'AI Systems Involved in Harmful Events: Liable Persons or Mere Instruments? An Interdisciplinary and Comparative Analysis', *BioLaw Journal - Rivista Di BioDiritto* 2023/1., https://doi.org/10.15168/2284-4503-2646.

La Vattiata F. C., 'AI-Based Medical Devices: The Applicable Law in the European Union', *BioLaw Journal - Rivista Di BioDiritto* 2022/4, https://doi.org/10.15168/2284-4503-2484.

La Vattiata F. C., 'Artificial Intelligence in Healthcare: Risk Assessment and Criminal Law', [in:] I. Beridze, S. van de Meulengraaf, O. McCarthy, A. Rodriguez Tamayo (eds.), *Special Collection on Artificial Intelligence*, Torino: UNICRI 2020.

LaFave W. R., Scott A. W., *Substantive Criminal Law*, St. Paul: West Pub. Co 1986.

Letendre L. A., 'Lethal Autonomous Weapon Systems: Translating Geek Speak for Lawyers', *International Law Studies* 2020/96.

Ligeti K. (ed.), *The European Public Prosecutor's Office at Launch: Adapting National Systems, Transforming EU Criminal Law*, Padova: CEDAM 2020.

Maiwald M., *Kausalität Und Strafrecht: Studien Zum Verhältnis von Naturwiss. u. Jurisprudenz*, Göttingen: Schwartz 1980.

Maiwald M., *L'evoluzione del diritto penale tedesco in un confronto con il sistema Italiano* (V. Militello ed.), Torino: Giappichelli 1993.

Mitsilegas V., Giuffrida F., 'The European Public Prosecutor's Office and Human Rights', [in:] W. Geelhoed, L. H. Erkelens, A. W. H. Meij (eds.), *Shifting Perspectives on the European Public Prosecutor's Office*, The Hague: T.M.C. Asser Press 2018.

Montavon G., Samek W., Müller K.-R., 'Methods for Interpreting and Understanding Deep Neural Networks', *Digital Signal Processing* 2018/73.

Naucke W., 'Über Das Regreßverbot Im Strafrecht', 76 *Zeitschrift Für Die Gesamte Strafrechtswissenschaft* 1964.

On-Road Automated Driving (ORAD) committee, *Taxonomy and Definitions for Terms Related to Driving Automation Systems for On-Road Motor Vehicles*, SAE International, https://doi.org/10.4271/J3016_201806.

Ordish J., Hall A., Murfet H., *Algorithms as Medical Devices*, Cambridge: PHG Foundation 2019.

Paliero C. E., 'La causalità dell'omissione: formule concettuali e paradigm prasseologici', *Rivista Italiana Di Medicina Legale* 1992/2.

Piergallini C., *Danno da prodotto e responsabilità penale: profili dommatici e politico-criminali*, Milano: A. Giuffrè 2004.

Pound R., 'Law in Books and Law in Action', *American Law Review* 1910/44(1).

Preuss W., *Untersuchungen Zum Erlaubten Risiko Im Strafrecht*, Berlin: Duncker und Humblot 1974.

Preziosi S., *La causalità penale: nell'orizzonte della 'scienza nuova'*, Napoli: Jovene 2021.

Price J. M., Gates Kelly G., 'Junk Science in the Courtroom: Causes, Effects and Controls', *Hamline Law Review* 1996/19.

Puppe I., *Die Erfolgszurechnung im Strafrecht: dargestellt an Beispielsfällen aus der höchstrichterlichen Rechtsprechung*, Baden-Baden: Nomos 2000.

Regulation 2017/1939/EU of the Council of October 12th, 2017 implementing enhanced cooperation on the establishment of the European Public Prosecutor's Office ('the EPPO'), available at https://eur-lex.europa.eu/legal-content/EN/TXT/?uri=celex%3A32017R1939.

Roberts P. (ed.), *Expert Evidence and Scientific Proof in Criminal Trials*, London: Routledge 2016.

Robinson P. H., *Structure and Function in Criminal Law*, Oxford-New York: Clarendon Press-Oxford University Press 1997.

Romano M., 'Nesso causale e concretizzazione delle leggi scientifiche in diritto penale' in: M. Bertolino, G. Forti (eds.), *Scritti per Federico Stella*, Napoli: Jovene 2007.

Romano M., *Commentario Sistematico Del Codice Penale*, vol. 1, Milano: Giuffrè 2004.

Ross J. E., Thaman S. C. (eds.), *Comparative Criminal Procedure*, Cheltenham-Northampton: Edward Elgar Publishing 2016.

Scherer M. U., 'Regulating Artificial Intelligence Systems: Risks, Challenges, Competencies, and Strategies', *SSRN Electronic Journal* 2015, https://doi.org/10.2139/ssrn.2609777.

Schurz G., 'Ceteris Paribus Laws: Classification and Deconstruction', *Erkenntnis* 2002/57(3).

Sicurella R., Mitsilegas V., Parizot R., Lucifora A. (eds.), *General principles for a common criminal law framework in the EU: a guide for legal practitioners*, Milano: Giuffrè 2018.

Sicurella R., *Per una teoria della colpevolezza nel sistema dello statuto della Corte Penale Internazionale*, Milano: Giuffrè 2008.

Stella F., *Giustizia e modernità: la protezione dell'innocente e la tutela delle vittime*, Milano: Giuffrè 2003.

Stella F., *Il giudice corpuscolariano: la cultura delle prove*, Milano: Giuffrè 2005.

Stella F., *La «descrizione» dell'evento. I: L'offesa – Il nesso causale*, Milano: Giuffrè 1970.

Stella F., *Leggi scientifiche e spiegazione causale nel diritto penale*, Milano: Giuffrè 1990.

Toepel F., *Kausalität Und Pflichtwidrigkeitszusammenhang Beim Fahrlässigen Erfolgsdelikt*, Berlin: Duncker & Humblot 1992.

Ulsenheimer K., *Das Verhältnis Zwischen Pflichtwidrigkeit Und Erfolg Bei Den Fahrlässigkeitsdelikten*, Bonn: Ludwig Röhrshceid Verlag 1965.

Wright R. W., 'Liability for Possible Wrongs: Causation, Statistical Probability and the Burden of Proof', *Loyola of Los Angeles Law Review* 2008/41.

Zweigert K., Kötz H., *Introduction to Comparative Law*, Oxford-New York: Clarendon Press-Oxford University Press 1998.

Dr. Marcin Galiński[1]

IX. Detection of usage deepfake technology in evidentiary proceedings on the ground of the Polish Code of Criminal Procedure

Abstract: The following paper discusses the issue of detecting the use of deepfake technology in evidentiary proceedings in Polish law, specifically under the Polish Code of Criminal Procedure. In this section, we will define deepfake and explore the possibilities and consequences of using this technology in criminal proceedings. We will also examine the relevant provisions of the Polish Code of Criminal Procedure that can be utilized to detect the use of deepfake technology for fabricating evidence. In conclusion, we find that the current provisions of the CCP offer significant possibilities for detecting the use of deepfake technology in evidentiary proceedings, but amendments to the provisions regulating the issue of examination are necessary.

Keywords: deepfake, evidentiary proceedings, Code of Criminal Procedure

1. Introduction

The modern era is characterised by the computerisation and digitalisation of every aspect of human life. The swift and profound changes brought about by advancing technologies offer numerous benefits and unprecedented opportunities to improve daily life. However, it's crucial to recognise the accompanying negative implications. From a legal standpoint, the latest technology serves as a source of emerging forms of criminal activity, leading to significant consequences in both substantive and procedural law.

One of the newest technologies which can be used for unlawful purposes is deepfake technology. Somewhat anticipating further considerations, let's note that the aforementioned technology allows for the realistic modification of video materials, raising the risk of fabricated video materials being used in court proceedings to unlawfully influence judicial decisions.

Given the continuous advancement of deepfake technology, which provides more opportunities for altering content, it is essential to establish measures that enable law enforcement to identify evidence tampering and appropriately address cases involving deepfake materials that may influence judicial decisions.

1 ORCID no. 0000-0001-5512-2249. Assistant at Jacob of Paradies University in Gorzów Wielkopolski and Institute of Justice in Warsaw.

In this article, I will briefly discuss the reasons and methods for Polish regulations to create a legal framework for detecting and addressing the use of deepfake technology in criminal proceedings. We will assess whether current regulations are adequate for detecting the use of deepfake technology in criminal proceedings or if amendments are necessary.

2. Definition of deepfake

The word "deepfake" is a combination of two words: "deep" and "fake". The word deep in this case means deep learning used for deepfake creation, and another AI-based technology, whereas the word fake indicates falsehood.[2]

The term deepfake has both narrow and broad definitions. In a narrow sense, deepfakes are: "created by techniques that can superimpose face images of a target person onto a video of a source person to make a video of the target person doing or saying things the source person does. This constitutes a category of deepfakes, namely faceswap".[3] In a broader definition, the term deepfake stands for: "artificial intelligence-synthesized content that can also fall into two other categories, i.e., lip-sync and puppet-master. Lip-sync deepfakes refer to videos that are modified to make the mouth movements consistent with an audio recording. Puppet-master deepfakes include videos of a target person (puppet) who is animated following the facial expressions, eye, and head movements of another person (master) sitting in front of a camera".[4] Thus, deepfake technology allows the creation of a lifelike montage which is a false presentation of the world. Nowadays, it is possible to create such a deepfake material, which, for most people, will be difficult to recognise as manipulation. Crucially, this technology is still being developed. As a consequence, it will lead to the creation of more advanced montages, which will be difficult to recognise as fake, even for professional developers and for AI applications. Moreover, it will be easier to use and, thus, more popular among casual users.

Deepfake technology offers plenty of possibilities for the manipulation of video content. Therefore, the abovementioned technology can be used for various

---

2 See J. Kietzman et al., 'Deepfakes: Trick or threat', *Business Horizons* 2020/63(2), Kelley School Business, Indiana University, Bloomington, p. 136; I. Ambrus, 'The new sexual offences in the light of digitalisation', *Studia Iuridica* 2022/93, Wydawnictwo Uniwersytetu Warszawkiego, Warsaw, p. 8.

3 T.T. Nguyen et. al., 'Deep Learning for Deepfakes Creation and Detection: A Survey', Cornell University, Ithaka 2022, available at: https://arxiv.org/pdf/1909.11573.pdf, p. 1, [accessed on May 3rd, 2023].

4 T.T. Nguyen et. al., *Deep Learning, op.cit.*, p. 1.

purposes such as entertainment, or education. However, deepfake technology can be used to spread disinformation, discredit a certain person or commit a crime, or create false pornography movies with a celebrity or acquaintance person (so-called pornography deepfake or deep porn).

3. The term evidence on the ground of the Polish Criminal Procedure

The Polish Code of Criminal Procedure[5] does not define the term evidence (*dowód*). The abovementioned act also does not express a catalogue of means of proof. That issue is solved by doctrine.

K. Witkowska indicated that CCP use the term "evidence" (*dowód*) in various aspects.[6] According to the author, evidence can be defined as the source of information about certain facts, which allows for establishing other important facts relevant to a particular case. Witkowska's view is that evidence serves as a means of proof (środek dowodowy). Another form of evidence is an evidentiary fact (fakt dowodowy), which enables the determination of other key facts. The term 'evidence' is considered ambiguous in this context. Furthermore, the author noted that the term 'evidence' encompasses every means or action provided by procedural law that is used to establish facts.[7]

K. Marszał et al. noticed that in procedural law, evidence means a source of information, a form of information, an evidentiary fact, every final procedural act connected to collecting information, entering and manifesting information in criminal proceedings, and a result of thought processes.[8]

T. Grzegorczyk understands the term "evidence" as every measure allowed by criminal procedure law to make certain arrangements, which is to determine circumstances relevant to pass a verdict.[9]

Thus, under Polish criminal procedure, evidence includes any legally permissible information, information carrier, personal or material source of information, and factual evidence that contributes to the knowledge of criminal proceedings. The purpose of evidence in pretrial proceedings is to establish facts for the prosecution

5 Act of July 6th, 1997. Code of Criminal Procedure in *Dziennik Ustaw* 1375/2022 with amendments. Hereinafter: CCP.

6 K. Witkowska, 'Dowody w procesie karnym a realizacja celów postępowania karnego', *Przegląd Sądowy* 2011/3, Wolters Kluwer, Warsaw, p. 51.

7 K. Witkowska, *Dowody w procesie*, *op.cit.*, p. 52.

8 K. Marszał et al., *Proces karny*, Wydawnictwo Volumen, Katowice 2003, p. 216.

9 T. Grzegorczyk, *Dowody w procesie karnym*, Wydawnictwo Prawnicze Sp. z o.o., Warsaw 1998, p. 3.

of a specific individual or to determine if a crime was committed, if it was committed by another person, or if a certain individual is not liable under the law.

In doctrine, evidence has various categories. For the purposes of this paper, it is important to distinguish personal and material evidence. The source of personal evidence is people. This category of evidentiary sources includes the testimony of witnesses or expert witness opinions. The source of material evidence is material objects sensu largo. Thus, material sources of evidence can be, for instance, the content of documents or audio and video recordings.[10]

4. Deepfake material as evidence in criminal proceedings

Based on the aforementioned understanding, in Polish criminal trial, video or pictures can be used as evidence in certain criminal proceedings. Consequently, montages created via deepfake technology can also be used as evidence.

When considering the purpose of the proceedings, it should be noted that the primary aim of using deepfake technology within the proceedings is to create a false impression of reality in the judge's mind. This could potentially lead to wrongful prosecution and result in unjust verdicts in some cases.

There is a wide range of deepfake methods within evidentiary proceedings. As the most important form, we should mention:

- presentation in the fabricated video situation that is real; nevertheless, video material contains changes in some element of reality (behaviour of a certain person, subject of behaviour, or circumstances of the presented situation etc.),
- eradicating proof of existing situations being the subject of certain proceedings by deepfake video,
- creating proof of the existence of facts that had not happened in reality.[11]

---

10 K. Witkowska, *Dowody w procesie*, *op.cit.*, p. 53.

11 See A. McPeak, 'The Threat of Deepfakes in Litigation: Raising the Authentication Bar to Combat Falsehood', *Vanderbilt Journal of Entertainment and Technology Law* 2021/2, Vanderbilt University Law School, Nashville, pp. 435–440; B.v.D. Sloot et al., '*Summary: Deepfakes: The Legal Challenge of a Synthetic Society*'. *Tilburg Institute for Law, Technology and Society*, Tilburg 2021, available at: https://www.tilburguniversity.edu/sites/default/files/download/Deepfake%20EN.pdf p. 3 et seq, [accessed on May 3rd, 2023]; R.A. Delfino, 'Deepfake on Trial: a Call to Expand the Trial Judge's Gatekeeping Role to Protect Legal Proceedings from Technological Fakery', *Hasting Law Journal* 2023/74(2), *UC Hasting Law, San Francisco*, p. 298 et seq.; M. Galiński, 'Deepfake Technology as a Threat and Challenge to the evidentiary proceeding', EJ Project Articles 2023, available at: https://www.effective-justice.com/post/deepfake-technology-as-a-threat-and-challenge-to-evidentiary-proceedings-ej-project-articles-vol-1, [accessed on May 3rd, 2023].

As a consequence, deepfake technology yields a negative impact on evidentiary proceedings. The abovementioned technology blurs the fine line between truth and lies. According to Article 2 § 2 of CCP, all decisions should be based on true factual findings. Because of deepfake technology, the realisation of the principle expressed in the quoted provision becomes difficult and, in some cases, even impossible. So, the issue of verification of trustworthy evidence cannot be nowadays omitted by the legislator and should be regulated by provisions of procedural law.

It should be noted that Polish criminal procedure provisions do not establish a hierarchy of evidence. Despite this, that video material can be treated as more trustworthy evidence than e.g., witness testimony, as before discovering and publishing deepfake tools, such type of evidence was difficult to counterfeit in that way the montage looks like realistic video material.

5. Anti-deepfake regulation - prerequisites

Before delving into the Polish criminal procedure regulations regarding the use of deepfake evidence in evidentiary proceedings, it is important to outline the prerequisites that must be met by procedural provisions aimed at preventing the use of deepfake evidence. These prerequisites pertain to the circumstances under which video material should be assessed for its reliability in evidentiary proceedings and the individuals who will be responsible for conducting such assessments.[12]

The question arises whether every piece of video evidence should be examined for trustworthiness in legal proceedings, or if such examination should only occur when there are doubts about the accuracy of the video.[13] Anticipating further

12 It has to be noted that the problem of the prerequisites above for anti-deepfake provision is very wide, and it is not possible to outlay them in this paper comprehensively. Thus, the following deliberations should be treated as signalling of key issues connected with these prerequisites. Nonetheless, such action is sufficient to present the issue duly included in the title. It should be noted that this fragment will omit issues such as prerequisites of the provision creating a legal framework reaction to the usage of fabricated video material as evidence and the consequences of using deepfake video by a particular subject to present it as the real record. The mentioned issues can be regulated by procedural law: the softest reaction is the ineffectiveness of evidence, and the strictest is criminal liability for video forgery. Forms of measures can differ in every legal order. Taking into account differences between particular legal orders (especially on the grounds of the axiology of punishment and criminal policy), the proposition of imposing one of the mentioned forms of legal reaction is not appropriate.

13 There is also the third option – video material veracity should not be verified within evidentiary proceedings. Nonetheless, that option must be rejected, because it makes detection of deepfake usage impossible.

deliberations, we must note that Article 7 CCP establishes the principle of free assessment of the evidence. Therefore, requiring verification of all video evidence may appear to contradict this principle. On the other hand, such a limitation could aid in achieving the goals of the legal process, particularly in establishing facts. The issue also extends to the economics of the legal process, as verifying the trustworthiness of every video evidence could prolong the proceedings and increase costs. This creates a conflict between two fundamental principles of criminal proceedings: the pursuit of truth and the economic efficiency of the process. To reconcile these principles, it may be necessary to establish both a minimal and maximal level of verifying video evidence. The minimal level could involve allowing judges or prosecutors to verify the accuracy of the video material, while the maximal level would require verification of all video evidence. For the purpose of this discussion, we will consider it sufficient to adhere to the minimum standard under Polish law, while treating the maximum standard as a soft guideline that should be followed as far as possible without contradicting the efficiency of the legal process.

Secondly, verification of the trustworthiness of the video should be limited not only to *ex officio* judge or prosecutor decision but also should be carried out at the participant's request. That solution allows for an increase in the ability to detect manipulated evidence.[14] This is because situations where the body conducting the procedure does not see a high probability of manipulation in certain video material admitted as evidence, and that is likely to be noticed by a party, should be an exception.

The next issue is, what should assess the video's veracity with evidentiary proceedings. As was mentioned in previous paragraphs, deepfake is an advanced IT technology. So, it cannot be excepted that a prosecutor or judge may be able to recognise every case of manipulation of video (evidence) in a particular proceeding. Hence, the legal system should enable organ conducting proceeding to call an expert witness or expert institutions to assess whether particular material is a deepfake or not. Within the pre-trial proceedings, legal provisions should except ordering verification of video veracity to organs such as police or border guards. These organs should be equipped with specialized tools dedicated to the detection

14 Of course, the party may carry out a request to verify the video trustworthiness when theyknow that video evidence is not a montage. It is the role of the judge in a court proceedings or the prosecutor in a pre-trial proceedings to assess whether a certain evidential request is based on real premises (not only based on the undoubtful fact of video fabrication, but also based on the high likelihood of that forgery), and what is only aimed to obstruction of the proceedings.

of video modification and allowed by law to use according to prosecutor resolution. However, in very obvious situations (e.g. deepfake material was prepared in such a way that it is possible *prima vista* to recognise it as a deepfake), calling an expert witness is not necessary, and judges ought to base on their own knowledge and life experience.

6. The most important provisions of CCP for issues of deepfake detection

We should start our considerations with Art. 7 CCP. According to this provision: "Proceeding organs form their belief on the basis of all evidence, freely assessed, taking into account the principles of correct reasoning and indications of knowledge and life experience". As D. Zalikowska noticed, Art. 7 CCP is the only provision in Polish criminal procedure which expresses what activities the court has to take within the analysis of evidence.[15] According to the mentioned principle, organs assess evidentiary materials freely. Hence, assessment of evidence stems from the belief of organ in certain evidentiary value (worth) of particular evidence.[16]

Nonetheless, this freedom has certain limitations. Firstly, an organ must justify its decision. Justification must contain reasoning why it treated particular evidence as trustworthy and why another piece of evidence was recognised as uncreditable. Secondly, evidentiary resolutions of an organ can be controlled within instance control.[17] Thus, the Polish legal system is realising the model of controlled assessment

15 D. Zalikowska, 'Zasada swobodnej oceny dowodów', *Kortowski Przegląd Prawniczy*, 2014/4, Wydawnictwo Uniwersytetu Warmińsko-Mazurskiego w Olsztynie, Olsztyn, p. 4.

16 Belief in doctrine is understood as more or less perpetuating judgements about some object and as an intellectual state of confidence about the rightness of notions about certain objects. See Z. Świda-Łagiewska, *Zasada swobodnej oceny dowodów w polskim procesie karnym*, Wydawnictwo Uniwersytetu Wrocławskiego, Wrocław 1983, p. 99. Thus, beliefs as base of evidence assessment are not objective knowledge about some part of reality, but subjective feelings about certain material. Nevertheless what will be presented further, mentioned subjective feelings must have an objective basis expressed in Article 7 of CCP.

17 D. Czerniak, 'Zasada swobodnej oceny dowodów', [in:] P. Hofmański (ed.), *System Prawa Karnego Procesowego. Tom VIII. Dowody*, Wydawnictwo Wolters Kluwer, Warsaw 2019, p. 3005.

of the evidence.[18] What is important is that limitations of free assessment of evidence are also expected in Article 7 of CCP. The first limitation is an obligation for the proceeding organ to assess every evidence allowed by procedural law.[19] Thus, an organ cannot base its resolution only on selected evidence, and omit another one. Indeed, it is allowed and necessary to assess the usefulness of evidence for the case, or credibility of certain evidence. Nonetheless, that assessment is mandatory, and believing in selected evidence or recognising evidence as trustworthy must review all of the collected evidence.[20] Moreover, evidence assessment must include the principles of correct reasoning, which is understood as using rules of logic and obeying the principle of consistency.[21] Organs have to form their beliefs taking into account indications of knowledge and life experience.

What is important is 'knowledge', which is based on art. 7 CCP is not only legal but also, e.g. psychological, medical, chemical informatics knowledge etc. The last requirement is using life experience. In Polish doctrine, life experience, as per the mentioned provision, is defined as all the information gained through personal observations, knowledge of life, things and people, skills, and practical knowledge acquired through human activities.[22] Consequently, the Polish legislator has imposed limitations on the assessment of evidence to ensure the best possible evaluation. In cases when it is necessary to verify whether video evidence is fake or not, it should be expected that the person assessing that content will have represented the best knowledge on the ground of the newest technologies and its impact on evidentiary proceedings (in case using as evidence deep fake material). Of course, Art. 7 CCP cannot make judges or prosecutors aware of the existence of certain newest technologies, such as the deepfake and the consequences of its

---

18 Polish doctrine distinguishes also a model of completely free assessment of evidence. In that model of proceedings organ assesses evidence freely, because the legal system does not except any rules of evidence assessment, and they have no duty to justify its decision. See e.g. D. Czerniak, *Zasada swobodnej oceny, op.cit.*, p. 3002; R. Kmiecik (ed.), *Prawo dowodowe. Zarys wykładu*, Wydawnictwo Wolters Kluwer, Warsaw 2008, p. 78 and K. Marszał et al., *Proces karny*, p. 82.

19 Procedural law limitations in the field of using evidence relate to the term inadmissibility of evidence (*zakazy dowodowe*). Examples of inadmissible evidence is evidence indicated in Article 178 of CCP: hearing of an advocate or attorney-at-law about facts disclosed to them during providing legal advice or managing a case, or a testimony of a priest about the facts he learned during confession.

20 D. Czerniak, *Zasada swobodnej oceny*, *op.cit.*, p. 3016.

21 D. Czerniak, *Zasada swobodnej oceny*, *op.cit.*, pp. 3021–3023; S. Waltoś, P. Hofmański, *Proces karny. Zarys systemu*, Wydawnictwo Wolters Kluwer, Warsaw 2020, p. 562.

22 Z. Świda-Łagiewska, *Zasada swobodnej oceny*, *op.cit.*, p. 107.

usage. However, organs lacking specialistic knowledge can call an expert witness. A partial conclusion should be expressed that Article 7 CCP does not exclude or shrink the possibilities of assessment video material for its fabrication. On the contrary, the mentioned provision creates a legal framework to assess video veracity by proceeding organs without calling another person, such as an expert witness.

According to Art. 167 CCP evidence is carried out *ex officio* or at the party's request. One should also pay attention to Art. 169 CCP, which is regulating the matter of evidence request (*wniosek dowodowy*). According to § 1, an evidence request should specify the designation of the evidence and the circumstances to be proved.[23] Such a request can also specify how evidence should be taken. In Art. 169 § 2 CCP legislator indicated that evidence requests can lead to the detection or assessment of appropriate evidence. In doctrine, the term evidence request is understood as the request of the participant to the proceedings to conduct evidence by appropriate proceeding organ, namely getting acquainted with the content of means of evidence on the circumstance which has to be proven.[24] An evidence request can be either written or oral.[25] Request for evidence (evidence request) must contain data indicated in Article 169 § 1 CCP. Evidence-request can be submitted both in pre-trial proceedings and in trial. Subjects allowed to submit evidence requests are parties to the proceedings and their representatives or persons who are attributed rights of parties in particular cases.[26] The proceeding organ can dismiss the evidence request if one of the premises expressed in Article 170 § 1 CCP will be fulfilled.[27] However, dismissing evidence request

---

23 Circumstances which have to be proven in doctrine are called evidential thesis (*teza dowodowa*). See e.g. S. Waltoś, P. Hofmański, *Proces karny*, *op.cit.*, p. 365.

24 K. Woźniewski, 'Wprowadzenie dowodów do postępowania karnego', [in:] P. Hofmański (ed.), *System Prawa Karnego, op.cit.*, p. 3507.

25 S. Waltoś, P. Hofmański, *Proces karny*, *op.cit.*, p. 365; J. Skorupka (ed.) et al., *Proces karny*, Wydawnictwo Wolters Kluwer, Warsaw 2020, p. 454.

26 An instance of an extension catalogue of subjects allowed to submit evidence requests can be indicated in Article 91b of CCP. According to mentioned provision: "The owner of the enterprise at risk of forfeiture, referred to in Article 44a § 2 of the Penal Code, the rights of the parties in the field of procedural activities relating to this measure."

27 According to Article 170 § 1 of CCP evidence request is dismissed if: the taking of evidence is inadmissible, the circumstance to be proved is irrelevant to the resolution of the case or has already been proved according to the applicant's claim, the evidence is useless to establish the given circumstance, the evidence cannot be taken, the evidence request is aimed at prolonging the proceedings, evidence request has been submitted after the date specified by the procedural authority, of which the party submitting the application has been notified.

should be treated as an exception, and as a rule, evidence requests should be taken it into account.[28] Given those forming provisions regulating the issue of submitting evidence request, it is allowed to express a request for verification for certain video material to verify its veracity.

Provisions of the CCP also regulate the issue of the participation of expert witnesses in criminal proceedings. According to Article 193 § 1 CCP if the finding of circumstances relevant to the resolution of the case requires special information, an expert or experts shall be consulted. On the grounds of the mentioned provision, it should be noted that calling an expert witness generally depends on the organ's opinion on whether a resolution of certain circumstances requires specialised knowledge.[29] An expert witness can be not only a natural person but also a scientific or specialised organisation.[30] As an example of the organisations mentioned above, we can refer to universities, laboratories, or institutes. An expert witness can be registered on a court list or called *ad hoc* (especially when a particular court's expert witness list does not have anyone in a certain field).[31] Expert witness prepares an opinion at a request of a court or prosecutor by passing an order. Such order – according to Article 194 CCP – shall indicate: the name, surname and speciality of the expert or experts, and in the case of an opinion of an institution, if necessary, the speciality and qualifications of persons who should take part in the expert opinion, the subject and scope of the expert opinion with, if necessary, formulation of detailed questions and the date of delivery of the opinion. Opinions can have both written form and oral form.[32] According to Article 201 CCP, if an expert witness's opinion is incomplete or unclear or there are contradictions in the content of the opinion or between opinions prepared in the same case, the same expert witness can be called again to prepare a supplementary opinion. Moreover, a new expert witness or expert witnesses can be called to prepare a new or supplementary opinion.

---

28 J. Skorupka (ed.) et al., *Proces, op.cit.*, p. 457.

29 C. Kulesza in: K. Dudka (ed.), *Kodeks postępowania karnego. Komentarz*, Wydawnictwo Wolters Kluwer, Warsaw 2020, pp. 407–408.

30 In Article 193 § 2 of CCP legislator indicated that to issue an opinion organ can turn to a scientific or specialistic institution. According to Article 193 § 2a provisions on experts shall apply accordingly to a scientific or specialist institution and to persons who participate in issuing the opinion of that institution.

31 According to Article 195 of CCP, an expert witness *ad hoc* is any person known to have relevant knowledge in a particular field.

32 In the case of oral form expert witness present content of opinion at the hearing.

Regarding the title issue, the key question is whether the court or prosecutor can bring in expert witnesses to confirm the truthfulness of the evidence. In simple terms, we need to determine if the creation of evidence can be considered as events that can be evaluated by an expert witness as part of a criminal proceeding. In the CCP, the legislator does not address this issue. As rightly noticed by R. Kmiecik, a subject of opinion is a fact or a set of facts understood as a fragment of objective reality whose explanation requires special knowledge.[33] That meaning of the opinion subject does not exclude the possibility of calling an expert witness or expert witness to prepare an opinion about the veracity of other evidence, such as video materials.

Regarding deepfake detection within the proceedings, we should present an institution of examination (*oględziny*). An examination (within a criminal proceeding) means sensory cognition (visual, auditory, oflactory, and tactile) of a particular object *sensu largo* (for example human, thing or object).[34] According to Article 207 § 1 CCP, if necessary, an examination of a place, person, or thing is made. The legislator in CCP does not set rules for making examinations, apart from more precise regulations about the examination of the body and the corpse. The question at hand is whether video material can be considered as evidence in criminal proceedings. First, we need to define what category video material falls into. It is clear that video material is neither a person nor a place. However, it is not a physical object that can be held or touched, like an item. Instead, it is the carrier of the video material, such as a hard drive, USB flash drive, or CD, that can be examined. When the carrier is examined, its contents are reviewed to determine if the video material has been manipulated, for instance, by using deepfake technology.

7. Fulfilment prerequisites by the provision of CCP

It should be noted that the first prerequisite is the legal possibility of a court verifying the veracity of video evidence. The minimal standard should consist of the organ's competence for that verification when necessary. The maximum standard is a warrant of verification of video evidence that is trustworthy for every inserted video evidence in the case. The Code of Criminal Procedure is realising the minimal standard. Precisely, Article 7 CCP grants prosecutors and judges the possibility of free assessment of the evidence. Thus, a procedural organ can assess the trustworthiness of video evidence single-handedly and is not obligated

33 R. Kmiecik (ed.), *Prawo*, *op.cit.*, p. 156.
34 R.A. Stefański, S. Zabłocki (eds.), *Kodeks*, *op.cit.*, p. 634.

to call in an expert witness or admit evidence from the examination in every case. Moreover, if a judge or prosecutor assesses whether it requires special knowledge, they decide on the premise of calling an expert witness or witnesses.

The second prerequisite is the possibility of submitting an evidence request by proceeding participants. As previously mentioned, Article 167 CCP gives participants the possibility to submit an evidence request, which can concern the verification of particular evidence (for instance, by an expert witness or by examination). Thus, such a prerequisite in the ground of CCP is fulfilled.

The third prerequisite is the possibility of calling an expert witness to verify the video's veracity. Provisions of CCP contain norms which order the proceeding organ, such as police or border guard, to call an expert witness or witnesses when specialised knowledge and/or verification of videos is necessary. As outlined above, CCP accepts the institution calling an expert witness or witnesses to draft an opinion in the case. The subject of the mentioned opinion can also be the issue of the video's veracity. Another possibility of video verification is examination. However, it is not an examination of video material but of a carrier containing video.

Thus, CCP creates legal frameworks allowing verification of whether video evidence is a deep fake montage or not. However, current legal standing cannot be treated as sufficient to ensure appropriate protection against the use of deep fake montage as evidence. In consequence, it is recommended that de lege ferenda postulates be supported.

Regarding such, one shall consider an amendment of regulations about examination. Nowadays, there are no provisions precisely regulating the procedure of examining videos for deepfake modifications. To appropriately detect deepfake videos, it is important to set rule-defining procedures for examining such content, especially via indication tools and computer programs, which should be used to examine it with the description of the technical requirements of the abovementioned measures.[35] The most appropriate organ for examining video content is the police. Thus, the mentioned group of provisions should be put not in CCP but in the Act of April 6th, 1990 on the Police.[36] To simplify the wording of provisions regulating the abovementioned issue, it would be suitable to introduce in Article 207 CCP a new category of a subject of examination – electronic files.[37]

---

35 The analyze issue of technical measures of deepfake detection, and in consequence legal provisions regulating that, exceeds the scope of this article.

36 Act of April 6th, 1990 on the Police in *Dziennik Ustaw* 171/2023 with amendments.

37 Alternatively, can be setting a broader category – video materials or electronic files containing video.

Nowadays, there is no necessity to change provisions for evidence requests or the calling of witnesses. On the grounds of discussed issues, it is not necessary to amend Article 7 CCP, and as a consequence, the meaning of the principle of free assessment of evidence. Nevertheless, deepfake technology is still developing. Hence, legislators should monitor the development of this technology. Also, practical usage deliberated provision by judges and prosecutors in situations of possible usage of deepfake material as evidence should be monitored.

8. Conclusions

Deepfake technology offers plenty of possibilities for manipulating video content. It can be used in many ways and for various purposes, including influencing resolution proceedings. As was presented, deep fake technology is a real threat to the reliability of criminal proceedings.

The current provisions of CCP provide several significant possibilities for detecting the usage of deepfake technology in evidentiary proceedings. CCP creates a legal framework for verifying the trustworthiness of video evidence. The major instruments that can be used for this purpose are the opinions of expert witnesses and the examination of carriers containing video material. It is also significant that the principle of free assessment of evidence expressed in Article 7 CCP allows the judge or prosecutor to freely assess all evidence in the case by considering the principles of correct reasoning and indications of knowledge and life experience.

Although the number of de lege ferenda postulates is relatively small, due to the persistent development of deepfake technology, legal acts will inevitably need to be updated to detect better and counteract the usage of this technology in proceedings. The current issue with using deepfake in evidentiary proceedings is not numerous, so there is no established practice of interpreting the CCP provision in this matter. However, this issue will likely become a more and more significant challenge for legal professionals in the relatively near future. Initially, the issue of deepfake should be addressed mainly by using the existing provisions proposed in this article.

Bibliography

Ambrus, I., 'The new sexual offences in the light of digitalisation', Studia Iuridica, 2002/93.

Delfino, R. A., 'Deepfake on Trial: a Call to Expand the Trial Judge's Gatekeeping Role to Protect Legal Proceedings from Technological Fakery', *Hasting Law Journal* 2023/74(2).

Dudka, K. (ed.), *Kodeks postępowania karnego. Komentarz*, Warsaw: Wydawnictwo Wolters Kluwer 2020.

Galiński, M., 'Deepfake Technology as a Threat and Challenge to the evidentiary proceeding', EJ Project Articles, <https://www.effective-justice.com/post/deepfake-technology-as-a-threat-and-challenge-to-evidentiary-proceedings-ej-project-articles-vol-1>, May 7th, 2023.

Grzegorczyk, T., *Dowody w procesie karnym*, Warsaw: Wydawnictwo Prawnicze Sp. z o.o., 1998.

Hofmański, P. (ed.), *System Prawa Karnego Procesowego*. Tom VIII. Dowody, Warsaw: Wydawnictwo Wolters Kluwer, 2019.

Kietzman, J., et al., 'Deepfakes: Trick or Threat', *Business Horizons*, 2020/63(2).

Kmiecik, R. (ed.), *Prawo dowodowe. Zarys wykładu*. Warsaw: Wydawnictwo Wolters Kluwer, 2008.

McPeak, A., 'The Threat of Deepfakes in Litigation: Raising the Authentication Bar to Combat Falsehood', *Vanderbilt Journal of Entertainment and Technology Law* 2021/ 2.

Marszał, K., et al., *Proces karny*, Katowice: Wydawnictwo Volumen, 2003.

Nguyen, T. T., et. al., 'Deep Learning for Deepfakes Creation and Detection: A Survey' 2022, arXiv, https://arxiv.org/pdf/1909.11573.pdf'.

Skorupka, J. (ed.) et al., *Proces karny*, Warsaw: Wydawnictwo Wolters Kluwer, 2020.

Sloot, B.v.D., et al., 'Summary: Deepfakes: The Legal Challenge of a Synthetic Society', Tilburg Institute for Law. Tilburg: *Technology and Society*, 2021, https://www.tilburguniversity.edu/sites/default/files/download/Deepfake%20EN.pdf.

Stefański, R. A., Zabłocki, S. (eds.), *Kodeks postępowania karnego. Tom I. Komentarz do art. 1–166*, Warsaw: Wydawnictwo Wolters Kluwer, 2017.

Świda-Łagiewska, Z., *Zasada swobodnej oceny dowodów w polskim procesie karnym*. Wrocław: Wydawnictwo Uniwersytetu Wrocławskiego, 1983.

Waltoś S., Hofmański, P., *Proces karny. Zarys systemu*, Warsaw: Wydawnictwo Wolters Kluwer, 2020.

Witkowska, K., 'Dowody w procesie karnym a realizacja celów postępowania karnego', *Przegląd Sądowy* 2011/3.

Zalikowska, D., Zasada swobodnej oceny dowodów', *Kortowski Przegląd Prawniczy* 2014/4.

Dr. Rodrigo da Silva Brandalise,[1] Décio Alonso Gomes[2]

X. Message Applications Mirroring, Jurisprudential Interpretation, and the Challenging Chain of Custody in a Criminal Case

Abstract: Regardless of the concept of chain of custody (by doctrine, jurisprudence, or law), all concur that it represents a procedural guarantee. It seems reasonable to believe that the essence of the chain of custody concept is to provide the integrity of the source of evidence and the evidence itself, enabling the exercise of contradictory and probative evaluation/valuation.

The present study is focused on a critical analysis of the Brazilian judicial decisions about the chain of "digital evidence", one of the most important pieces of evidence to combat current crimes. The encryption had a great impact: telephone and telematic interceptions lost effectiveness and were unable to access the content of the messages in an understandable and useful way to the criminal procedure. This scenario forced the investigation and intelligence agencies to seek alternatives to overcome this technological barrier. produced by other available means, which it expressly recognises.

Keywords: digital evidence, message applications mirroring, Brazilian criminal procedure, effective justice

---

1 Dr. FDUL in Juridical-Criminal Sciences from FDUL (Lisbon); Professor of Criminal Procedure in Law at Fundação Escola Superior do Ministério Público do Rio Grande do Sul; Public Prosecutor of Rio Grande do Sul, Brazil.

2 PhD in Criminal Procedure from Faculdade de Direito da Universidade do Estado do Rio de Janeiro; Doctor Criminal Procedure from Faculdade de Direito da Universidade de São Paulo; Master in Juridical-Criminal Sciences from Universidade Candido Mendes; Graduated in Strategic Inteligence from Escola Superior de Guerra of Ministério da Defesa; Professor of Criminal Procedure in Law at Fundação Escola Superior do Ministério Público do Rio Grande do Sul at IBMEC/RJ, ESMP/SP e EMERJ; Public Prosecutor of Rio de Janeiro, Brazil.

1. Introduction

In Brazil, due to the jurists' incentive,[3] the jurisprudential debate on the chain of custody (initial and generally linked to telephone and telematic[4] interception techniques) antecede[5] the Code of Criminal Procedure.[6]

Regardless of the concept of chain of custody (by doctrine, jurisprudence, or law), all concur that it represents a procedural guarantee that legitimises the penalty imposition, no matter which participant gives the evidence in court.

Moreover, the free experimentation before the normative discipline gave rise to a mismatch – between jurists and jurisprudence – related to the scope of the

3 For all: G. Prado, *Prova penal e sistema de controles epistêmicos: a quebra da cadeia de custódia das provas obtidas por métodos ocultos*, São Paulo: Marcial Pons 2014. However, the idea of the source's preservation of evidence is not an academic novelty, its conception being an old companion of the journey of scholars of the phenomena of procedural disconformities: "If this is so, it is evident that the party has the right to know and to pronounce on the results of the procedures for obtaining and producing evidence, in its entirety, because the unity is one of the fundamental principles of the evidentiary discipline. It means, in summary, that the evidentiary material forms a unit that, as such, must be examined by the judge together, to confront the various elements, verify their agreement or disagreement and thus reach the final conclusion". (A.P. Grinover, A.S. Fernandes, A.M. Gomes Filho, *As nulidades no processo penal*, 10ª ed., São Paulo: Revista dos Tribunais 2007, p. 155).

4 For all: Brazil, Superior Court of Justice, Ordinary Appeal in *Habeas Corpus* 66.741/SC, Brasília 2016. It should be noted, out of the duty of loyalty, that the subject was already defined by jurisprudence at an earlier time, however, without using the name "chain of custody", but with special emphasis on the issue of preserving the source of evidence, declaring inadmissible the evidence obtained through the breach of telephone and telematic secrecy, due to its fragmentation and the loss of part of the products of interceptions, within the investigative police. On the same basis: Brazil, Superior Court of Justice, *Habeas Corpus* 160.662/RJ, Brasília 2014.

5 "Although the specific arts. 158-A to 158-F of the Brazilian Code of Criminal Procedure (introduced by Law 13.964/2019) do not retroact, the need to preserve the chain of custody did not arise with them. After all, the idea of chain of custody is logically inseparable from the concept of crime, constant in the Brazilian Code of Criminal Procedure since the original Article 158. Therefore, even for events before 2019, it is necessary to assess the preservation of the chain of custody" (Brazil, Superior Court of Justice, Regimental Appeal in *Habeas Corpus* 143.169/RJ).

6 "Art. 158-A. Chain of custody is considered the set of all procedures used to maintain and document the chronological history of the evidence collected in places or in victims of crimes, to trace its possession and handling from its recognition until disposal". Included by Law 13.964, of December 24th, 2019.

guarantee and led to different perspectives and expectations about how the preservation of evidence should be carried out.

For no other reason, it seems reasonable the idea that the essence of the chain of custody concept is to provide the integrity of the source of evidence and the evidence itself, enabling the exercise of contradictory and probative evaluation/valuation. In other words, the "*main purpose of the chain of custody is to ensure that the evidence left in the material world by a criminal offence correspond exactly to those collected by the police, examined and presented in Court*".[7]

After all, the party should know and contradict the theses of his opponent. And, precisely for this reason, the integrality protected by the chain of custody must be a "qualitative integrality" of probative information.

This characteristic, of course, becomes modulated, casuistically, depending on the type of evidence generated by the conduct. In this regard, the Brazilian Superior Court of Justice (also called the Citizenship Court) decided that the quantitative real evidence divergence does not automatically break the chain of custody. Thus, situations like these should be analysed in each case because even if the defendant argued that there was an insufficient quantity of real evidence, the evidence could be admissible to prove the criminal conduct. Consequently, the defendant should demonstrate unfair prejudice in situations such as this before any nullity declaration.[8]

---

7 Brazil, Superior Court of Justice, Regimental Appeal in *Habeas Corpus* 143.169/RJ.

8 As stated in the judgment: "2. In case, although the divergence in the amount of cigarettes seized was recognized in the infraction report prepared by the *Receita Federal* (1,050 packs) and in the arrest and exhibition report of the civil police (10,050 packs), there is no break of the chain of custody, since there is sufficient evidence in the records for conviction, given that it was proven that the defendant kept at least 1,050 packs of foreign cigarettes in storage without legal documentation in national territory. Thus, this situation does not lead to the inadmissible evidence, because it was proven that the 1,050 packs actually belong to the defendant, which constitutes the crime. 3. In addition, it is important to note that the jurisprudence of this Superior Court was established in the sense that, in the field of nullity in criminal proceedings, the *pas de nulité sans grief* principle is applied, according to Article 563 of the CPP that states the recognition of nullity requires proof of effective damage. Thus, the contradiction in the number of cigarettes seized did not impair the demonstration of the real evidence of the crime, and there is no doubt that the defendant kept at least 1,050 packs of foreign cigarettes in storage without legal documentation of regular internalization in the national territory. Afterward, the defense failed to demonstrate damage due to the alleged nullity, since the conviction is sustained in the 1,050 seized packages" (Brazil, Superior Court of Justice, Regimental Appeal in Special Appeal 1.847.296/PR).

In summary, it is not any alteration of the chronological history documentation of the collected evidence that causes nullity. If the alteration – merely quantitative - does not affect the essence of the source or the evidence itself, the Court will not declare the violation of the procedural guarantee. However, if there is a qualitative alteration, it breaks the guarantee matrix, it does not assure the parties (and the judge) the integral knowledge of the evidence and it affects its analysis and the evaluation of the evidence and/or its effectiveness of the contradictory.

Considering these perceptions as premises, the present study is focused on a critical analysis of Brazilian judicial decisions regarding the chain of "digital evidence," one of the most important pieces of evidence to combat current crimes.

2. Technological Advances, Messaging Applications, and Collecting the Evidence

Technological advances show the importance of security and privacy factors when using electronic resources and devices, especially those used for instant messages. In the Information Technology Era, the certainty that its flow is secure constitutes an inalienable factor.

In the 2010s, BlackBerry's smartphone, from Research in Motion (RIM), was a success story since its emergence in the international market and conquering millions of users. In addition to the general features, the smartphones offered BlackBerry Messenger (BBM), which was exalted among users for its ability to keep end-to-end text messages private.[9]

However, this confidential element has generated controversy in several countries and has caused threats of partial suspension of the data traffic between smartphones as a result of the impossibility of monitoring the messages exchanged between smartphone users. After all, and as expected, the promised inviolability ended up being used for criminal purposes, hindering or making unfeasible the

9 At that time, the company offered the solution Enterprise Server, promising the inviolability of users' messages by making the data traffic pass through the common network and then to the manufacturer's servers in Canada, where it was encoded and returned to the smartphone (Correio Braziliense, *Codificação da BlackBerry gera polêmica na Ásia e no Oriente Médio*, Brasília 2010).

repressive action of the persecutory instances and, in the international scenario, it was used as a tool for terrorism.[10]

In the next chapter of the conflict, the countries managed to overcome this barrier and the intelligence and investigative agencies began to access the content of the messages. The consequence of the publicity of this government achievement was the gradual but unstoppable loss of users, who migrated to other smartphones or safer technologies.

It is inevitable to say that because of the commercial market objective, messaging application companies needed to develop and propagate efficient tools regarding data protection and ensuring user confidentiality.

Thus, the evolution and resurgence of encryption have again built an important barrier that affects criminal prosecution, blocks criminal investigations and how to know about them, considering that there is a technical inability to intercept end-to-end encrypted messages (encoded information with data protection at both ends of the process: sender and recipient).

Encryption had a great impact on criminal procedure: telephone and telematic interceptions lost effectiveness and were unable to access the content of the messages in an understandable and useful way.

This scenario forced the investigation and intelligence agencies to seek alternatives to overcome this technological barrier, such as mirroring or data replication, that is, the synchronous reflection of physical objects on a distinct monitor that allows access to a faithful copy of the data in another location (physical or logical). For prosecutorial purposes, mirroring permits the availability of data at the source without alerting the investigated person during the observation of exchange messages.

10 The jurists explain that the communication with protection known as *point to point* is an important means of planning and executing crimes, especially when it involves public resources. In addition, they bring people closer, who no longer need to be in person for the adjustments of criminal activities, since the technologic resources (audio, video, files) end up achieving a high degree of protection. The difficulties mentioned are known as *going dark problem* (A. G. Barreto, J. L. Andrade Júnior, 'Tecnologia, whatsapp e os desafios na atribuição de autoria delitiva nos crimes de corrupção', [in:] H.V.N. Jorge (ed.), *Enfrentamento da corrupção e investigação criminal tecnológica. Procedimentos, fontes abertas, estudos de casos e direito anticorrupção*, Salvador: JusPodivm 2020, pp. 256–257).

The first question must be answered directly: the mirroring service does not necessarily use a different smartphone because it must be limited to the visualization feature without interaction. Thus, data replication does not necessarily lead to editing or manipulating the source data.

There is conceptual corruption due to the wide use of a particular message application in Brazil instead of other apps:[11] the popular use of WhatsApp narrows the technology knowledge to the possibilities and limitations of this app.

In the current version of the WhatsApp Application, it is possible to use four connected smartphones voluntarily simultaneously without keeping the main user connected to the internet. The application portal clarifies that the primary user must access WhatsApp every fourteen days to keep the other smartphones connected to the same account.[12]

Even if this maximum option is adopted, individual media files and calls are still protected with end-to-end encryption because each smartphone is connected to WhatsApp independently and has the same level of privacy and security as the main smartphone.

In addition, the WhatsApp app for desktops can be used with a WhatsApp Web Version, an extension of the account used on smartphones. The sent and received messages are synchronised to allow access on both devices.

The mirroring procedure can take place through other routes, such as the spy app (stalkerware or spyware), which sends all actions performed by the user to third parties; mirroring by malware of the type Remote Administration Tool (RAT); or even the "theft" (invasion) of accounts, which does not necessarily use malware but, in most cases, simple actions of social engineering to obtain the users' access data.

This range of options that allow bilateral manipulation of the data content—both in the original and in the monitored application—produces the general understanding that mere visualization without controlling the actions or registering access would not be possible.

This misunderstanding contaminated Brazilian jurisprudence, which initially eliminated mirroring as a valid alternative to digital criminal prosecution.

---

11 WhatsApp is the most used application/social network in Brazil and in the world, reaching more than two billion users. See Sinch Engage, *Os aplicativos de mensagens mais usados no mundo: os dados atuais*, 2023, available at: https://engage.sinch.com/pt-br/blog/aplicativos-de-mensagens-mais-usados-no-mundo/, [accessed on December 3rd, 2023].

12 Whatsapp, *Help Center*, 2023.

3. The Jurisprudential Inflection on Mirroring

A judicial decision of the Brazilian Superior Court of Justice stood out for the alleged impossibility of mirroring implementation. This decision declared the nullity of a lower-court decision that allowed the mirroring of WhatsApp via QR Code. Thus, the evidence obtained by the mirroring was declared inadmissible.

The judicial procedure RHC 99.735/SC, which was ruled by Brazilian Justice Laurita Vaz,[13] is relevant to understanding the mirroring judicial decision because it considers that the WhatsApp Messages mirroring takes place on an electronic site provided by the WhatsApp Group, WhatsApp Web. On the platform, a specific type of barcode is generated, known as a QR Code (Quick Response), only for the smartphone user or for those who get, even for a short period, the monitored smartphone.

Specifically, the aforementioned decision considered that (a) WhatsApp allows unlimited access to all past, present, and future exchange messages; (b) the WhatsApp Web allows message performance whose access could be obtained by the smartphone itself; (c) what will be authorised for the user to chat on the smartphone and on the desktop, with (d) immediate message update on the unused smartphone.[14]

In this way, the judicial decision set up the two instruments used (desktop and smartphone) to allow total freedom to send and delete messages, regardless of whether they are sent or received before or after mirroring. For this reason, according to the Brazilian Court, there would be no evidence to be ascertained of the messages, which would not allow their recovery for the purposes of evidence (the group does not store the content of users' conversations and uses end-to-end encryption).[15]

---

13 Brazil, Superior Court of Justice, Appeal in *Habeas Corpus* 99.735/SC, Brasília 2018.

14 3. "More than just allowing unlimited access to all past, present, and future messages, the WhatsApp Web was developed to enable the user to carry out all the acts of communication to which they would have access on their smartphone. The pairing between smartphone and desktop authorises the user, if for some reason so desired, to chat within the application of the smartphone and, simultaneously, in the Internet Browser, when the messages are automatically updated on the platform that is not being used" (Brazil, Superior Court of Justice, Appeal in *Habeas Corpus* 99.735/SC, Brasília 2018).

15 "4. Both in the application and in the browser, it is possible, and completely free, to send new messages and delete old (registered before pairing) and recent (registered after) messages, whether the user sent them, whether they were received from a contact. Any deletion of a message sent (in the option "Delete only for Me") or of a message received (in any case) leaves absolutely no trace, either in the application or on the paired computer, and, therefore, can never be recovered for the purposes of evidence in criminal proceedings, because the company that provides the service, due to end-to-end encryption technology, does not store the content of users' conversations on any server" (Brazil, Superior Court of Justice, Appeal in *Habeas Corpus* 99.735/SC, Brasília 2018).

If evidence is lacking and not stored, the Brazilian Superior Court of Justice declares the police investigation absolute legitimacy because it would be devil's evidence if the Court required the defendant to demonstrate any legal violation of the State during the criminal investigation.[16]

This situation would not, therefore, resemble the possibilities of telephone interception since, in this case, there would be a passive conduct of the investigator, who is a mere observer of the conversations carried out. In cases of WhatsApp Web mirroring, a feature provided by the application itself, direct, broad, and unrestricted participation of the state agent is allowed, which would also reinforce the idea of the diabolical evidence for the defense.[17]

The Court concluded:

> *10. Third: unlike telephone interception, which is operationalised without the simultaneous need for a personal or home search for the telephone set, the mirroring with the QR Code depends on the person or his residence search, with the apprehension of his smartphone for a short period and subsequent return it without reporting the constrictive measure for the Police Authority, or even, perhaps - although there is no news that this has occurred in the specific case -, accompanied by a false statement that nothing was done.*[18]

---

16 "8. The fact of possible sent message deletion (in the "Delete for me" mode) or received (in any case) leaves no trace either for the user or for the recipient. The fact of such deleted messages, because of encryption end-to-end not be stored on any server, constitute sufficient grounds for the conclusion that the admission of such a means of obtaining evidence would imply undue absolute presumption of the legitimacy of the actions of the investigators since requiring adequate opposition on the part of the investigated would be equivalent to demanding the production of diabolical evidence" (Brazil, Superior Court of Justice, Appeal in *Habeas Corpus* 99.735/SC, Brasília 2018).

17 "7. First: unlike telephone interception, in which the police investigator acts as a mere observer of conversations undertaken by third parties, in WhatsApp Web mirroring, the police has the concrete possibility of acting as a participant in both the conversations that will be carried out and the conversations that are already registered on the smartphone, since he has the power, conferred by the online platform itself, to interact in the dialogues by sending new messages to any contact present on smartphone and deleting, with total freedom, and without leaving a trace, of any past, present or, if applicable, future message. (…) 9. Second: unlike telephone interception, which has as its object the listening of conversations only after judicial authorisation (*ex nunc*), the mirroring via QR Code allows the police investigator broad and unrestricted access to any messages before the aforementioned authorisation, operating retroactive effects (*ex tunc*)". (Brazil, Superior Court of Justice, Appeal in *Habeas Corpus* 99.735/SC, Brasília 2018).

18 Brazil, Superior Court of Justice, Appeal in *Habeas Corpus* 99.735/SC, Brasília 2018.

This argument was repeated in the Brazilian Citizenship Court,[19] making mirroring inadmissible as one of the persecutory investigations. Of all the decisions in this line, it is evident the perception that there would be the impossibility of affirming the integrity and reliability of the chain of custody of the evidence since the conversations could not be demonstrated in a judicial procedure.[20]

Therefore, a question is necessary here: without ignoring the relevance of freedom of expression and the guarantee of privacy, would it be correct to permit operating technologies that are entirely immune to prosecution?[21] Should the operation by information and communication technology companies that simply "wash their hands" of what their users do be tolerated? In this equation, the privacy factor has already demonstrated the dimension of its value. But should it override other equally constitutional guarantees?

In this regard, it is essential to follow Pezzotti's warning when he asserts that, currently, knowledge of the methods and concepts of Information Technology is fundamental for Prosecution Agencies and Courts in complex criminal cases. Although technological development enables new communication flows, it creates unprecedented channels to promote the information capture that must interest criminal investigations and proceedings.[22]

And the warning is extremely relevant. After all, the barriers of knowledge and technology only serve to increase conceptual confusion in the judicial decision field. Initially, it is necessary to clarify that the eventual message exclusion, by itself, does not make their recovery/restoration impossible because there are

---

19 As an example: Brazil, Superior Court of Justice, Regimental Appeal in *Habeas Corpus* 133.430/PE.

20 M.L. Dornelles, R.S. Brandalise, R.F. Silva, 'Tema: Estudo do MPRS - Cadeia de Custódia de whatsapp: breve considerações sobre decisões do Superior Tribunal de Justiça', [in:] Ministério Público de São Paulo, Centro de Apoio Criminal, *Boletim Criminal Comentado nº 200. São Paulo*, São Paulo 2022, p. 109.

21 While the prosecution depends on slow processes for the acquisition of technology, criminals find no barriers to using it, buying it and also developing it (A G. Barreto, J. L. Andrade Júnior, 'Tecnologia, whatsapp e os desafios na atribuição de autoria delitiva nos crimes de corrupção', [in:] H.V.N. Jorge (ed.), *Enfrentamento da corrupção e investigação criminal tecnológica. Procedimentos, fontes abertas, estudos de casos e direito anticorrupção*, Salvador: JusPodivm 2020, p. 263).

22 O. E. Pezzotti, 'Interceptação telemática, quebra de sigilo de dados e a resistência das big techs: alternativas disponíveis aos órgãos de persecução penal e ao poder judiciário' in: G. C. Paulino et al., *Técnicas avançadas de investigação*, vol. 2. Brasília: ESMPU 2022, p. 240.

extraction tools that allow access to it as long as the original deleted file has not been overwritten (it has not been replaced). This is called "*Universal Forensic Extraction Device*".[23]

Besides the technical question, there is also an effective misconception and misunderstanding of the evidence submitted to the Court. In the aforementioned appeal,[24] the account mirroring was obtained with judicial authorisation under certain conditions. Another important decision, which applied the effects of the mentioned decision, was the spontaneous presentation of the real evidence by one member of the message group.[25]

As is evident, the factual premises are distinct and do not allow the same final effect.[26]

After realising these situations, the Brazilian Superior Court of Justice recently revisited its precedents and overruled the illegitimacy of the mirroring decision. Several points arise from this new decision, which stands that, in covert action, virtual investigation, or infiltration in cyberspace, judicial authorisation must be required for WhatsApp Web mirroring:[27]

i. Mirroring is an investigation technique to collect evidence that must occur with the trust of the agents, especially the *agent provocateur*, who must obtain information from the rest of the people involved in the crime;

---

23 M.L. Dornelles, R.S. Brandalise, R.F. Silva, *Tema: Estudo do MPRS*, *op.cit.*, p. 109.

24 Brazil, Superior Court of Justice, Appeal in *Habeas Corpus* 99.735/SC, Brasília 2018.

25 As stated in it: "(…) 2. In the records, the WhatsApp messages prints would have been made effective by one of the members of the group, that is, it would be one of the interlocutors, given that it still appears in the judgment of the original Court that, as well punctuated by the prosecutor, (…) the defence's thesis that the evidence is inadmissible is opposed to the prosecution's thesis that the messages were leaked by one of the interlocutors and should be evidence in the proceeding" (Brazil, Superior Court of Justice, Regimental Appeal in *Habeas Corpus* 133.430/PE).

26 M.L. Dornelles, R.S. Brandalise, R.F. Silva, *Tema: Estudo do MPRS*, *op.cit.*, p. 110.

27 "2. It is possible to use, in the Brazilian legal system, covert actions, virtual control, or *agent provocateur* in cyberspace since the use of controlled action in criminal investigations is supported by judicial authorisation. The legal authorisation, therefore, enables legitimate monitoring, including WhatsApp Web mirroring, granting functionality to virtual prosecution, which is invaluable in today's world. The evidence obtained, via judicial control, is not inadmissible, like the derived evidence, departing from the theory of fruits of the poison tree in the case". (Brazil, Superior Court of Justice, Regimental Appeal in Special Appeal 2.309.888/MG).

ii. For this reason, the *agent provocateur* needs to perform direct action in crime preparation and execution;[28]
iii. The Brazilian Law also allows access to and interference in the so-called *communications flow* through the internet since it is duly authorised, in the same way as the breach of data communication confidentiality, and judicially justified;
iv. Therefore, there is a grant of legitimacy and rite to mirroring from the proper understanding of the current reality and the technological evolution;
v. As stated in the decision itself, the new forms of criminality will put the criminal procedure in check if criminal prosecution continues in traditional ways.[29]

---

28 The decision states: "(…) the controlled action, through the *agent provocateur*, results in action that aims to obtain evidence to incriminate the suspect, gain his trust, keeping abreast of the events, monitoring the execution of the facts and practising execution acts, if necessary, as a way to obtain the necessary information at the end of the investigation. The *agent provocateur*, therefore, has or may have, direct intervention in the preparatory and execution acts of the crime. The nature of *the agent provocateur*, therefore, influences how the crime is practised. In addition to the aforementioned Law against Criminal Organizations (Law 12.850/2013) that admits *agent provocateur* when there are indications of criminal organisation, other legislation, such as Law 11343/2006 (Law against Toxics), in its Article 53, item I, contemplates the *agent provocateur* (undercover operation) in the criminal investigation of illicit drug trafficking, as occurred in the hypothesis". (Brazil, Superior Court of Justice, Regimental Appeal in Special Appeal 2.309.888/MG).

29 The decision states: "4. In addition, the law that regulates the *Marco Civil da Internet* (Law 12965/2014), establishes principles, guarantees, rights, and duties for the use of the Internet in Brazil and assures access and interference in the "*flow of communications over the Internet, by judicial authorization*". Similarly, Law 12.850/2013 (…), redacted by Law 13.694/2019, expressly establishes the *agent provocateur* in cyberspace in Article 10-A. 5. On the other hand, Law 9.296/1996 (telephone interception), in its Article 1, sole paragraph, allows the breach of confidentiality of virtual data, after judicial authorisation. At this point lies the legal permission for the breach of confidentiality of virtual data, in the hypothesis, and, subsequently, the interaction, interception, and infiltration, including through cyberspace, consisting of the Whatsapp Web mirroring. The Telephone Interception Law, in combination with the Law against Criminal Organizations, in the hypothesis, grants legitimacy (legality) and dictates the rite (procedural rule), to the aforementioned mirroring, in progressive interpretation, by the current reality and technological evolution". (Brazil, Superior Court of Justice, Regimental Appeal in Special Appeal 2.309.888/MG).

The decision declared:

> 6. The criminal damaging of acts committed by criminal organisations through cyberspace, combined with the complexity and difficulty of criminal prosecution in the virtual environment, as in this case, should lead jurisprudence to admit controlled actions and cyber infiltration, as in the present case. In fact, in recent years, social networks and applications have become indispensable tools for communication, interaction, and exchange of information worldwide. However, this rapid expansion and influence also brought a series of challenges and problems in the cyberspace criminal investigation field, demanding the evolution of jurisprudence on the subject, which is an increasingly relevant and urgent issue.[30]

This recent decision presents that the use of covert actions or *agent provocateur* during criminal investigation, especially in virtual media, must be combined with proportionality (utility, necessity) and subsidiarity, that is when they cannot be produced by other available means, which it expressly recognises.[31] After all, the defendant's right not to self-incriminate (*against self-incrimination*) and the right to remain silent are conferred by the State to avoid any obligation for the defendant to produce the evidence that incriminates him, except if the defendant himself voluntarily carries it out.[32]

Regarding the authenticity of the conversation, the decision stated that the expert examination is unnecessary to verify the recording's reliability because they must presume authenticity, considering the public faith of state agents. For this reason, the chain of custody, per se, cannot decide about the inadequacy of the evidence. Like any other type of evidence, the WhatsApp Web's evidence

30 Brazil, Superior Court of Justice, Regimental Appeal in Special Appeal 2.309.888/MG.

31 Expressly: "(...) It is plausible, therefore, that the authorised WhatsApp Web mirroring by the prosecution is equivalent to the agent provocateur modality, which consists, as already stated, of an extraordinary but valid means of obtaining evidence. 12. In this way, the police can use the WhatsApp Web mirroring, since the parameters of proportionality, subsidiarity, judicial control, and legality are respected and based on judicial authorisation as occurred in the present hypothesis (...)". (Brazil, Superior Court of Justice, Regimental Appeal in Special Appeal 2.309.888/MG).

32 "13. It is possible to argue that the evidence obtained through WhatsApp Web mirroring, as a type of investigation through *agent provocateur*, would imply a violation of the defendant's prerogative not to produce evidence against himself (against self-incrimination) or the right to remain silent. However, respect for the defendant, as a procedural subject, only prevents the State from forcing the defendant to produce evidence against himself. Thus, if the defendant spontaneously produces evidence capable of corroborating his accusation, it should be valued in the process before its admissibility. This is what happens in the hypothesis of multi mentioned mirroring". (Brazil, Superior Court of Justice, Regimental Appeal in Special Appeal 2.309.888/MG).

analysis must be combined with the rest of the evidentiary context. Moreover, it is up to those who claim impropriety to demonstrate it in the Court since it cannot be presumed by the fact of inherent interaction resulting from controlled action and infiltration.[33]

In addition, the Brazilian Superior Court of Justice has recognized the maintenance of the source of the evidence when its content is still extractable and reviewed, including the evidence obtained via Whatsapp Web. If the source is maintained in its entirety, there is no need for a surprise to get its content since it is static data storage.[34]

This jurisprudence reveals the current concern with modern criminal practices and the increasing evidentiary uselessness of traditional ways of obtaining evidence.

4. The Mirroring Chain of Custody

How do we reconcile these two seemingly parallel universes? On one hand, there is an entirely open field without any specific discipline. On the other hand, there is a need to preserve the source of evidence against adulteration or harmful manipulations.

Of course, it is worth mentioning that the WhatsApp:

> "(…) informs the personal data of its users (smartphone and operating system information, App version, date and time of registration, connection status, last connection with date and time, name and email address if available, Web user information, etc.). (…) In this way, through the telematic interception of WhatsApp, it will be possible to discover the telephone numbers of the interlocutors that exchange messages with

33 "15. In the present case, there was no evidence of any adulteration in the course of the investigation; no element came to the record to demonstrate that there was adulterer evidence, alteration in the chronological order of the dialogues, or even interference by anyone to the point of turn inadmissible the evidence, except, of course, the eventual interference and interaction that arises from the performance in the controlled action by the agent provocateur recognised here, and such invalidity cannot be presumed" (Brazil. Superior Court of Justice. Regimental Appeal in Special Appeal 2.309.888/MG).

34 The jurist says: "(…) Since the vice of illegality often occurs when obtaining the source of evidence, the surprise factor disappears after its production and, in this case, with the subsequent judicial declaration of nullity. Years after an inadmissible telephone interception was carried out, it would be completely useless for the judge to authorise a new interception to try to capture the same content of the conversation between the same parties, but it would not be impossible. (…) However, in the breach of bank and tax secrecy, surprise is not a determining factor (…)". (G. H. Badaró, 'Epistemologia judiciária e prova penal', São Paulo: *Revista dos Tribunais* 2023, p. 173).

> the defendant (…), clarify the content that was sent during conversations (…), receive information about the device types, dates, times, IP addresses and logic gates of each conversation that the defendant has had and other relevant information to the criminal investigation[35]".

The importance lies in that, as can be seen, the application does not provide the content of the messages.

Brazil recently assumed new international obligations in the combat against cybercrime through Decree 11.491/2023 (Cybercrime Convention), more than twenty years after its signature on the international scene.[36] This international agreement requires a *positive procedural obligation*[37] (supranational criminal Policy situation) regarding the interception of content data.

Article 21, item 1, states that each party shall take legislative and other necessary measures, considering a set of serious crimes specified by domestic law and considering the content of specific communications that occurred in its territory by a computer system, to empower its competent authorities in real time to (a) collect or record such messages, by technical means, in the territory of that party; and (b) compel a service provider, within the limits of its technical capacity: (i) collect or record such communications, by technical means, in real-time; or (ii) to cooperate with or assist the competent authorities in obtaining or recording the content of such messages.

In another passage, the agreement mentions the search and apprehension of computer data (Article 19, item 1) and imposes: a) the apprehension or protection of a computer system or part of it or data storage; b) the data backup and storage in a computer; c) maintenance of the integrity of the relevant computer data.

If it is true that "unlike telephone interception, which has as its object the listening of conversations carried out only after judicial authorisation (*ex nunc*), the mirroring via QR Code allows the police broad and unrestricted access to any communication made before the authorisation, operating retroactive effects

---

35 A.D. Freitas Júnior, H.V.N. Jorge, O.C.F. Garzella, *Manual de interceptação telefônica e telemática – teoria, prática e legislação*, Salvador: JusPodivm, 2020, pp. 125–126.

36 Brazil ratified the Budapest Convention in 2022, promulgating it in 2023, with Decree 11.491/2023.

37 It consists "(…) in the requirement that their investigators who are legitimately in charge of an effective criminal prosecution must guarantee the safeguarding of these rights, preventing their violation and providing clarification of the crimes, as a way of effecting adequate and concrete repression, and not merely formal or symbolic, to the verified aggressions" (D. Fischer, F. Valdez Pereira, *As obrigações processuais penais positivas. Segundo as Cortes Europeia e Interamericana de Direitos Humanos*, Porto Alegre: Livraria do Advogado 2018, p. 81).

(*ex tunc*)[38]"; this hybrid characteristic of mirroring, before preventing its management, recommends the adoption of measures to guarantee both species of means of obtaining evidence.

Thus, after the necessity and legality of the invasive measure are established before judicial control of it, the company responsible for the communication tool, application, or operating system should provide the agencies responsible for criminal prosecution with access—in real time and synchronous—to the actions carried out on the target device in non-modifiable mode (read-only) to avoid the generic allegation of the possibility of manipulation.[39]

If the company's alleged technical inability to provide access in a non-modifiable mode is proven, the prosecution may adopt accreditation procedures to demonstrate that the means of obtaining evidence and sources of evidence have been properly accessed and recorded. After all, preserving the hygiene of the information obtained in the initial proceedings of the criminal prosecution constitutes an important concern for the State, including its accessibility to the technical defence.[40]

Data extraction instruments from smartphones and, more specifically, Whatsapp Web can be used in a third plane. After all, the smartphone where the application is installed is the source of evidence, and the file record is the content of the respective evidence. That is, the smartphone contains, inside, its own chain of custody.

Finally, in the absence or impossibility of using the evidence, carry out the records of the stages of access and analysis of the contents with the greatest possible description (for documents, certifications, and video recordings, among others),[41] in such a way that it is possible to make due confrontation in the face of future claims of nullity by the defence. This is important because this element

38 Brazil, Superior Court of Justice, Appeal in *Habeas Corpus* 99.735/SC, Brasília 2018.

39 In a similar situation: O. E. Pezzotti, 'Interceptação telemática, quebra de sigilo de dados e a resistência das big techs: alternativas disponíveis aos órgãos de persecução penal e ao poder judiciário', [in:] G. C. Paulino, et al., *Técnicas avançadas de investigação*, vol. 2. Brasília: ESMPU 2022, p. 261.

40 Brazil, Federal Supreme Court, Second Regimental Appeal in Extraordinary Appeal 1.343.875/RJ.

41 "It is more consistent with the principle of the presumption of innocence to have a posture of constant doubt in relation to the factual statements which bear the charge (…). However, this perspective should not reach the means or sources of evidence, as some authors argue. If there is no reason to doubt certain evidence, this should, as a rule, be considered minimally reliable". [D. Salgado, 'Fundamentos à admissibilidade da metaprova no processo penal', *Quaestio facti, Revista Internacional sobre Razoaniamento Probatório* 2023/5, Girona, p. 105].

of evidence must be confronted with the others to confer its reliability, even if it is still said that there is a break in the chain of custody.[42]

With an important warning: in the line expressed by the Brazilian Superior Court of Justice, it is up to those who allege the violation of the chain of custody to demonstrate it and, even more so, the adulteration of its contents,[43] notably, because there is a sequence that the conversation itself demonstrates, even when arising from screen capture.[44]

5. Conclusion

Afterwards, it is time to say that the chain of custody in digital evidence is always relevant because this evidence is presented as an important instrument for criminal prosecution today. After all, technology is increasingly present these days, including in the world of crime.

---

42 "7. The judge must weigh the position that maintains the constant irregularities of the chain of custody with all the elements produced in the procedure to assess whether the evidence is reliable (…)". (Brazil, Superior Court of Justice, *Habeas Corpus* 653.515/RJ, Brasília, 2021).

43 "Therefore, considering the *prima facie* validity of the procedural acts (…), the mere possibility of nullity does not diminish the value of the evidence, and it seems essential the effective demonstration of contamination or manipulation of the source of evidence that generates well-founded doubt, that is a question to enable the admission/production of *metaprova*. (…) With this, the unduly extended or paralysed procedure is avoided, and the right to a speedy process like before is mentioned (…)". [D. Salgado, *Fundamentos à admissibilidade*, *op.cit.*, p. 105].

44 "1. The breaking of the chain of custody concerns the suitability of the path that must be taken by the evidence until its analysis by the judge; any interference during the criminal proceeding may result in its inadmissibility. It aims to guarantee to all the defendants the due legal process and the resources inherent to it, such as ample defence, the contradictory, and especially the right to lawful evidence. 2. In the present case, the occurrence of a break in the chain of custody was not verified since at no time was shown any indication of adulterer evidence or changing the chronological order of the WhatsApp message obtained through the screen prints of the victim's cell phone" (Brazil, Superior Court of Justice, Regimental Appeal in Habeas Corpus 752.444/SC). Still: "4. In addition, 'it is the burden of the defence, when alleging violation of the provisions of Article 2, item II, of Law 9.296/1996, to demonstrate that there were, in fact, alternative investigative means to the authorities for the elucidation of the facts at the time in which the invasive measure was requested, under penalty of the use of telephone interception becoming absolutely unfeasible'. (…), which did not occur in the species. Absence of illegal constraint. Precedents". (Brazil, Superior Court of Justice, *Regimental Appeal in Habeas Corpus* 145.818/SP, Brasília 2023).

The intention is indeed to qualify the criminal prosecution and, therefore, the evidentiary findings even more.

On the other hand, criminal investigation and prosecution need to understand this universe. The judicial Power also needs to understand what each of the applications and resources available to users technically consists of so that it does not produce misconception and confusion. If the judges confuse the concepts, the investigation becomes unqualified.

In addition, it is essential to understand that there are procedural rules for evidence and decisions that are not removed by the virtual evidence. The features of WhatsApp tell a path of messages and exchange of information, and the smartphones and the application background register what is, in fact, the chain of custody, and there must be the responsibility of those who make the allegation of violation (who sustains it must exercise the burden of proving it).

No evidence is perfect in the world of facts, and its credibility must be extracted from a process and its complete content. Dismissing such relevant evidence without this understanding would be too simplistic.

Bibliography

Badaró, G. H., 'Epistemologia judiciária e prova penal', São Paulo, *Revista dos Tribunais*, 2023.

Barreto, A. G., Andrade Júnior, J. L., 'Tecnologia, whatsapp e os desafios na atribuição de autoria delitiva nos crimes de corrupção" [in:] H. V. N. Jorge (ed.), *Enfrentamento da corrupção e investigação criminal tecnológica. Procedimentos, fontes abertas, estudos de casos e direito anticorrupção*, Salvador, JusPodivm, 2020.

Correio Braziliense, *Codificação da BlackBerry gera polêmica na Ásia e no Oriente Médio*, Brasília, 2010, available at https://www.correiobraziliense.com.br/app/noticia/tecnologia/2010/09/17/interna_tecnologia,213360/codificacao-da-blackberry-gera-polemica-na-asia-e-do-oriente-medio.shtml.

Dornelles, M. L., Brandalise, R. S.; Silva, R. F., 'Tema: Estudo do MPRS - Cadeia de Custódia de whatsapp: breve considerações sobre decisões do Superior Tribunal de Justiça', [in:] Brasil, Estado de São Paulo, Ministério Público, Centro de Apoio Criminal, *Boletim Criminal Comentado nº 200*. São Paulo. São Paulo, 2022, available at https://mpspbr.sharepoint.com/sites/g_caocrim/Shared%20Documents/Forms/AllItems.aspx?ga=1&id=%2Fsites%2Fg%5Fcaocrim%2FShared%20Documents%2FSite%2FBoletim%20semanal%2FBoletim%20n%C2%BA%20200%2Epdf&parent=%2Fsites%2Fg%5Fcaocrim%2FShared%20Documents%2FSite%2FBoletim%20semanal.

Fischer, D., Valdez Pereira, F., *As obrigações processuais penais positivas. Segundo as Cortes Europeia e Interamericana de Direitos Humanos.* Porto Alegre, Livraria do Advogado, 2018.

Freitas Júnior, A. D., Jorge, H. V. N., Garzella, O. C. F., *Manual de interceptação telefônica e telemática – teoria, prática e legislação*, Salvador, JusPodivm, 2020.

Grinover, A. P., Fernandes, A. S., Gomes Filho, A. M., 'As nulidades no processo penal', 10ª ed., São Paulo, *Revista dos Tribunais*, 2007.

Pezzotti, O. E., 'Interceptação telemática, quebra de sigilo de dados e a resistência das big techs: alternativas disponíveis aos órgãos de persecução penal e ao poder judiciário' [in:] G. C. Paulino, *et al, Técnicas avançadas de investigação*, vol. 2. Brasília, ESMPU, 2022.

Prado, G., *Prova penal e sistema de controles epistêmicos: a quebra da cadeia de custódia das provas obtidas por métodos ocultos*, São Paulo, Marcial Pons, 2014.

Salgado, D., 'Fundamentos à admissibilidade da metaprova no processo penal', *Quaestio facti, Revista Internacional sobre Razoaniamento Probatório*, Girona, 2023/5.

Sinch Engage, *Os aplicativos de mensagens mais usados no mundo: os dados atuais*, 2023, available at https://engage.sinch.com/pt-br/blog/aplicativos-de-mensagens-mais-usados-no-mundo/.

Whatsapp, *Help Center*, 2023, available at https://faq.whatsapp.com/1317564962315842/?helpref=uf_share&cms_platform=web&cms_id=1317564962315842&draft=false.

Legislation and jurisprudence

Brazil. Decree n. 11.491, April 12th, 2023. Promulgates the Convention on Cybercrime, signed by the Federative Republic of Brazil, in Budapest, on November 23rd, 2001. Brasília, 2023, available at: https://www.planalto.gov.br/ccivil_03/_Ato2023-2026/2023/Decreto/D11491.htm.

Brazil. Decree n. 3.689, October 3rd, 1941. Criminal Procedure Code. Rio de Janeiro, 1941, available at: http://www.planalto.gov.br/ccivil_03/Decreto-Lei/Del3689.htm.

Brazil. Federal Law n. 3.689, December 24th, 2014. Brasília, 2019, available at: https://www.planalto.gov.br/ccivil_03/_ato2019-2022/2019/lei/l13964.htm [accessed on: 24 Nov 2023].

Brazil. Federal Supreme Court. Second Regimental Appeal in Extraordinary Appeal 1.343.875/RJ, Brasília, 2022, available at: https://portal.stf.jus.br/jurisprudencia/obterInteiroTeor.asp?idDocumento=763043675.

Brazil. Superior Court of Justice. Appeal in *Habeas Corpus* 99.735/SC, Brasília, 2018, available at: https://scon.stj.jus.br/SCON/GetInteiroTeorDoAcordao?num_registro=201801533498&dt_publicacao=12/12/2018.

Brazil. Superior Court of Justice. *Habeas Corpus* 160.662/RJ, Brasília, 2014, available at: https://processo.stj.jus.br/processo/revista/documento/mediado/?componente=ITA&sequencial=1297583&num_registro=201000153608&data=20140317&formato=PDF.

Brazil. Superior Court of Justice. *Habeas Corpus* 653.515/RJ, Brasília, 2021, available at: https://processo.stj.jus.br/processo/revista/documento/mediado/?componente=ITA&sequencial=2073941&num_registro=202100831087&data=20220201&formato=PDF.

Brazil. Superior Court of Justice. Motion for Clarification in *Reclamação* 36.734/MG, Brasília, 2021, available at: https://processo.stj.jus.br/processo/revista/documento/mediado/?componente=ITA&sequencial=1992838&num_registro=201802854798&data=20210222&formato=PDF [acessed on: 30 Nov 2023].

Brazil. Superior Court of Justice. Ordinary Appeal in *Habeas Corpus* 66.741/SC, Brasília, 2016, available at: https://scon.stj.jus.br/SCON/GetInteiroTeorDoAcordao?num_registro=201503161980&dt_publicacao=30/09/2016.

Brazil. Superior Court of Justice. *Reclamação* 36.734/MG, Brasília, 2021, available at: https://processo.stj.jus.br/processo/revista/documento/mediado/?componente=ITA&sequencial=1992838&num_registro=201802854798&-data=20210222&formato=PDF.

Brazil. Superior Court of Justice. Regimental Appeal in *Habeas Corpus* 143.169/RJ, Brasília, 2023, available at: https://scon.stj.jus.br/SCON/GetInteiroTeorDoAcordao?num_registro=202100573956&dt_publicacao=02/03/2023.

Brazil. Superior Court of Justice. Regimental Appeal in *Habeas Corpus* 133.430/PE, Brasília, 2021, available at: https://processo.stj.jus.br/webstj/Processo/justica/jurisprudencia.asp?valor=202002175828.

Brazil. Superior Court of Justice. *Regimental Appeal in Habeas Corpus* 145.818/SP, Brasília, 2023, available at: https://scon.stj.jus.br/SCON/GetInteiroTeorDoAcordao?num_registro=202101108653&dt_publicacao=14/06/2021.

Brazil. Superior Court of Justice. Regimental Appeal in Habeas Corpus 752.444/SC, Brasília, 2022, available at: https://scon.stj.jus.br/SCON/GetInteiroTeorDoAcordao?num_registro=202201976462&dt_publicacao=10/10/2022.

Brazil. Superior Court of Justice. Regimental Appeal in Special Appeal 1.847.296/PR, Brasília, 2021, available at: https://processo.stj.jus.br/processo/revista/documento/mediado/?componente=ITA&sequencial=2073099&num_registro=202100493816&data=20210628&peticao_numero=202100584037&formato=PDF.

Part II
Systems of Effective Remedies

Prof. UW Dr. hab. Szymon Pawelec[1]

I. The right to an effective remedy in the light of the length of the proceedings in the Polish criminal process according to the jurisprudence of the ECtHR

Abstract: Practical realisation of the right specified in Article 13 ECHR raises a number of issues stemming not only from the problematic general wording of that particular provision but also from its systemic position and relation to other regulations of the Convention. One such problem concerns violating the "reasonable time" requirement in criminal proceedings, which has been analysed by the European Court of Human Rights for decades. A landmark judgment in this regard was issued by the ECtHR in the case Kudła v. Poland. According to the position adopted therein, the right to an effective remedy under Art. 13 ECHR is distinct from the reasonable time requirement under Art. 6 § 1 ECHR.

The scope of the analysis will include especially the requirement that the domestic legal order must have adequate instruments for the realisation of the right from Article 13 of the ECHR, including, inter alia, the effectiveness of a complaint for protracted proceedings and the right to seek compensation and redress for damage caused by excessively long proceedings. In implementing the case Kudła v. Poland, Poland enacted the Law of June 17th, 2004 on a complaint about a breach of the right to have a case examined in judicial proceedings without undue delay. This law constructs the grounds for critical analysis presented in this chapter.

Keywords: effective remedy, length of the proceedings, Polish criminal procedure, human rights, ECHR

1 ORCID no. 0000-0001-7166-9180. Head of the Department of International Criminal Procedure, Faculty of Law and Administration, University of Warsaw.

1. Introduction

Practical realisation of the right specified in Article 13 of the European Convention on Human Rights[2] raises a number of issues stemming not only from the problematic general wording of that particular provision but also from its systemic position and relation to other regulations of the Convention. One such problem concerns the violation of the "reasonable time" requirement in criminal proceedings, which has been analysed by the European Court of Human Rights[3] for decades.

Despite the obvious importance of the right to an effective remedy in the human rights protection system, for a long time ECtHR did not see the need to separately assess the applicant's situation from the perspective of the violation of the right arising from Art. 13 ECHR, when a violation of the party's right to have the case heard within a reasonable time, specified in Art. 6 § 1 ECHR, was recognized.[4]

However, due to the constantly growing number of complaints submitted to the Court regarding excessive length of proceedings, the ECtHR was forced to introduce changes to its existing jurisprudence in that respect.[5] A landmark judgment in this regard was issued by the ECtHR in the case *Kudła v. Poland* on October 26th, 2000.[6]

According to the position adopted therein, the right to an effective remedy under Art. 13 ECHR is distinct from the reasonable time requirement under

---

2 Convention for the Protection of Human Rights and Fundamental Freedoms (hereinafter referred to as ECHR or European Convention on Human Rights), adopted under the auspices of the Council of Europe in Rome on November 4th, 1950, came into force on September 3rd, 1953, The Convention with all additional protocols is available on the website: https://www.echr.coe.int/documents/d/echr/convention_ENG [accessed on January 12th, 2024]; hereinafter as "*ECHR*".

3 As for the European Court of Human Rights, the abbreviation *ECtHR* and the terms *Tribunal* and *Court* will be used interchangeably.

4 See C. Teleki, *Due Process and Fair Trial in EU Competition Law*, Leiden-Boston 2021, p. 279.

5 See M. Kuijer, 'The Right to a Fair Trial and the Council of Europe's Efforts to Ensure Effective Remedies on a Domestic Level for Excessively Lengthy Proceedings', *Human Rights Law Review*, 2013/13(4), p. 786; K. Zombory, 'The right to an effective remedy: a key element for ensuring the effectiveness of the ECHR system – the example of Poland and Hungary', [in:] A. Mezglewski (ed.), *Efficiency of the Judiciary*, Warsaw: Wydawnictwo Instytutu Wymiaru Sprawiedliwości 2023, p. 209.

6 ECtHR, Case *Kudła v. Poland*, judgement of October 26th, 2000, Application no. 30210/96, HUDOC.

Art. 6 § 1 ECHR. Moreover, the national legal orders of the Member States must include remedies within the meaning of Art. 13 ECHR, enabling a challenge to the excessive length of the proceedings.[7]

The purpose of this paper is to analyse, on the basis of the judgments of the European Court of Human Rights, the realisation of the Strasbourg standard of the right to an effective remedy in the Polish criminal process stemming from the judgement in *Kudła v. Poland* case.

The scope of the analysis will include especially the requirement that the domestic legal order must have adequate instruments for the realisation of the right from Article 13 of the ECHR, including, *inter alia*, the effectiveness of a complaint for protracted proceedings and the right to seek compensation and redress for damage caused by excessively long proceedings.

2. The meaning of an effective remedy under Article 13 ECHR

According to Art. 13 ECHR "*Everyone whose rights and freedoms as set forth in [the] Convention are violated shall have an effective remedy before a national authority notwithstanding that the violation has been committed by persons acting in an official capacity.*" However, the ECHR does not provide any legal definition of a 'remedy' or an 'effective remedy'. The meaning of this concept, therefore, had to be developed by the doctrine and jurisprudence of the ECtHR.

Thus, the literature on the subject indicates that the term 'remedies' embraces two different aspects, the first being procedural and the other substantial.[8] In a procedural sense, remedies are the processes by which arguable human rights claims are considered and resolved. However, the essence of the meaning of "remedial measures" comes down to the outcome of such proceedings, which should end with the award of appropriate compensation to the complainant.[9]

7 *Kudła v. Poland*, paras 146–160.

8 See D. Shelton, *Remedies in International Human Rights Law*, Oxford 2015, p. 7; K. Zombory, *The right*, *op.cit.*, pp. 206–207; K. Gutman, 'The Essence of the Fundamental Right to an Effective Remedy and to a Fair Trial in the Case-Law of the Court of Justice of the European Union: The Best Is Yet to Come?', *German Law Journal*, 2019/20(6), pp. 887–888.

9 Cf. K. Zombory, *The right*, *op.cit.*, p. 206–207; see also S. Allegrezza, 'Judicial Review as a Fundamental Right' [in:] S. Allegrezza, V. Covolo (eds.), *Effective Defence Rights in Criminal Proceedings*, Milan 2018, p. 97–131; V. Covolo, 'Guarantees of Judicial Protection Under the ECHR: What Interactions With EU Law?', [in:] S. Allegrezza & V. Covolo (eds.), *Effective Defence Rights in Criminal Proceedings*, Milan 2018, p. 133–159.

As early as in 1978, in the case of *Klass and others v. Germany*, ECtHR explained that:

> 'Article 13 requires that where an individual considers himself to have been prejudiced by a measure allegedly in breach of the Convention, he should have a remedy before a national authority in order both to have his claim decided and, if appropriate, to obtain redress.'[10]

However, the Convention does not determine in any respect solutions regarding the remedy within the meaning of Art. 13 ECHR. In particular, it does not specify it nor what kind of measure it should be (complaint to a common court, constitutional complaint), nor in what manner it should be examined (in court proceedings, in administrative proceedings, or in a mode especially created for this purpose). Therefore, there is no uniform model of the measure or measures for an excessive length of proceedings, and from the Convention, only general assumptions regarding the features of this measure result. Parties to the convention, therefore, have a wide margin of freedom in choosing the means to implement the rights arising from the Convention. However, in each case, it must be an "effective" and "available" measure, both in practice and in theory, and the use of "remedies" cannot be unjustly prevented by the actions or omissions of state authorities.[11]

Nevertheless, it should be emphasised that the remedy within the meaning of Art. 13 ECHR does not constitute a measure as to which there is a certainty that it will bring a favourable result for the complainant. It only guarantees means of appeal to the state authority competent to hear the merits of the complaint.[12]

---

10 ECtHR, Case *Klass and others v. Germany*, judgement of September 6th, 1978, Application no. 5029/71, para. 64.

11 See M. Kłopocka, 'Skarga na przewlekłość w postępowaniu sądowym (ze szczególnym uwzględnieniem przepisów postępowania karnego)', [in:] L. Boguni (ed.), *Nowa kodyfikacja prawa karnego*, vol. XIX, Wrocław 2006, p. 149; see also: ECtHR, Case *Urbańczyk v. Poland*, decision of May 28th, 2006, Application no. 33777/96, HUDOC; Case *Jakub v. Slovakia*, judgement of February 28th, 2006, Application no. 2015/02, HUDOC.

12 see e.g. ECtHR. Case *Zawadka v. Poland*, decision of November 7th, 2002, Application no. 48524/99, Case *Peryt v Poland*, decision of November 30th, 2000, Application no. 42042/98, HUDOC. In both of the above-mentioned decisions, the ECtHR clearly stated that the remedy within the meaning of Article 13 does not mean a remedy bound to succeed, but simply an accessible remedy before an authority competent to examine the merits of the complaint (see ECtHR, Case *K. v. the United Kingdom*, decision of October 15th, 1986, application no. 11468/85, para. 199).

Within the meaning of the above-mentioned provision, an effective measure is a measure that interrupts the excessive length of proceedings or prevents further excessive length of proceedings, as well as leads to the provision of appropriate compensation for any delay in the proceedings.[13] It should be noted that in the Tribunal's opinion, such a measure should, first of all, speed up the proceedings and prevent their further unjustified prolongation.[14]

The ECtHR has repeatedly emphasised in its case law that Article 13 of the ECHR does not guarantee a successful outcome of the proceedings initiated by filing an appeal. In the case *Amann v. Switzerland*, the ECtHR pointed out that:

> '(..) Article 13 of the Convention requires that any individual who considers himself injured by a measure allegedly contrary to the Convention should have a remedy before a national authority in order both to have his claim decided and, if appropriate, to obtain redress (see the Leander judgment cited above, pp. 29–30, § 77). That provision does not, however, require the certainty of a favourable outcome (see the D. v. the United Kingdom judgment of May 2nd, 1997, Reports 1997-III, p. 798, § 71).'[15]

In turn, in the case *Soering v. Great Britain*, stating that pursuant to Art. 13, there is no requirement for the complainant to obtain a favourable decision, the Court emphasised that it was only a matter of the authority examining the case to issue such a decision if they accepted the complainant's arguments.[16] Article 13 of the ECHR requires the states which are parties to the Convention to ensure that the body that hears an appeal within the meaning of this provision has an opportunity to decide whether or not there has been a violation of freedom or right specified in the Convention as a result of an act or omission by persons exercising their official functions. Therefore, it must be a body with decision-making powers.[17]

---

13 See L. Garlicki, 'Implementacja orzecznictwa Europejskiego Trybunału Praw Człowieka w ustawodawstwie krajowym (problemy przewlekłości postępowania)', *Biuletyn Biura Informacji Rady Europy. Wybór orzecznictwa Europejskiego Trybunału Praw Człowieka w sprawach polskich*, 2002/2(1), pp. 7–8; see also ECtHR, Case *Dobrev v. Bulgaria*, judgement of August 10th, 2006, Application no. 190415, HUDOC.

14 See ECtHR, Case *Holzinger v. Austria*, judgment of January 30th, 2001, Application no. 23459/94, HUDOC.

15 ECtHR, Case *Amann v. Switzerland*, judgment of February 16th, 2000, Application no. 27798/95, para 88, HUDOC.

16 ECtHR, Case *Soering v. Great Britain*, judgement of July 7th, 1989, A 161, para 120, HUDOC.

17 See e.g. ECtHR *Jordan v. Great Britain*, judgement of May 4th, 2001, Application no. 24746/94. HUDOC.

In its case law, the ECtHR emphasises, however, that for an appeal to meet the requirements of Art. 13, that appeal must be ordinary, i.e. available to the entity whose rights were violated. Therefore, this criterion is not met by extraordinary remedies or the possibility of submitting applications to bodies such as the Minister of Justice or the Ombudsman. The decision of such bodies is undoubtedly discretionary. In case *Małasiewicz v. Poland*, ECtHR reminded that Article 35 of the ECHR, which sets out the rule on exhaustion of domestic remedies, provides for a distribution of the burden of proof. If a state argues that the applicant has not exhausted domestic remedies, it must demonstrate that the State has a remedy that is effective and available in theory and in practice in a timely manner, i.e. available and capable of compensating the applicant for damages in accordance with the applicant's claims and the one which has reasonable prospects of achieving success.[18]

3. The right to an effective remedy due to the length of the proceedings in the case law of the ECtHR

For decades, the ECtHR assumed in its jurisprudence that when a violation of the standard of considering a case "within a reasonable time" was found, a violation of the right to an effective remedy was no longer considered. The Tribunal assumed that the relationship between Art. 6 § 1 and Art. 13 ECHR is based on the principle of *lex specialis derogat legi generali*, as the guarantees of Art. 6 § 1 ECHR are stricter and more favourable from the point of view of the individual than the requirements for effective remedies within the meaning Art. 13 ECHR.[19]

---

18 ECtHR, Case *Małasiewicz v. Poland*, judgement of October 13th, 2003, Application no. 22072/02, para 31, HUDOC compare also: ECtHR, Case *Olczak v. Poland*, decision of November 7th, 2002, Application no. 30417/96, ECtHR, Case *Piechowicz v. Poland*, decision of October 21st, 1998, Application 38857/97, HUDOC. ECtHR, Case *Hajnrich v. Poland*, decision of May 31st, 2001, Application no. 44181/98, HUDOC.

19 See C. Kłak, 'Pojęcie skutecznego środka odwoławczego w odniesieniu do przewlekłości postępowania w rozumieniu art. 13 EKPC a polska skarga na przewlekłość postępowania karnego', [in:] P. Czubik, Z. Mach (eds.) *Hereditas Mercarture, Księga pamiątkowa dedykowana świętej pamięci profesorowi Stanisławowi Miklaszewskiemu*, Kraków: Instytut Multimedialny 2012, pp. 33–34 and the literature given there: T. Vospernik, 'Das Verhältnis zwischen Art. 13 und art. 6 EMRK – Absorption oder "Apfel und Birne"?', *Österreische Juristen-Zeitung*, 2001/56(10), pp. 361–368; F. Matscher, 'Zur Funktion und Tragweite der Bestimmung des Art. 13 EMRK' [in:] K.H. Böckstieger et al. (eds.), *Völkerrecht. Recht der Internationalen Organisationen. Weltwirtschaftsrecht. Festchrift für Ignaś Seidl- Hohenveldern*, Carl Heymanns Verlag KG 1988, pp. 315–337; M. Holoubek,'Das Recht auf eine wirksame Beschwerde bei einer nationaken Ibstanz. Zur Bedeutung des art. 13 EMRK', *Juristische Blätter* 1992/3, pp. 137–155.

The Tribunal took that position, for example, in the cases *Sporrong and Lönnorth v. Sweden*, or *Håkansson and Sturesson v. Sweden*.[20] Whereas in the case *Trojanowski and Rogosz v. Poland*, the ECtHR stated explicitly that the requirements of Art. 13 ECHR are less precise and are absorbed by Art. 6 § 1 ECHR.[21] While the role of the right to an effective remedy in the overall European system of human rights protection cannot be underestimated, Art. 13 ECHR received little attention from conventional bodies in their early case law. It was considered to be the "most obscure provision" of the ECHR.[22]

A breakthrough decision in the Tribunal's approach to the issue of protecting the right to an effective remedy under Art. 13 was ruled by the ECtHR in the already-mentioned case *Kudła v. Poland*.[23] In that judgment, the ECtHR changed its assessment of the relationship between Art. 6 § 1 and Art. 13 ECHR. Due to the importance of the above judgment and its impact on further judicial practice of the ECtHR, it is necessary to consider the facts of this case.

Andrzej Kudła was brought before the Cracow Regional Prosecutor on August 8th, 1991, charged with fraud and forgery, and detained on remand. He reported to the prosecutor that he was suffering from various ailments, so the authorities ordered that he be examined by a doctor. After the examination, Andrzej Kudła was found fit to be detained in temporary arrest.

From August 1991 to the end of July 1992, Andrzej Kudła filed thirty applications for release and appeals against decisions refusing to release him. In October 1991, he attempted to commit suicide. From November 4th, 1991, he went on a hunger strike for an unspecified period. Because of that, in November 1991 the authorities ordered that he must be examined by doctors. A report was made by experts, and they considered that Andrzej Kudła was not fit to be detained in an ordinary temporary arrest and recommended that, if his detention was to be continued, he should be confined in the psychiatric ward of a prison hospital. Andrzej Kudła was taken to Bytom Prison Hospital. On January 20th and February 27th, 1992, he was examined by specialists in forensic medicine who considered that he needed psychiatric treatment in prison but that it was not necessary to place him in the psychiatric ward of a prison hospital.

20 M.A. Nowicki, *Europejska Konwencja Praw Człowieka. Wybór orzecznictwa*, Warszawa 1998, p. 425.

21 ECtHR, Case *Trojanowski and Rogosz v. Poland*, decision of November 30th, 1999, Application no. 32731/96, HUDOC.

22 See C. Teleki, *Due Process*, *op.cit.*, p. 279; K. Zombory, *The right*, *op.cit.*, p. 208.

23 ECtHR, Case *Kudła v. Poland*.

On April 30th, 1992 an indictment against Kudła was lodged with the Cracow Regional Court with twenty-nine charges. After obtaining the opinion of doctors, the Cracow Regional Court quashed the detention order on July 27th, 1992.

The court held hearings in the case on 26, 27 and 28 October and on 14 and 15 December, 1992. A hearing listed for February 8th, 1993 was cancelled due to the applicant's illness. The court ordered that Kudła should, within three days, submit a medical certificate issued by a forensic expert. Andrzej Kudła did not submit the required certificate, but on February 12th, 1993, he informed the court that he was undergoing climatic treatment in Świnoujście and was to stay there until March 7th, 1993. The defendant had not informed the court of the address at which summonses could be served on him, so on February 18th, 1993, the court ordered that a "wanted" notice be issued with a view to locating and redetaining him on the ground that he had failed to attend hearings. The next hearing scheduled for March 16th, 1993 was also cancelled due to Andrzej Kudła's absence. On October 4th, 1993 he was arrested by the police in connection with a traffic offence and placed in detention. The Regional Court listed hearings for 6 October and 15 and 17 November 1993. All of them were cancelled because of the defendant's mental state (in particular, his difficulties in concentrating). According to an expert's report obtained by the court at the end of 1993, Andrzej Kudła was not suffering from mental illness at that time, and his mental state was not an obstacle to keeping him in detention. On October 18th, 1993, the defendant's lawyer unsuccessfully appealed against the detention order. Between October 1993 and November 1994, Andrzej Kudła made twenty-one further unsuccessful applications for release and appealed, likewise unsuccessfully, against each refusal. The court held hearings on 13, 14 and 16 December 1993, but further hearings – scheduled for January 1994 – were cancelled because Andrzej Kudła had attempted to commit suicide. The trial was able to continue on 14, 15 and 16 February 1994. The hearings listed for March 1994 were cancelled because of the illness of the presiding judge. Subsequent hearings took place on 14, 15 and 16 June 1994. In the meantime, Andrzej Kudła had undergone psychiatric observation in Wrocław Prison Hospital. The further course of the proceedings before the court of first instance was also full of various obstacles, such as a change of defence lawyer during the case or illnesses of other defendants. The last steps of the evidentiary proceedings were carried out by the Court on 13, 14 and 15 March, 3, 4 and 5 April, and 4, 5, 30 and 31 May 1995. Certain witnesses who had previously failed to appear were brought to the court by the police. Finally, on June 1st, 1995, the Cracow Regional Court convicted Andrzej Kudła of fraud and forgery and sentenced him to six years imprisonment and a fine of 5,000 zlotys (PLN). On June 2nd, 1995, both the applicant and his lawyer filed a notice of appeal. On August 1st, 1995, Andrzej Kudła complained to the Minister of Justice that the trial court had not prepared the statement of reasons for its judgment within the statutory time-limit of seven days. On August 28th, 1995, the Head of the Criminal Department of the Ministry of Justice, in reply to that complaint, informed him that it was likely that the statement of reasons for the judgment would exceed two hundred pages and that the failure to comply with the statutory time-limit was since the judge rapporteur had been on leave. Notwithstanding the above complaint, on August 14th, 1995, Andrzej Kudła requested to be released, arguing that his prolonged detention had had very harmful effects on his health and on the well-being of his family. On August 31st, 1995 the Cracow Court of Appeal upheld that decision and observed that his detention was warranted by the severity of the sentence imposed. On September 27th, 1995, at the Regional Court's request, the applicant was examined by forensic psychiatrists, who stated that if the legal proceedings required that the defendant spend a further period in prison, he should be sent to a hospital ward and be supervised by specialist staff. He should also be guaranteed access to a psychiatrist and a psychologist. On October 6th, 1995, Andrzej Kudła received the statement of the reasons for the judgment and, at some date thereafter, lodged an appeal. The case file was transferred to the Cracow Court of Appeal on November 14th, 1995. On February 22nd, 1996, the Court of Appeal quashed the conviction and ordered a retrial on the grounds that the trial court had been incorrectly constituted and that there had been numerous breaches of procedural provisions. However, the Court of Appeal did not revoke the pre-trial detention imposed on the accused.

In the repeated proceedings, the accused was still under pre-trial detention, but in May 1996, the Court agreed to lift the arrest of Andrzej Kudła if he paid a bail of PLN 10,000 within one month from the date of the delivery of the decision. On June 11th, 1996, the trial court received a report from a psychiatric expert who found that Andrzej Kudła was in a state of chronic depression accompanied by suicidal thoughts. He considered that the defendant was able to participate in hearings but that continuing detention could jeopardise his life because of the likelihood that he would attempt to commit suicide. The accused appealed against this decision. However, the Cracow Court of Appeal dismissed his appeal, holding that the sum set for bail was not excessive, given the cost of the damage resulting from the commission of the offences with which he had been charged and the serious nature of those offences. The Court of Appeal attached considerable importance to the fact that after the first order for his detention had been quashed in July 1992, Andrzej Kudła had absconded and had been redetained on that ground. Andrzej Kudła, therefore, filed a complaint to the Ombudsman (Rzecznik Praw Obywatelskich), who emphasised in response that it was primarily the accused who, through his own conduct, prolonged the criminal proceedings in his case. The accused again tried to convince the court to reduce the bail amount but to no avail. The retrial was to start on October 10th, 1996 but was postponed because one of the co-defendants had meanwhile been detained in connection with other criminal proceedings against him. On October 29th, 1996, the Cracow Regional Court quashed the detention order after Andrzej Kudła's family had paid bail of PLN 10,000 to the court. The next two hearings planned for March 1997 were postponed because of the illness of the co-defendant. The evidentiary proceedings then lasted from January to November 1998. On December 4th,1998, the Cracow Regional Court convicted Andrzej Kudła as charged and sentenced him to six years' imprisonment. The defendant appealed on April 19th, 1999. On October 27th, 1999, the Cracow Court of Appeal changed the trial court's judgment and reduced the applicant's sentence to five years' imprisonment.[24]

The proceedings in Andrzej Kudła's case lasted over nine years in total, and despite obvious health problems, he remained in pre-trial detention for a significant part of that time.

Andrzej Kudła's case was referred to the ECtHR by the European Commission of Human Rights. The complaint filed by him included the following allegations:

1. lack of proper psychiatric treatment during his stay in custody, which violated his rights under Art. 3 ECHR;
2. application of pre-trial detention contrary to Art. 5 § 3 ECHR;
3. the overall time of the trial violated the framework of reasonableness of time within the meaning of Art. 6 § 1 ECHR;
4. the accused had no legal opportunity to question the excessive length of the trial, which violated Art. 13 ECtHR.[25]

As regards the allegation of violation of Art. 13 ECHR, the applicant pointed out that an individual's entitlement to an effective remedy under Article 13 did not depend on whether or not a violation of his Convention rights had, in fact, been found but on whether he had an arguable claim that those rights had been violated. In his opinion, Polish legislation had not provided any legal remedy whereby he could have effectively contested the length of the criminal proceedings against him and have his right to a hearing within a reasonable time enforced.

24 ECtHR, Case *Kudła v. Poland*, paras 10–57.
25 ECtHR, Case *Kudła v. Poland*, paras 82–133.

Consequently, his right to an effective remedy before a national authority within the meaning of Article 13 had not been respected.[26]

Referring to the opinions of some members of the European Commission presented in the report in Mikulski v. Poland, the applicant argued that not in all cases may Art. 6 § 1 ECHR be perceived as *lex specialis* in relation to Art. 13 ECHR. In some situations, Art. 13 of the ECHR should apply regardless of whether a violation of Art. 6 § 1 of the ECHR had taken place or not.

In turn, Poland referred to the previous case law of the ECtHR, according to which the requirements of Article 13 are less strict than and are here absorbed by those of Article 6 or that the role of Article 6 § 1 in relation to Article 13 is a *lex specialis*, so those of Article 6 § 1 absorb the requirements of Article 13. Moreover, Poland also held that even if the Tribunal found it necessary to review the case under Article 13 ECHR, there had been no violation of that provision in Andrzej Kudla's case. In this respect, the State admitted that in Poland, there was no single, specific legal remedy by which a complaint could be made about delays in judicial proceedings. Still, they pointed out that in the criminal proceedings pending against him, the applicant could have raised the issue of their length in his complaints against the decisions extending his pre-trial detention or in applications for release submitted pursuant to Art. 214 of the Code of Criminal Procedure.

According to Poland, the Complainant could also submit a complaint to the president of the court handling his case or to the Minister of Justice, which would result in these persons placing his case under their administrative supervision. This supervision, in turn, could result in the imposition of disciplinary sanctions on the judge if he or she did not conduct the hearing effectively and efficiently.[27]

After hearing the case, the ECtHR admitted that in many previous cases, it had not noticed the need to assess the state of the case through the prism of Art. 13 ECHR, in particular in a situation where a violation of Article 6 § 1 was found. However, in Andrzej Kudła's case, the Tribunal took the position that there is no overlap and hence no absorption where, as in that case, the alleged Convention violation that the individual wishes to bring before a national authority is a violation of the right to trial within a reasonable time, contrary to Article 6 § 1.

The ECtHR emphasised that:

> 'The question of whether the applicant in a given case did benefit from trial within a reasonable time in the determination of civil rights and obligations or a criminal charge is a separate legal issue from that of whether there was available to the applicant under

26 ECtHR, Case *Kudła v. Poland*, paras 136–137.

27 ECtHR, Case *Kudła v. Poland*, para 138–145.

> domestic law an effective remedy to ventilate a complaint on that ground. In the present case, the issue to be determined before Article 6 § 1 "tribunals" was the criminal charges brought against the applicant, whereas the complaint that he wanted to have examined by a "national authority" for the purposes of Article 13 was the separate one of the unreasonable length of the proceedings.'[28]

The Tribunal clearly indicated that it was time to abolish the current line of jurisprudence and review its case-law in the light of the continuing accumulation of applications before it in which the only, or principal, allegation is that of a failure to ensure a hearing within a reasonable time in breach of Article 6 § 1. The ECtHR stated that the increasing frequency of findings of violations of this type must call attention to the "serious danger" that exists for the rule of law in national legal orders when "excessive delays in the administration of justice" occur "for which the parties to the dispute have no domestic remedy." In this regard, the Court referred to the cases: *Bottazzi v. Italy*,[29] *Di Mauro v. Italy*,[30] *A.P. v. Italy*[31] and *Ferrari v. Italy*.[32]

ECtHR, therefore, noticed that the approach to the application of Art. 13 ECHR should be changed. The Tribunal argued that neither the content of this provision nor the *ratio legis* of its introduction into the Convention implies the impossibility of its application in relation to any of the aspects of the right to a court contained in Art. 6 § 1. According to the Tribunal, the requirement for an effective remedy contained in Art. 13 ECHR should be understood to mean a remedy that is as effective as possible. The place of Art. 13 in the system of human rights protection established by the Convention should justify limiting its implied limitations to a minimum.

Moreover, it was indicated that under Art. 1 of the Convention, the primary responsibility for implementing and enforcing the guaranteed rights and freedoms rests with national authorities. In turn, Art. 35 § 1 of the Convention, which introduces the principle of exhaustion of domestic remedies, allows State Members to prevent or remedy violations alleged against them before such allegations are

---

28 ECtHR, Case *Kudła v. Poland*, para 147.

29 See ECtHR, Case *Botazzi v. Italy*, judgment of July 28th, 1999, Application no. 34884/97, HUDOC.

30 See ECtHR, Case *Di Mauro v. Italy*, judgment of July 28th, 1999, Application no. 34256/96, HUDOC.

31 See ECtHR, Case *A.P. v. Italy*, judgment of July 28th, 1999, Application no. 35265/97, HUDOC.

32 See ECtHR, *Ferrari v. Italy*, judgment of July 28th, 1999, Application no. 33440/96, HUDOC.

submitted to the ECtHR. In the opinion of the Tribunal, expressed in the case *Kudła v. Poland*, Art. 13 ECHR, therefore, obliges the states to protect human rights primarily within their own legal system, establishing an additional guarantee for the individual to ensure that he or she actually enjoys these rights. The subject of Article 13 is to provide a means by which individuals can obtain relief at the domestic level for violations of their Convention rights before they are required to trigger an international complaint mechanism before the Court. From this perspective, an individual's right to a fair trial within a reasonable time will be less effective if it is not possible first to present a Convention claim to a national authority. Requirements from Art. 13 ECHR should, therefore, be seen as reinforcing the requirements of Art. 6 § 1 and not absorbed by the general obligation imposed by that provision.[33]

The Tribunal did not share the position of Poland that the requirement for an appeal for excessive length of proceedings according to Art. 13 was tantamount to imposing a new obligation on the States to establish a "right of appeal", in particular the right to appeal on the merits, which, as such, is only guaranteed in criminal cases under Art. 2 of Protocol No. 7 to the Convention. It also did not accept the argument that providing such a remedy could, in practice, only lead to the prolongation of the proceedings before the national court. The Court emphasised that the remedy relating to the unjustified length of proceedings does not, as such, consist in challenging the "determination" of any criminal charge or civil rights and obligations, but only in the fact that the proceedings concerning their assessment by the national authorities lasted too long.

The ECtHR directly emphasised that:

> *'If Article 13 is, as the Government argued, to be interpreted as having no application to the right to a hearing within a reasonable time as safeguarded by Article 6 § 1, individuals will systematically be forced to refer to the Court in Strasbourg complaints that would otherwise, and in the Court's opinion more appropriately, have to be addressed in the first place within the national legal system. In the long term, the effective functioning, on both the national and international levels, of the human rights protection scheme set up by the Convention is liable to be weakened. In view of the foregoing considerations, the Court considers that the correct interpretation of Article 13 is that that provision guarantees an effective remedy before a national authority for an alleged breach of the requirement under Article 6 § 1 to hear a case within a reasonable time.'*[34]

33 ECtHR, Case *Kudła v. Poland*, para 150–152.
34 ECtHR, Case *Kudła v. Poland*, para 155–156.

Therefore, pointing out that the Polish government had not demonstrated in the circumstances of the case under consideration that Polish law allowed Andrzej Kudła to lodge one specific or a combination of different but effective remedies against the length of his proceedings, the ECtHR found that in this case there had been a violation of Article 13 of the Convention, in that the applicant did not have a domestic remedy by which he could have enforced his right to a "hearing within a reasonable time" guaranteed by Article 6 § 1 of the Convention.

As indicated above, the ECtHR's judgment in the *Kudła v. Poland* case undoubtedly had a precedent-setting nature regarding the relationship between Art. 6 § 1 and Art. 13 ECHR. As a result, there can be no doubt that there must be an effective remedy to bring before the national authorities a breach of the guarantees arising from Article 6 § 1 ECHR, including the right to have the case heard "within a reasonable time", and additionally that the ECtHR has the power to assess whether such a legal remedy in a given legal system is effective within the meaning of Art. 13 ECHR.[35]

The view expressed by the ECtHR in the *Kudła v. Poland* case was fully accepted and is still adopted in its case law.[36] There is no longer any doubt that there must be a remedy for an excessive delay of proceedings in the Member States' national laws.[37]

---

35 C. Kłak, *Pojęcie skutecznego środka odwoławczego*, *op.cit.*, pp. 32–33; M. Balcerzak, 'Projekt ustawy o skardze na przewlekłość postępowania sądowego – w celu wykonania wyroku Europejskiego Trybunału Praw Człowieka w sprawie Kudła v. Polska (skarga nr 30210/96, wyrok – 26.10.2000)', *Biuletyn Biura Informacji Rady Europy. Ochrona Praw Człowieka w Systemie Prawa Europejskiego*, 2003/3, p. 94.

36 Guide on Article 13 of the European Convention on Human Rights – Right to an effective remedy, updated od August 2022, Council of Europe/European Court of Human Rights, 2022, p. 7–8, 45, available at: https://www.echr.coe.int/documents/d/echr/guide_art_13_eng [accessed on January 12th, 2024].

37 See ECtHR, Case *Horvat v. Croatia*, judgment of July 26th, 2001, Application no. 51585, HUDOC. In the case *Horvat v. Croatia*, the Court, referring to the judgment in the case *Kudła v. Poland*, recalled that the correct interpretation of Art. 13 ECHR is such that this article guarantees a remedy before a national authority in the event of allegation of violation under Art. 6 § 1 ECHR, the requirement to hear the case within a "reasonable time"; see also: ECtHR, Case *Bukowski v. Poland*, decision of June 11th, 2002, Application no. 38665/97, HUDOC.

ECtHR, Case *D.M. v. Poland*, judgment of October 14th, 2003, Application no. 13557/02, HUDOC; ECtHR, Case *Petkov v. Bulgaria*, judgment of September 2nd, 2010, Application no. 65417/01, HUDOC. ECtHR, Case *Rumpf v. Germany*, judgment of September 2nd, 2010, Application no. 46344/06, HUDOC.

It should be noted that, according to the Tribunal, pursuant to Art. 13 ECHR, does not imply that only a single measure may be considered effective within the meaning of that provision. The state may introduce a "set" of remedies that together will meet the requirement of "effectiveness", even if the legal remedies offered are not "effective" taken individually.[38] However, as the Court adopted in the case *Krawczak v. Poland*, an appeal against excessive length of proceedings must enable the assessment of not only the court proceedings but also the proceedings in progress before the case came to court. If this is not the case, the national "redress" does not meet the requirements referred to in Art. 13 ECHR.[39]

4. The right to an effective remedy due to the length of the proceedings in the Polish criminal process

Poland, ratifying the ECHR, has accepted the guarantees resulting from these legal acts, both in the sphere of law-making and its application.[40]

It should be noted that long before Poland signed the ECHR and before the entry into force of the Constitution of the Republic of Poland of 1997, Polish jurisprudence repeatedly drew attention to the issue of trial time, recommending that from the moment of initiation of proceedings to the moment of issuing a final decision it did not take longer than necessary for a substantively correct decision.[41]

Already in the 1980s, the Supreme Court emphasised that the length of proceedings may lead to the adjudicating court's memory of the course of the event subject of judgment being blurred and lead to findings that are inconsistent with

38 See e.g. ECtHR, Case *Lukenda v. Slovenia*, judgment of October 6th, 2005, Application no. 23032/02, HUDOC.

39 ECtHR, *Case Krawczak v. Poland*, judgment of April 8th, 2008, Application no. 40387/06, HUDOC.

40 J. Bielasiński, 'Prawo do rozsądnego czasu postępowania. Uwagi na tle uregulowań Europejskiej Konwencji Praw Człowieka, Konstytucji RP oraz nowego kodeksu postępowania karnego', [in:] L. Boguni (ed.), *Nowa kodyfikacja prawa karnego*, vol. V, Wrocław 2000, p. 70; Z. Świda, 'Właściwość sądu i prawo strony do rozstrzygnięcia sprawy „w rozsądnym terminie"', *Państwo i Prawo*, 2005/10, p. 37; E. Morawska, 'The Principles of Subsidiarity and Effectiveness: Two Pillars of an Effective Remedy for Excessive Length of Proceedings within the Meaning of Article 13 ECHR', *Polish Yearbook of International Law*, 2019/39, pp. 159–185.

41 See Supreme Court Resolution of July 15th, 1974, KwPr 2/74 (Poland), *Orzecznictwo Sądu Najwyższego Izba Cywilna* 1974/12, item 203.

the evidence.[42] In turn, in the field of pre-trial detention, already in the decision of February 1st, 1975, the Supreme Court explicitly stated that the extension of pre-trial detention cannot be automatic as a result of the length of preparatory proceedings.[43]

However, there were no provisions in Polish legislation regulating this problem. There was no one effective legal remedy allowing a party who believes that a given proceeding is "sluggish" or "too long" to raise the objection about excessive length of proceedings in the course of it.[44]

The judgment of ECtHR in the *Kudła v. Poland* case obliged Poland to introduce into its national legal systems a measure enabling a challenge to the excessive length of proceedings. In implementation of this judgment Poland enacted the Law of June 17th, 2004 on complaint about breach of the right to have a case examined in judicial proceedings without undue delay (ustawa o skardze na naruszenie prawa strony do rozpoznania sprawy w postępowaniu sądowym bez nieuzasadnionej zwłoki – "*the 2004 Act*"). This 2004 Act was subsequently amended by the Act of February 20th, 2009 amending the Act on complaints regarding violation of the right to have a case heard in court proceedings without undue delay (ustawa o zmianie ustawy o skardze na naruszenie prawa strony do rozpoznania sprawy w postępowaniu sądowym bez nieuzasadnionej zwłoki – "*amendment of 2009*"). First of all, it changed the name of the 2004 Act itself to the Act on a complaint on a violation of the right to have a case heard in an investigation conducted or supervised by a prosecutor and in court proceedings without undue delay (ustawa o skardze na naruszenie prawa strony do rozpoznania sprawy w postępowaniu przygotowawczym prowadzonym lub nadzorowanym przez prokuratora i postępowaniu sądowym bez nieuzasadnionej zwłoki – "*the Act*").[45]

---

42 Supreme Court, Judgement of April 18th, 1985, II KR 70/85 (Poland), *Orzecznictwo Sądu Najwyższego, Wydawnictwo Prokuratury Generalnej*, 1986/5, item 67.

43 Supreme Court, Order of February 1st, 1975, IV KZ 26/75 (Poland), 3–4 *Orzecznictwo Sądu Najwyższego Izba Karna i Wojskowa* 1975, item 45.

44 M. Romańska, 'Skarga na przewlekłość postępowania sądowego', *Przegląd Sądowy*, 2005/11–12, p. 39; E. Bagińska, 'Skarga na przewlekłość postępowania i prawo do „odpowiedniej sumy pieniężnej" z tytułu naruszenia prawa strony do procesu w rozsądnym czasie – fiasko polskiego modelu kompensacyjnego?', XXXVI *Gdańskie Studia Prawnicze* 2016, p. 27.

45 Polish Journal of Laws no. 179, item 1843 z późn. zm; see P. Grzegorczyk, 'Skutki wyroków Europejskiego Trybunału Praw Człowieka w krajowym porządku prawnym', *Przegląd Sądowy*, 2006/6, p. 25.

Moreover, the amount that could be awarded at the request of the complainant if it was found that the proceedings were excessive was increased to PLN 20,000. This Act was amended twice more, most recently on August 2nd, 2023,[46] but despite the passage of many years, the conclusions arising from the ECtHR's case law and obvious economic changes in the country and around the world, the Polish legislator did not decide to increase the above amount further.

In the light of Art. 2 section 1 of the Act, a party may file a complaint for a declaration that in the proceedings to which the complaint relates, there has been a violation of its right to have the case heard without undue delay, if the proceedings aimed at issuing a decision concluding the proceedings in the case last longer than necessary to clarify the relevant factual circumstances and legal proceedings or longer than necessary to settle an enforcement matter or another matter related to the execution of a court decision (excessive length of proceedings). This provision applies *mutatis mutandis* to preparatory proceedings (Article 2 section 1a of the Act).

In turn, according to Art. 2 Section 2 of the Act, in order to determine whether the case was excessive in the length of proceedings, it is necessary to, in particular, assess the timeliness and correctness of the actions taken by the court to issue a decision ending the proceedings in the case or the actions taken by the prosecutor conducting or supervising the preparatory proceedings to end the preparatory proceedings or actions undertaken by a court or a court bailiff in order to conduct and complete an enforcement case or other case related to the execution of a court decision. When making this assessment, the total time of the proceedings from its initiation to the moment of considering the complaint is taken into account, regardless of the stage at which the complaint was filed, as well as the nature of the case, the degree of its factual and legal complexity, the importance for the party that filed the complaint, the resolution issues therein and the conduct of the parties, in particular the party who alleged that the length of the proceedings was unduly excessive.[47]

As a rule, the entity authorised to submit a complaint must be the party to the proceedings. However, in Art. 3 of the Act, the legislator also indicated other persons who are entitled to do so in a given proceeding. In terms of criminal proceedings, these are: 1) in proceedings regarding the liability of collective entities

46 Polish Journal of Laws 2023 r. item 1725.

47 See C.P. Kłak, 'Pojęcie przewlekłości postępowania sądowego', *Prokuratura i Prawo*, 2008/12, p. 63.

for acts prohibited under penalty – the applicant; 2) in criminal proceedings – the injured party (even if he is not a party to the proceedings).[48]

From a formal point of view, the complaint should be submitted to the court before the proceedings are pending and in the event of preparatory proceedings to the leading or supervising prosecutor's office (Art. 5 section 1 of the Act). The court competent to hear the submitted complaint will take precedence over the one who is accused of lengthy "processing" (Art. 5 section 2 and 5 section 4 of the Act).

As far as the formal requirements of the complaint are concerned, it should meet the requirements set out for a procedural document and should also contain a request for a declaration of the excessive length of proceedings in the case to which the complaint relates and a quotation of the circumstances justifying the request (Article 6 section 1 and Article 6 section 2 of the Act). The complaint may also include a request to issue to the court hearing the case or the prosecutor conducting or supervising the preparatory proceedings a recommendation to take appropriate actions within a specified period and to award an appropriate sum of money referred to in Art. 12 section 4 of the Act. The complaint is subject to a fixed fee of PLN 200 (Art. 17 section 1 of the Act).

An important circumstance proving a significant relaxation of the formal requirements for filing a complaint about the excessive length of proceedings is the lack of a requirement that the party be represented by a lawyer or legal advisor if the complaint is subject to examination before the Supreme Court (Art. 6 section 4 of the Act).[49]

---

48 It should be noted that in Polish criminal proceedings, the injured party is only a party to the preparatory proceedings. However, if the injured party wants to exercise the rights of a party in court proceedings, he or she must submit a declaration of acting as an auxiliary prosecutor before the commencement of the trial (see Articles 49, 299 and 54 of the Polish Code of Criminal Procedure, Polish Journal of Laws 2022, item 1375)

49 As a rule, filing and supporting appeals that are heard by the Supreme Court is covered by the so-called compulsory representation by a lawyer. This scope covers, among others, the following process steps:

a) filing a cassation appeal if it does not come from the prosecutor, the Prosecutor General, the Ombudsman or the Ombudsman for Children (Article 526 § 2 of the Polish Code of Criminal Procedure); b) filing a complaint against the judgment of the appellate court overturning the judgment of the court of first instance (Article 539f of the Polish Code of Criminal Procedure in connection with Article 526 § 2 of the Polish Code of Criminal Procedure); c) submitting an application to reopen the proceedings, if it does not come from the prosecutor (Article 545 § 2 of the Code of Criminal Procedure).

After considering the case, the court accepts the complaint and states that the proceedings concerned were excessively long or dismisses the complaint if it considers it unfounded (Article 12 section 1 and Article 12 section 2 of the Act). If the court accepts a complaint about the length of criminal proceedings, at the request of the complainant, it awards him a sum of money from the State Treasury ranging from PLN 2,000 to PLN 20,000. At the same time, the legislator specifies that the sum of money, within the above limits, is no less than PLN 500 for each year of the current duration of the proceedings, regardless of how many stages of the proceedings the excessive length of the proceedings concerns. The court may award a sum of money higher than PLN 500 for each year of the current duration of the proceedings if the case is of particular importance to the complainant whose attitude has not culpably contributed to the extension of the duration of the proceedings (Art. 12(4) of the Act).

A very significant right, included in the requirements of the ECtHR's jurisprudence, is introduced by Art. 15 of the Act. The Polish legislator states that the party whose complaint has been upheld may, in separate proceedings, seek compensation from the State Treasury for the damage resulting from the identified delay (Article 15 section 1 of the Act). Moreover, the decision to accept the complaint is binding on the court in civil proceedings for compensation or redress as to the excessive length of the proceedings (Article 15 section 2 of the Act). This is important because when filing such a lawsuit for compensation, a party no longer has to demonstrate to a civil court the circumstances confirming that the proceedings in its case were excessively long. It is only sufficient to submit a court decision stating this fact. It should only be remembered that if a party files such a lawsuit, the compensation or compensation due is reduced by the amount of the sums awarded under Art. 12 section 4 of the Act for the same period (Article 15 section 3 of the Act).

It should be emphasised that the Act allows a party to repeatedly appeal against the excessive length of proceedings and apply for an appropriate sum of money. The complainant may submit a new complaint in the same case after 12 months, and in preparatory proceedings in which pre-trial detention is applied and in an enforcement or other case concerning the execution of a court decision, after 6 months from the date of issuance of the judgment by the court (Article 14 section 1 of the Act).

Since the entry into force of the Act, the ECtHR has repeatedly had an opportunity to comment on the nature of its individual elements in terms of their compliance with the principles developed in the case law of the Tribunal. In principle, the Court found that the measures introduced by Polish legislation meet the requirements of Art. 13 and Art. 35 § 1 of the Convention and found that they were "effective" within the meaning of those provisions. In this respect, reference should be made to the ECtHR's decision in the case *Charzyński v. Poland.*

In that judgement, the Court explicitly stated that:

> 'The Court noted that the criminal proceedings against the applicant had been pending before the domestic courts, and the Court had not yet adopted a decision concerning the admissibility of his case. Accordingly, he was entitled to lodge a complaint under the 2004 Act. As to the effectiveness of the new remedy, the court fee did not appear to be excessive and did not constitute an unreasonable restriction on the applicant's right to complain about the new legislation. In any event, the court fee would be reimbursed should his complaint be considered justified. The limitation that a fresh complaint could be filed at one-year intervals did not seem unreasonable. In addition to the maximum amount of just satisfaction which could be awarded under the 2004 Act, the complainant could file a civil claim for further compensation. In sum, a complaint under the 2004 Act was capable of preventing the alleged violation of the right to a hearing within a reasonable time or its continuation and of providing adequate redress for any violation that had already occurred and thus satisfied the "effectiveness" test established in the Kudła judgment. Hence, the applicant was required by Article 35 § 1 to lodge such a complaint and to ask for the expedition of the proceedings and just satisfaction.'[50]

The Tribunal was aware that only the judicial practice of national courts would allow for a correct assessment of the effectiveness of the new provisions. However, it assumed that since the delay complaint was intended to speed up the proceedings and remedy the delays, it should be assessed positively[51] – in particular in view of the resolution of the Supreme Court of January 19th, 2005, which clearly stated that the provisions of the introduced Act should be interpreted as applying retroactively also to delays that occurred before its entry into force and which are still ongoing.[52]

The formal requirements of the complaint as a procedural document were also subject to a detailed analysis by the ECtHR. In this regard, e.g. in the case of *Wende and Kukówka v. Poland*, the ECtHR accepted the requirements of the complaint set out in Art. 6(2) of the Act, i.e. the need to include in it a request to establish excessive length of the proceedings in the case to which the complaint relates and cite the circumstances justifying the request. However, the Tribunal emphasised

---

50 ECtHR, Case *Charzyński v. Poland*, decision of March 1st, 2005, Application no. 15212/03, HUDOC.

51 ECtHR, Case *Rutkowski v. Poland.*

52 Supreme Court Resolution of January 19th, 2005, III SPP 113/04 (Poland), available at: http://www.sn.pl/sites/orzecznictwo/Orzeczenia1/III%20SPP%20113-04.pdf [accessed on January 12th, 2024].

that the practice of Polish courts, which requires a clear formulation of the request for a declaration of excessive length of proceedings, is defective. The ECtHR found that when it comes to requesting a declaration of excessive length of proceedings, the wording contained in the justification of the complaint, which shows the applicant's intention, is sufficient.[53] According to the Tribunal, however, the demanding practice of Polish courts is defective, directly expressing the request for a declaration of excessive length of proceedings. In this spirit, in the case of *Wawrzynowicz v. Poland*, the Court even found that the mere indication by the complainant in the justification of the complaint that the court proceedings lasted over eight years was sufficient to exhaust the statutory requirement to indicate the circumstances justifying the complaint. The Court, therefore, accepted that it was sufficient for the applicant to challenge only the overall duration of the proceedings. However, it does not have to demonstrate specific actions or omissions of the court or prosecutor that led to the excessive length of the proceedings.[54]

Unfortunately, despite many years that have passed since the Act entered into force, there is still a problem in Poland with the lengthiness of court proceedings and the possible ineffectiveness of the created measure. This is noticeable, among other things, in the number of complaints about unfinished proceedings taken into consideration by the ECtHR and submitted after using national measures to counteract excessive length of proceedings. One of the key decisions in this regard is the judgment issued by the ECtHR in the case *Rutkowski v. Poland*.[55]

In that case, the ECtHR faced the need to assess the fact that the proceedings before the first instance criminal court lasted 7 years and 10 months.[56] There were numerous procedural irregularities in the course of the proceedings, and there were significant periods of inactivity to which the complainant did not contribute in any way. The first hearing in that case took place only 4 years after

---

53 ECtHR, Case *Wende i Kukówka v. Poland*, judgment of May 10th, 2007, Application no. 56026/00, HUDOC.

54 ECtHR, Case *Wawrzynowicz v. Poland*, judgment of July 17th, 2007, Application no. 73191/01, HUDOC.

55 ECtHR, Case *Rutkowski and others v. Poland*, judgment of July 7th, 2015, Applications nos. 72287/10, 13927/11 and 46187/11, HUDOC.

56 It should be noted that, together with the *Rutkowski* case, the ECtHR heard cases initiated by complaints of two other Polish citizens: Mariusz Orlikowski and Aleksandra Grabowska. In these cases, the periods of excessive length of time examined were even longer than in the case of Wiesław Rutkowski, as they amounted to 11 years and 8 months and 13 years and 2 months, respectively. However, both of these cases concerned civil proceedings.

the indictment was received by the court, and the long delay led to a dispute as to the court's jurisdiction to hear the case. Ultimately, in 2010, the accused was acquitted. Given the above circumstances, the accused filed a complaint about the excessive length of the proceedings under Polish law. It was accepted, and he was awarded a sum of PLN 2,000 as compensation.[57]

Based on this case, apart from stating that there was obviously a violation of Art. 6 § 1 ECHR, the Court further emphasised that the violation of Article 13 of the Convention had occurred due to the defective functioning of the complaint brought under the 2004 Act, in that it had failed to provide the applicants with appropriate and sufficient redress for the violation of Article 6 § 1 of the ECHR. The Tribunal pointed out that Polish courts do not apply the ECtHR's case law in assessing the reasonable length of proceedings and appropriate and sufficient compensation for a breach of the right to have a case heard within a reasonable time. Ultimately, he ruled that Poland must use appropriate means, legal or otherwise, to ensure that national courts apply the appropriate principles set out in Article 6 § 1 and Article 13 of the Convention.[58]

Most importantly, based on the *Rutkowski v. Poland* case, the ECtHR not only found that there had been a violation of Art. 6 § 1 and Art. 13 ECHR in this specific case but also noticed a general systemic problem in Poland regarding the length of court proceedings. Regarding Art. 6 § 1 ECHR violations, the Court noted that they are most often related to too slow submission of opinions by court experts and defective process management – in particular, too frequent postponements of hearings and long breaks between subsequent hearings. In turn, under Art. 13 of the Convention, the Court noticed a structural problem in the functioning of the remedy created in the form of a complaint about excessive length. According to the Tribunal, it is wrong to limit the assessment of excessive length to the phase of a given procedure in which a complaint about excessive length is filed. Moreover, underestimating the amount of monetary compensation granted to applicants for excessive length limits the compensatory function of this remedy.[59]

Then, in the case *Lewandowski v. Poland*, the Tribunal recalled that, in light of the ECtHR's case law, a complaint brought under the Polish Act of June 17th, 2004

---

57 ECtHR, Case *Rutkowski v. Poland*; see also: A. Pietryka, 'Przewlekłość jako problem strukturalny w Polsce – analiza wyroku Rutkowski i inni przeciwko Polsce', [in:] Helsińska Fundacja Praw Człowieka, *Analizy i Rekomendacje*, 2015/9, pp. 1–2.

58 Ibidem.

59 See also P. Ostaszewski, E. Melaniu, *Sprawy ze skargi*, *op.cit.*, p. 141.

should provide the applicant with appropriate and sufficient redress in the form of compensation for the excessive length of the proceedings in his case.[60]

The ECtHR addressed the issue of the appropriate amount of compensation awarded in connection with the finding of excessive length of proceedings, e.g. in the case *Ković and others v. Serbia*. The Tribunal stated that the amount of sufficient compensation depends in particular on the characteristics and effectiveness of the measure. In the countries where a remedy has been introduced for the purposes of both expediting proceedings and awarding damages, these amounts may be less than those awarded by the Court, provided they are not unreasonably low. Whether the amount awarded can be considered reasonable must be assessed in light of all the circumstances of the case, such as the duration of the proceedings in a particular case. The value of compensation should also be viewed in the light of the standard of living in the country concerned and the fact that under national systems, compensation will generally be awarded and paid more quickly than if the case had been referred to the Court under Article 41 of the Convention.[61]

5. Final remarks

There can be no doubt that the right to an effective remedy, as referred to in Art. 13 of the ECHR, constitutes an important guarantee function in the system of human rights protection. The *Kudła v. Poland* judgment confirmed that importance through finding by the Tribunal that possible violations of Art. 13 of the ECHR should be assessed separately from the issue of assessing the violation of a party's right to have his case heard within a reasonable time within the meaning of Art. 6 § 1 of the ECHR.

As a result of the above judgement, the institution of complaint about excessive length of proceedings was introduced into the Polish legal system. By filing such a complaint with the competent national court, the complainant may demand not only a declaration of the excessive length of proceedings in a given case and an obligation for the relevant authorities to take appropriate procedural steps within a specified period but also demand an award of a sum of PLN 2,000–20,000. If the complaint is upheld, the complainant may also seek compensation exceeding this amount, but in separate proceedings. However, he is then obliged to prove the

60 ECtHR, Case *Lewandowski v. Poland*, judgment of March 18th, 2021, Application no. 29848/17, HUDOC.

61 ECtHR, Case *Ković and others v. Serbia*, judgment of April 4th, 2017, Application no. 39611/08, HUDOC; see also *Guide on Article 13*… pp. 44–45 and the case law cited therein.

occurrence of damage and harm and its amount, as well as the causal relationship between the excessive length of the proceedings and their occurrence.[62]

During the initial period after the entry into force of the Polish Act on complaints about excessive length of proceedings, the ECtHR considered that its provisions created a standard of an effective remedy in relation to the purpose of its introduction. Therefore, in 2005 alone, the ECtHR rejected over 600 complaints about the excessive length of proceedings brought against Poland.[63]

Unfortunately, complaints against Poland on this subject are constantly referred to the Tribunal despite the previous use of domestic remedies in this respect. In the case *Rutkowski v. Poland*, the ECtHR found that a violation of Art. 13 of the Convention may also occur through failure to provide appropriate and sufficient redress for a violation of Art. 6 § 1 of the ECHR, even if the complaint about the excessive length of proceedings was positively recognised in the domestic legal system.[64]

As regards the above position of the Tribunal on the amount that can be awarded by Polish courts to the complainant if a complaint about the length of proceedings is upheld, there seems to be a clear necessity of changes in the Polish provisions. Additionally, taking into account the jurisprudence of Polish courts reaching for amounts closer to the lower limit of the range specified in Art. 12 section 4 of the Act of June 17th, 2004, it should be considered that they do not in any way correspond to the current economic realities and therefore cannot meet the purpose they are intended to serve.[65]

Firstly, there can be no dispute that over the 20 years when the Act has been in force, the purchasing value of money has changed significantly. It is worth emphasising that due to the events of recent years (starting with the pandemic crisis and ending with the economic consequences of Russia's aggression against Ukraine), the scale of inflation in Poland has reached levels not seen since the second half

62 e.g. ECtHR, Case *Charzyński v Poland*; ECtHR Case *Ratajczyk v. Poland.*

63 ECtHR, Case *Rutkowski v. Poland.*

64 Ibidem.

65 According to statistical data presented by the Polish Ministry of Justice, in the years 2010–2022, the average amount of compensation awarded in this respect by district courts was approximately PLN 3-3.5 thousand, and by appellate courts was approximately PLN 5-8 thousand. Data available for download on the website: https://isws.ms.gov.pl/pl/baza-statystyczna/opracowania-wieloletnie/ [accessed on January 15th, 2024].

of the 1990s. The annual inflation level in 2023 (still lower than its peak in 2022) was comparable to that recorded for the last time in 1998.[66]

Thus, continuing to maintain the statutory amount that can be awarded by national courts at the level specified in Art. 12 section 4 of the Act of June 17th, 2004, will most likely result in an increasing number of complaints being filed against Poland regarding violations of Art. 13 ECHR in the scope indicated above.

It should be emphasised here that in a situation when a party considers that the amount awarded by the national court in proceedings to determine the excessive length of proceedings is abnormally low, filing a complaint to the ECtHR – in particular in the light of its well-established case law in this area – appears to be much more effective procedurally than taking the risk of starting with filing a lawsuit against the State Treasury pursuant to Art. 15 section 1 of the Act of June 17th, 2004. In such proceedings, the plaintiff would not only have to prove the occurrence of damage or harm, its amount and the causal relationship between the established length of the proceedings and their occurrence but also pay an appropriate court fee for the lawsuit, risking its loss if the lawsuit is dismissed. Meanwhile, proceedings before the ECtHR are exempt from fees.

In order to limit the risk of issuing by the ECtHR further decisions against Poland finding a violation of Art. 13 of the ECHR, which consists in awarding too low amounts to applicants in proceedings based on complaints about the excessive length of proceedings, an amendment to Art. 12 section 4 of the Act of June 17th, 2004, should be considered, which would increase the amount of money that can be awarded in proceedings under this Act. Obviously, the issue of choosing a specific amount from within the statutory range will always be left to an individual court decision. Due to the specific wording of the Act, it is a subject of dogmatic discussion whether the sum of money that can be awarded (i.e. the sum in the range of 2.000–20.000 PLN) should be treated as compensation in the civil law meaning of that category. Even without resolving the problem of the compatibility of that specific lump sum instrument with the nature of the compensatory measures, two things seem apparent. Firstly, as has been presented, the ECtHR does not support the practice of awarding arbitrarily low sums, which in itself allows for linking those sums with the elements of at least some adequacy and compensation for the harm suffered due to the excessive length of the proceedings. Secondly, even due to the sole economic factors observed presently – i.e. inflation

66 For more detalis see: https://stat.gov.pl/obszary-tematyczne/ceny-handel/wskazniki-cen/wskazniki-cen-towarow-i-uslug-konsumpcyjnych-pot-inflacja-/roczne-wskazniki-cen-towarow-i-uslug-konsumpcyjnych/ [accessed on January 17th, 2024].

rates unobserved in Poland for more than a quarter of a century – it would be difficult to argue about any adequacy of the old statutory ranges for the sums that can be awarded under the Act to the current value of money.

Bibliography

Allegrezza S., 'Judicial Review as a Fundamental Right', [in:] S. Allegrezza & V. Covolo (eds.), *Effective Defence Rights in Criminal Proceedings*, Milan 2018.

Bagińska E., 'Skarga na przewlekłość postępowania i prawo do „odpowiedniej sumy pieniężnej" z tytułu naruszenia prawa strony do procesu w rozsądnym czasie – fiasko polskiego modelu kompensacyjnego?', *Gdańskie Studia Prawnicze*, 2016, t. XXXVI.

Balcerzak M., 'Projekt ustawy o skardze na przewlekłość postępowania sądowego – w celu wykonania wyroku Europejskiego Trybunału Praw Człowieka w sprawie Kudła v. Polska (skarga nr 30210/96, wyrok – 26.10.2000)', *Biuletyn Biura Informacji Rady Europy. Ochrona Praw Człowieka w Systemie Prawa Europejskiego* 2003.

Bielasiński J., 'Prawo do rozsądnego czasu postępowania. Uwagi na tle uregulować Europejskiej Konwencji Praw Człowieka, Konstytucji RP oraz nowego kodeksu postępowania karnego', *Nowa kodyfikacja prawa karnego*, L. Boguni (ed.), Wrocław 2000/5.

Covolo V., 'Guarantees of Judicial Protection Under the ECHR: What Interactions With EU Law?', [in:] S. Allegrezza & V. Covolo (eds.), *Effective Defence Rights in Criminal Proceedings*, Milan 2018.

Garlicki L., 'Implementacja orzecznictwa Europejskiego Trybunału Praw Człowieka w ustawodawstwie krajowym (problemy przewlekłości postępowania)', *Biuletyn Biura Informacji Rady Europy. Wybór orzecznictwa Europejskiego Trybunału Praw Człowieka w sprawach polskich* 2002.

Grzegorczyk P., 'Skutki wyroków Europejskiego Trybunału Praw Człowieka w krajowym porządku prawnym', *Przegląd Sądowy*, 2006/6.

Guide on Article 13 of the European Convention on Human Rights – Right to an effective remedy, updated on August 2022, Council of Europe/European Court of Human Rights, 2022.

Gutman K., 'The Essence of the Fundamental Right to an Effective Remedy and to a Fair Trial in the Case-Law of the Court of Justice of the European Union: The Best Is Yet to Come?', *German Law Journal*, Special Issue, 2019/20 (6).

Holoubek M., *Das Recht auf eine wirksame Beschwerde bei einer nationaken Ibstanz. ZurBedeutung des Art. 13 EMRK*, Juristische Blätter, Heft 3, März 1992.

Kłak C. P., 'Pojęcie skutecznego środka odwoławczego w odniesieniu do przewlekłości postępowania w rozumieniu art. 13 EKPC a polska skarga na przewlekłość postępowania karnego', [in:] Czubik P., Mach Z. (eds.) *Hereditas Mercarture, Księga pamiątkowa dedykowana świętej pamięci profesorowi Stanisławowi Miklaszewskiemu*, Instytut Multimedialny, Kraków 2012.

Kłak C. P., 'Pojęcie przewlekłości postępowania sądowego', *Prokuratura i Prawo*, 2008/12.

Kłopocka M., 'Skarga na przewlekłość w postępowaniu sądowym (ze szczególnym uwzględnieniem przepisów postępowania karnego)', *Nowa kodyfikacja prawa karnego*, t. XIX, Bogunia L. (ed.), Wrocław 2006.

Kuijer M., 'The Right to a Fair Trial and the Council of Europe's Efforts to Ensure Effective Remedies on a Domestic Level for Excessively Lengthy Proceedings', *Human Rights Law Review*, 2013/13(4).

Matscher F., ‚Zur Funktion und Tragweite der Bestimmung des Art. 13 EMRK', [in:] K. H. Böckstieger et al. (eds.), *Völkerrecht. Recht der Internationalen Organisationen. Weltwirtschaftsrecht. Festchrift für Ignaś Seidl- Hohenveldern*, Carl Heymanns Verlag KG 1988.

Morawska E., 'The Principles of Subsidiarity and Effectiveness: Two Pillars of an Effective Remedy for Excessive Length of Proceedings within the Meaning of Article 13 ECHR', *Polish Yearbook of International Law*, 2019/39.

Nowicki M. A., *Europejska Konwencja Praw Człowieka. Wybór orzecznictwa*, Warszawa 1998.

Ostaszewski P., Melaniuk E., *Kwerenda spraw ze skargi na przewlekłość postępowania sądowego*, Warszawa 2019.

Ostaszewski P., Melaniuk E., 'Sprawy ze skargi na przewlekłość postępowania sądowego w 2018 r.', *Prawo w Działaniu, sprawy cywilne*, 2020/42.

Romańska M., 'Skarga na przewlekłość postępowania sądowego', *Przegląd Sądowy*, 2005/11–12.

Shelton D., *Remedies in International Human Rights Law*, Oxford 2015.

Świda Z., 'Właściwość sądu i prawo strony do rozstrzygnięcia sprawy „w rozsądnym terminie"', *Państwo i Prawo*, 2005/10.

Teleki C., *Due Process and Fair Trial in EU Competition Law*, Leiden-Boston 2021.

Vospernik T., *Das Verhältnis zwischen Art. 13 und Art. 6 EMRK – Absorption oder "Apfel und Birne"?*, Österreische Juristen-Zeitung, vol. 56, Heft 10 (2001).

Zombory K., 'The right to an effective remedy: a key element for ensuring the effectiveness of the ECHR system – the example of Poland and Hungary' [in:] *Efficiency of the Judiciary*, Wydawnictwo Instytutu Wymiaru Sprawiedliwości Warszawa 2023.

Dr. Lorenzo Bernardini[1]

II. Fair trial rights violations and effective remedies in criminal proceedings—The ECHR perspective

Abstract: This chapter offers a thorough exploration of the concept of 'effective remedy' as outlined in Article 13 ECHR. It then focuses on its application in the context of criminal proceedings, analyzing how the ECtHR approaches cases where fair trial rights are allegedly breached. Specifically, it offers an updated analysis of the ECtHR's legal reasoning regarding the necessity of guaranteeing effective remedies in cases involving violations of Article 6(1) ECHR (right to a trial within a reasonable time) and Article 6(2) ECHR (presumption of innocence). The chapter concludes by addressing any lingering unresolved questions in this regard.

Keywords: Fair trial rights, effective remedy, criminal proceedings, Article 6 ECHR, Article 13 ECHR, Article 47 CFREU

1. Introduction

From a theoretical perspective, the precise definition of 'effective remedy' in the context of criminal proceedings has been significantly investigated in doctrinal circles.[2] Yet, there are some issues that still seem unresolved. To name a few examples – which specific measures must domestic systems establish in order to qualify as a 'remedy'? What types of authorities (including judicial, administrative, political, and disciplinary bodies) are capable of providing an

---

1 ORCID no. 0000-0002-9768-7579. Postdoctoral Researcher in Criminal Law and Criminal Procedure at the University of Luxembourg. Currently, he is Visiting Scholar at Columbia Law School, Columbia University in the City of New York (spring semester 2025).

2 For a European perspective, see the comprehensive work of S. Allegrezza, 'Judicial Review as a Fundamental Right', [in:] S. Allegrezza, V. Covolo (eds.), *Effective Defence Rights in Criminal Proceedings*, Milan 2018, pp. 97–131 and V. Covolo, 'Guarantees of Judicial Protection Under the ECHR: What Interactions With EU Law?' in: S. Allegrezza, V. Covolo (eds.), *Effective*, *op.cit.*, pp. 133–159. For an in-depth analysis not only related to criminal procedure, see M. Reiertsen, *Effective Domestic Remedies and the European Court of Human Rights*, Oxford 2022, *passim.*

effective remedy? What attributes define an 'effective remedy' in the context of criminal proceedings, and how can its efficacy be quantified? Can the mere acknowledgement of a violation suffice as an 'effective remedy', or must such a remedy offer redress or relief for the contested circumstance? And, in this latter case, what may constitute the suitable form of redress for a violation of fundamental rights?

This chapter aims to comprehensively examine the concept of 'effective remedy' within the ECHR legal framework (§ 2.1) and subsequently delve into its scope of application within the context of criminal proceedings (§ 2.2). Against this backdrop, a detailed analysis of the approach adopted by the ECtHR in cases involving a breach of fair trial rights will be presented (§ 3). Some concluding remarks will delve into any unresolved questions that may persist (§ 4).

2. Granting effective remedies in criminal proceedings

2.1. General considerations

The right to an effective remedy is extensively acknowledged as a fundamental right and is indeed enshrined in all major human rights instruments, with slight divergencies in the wording adopted: the European Convention on Human Rights (ECHR),[3] the Charter of Fundamental Rights of the European Union (CRFEU or 'the Charter'),[4] the American Convention on Human Rights (ACHR),[5] the International Covenant on Civil and Political Rights (ICCPR)[6] and the Universal Declaration of Human Rights (UDHR).[7]

Centering attention on the ECHR legal framework, the focus is on Article 13 ECHR, which reads as follows: 'everyone whose rights and freedoms as set forth in [the] Convention are violated shall have an effective remedy before a national authority notwithstanding that the violation has been committed by persons acting in an official capacity'. The examination of such a prerogative can be approached from three distinct perspectives, which are worth to be developed

3 Article 13 ECHR.
4 Article 47(1) CFREU.
5 Article 25 ACHR.
6 Article 2(3)(a) ICCPR.
7 Article 8 UDHR.

at some length.[8] Firstly, it possesses an adaptable nature that aligns itself with the circumstances of material cases – its substantive characterisation carries subtle *nuances*. Secondly, it assumes the character of an *ancillary* and *teleological* right, as it is not an isolated entity within the scheme of human rights enshrined in the Convention but rather serves the purpose of actively enforcing these guarantees in practical terms. Thirdly, it stands as a notable embodiment of the principle of *subsidiarity*, exemplifying the States' obligation to safeguard human rights within its own domestic systems primarily.

Concerning the nuanced characterisation of the right to an effective remedy, it is apparent that the scope of application of Article 13 ECHR is not narrowly confined to criminal proceedings. Instead, it pertains to all the rights and freedoms laid down in the ECHR. In the words of the ECtHR, 'the scope of the obligation under Article 13 varies depending on the nature of the Convention right relied on'.[9] This feature is pivotal for depicting the kernel of that provision – a universal prototype of 'effective remedy' cannot be uniformly established across all branches of law. Its definition will inevitably fluctuate based on a case-by-case approach to the point that, for instance, what constitutes an effective remedy in civil or administrative law contexts might not necessarily be so in criminal proceedings and *vice versa*. Hence, the guarantees enshrined in Article 13 ECHR conform to the specific legal domain within which they are invoked.

This is not surprising, given that the right to an effective remedy is inherently teleological in nature. Indeed, this guarantee is not an end in itself; rather, its existence hinges on its purpose, which is fundamentally to guarantee the practical enforcement of the rights and freedoms enshrined in the Convention.[10]

---

8 For the purposes of this contribution, the term 'remedy' is used to encompass both of its distinct aspects. The first one is *procedural*, where remedies represent the procedures through which arguable human rights claims are heard and adjudicated. In other words, it pertains to the procedure by which individuals have their claims determined. The second aspect is *substantial*, where remedies denote the actual outcomes of such proceedings, that is, the range of available legal *mechanisms* that can provide redress or relief to the claimant, such as monetary compensation. In this regard, cf. D. Shelton, *Remedies in International Human Rights Law*, Oxford 2015, p. 16 et seq.. referring to the 'dual meaning of remedies' and, with reference to international law, S. Haasdijk, 'The Lack of Uniformity in the Terminology of the International Law of Remedies', *Leiden Journal of International Law* 1992/5(2), pp. 245–264.

9 *Hasan and Chaush v. Bulgaria* App no. 30985/96 (ECtHR, October 26th, 2000) § 98.

10 See C. Grabenwarter, *European Convention on Human Rights: Commentary*, Munich/Oxford/Baden-Baden 2014, p. 328; and W.A. Schabas, *The European Convention on Human Rights: A Commentary*, Oxford 2015, pp. 550–552.

This explains why Article 13 ECHR lacks autonomous substantive significance. Besides, it holds an ancillary nature, as it inherently 'complements' the remaining provisions of the Convention, functioning in conjunction with them.[11] To put it simply, to seek an effective remedy implies that the applicant should also possess a valid claim under another provision of the Convention for which such a remedy is invoked. This aligns with the main goal of the ECHR, which seeks to secure neither abstract nor illusory rights but practical and enforceable ones.[12] The existence of domestic remedies unequivocally serves this purpose.

Depending on the prerogative at stake, that remedy can be structurally conceived in varying forms. For instance, it can manifest as an appeal before an administrative entity or as a specialised procedure before a judicial body. Furthermore, it can adopt either a preventive character (intended to avert the breach from occurring) or a compensatory character (aimed at providing retrospective relief once the violation has occurred). In any case, mandating State Parties to establish a remedy within their domestic frameworks is evidently intended to ensure that rights and freedoms safeguarded by the ECHR are, first and foremost, upheld at the national level.[13] This reveals that the Convention has bestowed upon State Parties the primary duty of acting as guardians for the rights and freedoms enshrined within its provisions, in the light of the principle of subsidiarity,[14] which is one of the basic – albeit implicit – principles of the Convention mechanism.[15] As a result, the ECtHR holds a supervisory role towards national systems.[16] Against this background, the concept of the 'margin of appreciation' afforded to State Parties

---

11 *Dmitrijevs v. Latvia* App no. 37467/04 (ECtHR, September 7th, 2010) § 93.

12 *Airey v. Ireland* App no. 6289/73 (ECtHR, October 9th, 1979) § 24.

13 *Kudła v. Poland* App no. 30210/96 (ECtHR, October 26th, 2000) § 152 and the further references cited therein.

14 *S.H. v. Malta* App no. 37241/21 (ECtHR, December 20th, 2022) § 100. Additionally, the Court has asserted that Article 13 ECHR maintains a strong connection with Article 35(1) thereof, wherein the Court can only address the issue at stake once all domestic remedies have been exhausted, provided there exists an effective remedy within the national system pertaining to the alleged violation. See, among others, *Y.B. v. Russia* App no. 71155/17 (ECtHR, July 20th, 2021) § 32.

15 E. Morawska, 'The Principles of Subsidiarity and Effectiveness: Two Pillars of an Effective Remedy for Excessive Length of Proceedings within the Meaning of Article 13 ECHR', *Polish Yearbook of International Law* 2019/39, p. 163 et seq.

16 See *Z.A. and Others v. Russia* App no. 29392/95 (ECtHR, May 10th, 2001) § 103; *A.K. v. Latvia* App no. 33011/08 (ECtHR, June 24th, 2014) § 86 and, more recently, *M.K. v. Ukraine* App no. 24867/13 (ECtHR, September 15th, 2022) Joint Dissenting Opinion on Judges O'Leary, Chanturia and Bårdsen § 7 and the case-law cited therein.

gains significance – as repeatedly emphasised by the Court, the safeguards laid down in Article 13 ECHR do not extend to mandating a specific form of remedy.[17] State Parties retain the autonomy to devise the remedy that they consider most suitable to qualify as an effective means of upholding Convention rights. Still, such legal tool shall be 'effective' in practice as well as in law.[18]

A rich body of case-law from the Strasbourg Court has provided an interpretation of the notion of 'effective remedy' in concrete terms. Noteworthy topics scrutinised by the Court include the definition of 'remedy', 'effectiveness' of the latter, 'national authority' and 'violation' as stipulated in Article 13 ECHR.

Firstly, according to the ECtHR, a 'remedy' is mandated to empower competent domestic authorities to address the core issue, i.e., the merit of the relevant Convention grievance, and to grant suitable redress to the applicant concerned.[19] Thus, the inherent capability to directly offer redress for the challenged circumstance stands as a fundamental criterion in categorising a remedy as 'effective'. Furthermore, the Court has emphasised that the effectiveness of a remedy hinges upon its accessibility,[20] adequacy[21] and shall be sufficient for its purpose.[22] Beyond mere theoretical viability, it must also possess practical feasibility and effectiveness in both legal and practical terms,[23] all while considering the material circumstances of the case.[24] Significantly, the Court reiterated that the crux for Article 13 ECHR is ensuring a tangible legal tool for the individual in question – neither the potential positive outcome for the applicant[25] nor the existence of a prior Convention

---

17 *S.W. v. the United Kingdom* App no. 87/18 (ECtHR, June 22nd, 2021) § 59.

18 *Irodotou v. Cyprus* App no. 16783/20 (ECtHR, May 23rd, 2023) § 48. For a comparative analysis with the EU legal framework see S. Prechal, R. Widdershoven, 'Redefining the Relationship between Rewe-effectiveness and Effective Judicial Protection', *Review of European Administrative Law* 2011/4(2), pp. 31–52.

19 See *Darboe and Camara v. Italy* App no. 5797/17 (ECtHR, July 21st, 2022) § 193 and *M.S.S. v. Belgium and Greece* App no. 30696/09 (ECtHR, January 21st, 2011) § 288.

20 *Paulino Tomás v. Portugal* App no. 58698/00 (ECtHR, March 27th, 2003).

21 See *Kudła v. Poland* (n 13) § 158 and C. Grabenwarter, *European Convention, op.cit.*, p. 334.

22 *Šulcas v. Lithuania* App no. 35624/04 (ECtHR, January 5th, 2010) § 59.

23 *Z.A. v. Ireland* App no. 19632/20 (ECtHR, March 9th, 2023) § 108.

24 *Leander v. Sweden* App no. 9248/81 (ECtHR, March 26th, 1987) §§ 76–84.

25 *Vilvarajah and Others v. the United Kingdom* App nos. 13163/87, 13164/87, 13165/87, 13447/87 and 13448/87 (ECtHR, November 30th, 1991) § 122 and the case-law cited therein.

violation[26] hold relevance (and are thus not prerequisites) for the assessment of the 'effectiveness' of a remedy. Besides, in evaluating efficacy, not only formal remedies but also their operation within the broader legal and political context, as well as the personal circumstances of the applicant, must be considered.[27] The characteristics outlined by the Court thus delineate the "outer boundaries" of the concept of 'effective remedy', which, on the one hand, must allow for thorough and comprehensive scrutiny of the alleged violation claimed by the applicant and, on the other hand, if necessary, shall provide for appropriate redress. In this regard, overly stringent requirements for accessing such a remedy, as well as excessively prolonged timeframes for obtaining a decision, should be avoided.[28] Nevertheless, within these "outer boundaries", State Parties retain a degree of flexibility to institute a system of remedies to fulfil their obligations under the Convention.

Secondly, the ECtHR has provided clarification that the 'national authority' mentioned in Article 13 ECHR does not inherently have to be a judicial body.[29]

---

26 *Boyle and Rice v. the United Kingdom* App nos. 9659/82 and 9658/82 (ECtHR, April 27th, 1988) § 52.

27 See *Đorđević v. Croatia* App no. 41526/10 (ECtHR, July 24th, 2012) § 101, referring to *Akdivar and Others v. Turkey* App. no. 21893/93 (ECtHR, September 16th, 1996) § 69. This case-by-case approach, developed within the context of Article 35 ECHR relevant case-law, depicts the adaptable nature of effective remedies within the ECHR legal framework. Notably, it highlights the significance of considering individual circumstances, the legal context, and the specific nature of the violated right when determining the appropriate form of remedy. For a recent application of the ECtHR case-specific approach in this field, see *Tapayeva v. Russia* App no. 24757/18 (ECtHR, November 23rd, 2021) §§ 69–74.

28 *Wikimedia Foundation Inc. v. Turkey* App no. 25479/19 (ECtHR, March 1st, 2022) § 46: '*Un recours inapte à prospérer en temps utile n'est ni adéquat ni effectif*'.

29 *P.C. v. Ireland* App no. 26922/19 (ECtHR, September 1st, 2022) § 104. Conversely, Article 47 CFREU provides individuals whose rights and freedoms, as guaranteed by Union law, are infringed with an effective remedy 'before a tribunal'. For a comparative perspective, see S. Allegrezza, *Judicial Review*, *op.cit.*, p. 100 et seq.; V. Covolo, *Guarantees*, *op.cit.*, pp. 133 et seq.; C. Thiele, 'Das Recht auf einen wirksamen Rechtsbehelf in vergleichender europäischer Perspektive', *ERA Forum* 2015/16, pp. 511–527; K. Zombory, 'The right to an effective remedy: a key element for ensuring the effectiveness of the ECHR human rights system', [in:] A. Mezglewsky (ed.), *Efficiency of the Judiciary*, Warsaw 2023, pp. 213–215. On the content of Article 47 CFREU see H. Hofmann, 'Article 47. Specific Provisions (Meaning)', [in:] S. Peers et al. (eds.), *The EU Charter of Fundamental Rights: A Commentary*, Portland/Oxford 2014, p. 1211 et seq.; M. Safian, D. Düsterhaus, 'A Union of Effective Judicial Protection: Addressing a Multi-Level Challenge through the Lens of Article 47 CFREU', *Yearbook of European Law* 2014/33, pp. 3–40; A. Arnull, 'The Principle of Effective Judicial Protection in EU Law: An Unruly Horse?', *European Law Review*, 2011/36, pp. 51–70.

Yet, if it is not a judicial authority, the extent of its powers and the level of guarantees it provides are significant factors in assessing the effectiveness of the remedy available before it. Hence, where a non-judicial authority is said to be the 'national authority' as per Article 13 ECHR, a thorough assessment on its powers, prerogatives, competences and procedural safeguards is normally carried out by the ECtHR.[30] This may illustrate the clear preference of the Court for judicial authorities, which are rightfully regarded as traditionally characterised by strong guarantees of independence from political influence, accessibility to victims and their families, and the capacity to render binding decisions,[31] albeit Article 13 ECHR does not require such authority to be a judicial institution in the strict sense envisaged in Article 6 ECHR.[32] Still, when a judicial body is appointed as the 'national authority', the Court's scrutiny is not entirely absent, although it may be less rigorous in comparison to assessments involving non-judicial bodies. Broadly speaking, this may imply that considering the characteristics that the ECtHR expects a 'national authority' to possess (e.g., the ability to render binding decisions and offer adequate procedural safeguards), State Parties are somewhat encouraged to establish judicial bodies to address fundamental rights violations.

Besides this shareable standpoint, nonetheless, there seems to be some ambiguity in the ECtHR's approach regarding the substantive features of the procedure before such domestic bodies. The Court emphasised that the requirements of fairness stemming from Article 6 ECHR *may* be relevant for the assessment of the effectiveness of the remedy at stake.[33] However, it appears to be merely a factor for consideration rather than a mandatory aspect of the procedure in question. In this vein, it has been highlighted that the requirement for an oral hearing before such a 'national body' does not appear to be an absolute necessity for a remedy to conform to Article 13 ECHR.[34] Whereas scholars have correctly asserted that,

---

30 See C. Grabenwarter, *European Convention*, *op.cit.*, p. 333 and the case-law cited therein.

31 *Z. and Others v. the United Kingdom* (n 15) § 110. To be effective, a remedy necessitates that the national authority must possess the power to issue legally binding decisions and is not limited to providing mere recommendations, as pointed out by C. Grabenwarter, *European Convention*, *op.cit.*, p. 334.

32 *Adbilla v. Malta* App no. 36199/15 (ECtHR, July 17th, 2018) § 62. This perspective has been established in *Klass and Others v. Germany* App no. 5029/71 (ECtHR, September 6th, 1978), § 67.

33 *Csüllög v. Hungary* App no. 30042/08 (ECtHR, June 7th, 2011) § 46.

34 As rightly noted by C. Grabenwarter, *European Convention*, *op.cit.*, p. 338. Regarding the non-absolute nature of the right to an oral hearing as per Article 6 ECHR, see *Jussila v. Finland* App no. 73053/01 (ECtHR, November 23rd, 2006) §§ 40–43 and the case-law cited therein.

in any case, remedy proceedings should be 'formal, and the person concerned must be heard',[35] the wording of Article 13 ECHR seems to lean more towards the idea that even a procedure based only on written submissions can comply with it.

Thirdly, it is noteworthy that the right to an effective remedy is not absolute, as there might be claims which may appear ill-founded, abusive or 'fanciful'.[36] Indeed, Article 13 ECHR does not mandate the provision of a domestic remedy for every alleged grievance, irrespective of its merit; instead, it requires the claim of a violation to be 'arguable'.[37] This threshold enables State Parties to provide an effective remedy exclusively for those claims that can be considered to possess a certain level of merit.[38] The Court has not furnished a comprehensive definition of what constitutes *arguability*. Conversely, it has emphasised that the determination of whether a claim is arguable should be made based on the specific facts of the case and the nature of the legal issues raised.[39] Taking a case-by-case approach, the ECtHR has primarily shaped the concept of arguability "in the negative", that is, delineating when a complaint *is not arguable*. For example, this occurs when the evidence presented by the applicants fails to reveal any signs of a violation or refer to the considerations that led the ECtHR to conclude that there was no violation of the relevant provision.[40] Consequently, when a complaint is evidently ill-founded or is inadmissible, the ECtHR does not recognise such a claim as 'arguable' for the purposes of Article 13 ECHR.[41] Differently, the Strasbourg Court has offered little guidance in defining "in the positive" the concept of arguability, which may

35 C. Grabenwarter, *European Convention*, *op.cit.*, p. 338.

36 A. Lee, 'Focus on Article 13 ECHR', *Judicial Review* 2015/20(1), p. 33.

37 *Leander v. Sweden* (n 23) § 77. For a historical analysis of the 'arguability' threshold as developed through the ECtHR case-law, see F.J. Hampson, 'The Concept of An "Arguable Claim" Under Article 13 of the European Convention on Human Rights', *The International and Comparative Law Quarterly*, 1990/39(4), pp. 891–899 and G. Malinverni, 'Variations sur un thème encore méconnu: L'article 13 de la Convention européenne des droits de l'homme', *Revue Trimestrielle de Droits de l'Homme*, 1998/33(9), p. 650 et seq.

38 This aspect is emphasized by C. Grabenwarter, *European Convention*, *op.cit.*, p. 332 and W.A. Schabas, *The European*, *op.cit.*, p. 552.

39 *Bastys v. Lithuania* App no. 80749/17 (ECtHR, February 4th, 2020) § 51.

40 See, respectively, *Hüsniye Tekin v. Turkey* App no. 50971/99 (ECtHR, October 25th, 2005) § 55 and *Sevgin and İnce v. Turkey* App no. 46262/99 (ECtHR, September 20th, 2005) § 87.

41 *Sukachov v. Ukraine* App no. 14057/17 (ECtHR, January 30th, 2020) § 110.

apply, in principle, when a Convention violation has been previously established on merit or when a complaint has been deemed admissible.[42]

2.2. Article 13 ECHR and criminal proceedings: A narrow positioning

Whereas Article 13 ECHR is applicable across all legal domains, its scope of application within criminal proceedings does appear to be more limited. However, this does not imply that Article 13 ECHR lacks autonomous relevance in certain areas of criminal procedure.

For instance, it can be invoked in conjunction with Article 3 ECHR in cases of ineffective domestic judicial remedies for complaints as to inadequate conditions of detention,[43] indicating appropriate means of relief.[44] Similarly, the Court has consistently allowed the combination of Article 13 ECHR with Article 8 ECHR concerning the absence of an effective remedy in cases involving alleged violations of the right to private life in matters related to surveillance measures[45] or searches and seizures of electronic devices.[46] Moreover, a growing body of case law has emerged that links Articles 2 (right to life) and 3 (prohibition of torture) of the Convention with Article 13 thereof in the context of criminal proceedings.[47]

However, the limitation in the scope of application of Article 13 ECHR in the context of criminal proceedings becomes apparent in two specific areas that hold particular significance within the realm of criminal justice – the right to personal liberty and the right to a fair trial.

With regard to the former, this outcome arises from a comprehensive interpretation of other provisions of the Convention, which themselves contain tailored provisions outlining specialised procedures in the event of their violations. In a nutshell, while Article 13 ECHR establishes a general framework for an effective

---

42 Ibid., § 111.

43 *Volodya Avetisyan v. Armenia* App no. 39087/15 (ECtHR, May 3rd, 2022) §§ 27–29 and the case-law cited therein.

44 *Sukachov v. Ukraine* (n 41) § 113.

45 *İrfan Güzel v. Turkey* App no. 35285/08 (ECtHR, February 7th, 2017) §§ 90–109.

46 *Posevini v. Bulgaria* App no. 63638/14 (ECtHR, January 19th, 2017) §§ 82–87. On the broad relevance of Article 8 ECHR in the field of searches and seizures of electronic devices, see L. Bernardini, F. Sanvitale, 'Searches and seizures of electronic devices in European criminal proceedings: A new pattern for independent review?', *Revista Ítalo-española De Derecho Procesal*, 2023/1, pp. 73–119.

47 *Tagayeva and Others v. Russia* App nos. 26562/07, 14755/08, 49339/08, 49380/08, 51313/08, 21294/11 and 37096/11 (ECtHR, April 13th, 2017) § 619.

remedy in cases of alleged violations of fundamental rights protected by the Convention (*lex generalis*), there exist additional ECHR provisions that prescribe distinct remedies with *ad hoc* characteristics (such as the requirement for a judicial authority to adjudicate the matter) for particular fundamental rights that are pertinent in the context of criminal proceedings (*lex specialis*). Because these specialised remedies are more stringent and offer more detailed provisions compared to those outlined in Article 13 ECHR, the latter does not apply in such cases.[48]

This scenario is exemplified by the scope and content of the *right to liberty and security* laid down in Article 5 ECHR, which incorporates the comparatively less rigorous procedural standards of Article 13 thereof,[49] with specific reference to the procedural guarantees enshrined in Article 5(3), (4) and (5) of the Convention.

Indeed, these latter provisions apply to all circumstances involving the lawfulness of the deprivation of an individual's personal liberty. Accordingly, the ECtHR has consistently held that Article 5(4) and (5) constitutes *lex specialis* in relation to the more general requirements of Article 13 ECHR and absorbs the latter.[50] Given the prevalence of such situations and their structural role in criminal proceedings, the relevance of Article 13 ECHR is entirely superseded in this context, whereas the Court must evaluate the effectiveness of the remedy at stake solely in the light of Article 5 ECHR.[51]

In the context of the right to a fair trial, Article 6(1) ECHR is likewise considered *lex specialis* in relation to Article 13 ECHR. This viewpoint is grounded in a similar rationale to what has been previously explained. The provisions of Article 13 ECHR are less stringent compared to those articulated in Article 6(1) ECHR.[52] For instance, the latter not only explicitly references a 'tribunal' but also encompasses several robust procedural safeguards, including effective access to a court, assurances of independence and impartiality of the adjudicating body, equality of arms, adversarial proceedings, the provision of a reasoned decision allowing the defendant to comprehend the grounds for the judgment and the opportunity to pursue subsequent available remedies.[53] Consequently, when the matter pertains to the 'determination … of any criminal charge', any individual

48 C. Grabenwarter, *European Convention*, *op.cit.*, pp. 329–330.

49 V. Covolo, *Guarantees*, *op.cit.*, p. 139.

50 *Andrei Georgiev v. Bulgaria* App no. 61507/00 (ECtHR, July 26th, 2007) § 70. By analogy, the same principle applies with respect to Article 5(3) ECtHR, although the ECtHR has not issued a specific decision on this matter.

51 *Voykin and Others v. Ukraine* App no. 47889/08 (ECtHR, March 27th, 2018) § 124.

52 F. Kuty, *Justice pénale et procès équitable*, Bruxelles 2006, p. 281 et seq.

53 W.A. Schabas, *The European*, *op.cit.*, p. 284 ff. and the case-law cited therein.

is inherently entitled to the guarantees laid down in Article 6(1) ECHR. In such a circumstance, as this entitlement encompasses the full spectrum of judicial procedures and is more rigorous than those outlined in Article 13 ECHR, only Article 6(1) ECHR applies as the *lex specialis*, and Article 13 is typically rendered inapplicable.[54] In a nutshell, Article 13 ECHR holds limited significance in relation to the procedural guarantees established by Article 6(1) ECHR.[55]

3. Glancing at fair trial rights violations

The limited scope of application of Article 13 ECHR in the context of criminal proceedings implies that there are few situations where the right to an effective remedy can be invoked in conjunction with other provisions of the Convention.[56] Notably, there are at least two frequent circumstances in which such prerogative is invoked pending criminal proceedings, that is, should a breach of the right to be tried within a reasonable time (§ 3.1) or of the right to be presumed innocent (§ 3.2) allegedly occur in the material case.

3.1. The right to be tried within a reasonable time: A functionalistic approach to effective remedies

The right to be tried within a reasonable time, as articulated in Article 6(1) ECHR, serves both as a manifestation of the effective and smooth administration of (criminal) justice and as a fundamental right granted to all individuals engaged in proceedings conducted within the scope of application of Article 6 ECHR, which notably mandates that such proceedings be 'fair'.[57] Within the sphere of criminal proceedings, this right safeguards individuals from being subject to interminable procedures without a final determination of the criminal charges against them. Moreover, an efficient criminal justice system reinforces the public's trust in governmental institutions, whereas protracted decision-making periods can erode confidence in the entire system and, importantly, may harm the reputation of the alleged offender. Between two competing imperatives – the (time-consuming) need for the effective administration of justice and the right to be tried within a reasonable time – the ECtHR examines whether a fair balance has been struck among the different facets of this guarantee. This evaluation comes into play

54 As famously found in *Airey v. Ireland* (n 12) § 35.

55 C. Grabenwarter, *European Convention*, *op.cit.*, p. 331.

56 See, for instance, *Blaj v. Romania* App no. 36259/04 (ECtHR, April 8th, 2014) § 67.

57 *Faysal Pamuk v. Turkey* App no. 430/13 (ECtHR, January 18th, 2022) § 44.

when determining whether a trial has exceeded a duration deemed 'reasonable',[58] a notion whose meaning is to be found on a case-by-case basis,[59] depending on the material circumstances of the case under scrutiny.[60]

Without delving into details, it is worth recalling that the ECtHR typically excluded Article 13 ECHR from being applicable where breaches of the reasonable time requirement are found.[61] This might be seen as the expression of a legal approach arguably based on the stronger character of the guarantees laid down in Article 6(1) ECHR.[62] This essentially meant that the Court did not view any legal interest in re-examining the same subject matter of complaint under Article 13 ECHR.[63]

Still, such a standpoint was incongruous for three distinct reasons. Firstly, Article 6(1) and Article 13 ECHR are autonomous provisions, and there is no indication in their respective wording that suggests their concurrent application is hindered by the Convention, particularly in cases involving a breach of the reasonable time requirement. It is crucial to distinguish between, on the one hand, evaluating whether the trial's duration was reasonable and, on the other hand, ascertaining whether the applicant had an effective means to challenge such a violation. These constitute separate considerations that should deserve separate analysis before the ECtHR. Secondly, a complaint under Article 13 ECHR grounded on an alleged breach of the reasonable time requirement, seems to encompass a different scope of application compared to that of Article 6(1) ECHR, which specifically relates to the determination of a criminal charge. Consequently, the two fundamental rights differ in their scope of application and no overlapping between them may occur *in concreto*. Thirdly, and importantly, in recent leading cases that supported the assertion of Article 13 ECHR non-applicability in this field, the Court did not provide any explicit rationale for this stance. Instead, it limited itself to asserting that it 'does not consider it necessary also to examine

58 *Boddaert v. Belgium* App no. 12919/87 (ECtHR, October 12th, 1992) § 39.

59 M. Henzelin, H. Rordorf, 'When Does the Length of Criminal Proceedings Become Unreasonable According to the European Court of Human Rights?', *New Journal of European Criminal Law*, 2014/5(1), pp. 78–109.

60 *Pélissier and Sassi v. France* App no. 25444/94 (ECtHR, March 25th, 1999) § 67.

61 *Giuseppe Tripodi v. Italy* App no. 40946/98 (ECtHR, January 25th, 2000) § 15.

62 B. Delaunay, 'Le droit au juge et à un recours effectif selon la Convention européenne de sauvegarde des droits de l'homme et des libertés fondamentales (Art. 13)', *Zbornik radova Pravnog fakulteta u Splitu*, 2015/52(1), p. 4.

63 In this vein, see, in the context of civil proceedings, *Pizzetti v. Italy* App no. 12444/86 (ECtHR, February 26th, 1993) § 21.

the case under Article 13'[64] or that it '*ne croit pas nécessaire de se placer de surcroît sur le terrain de l'article 13*'.[65] In prior rulings, nonetheless, the position held was that the underlying justification could be traced to the comparatively more lenient safeguards established in Article 13 ECHR. Yet, this explanation is absent in recent decisions, casting doubt upon its validity.

These shortcomings had a role in prompting the Court to overturn its prior case law, as exemplified in the landmark *Kudła* judgment.[66] For the first time, the autonomous importance of the right to an effective remedy for a breach of the reasonable time requirement stemming from Article 6(1) ECHR was expressly acknowledged.[67] Yet, this review was motivated not only by the reasons previously outlined but also by the ECtHR's heightened consideration of pragmatic factors.[68] Specifically, it cited 'the continuing accumulation of applications before it in which the only, or principal, allegation is that of a failure to ensure a hearing within a reasonable time'.[69] Additionally, the Court pointed out the increasing frequency with which violations in this regard were being discovered, highlighting the significant risk to the rule of law within national legal systems when excessive delays in the administration of justice occur without domestic remedies available to litigants.[70] Finally, it was noted that if Article 13 ECHR is deemed inapplicable in conjunction with Article 6(1) in this context, individuals would consistently be compelled to resort to the ECtHR, whereas their issues would be more suitably addressed initially within the national legal system.[71] As has been aptly emphasised, 'the ECtHR [...] attempts to preserve its efficiency and forestall the collapse of the ECHR legal order by enforcing the role of Article 13'[72] which, in turn, underpins the effectiveness of Article 6(1) ECHR.[73] Against this background, whereas *Kudła* is commendable for enhancing procedural safeguards for individuals who claim a violation of their right to a timely trial, pragmatic considerations – although

64 *Giuseppe Tripodi* (n 61) § 15.
65 *Pizzetti* (n 63) § 21 and, with the same wording, *Bouilly v. France* App no. 38952/97 (ECtHR, December 7th, 1999) § 27.
66 *Kudła* (n 13) § 147.
67 K. Zombory, *The right*, *op.cit.*, p. 209 and B. Delaunay, *Le droit*, *op.cit.*, pp. 5–7.
68 Labelled as grounds stemming from 'legal practice' by V. Covolo, *Guarantees*, *op.cit.*, p. 139.
69 *Kudła* (n 13) § 148, first paragraph.
70 *Kudła* (n 13) § 148, second paragraph.
71 *Kudła* (n 13) § 155.
72 K. Zombory, *The right*, *op.cit.*, p. 209.
73 C. Thiele, *Das Recht*, *op.cit.*, p. 515.

shareable and deserving of serious consideration[74] – seem to carry limited weight when determining the applicability of Article 13 ECHR in conjunction with Article 6(1) thereof in this context.[75] As previously indicated, a literal and contextual analysis of both provisions could have led to this conclusion without necessitating reference to the significant caseload of the Court concerning breaches of the reasonable time requirement. Arguably, relying on practical considerations when addressing fundamental rights might be risky, as it may, at times, weaken rather than enhance the protections afforded by the Convention.[76]

As for the effective remedies to be provided to the applicant for a breach of the reasonable time requirement, the Court has expressed a strong preference for *preventive* remedies – these are remedies designed to expedite legal proceedings and prevent them from becoming excessively lengthy.[77] While these preventive remedies are preferred, their establishment is not mandatory for State Parties. Indeed, States can also offer effective *compensatory* remedies, that is, legal means that offer redress for delays that have already occurred, whether the legal proceedings are still ongoing or have concluded (e.g., a monetary compensation, the distribution of a milder penalty or the *ex officio* discontinuance of the case at stake).[78]

3.2. The right to be presumed innocent: A blurred reading of Article 13 ECHR

The foundational tenet of the presumption of innocence is enshrined within Article 6(2) ECHR, according to which 'everyone charged with a criminal offence shall be presumed innocent until proved guilty according to law'.

74 See E. Morawska, *The principles*, *op.cit.*, p. 167, who highlights that the ECtHR's standpoint in *Kudła* 'largely' relies on the principle of subsidiarity.

75 Cf. the Partly Dissenting Opinion of Judge Casadevall in *Kudła* (n 13) §§ 3–4.

76 A notable example (although not the only one) of this "concrete situation approach" can be observed in the ECtHR's case-law concerning collective expulsions. In these cases, the Court's consideration of practical situations at the borders of State Parties led to a restriction in the application of Article 4, Protocol 4 to the ECHR. See, for instance, *Asady v. Slovakia* App no. 24917/15 (ECtHR, March 24th, 2020) § 59, where the ECtHR mentioned the 'challenges facing European States in terms of immigration control as a result of the economic crisis and recent social and political changes which have had a particular impact on certain regions of Africa and the Middle East'.

77 *Scordino v. Italy (No. 1)* App no. 36813/97 (ECtHR, March 29th, 2006) § 183.

78 See, respectively, *Hiernaux v. Belgium* App no. 28022/15 (ECtHR, January 24th, 2017) §§ 57–62; *Chiarello v. Germany* App no. 497/17 (ECtHR, June 20th, 2019) §§ 54–59; *Panju v. Belgium (No. 2)* App no. 49072/21 (ECtHR, May 23rd, 2023) § 72.

The well-established ECtHR's case-law has consistently upheld the admissibility of combining this aforementioned provision with Article 13 ECHR.[79] Consequently, the right to an effective remedy has consistently preserved its substantive autonomy where breaches of the presumption of innocence are alleged. Against this background, whereas the ECtHR's case-law has not followed a uniform standpoint, the Court nonetheless tried to delineate the fundamental grounds that a remedy must satisfy to be deemed 'effective' within the framework of Article 13 ECHR in light of Article 6(2) ECHR. In this regard, at least three features may be mentioned.

Firstly, the Court has explicitly acknowledged that, given the nature of the right protected by Article 6(2) ECHR, any effective domestic remedy aimed at addressing an alleged violation of the presumption of innocence during ongoing criminal proceedings must be *immediately accessible* to the individual and should not be contingent upon the outcome of their trial.[80] To suggest otherwise, the ECtHR has argued, would undermine the very principle of the presumption of innocence.[81] This means that the applicant should not be required to await the conclusion of the proceedings before seeking redress for violating their presumption of innocence.[82] Consequently, *compensatory* remedies shall be foreseen in domestic law, and they must be promptly accessible to the defendant, even when investigations (or, should it be the case, the trial) are still in progress.[83]

Secondly, regarding the *substance* of such a remedy, the Court has emphasised that 'in principle' a civil law remedy can be deemed 'effective' against alleged violations of the presumption of innocence.[84] Nevertheless, and importantly, the Court has consistently held that mere monetary compensation *would not suffice* in such cases. In *Konstas*, the Court set forth that, under Article 13 ECHR, a claim for civil damages arising from a breach of the presumption of innocence could only serve as a partial remedy, as it could not 'fully' redress the alleged infringement.[85] Thus, for a civil law remedy to be considered 'effective', it must be complemented

79 See, for instance, *Konstas v. Greece* App no. 53466/07 (ECtHR, May 24th, 2011) §§ 48–57.

80 *Gutsanovi v. Bulgary* App no. 34529/10 (ECtHR, October 15th, 2013) § 176.

81 *Banevi v. Bulgary* App no. 25658/19 (ECtHR, October 12th, 2021) § 139.

82 In this regard, see *Lolov and Others v. Bulgary* App no. 6123/11 (ECtHR, February 21st, 2019) § 47.

83 Indeed, preventive remedies seems not feasible in this field – while it is possible to urge courts to expedite their actions, there is no legal mechanism that, in advance, can preempt authorities from violating the presumption of innocence of individuals.

84 *Gutsanovi* (n 80) § 178.

85 *Konstas* (n 79) § 29.

by *additional procedures* aimed at recognising or rectifying the violation of the presumption of innocence.[86] Reference can be made to the retraction of the contested statements through a subsequent declaration[87] or the inclusion of a communication (in the publication where the contested statements were originally reported) aiming at putting an end to the infringement of the presumption of innocence.[88] While the case law in this regard appeared to be well-established before the Court, a recent decision in the *Januškevičienė* case suggests a different line of reasoning. In that judgement, the ECtHR considered a purely monetary remedy to be 'effective' as per Article 13 ECHR in conjunction with Article 6(2) thereof, sparking a powerful – and shareable – Dissenting Opinion from the minority of judges.[89] Very recently, a concise decision taken by a Committee of the Court has recognised that a civil law remedy is *inherently* incapable of fully remedying ('*de nature pas à remédier pleinement*') the alleged violation of the presumption of innocence, raising the possibility that *Januškevičienė* was hopefully an isolated judgement.[90] Therefore, it appears rightly established that only a combination of civil law remedies and the aforementioned 'additional procedures' can be considered an 'effective remedy' in accordance with the Convention.

Lastly, as for the *national authority* responsible for evaluating the alleged violation of the presumption of innocence, the ECtHR has interestingly departed from its established case law on Article 13 ECHR, specifying that it will be the task of *criminal courts* to address the applicant's claims and assess any alleged infringement of Article 6(2) ECHR *from a procedural perspective*. More specifically, in rejecting the effectiveness of purely monetary compensation as per Article 13 ECHR, the Court pointed out that 'the Government did not refer to *any remedy that would have enabled the applicant to invite the criminal court concerned to find a violation of the presumption innocence from the procedural standpoint*. That being so, the claim for damages […] to which the Government referred could only be related to the alleged violation and *sufficient in part*; it could not

86 *Januškevičienė v. Lithuania* App no. 69717/14 (ECtHR, September 3rd, 2019) § 59 and the case-law cited therein.

87 *Babjak and Others v. Slovakia* App no. 73693/01 (ECtHR, March 30th, 2004) § 2 ('The Law' part of the judgement).

88 *Marchiani v. France* App no. 30392/03 (ECtHR, May 27th, 2008) § 1 ('The Law' part of the judgement).

89 See *Januškevičienė* (n 86) §§ 56–63 and Dissenting Opinion of Judges Pinto de Albuquerque, Kūris and Paczolay, §§ 34–44.

90 *Savvaidou v. Greece* App no. 58715/15 (ECtHR, January 31st, 2023) § 11, recalling *Konstas* (n 79) §§ 28–31.

fully remedy the alleged infringement of the presumption of innocence'.[91] This implies that civil law remedies should be accessible through civil courts, whereas the 'additional procedures' mentioned earlier ought to be accessible *through criminal courts only*. Thus, the broad notion of a 'national authority' stipulated in Article 13 ECHR appears to refer specifically to 'criminal courts' (and not to any other entity) where those 'additional procedures' are to be implemented *vis-à-vis* the individual concerned.

4. Concluding remarks

As has been evocatively claimed, addressing Article 13 ECHR entails grappling with 'the most obscure provision of the ECHR'.[92] Initially overlooked during the early years of the ECtHR's activities – to the extent that it was dubbed a 'dormant effective remedy clause'[93] – Article 13 ECHR has regained momentum within the recent ECtHR case-law. Nonetheless, in the specific context of criminal proceedings, the significance of that provision appears to be still underestimated. While Article 5(3), (4), and (5) ECHR can be legitimately regarded as *lex specialis vis-à-vis* Article 13 ECHR,[94] the same does not seem to hold true for Article 6 ECHR. If my reading is correct, there is nothing in the wording of the latter provision that implies that the less stringent requirements of Article 13 ECHR should be absorbed, in any case, by those of Article 6 ECHR.[95] A distinction may – and seemingly should – be drawn between the violation of a specific fair trial right and the lack of an effective remedy to rectify such a breach (as currently happens, for instance, with the right to be presumed innocent). In this vein, there has been growing argumentation that the relationship between these two prerogatives should be more thoroughly considered, with some scholars sharply criticising the stance taken by the ECtHR.[96]

---

91 *Konstas* (n 79) § 29, emphasis added.

92 *Malone v. the United Kingdom* App no. 8691/79 (ECtHR, August 2nd, 1984), Partly Dissenting Opinion of Judges Matscher and Pinheiro Farinha.

93 H. Keller, A. Stone Sweet, 'Assessing the Impact of the ECHR on National Legal System', [in:] H. Keller (ed.), *A Europe of Rights: The Impact of the ECHR on National Legal System*, Oxford 2008, p. 708.

94 This consideration stems from the wording of those provisions which allows for *ad hoc* effective remedies for the breach of the right to personal liberty and security.

95 In this regard, see *W. v. the United Kingdom* App no. 9749/82 (ECtHR, July 8th, 1987), Joint Separate Opinion of Judges Pinheiro Farinha and De Meyer.

96 See T. Barkhuysena, *Artikel 13 EVRM effectieve nationale rechtsbescherming bij schending van mensenrechten*, Lelystad 1998, *passim*.

Since *Kudła*, the Court embraced an alternative viewpoint. Regarding the breach of the reasonable time requirement, it recognised that Article 6(1) ECHR and Article 13 thereof could be regarded as distinct and separate. This perspective is defensible, although it has been (also) rooted in pragmatic considerations that arguably should not be employed to shape the ECtHR's case-law. Instead, the Court's decisions should be grounded in a thorough examination of the relevant provisions, considering their literal meaning, their context and their purpose.

Nevertheless, if the Court continues to embrace this functionalistic approach, it appears that there is still room within the realm of fair trial rights to recognise the significance of Article 13 ECHR fully. This is particularly evident when considering the rights of the defence outlined in Article 6(3) ECHR, which are a specific manifestation of the right to a fair trial as articulated in Article 6(1) thereof. While the ECtHR has previously ruled out the autonomous relevance of Article 13 ECHR in this context,[97] it remains possible that the Court may, in the future, acknowledge the necessity of finding a violation of the right to an effective remedy in conjunction with a violation of the defence rights in question. Or, at the very least, there would be no hindrance to the ECtHR advocating for such a line of reasoning. Ultimately, *Kudła* served as a sort of "call to action" for State Parties, urging them to effectively fulfill their role as guardians of the Convention. This potentially reveals that the matter of providing effective remedies for violations of fair trial rights is an evolving concern before the ECtHR amidst, on one hand, the need for ensuring effective remedies for all individuals alleging a breach of Convention rights and, on the other hand, the principle of subsidiarity, which suggests that national courts are better positioned to identify violations of Convention provisions and, crucially, they serve as the most appropriate avenue for effective remedies for European citizens involved in criminal proceedings.[98]

Bibliography

Allegrezza S., 'Judicial Review as a Fundamental Right' in: S. Allegrezza, V. Covolo (eds.), *Effective Defence Rights in Criminal Proceedings*, Milan 2018.

Arnull A., 'The Principle of Effective Judicial Protection in EU Law: An Unruly Horse?', *European Law Review*, 2011/36.

97 As of 2023, no judgement concerning the violation of Article 13 ECHR in conjunction with Article 6(3) thereof has been rendered by the ECtHR.

98 In the sense that domestic judges are able to – and should – influence the ECtHR case-law, see R. Carnwath, 'E.C.H.R. Remedies From a Common Law Perspective', *International and Comparative Law Quartetly* 2000/49, p. 527.

Barkhuysena T., *Artikel 13 EVRM effectieve nationale rechtsbescherming bij schending van mensenrechten*, Lelystad 1998.

Bernardini L., Sanvitale F., 'Searches and seizures of electronic devices in European criminal proceedings: A new pattern for independent review?', *Revista Ítalo-española De Derecho Procesal*, 2023/1.

Carnwath R., 'E.C.H.R. Remedies From a Common Law Perspective', *International and Comparative Law Quartetly*, 2000/49.

Covolo V., 'Guarantees of Judicial Protection Under the ECHR: What Interactions With EU Law?', [in:] S. Allegrezza, V. Covolo (eds.), *Effective Defence Rights in Criminal Proceedings*, Milan 2018.

Delaunay B., 'Le droit au juge et à un recours effectif selon la Convention européenne de sauvegarde des droits de l'homme et des libertés fondamentales (Art. 13)', *Zbornik radova Pravnog fakulteta u Splitu*, 2015/52(1).

Grabenwarter C., *European Convention on Human Rights: Commentary*, Munich/Oxford/Baden-Baden 2014.

Haasdijk S., 'The Lack of Uniformity in the Terminology of the International Law of Remedies', *Leiden Journal of International Law*, 1992/5(2).

Hampson F. J., 'The Concept of An "Arguable Claim" Under Article 13 of the European Convention on Human Rights', *The International and Comparative Law Quarterly*, 1990/39(4).

Henzelin M., Rordorf H., 'When Does the Length of Criminal Proceedings Become Unreasonable According to the European Court of Human Rights?', *New Journal of European Criminal Law*, 2014/5(1).

Hofmann H., 'Article 47. Specific Provisions (Meaning)', [in:] S. Peers et al. (eds.), *The EU Charter of Fundamental Rights: A Commentary*, Portland/Oxford 2014.

Keller H., Stone Sweet A., 'Assessing the Impact of the ECHR on National Legal System' [in:] H. Keller (ed.), *A Europe of Rights: The Impact of the ECHR on National Legal System*, Oxford 2008.

Kuty F., *Justice pénale et procès équitable*, Bruxelles 2006.

Malinverni G., 'Variations sur un thème encore méconnu: L'article 13 de la Convention européenne des droits de l'homme', *Revue Trimestrielle de Droits de l'Homme*, 1998/33(9).

Morawska E., 'The Principles of Subsidiarity and Effectiveness: Two Pillars of an Effective Remedy for Excessive Length of Proceedings within the Meaning of Article 13 ECHR', *Polish Yearbook of International Law*, 2019/39.

Prechal S., Widdershoven R., 'Redefining the Relationship between Rewe-effectiveness and Effective Judicial Protection', *Review of European Administrative Law*, 2011/4(2).

Reiertsen M., *Effective Domestic Remedies and the European Court of Human Rights*, Oxford 2022.

Safian M., Düsterhaus D., 'A Union of Effective Judicial Protection: Addressing a Multi-Level Challenge through the Lens of Article 47 CFREU', *Yearbook of European Law*, 2014/33.

Schabas W. A., *The European Convention on Human Rights: A Commentary*, Oxford 2015.

Shelton D., *Remedies in International Human Rights Law*, Oxford 2015.

Thiele C., 'Das Recht auf einen wirksamen Rechtsbehelf in vergleichender europäischer Perspektive', *ERA Forum*, 2015/16.

Zombory K., 'The right to an effective remedy: a key element for ensuring the effectiveness of the ECHR human rights system', [in:] A. Mezglewsky (ed.), *Efficiency of the Judiciary*, Warsaw 2023.

Dr. Aleksandra Komar-Nalepa[1]

III. Non-appealable nature of evidentiary decisions in appeal proceedings in Polish criminal trial from the perspective of the right to an effective remedy under Art. 13 ECHR

Abstract: The purpose of this paper is to draw attention to the issue of the lack of appealability of evidentiary decisions at the stage of appeal proceedings in the Polish criminal trial through the prism of the right to an effective remedy resulting from Art. 13 ECHR. With a significant expansion of the scope of evidentiary proceedings that may be conducted before an appellate court, the Polish legislator has also introduced new evidentiary restrictions. The most important of them is certainly the inability to present evidence that could have been called by the applicant before the first-instance court, or if the circumstance to be proven by a given evidence concerns a new fact that is not the subject of the proceedings before the first-instance court, and the applicant could then indicate.

The Author argues that a party who believes that his or her right to a fair criminal trial has been violated should, therefore, have access to at least one effective legal remedy to appeal against an unfavourable court's evidentiary decision. In this context, the inability to appeal in Polish criminal proceedings against the decision to dismiss an application for evidence by the appellate court at the stage of the pending proceedings, should be assessed as inconsistent with Art. 13 ECHR.

Keywords: Polish criminal procedure, effective justice, effective remedy, art. 13 ECHR, evidentiary decisions

1. Introduction

This chapter aims to draw attention to the issue of evidentiary decisions' inability to be appealed at the appeals stage in the Polish criminal trial through the prism of the right to an effective remedy resulting from Art. 13 ECHR.[2]

---

1 ORCID no. 0000-0001-5338-9935. Adjunct Professor at Department of International Criminal Procedure, Faculty of Law and Administration, University of Warsaw.

2 Convention for the Protection of Human Rights and Fundamental Freedoms (hereinafter referred to as ECHR or European Convention on Human Rights), adopted under the auspices of Council of Europe in Rome on November 4th, 1950, came into force on September 3rd, 1953, The Convention with all additional protocols is available on the website: https://www.echr.coe.int/documents/d/echr/convention_ENG [access on 24.01.2024]; hereinafter as "*ECHR*".

With a significant expansion of the scope of evidentiary proceedings that may be conducted before an appellate court, the Polish legislator has also introduced new evidentiary restrictions. The most important of them is certainly the inability to present evidence that the applicant could have called before the first-instance court or if the circumstance to be proven by a given evidence concerns a new fact that is not the subject of the proceedings before the first-instance court, and the applicant could then indicate it (Article 452 § 2 point 2 CCP[3] in connection with Article 427 § 3 CCP).

However, it is strictly stipulated that the request for evidence cannot be dismissed on the basis of the above premises in a situation where the circumstance to be proven, within the limits of the consideration of the case by the appellate court, is of significant importance for determining whether a prohibited act was committed at all, and if so, under what conditions it was committed, in order to impose an appropriate penalty or order stay in a psychiatric facility, the Polish legislator did not decide to provide the party with any remedy in this respect.

Meanwhile, there cannot be the slightest doubt that a possible incorrect assessment by the appellate court regarding the occurrence of any of the above-mentioned circumstances may directly affect the correctness of the substantive decision of the court. Thus, it may clearly and directly violate the principle of fairness of the criminal process specified in Art. 6 ECHR.

Therefore, ensuring an appropriate procedure for possible verification of the appellate court's position in the above respect seems necessary. In particular, as a rule, the party is no longer entitled to any further remedies against the substantive decision of the appellate court. Extraordinary remedies, such as cassation or a motion to reopen proceedings, may be brought in Polish criminal proceedings only in very limited subjective and objective situations.

Therefore, it is necessary to make de lege ferenda comments so that the Polish legal system has appropriate instruments to realize the right arising from Art. 13 ECHR.

2. The nature of evidentiary proceedings at the appeal stage in Polish criminal trial

As a result of changes introduced to Polish criminal procedure in 2015–2019, the scope of evidentiary proceedings in the appellate instance was significantly

---

3 Ustawa z dnia 6 czerwca 1997 r. - Kodeks postępowania karnego (Journal of Laws 1997, No. 89, Issue 555 with the amends.); hereinafter as "*Code of Criminal Procedure*", "*CCP*".

expanded. A fundamental change in the conduct of evidence before the appellate court was introduced by the amendment to the Code of Criminal Procedure of September 27th, 2013, which entered into force on July 1st, 2015.[4] Until that moment, the legislator had excluded the possibility of conducting evidentiary proceedings before the appellate court regarding the substance of the case.[5] After the amendment of March 11th, 2016,[6] entered into force,[7] the scope of evidentiary proceedings before the appellate court was further expanded.

A significant change in the content of Art. 452 CCP was also brought by the amendment of July 19th, 2019.[8] On the one hand, this act introduced a new, independent basis for rejecting an application for evidence, which is the fact that the evidence was not presented before the court of first instance, even though the applicant could have presented it at that time, or a circumstance which to be proven, concerns a new fact that is not the subject of the proceedings before the court of first instance, and the applicant could then indicate it (Article 452 § 2 point 2 CCP). On the other hand, pointing out that even if an application for evidence is submitted under the conditions specified above, it cannot be dismissed if the circumstance to be proven, within the limits of the consideration of the case by the appellate court, is significant for determining whether a prohibited act has been committed, whether it constitutes a crime and what it is, whether the prohibited act was committed in the conditions referred to in Art. 64 or art. 65 CC, or whether there are conditions for a stay in a psychiatric facility pursuant to Art. 93g CC (Article 452 § 3 CCP).

Currently, the ability of the appellate court to conduct evidentiary proceedings is limited only by the inadvisability of taking evidence for the reasons specified in Art. 437 § 2 sentence 2 CCP; the existence of a general basis for rejecting an application for evidence under Art. 170 CCP; or the existence of a specific basis for rejecting an application for evidence under Art. 452 § 2 point 2 in connection with § 3 CCP, which will be described in detail in further consideration.

---

4 Ustawa z dnia 27 września 2013 r. o zmianie ustawy - Kodeks postępowania karnego oraz niektórych innych ustaw (Journal of Laws 2013, issue 1247).

5 Article 452 § 1 of the CCP read as follows: "*The appellate court cannot conduct evidentiary proceedings as to the substance of the case.*" („*Sąd odwoławczy nie może przeprowadzić postępowania dowodowego co do istoty sprawy.*").

6 Ustawa z dnia 11 marca 2016 r. o zmianie ustawy - Kodeks postępowania karnego oraz niektórych innych ustaw (Journal of Laws 2016, issue 437).

7 April 15th, 2016.

8 Ustawa z dnia 19 lipca 2019 r. o zmianie ustawy - Kodeks postępowania karnego oraz niektórych innych ustaw (Journal of Laws 2019, issue 1694).

Therefore, actually, in Polish criminal trials, appeal proceedings are substantive in nature, not only of a control-oriented nature. The doctrine rightly emphasises that under Art. 437 § 2 sentence 2 CCP, the obligation of the appellate court is to rule in a reformatory manner. This obligation, combined with the power to conduct extensive evidentiary proceedings, means that the burden of substantive examination of the case also rests with the court of second instance.

However, this court's function is not to repeat the entire evidentiary proceedings but only to renew or supplement the evidence to the extent necessary for the proper conduct of the appellate review and to make truthful factual findings.[9]

Therefore, the appellate court is, in principle, supposed to adjudicate substantively,[10] including reforms, and can only issue a cassation judgment in three

---

9 D. Świecki [in:] D. Świecki, *KPK. Komentarz*, vol. 2, 2018, pp. 327–328; K. Woźniewski, 'Oddalenie wniosku dowodowego przez sąd odwoławczy na podstawie art. 452 § 2 k.p.k.', [in:] T. Grzegorczyk, R. Olszewski (eds), *Verba volant, scripta manent: proces karny, prawo karne skarbowe i prawo wykroczeń po zmianach z lat 2015–2016: księga pamiątkowa poświęcona Profesor Monice Zbrojewskiej*, Warszawa 2017, passim.

10 See judgement of the Polish Supreme Court – Criminal Law Section, 18.05.2023r., I KS 3/23. The Supreme Court stated that:

> '*1. The currently applicable provisions of criminal procedure (Article 437 § 1 and 2 of the Code of Criminal Procedure) establish the rule that the appellate court, after examining the case, issues a substantive judgment (upholding the contested judgment or amending the contested judgment), and not a cassatory judgment (reversing the contested judgment and transferring the case to the court of first instance for reconsideration). The possibility for the appellate court to issue the latter judgment is an exception, justified either by procedural limitations of the appellate court's adjudication freedom or by the occurrence of such gross irregularities in the proceedings of the first-instance court that even disqualify the proceedings before the court a quo as the basis for resolving the issue of the accused's criminal liability. This position and tasks of the appellate court, combined with the granting of broad powers in the field of evidentiary proceedings, was justified by the need to limit the number of cassatory judgments to situations in which remitting the case to the merits court was necessary to achieve the objectives of the criminal proceedings. 2. The finding of shortcomings in the evidentiary proceedings, which boil down to an incorrect assessment of some of the personal evidence, obliges the court of the second instance to independently correct these shortcomings by carrying out certain evidentiary activities on its own or by assessing them correctly, since the applicable regulations of the appeal procedure, including those resulting from Art. 452 of the Code of Criminal Procedure grant the appellate court broad powers to adjudicate, including on the basis of evidence conducted exclusively in this phase of the proceedings. Such a procedure would be out of the question only if the entire judicial process had to be conducted in the appeal proceedings.*'

cases precisely defined by the legislator (Article 437 § 2 sentence 2 CCP). These are the following situations: 1) when one of the absolute grounds for appeal specified in Art. 439 CCP,[11] 2) when it is necessary to convict the accused who was acquitted by the court of first instance (Article 454 § 1 CCP),[12] and

---

11 Absolute grounds for appeal are the most serious shortcomings which, while burdening the judgment, must always lead to its repeal. Their exhaustive catalogue is listed in Art. 439 § 1 CCP, which stipulates that regardless of the limits of the appeal and the allegations raised and the impact of the infringement on the content of the judgment, the appeal court shall repeal the contested judgment at a meeting if:

1) a person who was unauthorised or incapable of adjudicating or was subject to exclusion pursuant to Art. 40 CCP (iudex inhabilis),
2) the court was improperly staffed or any of its members were not present at the entire hearing,
3) a common court ruled in a case falling within the jurisdiction of a special court or a special court ruled in a case falling within the jurisdiction of a common court,
4) a lower court ruled on a case falling within the jurisdiction of a higher court,
5) a penalty, punitive measure, compensatory measure or security measure unknown to the law was imposed,
6) it was adopted in violation of the majority vote rule or was not signed by any of the persons involved in its issuance,
7) there is a contradiction in the content of the judgment that makes its execution impossible,
8) was issued despite the fact that criminal proceedings relating to the same act by the same person have already been legally concluded,
9) one of the circumstances excluding the proceedings specified in Art. 17 § 1 points 5, 6 and 8–11 CCP,
10) the accused in court proceedings did not have a defence lawyer in the cases specified in Art. 79 § 1 and 2 CCP and art. 80 CCP (obligatory defense), or the defender did not participate in activities in which his participation was mandatory,
11) the case was heard in the absence of the accused, whose presence was mandatory.

However, the legislator stipulates that the annulment of the judgment only for the reasons specified in § 1, points 9–11 may only be to the benefit of the accused (Article 439 § 2 CCP).

12 In the same judgment as above, the Supreme Court indicated that: '*The possibility of overturning an acquittal and remitting the case for retrial is related to the ne peius rule specified in Art. 454 § 1 of the Code of Criminal Procedure (Article 437 § 2, second sentence of the Code of Criminal Procedure) occurs only when the appellate court - as a result of removing the identified deficiencies constituting one of the grounds for appeal specified in Art. 438 points 1–3 of the Code of Criminal Procedure (e.g. after completing the evidentiary proceedings, properly assessing the evidence, and making correct factual findings) - states that there are grounds for issuing a conviction, which is, however, prevented by the prohibition specified in Art. 454 § 1 Code of Criminal Procedure.*'

3) when it is necessary to conduct the entire trial again (Article 437 § 2 sentence 2 CCP).[13]

As to what specific evidence may be taken before the appellate court, the catalogue is open, just like before the court of first instance. Most often, the judicial proceedings may be supplemented with evidence from personal evidence sources as well as from material sources. During evidentiary proceedings before the court of appeal, it is also permissible to read reporting documents (protocols) with the content of evidentiary statements (explanations and testimonies) recorded therein. If a party or the appellate court hears a witness, they not only can but should refer to the record of his testimony given earlier if, for example, the witness testifies clearly differently or declares that he does not remember certain circumstances (see Article 391 § 1 CCP). The same applies to the accused (Article 389 § 1 CCP) or the expert (Article 393 § 1 CCP), respectively.

It should be emphasised, however, that due to the complaint principle, evidentiary proceedings before the appellate court are limited by the limits of the appeal. This also means that if specific allegations are indicated in the appeal, evidentiary applications may also be submitted within the limits of these allegations. The appellate court is bound by the complaint both positively and negatively. On the one hand, it must thoroughly examine the appeal filed and address all the allegations contained therein. On the other hand, the content and scope of the appeal are limited by the appellate court as to the possibility of conducting an inspection.[14] The purpose of the appellate court is not to re-examine the case, but to review the judgment of the court of first instance, within which it may

---

13 See judgement of the Polish Supreme Court – Criminal Law Section, 4.07.2023r., II KS 16/23, *Prokuratura i Prawo*, 2023/11/61. The Supreme Court stated that: '*The appellate court conducting its own evidentiary proceedings is a rule, especially in the light of Art. 452 § 2 of the Code of Criminal Procedure Only exceptionally, when it is not possible to issue an accurate decision without renewing all the evidence, the appellate court may repeal the judgment of the court of first instance and refer the case for reconsideration.*'

14 Z. Doda, 'Konstrukcja granic środka odwoławczego w polskim prawie karnym procesowym', *Krakowskie Studia Prawnicze*, 1975/8, p. 52; see also S. Steinborn, 'O konsekwencjach nowego przepisu art. 447 § 3 k.p.k. dla wyznaczania granic zaskarżenia wyroku i dopuszczalności zaskarżania rozstrzygnięć negatywnych', *Kwartalnik Sądowy Apelacji Gdańskiej*, 2014/1, pp. 45 et seq.

and should carry out additional specific evidentiary activities to be able to issue a substantive decision.[15]

Therefore, issues that the parties do not make the subject of an appeal and possibly an appeal will be beyond the scope of the appeal court's decision in the appeal proceedings. In the doctrine of criminal proceedings, it is argued that this leads to the correct conclusion that strict evidence that may be admitted and then conducted before the appellate court may only serve to verify the validity of the appeal and the allegations raised therein.[16]

As in the proceedings before the court of first instance, the court may also take evidence both at the request of the parties and ex officio in the appeal proceedings. However, the parties must remember the evidentiary exclusion introduced by the legislator. Pursuant to Art. 427 § 3 CCP, the appellant may indicate new facts or evidence, but only if he was unable to present them in the proceedings before the court of first instance. As a rule, a party should not leave key, favourable evidence for appeal, as it may be dismissed for this reason.

As it was already mentioned in the proceedings before the court of first instance, an application for evidence may be dismissed only in situations indicated explicitly by the legislator, specified in Art. 170 § 1 CCP - i.e. when: 1) taking evidence is inadmissible; 2) the fact to be proven is irrelevant to the resolution of the case or has already been proven in accordance with the applicant's claim; 3) the evidence is useless to establish a given circumstance; 4) the evidence cannot be taken; 5) the request for evidence clearly aims to prolong the proceedings; 6) the request for evidence was submitted after the deadline set by the procedural authority, about which the party submitting the request was notified.

At the same time, however, the court cannot dismiss a request for evidence since it obviously aims to prolong the proceedings or that it was submitted after the deadline set by the procedural authority if the fact to be proven is important for determining whether a prohibited act has been committed, whether it constitutes a crime and what kind, whether the prohibited act was committed in the

15 See Decision of the Polish Supreme Court, 17.12.2020 r., V KK 280/19, OSNKW 2021, No 2, item 9. The Supreme Court stated that: '*In the current model of appeal proceedings, the court of second instance does not re-examine the case, but reviews (essentially within the limits of the appeal and - if indicated - the allegations raised) the judgment of the court of first instance. Therefore, the appellate court only takes supplementary evidence because it does so - as a rule - within the limits of appellate review (Article 433 § 1 of the Code of Criminal Procedure).*'

16 S. Steinborn, *Postępowanie*, *op.cit.*, pp. 155–156; A. Sakowicz, *Postępowanie*, *op.cit.*, p. 463.

context of recidivism or obtaining a permanent source of income from committing crimes, or whether there are conditions for a stay in a psychiatric facility as part of the need to apply a protective measure against the perpetrator, to whom no blame can be assigned (art. 170 § 1a CCP). Moreover, the court cannot dismiss an evidentiary request on the grounds that the evidence so far has shown the opposite of what the applicant intends to prove. The appellate court, in turn, in addition to the grounds for dismissing the evidence application described above, should also refuse to take evidence when it would be pointless due to the need to overturn the judgment and refer the case for reconsideration to the first-instance court[17] or if the evidence was not called before the first-instance court, even though the applicant could then have cited it, or the fact to be proven concerns a new fact which is not the subject of the proceedings before the court of first instance, and the applicant could then have indicated it (Article 452 § 2 of the CCP). Content of article 452 § 2 of the Code of Criminal Procedure, therefore, refers to the evidentiary exclusion resulting from Art. 427 § 3 CCP, according to which the appellant may indicate new facts or evidence in the appeal if he was unable to present them in the proceedings before the court of first instance.

These provisions also define the terms "new facts" and "new evidence". The doctrine emphasises that: 1) only evidence that could not be adduced before the court of first instance should be considered new evidence that may be admitted in the appeal proceedings at the request of a party; 2) a new fact subject to proof in the appellate instance will be one that could not be indicated before the court of first instance. Therefore, it will be entirely possible and justified to submit an evidentiary request for additional taking of evidence in the appellate instance for a circumstance that could not be established during the proceedings before the first-instance court, e.g. the questioned witness learned about new facts after the hearing. However, it is excluded to request a supplementary hearing of a witness regarding facts that he knew about during the hearing before the court of first instance but was not asked about them at that time. The reasons why the

17 See judgement of the Polish Supreme Court – Criminal Law Section, 4.07.2023r., II KS 16/23, *Prokuratura i Prawo*, 2023/11/61. The Supreme Court stated that: '*The premise of "the need to re-run the proceedings in their entirety" is only valid when, in the first-instance proceedings, there has been a violation of the norms of procedural law which, in the circumstances of a specific case, undermines the reliability of the entire proceedings, which argues for repeating (re-conducting) all procedural activities. constituting the judicial proceedings in the court of first instance.*'

complainant did not ask the witness about these circumstances at that time are irrelevant.[18]

It should be recalled, however, that the appellate court may never dismiss an evidentiary request on the basis described above if the circumstance to be proven is important for determining whether a prohibited act has been committed, whether it constitutes a crime and what, whether the prohibited act was committed under conditions recidivism or obtaining a permanent source of income from committing crimes, or whether there are conditions for a stay in a psychiatric facility as part of the need to apply a protective measure to a perpetrator who cannot be blamed.

3. The right to an effective remedy stated in art. 13 ECHR

The right to an effective remedy, specified in Art. 13 ECHR, should be read in procedural and substantive terms. Due to the fact that the ECHR does not introduce any legal definition in this respect, the nature and scope of application of Art. 13 ECHR had to be developed by the doctrine and case law of the ECtHR.[19]

Thus, an effective remedy in the procedural aspect is the possibility of appealing against decisions that, in the complainant's opinion, violate his rights under the Convention. In turn, the substantive aspect comes down to the possible result of examining such an appeal.[20]

---

18 See A. Komar, S. Pawelec, 'Zakres postępowania dowodowego w postępowaniu odwoławczym. Uwagi de lege lata i de lege ferenda', [in:] A. Lach (ed.), *Postępowanie dowodowe w świetle nowelizacji kodeksu postępowania karnego*, Warszawa 2014, p. 194.

19 See: D. Shelton, *Remedies in International Human Rights Law*, Oxford 2015, p. 7; K. Zombory, 'The right to an effective remedy: a key element for ensuring the effectiveness of the ECHR system – the example of Poland and Hungary', [in:] *Efficiency of the Judiciary*, Wydawnictwo Instytutu Wymiaru Sprawiedliwości, Warszawa 2023, pp. 206–207; K. Gutman, 'The Essence of the Fundamental Right to an Effective Remedy and to a Fair Trial in the Case-Law of the Court of Justice of the European Union: The Best Is Yet to Come?', *German Law Journal*, 2019/20(6), pp. 887–888.

20 Cf. K. Zombory, 'The right', *op.cit.*, pp. 206–207; see also S. Allegrezza, 'Judicial Review as a Fundamental Right', [in:] S. Allegrezza, V. Covolo (eds.), *Effective Defence Rights in Criminal Proceedings*, Milan 2018, pp. 97–131; V. Covolo, 'Guarantees of Judicial Protection Under the ECHR: What Interactions With EU Law?', [in:] S. Allegrezza, V. Covolo (eds.), *Effective*, *op.cit.*, pp. 133–159.

Unfortunately, the Convention does not specify in any respect what remedies must be provided in national legal systems in the light of Art. 13 ECHR. It does not even specify what general nature the measure is to be (complaint to a common court, constitutional complaint) or how it should be considered (in court proceedings, in administrative proceedings or in a procedure specially created for this purpose).

However, the ECtHR has repeatedly emphasised that the content of Art. 13 ECHR requires that where a person considers that he has suffered prejudice as a result of a measure allegedly in breach of the Convention, he must have recourse to a remedy before a national authority in order both to consider his claim and, where appropriate, to obtain appropriate redress.[21]

States parties, therefore, have a wide degree of freedom in selecting appropriate legal remedies in their domestic domestic systems. However, it must be an "effective" and "available" measure both in practice and theory and the use of "measures" cannot be unjustifiably prevented by actions or omissions of state authorities.[22]

In the light of the Tribunal's case law, the remedy within the meaning of Art. 13 ECHR must also provide minimum guarantees for the speed of proceedings because a measure that does not bring results in due time is insufficient and ineffective.[23] However, this remedy does not have to guarantee the certainty of a favourable decision for the complainant. The only important thing is that the body examining the appeal is competent to make a substantive decision in a given scope.[24]

---

21 ECtHR, Case *Klass and others v. Germany*, judgement of September 6th, 1978, Application no. 5029/71, para. 64.

22 ECtHR, Case *Urbańczyk v. Poland*, decision of May 28th, 2006, Application no. 33777/96, HUDOC; ECtHR, Case *Jakub v. Slovakia*, judgement of February 28th, 2006, Application no. 2015/02, HUDOC.)

23 ECtHR, Case *Pine Valley Developments Ltd and Others v. Ireland*, judgment of November 29th, 1991; ECtHR Case *Payet v. France*, judgment of January 20th, 2011, Application no. 19606/08, HUDOC.

24 In the case *Soering v. Great Britain*, stating that pursuant to Art. 13, there is no requirement for the complainant to obtain a favourable decision, the Tribunal emphasised that it was only a matter of the authority examining the case to issue such a decision if they accepted the complainant's arguments. ECtHR, Case *Soering v. Great Britain*, judgement of July 7th, 1989, A 161, para 120, HUDOC.)

Moreover, the Tribunal emphasises that in light of Art. 13 ECHR, a complaint must be an ordinary remedy, i.e., it must be available to the entity whose rights have been violated. Therefore, extraordinary remedies or the possibility of submitting a request to bodies such as the Minister of Justice or the Ombudsman do not meet this criterion. The decision of such bodies is discretionary.

4. Non-appealability of decisions rejecting evidence applications in appeal proceedings and the guarantees arising from Art. 13 ECHR

There can be no doubt that the changes introduced in Polish criminal procedure in recent years, particularly the extension of the scope of evidentiary proceedings that can be conducted before the appellate court, were aimed at streamlining and speeding up the proceedings.[25]

The new model of appeal proceedings, aimed primarily at reformative adjudication and thus limiting the possibility of cassation adjudication only to circumstances specifically indicated by the legislator, is intended to limit the lengthiness of criminal proceedings. The frequent use by appellate courts of cassation judgments and remitting cases for reconsideration by courts of first instance, in the legal status before July 1st, 2015, was undoubtedly one of the main factors contributing to the prolongation of the proceedings.[26]

It is necessary to point out that the above-described significant extension of the scope of evidentiary proceedings before the appellate court, the purpose of which is to issue a reform judgment, is consistent with the standard of two-instance proceedings specified in Art. 78 and art. 176 Section 1 of the Constitution of the Republic of Poland.[27] On constitutional grounds, this principle is understood in a formal, not substantive, sense. This means that there is no requirement for each

25 T. Grzegorczyk, 'Ku usprawnieniu postępowania apelacyjnego i szerszemu reformatoryjnemu orzekaniu przez sąd odwoławczy', [in:] P. Hofmański (ed.), *Fiat iustitia pereat mundus. Księga jubileuszowa poświęcona Sędziemu Sądu Najwyższego Stanisławowi Zabłockiemu z okazji 40-lecia pracy zawodowej*, Warszawa 2014, pp. 154–155.

26 See justification of the draft amendment act, parliamentary form 870/VII; T. Grzegorczyk, 'Podstawowe kierunki projektowanych zmian procedury karnej', *Państwo i Prawo*, 2012/11, p. 26;

27 Konstytucja Rzeczypospolitej Polskiej z dnia 2 kwietnia 1997 roku, Polish Journal of Laws, No. 78, Issue. 483.

factual finding to be made by the first-instance court and then subject to review by the appellate court.[28]

In the above context, however, an important circumstance should be mentioned. In the light of Art. 170 § 3 CCP, rejection of an application for evidence must be made in the form of a decision[29] that is not subject to appeal (Article 459 § 1 CCP). This decision does not have substantive finality,[30] and therefore, it is possible to repeat the same evidence requests even many times, but it is impossible to cause any review of the court's decision in this respect by another independent court or only by another composition of the same court.

While in the case of evidentiary decisions issued in proceedings before the court of first instance, the inability to appeal against them by filing a complaint is compensated by the possibility of formulating appropriate appeal grounds in this respect (Article 447 § 4 CCP), in the case of decisions rejecting the application evidence at the stage of appeal proceedings, the inability to file a complaint against it should be considered problematic.

---

28 S. Steinborn, *Postępowanie dowodowe w instancji apelacyjnej w świetle nowelizacji kodeksu postępowania karnego*, 1–2 Prokuratura i Prawo 2015, pp. 161–165; D. Świecki, 'Konstytucyjna zasada dwuinstancyjności postępowania sądowego a możliwość reformatoryjnego orzekania w instancji odwoławczej w świetle wchodzącej w życie 1 lipca 2015r. nowelizacji kodeksu postępowania karnego', [in:] T. Grzegorczyk (ed.) *Polski proces karny i materialne prawo karne w świetle nowelizacji z 2013 roku. Księga jubileuszowa dedykowana Profesorowi Januszowi Tylmanowi z okazji Jego 90. Urodzin*, Warszawa 2014, pp. 222–223; P. Hofmański, S. Zabłocki, 'Dowodzenie w postępowaniu apelacyjnym i kasacyjnym – kwestie modelowe', [in:] T. Grzegorczyk (ed.), *Funkcje procesu karnego. Księga jubileuszowa Profesora Janusza Tylmana*, Warszawa 2011, pp. 473–474; W. Hermeliński, B. Nita, 'Orzekanie reformatoryjne na podstawie nowych ustaleń faktycznych w postępowaniu karnym', *Państwo i Prawo* 2009/9, p. 167.

29 Sąd Najwyższy (The Supreme Court) has repeatedly emphasised in its jurisprudence that failure to issue a decision to reject a request for evidence is always a gross violation of Art. 170 § 3 CCP, as it makes it impossible to learn the position of the procedural authority in this regard. Proper handling of the parties' requests for evidence is a very important element of the substantive right to defence and the guarantee of an adversarial form of a fair trial (see judgement of the Polish Supreme Court – Criminal Law Section, 11.1.2012 r., III KK 182/11, Legalis; judgement of Polish Supreme Court, 14.5.2019 r., II KK 284/18, Legalis).

30 See judgement of the Polish Supreme Court – Criminal Law Section, 28.04.2011r., V KK 316/10, Legalis. The Supreme Court expressis verbis stated that: '*The decision on taking evidence, whether positive or negative, does not become substantive final and may be changed by the adjudicating court. This is especially justified when new circumstances become known after the decision is issued.*'

In particular, the purpose of the evidentiary proceedings conducted by the appellate court is to issue a judgment of a reformatory nature, which may be different from the judgment of the court of first instance, against which the parties are no longer entitled to any other ordinary means of appeal. The pursuit of ensuring the speed and efficiency of the proceedings cannot, under any circumstances, be at the expense of the reliability of the process and the truthfulness of the factual findings made. The criminal trial should, of course, be as short as possible, but above all, it must be reliable and fair, which is impossible without true factual findings. This was emphasised many times in the case law of the ECtHR.

For example, in the case of *Boddaert v. Belgium*, the Tribunal emphasised that the speed of adjudication cannot constitute an obstacle to the proper functioning of the justice system. However, the Tribunal considers it unnecessary to care that the decision is based on the correct basis factual findings made in compliance with the requirements of fairness of the proceedings.[31] The ECtHR also indicated, among other things, that the proceedings must be speedy "reasonable" (so "reasonable haste" is required), therefore, cannot take place at the expense of factual findings made;[32] haste in conducting proceedings must be "moderate" and speed of proceedings cannot be an end in itself;[33] the speed of proceedings cannot be achieved at any cost, at the expense of the reliability of the examination of the case, because the reliability of the proceedings is the overriding requirement resulting from Art. 6 ECHR.[34]

31 ECtHR, Case *Boddaert v. Belgium*, judgment of October 12th, 1992, HUDOC.

32 ECtHR, Case *Ognyanova i Choban v. Bulgary*, judgment of February 23rd, 2006, Application no. 46317/99, HUDOC; ECtHR, Case *Şeker v. Turkey*, judgment of February 21st, 2006, Application no. 52390/99, HUDOC, ECtHR, Case *Toğcu v. Turkey*, judgment of May 31st, 2005, Application no. 27601/95, HUDOC, ECtHR, Case *Nesibe Haran v. Turkey*, judgment of October 6th, 2005, Application no. 28299/95, HUDOC.

33 ECtHR, Case *Mojsiejew v. Poland*, judgment of March 24th, 2009, Application no. 11818/02, HUDOC.

ECtHR, Case *Dizman v. Turkey*, judgment of September 20th, 2005, Application no. 27309/05, HUDOC.

34 ECtHR, Case *Laskowska v. Poland*, judgment of March 13th, 2007, Application no. 77765/01, HUDOC.

As already mentioned above, in Polish criminal procedure, any decision to dismiss an application for evidence issued by the court of first instance may be used by a party dissatisfied with the judgment to formulate an appropriate appeal. Raising a violation of the provisions of procedural law in this respect, i.e. an allegation of violation of a specific point of Art. 170 § 1 CCP, the party should request that the appellate court take evidence that the court of first instance refused to take. Therefore, despite the lack of a separate complaint against the decision to reject the request for evidence, the party has the means to verify the decision of the court of first instance in this matter. It should be noted that this method meets the requirement that the complaint be of an ordinary nature. In Polish criminal proceedings, each judgment issued by the court of first instance may be subject to an ordinary means of appeal in the form of an appeal. This procedure, therefore, meets the requirements of Art. 13 ECHR.

Unfortunately, the situation is different in the context of appeal proceedings. With the extension of the scope of appeal proceedings before this court and at the same time with the introduction of new grounds for dismissing evidence applications, there is undoubtedly also a risk of erroneous court decisions in this respect. A decision to dismiss a request for evidence, the purpose of which is, in principle, always to contribute to correct factual findings, may certainly violate the party's right to a fair criminal trial. In this respect, there can be no doubt that the party should be provided with an appropriate remedy that would enable it to subject the evidentiary decision of the appellate court to review in accordance with the standards resulting from Art. 13 ECHR.

Meanwhile, in the current legal situation, there is no such right. The appellate court's judgment is final upon announcement and is not subject to further appeal under ordinary appeals. Although Polish criminal procedure is familiar with extraordinary remedies - cassation,[35] motion to reopen

---

35 Cassation is an extraordinary remedy available against a final judgment of the appellate court ending the proceedings and against a final decision of the appellate court to discontinue the proceedings and apply a protective measure specified in Art. 93a of the Penal Code, a cassation appeal may be filed (art. 519 CCP). What is very important, however, is that, as a rule, a cassation appeal in favour of the accused may be filed only if he is sentenced for a crime or a fiscal offence and is sentenced to imprisonment without conditional suspension of its execution, while a cassation appeal to the detriment of the accused may only be filed if he is acquitted or the proceedings are discontinued (art. 523 § 2 and 3 CCP). Moreover, a party that has not appealed against the decision of the Court of First Instance cannot file a cassation appeal against the decision of the Court of Appeal if the decision of the Court of First Instance has been upheld or changed in its favour (art. 520 § 2 CCP).

proceedings[36] and complaint against the judgment of the appellate court[37] - the legislator has introduced numerous subjective and objective restrictions in the procedure for filing them. However, apart from purely formal issues, in none of the extraordinary remedies known to the Polish procedure can an allegation of error in determining the facts be raised, which in practice must ultimately amount to the failure to use specific means of evidence. The subject of cassation may only concern circumstances constituting the so-called absolute reasons for appeal or other gross violations of law if it could have a significant impact on the content of the judgment. In turn, the subject of an application to reopen proceedings may be new facts or evidence, but only those disclosed after the issuance of a final judgment and indicating that the convicted person did not commit an act or his act did not constitute a crime or was not subject to punishment; he was convicted of an offence punishable by a more severe penalty, or the circumstances

---

36 An application to reopen proceedings is an extraordinary means of appeal that serves to reopen proceedings ended with a final court judgment in situations where:

1) an offense was committed in connection with the proceedings, and there are reasonable grounds for assuming that this could have influenced the content of the judgment;
2) after the judgment is issued, new facts or evidence are revealed indicating that:
   a) the convicted person did not commit an act or his act did not constitute a crime or was not subject to punishment,
   b) he was convicted of an offense punishable by a more severe penalty, or the circumstances requiring extraordinary leniency of the penalty were not taken into account, or the circumstances leading to an extraordinary tightening of the penalty were incorrectly assumed,
   c) the court discontinued or conditionally discontinued the criminal proceedings, wrongly assuming that the accused had committed the offense with which he was charged. Moreover, the proceedings are resumed in favor of the party: 1) if the Constitutional Tribunal has ruled that the legal provision on the basis of which the judgment was issued is inconsistent with the Constitution, a ratified international agreement or an act; the reopening cannot be to the detriment of the accused; 2) when such a need results from a decision of an international body acting under an international agreement ratified by the Republic of Poland (art. 540 CCP). In addition, the legislator provides specific grounds for renewal specified in Art. 540a and 540b CCP.

37 An appeal against the judgment of the appellate court overturning the judgment of the first instance court and remitting the case for reconsideration may be brought by the parties to the Supreme Court. However, it may only be brought due to a violation of Art. 437 CCP or due to deficiencies specified in Art. 439 § 1 CCP.

requiring extraordinary leniency of the penalty were not taken into account, or the circumstances leading to an extraordinary tightening of the penalty were incorrectly assumed; the court discontinued or conditionally discontinued the criminal proceedings, wrongly assuming that the accused had committed the offence he was charged with.

Therefore, it should be held that the extension of the scope of evidentiary proceedings before the appellate court, aimed primarily at enabling appellate courts to issue reform judgments, while at the same time failing to provide the parties to the proceedings with appropriate means to challenge the evidentiary decisions of the appellate court (and therefore the court of last instance), remains incompatible with the standards resulting from Art. 13 ECHR. The parties to a criminal trial do not have any means of appeal in the national legal system regarding the evidentiary decisions of the appellate court, which may violate their right to a fair criminal trial.

5. Final remarks - in search of an effective remedy

To sum up the considerations so far, it should be stated that any incorrect decision regarding the admission and taking of evidence by the court, whose task is to issue a judgment on the merits of the case, should have its consequences. A party who believes that his or her right to a fair criminal trial has been violated should, therefore, have access to at least one effective legal remedy to appeal against an unfavourable court's evidentiary decision.

As follows from the above-mentioned case law of the ECtHR, an appeal must provide minimum guarantees for the speed of proceedings in order to meet the standards of effectiveness established by Art. 13 ECHR. A measure that does not bring results in due time is insufficient and ineffective.

In this context, the inability to appeal in Polish criminal proceedings against the decision to dismiss an application for evidence by the appellate court at the stage of the pending proceedings should be assessed as inconsistent with Art. 13 ECHR. Since the appellate court may also take evidence unknown to the first-instance court and, on its basis, issue a substantive decision in the case, the party should be able to have the court's specific position in the above respect verified by another independent body. It is important that an appropriate appeal can be brought during this particular proceeding so as to remedy the effects of the defective decision as quickly as possible.

In view of the above, it seems absolutely necessary to introduce a separate incidental appeal into the Polish criminal process, which will enable an appeal against a decision of evidence unfavourable to a party. Due to the nature of the decision to be appealed against, it would be advisable to consider making a complaint to another panel of judges within the same court. Moreover, it would be necessary to specify the time within which the complaint should be examined, provided that until it is examined, no substantive decision in the main case can be made.

Bibliography

Allegrezza S., '*Judicial Review as a Fundamental Right*', [in:] S. Allegrezza & V. Covolo (eds.), *Effective Defence Rights in Criminal Proceedings*, Milan 2018.

Covolo V., 'Guarantees of Judicial Protection Under the ECHR: What Interactions With EU Law?', [in:] Allegrezza S. & Covolo V.(eds.), *Effective Defence Rights in Criminal Proceedings*, Milan 2018.

Doda Z., 'Konstrukcja granic środka odwoławczego w polskim prawie karnym procesowym', *Krakowskie Studia Prawnicze*, 1975/8.

Garlicki L., *Implementacja orzecznictwa Europejskiego Trybunału Praw Człowieka w ustawodawstwie krajowym (problemy przewlekłości postępowania)*, Biuletyn Biura Informacji Rady Europy. Wybór orzecznictwa Europejskiego Trybunału Praw Człowieka w sprawach polskich 2002.

Guide on Article 13 of the European Convention on Human Rights – Right to an effective remedy, updated on August 2022, Council of Europe/European Court of Human Rights, 2022.

Gutman K., 'The Essence of the Fundamental Right to an Effective Remedy and to a Fair Trial in the Case-Law of the Court of Justice of the European Union: The Best Is Yet to Come?', *German Law Journal*, 2019/ 20 (6), Special Issue.

Grzegorczyk T., 'Ku usprawnieniu postępowania apelacyjnego i szerszemu reformatoryjnemu orzekaniu przez sąd odwoławczy', [in:] P. Hofmański (ed.), *Fiat iustitia pereat mundus. Księga jubileuszowa poświęcona Sędziemu Sądu Najwyższego Stanisławowi Zabłockiemu z okazji 40-lecia pracy zawodowej*, Warszawa 2014.

Grzegorczyk T., 'Podstawowe kierunki projektowanych zmian procedury karnej', *Państwo i Prawo*, 2012/11.

Hermeliński W., Nita B., 'Orzekanie reformatoryjne na podstawie nowych ustaleń faktycznych w postępowaniu karnym', *Państwo i Prawo*, 2009/9.

Hofmański P., Zabłocki S., 'Dowodzenie w postępowaniu apelacyjnym i kasacyjnym – kwestie modelowe', [in:] Grzegorczyk T. (ed.), *Funkcje procesu karnego. Księga jubileuszowa Profesora Janusza Tylmana*, Warszawa 2011.

Holoubek M., ‚Das Recht auf eine wirksame Beschwerde bei einer nationaken Ibstanz. ZurBedeutung des Art. 13 EMRK', *Juristische Blätter*, Heft 3, März 1992.

Komar A., Pawelec S., 'Zakres postępowania dowodowego w postępowaniu odwoławczym. Uwagi de lege lata i de lege ferenda', [in:] A. Lach (ed.), *Postępowanie dowodowe w świetle nowelizacji kodeksu postępowania karnego*, Warszawa 2014.

Kuijer M., 'The Right to a Fair Trial and the Council of Europe's Efforts to Ensure Effective Remedies on a Domestic Level for Excessively Lengthy Proceedings', *Human Rights Law Review*, 2013/ 4.

Morawska E., 'The Principles of Subsidiarity and Effectiveness: Two Pillars of an Effective Remedy for Excessive Length of Proceedings within the Meaning of Article 13 ECHR', *Polish Yearbook of International Law*, 2019/39.

Nowicki M. A., *Europejska Konwencja Praw Człowieka. Wybór orzecznictwa*, Warszawa 1998.

Shelton D., *Remedies in International Human Rights Law*, Oxford 2015.

Steinborn S., 'O konsekwencjach nowego przepisu art. 447 § 3 k.p.k. dla wyznaczania granic zaskarżenia wyroku i dopuszczalności zaskarżania rozstrzygnięć negatywnych', *Kwartalnik Sądowy Apelacji Gdańskiej*, 2014/1.

Steinborn S., 'Postępowanie dowodowe w instancji apelacyjnej w świetle nowelizacji kodeksu postępowania karnego', *Prokuratura i Prawo*, 2015/1–2.

Świda Z., 'Właściwość sądu i prawo strony do rozstrzygnięcia sprawy „w rozsądnym terminie"', *Państwo i Prawo*, 2005/10.

Świecki D. [in:] D. Świecki, *KPK. Komentarz*, vol. 2, 2018.

Świecki D., 'Konstytucyjna zasada dwuinstancyjności postępowania sądowego a możliwość reformatoryjnego orzekania w instancji odwoławczej w świetle wchodzącej w życie 1 lipca 2015r. nowelizacji kodeksu postępowania karnego', [in:] T. Grzegorczyk (ed.), *Polski proces karny i materialne prawo karne w świetle nowelizacji z 2013 roku. Księga jubileuszowa dedykowana Profesorowi Januszowi Tylmanowi z okazji Jego 90. Urodzin*, Warszawa 2014.

Teleki C., *Due Process and Fair Trial in EU Competition Law*, Leiden-Boston 2021.

Woźniewski K., '*Oddalenie wniosku dowodowego przez sąd odwoławczy na podstawie art. 452 § 2 k.p.k.*', [in:] Grzegorczyk T., Olszewski R. (eds.), *Verba volant, scripta manent: proces karny, prawo karne skarbowe i prawo wykroczeń po zmianach z lat 2015–2016: księga pamiątkowa poświęcona Profesor Monice Zbrojewskiej*, Warszawa 2017.

Vospernik T., *Das Verhältnis zwischen Art. 13 und Art. 6 EMRK – Absorption oder "Apfel und Birne"?*, Österreische Juristen-Zeitung, vol. 56, Heft 10 (2001)

Zombory K., 'The right to an effective remedy: a key element for ensuring the effectiveness of the ECHR system – the example of Poland and Hungary', [in:] *Efficiency of the Judiciary*, Wydawnictwo Instytutu Wymiaru Sprawiedliwości: Warszawa 2023.

Dr. Emanuele Toma[1]

IV. Evidentiary misbehaviors and their consequences

Abstract: The main objective of this study will be to examine how to find an effective remedy to this kind of evidentiary misbehaviour, and, to do so, we will examine the implication of fair trial and due process principles and of Constitutional exclusionary rules. Finding a good compromise between limiting unlawful intermissions with the individual's fundamental rights and the collectivity's need to prosecute crimes and punish their perpetrators is a hard task. This balance is found in the remedies provided by the system. These remedies should be differently shaped depending on the country's system, but always consider that a constitution, as any other law, is, in the first place, a source of rules. If the law provides for the procedure for taking evidence, it should also provide for the consequences of its violations.

Keywords: evidence, Italian criminal procedure, exclusionary rules, effective remedy, fair trial

1. An introduction about criminal systems

Defining evidentiary rules often means shaping the essence of a criminal trial, and it represents one of the most immediate applications of its general principles. Allowing the judge to take the initiative, giving the prosecution and the defence the same powers, electing which should be the conditions to admit a piece of evidence and exclude another, or settling the evidentiary procedure and the consequences of its violation are all clear examples of how much that choice may condition the overall structure of a trial.[2]

When studying the founding principles of a criminal proceeding, many scholars have wondered: "*What distinguishes an adversarial system from an inquisitory*

1 ORCID no. 0000-0002-6114-2120. Assistant Professor at University of Rome La Sapienza.

2 On this subject, see, among many others, K. Ambos, 'International Criminal Procedure: 'Adversarial', 'Inquisitorial' or Mixed?', *Third International Criminal Law Review*, 2003/3, pp. 1–37; P. Ferrua, Processo penale tra modello inquisitorio e modello accusatorio, *Penale diritto e procedura*, May 24th, 2022.

system?". This question, which some nowadays deem obsolete,[3] reveals itself as a valuable understanding tool. An adversarial system may be defined as "*characterised by an impartial decision-maker who evaluates contrasting presentations by adversaries to a dispute, evaluates the merits of those presentations, and renders a decision that distributes a positive outcome to one party and a corresponding negative outcome to the other*",[4] the inquisitorial system "*is characterised by a decision-maker who retains substantial power to elicit evidence in an inquiry aimed at discovering the facts underlying a dispute*".[5] Still, a question remains: "*Why do many give such a definitive value to whether the judge withholds any evidentiary power and to what extent he does?*".[6]

Even if it's unlikely – or probably impossible – to find those systems in their pure forms, it can't be denied how useful it is to understand that what's the ideological choice that seems to build the two systems. That choice appears to be based on the different premise that the "*truth*" may or may not always be achieved through a trial. An inquisitorial system assumes the truth may always be reached in a Court of law, consequently making it indispensable to give significant evidentiary powers to the decision-maker: taking one away means risking the exclusion of one of the tools the judge may employ to reach that truth. On the contrary, an adversarial system revolves around the idea that a trial held may always be fallacious to some degree, and – because of that – one must keep in mind that the "truth" achieved may not be the correct reconstruction of the facts. Nonetheless,

---

3 See K. Ambos, 'International Criminal Procedure', loc.cit. The author highlights how it may be anachronistic to try to differentiate the systems based on this distinction nowadays since trials in common law and civil law countries should only consider whether the system assists the Tribunals in accomplishing their tasks and whether it complies with fundamental fair trial standards.

4 See J. Sevier, 'The truth-justice tradeoff: Perceptions of decisional accuracy and procedural justice in adversarial and inquisitorial legal systems', *Psychology, Public Policy, and Law*, 2014/20(2), pp. 212–224, available at: https://doi.org/10.1037/law0000009. See also J. Thibaut, L. Walker, 'A theory of procedure', *California Law Review*, 1978/66, pp. 541–566.

5 See, J. Sevier, *The truth-justice*, *op.cit.*, pp. 212–224. See also H.F.M. Crombag, 'Adversarial or inquisitorial: Do we have a choice?', [in:] P.J. Van Koppen, S.D. Penrod (eds.), *Adversarial versus Inquisitorial Justice: Psychological perspectives on criminal justice systems*, New York 2003, pp. 21–25.

6 The evidence's discipline (initiative, equal powers between prosecution and defence, *etc.*) isn't the only feature distinguishing the two systems. Considering that no country ever adopted a purely adversarial or inquisitorial system, many believe other distinguishing features to be the possibility of preventive custody of the perpetrator, the presumption of guilt, the secrecy of the trial, or the distinction between decision-maker and prosecutor.

given the primary importance of a well-functioning crime prevention and punishment system, adversarial systems aim to correct this flaw by providing stricter rules for the evidence acquisition process. This brings a tendency to exclude all evidence obtained without evaluating the contrasting presentation of the parties: the facts that are the object of dispute between two parties with the same powers are the only ones reliable enough to justify a conviction.

Ultimately, adversarial systems put the relevance of the quality of evidence above its quantity.[7]

To better understand the concept, Professor Giostra[8] used a clever metaphor to describe a criminal trial as a precarious Tibetan bridge connecting the *res iudicanda* (thing to be judged) to the *res iudicata pro veritate habetur* (the thing judged as if it were the truth). This also highlights another feature of adversarial systems that may otherwise seem secondary. Given the fundamental impossibility of being certain that the reached reconstruction of the events is, in fact, correct, the means employed to get the truth must be carefully selected and must respect many rules. This makes it so that the evidence collected may be more reliable, which is what the statute of an adversarial principle tends to do.[9]

Given these premises, it should now be easy for the reader to understand how central the discipline of evidence in a criminal trial is, how potentially dangerous the misbehaviors in the procedures are, and how necessary it is to identify the flaws and their consequences.

---

7 On the specific subject of the differences between adversarial and inquisitorial systems, in relation to the Italian and Brazilian experiences, see B. Cunha Souza – E. Toma, 'Il contraddittorio, il giudice e i fascicoli nei sistemi processuali penali del brasile e d'italia', *Revista Antinomias*, 2023/1, p. 8.

8 G. Giostra, *Prima lezione sulla giustizia penale*, Rome 2022.

9 Which can be resumed in the right of each party concerned in a legal procedure to be duly summoned and given a chance to assert their rights and present their arguments. Many Scholars have tried to give their interpretation of the principle, distinguishing between a 'full contradictory' and a 'weak contradictory' between the parties (see G. Giostra, 'Contraddittorio (principio del)', *Enceclopedia giuridica Treccani*, 2021/3, p. 1; and G. Lozzi, 'I principi dell'oralità e del contraddittorio nel processo penale', *Rivista Italiana di Diritto e procedura penale*, 1997/3, p. 690) or, in an even more interesting categorisation, between 'contradictory for the evidence' and 'contradictory about the evidence' (conceived by D. Siracusano, 'Il contraddittorio tra Costituzione e legge ordinaria', *Diritto penale e processo* 2000/11, p. 1425). In this last reconstruction, the Professor differentiates between an imperfect realisation of the principle, where parties would only be able to contradict each other regarding the meaning to be given to evidence, and a perfect one, in which parties are opposed and called to intervene since the preliminary phases of the evidentiary process, opposing to its admissibility and conducting the taking in itself.

Nonetheless, even in adversarial systems, extending too much the possibility of losing a valid piece of evidence is rightfully regarded with concern. Like so, in many countries, judges tend to give very restrictive interpretations of the exclusionary rules while extending the ones of their exceptions. The situation becomes even more complicated when the law doesn't provide a rule for taking the evidence and its exclusion from the trial, leaving the interpreter with the difficult task of finding a delicate solution. In particular, this Author will try to indicate the path to reach a satisfactory balance between the opposing interests and an adequate – and effective – remedy to evidentiary misbehaviors that the lawmaker has yet to sanction.

2. The Constitution as a source of exclusionary rules

To further develop the thoughts in the premise, we will first consider the evolution of case law in Italy, which went from an inquisitorial system (Rocco Code from 1930) to one (still in force) that leans towards adversarial.[10]

In the previous system, the law stated nothing explicitly about whether the evidence should have been subject to the principle of legality, quickly becoming the dominant opinion among judges and Scholars that evidence not provided by the code could also be admitted in a trial. This was consequential to the constant expansion that judges gave to the principle of "*libero convincimento*",[11] which was

10 Regarding the events that concerned the new code since its promulgation, see P. Ferrua, 'La lenta agonia del processo accusatorio a trent'anni dall'entrata in vigore: trionfante nella Carta costituzionale, moribondo nel reale', *Processo penale e giustizia*, 2020/1, p. 7. The system is the result of the discipline provided by the new code of 1988, which was more openly adversarial after it was changed because of a series of bombings by the Mafia that led the public opinion to pressure the Parliament into giving back most of the evidentiary powers to the prosecutors. After this, it was the Constitutional Court itself who ruled that in the Italian system would be implied a principle of non-dispersion of evidence collected during the investigation, which strongly limited many of the new rules aimed to distinguish clearly between the phases of a criminal proceeding (see Constitutional Court, October 14th, 1998, p. 368, [in:] *Diritto penale e processo* 1998, p. 1493, commented by P. Tonini, 'Il diritto a confrontarsi con l'accusatore', *op.cit.*, p. 1506, and E. Marzaduri, 'Il diritto al silenzio del coimputato', *op.cit.*, p. 1512. For a more ample commentary, see I. Frioni, 'Equilibrismi e improbabili in simmetrie nella sentenza n. 361/1998 della Corte costituzionale, in *Cassazione Penale* 1999, p. 431. After this sentence, the lawmaker understood that a true change wasn't possible without a reform of the Constitution itself and law n. 2 of 1999 specifically intervened, adding 4 new paragraphs to article 111 Cost., so that the principle of contradiction between opposed parties, equally armed, had become one of the main pillars of a fair trial.

11 Italian for: "*Inner conviction*". Other viable translations may be: "*free persuasion*", "*freedom of conscience*" or simply "*discretion*".

interpreted in such an extensive manner that it ended up signifying the "*rejection of any kind of limitation of the free evaluation of evidence*" aiming to "*let the judge free from the medieval evidence system, seen as an instrument of humiliation to the rationality of the judicial determination*".[12] This had relevant consequences.

Finding a way to prevent judges from introducing evidence in a trial, disregarding any prior delimitation stated by law, became a fundamental matter. Because of this, some scholars have suggested that thorough respect for a lawful evidentiary procedure should be considered a mandatory implication of the same *libero convincimento* principle since it avoids degeneration.[13] Others[14] focused on the distinction between *unnamed evidence* and *named evidence unlawfully acquired*, which are inadmissible in trial. Even so, the concept of *libero convincimento* kept expanding, becoming a true loophole for judges to exploit, admitting evidence that should have been excluded from trials.

This led some to elaborate a theory aimed at filling the void left by the lawmaker, using the Constitution: all evidence obtained in violation of a fundamental right should not be admitted in a trial.[15] The introduction of a new set of exclusionary rules, which weren't provided by the law but by the Constitution itself,

---

12 E. Amodio, 'Libero convincimento e tassatività dei mezzi di prova: un approccio comparativo', *Rivista italiana diritto e procedura penale* 1999, p. 3.

13 M. Nobili, *Il principio del libero convincimento del giudice*, Milan 1974, p 27–28.

14 See, again, F. Cordero, *Tre studi sulla prova penale*, *passim*.

15 As we'll see, the discipline of the flaws of evidence in Italy is largely based on the exclusionary rules' doctrine from the US, where the possibility of sanctioning illicit evidence because of the violation of Constitutional fundamental rights has been affirmed by the Supreme Court since the 60s (see below, § 3.2). One of the first comments to this theory was given by F. Cordero, *Tre studi sulle prove penali*, *op.cit.*, p. 153–155, who highlighted how this doctrine developed starting from the works of German Scholars such as H. Sendler, 'Die Verwertung rechtswidrig erlangter Beweismittel im Strafprozess mit Berücksichtigung des anglo-amerikanischen und des franzosichen Rechts', *Jur. Diss.*, Berlin 1956, who proposed the constitution as a never-ending source of extra-procedural prohibitions. For a more recent overview of this doctrine in Italy, see, N. Galantini, 'L'art. 191 CPP a confronto con la "inutilizzabilità derivata" in un nuovo giudizio costituzionale', *Sistema Penale*, January 18th, 2022, and A. Camon, 'Le riprese visive come mezzo di indagine: spunti per una riflessione sulle "prove incostituzionali"', *Cassazione Penale* 1999. From the perspective of Italian case law, see Constitutional Court, June 4th, 1973, n. 34, which first employed the term "uncostitutional evidence", available at: https://giurcost.org/decisioni/1973/0034s-73.html, commented by V. Grevi, 'Insegnamenti, moniti e silenzi della Corte costituzionale in tema di intercettazioni telefoniche', *Giurisprudenza Costituzionale* 1974, p. 317. See also R. Casiraghi, 'Prove vietate e processo penale', *Rivista Italiana di Diritto e Procedura Penale* 2009/4, p, 1768.

was based on the assumption that some fundamental rights would necessarily imply them. The theory, in its essence, suggests that the provision of a right as fundamental must necessarily imply an exclusionary rule for any evidence taken in its disregard without the need for a specific implementation by the lawmaker. Furthermore, according to this doctrine, the remedy to such violations should be found within the same criminal trial where the misbehaviour occurred, as judges should be able to apply the constitutional provisions directly: after all, a constitution is, firstly, a source of law.

Nonetheless, many oppose this conclusion. Professor Franco Cordero, for example, claimed that, in an inquisitorial system, the evidence unlawfully obtained by the police would later be – if relevant – lawfully re-introduced into the trial by the judge, even if the misconduct harmed the fundamental rights of the citizen. Because of this, "*the equation* [didn't] *add up, when the intromission in someone else's privacy, arbitrarily carried by an official, is consented to the judge: it was obtained nothing more than what would have been sine injuria*",[16] and thus the evidence shouldn't be excluded.

In 1988, as anticipated, Italy tried to turn into a purely adversarial system but, ultimately, ended up with a mixed one.[17] The new code explicitly allowed *unnamed evidence* in trials, under the new definition of "*prova atipica*", thanks to the introduction of article 189 CCP, which – while expressly stating that evidence could be "atypical" – ended up reinforcing the very same principle of legality.[18] Many scholars soon realised that the new discipline implied a prohibition concerning typical evidence taken in non-typical forms, which should always be excluded from the trial.

Moreover, most of the evidentiary powers are now held by the parties,[19] while the judge has an autonomous power when the law expressly states so.[20]

However, new problems soon arose concerning the lack of sanctions, specifically the recently born "digital evidence" category. With the fast progress science has made in the 40 years since the Italian CPP was written, it became self-evident that the provisions in articles 189 and 191 of the CPP couldn't prevent

16 Once again, see F. Cordero, *Tre studi sulla prova penale, op.cit.*, p. 125.

17 See note 7.

18 Article 189 CPP today states that "1. *When the admission of evidence non-provided by the law is demanded, the judge may allow it if it seems suitable for the ascertainment of facts and doesn't harm the moral freedom of the individual. 2. The judge proceeds to its admission, having heard both parties about the procedure for its taking*".

19 Article 190, co. 1, CPP.

20 Article 190, co. 2, CPP.

illicit evidence from being admitted and used in trial. Anyway, it couldn't seem to protect the individual rights threatened by the employment of the new and formidable means of investigation satisfyingly.

Unnamed evidence, in today's Italian criminal procedure, still has close to no discipline, and when it comes to identifying a prohibition relevant under article 191 CPP as a cause of exclusion of evidence, article 189 only requires it to (i) be suitable for the ascertainment of facts and (ii) not to affect "moral freedom". Both requirements seem, sadly, insufficient:

i) The first requirement says nothing about the lawfulness of the evidence itself and would only exclude the unreliable ones;
ii) Furthermore, the definition of *moral freedom* – which sounds wide and flexible enough to include the concept of fundamental rights – is clearly given by Article 188 CPP as "*methods or techniques able to influence the freedom of self-determination or to alter the ability to remember and evaluate facts*".[21]

Like so, new life was brought to the debate about constitutional exclusionary rules. Even if many Scholars and most judges kept opposing it, denying its very existence, many others thought it could have been the key to completing the new system, setting strict boundaries that not even Article 189 CPP could break. Because of this, the case law and the Scholars were brought to reconsider the meaning of the concept of "*evidentiary prohibition*", which is the pivot of Article 191 CCP.[22]

On one side, many Scholars[23] and judges[24] kept arguing that the existence of a principle of legal certainty of the sanctions imposed to follow the traditional

21 For a different point of view regarding the possibility of including fundamental rights in the concept of "moral freedom", see L. Annunziata, *Questioni probatorie tra "male captum bene retentum" e "theory of the fruit of the poisonous tree"*, Pisa 2017, p. 40. Italian Court of Cassation recently re-affirmed this restrictive interpretation in sentencing no. 31604 of September 30th, 2020, commented by E. Toma [in] *Cassazione Penale*, 2021/6, p. 2133. In this ruling, it was expressly stated that the *Trojan horse virus*, when used to gather evidence, doesn't affect the *moral freedom* of people "*because it's not possible to identify it as a mean capable of affecting [their] self-determination.*"

22 See N. Galantini, *L'inutilizzabilità della prova nel processo penale*, Milan 1992, p. 255.

23 See, among many, P. Ferrua, 'Ammissibilità della prova e divieti probatori', *Revista Brasileira de Direito Processual Penal* 2021/7, 1, pp. 237–238; F. Caprioli, *Colloqui riservati e prova penale*, Turin 2000, p. 236; F. Cordero, *Procedura penale*, Giuffré 2012, p. 639; N. Galantini, *L'inutilizzabilità della prova*, *op.cit.*, p. 204.

24 Court of Cassation, Sez. III, October 4th, 2006, n. 37402, available in C.E.D. Cass., n. 235034; Court of Cassation, Sez. III, November 13th, 2007, n. 2001, R., available in C.E.D. Cass., n. 238846.

approach and kept giving a strict interpretation to new article 191, co. 1, CPP,[25] arguing that an "*evidentiary prohibition*" may be exclusively found in *laws of criminal procedure*. Even when admitting that the Constitution may provide exclusionary rules,[26] Scholars claimed it to be impossible to deduct and apply an exclusionary rule directly from the provision of any fundamental right. Fundamentally, they rejected the idea that such rules may be implied and had to be explicit. Instead, when the Constitution doesn't provide an explicit sanction, the lawmaker must translate the Constitutional provision into an "evidentiary prohibition" in the Italian CPP.

At the same time, those conclusions fundamentally negated any possibility for this kind of evidentiary flaw to find an immediate remedy inside the trial. On the contrary, a remedy should only be found outside of the trial, before the Constitutional Court, which should be explicitly questioned about the possible damage to fundamental rights that may be suffered because of the absence of such sanction.

Other Scholars argue that the new code of 1988 should have led to a new interpretation of the system of evidentiary sanctions, especially considering that a more flexible interpretation may be more adequate for the new balance of powers among the parties and the judge. Under this perspective, it started to seem like some previously examined opinions had partly lost their foundation. If Professor Franco Cordero found one of the main reasons to oppose this theory in the possibility the judges had to reintroduce the same evidence in the trial, and this power has now been taken from them, it seemed safe to assume that a revision of the whole system was implied, bringing the "*equation*" to add up again. Moreover, many Scholars[27] pointed out that the Court of Cassation hasn't always been cautious about affirming the principle of legal certainty, leading some to believe the Italian system may be going in the opposite direction. For instance, the Court of Cassation stated that an exclusionary rule could be implied and not expressly

25 "Evidence obtained in violation of an evidentiary prohibition shall not be used".

26 In fact, it's accepted by all that, for example, article 111, sections 4 and 5 of the Italian Constitution state more than one prohibition.

27 C. Conti, 'Il principio di non sostituibilità: il sistema probatorio tra costituzione e legge ordinaria', *Cassazione Penale*, 2024/2, p. 461; Id., *Accertamento del fatto e inutilizzabilità nel processo penale*, Cedam 2007; G. Illuminati, 'L'inutilizzabiltà della prova', *Rivista Italiana di Diritto e Procedura Penale*, 2010, p. 521–546.

provided when it concerns the nature or the object of the evidence,[28] and they are "deducible from the system".[29]

2.1. A few words about a recent decision

In a recent ruling,[30] the Court of Cassation seemed to open to a new approach, expressly stating that violations of fundamental rights have an effective and immediate remedy within the trial. Violations of constitutional rights would lead to the un-usability of evidence provided by article 191 CPP, which is irremediable. In this case, data intercepted thanks to a cell phone's monitoring were acquired in the trial without a warrant, imposed by Article 132 Legislative Decree no. 196/20023 (privacy code). The problem is that if the perpetrators request to be judged in the form of abbreviated proceedings, they effectively renounce the right to complain about un-usabilities other than those provided by Article 191 CPP, which, in the opinion of the Court of Appeal, was not the case with the violation of Article 132 in the statutory law. The Court of Cassation, nonetheless, argued that violations of fundamental rights should constitute misbehaviours relevant under Article 191; at least in all instances, they are further guaranteed by a rule of law or a reserve of jurisdiction. In the opinion of the Court of Cassation, the violation of such guarantees, more than of the right, should always force the judge to exclude their results from the trial.

The reasoning is interesting, but the premise should not be shared even if the conclusions reached are acceptable.

To better understand the conclusions of the Court of Cassation, it's essential to introduce the traditional theory concerning the possibility of finding an implied exclusionary rule CPP relevant under the provision of Article 191 CCP

---

28 Court of Cassation, Sez. I, October 25th, 2004, n. 1594, in C.E.D. *Cass.*, n. 230774.

29 Court of Cassation, Sez. U, *Sala*, March 27th, 1996, n. 5021, commented by M. Vessichelli, 'Sui limiti alla utilizzabilità del sequestro conseguente a una perquisizione illegittima', *Cassazione penale*, 1996/11, p. 3268; Court of Cassation, Sez. U, *Gallieri*, July 13th, 1998, n. 21, commented by G. Melillo, 'L'acquisizione dei tabulati relativi al traffico telefonico fra limiti normativi ed equivoci giurisprudenziali', *Cassazione Penale*, 1998/2, p. 465.

30 Court of Cassation, 1.11.2023, n. 15836, commented by C. Marinelli: "Non sono utilizzabili neppure in sede di giudizio abbreviato i dati di geolocalizzazione relativi a cellulari, contenuti nei tabulati telefonici, acquisiti dalla polizia giudiziaria in assenza del decreto di autorizzazione dell'autorità giudiziaria [Nota a sentenza] Sez. VI, 11/1/2023 (dep. 14/4/2023), n. 15836", *Cassazione Penale*, 2023/7–8, p. 2279.

in the statutory law. The Scholars that support this theory[31] sustain that while a violation concerning the forms of the evidentiary procedure (*quomodo*) should only be sanctioned when the lawmaker provides so, the violations that disregard a condition of admissibility of specific evidence (*an*) are always sanctioned by article 191 CPP, and the Court of Cassation seemed to follow this principle.[32] Thus, the violation of Article 132 of the Legislative Decree No. 193/2003 should have been considered relevant directly under the provision of Article 191 CPP without any relevance concerning the constitutional exclusionary rules. This is because Article 132 of the Legislative Decree no. 193/2003, which provides that "*data is acquired from the provider through a reasoned decree of the Judge, issued on the Prosecutor's request*", quite obviously poses a rule concerning the possibility itself of taking the evidence.

3. In search of an effective remedy

Such problems, perfectly exemplified by the Italian situation, are common in most countries. The main reasons that bring judges to oppose a broader application of exclusionary rules usually lie in the struggle to find a good balance between the

31 Among all, see F. Cordero, *Procedura penale*, Milan 2003, p. 612; N. Galantini, 'Inutilizzabilità della prova', *op.cit.*, p. 65–66. Many Italian Scholars, nowadays, seem to abandon this theory and claim that violations of the *quomodo* might still be relevant under the provision of article 191 CPP at some conditions. See M. Nobili, 'Divieti probatori e sanzioni', *Giustizia penale*, 1991/3, p. 64. See also G. Pierro, 'Una nuova specie d'invalidità l'inutilizzabilità degli atti processuali penali', *Università degli Studi di Salerno Pubblicazioni - Sezione Studi Giuridici* 1989, p. 148.

32 See Court of Cassation, Sez. VI, October 8th, 2008, n. 40973, 241318 *C.E.D. Cass.* At the same time the Court of Cassation has sometimes expressed doubts about a "spreading discomfort" felt because of the excessive rigor the lawmaker employs when it comes to sanction violations concerning the *quomodo* (see Court of Cassation, Sez. U, *Cagnazzo*, March 25th, 2010, n. 13426, commented by S. Beltrani, 'Intercettazioni inutilizzabili e procedimento di prevenzione: la fine di un equivoco', *Cassazione Penale* 2010/9, p. 3049). Even so, and fundamentally disregarding the system's evolution during the '90 and early 2000 (see note § 7), the case law still seems to favor the conservation of evidence over the interpretation principles stated by the Constitutional Court and the international Courts. About this, see A. Balsamo - S. Recchione, 'La costruzione di un modello europeo di prova dichiarativa: 'il nuovo corso' della giurisprudenza e le prospettive aperte dal Trattato di Lisbona', *Cassazione penale* 2010, p. 3620.

collective interests and the fundamental rights of the citizens,[33] further complicated by the moral dilemmas implied by the choice between admitting unlawfully obtained evidence and letting a guilty person free. From now on, the main objective of this article will be to examine the experiences of various countries and the remedies they provided for this kind of evidentiary misbehaviour.

Starting from the double assumption that evidentiary misbehaviors should be sanctioned and that whoever is interested should have access to an effective remedy, we'll also keep in mind that no solution would be able to fit any system, so a secondary aim of this piece will be that of finding at which conditions they would be viable.

3.1. Exclusionary rules as a fair trial or due process remedy

As we previously said, some Scholars think that the distinction between inquisitorial and adversarial systems has already become obsolete since the only characteristic that should be considered is whether a system complies with the requirements of a fair trial.[34]

Following similar reasoning, some[35] considered – but ultimately excluded – that the ECHR may provide some "conventional" exclusionary rule relevant to the countries' criminal justice systems. Meanwhile, in the US, Scholars[36] have examined the possibility of inferring an exclusionary rule from the due process clause provided by the Fifth Amendment.[37] It is interesting to note that this last

33 On this subject, cf. R. Cross, *Evidence*, London: Butterworth 1858; J. B. Dawson, 'The Exclusion of Unlawfully Obtained Evidence: A Comparative Study', *The International and Comparative Law Quarterly*, 1982/31(3), pp. 513–549, available at: http://www.jstor.org/stable/759004 [accessed on February 10th, 2024]; M.E. Cammack, 'The Rise and Fall of the Constitutional Exclusionary Rule in the United States', 58 *The American Journal of Comparative Law* 2010, p. 631–658, available at: http://www.jstor.org/stable/20744557 [accessed on February 10th, 2024]; F. Cordero, *Tre studi*, loc.cit.

34 See note § 1.

35 M. Daniele, 'Indagini informatiche lesive della riservatezza. Verso un'inutilizzabilità convenzionale?', *Cassazione Penale*, 2013/1, p. 367.

36 M.R. Richard, 'The due process exclusionary rule', *Harvard Law Review* 2014/127(7), pp. 1885–1966, available at: https://www.jstor.org/stable/23741971.

37 "No person shall be […] nor be deprived of life, liberty, or property, without due process of law".

theory moves the focus from the provisions of the Fourth Amendment,[38] which is usually believed to be the source of the exclusion, considering that condemning someone in consequence of a search in the absence of a warrant translates to a "*limitation of liberty without due process*".[39] In this perspective, the Fourth Amendment fundamentally loses its status as a source of exclusionary rules and is seen as a rule governing the pre-trial process of evidence acquisition.[40]

A similar concept may be applied to the ECHR's system, considering the correlation between Articles 6[41] and 8.[42] The European Court often examined complaints regarding the unlawful violation of one's private life to gather evidence both under Article 6 and Article 8,[43] while some other times only under Article 8,[44] determining whether the intermission in someone's privacy might have had a direct repercussion on the overall fairness of the trial. This doesn't exclude violations of other rights to render the whole trial unfair, but this should be decided depending on the concrete circumstances of the specific case.

It is well known that the function of exclusionary rules is still discussed among Scholars: "*Should they (a) discipline police or the prosecution service, (b) protect the legal system, human rights or the integrity of court proceedings, (c) maintain legal certainty or justice or (d) ensure that the trial court does not consider inherently unreliable evidence?*".[45] However, it should be safe to assume that they have a

38 "The right of the people to be secure in their persons, houses, papers, and effects, against unreasonable searches and seizures, shall not be violated, and no Warrants shall issue, but upon probable cause, supported by Oath or affirmation, and particularly describing the place to be searched and the persons or things to be seized".

39 M.R. Richard, *The due process exclusionary rule, op.cit.*, pp. 1917–1918.

40 Ibidem, pp. 1918–1925.

41 Right to a fair trial.

42 Right to respect for private and family life.

43 Cf. ECHR, *O. v. the United Kingdom*, §§ 65–67; *Golder v. the United Kingdom*, §§ 41–45; *Macready v. the Czech Republic*, § 41; *Bianchi v. Switzerland*, 2006, § 113, HUDOC.

44 Cf. ECHR, *Soares de Melo v. Portugal*, § 65; *Santos Nunes v. Portugal*, § 56; *Havelka and Others v. the Czech Republic*, §§ 34–35; *Wallová and Walla v. the Czech Republic*, § 47; *Kutzner v. Germany*, § 56; *McMichael v. the United Kingdom*, § 87; and *Mehmet Ulusoy and Others v. Turkey*, 2019, § 109, HUDOC.

45 See S. Knickmeier, 'Securing a Fair Trial Through Exclusionary Rules: Do Theory and Practice Form a Well-Balanced Whole?', [in:] S. Gless, T. Richter (eds.), *Do Exclusionary Rules Ensure a Fair Trial? A Comparative Perspective on Evidentiary Rules*, Springer Open 2019, Ius Gentium: Comparative Perspectives on Law and Justice Vol. 74, p. 334–335.

complex function that tends to realise more than one aim,[46] and this means that at least some relevance might always be given to the principle of fair trial. The main unanswered question is: "*What remedy may be carried to enforce the violation?*". We'll focus on the matter further below (§ 4).

3.2. Constitutional Exclusionary Rules around the world

Other countries explicitly admit the possibility of excluding evidence because of a fundamental right violation.

In Spain, for instance, article 11 of the "*Ley Orgànica del Poder Judicial*" (LOPJ) provides that "*evidence obtained in direct or indirect violation of fundamental rights or freedoms will have no effect*". The main problem Spain and other countries with similar provisions had to deal with was balancing them with the need for efficiently prosecuting crimes.[47] The *Tribunal Constitucional* was, for the most time, against admitting evidence obtained in violation of a fundamental right, even if it always claimed it was abstractly possible.[48] In particular, the *Tribunal Constitucional* considers that "*the need for safeguard is more when the employed mean of proof harms directly a fundamental right*"[49] and "*when the mean of proof employed represents a direct materialisation of the harm to the right* […] *the prohibition of validity* […] *becomes indispensable to make so that the trial doesn't turn out to be unbalanced against the accused person because of the limitation of his fundamental rights*",[50] connecting the necessity for the application of exclusionary rules to the inequality of arms that the violation may have caused in the trial. This ultimately brought, for the first time in 2003, the *Tribunal Constitucional* to rule that *bona fides* of the prosecution may allow the use of unconstitutional evidence as long as "*The statute of the defendant couldn't prevent the taking of evidence if the*

46 Lawmakers often tend to provide exclusionary rules for different reasons. See G. Giostra, *Prima lezione…*, who highlights that, in Italian criminal proceedings, evidence is usually excluded for one of two reasons: because they are unreliable (epistemological limitation) or because they are contrary to the country's values (value limitation). In some instances, the exclusionary rule is provided because of both reasons: that's the case with torture-induced confessions.

47 On this subject, see M. Cinta Costa Torne, 'La prueba ilícita por violación de Derechos Fundamentales y sus excepciones', *Revista de Derecho UNED* 2012/11, p. 137, available at: http://revistas.uned.es/index.php/RDUNED/article/view/11128 [accessed on February 10th, 2024].

48 Tribunal Constitucional, April 2nd, 1998, n. 81.

49 Tribunal Constitucional, April 5th, 1999, n. 49.

50 Tribunal Constitucional, May 31st, 1999, n. 94.

Prosecutor had acted accordingly to the Constitution and, in this way, it's impossible to say that there has been any kind of harm to the principle of the equality of arms".[51]

In other countries, such as the United States, the Constitution has been considered a source of exclusionary rules since the end of the 19th century. They were found, specifically, in the provisions regarding the self-incrimination right[52] and the due process clause[53] (as already seen). At first, the US Constitution "*served as the primary standard of admissibility of illegally obtained evidence*", imposing on the States to honour the minimum guarantees it provides but letting them be free to require more comprehensive protection for the same rights. However, the theory had a downfall since, in more recent times, Scholars studied the approach of the Supreme Court towards it, noticing a transformation that was gradually demoting the Constitutional exclusionary rules from the status of "right" to that of "remedy".[54] Consequently, it brought a restriction on the exclusion of evidence as a response to violations of the Constitution.

As widely known, in 1961,[55] the Supreme Court stated that "*exclusion of evidence obtained as a result of an unconstitutional search or seizure is required in state criminal trials as a matter of federal constitutional law*". Briefly after that, in 1964,[56] the Sixth Amendment was held as a valid source of exclusion for evidence consisting in statements elicited from the accused in the absence of his lawyer and, in 1966, the Fifth Amendment excluded from the trial all the evidence gathered in violation of the right against compelled self-incrimination.[57]

All those cases didn't represent the first time the Supreme Court had ruled that an Amendment could require illegally obtained evidence to be excluded. Instead, they contributed to setting the minimum standards the US Constitution imposed on the federated states. Nonetheless, the possibility of an amendment excluding evidence has always been discussed, and over the past few decades, it has undergone a severe transformation. Although the Constitutional exclusionary remedy

---

51 Tribunal Constitucional, 2.10.2003, n. 22.

52 Fifth Amendment.

53 Fourteenth Amendment expressly states that "*No State shall make or enforce any law which shall abridge the privileges or immunities of citizens of the United States; nor shall any State deprive any person of life, liberty, or property, without due process of law; nor deny to any person within its jurisdiction the equal protection of the laws*".

54 See M. E. Cammack, *The Rise*, *op.cit.*, pp. 631–658.

55 *Mapp v. Ohio*, 367 U.S. 643 (1961).

56 *Massiah v. United States*, 377 U.S. 201 (1964).

57 *Miranda v. United States*, 384 U.S. 436 (1966), from which the "Miranda Warnings" were derived.

retains, to this day, central importance in US criminal proceedings, the views represented in the *Mapp*, *Massiah*, and *Miranda* decisions[58] slowly deteriorated. The Supreme Court has adopted a more prudent conception of rights based on a textualist approach. Because of this, the exclusion of the evidence is no longer a "right" of the individual but a mere "remedy" to be actioned in balance with the cost of the exclusion, measured in terms of "lost evidence".[59]

The idea that constitutional rights should be deducted from a strict textualist interpretation of the Constitution resembles the theories nowadays dominating Italian case law. One of the main reasons brought by judges to confute Constitutional exclusionary rules is, as we previously said, that such a consequence may only be provided by formal procedural laws because of the alleged existence of a principle of legal certainty of procedural sanctions. Following this reasoning, Scholars[60] have argued that the Italian Constitution directly states close to no procedural rule.[61] This possibility was rejected even if the Constitutional Court[62] expressly recognised that violations of fundamental rights, even when regarding an evidentiary act exclusively, should find an immediate remedy within the trial, and this implied that a judge might find the source of an exclusionary rule through a direct application of the provisions stated in the Constitution, without the need of a translation of that principle in an express sanction by the lawmaker.

Like so, the ruling no. 34/1973 remained an isolated case in the Italian constitutional case law. Most Scholars now claim that this theory should be considered abandoned and that the only way evidence may be deemed unconstitutional is through a direct appeal to the Constitutional Court, aimed to introduce a sanction that the lawmaker should have already provided, and in not doing so has provoked a violation of a fundamental right.[63] Nonetheless, the conclusion has the added value of establishing (or re-establishing) a clear separation between

58 Which generally reflected the idea that evidence derived through illegal means should be eliminated from the trial.

59 M. E. Cammack, *The Rise*, *op.cit.*, p. 633.

60 P. Ferrua, 'Ammissibilità della prova e divieti probatori', *Revista Brasileira de Direito Processual Penal*, 2021/7(1), pp. 215–246.

61 Except for article 111 Cost., about which see notes 7 and 24.

62 Constitutional Court, n. 34/1973, cited above.

63 P. Ferrua, 'Ammissibilità', *op.cit.*, p. 238.

the powers of the constitutional court and the judiciary and from this last one and the lawmaker.[64]

4. Conclusion. An effective remedy to evidentiary misbehaviours

Finding a good compromise between limiting unlawful intermissions with the individual's fundamental rights and the collective's need to prosecute crimes and punish their perpetrators is a challenging task, which – with no doubt – should be left primarily to the lawmakers. Nonetheless, judges and scholars are called to find a balance every time lawmakers are lazy or forgetful since there is no correct procedure, and there is always the theoretical problem of defining what may constitute misbehaviour. This balance might be found in the remedies provided by the system.

These remedies should be shaped differently depending on the country's system, but always consider that the Constitution, like any other law, is a source of rules.[65]

In a country where evidence is subject to the principle of legality, the remedy appears simple and should be its inadmissibility. If the law provides for the procedure for taking evidence, it should also provide for the consequences of its violations. But *quid juris* if it doesn't? In this case, we must distinguish whether the misbehaviour is a violation that harms a fundamental right guaranteed by the country's Constitution. There is the possibility of appealing to the Constitutional Court that it will be possible to proceed by bringing ordinary law to its attention, arguing that it is illegitimate because it poses a threat to the rights protected by the Constitution. Like so, there would be an effective remedy to the violation, which would have to operate indirectly, and that – depending on the country – may be actioned by an individual in his interest or to reach the elimination of the anti-constitutional provisions (*erga omnes* effect).

Suppose the violation renders the trial "unfair as a whole". In that case, an effective remedy should be found in challenging the decision before a domestic (if possible) or a supranational court (the ECHR, for all countries that recognise the Convention). This should always lead to the consequence of a reopening of the trial, excluding the evidence of which the taking had conflicted with Articles 6 and 8 ECHR.

---

64 Some Italian Scholars see the balance between those powers as precarious already. On the subject see M. Luciani, *Ogni cosa al suo posto. Restaurare l'ordine costituzionale dei poteri*, Giuffré 2023.

65 V. Crisafulli, 'Introduzione a La Costituzione e le sue disposizioni di principio', *Quaderni della Costituzione* 1952.

In countries where evidence can be admitted in a trial without a predetermined procedure, the same logic generally continues to apply, with some additional considerations needing to be made regarding unnamed evidence. In criminal systems based on the inquisitorial model, this Author shares the objection that, since a judge may still admit the evidence later (all the time, it's not radically excluded as such) even if it caused a violation of fundamental rights, it would be pointless to cause a useless delay in the times of conclusion of the trial. Even in these circumstances, though, evidence should still be excluded when the violations rendered the trial "unfair as a whole" and if there isn't a sanction provided by the lawmaker, only as long as a supernational remedy is provided.

However, a new problem is soon to arise. In an increasingly globalised world, where the web helps make borders uncertain, the nearest future will see evidence obtained in one country being used in another country's tribunal. But what if their values don't align? What if something that constitutes a clear violation of human rights in country A is deemed acceptable in uncivilised countries? In these situations, a new effective remedy will need to be found.

Bibliography

Ambos K., 'International Criminal Procedure: 'Adversarial', 'Inquisitorial' or Mixed?', *Third International Criminal Law Review*, 2003/3, Available at SSRN: https://ssrn.com/abstract=1972235.

Amodio E., 'Libero convincimento e tassatività dei mezzi di prova: un approccio comparativo', *Rivista italiana diritto e procedura penale*, 1999.

Annunziata L., *Questioni probatorie tra "male captum bene retentum" e "theory of the fruit of the poisonous tree"*, Pisa, 2017.

Balsamo A., S. Recchione, 'La costruzione di un modello europeo di prova dichiarativa: 'il nuovo corso' della giurisprudenza e le prospettive aperte dal Trattato di Lisbona', *Cassazione Penale* 2010.

Cammack M. E., 'The Rise and Fall of the Constitutional Exclusionary Rule in the United States', *The American Journal of Comparative Law*, 2010/58. Available on JSTOR, at http://www.jstor.org/stable/20744557.

Camon A., Le riprese visive come mezzo di indagine: spunti per una riflessione sulle "prove incostituzionali".

Caprioli F., 'Riprese visive nel domicilio e intercettazione «per immagini»', *Giurisprudenza Costituzionale* 2002.

Caprioli F., *Colloqui riservati e prova penale*, Turin 2000.

Casiraghi R., 'Prove vietate e processo penale', *Rivista Italiana di Diritto e Procedura Penale*, 2009/4.

Cintia Costa Torné M., 'La prueba ilícita por violación de Derechos Fundamentales y sus excepciones', *Revista de Derecho UNED*, 2012/11. Available at http://revistas.uned.es/index.php/RDUNED/article/view/11128.

Cordero F., *Procedura penale*, Milano, 2003.

Cordero F., *Tre studi sulla prova penale*, Varese, 1969.

Crisafulli V., 'Introduzione a La Costituzione e le sue disposizioni di principio', *Quaderni della Costituzione*, 1952.

Crombag H. F. M., 'Adversarial or inquisitorial: Do we have a choice?', [in:] P. J. Van Koppen & S. D. Penrod, *Adversarial versus Inquisitorial Justice: Psychological perspectives on criminal justice systems*, New York, 2003.

Cross R., Evidence, *London: Butterworth*, 1858.

Cunha Souza – E. Toma, 'Il contraddittorio, il giudice e i fascicoli nei sistemi processuali penali del brasile e d'italia', *Revista Antinomias*, 2023/1.

Daniele M., 'Digital investigations in breach of the right to respect for private life. Towards an ECHR's exclusionary rule?', *Cassation Penale*, 2013/1.

Dawson J. B., 'The Exclusion of Unlawfully Obtained Evidence: A Comparative Study', *The International and Comparative Law Quarterly*, 1982/31(3). Available on JSTOR, at http://www.jstor.org/stable/759004.

Ferrua P., 'Ammissibilità della prova e divieti probatori', *Revista Brasileira de Direito Processual Penal*, 2021/7(1).

Ferrua P., 'La lenta agonia del processo accusatorio a trent'anni dall'entrata in vigore: trionfante nella Carta costituzionale, moribondo nel reale', *Processo penale e giustizia* 2020/1.

Ferrua P., 'Processo penale tra modello inquisitorio e modello accusatorio', *Penale diritto e procedura*, May 24th, 2022.

Frioni I., 'Equilibrismi e improbabili in simmetrie nella sentenza n. 361/1998 della Corte costituzionale', *Cassazione Penale*, 1999.

Galantini N., 'L'art. 191 CPP a confronto con la "inutilizzabilità derivata" in un nuovo giudizio costituzionale', *Sistema Penale*, January 18th, 2022.

Galantini N., *L'inutilizzabilità della prova nel processo penale*, Milan 1992.

Giostra G., 'Contraddittorio (principio del)', *Enceclopedia giuridica Treccani*, 2021/3.

Giostra G., *Prima lezione sulla giustizia penale*, Roma, 2022.

Grevi V., 'Insegnamenti, moniti e silenzi della Corte costituzionale in tema di intercettazioni telefoniche', *Giurisprudenza Costituzionale* 1974.

Knickmeier S., 'Securing a Fair Trial Through Exclusionary Rules: Do Theory and Practice Form a Well-Balanced Whole?' [in:] *Do Exclusionary Rules*

Ensure a Fair Trial?', A Comparative Perspective on Evidentiary Rules, Cham, 2019 vol. 74.

Laronga A., *Le prove atipiche nel processo penale*, Milan, 2002.

Lozzi G., 'I principi dell'oralità e del contraddittorio nel processo penale', *Rivista Italiana di Diritto e Procedura Penale*, 1997/3.

Luciani M., Ogni cosa al suo posto. Restaurare l'ordine costituzionale dei poteri, *Giuffré*, 2023.

Marinelli C., 'The geolocation data relating to mobile phones, contained in telephone records, acquired by the judicial police without the decree of authorisation by the judicial authority, are not usable, even in the course of short judgment', *Cassation Penale*, 2023, 7/8.

Marzaduri E., 'Il diritto al silenzio del coimputato', *Diritto penale e processo* 1998.

Melillo G., 'L'acquisizione dei tabulati relativi al traffico telefonico fra limiti normativi ed equivoci giurisprudenziali', *Cassazione Penale*, 1998/2.

Nobili M., 'Divieti probatori e sanzioni', *Giustizia penale* 1991/3.

Nobili M., *Il principio del libero convincimento del giudice*, Milan, 1974.

Pierro G., 'Una nuova specie d'invalidità l'inutilizzabilità degli atti processuali penali', *Università degli Studi di Salerno Pubblicazioni - Sezione Studi Giuridici*, 1989.

Rafaraci T., 'Ricognizione informale dell'imputato e (pretesa) fungibilità delle forme probatorie, *Cassazione Penale*, 1998/6.

Richard M. R., The due process exclusionary rule, *Harvard Law Review*, 2014/127(7). Available on JSTOR, at https://www.jstor.org/stable/23741971.

Ruotolo M., 'L'interpretazione conforme a Costituzione torna a casa?', 3 Consulta online 2019.

Sevier J., 'The truth-justice tradeoff: Perceptions of decisional accuracy and procedural justice in adversarial and inquisitorial legal systems', *Psychology, Public Policy, and Law*, 2014/20(2). Available at: https://doi.org/10.1037/law0000009.

Siracusano D., 'Il contraddittorio tra Costituzione e legge ordinaria', *Diritto penale e processo*, 2000/11.

Thibaut J., & Walker T., 'A theory of procedure', *California Law Review*, 1978/66.

Toma E., 'Osservazioni a Sent. 31604 del 30 settembre 2020', *Cassazione Penale*, 2021/6.

Tonini P., 'Il diritto a confrontarsi con l'accusatore', *Diritto penale e processo*, 1998.

Vessichelli M., 'Sui limiti alla utilizzabilità del sequestro conseguente a una perquisizione illegittima', *Cassazione penale*, 1996/11.

Michał Wawrzyńczak[1]

V. Securing Effective Collection of Evidence: An Overview of Various Approaches to Interrogation Techniques

Abstract: Although a suspect's confession is no longer the 'queen of evidence' one cannot overestimate the value of testimony provided by personal sources of evidence in criminal proceedings. After all, defendants and witnesses, including expert witnesses, are the primary source of factual findings in the vast majority of pending cases. Only the correct reconstruction of events makes it possible to establish the real culprit and the basis of their responsibility. For that purpose, it is essential to obtain statements that are truthful.

This article focuses on the analysis of the interrogation techniques used to obtain evidence in the form of testimony at the pre-trial proceedings. Typically, interrogation activities are carried out by police officers or their equivalent; less frequently, the prosecutor or other supervising or prosecuting authority will be responsible for the interrogation. There are many interrogation techniques and their variants; in this paper, we will focus on the most important proposals of the doctrine, practice and legislature. Both so-called coercive techniques and those based on the rapport&trust building mechanism will be analysed. The main idea of the paper is to evaluate the commonly used interrogation techniques and to identify those that should provide a universal basis for shaping the ways of interrogation in the future.

Keywords: effective justice, interrogation, criminal procedure, human rights, evidence

1. Introduction

Criminal proceedings are an extremely complex matter. Starting from the issues related to the organisation of the pre-trial stage, through the interim proceedings to the judicial and executive proceedings, a vast number of factors influence the issues of effective organisation of the work of the judiciary. Among all the procedural activities carried out in a single (even multi-stage) proceeding, we can point to repeatable and non-repeatable activities. It is obvious that the quality of non-repeatable activities will be directly related to its efficiency. Indeed, it may happen that a flawed performance of the activity will have such defects that its

---

1 ORCID no. 0000-0003-1234-7194. PhD candidate at Adam Mickiewicz University and Bolonia University.

effects cannot be used. In addition, by the nature of the activity, it cannot be remedied. The situation is somewhat different with regard to repetitive actions. If they are defective, they can be corrected in the course of the proceedings, usually by performing them again. However, some actions - although repetitive - are characterised by the occurrence of so-called cognitive errors, consisting of the influence of external factors on the source of the evidence. Consequently, the information extracted through the evidentiary means is altered in content in relation to the originally known reality, resulting in a reduction in the effectiveness of its execution. This most often affects interrogation as a procedural act, which - due to the specific nature of the human psyche - is subject to the risk of cognitive errors and suggestions. As the majority of hearings take place at the stage of pre-trial proceedings - because it is based on the evidence gathered there that the decision is made to move the proceedings to the court stage - in this work, I will focus on optimal solutions for the shaping of this activity in terms of its correct, initial conduct.

2. Perception of effectiveness in the criminal procedure: do process or effects matter more?

One cannot discuss how an activity should be carried out without establishing what effectiveness is in the context of criminal procedure. A detailed discussion of the meaning of the word 'effectiveness' can be found in the chapter by Prof. Barbara Janusz-Pohl in vol. II.[2] Let me cite only the most critical findings, namely that effectiveness is assessed through the prism of the overall goals assigned by the legislator, while efficiency is measured not through the goals but rather through measurable parameters.[3] Since we can assess both the effectiveness of the proceedings as a whole and the actions in a point-oriented manner, their goals don't have to be the same.

I would argue that the prism of effectiveness is shared across both elements. Since the procedural action is a mere point in the course of the proceedings, it should still aim to serve general purposes. Moreover, we are talking about an extremely meaningful, impactful activity belonging to the evidentiary law sphere rather than merely a formal activity. The quality of testimony degrades along with time passing from the moment the criminal act occurred as well as due to

---

2 Precisely: B. Janusz-Pohl, 'Perception of the Effectiveness (effectivity) and Its Interdisciplinary Dimension - Keynotes', [in:], D. Vicoli (ed.), *Effective Justice International and Comparative Approaches*, Vol. 1, PeterLang.

3 Ibidem.

the 'good witness paradox'. The latter occurs when the witness starts to provide factually wrong information (even subconsciously) because they are trying to fulfil the expectations of law enforcement. The quality of the given interview may also degrade due to the power of suggestion, which may impact the witnesses' minds and cause a change in their memory based on the questions they were asked prior. Therefore, researchers underline the need for a high-quality first interview with a witness, which should be comprehensive.

If modern criminal procedures shall be compliant with undertaken international obligations, for most of the European states the provisions of ECHR will apply. That means that the standards of the fair trial have to be observed, and we shall introduce regulations which prohibit torture and degrading or ill-treatment. In that sense, preserving human rights becomes one of the goals of the proceedings. Moreover, the punctual action (interview/interrogation) must be carried out in a way optimised for the procedure's purposes. In such regard, not only does the trial have to be fair (in the understanding of art. 6 ECHR), but the activity must bear results that are optimal for the purposes of conducting pre-trial and court proceedings.

Such an approach has several consequences when it comes to evidentiary activities. One may argue that effective performance of the interview/interrogation means that the perpetrator or crucial information was provided during the former, and a confession was obtained during the latter. Such an implication would, however, be only vaguely accurate. The focal point of the proceedings is bringing the guilty to justice. We have to remember that only those who are convicted can be convicted, whose guilt was determined beyond reasonable doubt. It is precisely evidentiary law and proceedings (during the trial) that is responsible for creating or removing reasonable doubt as to one's guilt. In the pre-trial stage, optimal (hence effective) performance of interviewing/interrogating a person should lead to obtaining maximum information with possibly a maximum amount of it being true. It is hard to argue that false confession fulfils the criterion of effective interrogating. However – if merely obtaining a confession would be the goal of this activity – formally, it would check out. However, if the goal of the criminal procedure is indeed a conviction of the real (and not perceived) perpetrator, then such a manner in which a false confession is obtained would indeed be counterproductive.

Hence, for this paper, I am defining the effectiveness of the procedural activity as providing the maximum amount of information along with the maximum amount of accurate information and enhancing the protection of human rights. This leads to both securing higher-quality pre-trial proceedings and enabling a trial that better responds to the challenges and objectives of the criminal process as a whole. The latter I define as seeking to punish the actual perpetrator, provide justice for the victims, and enhance and promote social trust in law enforcement.

3. An overview of the exploited interview and interrogation methods

In contemporary law enforcement practice, one can see a range of interrogation techniques in use. Although they vary due to systemic model solutions that allow or prohibit the use of certain modes of conduct, they usually tend to be simply variations of interrogation models proposed by practitioners and academics. In this respect, two types of models can be highlighted: those directed against the person (coercive methods) and those oriented towards cooperation (rapport building). In the latter group, we will also include information-oriented methods (regardless of the veracity of the information), since they emphasise the building of trust between the subject and the investigator, which leads to an increase in the amount of information provided during the activity.

Historically, due to the inquisitorial shaping of criminal procedural models, person-facing interrogation methods have assumed a dominant role. In working terms, these may be referred to as psychological methods, as the essence of their design was to create an environment that exerted psychological pressure on the interrogated person to maximise the likelihood of a confession. Such techniques were the so-called Third Degree and, currently, the Reid Technique (in its many variants). These originated in American law enforcement practice. The former dates back to the late 19th century and involved the use of often highly abusive methods, including psychological coercion.[4] This method was not accepted by American society or the judiciary and jurisprudence - as evidenced by the Fourth and Fifth Amendments to the US Constitution and the Supreme Court's decision in *Bram v. United States.*[5] Despite the clear position of the judiciary, in reality, officers cultivated the practices of Third Degree while taking utmost care to conceal its application from the public.[6] The final blow to the Third Degree technique came

---

4 R.A. Leo, *Police Interrogations and American Justice*, Cambridge, London: Harvard University Press 1st ed. 2008, pp. 47–70.

5 Bram v. United States, 168 US 532 (1897).

6 W. Kozinski, 'The Reid Inter rogation Technique and False Confessions: A Time for Change', *Seattle Journal for Social Justice*, 2018/16(2), pp. 306–309 and the literature quoted therein. Available at: https://digitalcommons.law.seattleu.edu/sjsj/vol16/iss2/10 [accessed on September 1st, 2024].

in the case of *Watts v. Indiana*,[7] after which knowledge of its continued use was disseminated - resulting in renewed, strong opposition, with attempts to replace the methodological gap in law enforcement efforts caused by the unequivocal disqualification of Third Degree.[8] We will discuss the relevance and effectiveness of the use of psychological techniques - the Reid method and thus, indirectly, the variants used - later in the text.

Later models, shaped by the controversy surrounding the application of psychological techniques, included a number of proposals operating on the assumption that the basis for obtaining better quality testimony is establishing a relationship based on trust. For this reason, they can provisionally be categorised as rapport-building techniques. They derive from different assumptions and backgrounds. For example, the most notable breakthrough from the use of psychological techniques by law enforcement arose from the imposition of the PEACE technique in the UK, created as a result of numerous scandals involving false confessions based on the Reid technique. This shift provided the basis for moving beyond psychological techniques, precisely providing the impetus for the search for a new framework for carrying out interrogation activities. Nowadays, there are several non-coercive techniques that may be used all at once since they do not provide a complex structure (much like Reid or PEACE does) but play a significant role in certain aspects of interrogation. We will focus on a few proposals: Strategic Disclosure of Evidence, Unanticipated Questions, Cognitive Interview, and KREATIV. We will discuss them in a separate subchapter.

One more thing needs to be analysed. Namely, the difference between 'interview' and 'interrogation' is much broader than just the semantics. The interview is geared towards non-accusatory information gathering, whereas interrogation is an accusatory phase aiming to obtain a confession.[9] If we are talking about efficiency, the question is whether it is necessary to separate the methodology of interviewing the witness and the suspect/accused. Secondly, it is crucial to establish what we give primacy to during the interrogation/interview activity, which will help answer the question of what techniques should be included in law enforcement training. Answering the questions posed this way will be crucial to resolving the dilemma of effectively securing evidence from personal evidence sources in criminal proceedings.

---

7 Watts v. Indiana, 338 US 49 (1949).

8 R.A. Leo, *Police Interrogations*, *op.cit.*, p. 63.

9 N. J. Gordon, W. L. Fleisher, *Effective Interviewing and Interrogation Techniques*, Academic Press 2010, pp. 27–28.

4. Is confession-seeking effective? An overview of Reid's technique and its impact on criminal proceedings

Perhaps the best-known and popularised interrogation technique is The Reid Method - also known as The FBI Technique. According to the John E. Reid and Associates organisation, John E. Reid began working on it as early as 1947. Still, he did not achieve real success until 1955 through his participation in the Darrell Parker case.[10] His technique became a subject of teaching in police forces, private security companies, the military, the FBI, the CIA, and the Secret Service.[11] The scale of Reid's success is enormous; John E. Reid and Associates (interchangeably: Reid's organisation) itself indicates that their technique is the most widely used approach to question subjects in the world;[12] a 2014 report by the Office of Legislative Research, Connecticut General Assembly indicated more than 500,000 people trained with Reid's technique;[13] after all, it is claimed to be a leading method in at least 28 countries, as shown on their website.[14] Therefore, the effec-

---

10 D. Starr, 'The Interview', New Yorker 2013. Available at: http://www.newyorker.com/magazine/2013/12/09/the-interview-7 [accessed on September 1st, 2024].

11 Ibidem.

12 John E. Reid and Associates website. Available at: https://reid.com/about [accessed on September 1st, 2024].

13 J. Orlando, 'Interrogation Techniques', OLR Research Report 2014, Connecticut General Assembly [Online]. Available at: https://www.cga.ct.gov/2014/rpt/2014-R-0071.htm [accessed on September 1st, 2024].

14 Among those are: Germany; Bosnia-Herzegovina; the Czech Republic; the United Arab Emirates; Singapore; Japan; Mexico; Canada; Belgium; Israel; India; South Korea; China; Luxembourg; Africa; Italy; Malaysia; Norway; Philippines; Saudi Arabia; the Netherlands; Brazil; Peru; Jamaica; Ecuador; El Salvador; Iraq; Slovakia. John E. Reid and Associates website. Available at: https://reid.com/about [accessed on September 1st, 2024].

The list is not complete though, as e.g. Poland's leading method taught during police training is, in fact, the Reid method. See: Załącznik do decyzji nr 272 Komendanta Głównego Policji z dnia 2 listopada 2017 r., Program nauczania na kursie specjalistycznym z zakresu taktyki i technik przesłuchań [*Appendix to Decision No. 272 of the Chief of Police dated November 2nd, 2017, Curriculum for the specialized course in interrogation tactics and techniques*], Dz. Urz. 2017.70. Available at: https://edziennik.policja.gov.pl/eli/DU_KGP/2017/70/ogl/pol/pdf [accessed on September 1st, 2024]. It seems that this list of 28 countries only includes those that have acquired the certified training from the organization, whereas the technique is being taught on a domestic level by certified professionals that are not part of the John E. Reid and Associates organization, thus cannot certify the graduates.

tiveness of this technique is the main focus of our interest. Given that it is the most widespread - one could say, unified - technique used by law enforcement agencies worldwide, it is an excellent starting point for assessing the quality of investigators' work. According to the information available on the organisation's website, its methods also dominate the practice of investigators working in the EU. The Reid technique is widely used in Germany, Belgium, Italy, Slovakia, the Netherlands, the Czech Republic, Luxembourg and Norway (although here it is being superseded by the KREATIV technique), but also in Poland, where the Code of Criminal Procedure only outlines the boundary framework for carrying out the activity, leaving the choice of technique to the person carrying it out.

Reid's technique constituted the first modern interrogation method – consisting of principles and guidelines – encompassing all kinds of instructions for officers conducting investigations. John E. Reid created a whole manual on how to design interrogation rooms, how to behave, and how techniques and psychological methods shall be used to create the most interrogator-friendly environment.[15] The technique has three components: Factual Analysis, Behavioral Analysis Interview (BAI), and Interrogation.[16] Following the original wording used by Reid's organisation "Factual Analysis can be defined as estimating the probability of a suspect's guilt or innocence based on investigative findings".[17]

The second component of the technique has ignited a debate between scholars and the Reid organisation, which has engaged in a polemic with academia.[18] The core of this heated discussion was not only the essence and mode of BAI but also the matter of the effectiveness of such an approach. Several scholars who conducted studies on human psychology and the possibility of detecting deception

15 Among the materials to study the technique, John E. Reid and Associates provide various books, e.g. The Reid Technique of Interviewing and Interrogation; Criminal Interrogations and Confessions; Essentials of the Reid Technique: Criminal Interrogation and Confessions. The books are periodically updated as the socio-legal reality changes; thus, the techniques, methods, or clues evolve. Several positions are available at https://reid.com/store/products [accessed on September 1st, 2024].

16 J. Orlando, 'Interrogation', loc.cit.

17 John E. Reid and Associates, 'Factual Analysis' [Online]. Available at: https://reid.com/resources/investigator-tips/factual-analysis 2017 [accessed on September 1st, 2024].

18 See John E. Reid and Associates, 'The Reid Behavior Analysis Interview' 2014 [Online]. Available at: https://reid.com/resources/investigator-tips/the-reid-behavior-analysis-interview [accessed on September 1st, 2024].

and lies during interviews have put the efficacy of Reid's BAI into question,[19] with Kassin, Appleby and Torkildson describing BAI as "(...) a non-confrontational interview that possibly transitions into an interrogation. The purpose of the interview is to provide a means by which investigators can determine if suspects are lying or telling the truth".[20] Conversely, Reid's organisation characterises BAI as a polygraph-rooted "non-accusatory question and answer session, involving both standard investigative questions and structured 'behaviour provoking' questions to elicit behaviour symptoms of truth or deception from the person being interviewed."[21] Nevertheless, this stage is intended to evaluate the likelihood of the interviewed person being the suspect in a given case and whether the suspect is lying;[22] if such a conclusion is made, the next phase begins.

The third and final component of the Reid technique is the interrogation. During this phase, the investigator will follow nine steps that aim to gain success as a final result. However, it is pointed out that these steps may be essentially reduced to three aspects/principles fundamental to this method: isolation, confrontation and minimisation.[23] The issue with this technique, even at first sight, is its suspect-driven approach. While Reid's organisation would argue otherwise, this method is no longer handy when it comes to interviewing the witnesses, as it aims at obtaining a confession.[24] In other words, although some elements of this technique may be helpful in general interviewing practices, it has a narrow scope in the broadest range of interrogations. At the end of the day, it is not feasible for the authorities to obtain several confessions when the perpetrator may only be one.

This stage of Reid's technique is highly accusatory, and the steps are calculated to create a confession-friendly environment; the isolation phase aims to create anxiety through various powerplays, such as the layout of the interrogation room

19 For a further reference on this topic, see S.M. Kassin, S.C. Appleby, and J.T. Perillo, 'Interviewing suspects: Practice, science, and future directions', *Legal and Criminological Psychology*, 2010/15, pp. 39–55 and the literature quoted therein.

20 Ibidem, pp. 40–41.

21 J. Orlando, 'Interrogation', loc.cit.; John E. Reid and Associates, 'The Reid Behavior Analysis Interview' 2014 [Online]. Available at: https://reid.com/resources/investigator-tips/the-reid-behavior-analysis-interview [accessed on September 1st, 2024].

22 B. Snook, J. Eastwood, M. Stinson, J. Tedeschini, J., & J.C. House, 'Reforming investigative interviewing in Canada', *Canadian Journal Of Criminology & Criminal Justice*, 2010/52(2), p. 217.

23 T.F. Moore, C.L. Fitzsimmons, 'Justice Imperiled: False Confessions and the Reid Technique', *Criminal Law Quarterly* 2010/57(4), pp. 512–513.

24 W. Kozinski, 'The Reid Inter rogation', *op.cit.*, p. 311 and literature quoted therein.

(described carefully by Reid's organisation), the order of entering the room or food, drink and sleep deprivation.[25] The isolation phase does not stop at creating such a psychological and non-verbal atmosphere; it also consists of enforcing the suspect to acknowledge that his guilt is already well-known to the interrogator, who shall not even allow the suspect to plead his innocence and cut off any possibility of denial.[26] The end goal is to create a whole isolation of the suspect's body and mind; the anxiety of loneliness and inevitable fate shall arise, preparing the ground for the next phase, which is confrontation. After preparing the ground for vulnerability, the interrogator presents undeniable evidence, which may be non-existent or even fabricated, but its strength is so overwhelming that the conviction is inevitable and not reliant on a mere guilty plea – which, however, may lead to "bettering" the procedural position of the suspect in terms of leniency.[27] Rearranging the perception of the procedural situation of the suspect from hopeless (isolation stage) to one in which there is a distant light in the tunnel (confrontation with suggestions of leniency or preferable treatment in case of confession) prepares the ground for the minimisation phase. In this stage, the interrogator looks for "excuses" regarding the criminal conduct; a variety of possible crime schemes are presented, and the interrogator pretends to sympathise with the suspect, even going as far as minimising their participation, role and guilt, as well as giving ethical and moral justification for that crime,[28] to accustom the suspect with the thought of a guilty plea being their best choice and the most excellent chance for leniency.

Reid's technique, however, faces a great deal of criticism. It is pointed out that its extremely accusatorial - even extractive - nature creates a state of mental coercion,[29] often violating the sphere of protection established by the prohibition of torture and degrading or inhuman treatment. Even when the law enforcement officer's actions do not result in inflicting physical pain, the psychological aspect – such as sleep deprivation or denial of food and drinks connected with highly stressful and accusatorial interrogation – often may lead to wrongful

25 S.A. Pieters, R.E. Frank, 'Police Interrogations and The Psychology of False Confessions', Canadian Legal Information Institute, 388 CanLIIDocs 2016, p. 4. Available at: https://canlii.ca/t/2bvw [accessed on September 1st, 2024], p. 4.

26 W. Kozinski, 'The Reid Inter rogation', *op.cit.*, p. 311.

27 Ibidem., pp. 311–312.

28 A.M. Coughlin, 'Interrogation Stories', *University of Virginia Law Review* (UVA L. Rev.) 2009/95(7), p. 1646.

29 On the coercive interrogation methods, including the Reid technique, see S.A. Pieters, R.E. Frank, 'Police Interrogations', *op.cit.*, pp. 1–25 and the literature quoted therein.

convictions due to a high number of forced confessions resulting from inhuman and degrading treatment. Just in the USA alone, a study within the Innocence Project has shown that from 1989 to 2020, almost 30% of the confessions were false; among these 30%, nearly half of the suspects were below 21 years of age.[30] Another research shows that 95% of felony convictions occur through guilty pleas, out of which 18% happen to be false pleas – with a majority of convicts being people of colour.[31] The statistics clearly point towards the ineffectiveness of this technique. If assessed through the prism of the proposed goals for the activity (punctual analysis), we see that there is a fundamental issue with each the amount of true information along with the enhancement of human rights. The technique does not promote rapport-building nor trust in law enforcement authorities; in that regard, according to the proposed metric, it is even counterproductive, as false information and false confessions extend the time of the proceedings or even require that they are retaken. The same goes for the use of tortures – it has been found that the increasing level of coercion negatively impacts the quality of obtained information.[32]

30 Innocence Project, 'DNA Exonerations in the United States (1989–2020)', [Online]. Available at: https://innocenceproject.org/dna-exonerations-in-the-united-states/ [accessed on September 1st, 2024].

31 https://guiltypleaproblem.org/#stats [accessed on September 1st, 2024].

32 This was particularly the case regarding the usage of the RDI (Rendition, Detention and Interrogation Program for CIA). For a further elaboration on the practices and their effects, see: J.P. Pfiffner, 'The Efficacy of Coercive Interrogation', [in:] T. Lightcap and J.P. Pfiffner (eds.), *Examining Torture: Empirical Studies of State Repression*, New York City: Palgrave Macmillan 2014, pp. 150–151. See also: L. Tyler and E. Epstein, 'Legacy of the "Dark Side": The Costs of Unlawful US Detentions and Interrogations Post-9/11', Costs of War. Watson Institute of International and Public Affairs at Brown University 2022, and the sources cited therein. Available at: https://watson.brown.edu/costsofwar/files/cow/imce/papers/2022/Costs%20of%20War%20-%20Legacy%20of%20the%20%27Dark%20Side%27%20-%20Tayler%20and%20Epstein%20-%20FINAL%20Jan%209%202022.pdf [accessed on September 1st, 2024]; A. Schmidt, and K. Sikkink, 'Partners in Crime: An Empirical Evaluation of the CIA Rendition, Detention, and Interrogation Program', *Perspectives on Politics*, Cambridge University Press 2018/16(4), pp. 1014–1033.

5. In search for the better future: non-coercive techniques development

Although the above-described interrogation techniques were formed on the grounds of American law enforcement practice, the problems of coercive methods resulting from the application of the Reid technique or its variants are universal. The problem with high rates of wrongful convictions based on false or coerced confessions was recognised in the UK as early as the 1980s. This provided the impetus for developing the first information-gathering-based method, completely changing the paradigm guiding interrogators. The technique is named PEACE after 5 main elements that also create the 5-stages of interrogation: Planning and Preparation, Engagement and Explanation, Account, Closure, and Evaluation. Instead of seeking confession through pressure on the suspect, it relies on building rapport and trust and gathering information through employing principles of cognitive interview.[33] Since adopting the model within the United Kingdom's legal framework in 1992, the PEACE method has received positive reception, resulting in its implementation (also in due variants) in Norway or New Zealand.[34]

The fundamental assumption behind this method is that the investigator's activity is focused on the search for information. Its goal is to avoid emotional involvement in the "accusatorial" model of interrogation, in which the phenomenon of so-called tunnel vision bias is widespread.[35] Instead, this model promotes asking open-ended questions, reducing the officer's engagement to the role of a journalist rather than an interrogator, encouraging the interviewee to do most of the talking, and prohibiting false and non-existent evidence or deceit.[36] Although, as mentioned, this technique does not strive for confession, research shows that the confession rates are, in fact, higher than those obtained with Reid's technique.[37] Crucially, although the confession rates are higher, there is a significant

---

33 T.F. Moore, C.L. Fitzsimmons, 'Justice Imperiled', *op.cit.*, pp. 539–542.

34 Ibidem, p. 540.

35 S.A. Pieters, R.E. Frank, 'Police Interrogations', *op.cit.*, p. 4 and the sources cited therein; T.F. Moore, C.L. Fitzsimmons, 'Justice Imperiled', *op.cit.*, pp. 540–541 and the sources cited therein.

36 See, e.g. S.A. Pieters, R.E. Frank, 'Police Interrogations', *op.cit.*, p. 18; T.F. Moore, C.L. Fitzsimmons, 'Justice Imperiled, *op.cit.*, p. 540; J. Orlando, 'Interrogation', loc.cit., S.M. Kassin, S.C. Appleby, and J.T. Perillo, 'Interviewing suspects', *op.cit.*, pp. 46–47.

37 A, Spierer, 'The Right to Remain a Child: The Impermissibility of the Reid Technique in Juvenile Interrogations', *New York University Law Review*, 2017/92, pp. 1749–1750 and the literature quoted therein.

difference in the false confession rates.[38] Hence, from the effectiveness-oriented point of view, one can argue that PEACE is a much more effective technique than Reid's. Firstly, it is shaped in a way that promotes trust towards law enforcement. Secondly, it is a more effective way of gathering evidence, along with confessions, given the lower likelihood of them being false.

However, PEACE is not the only non-coercive model of investigative interviewing. Several developments of more or less structured propositions on how to conduct interviews have been made. Due to their clear opposition to psychological approaches, we will overview them in a single group.

Regarding Strategic Disclosure or Strategic Use of Evidence, much of the interrogation tactic relies on withholding information from the suspect rather than fabricating incriminating one.[39] The main idea of this lies detection technique is catching the lying suspect in the act – instead of forcing them into confession through bogus evidence or presenting them with all facts with a request to elaborate on it, their knowledge and reactions are being tested. This allows the investigator to go through all related facts without prior elaboration on them. Asking Unanticipated Questions as a technique refers to joint-involvement crimes; it requires that at least two suspects are concurrently interrogated regarding their participation in the crime. A group of researchers found out that it is possible to detect deceit based on the responses to the questions that are unlikely to be discussed between the guilty perpetrators.[40] Cognitive Interview techniques are twofold: some of them serve to detect lies in the testimonies, while some aim to enhance the reliability and the quality of the testimonies, especially the eyewitness ones. The first strand of cognitive interviews refers to imposing cognitive load; however, it is a theory that has been tested in academia and has no real impact on the practice of law enforcement agents.[41] The other strand is the

38 Ibidem and the literature quoted therein.

39 For further elaboration, see M. Hartwig, P.A. Granhag, L.A. Strömwall and A. Vrij, 'Detecting deception via strategic disclosure of evidence', 29(4) Law and Human Behavior 2005, pp. 469–484; T.J. Luke, M. Hartwig, E. Joseph et al., 'Training in the Strategic Use of Evidence technique: Improving deception detection accuracy of American law enforcement officers', 31 J Police Crim Psych 2016, pp. 270–278; M. Hartwig, P.A. Granhag, L.A. Strömwall and O. Kronkvist, 'Strategic use of evidence during police interviews: When training to detect deception works', 30(5) Law and Human Behavior 2006, pp. 603–619.

40 A. Vrij, S. Leal, P.a. Granhag et al., Outsmarting the Liars: The Benefit of Asking Unanticipated Questions, 33 Law Hum Behav 2009, pp. 159–166.

41 For a further elaboration on this technique, T.F. Moore, C.L. Fitzsimmons, 'Justice Imperiled', *op.cit.*, pp. 539–540.

cognitive interviews based on memory-retrieval mnemonics.[42] This approach is also multi-folded, as before the creation of the Cognitive Interview (CI) model in 1985, it was already recommended that the questions should be posed only after the witness is requested to describe the situation of interest,[43] thus compliant with the method of spontaneous relation evident, e.g. in the Polish criminal procedure.

Geiselman et al., within their model, rely on four interview stages posed in a particular order. The first one relies on reinstating the context surrounding the incident; the second demands to report everything, all memories regarding the incident, regardless of their perception as to their utility; the third asks to recall the event in different orders; the fourth relies on changing perspectives, e.g. asking the witness to report the incident from a victim's perspective.[44] The results of the laboratory study performed by the researchers have shown that the Cognitive Interview technique is an effective tool to enhance memory retrieval, particularly when it comes to recalling rapidly happening events with multiple details.[45] It also has been proven to be much more effective in comparison to standard interviews, vastly improving the number of recalled details and their accuracy.[46] It has been noted, however, that based on the practices and demands under the given tradition and requirements of law, the impact of using the Cognitive Interview method may be greater or smaller, e.g. European law enforcement employed structured interviews instead of standard interviews, contrary to their American counterpart.[47]

The next step in developing the CI was broadening its application scope to cover the entire interview. This happened through the development of the Enhanced Cognitive Interview (ECI) method, which comprised 7 steps instead of 4, as is in the case of the Cognitive Interview. The phases are as follows: (1) Greeting

---

42 A group of US academics developed this method as an alternative to the so-called standard interview practice within US law enforcement. For a further elaboration on this method, see R.E. Geieselman, R.P. Fisher, D.P. MacKinnon and HL Holland, 'Eyewitness memory enhancement in the police interview: Cognitive retrieval mnemonics versus hypnosis', *Journal of Applied Psychology*, 1985/70(2), pp. 401–412.

43 See R.E. Geiselman, R.P. Fisher, I. Firstenberg, L.A. Hutton, S. Sullivan, I. Avetissian and A. Prosk, 'Enhancement of eyewitness memory: An empirical evaluation of the cognitive interview', *Journal of Police Science and Administration*, 1984/12, pp. 74–80.

44 R.E. Geieselman, R.P. Fisher, D.P. MacKinnon and HL Holland, 'Eyewitness memory', *op.cit.*, p. 404.

45 Ibidem, pp. 409–410.

46 R.P. Fisher, D.M. Chin and M.R. McCauley, 'Enhancing eyewitness recollection with the cognitive interview', 6 National Police Research Unit Review 1990, p. 11.

47 Ibidem, p. 23–24.

and establishing rapport; (2) explaining the aims of the interview, exploring the second stage of CI – report everything; (3) initiating a free report through context reinstatement and open-ended questions; (4) questioning, again with report everything stage, through open and closed questions, but without fabrication of evidence; (5) varied and extensive retrieval, employing third and fourth stage of CI, namely changing perspectives and changing the temporal order; (6) summary; (7) closure.[48] Similarly to its predecessor, ECI also produced a significant increase in the effectiveness of collected testimony.[49]

Lastly, let us discuss the Norwegian creation, which is the KREATIV interviewing model. The acronym reflects the values and principles of the method, which are based upon communication, the rule of law, ethics and empathy, active consciousness, trust through openness, and information. The vantage point is science.[50] This model is based on PEACE, essentially being a variable of this model;[51] created in 2002, the technique relies on information-gathering techniques and plays an essential role in the basic training of Norwegian law enforcement officers.[52] Again, the focus is placed on obtaining reliable information instead of seeking confessions. The usage of deceit, fabricated evidence, sleep deprivation or any other coercive techniques is prohibited; although the same prohibitions exist under the Swedish law (which does not use PEACE or KREATIV models *per se*), there was a visible difference in the extent of confrontational/accusatorial interrogation tactics usage compared to KREATIV-trained Norwegian counterparts.[53]

All techniques described above share similar characteristics. Refraining from any kind of coercion, respect for human rights, and the central role of trust and

48 R. Milne, R. Bull, *Investigative Interviewing: psychology and practice*, Chichester: John Wiley and Sons Ltd. 1999, p. 40.

49 For a further elaboration, see M. Schollum, *Investigative Interviewing: The Literature*, Wellington: Review of Investigative Interviewing, Office of the Commissioner New Zealand Police 2005, pp. 61–62. Available at: https://www.police.govt.nz/sites/default/files/publications/investigative-interviewing-literature-2005.pdf [Accessed: December 3rd, 2023].

50 Norwegian Centre For Human Rights, Investigative Interviewing. 2020. Available at: https://www.jus.uio.no/smr/english/about/id/law/Investigative%20Interviewing/ [accessed on September 1st, 2024].

51 Ibidem.

52 M. Magnusson, M. Joleby, T.J. Luke, K. Ask and M. Lefsaker Sakrisvold, 'Swedish and Norwegian Police Interviewers' Goals, Tactics, and Emotions When Interviewing Suspects of Child Sexual Abuse', *Front. Psychol.*, 2021/12, p. 3 and the literature cited therein.

53 Ibidem, p. 3; 11.

rapport in effective interviewing play a vital role in each of them, regardless of any noticeable differences. They are much more intertwined, though. It is easily noticeable that each model is based on scientific grounds, namely laboratory or practical studies, contrary to Reid's technique – under which "lie detection" techniques are based on the gut and experience of the investigator instead.[54] Although these techniques tend to focus on gathering information, the confession and false confession rates are still an important determinant of their effectiveness; however, it has been raised in the academia that not only "pure" confession fulfils such criteria but also obtaining information which is inevitably linking the suspect with the perpetration of the crime.[55] Another factor that has to be accounted for is the relationship between the society/citizens and the law enforcement/judiciary. Fundamental human rights granted under international law aim to provide individuals with much-needed protection; its sometimes overlooked aspect is that their rigorous preservation also leads to the enhancement of trust towards state agents. Hence, in that manner, these techniques also promote building trust towards law enforcement, fulfilling one of the proposed criteria for effective performance of this procedural action.

6. Concluding remarks

Given that the single procedural action must always lead to the positive conclusion of the proceedings as a whole – meaning that the goals of the proceedings set forth by the legislator must be fulfilled – we have to include this element into the puzzle. If the non-coercive methods are providing us with more information – and, on top of that, less false information – then they prove to be much more effective than the coercive methods. On top of that, they were intended to enhance the human rights protection standard. Consequently, it leads to much more feasible and desirable outcomes, incredibly limiting situations where procedural actions may undermine social trust.

54 T.F. Moore, C.L. Fitzsimmons, 'Justice Imperiled', *op.cit.*, p. 541.

55 Although such statements are not treated as confessions *per se*, they play a vital role in the work of investigative forces within law enforcement. In fact, it is argued that the importance of such evidentiary-tied statements has impacted the significance and placing of information-gathering methods at the center of investigative interviewing studies. See A. Bergeron, F. Fortin, N. Deslauriers-Varin, 'Toward a new theoretical and methodological understanding of investigative interviews', *Investigative Interviewing: Research & Practice*, 2023/13(1), p. 61.

Based on the provided criteria for effectiveness assessment, we can observe that the psychologically coercive techniques are not really effective. Although they provide a fair number of confessions, which may simplify and expedite the proceedings, at the same time, almost a third of them are false. As personal freedom is one of the most fundamental human rights, every case in which a person was wrongfully convicted damages trust to the law enforcement and judiciary. Moreover, procedural errors may indeed lead to a significantly extended process, bearing more financial costs (including damages for wrongful imprisonment) and last longer, negatively impacting the assessment of procedural efficacy. On top of that, the person performing the activity must differentiate the style in which the conversation is happening, as interviews and interrogations vary greatly and are meant to produce different outcomes.

However, non-coercive (cognitive) interviews have proven to be equally effective when it comes to obtaining confessions. Ahead of the pack in this regard is the PEACE technique, employed in the UK. Moreover, this technique leads to fewer false confessions, even though it often produces better results. The most significant advantage of employing this group of techniques is that they are non-contradictory but indeed complement each other and may be employed concurrently. Treating every person participating in the activity equally, seeking information, and building rapport may also prove more accessible in terms of standardising the training of law enforcement officers, although proper preparation to conduct this type of interview is not straightforward.

Given the above, it becomes clear that non-coercive interviews are more effective and efficient when it comes to questioning people for the purposes of criminal proceedings. Appreciation of non-coercive techniques development was further emphasised by the creation of The Principles on Effective Interviewing for Investigations and Information Gathering[56] (so-called Méndez Principles), which are intended to serve as a universal standard of conduct for law enforcement agents. They have both a theoretical-dogmatical dimension, exposed in the sphere of legislation, where their implementation would lead to the creation of clearly defined procedural standards - and a practical dimension, providing guidance and a basis for training officers to achieve the best results. These Principles have been drafted by experts in the fields of interviewing, law enforcement, criminal investigations, national security, military, intelligence, psychology, criminology and human rights from around the world and were consulted with more than

56 Principles on Effective Interviewing for Investigations and Information Gathering [Méndez Principles], 2021.

80 experts from 40 countries during the 4-years long working process. The principles aim to transform the relationship between States and their citizens and are intended to change how public authorities conduct interviews, improving trust in the State. They also aim to enhance the quality of interrogations– as the first interrogation is crucial for information-gathering as the questions and possible influence of the suggestion may further impact the witness' memory.[57] A uniform approach and application of these rules should be shared and promoted, as coercive methods have proven to be highly ineffective in comparison to rapport-based techniques.

Bibliography

Bergeron, A., Fortin, F., Deslauriers-Varin, N., 'Toward a new theoretical and methodological understanding of investigative interviews', *Investigative Interviewing: Research & Practice*, 2023/13(1).

Coughlin, A. M., 'Interrogation Stories', *University of Virginia Law Review* (UVA L. Rev.), 2009/95(7).

Fisher, R. P., Chin, D. M., and McCauley, M. R., 'Enhancing eyewitness recollection with the cognitive interview', *National Police Research Unit Review* 1990/6.

Geiselman, R. E., Fisher, R. P., Firstenberg, I., Hutton, L. A., Sullivan, S , Avetissian, I. and Prosk, A., 'Enhancement of eyewitness memory: An empirical evaluation of the cognitive interview', *Journal of Police Science and Administration* 1984/12.

Geieselman, R. E., Fisher, R. P., MacKinnon, D. P. and Holland, HL, 'Eyewitness memory enhancement in the police interview: Cognitive retrieval mnemonics versus hypnosis', *Journal of Applied Psychology* 1985/70(2).

Gordon, N. J., Fleisher, W. L., *Effective Interviewing and Interrogation Techniques*, Academic Press 2010.

Hartwig, M., Granhag, P. A., Strömwall, L. A., and Vrij, A., 'Detecting deception via strategic disclosure of evidence', *Law and Human Behavior*, 2005/29(4) https://doi.org/10.1007/s10979-005-5521-x.

Hartwig, M., Granhag, P. A., Strömwall, L. A., and Kronkvist, O., 'Strategic use of evidence during police interviews: When training to detect deception

57 On the importance of timely disclosure of evidence, see e.g. S. Oleszkiewicz, & S.J. Watson, 'A meta-analytic review of the timing for disclosing evidence when interviewing Suspects', *Applied Cognitive Psychology*, 2020/35 (2). Available at: https://onlinelibrary.wiley.com/doi/full/10.1002/acp.3767 [accessed on September 1st, 2024].

works', *Law and Human Behavior*, 2006/30(5); https://doi.org/10.1007/s10979-006-9053-9.

Innocence Project, 'DNA Exonerations in the United States (1989–2020)', [Online]. Available at: https://innocenceproject.org/dna-exonerations-in-the-united-states/.

Janusz-Pohl, B., 'Perception of the Effectiveness (effectivity) in its Interdisciplinary Dimention - Keynotes', [in:] D. Vicoli (ed.), Effective Justice International and Comparative Approaches, Vol. 1, Peter Lang.

John E. Reid and Associates website (no date a). Available at: https://reid.com/about.

John E. Reid and Associates, 'The Reid Behavior Analysis Interview', 2014 [Online]. Available at: https://reid.com/resources/investigator-tips/the-reid-behavior-analysis-interview.

John E. Reid and Associates, 'Factual Analysis' 2017 [Online]. Available at: https://reid.com/resources/investigator-tips/factual-analysis.

Kassin, S. M., Appleby, S. C. and Perillo, J. T., 'Interviewing suspects: Practice, science, and future directions', *Legal and Criminological Psychology*, 2010/15, https://doi.org/10.1348/135532509X449361.

Kozinski, 'The Reid Interrogation Technique and False Confessions: A Time for Change', *Seattle Journal for Social Justice*, 2018/16(20. Available at: https://digitalcommons.law.seattleu.edu/sjsj/vol16/iss2/10.

Leo, R. A., *Police Interrogations and American Justice*, Cambridge, London: Harvard University Press 1st ed., 2008.

Luke, T. J., Hartwig, M., Joseph, E. *et al.*, 'Training in the Strategic Use of Evidence technique: Improving deception detection accuracy of American law enforcement officers', *J Police Crim Psych*, 2016/31, https://doi.org/10.1007/s11896-015-9187-0.

Magnusson M., Joleby M., Luke T. J., Ask K. and Lefsaker Sakrisvold M., 'Swedish and Norwegian Police Interviewers' Goals, Tactics, and Emotions When Interviewing Suspects of Child Sexual Abuse', *Front. Psychol.*, 2021, 12:606774, doi: 10.3389/fpsyg.2021.606774.

Milne, R. and Bull, R., *Investigative Interviewing: psychology and practice*, Chichester: John Wiley and Sons Ltd, 1999.

Moore, T. F., and Fitzsimmons, C. L., 'Justice Imperiled: False Confessions and the Reid Technique', *Criminal Law Quarterly*, 2011/57(4).

Norwegian Centre For Human Rights, *Investigative Interviewing*, 2020 [Online]. Available at: https://www.jus.uio.no/smr/english/about/id/law/Investigative%20Interviewing/.

Orlando, J., 'Interrogation Techniques', *OLR Research Report*, Connecticut General Assembly, 2014 [Online]. Available at: https://www.cga.ct.gov/2014/rpt/2014-R-0071.htm.

Pfiffner, J. P., 'The Efficacy of Coercive Interrogation', [in:] Lightcap T. and Pfiffner J. P. (eds.), *Examining Torture: Empirical Studies of State Repression*, New York City: Palgrave Macmillan 2014.

Pieters S. A. and Frank R. E., 'Police Interrogations and The Psychology of False Confessions', *Canadian Legal Information Institute*, CanLIIDocs 388, 2016, Available at: https://canlii.ca/t/2bvw.

Principles on Effective Interviewing for Investigations and Information Gathering [Méndez Principles] (2021). Available at: www.interviewingprinciples.com.

Schmidt, A. and Sikkink, K., 'Partners in Crime: An Empirical Evaluation of the CIA Rendition, Detention, and Interrogation Program', *Perspectives on Politics*, 2018/16(4), Cambridge University Press, doi: 10.1017/S1537592717004224.

Schollum, M., *Investigative Interviewing: The Literature*, Wellington: Review of Investigative Interviewing, Office of the Commissioner New Zealand Police, 2005 [Online]. Available at: https://www.police.govt.nz/sites/default/files/publications/investigative-interviewing-literature-2005.pdf.

Snook, B., Eastwood, J., Stinson, M., Tedeschini, J., & House, J. C., 'Reforming investigative interviewing in Canada', 52(2) *Canadian Journal Of Criminology & Criminal Justice* 2010/52(2).

Spierer, A., 'The Right to Remain a Child: The Impermissibility of the Reid Technique in Juvenile Interrogations', 92 *New York University Law Review* 2017.

Starr, D., 'The Interview', New Yorker 2013 [Online]. Available at: http://www.newyorker.com/magazine/2013/12/09/the-interview-7 [access: 1.09.2024].

Tyler, L. and Epstein, E., 'Legacy of the "Dark Side": The Costs of Unlawful US Detentions and Interrogations Post-9/11', *Costs of War. Watson Institute of International and Public Affairs at Brown University*, 2022. Available at: https://watson.brown.edu/costsofwar/files/cow/imce/papers/2022/Costs%20of%20War%20-%20Legacy%20of%20the%20%27Dark%20Side%27%20-%20Tayler%20and%20Epstein%20-%20FINAL%20Jan%209%202022.pdf.

Vrij, A., Leal, S., Granhag, P. A. et al., 'Outsmarting the Liars: The Benefit of Asking Unanticipated Questions', *Law Hum Behav* 2009/33, https://doi.org/10.1007/s10979-008-9143-y.

Dr. Katarzyna Zombory[1]

VI. Effective Remedies for the Violation of Cultural Human Rights under International Law

Abstract: In this paper, the author first briefly presents the concept of effective remedies and the international framework for protecting cultural rights. In the second part, the author identifies different approaches to remedies for violating cultural rights in the jurisprudence of the international treaty bodies at the universal and regional levels, specifically within the Inter-American, African, and European systems for human rights protection. Cultural rights form an integral part of the international human rights framework. The right to participate in cultural life has been recognised in all key human rights instruments on the universal and regional levels (ICESCR, ICCPR, ACHR, ACHPR).

In Europe, the ECtHR is more restrained towards awarding redress for cultural rights violations and leaves it to the requested state to decide on how to remedy the wrongful situation. Remedies ordered by the ECtHR in cases involving cultural rights commonly amount to moderate compensation.

Keywords: effective remedy, cultural human rights, effective justice, human rights

1. Introduction

The concern for cultural rights and the preservation of cultural identity has many roots. Nowadays, it has been catalysed by rapid globalisation and industrialisation. Cultural rights are part of the universal human rights framework and have remained thus since the adoption of the Universal Declaration of Human Rights in 1948.[2] They constitute the least developed category of human rights, both in

1 ORCID no. 0000-0002-0750-7555. University of Miskolc - Central European Academy, Director of Research Center.

2 The Universal Declaration of Human Rights, adopted by UN General Assembly Resolution 217 A(III) of December 10th, 1948.

terms of normative content and the possibility of assertion.[3] One reason for the uneven development of cultural rights is their specific aim: to protect the distinctive identity of particular communities. Other categories of human rights are concerned with the universal concept of protecting the humanity and dignity of all human beings.

The issue of enforceability and the provision of remedies are the main challenges related to protecting cultural rights, the effective realisation of which cannot be underestimated. The implementation of cultural rights is an essential component of the respect for every person's human dignity. However, it is an equally important aspect of international conflict prevention, given that culture is rooted in most international and domestic conflicts. In this paper, the author first briefly presents the concept of effective remedies and the international framework for protecting cultural rights. In the second part, the author identifies different approaches to remedies for violating cultural rights in the jurisprudence of the international treaty bodies at the universal and regional levels, specifically within the Inter-American, African, and European systems for human rights protection.

2. Effective remedy under international human rights law

The term 'legal remedies' has two meanings: the procedural meaning is that they are processes by which arguable human rights claims are heard and decided, whereas the substantial meaning refers to the outcome of such proceedings and the relief afforded to the successful claimant.[4] The existence of a legal remedy, understood in the sense of providing a procedural remedy when a violation has occurred or is imminent, and the process of awarding adequate reparations to the victim are intrinsic features of full-fledged human rights.[5] Under international human rights law, the concept of legal remedies and the corresponding right to an effective remedy forms part of a broader scheme that aims to secure the implementation and enforceability of human rights. Through its various universal

3 J. Symonides, 'Cultural Rights' in: J. Symonides (ed.), *Human Rights: Human Rights: Concept and Standards*, Aldershot: Ashgate 2000, p. 175. See also H. Nieć, 'Casting the foundation for the implementation of cultural rights', [in:] H. Nieć (ed.) *Cultural rights and wrongs: a collection of essays in commemoration of the 50th anniversary of the Universal Declaration of Human Rights*, Paris: UNESCO Publishing 1998, p. 176.

4 D. Shelton, *Remedies in International Human Rights Law. Third Edition*, Oxford: Oxford University Press 2015, p. 16.

5 International Commission of Jurists, *Courts and the Legal Enforcement of Economic, Social and Cultural Rights. Comparative Experiences of Justiciability*, Geneva 2008, p. 6.

and regional instruments, international human rights law imposes on states the obligation to ensure the effective enjoyment of human rights for all within their jurisdictions, and cultural rights are no exception. States must adopt all necessary legislative and other measures to give effect to the rights guaranteed under international law.[6] The right to an effective remedy and reparation is a consequence of the state's responsibility for human rights violations, the legal basis of which derives from the breach of a human rights treaty or norm of customary international law.[7]

The right to an effective remedy, which guarantees adequate redress for victims of human rights violations and imposes correlative obligations on states to make such remedies available, applies primarily to domestic legal remedies at the national level.[8] The role of international human rights bodies is subsidiary, which is well reflected by the rule of the exhaustion of domestic remedies, included among procedural requirements (admissibility criteria) of complaint procedures before the human rights treaty bodies. Notwithstanding the principle of subsidiarity, the right to effective remedy can be interpreted vis-à-vis the jurisprudence of international courts and quasi-judicial treaty bodies because, as Teshome noted, the competence to receive complaints and communications goes hand in hand with the obligation to provide effective remedies.[9] The role of international tribunals becomes all the more relevant and essential to the integrity of the human rights system when states deliberately and consistently deny domestic remedies.[10]

The right to an effective remedy has been recognised by all major universal and regional human rights treaties. At the universal level, the 1966 International Covenant on Civil and Political Rights (ICCPR) under Article 2, paragraph 3 guarantees any person whose rights or freedoms recognised therein are violated the right to have an effective remedy before competent national authorities.[11] The right to a legal remedy is recognised and well-established under the 1966 International

6 International Commission of Jurists, *The Right to a Remedy and Reparation for Gross Human Rights Violations. A Practitioners' Guide*, Geneva 2018, p. 19.
7 Ibidem, p. 15; D. Shelton, *Remedies in International*, *op.cit.*, p. 58.
8 R.G. Teshome, 'Provision of Remedies for Violation of Economic, Social and Cultural Rights: A Comparative Study of the United Nations, Inter-American and African Human Rights Systems', *African Journal of International and Comparative Law*, 2020/28(2), p. 302.
9 Ibidem, p. 303.
10 D. Shelton, *Remedies in International*, *op.cit.*, p. 59.
11 International Covenant on Civil and Political Rights, adopted in New York on December 16th, 1966, UN Treaty Series No. 14668.

Covenant on Economic, Social and Cultural Rights (ICESCR). However, the document does not explicitly refer to the states parties' obligation to ensure effective redress.[12] In the regional human rights systems, the right to an effective remedy has been enshrined in the European Convention on Human Rights[13] (Article 13) and in the American Convention on Human Rights (Article 25),[14] both of which guarantee the right to effective redress for human rights violations before competent national authorities. The right to effective remedy can be derived from the African Charter on Human and Peoples' Rights provisions.[15]

The universal and regional treaty bodies have developed a relatively uniform approach concerning domestic remedies required from state parties to give effect to human rights: Such remedies shall be accessible, affordable, timely, and effective.[16] At the same time, the international organs lack a coherent practice concerning remedies available in complaint procedures under different international monitoring mechanisms. According to Shelton, human rights tribunals appear to be unsure about the scope of their power to design and award remedies.[17] International instruments endowing treaty bodies with the competence to hear individual complaints (in many cases, optional protocols to principal human rights treaties) do not set out the types of remedies that should be provided in case of specific human rights violations. They do not provide for any rules that should be considered while awarding remedies, either. Treaty bodies have developed such rules in their jurisprudence, mainly based on the law of state responsibility, domestic legal systems, and legal traditions of states parties. A morally adequate

---

12 Committee on Economic, Social and Cultural Rights (CESCR), *General Comment No. 9, The domestic application of the Covenant*, December 3rd, 1998, E/C.12/1998/24, para. 2.

13 Convention for the Protection of Human Rights and Fundamental Freedoms (European Convention on Human Rights, ECHR), adopted in Rome on November 4th, 1950 under the auspices of the Council of Europe, UN Treaty Series No. 2889.

14 American Convention on Human Rights, adopted in San José on November 22nd, 1969 under the auspices of the Organization of American States, UN Treaty Series No. 17955.

15 African Commission on Human and Peoples' Rights (ACHPR), *Principles and Guidelines on the Implementation of Economic, Social and Cultural Rights in the African Charter on Human and People's Rights*, available at: http://archives.au.int/handle/123456789/2063, para. 21–22, [accessed on April 6th, 2023].

16 See e.g. CESCR, *General Comment No. 9*, para. 9; ACHPR, *Principles and Guidelines…*, para. 22; Human Rights Committee (CCPR), *General Comment No. 31 [80], The Nature of the General Legal Obligation Imposed on States Parties to the Covenant*, March 29th, 2004, CPR/C/21/Rev.1/Add. 13, paras 15–16.

17 D. Shelton, *Remedies in International*, *op.cit.*, pp. 1–2.

remedy should seek to restore the victim's position, that is, to place the victim in the same position as they would have been had no injury occurred.[18] Remedies should be able to address the systemic problem in the responsible state that has led to the given human rights violation in order to prevent similar infringements from taking place in the future.[19]

3. Effective remedies vis-à-vis the protection and enforcement of cultural rights

3.1. Cultural rights as human rights

Notwithstanding the conceptual nuances in different legal and academic sources, cultural rights aim at the preservation, maintenance, and development of culture, which are the specific elements of the social or cultural life of a group that contributes to its separate identity.[20] As Francioni noted, cultural rights rest on the uniqueness of a legacy that binds a group or community to a shared memory upon which the powerful sentiment of belonging and identity is built.[21] Central to cultural human rights is the protection of cultural identity and the enjoyment and preservation of cultural heritage.[22] The effective legal protection of cultural rights is important for national minorities and Indigenous people, who struggle to preserve their own unique cultural identity and heritage, unlike the dominant 'majority' culture.

Cultural, economic, and social rights traditionally belong to the second generation of human rights.[23] As seen in the case laws of several international bodies, the effective enjoyment of cultural rights is inextricably linked to the

---

18 Ibidem, pp. 19–20.

19 R.G. Teshome, *Provision of Remedies*, *op.cit.*, p. 308.

20 W. Mannens, 'The International Status of Cultural Rights for National Minorities', [in:] P. Cumber, S. Wheatley (eds), *Minority Rights in the "New" Europe*. The Hague: Martinus Nijhoff Publishers 1999, pp. 185–186.

21 F. Francioni, 'Culture, Heritage and Human Rights', [in:] F. Francioni, M. Scheinin (eds), *Cultural Human Rights*, Boston-Leiden: Brill 2008, p. 3. See also: L. Riedel, 'What are Cultural Rights? Protecting Groups with Individual Rights' in: M. Ssenyonjo (ed.), *Economic, Social and Cultural Rights*, London: Routledge 2011, pp. 411–427.

22 J. Symonides, *Cultural*, *op.cit.*, p. 187; K. Zombory, 'The Protection of Cultural Heritage in International Law', [in:] A. Raisz (ed.), *International Law From a Central European Perspective*, Budapest-Miskolc: Central European Academic Publishing 2022, pp. 255–256.

23 S. Domaradzki, M. Khvostova, D. Pupovac, 'Karel Vasak's Generations of Rights and the Contemporary Human Rights Discourse', *Human Rights Review*, 2019/20, p. 424.

proper implementation of first-generation human rights, such as the freedoms of expression, peaceful assembly and association, and thought, conscience, and religion, the right to respect for private and family life, as well as third-generation 'solidarity rights', such as the right to a healthy environment.[24] The protection of cultural rights imposes a range of positive and negative obligations on states, which can be pinned down to three levels of obligation: respect, protection, and fulfilment.[25] Safeguarding cultural rights often remains at the level of political commitments, which are not followed by legal measures. States adopt a reserved approach to the implementation of cultural rights, not the last place, out of the fear that empowering communities with distinct cultural identities (national minorities or Indigenous peoples) through the recognition of their cultural rights can provoke secessionist demands and endanger the territorial integrity of the state.

3.2. Universal framework for the protection and enforcement of cultural rights

At the universal level, everyone's right to participate in cultural life, as proclaimed under Article 15, paragraph 1(a) of the ICESCR, is most relevant for the protection of cultural rights. It refers to 'culture' and 'cultural life', and these terms are understood broadly, including *inter alia* ways of life, language, religion, natural and man-made environments, and customs and traditions through which individuals and communities express themselves.[26] To comply with the obligations under this provision, states should take all appropriate measures to ensure the respect for and protection of cultural freedoms and the necessary steps towards fully realising the right to participate in cultural life within their maximum available resources.[27] According to the Committee on Economic, Social and Cultural Rights (CESCR), which is the treaty body mandated to monitor the implementation of the ICESCR, violations of the right to take part in cultural life can take place through the direct action of a state party or of other entities that are insufficiently regulated by the

---

24 F. Shaheed, *Report on the Access to and Enjoyment of Cultural Heritage*, submitted in Accordance with Human Rights Council resolution 10/23, March 21st, 2011, A/HRC/17/38, paras 44–48.

25 CESCR, *General Comment No. 21: Right of everyone to take part in cultural life (article 15, para. 1 (a), of the International Covenant on Economic, Social and Cultural Rights)*, 2009, E/C.12/GC/21, para. 60. See also: International Commission of Jurists, *Courts and the Legal Enforcement*, *op.cit.*, p. 10.

26 CESCR, *General Comment No. 21*, *op.cit.*, para. 13.

27 Ibidem, para. 60.

state, particularly those in the private sector.[28] Preventing individuals and communities from accessing cultural life, practices, goods, and services amounts to violating Article 15, paragraph 1(a) of the ICESCR. The infringement of the right to take part in cultural life may equally take place through omission when a state party fails to take appropriate steps to achieve the full realisation of the right of everyone to take part in cultural life and the failure to enforce relevant laws or provide administrative, judicial, or other appropriate remedies to enable people to exercise in full the right to take part in cultural life.[29]

In General Comment No. 26 on land and economic, social, and cultural rights,[30] the CESCR took a far-reaching approach to implementing Article 15 paragraph 1(a) of the ICESCR and effective remedies for violating cultural rights. For many communities worldwide, land constitutes the foundation for social, cultural, and religious practices to express cultural identity and enjoy the right to participate in cultural life, aside from 'merely' being a resource for producing food or generating income.[31] The CESCR urged states to ensure that they have administrative and judicial systems to implement policy and legal frameworks relating to land effectively. According to the CESCR, access to justice is of crucial importance: it should be accessible and affordable, even in remote areas, and particularly for disadvantaged and marginalised individuals and groups. Judicial remedies should be tailored to suit the conditions of rural areas and the needs of victims of violations, giving them access to all relevant information and adequate redress and compensation, including, whenever appropriate, the restitution of land and return of refugees and internally displaced persons.[32] Regarding violations of indigenous peoples' cultural rights, the CESCR considers land restitution the primary remedy. States should build the capacity of their administrative and judicial authorities in such a way as to ensure access to timely, affordable, and effective means of resolving disputes over tenure rights through impartial and competent judicial and administrative bodies.[33] According to the CESCR, effective remedies are crucial when it comes to the protection of secure and equitable access to, the use of, and

---

28 Ibidem, para. 62.

29 Ibidem, para. 63.

30 CESCR, *General comment No. 26 (2022) on land and economic, social and cultural rights*, January 24th, 2023, E/C.12/GC/26.

31 Ibidem, para. 1 and 10.

32 Ibidem, para. 60.

33 Ibidem, para. 61.

control over land, which are the preconditions for the enjoyment of many of the rights guaranteed by the ICESCR.[34]

The CESCR is competent to receive individual communications concerning alleged violations of the ICESCR, vis-à-vis states that have recognised the ICESCR's competence by ratifying its Optional Protocol (OP-ICESCR).[35] The OP-ICESCR reaffirms under Article 3, paragraph 1 that for all rights violations, there should be a domestic remedy first, except when the application of domestic remedies is unreasonably prolonged. The communication procedure before the CESCR is still of limited practical significance, given that relatively few states have ratified or acceded to the OP-ICESCR so far. Nonetheless, the adoption of the OP-ICESCR has the crucial symbolic value of granting an equal footing to the rights guaranteed by the ICCPR and ICESCR regarding the enforcement and protection they offer internationally.[36] The case law of the CESCR includes only one communication about an alleged violation of Article 15 paragraph 1(a) of the ICESCR, which was declared inadmissible owing to the non-exhaustion of domestic remedies. *A.M.B. v. Ecuador*[37] was brought by a Colombian national living in Ecuador, who claimed that her son's right to participate in cultural life had been violated by the repeated refusal to register him in youth football tournaments. The author of the communication had not filed a complaint in the domestic administrative courts, arguing that the administrative dispute-settlement procedures were too slow in Ecuador. The fact that the author had not submitted a domestic complaint did not allow the ICESCR to evaluate whether an eventual undue delay by the authorities in resolving the matter would have left the author's son without protection and rendered the remedy ineffective in practice. According to the ICESCR, 'mere perception that domestic remedies are ineffective is insufficient to exempt the author of a communication from the requirement to try them'.[38]

Apart from the right of *everyone* to take part in cultural life, guaranteed under Article 15 paragraph 1(a) of the ICESCR, the universal human rights system provides for specific protections to be enjoyed only by cultural minorities and indigenous people, directed to ensure the survival and continued development of the cultural, religious, and social identities of such groups. Article 27 of the

34 Ibidem.

35 Optional Protocol to the International Covenant on Economic, Social and Cultural Rights, adopted on December 10th, 2008 by General Assembly resolution A/RES/63/117, entered into force on May 5th, 2013 (OP-ICESCR).

36 International Commission of Jurists, *Courts and the Legal Enforcement…*, p. 102.

37 CESCR, *A.M.B. v. Ecuador*, views adopted on June 20th, 2016, communication no. 3/2014.

38 *A.M.B. v. Ecuador*, para. 7.6.

ICCPR establishes the right of persons belonging to ethnic, religious, and linguistic minorities to enjoy their own culture, to profess and practise their own religion, and to use their own language in community with other members of their group. Under Article 27, culture can manifest in many forms, including a particular way of life associated with the use of land resources, especially for indigenous people.[39] According to the Human Rights Committee (CCPR), that is, the treaty body that monitors state parties' compliance with the ICCPR, the enjoyment of cultural rights under Article 27 of the ICCPR imposes on states the obligation to ensure that the existence and exercise of these rights are protected against their denial or violation. Positive measures for protection are required against the acts of the state, its legislative, judicial, or administrative authorities, and other persons within the state.[40] The enjoyment of cultural rights requires measures to ensure the effective participation of members of minority communities in decisions that affect them.[41]

Compared to the ICESCR, the individual complaint mechanism before the CCPR for the alleged violations of the ICCPR rights has received greater international recognition and is, therefore, better developed. The first Optional Protocol to the ICCPR from 1966 (OP1-ICCPR)[42] places the exhaustion of domestic remedies among the admissibility criteria under Article 5, paragraph 2 (b), except where the application of domestic remedies is unreasonably prolonged. The CCPR's rather extensive case law regarding the rights of persons belonging to ethnic, religious, or linguistic minorities under Article 27 of the ICCPR sheds light on the CCPR's approach to remedies for violations of cultural human rights.

In *Sandra Lovelace v. Canada*,[43] the CCPR concluded that the Canadian legislation preventing the author from being officially recognised as a member of Maliseet Indians and allowed to live on a reserve together with other members of her tribe was tantamount to a denial of her minority rights under Article 27 of the ICCPR.[44] However, the CCPR refrained from specifying the remedies expected

39 CCPR, *General Comment No. 23: Article 27 (Rights of Minorities)*, April 26th, 1994, CPR/C/21/Rev.1/Add.5, para. 7.

40 Ibidem, para. 6.1.

41 Ibidem, para. 7.

42 Optional Protocol to the International Covenant on Civil and Political Rights, adopted on December 16th, 1966 by General Assembly resolution 2200A (XXI), entered into force on March 23rd, 1976 (OP1-ICCPR).

43 CCPR, *Sandra Lovelace v. Canada*, views adopted on July 30th, 1981, communication no. R.6/24.

44 *Sandra Lovelace v. Canada*, para. 17.

from the state to rectify this infringement. In *Ángela Poma Poma v. Peru*,[45] the CCPR held that there was a violation of cultural rights under Article 27 ICCPR on the grounds that the interference with natural resources had affected the traditional economic activity and way of life that were essential elements of the culture of the Indigenous community to which the author belonged.[46] The CCPR considered that the state's action had substantively compromised the way of life and culture of the author and of the entire community.[47] Nevertheless, while ordering remedies, the treaty body limited itself to a vague statement that the state had to provide an effective remedy and reparation measures commensurate with the harm sustained.[48]

In two recent cases, *Sanila-Aikio v. Finland*[49] and *Käkkäläjärvi v. Finland*,[50] the CCPR ordered more specific remedies to rectify the violation of the authors' cultural rights under Article 27 of the ICCPR. Both cases were filed by the members of the Sami indigenous community, who claimed that Finland had violated the Sami people's rights to political participation under Article 25 of the ICCPR by granting the right to vote in elections for the Sami Parliament to those who had been found ineligible to vote by the Sami community. The authors claimed that as the Sami Parliament guarantees the Sami linguistic and cultural autonomy, diluting the indigenous community's vote in parliamentary elections also diluted their right to enjoy their own culture and language, and as such was tantamount to the violation of Article 27 of the ICCPR. The CCPR found that there had been an infringement of Article 25 of the ICCPR, read alone and in conjunction with Article 27 of the ICCPR.[51] As the violation was a direct consequence of a wrongful interpretation by Finnish courts of the Act on Sami Parliament, the CCPR ordered Finland to review the provisions of the Act to ensure that the criteria for eligibility to vote in Sami Parliament elections are defined and applied in a manner that

45 CPPR, *Ángela Poma Poma v. Peru*, views adopted on March 27th, 2009, communication no: 1457/2006.

46 Ibidem, para. 7.3.

47 Ibidem, para. 7.7.

48 Ibidem, para. 9.

49 CCPR, *Tina Sanila-Aikio v. Finland*, decision on admissibility adopted on March 28th, 2017, communication no.: 2668/2015, and *Tina Sanila-Aikio v. Finland*, views adopted on November 1st, 2018, communication no.: 2950/2017.

50 CCPR, *Klemetti Käkkäläjärvi et al. v. Finland*, views adopted on November 2nd, 2018, communication number: 2950/2017.

51 *Tina Sanila-Aikio v. Finland*, views, para. 6.11; *Klemetti Käkkäläjärvi et al. v. Finland*, para. 9.11.

respects the right of the Sami people to exercise their internal self-determination by Articles 25 and 27 of the ICCPR.[52] The CCPR added that the state is under an obligation to take all steps necessary to prevent similar violations from occurring in the future. The CCPR concluded that the state's commitment to providing the authors with an effective remedy, stemming from Article 2 Paragraph 3 (a), requires it to make full reparation to individuals whose ICCPR rights have been violated, albeit without giving any indication as to how to assess the amount of reparation. The CCPR noted that under Article 2 of the ICCPR, states have undertaken to ensure to all individuals within their territory the rights recognised in the ICCPR and to provide an *effective and enforceable* remedy when it has been determined that a violation has occurred.[53]

In *Sanila-Aikio v. Finland* and *Käkkäläjärvi v. Finland*, the CCPR dealt equally with the substantive and procedural aspects of effective remedies in the context of alleged violations of cultural rights under Article 27 of the ICCPR. In both cases, the procedural aspect of remedies implied access to justice vis-à-vis standing requirements under Article 2 of the OP1-ICCPR, in terms of which only individuals who claim that their rights under the ICCPR have been violated can submit communications to the CCPR. The state argued that the communications were inadmissible as the authors had no standing to collectively act on behalf of the Sami indigenous people. According to the state, the authors did not allege violations of their individual rights, and their claims equated to an *action popularis*, involving indirect or even hypothetical breaches of the rights of the Sami people in general. The CCPR considered that by submitting the communication on their own behalf, the authors brought the claims as members of the Sami indigenous people and as voters for the Sami Parliament (or, in the case of Tina Sanila-Aikio, as a member of the Sami Parliament). In their individual capacities, they were affected by issues concerning the functioning of the Sami Parliament and the elections.[54] Therefore, the authors were granted standing before the CCPR and an effective remedy, understood in its procedural aspect of access to justice.

52 *Tina Sanila-Aikio v. Finland*, views, para. 8; *Klemetti Käkkäläjärvi et al. v. Finland*, para. 11.

53 *Tina Sanila-Aikio v. Finland*, views, para. 9; *Klemetti Käkkäläjärvi et al. v. Finland*, para. 12.

54 *Tina Sanila-Aikio v. Finland*, decision on admissibility, para. 8.5; *Klemetti Käkkäläjärvi et al. v. Finland*, para. 8.5.

3.3. Regional frameworks for the protection and enforcement of cultural rights

The first inter-state instrument presenting a catalogue of cultural rights was adopted within the Inter-American human rights system. Article XIII of the American Declaration of the Rights and Duties of Man of 1948[55] recognised the right of every person to take part in the cultural life of the community, which acquired a binding character under Article 14 of the Additional Protocol to the American Convention on Human Rights in the area of Economic, Social and Cultural Rights (Protocol of San Salvador).[56] The American Convention on Human Rights (ACHR)[57] contains few provisions on cultural rights, notably Article 26, which imposes on state parties the obligation to adopt measures to progressively achieve the full realisation of the rights implicit in the economic, social, educational, scientific, and cultural standards outlined in the Charter of the Organization of American States. The ACHR empowers two bodies to ensure the state's parties' compliance with human rights and freedoms under the Convention, namely the Inter-American Commission on Human Rights (IACmHR) and the Inter-American Court of Human Rights (IACtHR). The latter is competent to issue binding decisions and has expansive formal powers to order reparations stemming from Article 63, paragraph 1 of the ACHR. Although the IACtHR does not have jurisdiction *ratione materiae* over the alleged violations of the cultural rights recognised in the Protocol of San Salvador,[58] over the years, the IACtHR has nevertheless created far-reaching standards for the protection of cultural rights based on the normative content of the ACHR, notably the rights to property (Article 21 of the ACHR) vis-à-vis land rights; to life (Article 4 of the ACHR), and Article 26 of the ACHR, referring to the progressive realisation of economic, social and cultural rights.

The IACtHR's case law on cultural rights has developed in connection with the rights of indigenous peoples in Latin America, who constantly face forced

55 American Declaration of the Rights and Duties of Man, adopted by the 9th International Conference of American States in Bogotá on May 2nd, 1948.

56 Additional protocol to the American Convention on Human Rights in the area of Economic, Social and Cultural Rights (Protocol of San Salvador), adopted on November 17th, 1988 under the auspices of the Organization of American States.

57 American Convention on Human Rights, adopted in San José on November 22nd, 1969, UN Treaty Series No. 17955.

58 According to Article 19 para. 6 of the Protocol of San Salvador, only violations of the trade union rights and the right to education set forth in Articles 8 para. a) and 13 of the Protocol can be claimed through the application of the system of individual petitions.

assimilation, displacement, expropriation, and the denial of rights to native lands, all of which endanger their cultural identity.[59] The effective protection of the cultural rights of Indigenous communities requires the efficient enforcement of and respect for the (communal) property rights guaranteed by Article 21 of the ACHR, given that the spiritual relationship these communities have with the land they live on forms an essential part of their cultural identity. This approach to the protection of indigenous people, based on the interrelation between cultural and land rights, has been adopted by the IACtHR, and has consequently developed over the last two decades. It has also been reflected in the following cases: *Mayagna (Sumo) Awas Tingni Community v. Nicaragua,*[60] *Yakye Axa Indigenous Community v. Paraguay,*[61] *Sawhoyamaxa Indigenous Community v. Paraguay,*[62] *Saramaka People v. Suriname,*[63] *Kichwa Indigenous People of Sarayaku v. Ecuador,*[64] *Kaliña and Lokono peoples v. Suriname,*[65] *Indigenous Communities of the Lhaka Honhat (Our Land) Association v. Argentina.*[66]

According to the IACtHR, the reparation of the damages caused by the infringement of human rights, whenever possible, shall aim for the full restitution (*restitutio in integrum*) and removal of the effects of the violation.[67] Where this is not possible, other measures may be determined to guarantee the observance of human rights and to remedy the consequences of their breach. The

59 T.M. Antkowiak, 'Rights, Resources, and Rhetoric: Indigenous Peoples and the Inter-American Court', *University of Pennsylvania Journal of International Law*, 2013/35(1), pp. 115–118; A. Raisz, 'Indigenous Communities before the Inter-American Court of Human Rights – New Century, New Era?', *Miskolc Journal of International Law* 2008/5(2), pp. 40–41.

60 IACtHR, *Mayagna (Sumo) Awas Tingni Community v. Nicaragua*, Judgment of August 31st, 2001 (Merits, Reparations and Costs), paras 148–149.

61 IACtHR, *Yakye Axa Indigenous Community v. Paraguay*, judgment of June 17th, 2005 (Merits, Reparations and Costs), para. 137.

62 IACtHR, *Sawhoyamaxa Indigenous Community v. Paraguay*, judgment of March 29th, 2006 (Merits, Reparations and Costs), para. 118.

63 IACtHR, *Saramaka People v. Suriname*, Judgment of November 28th, 2007 (Preliminary Objections, Merits, Reparations, and Costs), see para. 120.

64 IACtHR, *Kichwa Indigenous People of Sarayaku v. Ecuador*, Merits and Reparations. Judgment of June 27th, 2012. Series C No. 245.

65 IACtHR, *Kaliña and Lokono peoples v. Suriname*, Judgment of November 25th, 2015 (Merits, Reparations and Costs).

66 IACtHR, *Indigenous Communities of the Lhaka Honhat (Our Land) Association v. Argentina*, judgement of February 6th, 2020 (Merits, reparations and costs).

67 *Sawhoyamaxa Indigenous Community v. Paraguay*, para. 197.

nature and amount of reparations depend on the specifics of the violation and damage inflicted at the financial and non-pecuniary levels.[68] In cases involving the infringement of land rights protected under Article 21 of the ACHR, the reparations ordered by the IACtHR comprise a variety of different actions aimed at securing the effective enjoyment of property rights over traditional lands, such as the official recognition of communal property of Indigenous people, granting collective title over the traditional territory, the demarcation of Indigenous lands, handing over of traditional territory to Indigenous communities, and relocating non-indigenous settlers from traditional lands (e.g. *Mayagna Awas Tingi v. Nicaragua, Yakye Axa v. Paraguay, Saramaka v. Suriname, Kaliña and Lokono v. Suriname, Lhaka Honhat v. Argentina*). The IACtHR orders the state to abstain from acts that may lead the agents of the state or third parties to interfere with indigenous lands and natural resources (e.g. *Mayagna Awas Tingni v. Nicaragua, Saramaka v. Suriname*). In cases involving the exploitation of Indigenous lands without prior consultation with Indigenous communities affected, the IACtHR does not hesitate to order specific actions necessary to remove the effects of human rights violations. When a private oil company carrying out oil exploration introduced high-powered explosives on Indigenous territory, the IACtHR, while holding the state responsible for granting a permit in breach of Article 21 of the ACHR, ordered it to neutralise, deactivate and completely remove the explosives (*Kichwa Indigenous People of Sarayaku v. Ecuador*). The IACtHR gave precise instructions relating to the removal and neutralisation of the explosives and ordered the state to consult with the indigenous communities so that they could authorise the means of removal and the presence of the technical equipment and people required in this regard on their territory.[69]

According to the IACtHR, 'reparation should help strengthen the cultural identity of the indigenous peoples, guaranteeing the control of their own institutions, cultures, traditions and territories to contribute to their development in keeping with their life projects, and present and future needs'.[70] It considers the guarantees of non-repetition a form of reparations, especially in cases of repeated violations, which requires the adoption of legal, administrative, and/or other types of measures on the part of the state to ensure the effective exercise of the rights of indigenous peoples.[71] The IACtHR considers that the judgment is a form of

68 IACtHR, *Case of La Cantuta v. Perú*, Judgment of November 29th, 2006 (Merits, Reparations and Costs), para. 202.

69 *Kichwa Indigenous People of Sarayaku v. Ecuador*, paras 289–295.

70 *Kaliña and Lokono peoples v. Suriname*, para. 272.

71 Ibidem, para. 300.

reparations that should be understood as a form of satisfaction that recognises that the rights of the members of the Indigenous community have been violated by the state.[72]

In cases involving violations of cultural rights, the IACtHR orders generous pecuniary compensation, which includes material and immaterial damages inflicted (e.g. *Sawhoyamaxa v. Paraguay, Saramaka v. Suriname*). For example, the IACtHR said that the indigenous population had to be compensated for the significant property damage to ancestral territories caused by logging concessions awarded by the state. Aside from material damage, the IACtHR considered the suffering and distress that the members of the Indigenous community had endured as a result of the long struggle for the legal recognition of their land rights and their frustration caused by the lack of an effective domestic remedy, constituted a denigration of their basic cultural and spiritual values, which entitled them to just compensation.[73]

In several cases involving harm to Indigenous cultural identity, the IACtHR has ordered, as a form of compensation, the creation of a special fund for community development. The state must allocate a significant sum to this fund, earmarked for actions addressing indigenous cultures' recovery (see, e.g. *Saramaka v. Suriname, Kaliña and Lokono v. Suriname, Lhaka Honhat v. Argentina*). Another form of just compensation, applied when a violation of Article 21 of the ACHR involves the exploitation of natural resources on Indigenous territories, is the obligation of the state to reasonably share with the Indigenous community the benefits of such economic activity, provided that the community determines who the beneficiaries of the compensation should be.[74]

In Africa, the African Charter on Human and Peoples' Rights of 1981 (Banjul Charter)[75] formulates the right of every person to take part in the cultural life of his community freely (Article 17 paragraph 2), as well as the collective right of all peoples to their economic, social, and cultural development vis-à-vis their freedom and identity and in the equal enjoyment of the common heritage of mankind (Article 22 paragraph 1). Both the African Commission on Human and Peoples' Rights (ACmHPR), established by the Banjul Charter, and the African Court of Human and Peoples' Rights (ACtHPR), established by the Protocol to the Banjul

72 *Saramaka People v. Suriname*, para. 195.

73 Ibidem, paras 198–200.

74 *Kaliña and Lokono peoples v. Suriname*, para. 7.

75 African Charter on Human and Peoples' Rights, adopted on June 27th, 1981 under the auspices of the Organization of African Unity, OAU Doc. CAB/LEG/67/3 rev. 5 (the Banjul Charter).

Charter,[76] are competent to receive and consider individual communications. The case law of the ACmHPR is more prosperous and developed than that of the ACtHPR because the ACmHPR began its activities much earlier than the ACtHPR and because it is more accessible owing to different standing requirements.

In a pathbreaking case for the protection of cultural rights in Africa, namely *Centre for Minority Rights Development (Kenya) and Minority Rights Group (on behalf of Endorois Welfare Council) v. Kenya*, the ACmHPR examined a complaint filed by an NGO on behalf of the Endorois people. The state forcibly removed this Indigenous community from their ancestral lands without proper consultations or adequate and effective compensation. The complainants alleged that the state had impaired their freedom to practice their religion and culture, as their health, livelihood, religion, and culture were connected with their traditional land. The ACmHPR held that the Endorois culture, religion, and traditional way of life were intimately intertwined with their ancestral lands and found the government of Kenya in violation of several rights guaranteed by the Banjul Charter, including the cultural rights set forth under Article 17. The ACmHPR recommended that the state took several restitutive and compensatory remedies and urged it to: (i) recognise the rights of ownership over the Indigenous community and ensure the restitution of their ancestral land, (ii) ensure that the Indigenous community has unrestricted access to the traditional lands for religious and cultural rites and for grazing their cattle, (iii) pay adequate compensation to the community for all the loss suffered, (iv) pay royalties to the indigenous community from existing economic activities and ensure that they benefit from employment possibilities within the reserve, (v) grant registration to the Endorois Welfare Committee, (vi) engage in dialogue with the indigenous community for the effective implementation of the recommendations, and finally, to (vii) report on the implementation of these recommendations.[77] According to the ACmHPR, the right to obtain 'just compensation' in the spirit of the Banjul Charter translates into a right of the members of the Indigenous community to reasonably share in the benefits made as a result of a restriction or deprivation of their right to the use and enjoyment of their traditional lands and of those natural resources necessary for their survival.[78] While formulating the recommendations, the ACmHPR drew upon the considerations and remedies adopted by the Inter-American Court of

76 Protocol to the African Charter on Human and Peoples' Rights on the Establishment of an African Court on Human and Peoples' Rights, adopted on June 10th, 1998, OAU Doc. OAU/LEG/AFCHPR/PROT (III).

77 Ibidem, part: Recommendations of the African Commission.

78 Ibidem, para. 295.

Human Rights (IACtHR) in *Yakye Axa v. Paraguay* and *Saramaka v. Suriname*.[79] The IACtHR's case law was generously cited by the African Court of Human and People's Rights in its first judgement relating to the protection of indigenous rights (*African Commission on Human and Peoples' Rights v. Kenya*[80]), brought about by the Ogiek indigenous community in connection with forced eviction from their ancestral lands. The ACtHPR held that the state violated the rights to culture of the Ogiek population, guaranteed by Article 17, paragraphs 2 and 3 of the Banjul Charter, by evicting them from their traditional territory, which resulted in restricting them from exercising their cultural practices.[81] In a judgement concerning reparations, the ACtHPR, in line with Article 27 Paragraph 1 of the Protocol to the Banjul Charter, ordered extensive reparations, including pecuniary and non-pecuniary reparations for material and moral damage,[82] and including a variety of actions, such as the restitution of Ogiek's ancestral land and their full recognition as an Indigenous community, respectively.[83] The ACtHPR ordered the state to establish mechanisms for consultation and dialogue with the Ogiek on all matters affecting their ancestral land.[84] The ACtHPR urged the state to adopt appropriate measures to avoid the recurrence of the violations established by the court, as guarantees of non-repetition.[85] Drawing on the practice of the IACtHR, the ACtHPR ordered the creation of a community development fund, which was intended to serve as a repository of all funds ordered as reparations, and used

79 Ibidem, paras 284–294.

80 ACtHPR, *The African Commission on Human and Peoples' Rights v. Republic of Kenya*, judgement of May 26th, 2017 (Merits), application no. 006/2012, para. 153 and 186; ACtHPR, *The African Commission on Human and Peoples' Rights v. Republic of Kenya*, judgement of June 23rd, 2022 (Reparations), application no. 006/2012, paras 67, 72–74, 91–92, 142.

81 *African Commission on Human and Peoples' Rights v. Kenya* (Merits), paras 176–190.

82 *The African Commission on Human and Peoples' Rights v. Republic of Kenya* (Reparations), paras 47–93.

83 *The African Commission on Human and Peoples' Rights v. Republic of Kenya* (Reparations), paras 94–126.

84 *The African Commission on Human and Peoples' Rights v. Republic of Kenya* (Reparations), para. 144.

85 *The African Commission on Human and Peoples' Rights v. Republic of Kenya* (Reparations), paras 146–150.

to support projects for the benefit of the Ogiek in the fields of health, education, food security, and natural resource management.[86]

The European Convention on Human Rights (ECHR), does not explicitly protect cultural rights. Nevertheless, the European Court of Human Rights (ECtHR) has gradually recognised the right to the protection of cultural identity through an evolutionary interpretation of different provisions of the ECHR. The provisions mostly invoked in cases relating to the protection of cultural rights include Articles 8 (right to respect for private and family life),[87] 9 (freedom of thought, conscience, and religion),[88] 11 (freedom of assembly and association),[89] and 14 and Article 1 of Protocol No. 12 (prohibition against discrimination),[90] and Article 2 of Protocol No. 1 (right to education).[91] The growing importance of cultural rights in the ECtHR's case law is linked to the number of cases brought forth by persons belonging to national minorities, including cultural, linguistic, or ethnic ones, seeking the right to maintain a minority identity and to lead their private and family lives in line with the traditions and culture of that identity. The ECtHR has jurisdiction to receive applications from any person, group of persons, or NGO claiming to be the victim of a violation by a state party to the ECHR and the rights set forth therein (Article 34) on the condition that all domestic remedies have been exhausted (Article 35, paragraph 1). The ECHR gives the ECtHR the explicit competence to afford remedies when it determines there has been a breach of the ECHR (Article 41). However, examining the remedies for violating

86 *The African Commission on Human and Peoples' Rights v. Republic of Kenya* (Reparations), paras 154–156. The applicants requested a public apology from the state and sought the erection of a public monument, which the ACtHPR refused to order, saying that the judgement was a sufficient form of reparation and satisfaction, see: para. 129 and 133.

87 See e.g. ECtHR, *Chapman v. the United Kingdom*, judgement of January 18th, 2001, application no. 27238/95; ECtHR, *Ciubotaru v. Moldova*, judgement of April 27th, 2010, application no. 27138/04.

88 See e.g. ECtHR, *Cyprus v. Turkey*, judgement of May 10th, 2001, application no. 25781/94.

89 See e.g. ECtHR, *Sidiropoulos and others v. Greece*, judgement of July 10th, 1998, applications no: 57/1997/841/1047; ECtHR, *Yazar, Karatas, Aksoy and the People's Labour Party (HEP)*, judgement of April 9th, 2002, applications nos. 22723/93, 22724/93 and 22725/93.

90 See e.g. ECtHR, *Ádám and others v. Romania*, judgement of October 13th, 2020, applications nos. 81114/17, 49716/18, 50913/18, 52370/18, 54444/18, 54475/18.

91 See e.g. ECtHR, *Cyprus v. Turkey*, judgement of May 10th, 2001, Application no. 25781/94; ECtHR, *İrfan Temel and others v. Turkey*, judgement of March 3rd, 2009, application no. 36458/02.

cultural rights in the ECtHR's jurisprudence is not without challenges, as in many cases, the ECHR does not rule in favour of cultural minorities, and even when it does, it has a restrained approach. The ECtHR does not deem it its task to indicate what means a state should utilise to perform its obligations under the ECHR.[92]

In *Ciubotaru v. Moldova*, the ECtHR found that Moldova's refusal of the applicant's request to change his ethnicity (from Moldavian to Romanian) in his identity documents violated Article 8 of the ECHR (right to private and family life). The ECtHR considered that an award of compensation for non-pecuniary damage justified, and made the assessment on an equitable basis and awarded the applicant half the amount he requested.[93] In *Tasev v. North Macedonia*, the ECtHR held that the state's refusal to register the applicant's declared ethnicity infringed on Article 8 of the ECHR, and for that considered an award of compensation for non-pecuniary damage justified, although only to the extent of 1/13 of the amount requested by the applicant.[94]

In *Yazar, Karatas, Aksoy and the People's Labour Party (HEP) v. Turkey*, the ECtHR found that dissolving a political party advocating the right of self-determination and recognition of Kurdish language rights, which had not advocated any policy that could have undermined the country's democratic regime, breached Article 11 of the ECHR. The ECtHR considered that because of the dissolution of the party, the applicants sustained non-pecuniary damage. Assessing on an equitable basis, the ECtHR awarded compensation to each applicant and set a default interest rate in case of the state's late payment.[95] In *Sidiropoulos and others v. Greece*,[96] the ECtHR held that Greek courts' refusal to register a Macedonian cultural association on the ground that it supposedly intended to dispute the Greek identity of Macedonia and to undermine Greece's territorial integrity violated Article 11 of the ECHR. According to the ECtHR, 'the existence of minorities and different cultures in a country was a historical fact that a democratic society had to tolerate and even protect and support according to the principles of international law'.[97] The applicants pleaded non-pecuniary damage vis-à-vis the sadness caused to them by the refusal of their application to register the association and

92 D. Shelton, *Remedies in International*, *op.cit.*, pp. 215–216

93 *Ciubotaru v. Moldova*, para. 64.

94 ECtHR, *Tasev v. North Macedonia*, judgement of May 16th, 2019, application no. 9825/13, para. 55.

95 *Yazar and others v. Turkey*, para. 74 and 80.

96 ECtHR, *Sidiropoulos and others v. Greece*, judgement of July 10th, 1998, applications no: 57/1997/841/1047.

97 *Sidiropoulos and others v. Greece*, para. 41.

by its social and political consequences. The ECtHR considered that the judgment constitutes sufficient just satisfaction for the non-pecuniary damage sustained by the applicants and refused to order additional compensation.[98]

In *Cyprus v. Turkey*, the ECtHR found numerous violations of the ECHR, arising out of the military operations Turkey had conducted in northern Cyprus in 1974, the continuing division of the territory of Cyprus, and the activities of the 'Turkish Republic of Northern Cyprus'. No appropriate secondary school facilities were available to children of Greek-Cypriot parents in northern Cyprus wishing to pursue a secondary education in the Greek language. This amounted, according to the ECtHR, to a violation of the right to education (Article 2 of Protocol No. 1).[99] As many as 13 years after the principal judgement, the ECtHR issued a separate decision on just satisfaction, in which it ordered Turkey to pay 60,000,000 EUR, in respect of non-pecuniary damage suffered by the enclaved Greek-Cypriot residents of the Karpas peninsula, plus any tax that may be chargeable, and set a default interest rate in case of late payment.[100] The ECtHR instructed the Cypriot government to set up, under the supervision of the CoE's Committee of Ministers, an effective mechanism to distribute the compensation to individual victims within 18 months from the date of the payment or within any other period considered appropriate by the Committee of Ministers. The ECtHR assessed the amount of compensation on an equitable basis, taking into account the protracted feelings of helplessness, distress, and anxiety among the Karpas residents whose ECHR rights, including those under Article 2 of Protocol No. 1, were found to have been violated.[101]

4. Conclusions

Cultural rights form an integral part of the international human rights framework. The right to participate in cultural life has been recognised in all key human rights instruments on the universal and regional levels (ICESCR, ICCPR, ACHR, ACHPR). Although the ECHR does not explicitly protect cultural rights, it allows for the protection of cultural rights by the evolutionary interpretation of some of its other provisions. Cultural human rights, either recognised explicitly or

---

98 *Sidiropoulos and others v. Greece*, para. 62.

99 ECtHR, *Cyprus v. Turkey*, judgement of May 10th, 2001, application no. 25781/94, paras 277–280.

100 ECtHR, *Cyprus v. Turkey*, judgement of May 12th, 2014 on just satisfaction, application no. 25781/94, paras 58–59.

101 *Cyprus v. Turkey*, judgement on just satisfaction, paras 57–58.

implicitly, need to be given effect in the first place at the domestic level, which is the idea embodied in the concept of the right to an effective remedy and manifested by the subsidiary role of human rights treaty bodies. The state parties' failure to ensure the effective enjoyment of cultural human rights and/or effective remedies within their jurisdiction empowers international organs to provide remedies, understood both as access to justice and redress if a violation has been found.

International mechanisms to secure the effective enjoyment of cultural human rights comprise inter-state and individual complaint procedures before the human rights treaty bodies (CCPR, CESCR, IACtHR, ACmHPR and ECtHR). The case laws of different universal and regional organs vary significantly in terms of the scope and types of redress awarded, ranging from declaratory judgments and compensation to specific actions and non-monetary remedies. The CCPR has developed significant case laws dedicated to protecting the rights of people belonging to cultural minorities, initially without major contributions to the discussion on the remedies for cultural rights violations. In its recent case law, the CCPR has recommended the adoption of specific legislative amendments to prevent additional wrongdoings and required the state to make full reparations to applicants whose cultural rights have been violated. The CESCR, competent to receive complaints on violating everyone's right to participate in cultural life, has not yet developed its jurisprudence on cultural rights.

The regional treaty bodies' case-laws related to cultural rights show several interactions and cross-influences, albeit the approach to remedies has not developed on different continents equally. The most specific and far-reaching remedies for cultural rights violations can be found in the jurisprudence of the IACtHR and have been developed in the context of protecting indigenous people in Latin America. In the IACtHR's case law, the effective enjoyment of the right to cultural identity, requiring effective protection of the traditional way of life and land rights, is promoted by a combination of restitutive and compensatory remedies. The IACtHR orders different actions aimed at securing the effective enjoyment of property rights over traditional lands, awards generous pecuniary compensation for material and non-material damages, and orders the creation of a special fund for the benefit of indigenous communities. In Africa, the ACmHPR and the ACtHPR draw upon the case laws of the IACtHR, when they order the adoption of restitutive and compensatory remedies to ensure the effective enjoyment of cultural rights, including the recognition of the traditional land rights of indigenous communities. In Europe, the ECtHR is more restrained towards awarding redress for cultural rights violations and leaves it to the requested state to decide how to remedy the wrongful situation. Remedies ordered by the ECtHR in cases involving cultural rights commonly amount to moderate compensation. While ordering compensation, the ECtHR is specific about the payment modalities, such as the default interest rate. At other times, the ECtHR does not hesitate to refuse the applicants' claim for compensation, in which case, the declaratory judgement must suffice for a just satisfaction for non-pecuniary damage.

The proper implementation of cultural human rights is of utmost importance for the peaceful coexistence of different cultures, which cannot be achieved without the existence of effective remedies at the domestic and supra-national levels. Several human rights bodies have recognised the significance of reparations for victims of cultural rights violations and do not hesitate to order specific measures to remove harmful consequences and prevent further systemic violations. This approach is yet to be translated into significant international practice. However, it undoubtedly signals that the issue of effective enjoyment and enforceability of cultural rights has finally come to age.

Bibliography

African Commission on Human and Peoples' Rights (ACHPR), *Principles and Guidelines on Implementing Economic, Social and Cultural Rights in the African Charter on Human and People's Rights*. Available at: http://archives.au.int/handle/123456789/2063 [accessed September 1st, 2024].

Antkowiak, T. M., 'Rights, Resources, and Rhetoric: Indigenous Peoples and the Inter-American Court', 35(1) *University of Pennsylvania Journal of International Law*, 2013/35(1).

CCPR, *General Comment No. 23: Article 27 (Rights of Minorities)*, April 26th, 1994, CPR/C/21/Rev.1/Add.5.

CESCR, *General Comment No. 21: Right of everyone to take part in cultural life (article 15, para. 1 (a), of the International Covenant on Economic, Social and Cultural Rights)*, 2009, E/C.12/GC/21.

CESCR, *General Comment No. 26 (2022) on land and economic, social and cultural rights*, January 24th, 2023, E/C.12/GC/26.

Committee on Economic, Social and Cultural Rights (CESCR), *General Comment No. 9, The domestic application of the Covenant*, December 3rd, 1998, E/C.12/1998/24.

Francioni, F., 'Culture, Heritage and Human Rights', [in:] F. Francioni, M. Scheinin (eds), *Cultural Human Rights*, Boston-Leiden: Brill 2008.

General Legal Obligation Imposed on States Parties to the Covenant, March 29th, 2004, CPR/C/21/Rev.1/Add. 13.

Human Rights Committee (CCPR), *General Comment No. 31 [80], The Nature of the* Domaradzki, S., Khvostova, M., Pupovac, D., 'Karel Vasak's Generations of Rights and the Contemporary Human Rights Discourse', *Human Rights Review*, 2019/20.

International Commission of Jurists, *Courts and the Legal Enforcement of Economic, Social and Cultural Rights. Comparative Experiences of Justiciability*, Geneva 2008.

International Commission of Jurists, *The Right to a Remedy and Reparation for Gross Human Rights Violations. A Practitioners' Guide*, Geneva 2018.

Mannens, W., 'The International Status of Cultural Rights for National Minorities', [in:] P. Cumber, S. Wheatley (eds), *Minority Rights in the "New" Europe*, The Hague: Martinus Nijhoff Publishers 1999.

Nieć, H., 'Casting the foundation for the implementation of cultural rights', [in:] H. Nieć (ed.) *Cultural rights and wrongs: a collection of essays in commemoration of the 50th anniversary of the Universal Declaration of Human Rights*, Paris: UNESCO Publishing 1998.

Raisz, A., 'Indigenous Communities before the Inter-American Court of Human Rights – New Century, New Era?', *Miskolc Journal of International Law* 2008/5(2).

Riedel, L., 'What are Cultural Rights? Protecting Groups with Individual Rights', [in:] M. Ssenyonjo (ed.), *Economic, Social and Cultural Rights*, London: Routledge 2011.

Shaheed, F., *Report on the Access to and Enjoyment of Cultural Heritage*, submitted in Accordance with Human Rights Council resolution 10/23, March 21st, 2011, A/HRC/17/38.

Shelton, D., *Remedies in International Human Rights Law. Third Edition*, Oxford: Oxford University Press 2015.

Symonides, J., 'Cultural Rights', [in:] J. Symonides (ed.), *Human Rights: Human Rights: Concept and Standards*, Aldershot: Ashgate 2000.

Teshome, R. G., 'Provision of Remedies for Violation of Economic, Social and Cultural Rights: A Comparative Study of the United Nations, Inter-American and African Human Rights Systems', *African Journal of International and Comparative Law*, 2020/28(2).

Zombory, K., 'The Protection of Cultural Heritage in International Law', [in:] A. Raisz (ed.), *International Law From a Central European Perspective*, Budapest-Miskolc: Central European Academic Publishing 2022.

Ius, Lex et Res Publica

Studies in Law, Philosophy and Political Cultures

Edited by

Barbara Janusz-Pohl

Vol. 1 Anna Jaron: Socio-Economic Constitutional Rights in Democratisation Processes. An Account of the Constitutional Dialogue Theory. 2012.

Vol. 2 Stanisław Filipowicz: Democracy – The Power of Illusion. 2013.

Vol. 3 Teresa Dukiet-Nagórska (ed.): The Postulates of Restorative Justice and the Continental Model of Criminal Law. As Illustrated by Polish Criminal Law 2014.

Vol. 4 Agnieszka Kupzok: Enforcement of Patents on Geographically Divisible Inventions. An Inquiry into the Standard of Substantive Patent Law Infringement in Cross-Border Constellations. 2015.

Vol. 5 Alicja Jagielska-Burduk / Wojciech Szafrański: Legal Issues in Cultural Heritage Management. A Polish Perspective. 2016.

Vol. 6 Maciej Mataczyński (ed.): The Takeover of Public Companies as a Mode of Exercising EU Treaty Freedoms. 2017.

Vol. 7 Maciej Barczewski (ed.): Value of Information. Intellectual Property, Privacy and Big Data. 2018.

Vol. 8 Pawel Smoleń, Marcin Burzec: Introduction to Polish Tax Law. 2018.

Vol. 9 Łukasz Pohl, Konrad Burdziak: Judicial Interpretation of the 1997 Criminal Code Provisions on Self-Defence. 2019.

Vol. 10 Adam Szot: Judicial Review of Administrative Discretion. The Influence of Court Decisions on Administrative Actions. 2019.

Vol. 11 Michał Peno / Konrad Burdziak (eds.): The Concept of Modern Law. Polish and Central European Tradition. 2019.

Vol. 12 Leszek Leszczyński / Bartosz Liżewski / Adam Szot (eds.): Potential of Precedent in the Statutory Legal Order. 2019.

Vol. 13 Łukasz Bolesta: In Search of a Model for the Legal Protection of a Whistleblower in the Workplace in Poland. A legal and comparative study. 2020.

Vol. 14 Paweł Chmielnicki / Adam Sulikowski (eds.): New Perspectives on Legislation. A Comparative Approach. 2020.

Vol. 15 Marcin Burzec / Beata Kucia-Guściora / Paweł Smoleś: Agricultural Activity in Poland: A Fiscal and Legal Study. 2020.

Vol. 16 Magdalena Półtorak / Ilona Topa (eds.): Women, Children and (Other) Vulnerable Groups. Standards of Protection and Challenges for International Law. 2021.

Vol. 17 Josef Albert Fox: Die polnische Verfassung vom 3. Mai 1791. Hintergründe der Entstehung und der Außerkraftsetzung. Stellung Polens im Zeitalter der Aufklärung. 2021.

Vol. 18 Barbara Janusz-Pohl (ed.): Juvenile Justice Systems: Poland-Brazil-Portugal. 2021.

Vol. 19 Leszek Leszczyński: General Reference Clauses in the Judicial Process. Context of Legislative Intentions Interpretative Discretion. 2021.

Vol. 20 Francisco J. Campos Zamora: Das Problem der Begründung richterlicher Entschei- dungen. Eine Analyse auf der Grundlage der Theorie der juristischen Argumentation. 2021.

Vol. 21 Aneta Skorupa-Wulczyńska: Language Rights of the Citizen of the European Union. 2022.

Vol. 22 Mateusz Osiecki: International Legal Aspects of Aerial Terrorism. Methods of Law Enforcement in Avia-tion. 2022.

Vol. 23 Vladimír Sharp / Gabriela Blahoudková / Jakub Handrlica (eds.): Law, Pandemics and Ownership Restrictions. 2022.

Vol. 24 Piotr Kasprzyk / Anna Konert: Drones – Future of Aviation Law? Interference of Public Law in Private Law. 2023.

Vol. 25 Szymon Pawelec (ed.): Consensual Mechanisms in Criminal Proceedings – Integrative and Comparative Perspective. 2023.

Vol. 26 Dorota Pudzianowska: Statelessness in Public Law. 2023.

Vol. 27 Boguslaw Przywora / Aleksander Wróbel: Formalised Access to Pre-jurisdictional Free Legal Aid. 2023.

Vol. 28 Ewa Dawidziuk / Patricia Panero / Anny Tarwacka (eds.): Family, Law, and Society: from Roman Law to the Present Day. 2024.

Vol. 29 Marian Grzybowsk / Boguslaw Przywora / Aleksandra Syryt (eds.): Free Legal Aid, Theory, Legal Basis and Practice. European Standards. 2024.

Vol. 30 Karolina Gmerek: Trial as a Social Communication Occurrence. 2024.

Vol. 31 Pawel Wiliński (ed.): Effective Legal Remedies in Criminal Justice System. European Perspective. 2024.

Vol. 32 Jakub Hanc / Olga Sitarz / Anna Jaworska-Wieloch: On the (non)existence of the right to religious freedom of persons deprived of liberty. 2024.

Vol. 33 Marian Grzybowsk / Boguslaw Przywora / Aleksandra Syryt (eds.): Free Legal Aid – A Comparative Approach. 2024.

Vol. 34 Dominik Gajewski (ed.): Functioning of Administrative Judiciary in the Context of Economic Changes. 2024.

Vol. 35 Mikołajczyk, Barbara: Older Migrants – Vulnerable and Excluded. 2024.

Vol. 36 Świder, Maciej: The Exercise of the Right to a Fair Trial in the Era of the COVID-19 Pandemic. 2024.

Vol. 37 Tomasz Barankiewicz / Boguslaw Przywora (eds): Public and Civil Service in Poland. 2024.

Vol. 38 Daniele Vicoli (ed.): Effective Justice 1. Effective Justice. International and Comparative Approaches. 2025.

Vol. 39 Barbara Janusz-Pohl (ed.): Effective Justice 2. Effective Justice. International and Comparative Approaches. 2025.

www.peterlang.com

www.ingramcontent.com/pod-product-compliance
Ingram Content Group UK Ltd.
Pitfield, Milton Keynes, MK11 3LW, UK
UKHW021830100926
8556IPUK00004B/259

9 783631 901427